FUNDAMENTALS OF COMPUTER PROGRAMMING AND IT

Salient Features of the Present Edition

- **Motivates the unmotivated** and provides the teachers an unequaled approach that allows them to teach students with a disparity of computer experience backgrounds.
- Covers **detailed theory** supplemented with **appropriate figures** and **examples.**
- Introduces **Computer Organization.**
- Introduces **Operating System.**
- Introduces **Word Processor, PowerPoint** and **Spreadsheets.**
- Covers evolution of Internet and its applications and services.
- Covers Problem Solving and Program Planning.
- Provides the Basics of Programming using C++.
- Covers abundance of C++ programming examples with proper testing on Turbo C++ Compiler.
- Covers **adequate number of exercises and review questions** of all types.
- Provides **user friendly approach.**

Other Books by the Same Author :

1. Mastering C++ Programs (*Published by Firewall Media*)
2. Fundamentals of Computers
3. Programming in C and Numerical Analysis (For B.A. / B.Sc. III)
4. Solutions to Numerical Analysis
5. Excel with Objective Book for NIMCET (MCA Entrance Examination) (*Published by Golden Bells*)
6. Computer Concepts and Programming in C (B.E./B.Tech./MCA U.P. Tech. Univ. Lucknow)
7. Fundamentals of Computers and Programming in C
8. Mastering C Programs (*Published by Firewall Media*)
9. Programming in C (*Published by Firewall Media*)
10. Programming in C++ (*Published by Firewall Media*)
11. Programming in C and Numerical Analysis (*Published by Firewall Media*)
12. Computer Fundamentals and Programming in C (For B.Sc. I)
13. Digital Design and Computer Organisation (*Published by University Science Press*)
14. Structured System Analysis and Design
15. Information Technology in Business Management
16. *Excel with* Information and Communications Technology
17. Computer Programming and Utilization
18. Mastering Data Structures Through 'C' Language
19. Intelligent Instrumentation for Engineers
20. Fundamentals of Computing and Programming
21. Mastering Java Programs
22. Introduction to Computing
23. Electrical Power Quality
24. Numerical Methods
25. Presentation Software and Computer Communication
26. Object Oriented Programming Using C++
27. Fundamentals of Computing and Programming.

FUNDAMENTALS OF COMPUTER PROGRAMMING AND IT

By

J.B. DIXIT

UNIVERSITY SCIENCE PRESS

(An Imprint of Laxmi Publications Pvt. Ltd.)

**BANGALORE • CHENNAI • COCHIN • GUWAHATI • HYDERABAD
JALANDHAR • KOLKATA • LUCKNOW • MUMBAI • PATNA
RANCHI • NEW DELHI**

Published by :
UNIVERSITY SCIENCE PRESS
(An Imprint of Laxmi Publications Pvt. Ltd.)
113, Golden House, Daryaganj,
New Delhi-110002

Phone : 011-43 53 25 00
Fax : 011-43 53 25 28

www.laxmipublications.com
info@laxmipublications.com

Edited by : **Sangeeta Dixit**

Third Edition : 2011

OFFICES

✆ **Bangalore**	080-26 75 69 30	✆ **Chennai**	044-24 34 47 26
✆ **Cochin**	0484-237 70 04, 405 13 03	✆ **Guwahati**	0361-251 36 69, 251 38 81
✆ **Hyderabad**	040-24 65 23 33	✆ **Jalandhar**	0181-222 12 72
✆ **Kolkata**	033-22 27 43 84	✆ **Lucknow**	0522-220 99 16
✆ **Mumbai**	022-24 91 54 15, 24 92 78 69	✆ **Patna**	0612-230 00 97
✆ **Ranchi**	0651-220 44 64		

UCP–9362–350–FUND COMP PROG INFO TEC–DIX **C—**592/09/09

Typeset at : ABRO Enterprises, Delhi. Printed at : Repro Knowledgecast Limited, Thane

Dedicated to

All Beloved Readers, Friends

and

Family Members

CONTENTS

PREFACE TO THE THIRD EDITION

I am highly delighted to place in the hands of my esteemed readers the text of **"FUNDAMENTALS OF COMPUTER PROGRAMMING AND IT"** in its revised form.

This book is written for Engineering, M.Tech., M.C.A., M.Sc. (Computer Science), B.C.A., B.I.T., B.Sc., P.G.D.C.A. and other diploma course students.

PART A of the book presents **Fundamentals of Computer and IT** in a simple and easy to understand style. The subject matter thoroughly clears the doubts (if any) of both a novice or an experienced computer user.

PART B of this book covers **Basics of Programming Using C++.** It presents all the C++ programming topics from elementary to basics of file handling with properly tested programming examples.

I have put my sincere efforts and knowledge to make you understand the subject matter in simplest and easiest form. Valuable suggestions are always most welcome.

WISH YOU A GRAND SUCCESS in your examination, and a very bright future in the field of Computer Science.

—AUTHOR

ACKNOWLEDGEMENTS

It is with a great sense of satisfaction that I acknowledge the help and support rendered to me by many people in bringing this book in its current form.

My heartiest thanks to Mr. Raman Sharma (Manager—WIPRO) for his creative and thoughtful association in the preparation of this book.

My lovely children Apoorva, Aanchal and Vansh always remind me about the work to be completed with their ever smiling faces. So, a special thank to them also.

I would like to thank all my teachers, members of my family, students and well wishers whose blessing, knowledge, advice and interaction have made this project a possible venture in my life.

—AUTHOR

SYLLABUS

BTCS 101 Fundamentals of Computer Programming and IT

Part A (Fundamentals of Computer and IT) (25%)

1. Introduction to Computers

Define a Computer System, Block diagram of a Computer System and its working, associated peripherals, memories, RAM, ROM, secondary storage devices, Computer Software and Hardware. **(2)**

2. Working Knowledge of Computer System

Introduction to the operating system, its functions and types, working knowledge of GUI based operating system, introduction to word processors and its features, creating, editing, printing and saving documents, spell check, mail merge, creating power point presentations, creating spreadsheets and simple graphs, evolution of Internet and its applications and services. **(3)**

3. Problem Solving and Program Planning

Need for problem solving and planning a program; program design tools–algorithms, flow charts, and pseudocode; illustrative examples. **(2)**

Part B (Basics of Programming Using C++) (75%)

4. Overview of C++ Language

Introduction to C++ language, structure of a C++ program, concepts of compiling and linking, IDE and its features; Basic terminology–character set, tokens, identifiers, keywords, fundamental data types, literal and symbolic constants, declaring variables, initializing variables, type modifiers. **(3)**

5. Operators and Expressions

Operators in C++, precedence and associativity of operators, expressions and their evaluation, type conversions. **(2)**

6. Beginning with C++ Program

Input/output using extraction (>>) and insertion (<<) operators, writing simple C++ programs, comments in C++, stages of program execution. **(4)**

7. Control Structures

Decision-making statements: if, nested if, if—else. Else if lader, switch, Loops and iteration: while loop, for loop, do-while loop, nesting of loops, break statement, continue statement, goto statement, use of control structures through illustrative programming examples. **(4)**

8. Functions

Advantages of using functions, structure of a function, declaring and defining functions, return statement, formal and actual arguments, const argument, default arguments, concept of reference variable, call by value, call by reference, library functions, recursion, storage classes. Use of functions through illustrative programming examples. **(4)**

9. Arrays and Strings

Declaration of arrays, initialization of array, accessing elements of array, I/O of arrays, passing arrays as arguments to a function, multidimensional arrays. String as array of characters, initializing string variables, I/O of strings, string manipulation functions (strlen, strcat, strcpy, strcmp), passing strings to a function. Use of arrays and strings through illustrative programming examples. **(4)**

10. Concepts of Object Oriented Programming

Introduction to Classes, Objects, Data abstraction, Data encapsulation, inheritance and polymorphis. **(2)**

11. Classes and Objects

Defining classes and declaring objects, public and private keywords, constructors and destructors, defining member functions inside and outside of a class, accessing members of a class, friend function. Use of classes and objects through illustrative programming examples. **(4)**

12. Basics of File Handling

Opening, reading, and writing of files, error handling during files operation. **(2)**

Part
A

FUNDAMENTALS OF COMPUTER AND IT

CHAPTER 1

Introduction to Computers

1.1 Introduction

Computer is perhaps the most powerful and versatile tool ever created by human being. In today's world, the use of computers has increased so rapidly that we can no longer ignore them. Computers influence our lives in one way or the other. These days we see computers being used to perform several functions that have made our life easy. The list of services for which computers are used is a long one.

The computer mainly consists of hardware and software. Both of these components work together to process data. Figure 1.1 illustrates these two components.

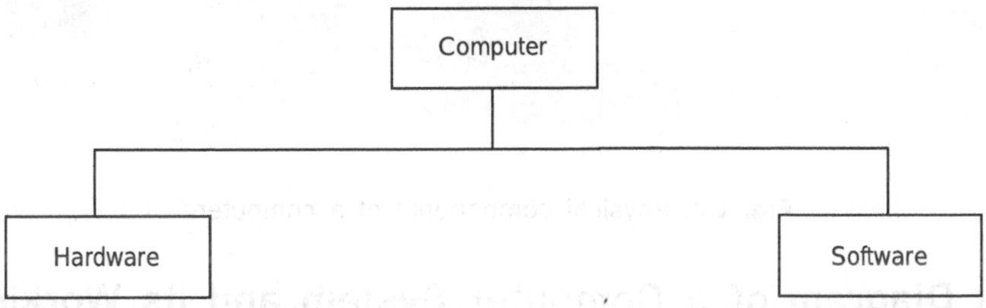

Fig. 1.1. Computer components (Hardware and software).

The parts of computer that can be touched and have some weight are called as hardware. The term hardware is used to refer to all the components inside or outside the computer. In addition to this, components used to interconnect two or more components, for example, wires, are also regarded as hardware. We have several hardware devices that are used at various phases of data processing cycle. The hardware that are used to supply input to computer are called as *input devices.* The hardware that are used to process the data, are called as *processing devices* and the devices that are used to present output of computer, are called as *output devices.* Each of these category has a broad variety of devices of various brands and qualities. The Input/Output Ports/Connections are used for connecting various devices with the motherboard of a computer.

1.2 What is a Computer ?

Computer is an electronic device that can accept, store and process data under the control of a set of instructions. The instructions, called a program, are stored in the computer when in use, so they can be executed automatically.

A computer appears to be far more intelligent and informed than human beings but the fact is, it cannot perform any task on its own. We need to give the computer instructions on exactly what it has to do.

If an unanticipated situation arises, computers will either produce wrong results or abandon the task altogether. They do not have the potential to work out alternative solutions.

Figure 1.2 shows some of the physical components of a computer :

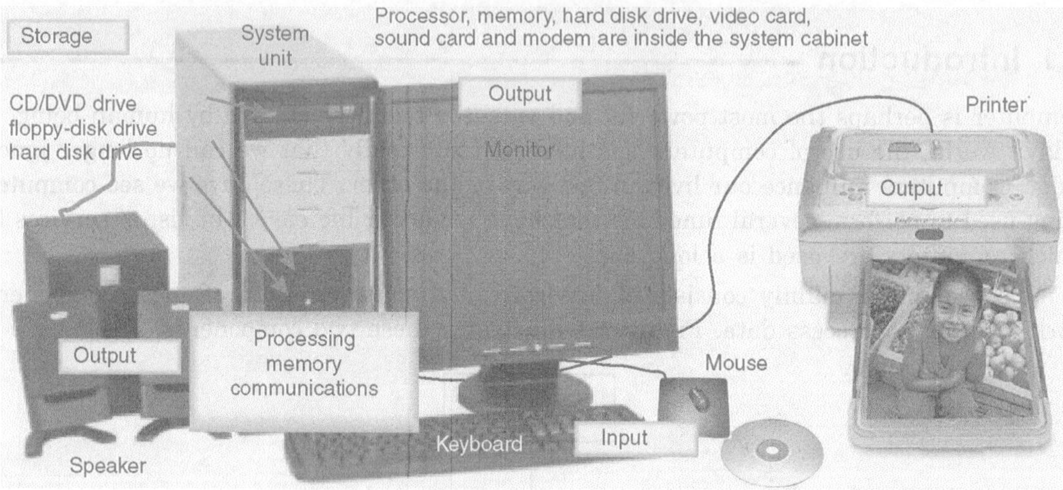

Fig. 1.2. Physical components of a computer.

1.3 Block Diagram of a Computer System and its Working

Regardless of type and size, *all computers follow the same four basic operations :*

1. Input
2. Processing
3. Storage, and
4. Output

In addition to these one more important operation is also performed, that is,

5. Communications.

Figure 1.3 summarizes these five operations :

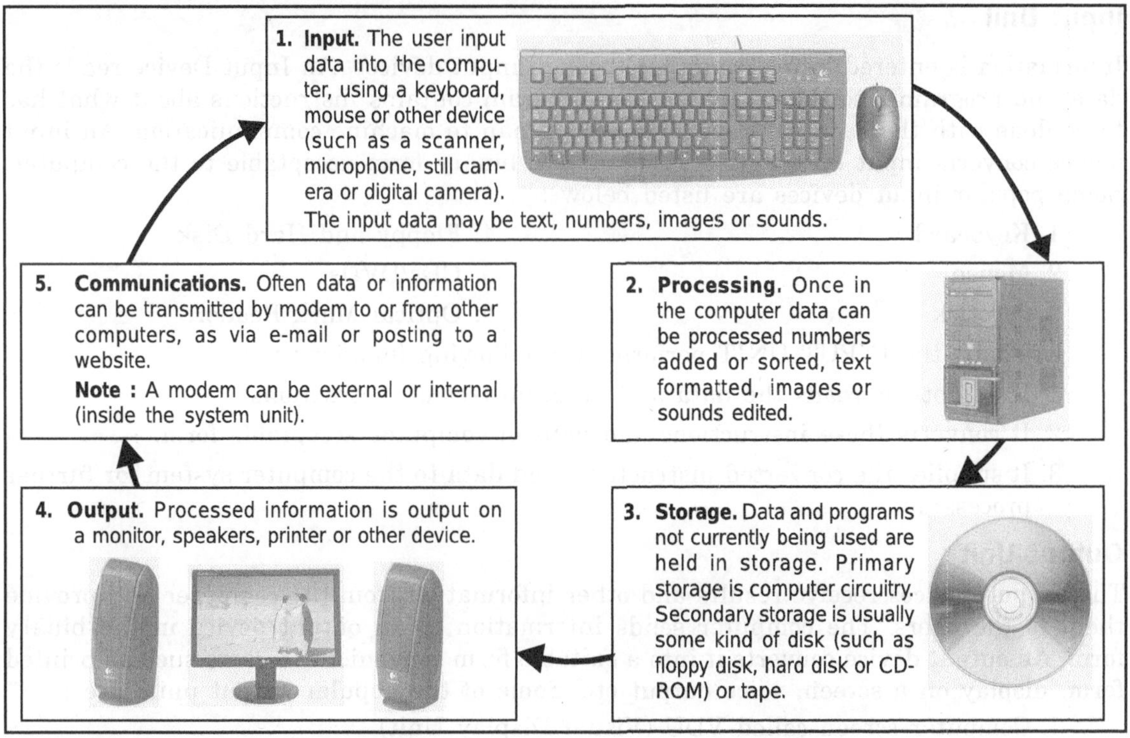

Fig. 1.3. The basic operations of a computer.

All these above operations are performed by some functional units which form the basic building blocks of any computer system.

Figure 1.4 shows the block diagram of a computer system. In this figure, the solid lines are used to indicate the flow of instructions and data, and the dotted lines represent the control exercised by the control unit.

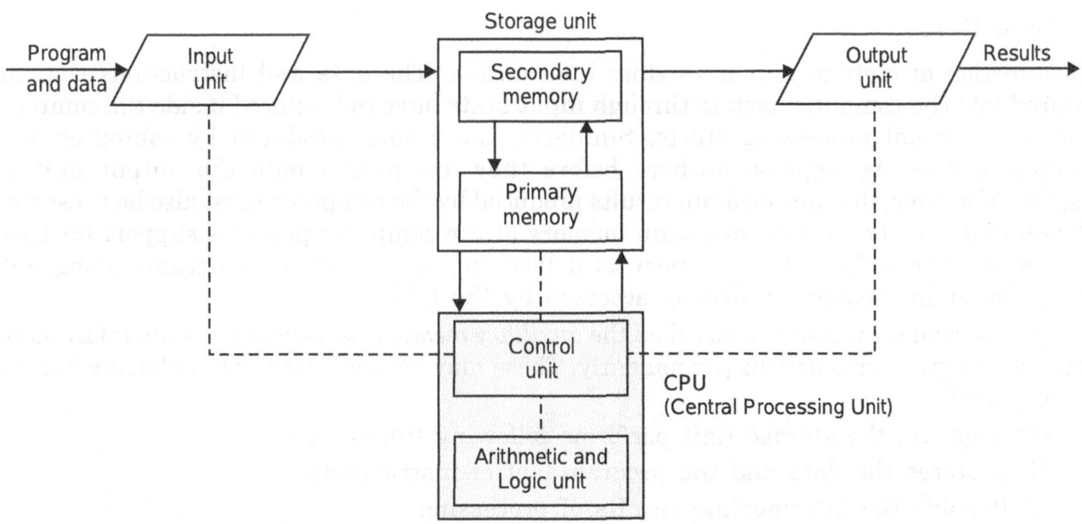

Fig. 1.4. Block diagram of a computer system.

The function of each of these units is described below :

Input Unit

Information is entered into a computer through input devices. An Input Device reads the data and program into the computer. The program contains instructions about what has to be done with the data. It provides a way of man to machine communication. An input device converts input information into suitable binary form acceptable to the computer. Some popular input devices are listed below :

1. Keyboard
2. Mouse
3. Joystick
4. Floppy and Hard Disk
5. CDs/DVDs
6. Optical Mark Reader.

In short, the INPUT UNIT performs the following functions :

1. It accepts or reads the data and program (set of instructions).
2. It converts these instructions and data in computer acceptable form.
3. It supplies the converted instructions and data to the computer system for further processing.

Output Unit

The output devices receive results and other information from the computer and provide them to the users. The computer sends information to an output device in the binary form. An output device converts it into a suitable form convenient to users such as printed form, display on a screen, voice output etc. Some of the popular output units are :

1. Computer screen called VDU (Visual Display Unit)
2. Printer
3. Plotter

In short, the following functions are performed by an output unit :

1. It accepts the results produced by the computer which are in coded form.
2. It converts these coded results to human acceptable form.
3. It supplies the converted results to the outside world.

Storage Unit

The function of storage unit is to store information. The data and instructions that are entered into the computer system through input units have to be stored inside the computer before the actual processing starts. Similarly, the results produced by computer after processing must be kept somewhere before they are passed onto the output unit for display. Moreover, the intermediate results produced by the computer must also be preserved. The storage unit or the primary/main memory of the computer provides support for these storage functions. The main memory is a fast memory. It stores programs along with data. The main memory is directly accessed by the CPU.

The secondary memory, also called the *auxiliary memory,* is used to store the information, data and program instructions permanently. These may be used later on or deleted whenever not required.

To sum up, the storage unit performs following functions :

1. It stores the data and the program (set of instructions).
2. It holds the intermediate results of processing.
3. It stores the final results of processing before they are passed onto the output unit.

Central Processing Unit

The CPU is the brain of a computer. Its primary function is to execute programs. Besides executing programs, the CPU also controls the operation of all other components such as memory, input and output devices. The major sections of a CPU are :

(*i*) Arithmetic and Logic Unit (ALU)

(*ii*) Control Unit (CU).

(*i*) **ALU.** The function of an ALU is to perform arithmetic and logic operations such as addition, subtraction, multiplication and division : AND, OR, NOT, EXCLUSIVE OR Operations. It also performs increment, decrement, left shift and clear operations.

(*ii*) **Control Unit.** The control unit is the most important part of the C.P.U. as it controls and co-ordinates the activities of all other units such as ALU, memory unit, input and output unit. Although, it does not perform any actual processing on the data, the CU acts as a central nervous system.

To sum up, it performs the following functions :

1. It can get instructions out of the memory unit.
2. It can decode the instructions.
3. It sets up the routing, through the internal wiring of data to the correct place at the correct time.
4. It can determine the storage location from where it is to get the next instruction after the previous instruction has been executed.

1.4 Input and Output Devices (Peripherals)

Input refers to data entered into a computer for processing—for example, from a keyboard or from a file stored on disk. Input includes program instructions that the CPU receives after commands are issued by the user. *Output* refers to the results of processing— that is, information sent to the screen or the printer or to be stored on disk or sent to another computer in a network. Figure 1.5 illustrates the common input and output devices used with a computer.

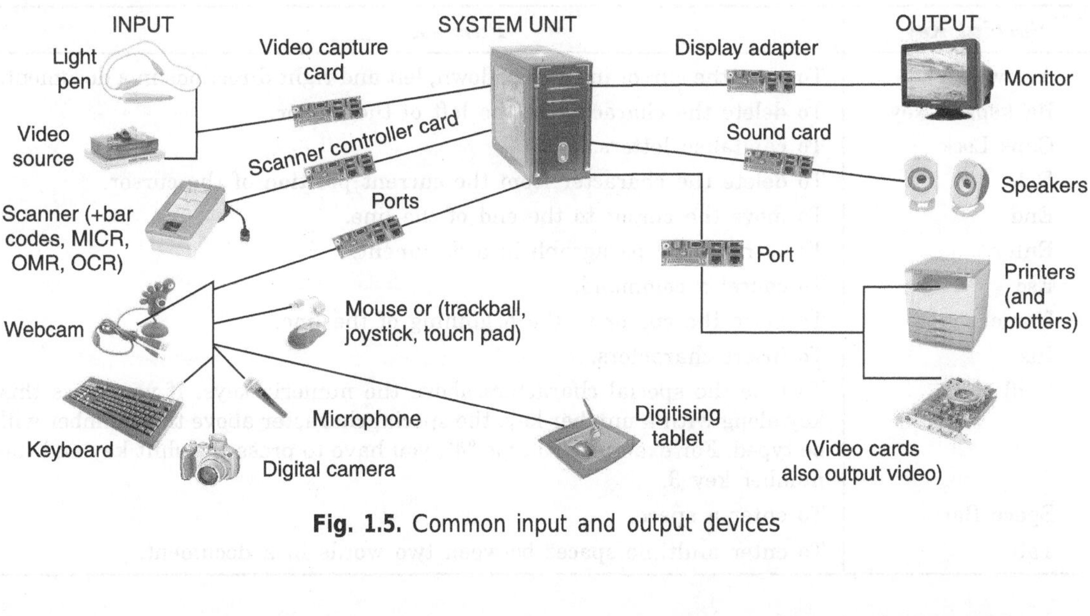

Fig. 1.5. Common input and output devices

- **Input Devices**

Any device that allows information from outside the computer to be communicated to the computer is considered an input device. Since, the Central Processing Unit (CPU) of a digital computer can understand only discrete binary information, all computer input devices and circuitry must eventually communicate with the computer in this form. Many devices are capable of performing this task. Some common computer input devices are:

1. Keyboard
2. Mouse
3. Light Pen
4. Touch Screens
5. Graphics Tablets (Digitisers)
6. Joystick
7. Trackball
8. MICR
9. OCR
10. Scanner
11. Smart Card Reader
12. Barcode Reader
13. Biometric Sensor
14. Web Camera
15. Digital Camera

Let us discuss some of the input devices and their functions:

Keyboard

Keyboard is perhaps the most popular and widely used device for entering data and instructions in a computer system (See Figure 1.6). A keyboard is similar to the keyboard of a typewriter. It contains alphabets, digits, special characters and some control keys. A general purpose keyboard normally contains cursor control keys and function keys. Function keys allow user to enter frequently used operations in a single keystroke, and cursor-control keys can be used to select displayed objects or co-ordinate positions by positioning the cursor on the screen.

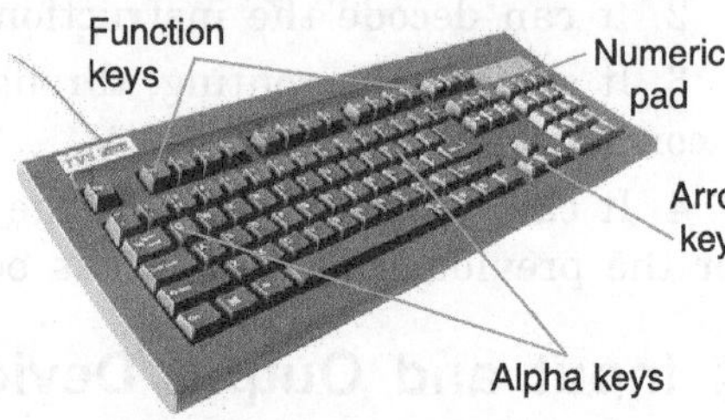

Fig. 1.6. A Keyboard

Some of the special keys on a keyboard are given in Table 1.1.

Table 1.1. Special Keys on a Keyboard and their Purpose

Special Key	*Purpose*
Arrow Key	To move the cursor in the top, down, left and right directions in a document.
Backspace Key	To delete the character on the left of the cursor.
Caps Lock	To capitalise letters.
Del	To delete the character from the current position of the cursor.
End	To move the cursor to the end of the line.
Enter	To start a new paragraph in a document.
Esc	To cancel a command.
Home	To move the cursor to the beginning of the line.
Ins	To insert characters.
Shift	To type the special characters above the numeric keys. If you press this key along with a number key, the special character above that number will be typed. For example: To type "#", you have to press the shift key and the number key 3.
Space Bar	To enter a space.
Tab	To enter multiple spaces between two words in a document.

Mouse

A mouse is a pointing device (See Figure 1.7). It is a small hand held box and it is used to position the cursor on the screen. The amount and the direction of movement can be detected by the wheels or the rollers on the bottom of the mouse. The wheels have their axes at right angles. Each wheel is connected to a shaft encoder and whenever the wheel moves this shaft encoder emits electrical pulses. The distance moved is determined by the number of pulses emitted by the mouse.

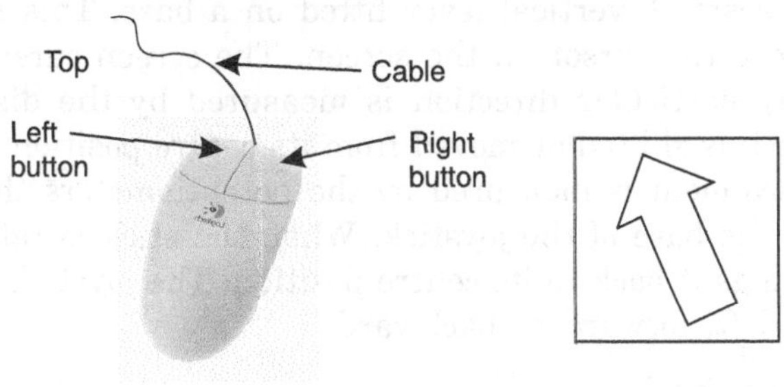

Fig. 1.7. A mouse and standard mouse pointer

The movements of the mouse cursor always match that of the mouse. There are three kinds of clicks. They are left-click, right-click and double click. The mouse can be used to drag and drop objects on the screen. Cordless mice are also available.

Advantages:

1. It is a simple device and very easy to use.
2. It is not very expensive.
3. It moves the cursor faster than the arrow keys of the keyboard.

Disadvantages:

1. The movement of the cursor is not very sensitive to the movement of mouse.
2. If the contact between wheels and mouse pad is lost, the cursor does not move.

> ***Note :*** *It is a good practice to use the mouse pad instead of just any flat surface for movement of the mouse.*

Scanner

Scanners, or *optical scanners*, use light-sensing (optical) equipment to translate images of text, drawings, photos, and the like into digital form (See Figure 1.8).

The images can then be processed by a computer, displayed on a monitor, stored on a storage device, or transmitted to another computer. Scanners are similar to photocopy machines except they create electronic files of scanned items instead of paper copies.

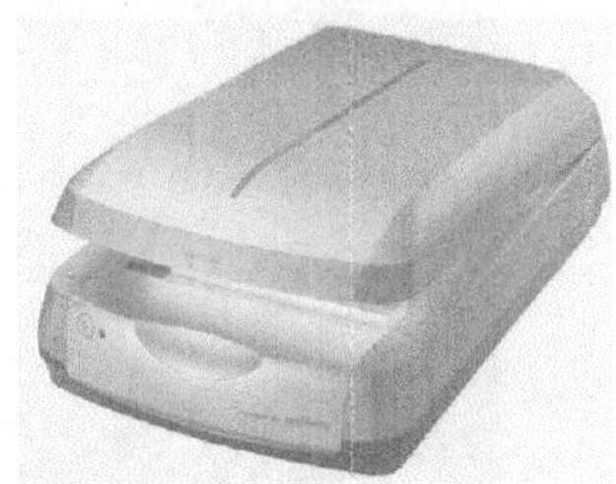
Fig. 1.8. A desktop scanner

Scanners vary in resolution. *Resolution*, refers to the clarity and sharpness of an image and is measured in *dots per inch (dpi)*—the number of columns and rows of dots per inch. The higher the number of dots, the clearer and sharper the image.

One of the most popular types of scanners is the *flatbed scanner*, or *desktop scanner*, which works much like a photocopier—the image being scanned is placed on a glass surface, where it remains stationary, and the scanning beam moves across it. Three other types of scanners are *sheet-fed, handheld* and *drum*.

Joystick

Fig. 1.9. A joystick

A joystick is also a pointing device (See Figure 1.9). It consists of a small, vertical lever fitted on a base. This lever is used to move the cursor on the screen. The screen-cursor movement in any particular direction is measured by the distance that the stick is shifted or moved from its centre position. The amount of movement is measured by the potentiometers that are plugged at the base of the joystick. When the stick is released, a spring brings it back to its centre position. The joystick can move right or left, forward or backward.

Trackball

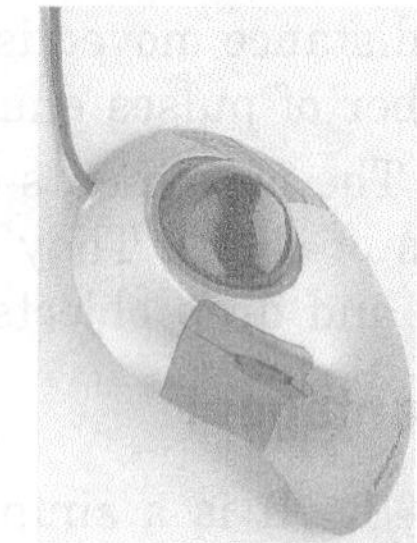

Fig. 1.10. Trackball

The *trackball* is a movable ball, mounted on top of a stationary device, that can be rotated using your fingers or palm (See Figure 1.10). In fact, the trackball looks like the mouse turned upside down. Instead of moving the mouse around on the desktop, you move the trackball with the tips of your fingers. A trackball is not as accurate as a mouse, and it requires more frequent cleaning, but it is a good alternative when desktop space is limited. Trackballs come in wired and wireless versions, and newer optical trackballs use laser technology.

Bar code Reader

Bar codes are the vertical, zebra-striped marks you see on most manufactured retail products–everything from candy to cosmetics to books.

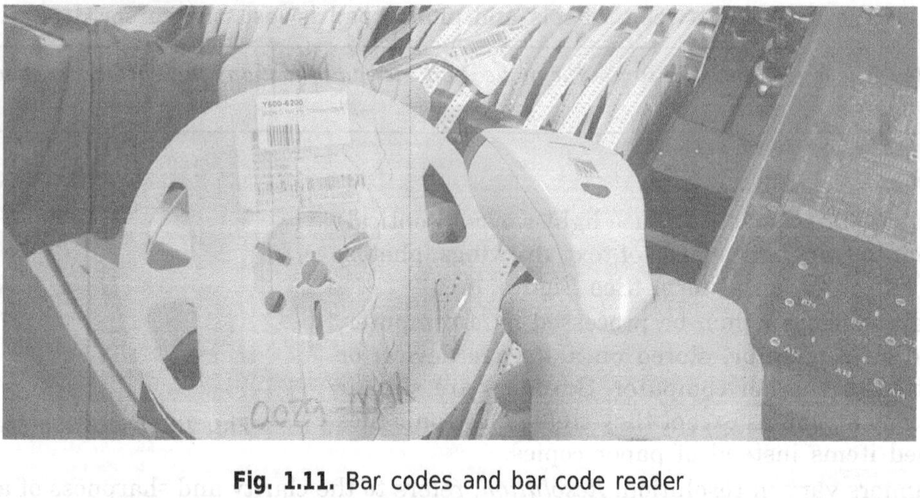

Fig. 1.11. Bar codes and bar code reader

Bar code readers are photoelectric (optical) scanners that translate the symbols in the bar code into digital code (See Figure 1.11). In this system, the price of a particular item is set within the store's computer. Once the bar code has been scanned, the corresponding price appears on the sales clerk's point-of-sale terminal and on your receipt. Records of sales from the bar code readers are input to the store's computer and used for accounting, restocking store inventory, and weeding out products that do not sell well.

- **Output Devices**

An output device is a device which accepts results from the computer and displays them to the user. The output device also converts the binary code obtained from the computer into human readable form. The principal kinds of output are hardcopy and softcopy. Table 1.2 illustrates the types of output devices.

Table 1.2. Types of Output Devices

Type	*Example*
Soft copy Devices	CRT display screens, Flat-panel display screen (*e.g.*, liquid crystal display)
Hard copy Devices	Impact printers: dot-matrix printer
	Non impact printers: laser, ink-jet, thermal
Other Devices	Sound output, Voice output, Video output

Let us discuss some of the output devices and their functions:

Monitors

These are also known as **Visual Display Unit (VDU)** or simply screens. They are output devices that show programming instructions and data as they are being input and information after it is processed. The size of a computer screen is measured diagonally from corner to corner in inches. For desktop microcomputers, the most common sizes are 13, 15, 17, 19, 21 and 24 inches; for laptop computers, 12.1, 13.3, 14.1 and 15.1 inches. Figure 1.12 illustrates some sizes of computer screen.

Monitor screen size	Viewable image area
15 inches	14 inches
17 inches	16 inches
21 inches	20 inches
24 inches	23 inches

Fig. 1.12. Illustrating sizes of computer screen

Type of Monitors

The two types of monitors are CRT and flat-panel.

CRT

A CRT, for cathode-ray tube, is a vacuum tube used as a display screen in a computer or video display terminal. These are the most common type of computer display, at least for desktop systems. Figure 1.13 illustrates CRT display.

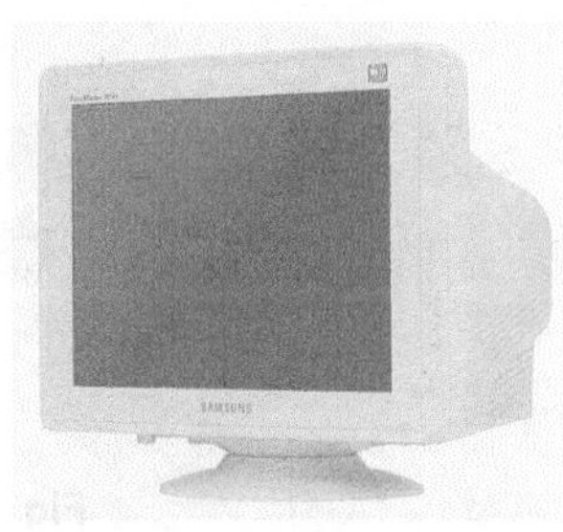

Fig. 1.13. CRT display

Flat-panel Displays

Compared to CRTs, flat-panel displays are much thinner, weigh less and consume less power. Thus, they are better for portable computers, although they are available for desktop computers as well. Figure 1.14 illustrates a flat-panel display.

Flat-panel displays are made up of two plates of glass separated by a layer of a liquid crystal display in which light is manipulated.

Fig. 1.14. A flat-panel display

Advantages:

1. Lower power consumption.
2. Cover less space than conventional monitors.
3. Reduction in cooling load (as these radiate less heat).
4. High performance monitors.
5. Flexibility of usage.
6. More viewing area.

Printers

A *printer* is an output device that prints characters, symbols, and perhaps graphics on paper or another hardcopy medium. The resolution, or quality of sharpness, of the printed image is indicated by *dpi* (*dots per inch*), which is a measure of the number of rows and columns of dots that are printed in a square inch. For microcomputer printers, the resolution is in the range of 60–1,500 dpi.

Printers can be separated into two categories, according to whether or not the image produced is formed by physical contact of the print mechanism with the paper. *Impact printers* have contact with paper; *nonimpact printers* do not.

Impact printers: An *impact printer* forms characters or images by striking a mechanism such as a print hammer or wheel against an inked ribbon, leaving an image on paper. A *dot-matrix printer* contains a print head of small pins that strike an inked ribbon against paper, to form characters or images (See Figure 1.15). Now-a-days impact printers are more commonly used with mainframes than with personal computers.

Note that dot matrix printers are the only desktop printers that can use multilayered forms to print "carbon copies."

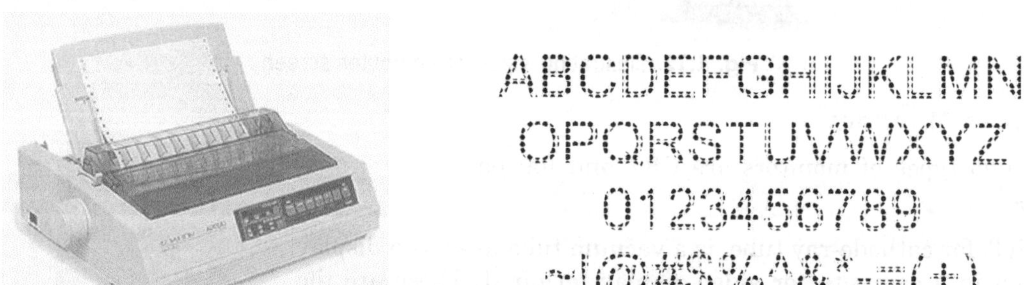

Fig. 1.15. A dot-matrix printer and its character pattern

Advantages:

1. They are inexpensive and are used widely.
2. Other language characters can also be printed.
3. The width of characters can be doubled to get bolder characters for headings.

Disadvantages:

1. The speed of these printers is slow.
2. The quality of the printing is not so good.

Nonimpact printers: Nonimpact printers are faster and quieter than impact printers because no print head strikes paper. *Nonimpact printers* form characters and images without direct physical contact between the printing mechanism and the paper. Two types of nonimpact printers often used with microcomputers are *laser printers* (See Figure 1.16) and *ink-jet printers* (also called desk-jet printers). A third kind, the *thermal printer*, is seen less frequently.

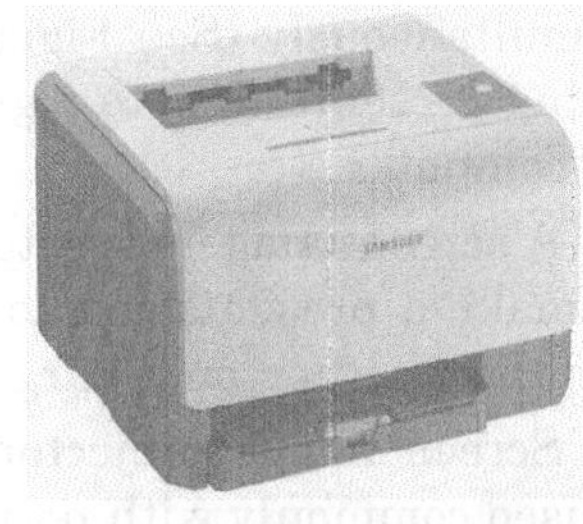

Fig. 1.16. A laser printer

Unlike a dot-matrix printer, a *laser printer* creates images and characters completely. As in a photocopying machine, these images are produced on a drum, treated with a magnetically charged ink-like toner (powder), and then transferred from drum to paper.

Advantages:

1. Very high speed.
2. Low noise level.
3. Low maintenance requirements.
4. Very high image quality.
5. Excellent graphics capabilities.
6. A variety of type sizes and styles.

Ink-jet printers spray on to the paper small, electrically charged droplets of ink from four nozzles through holes in a matrix at high speed. Figure 1.17 shows an ink-jet printer.

Fig. 1.17. An ink-jet printer

Speakers

Speakers are the devices that play sounds transmitted as electrical signals from the sound card (See Figure 1.18). Most PCs are now multimedia computers, capable of outputting not only text and graphics but also sound, voice, and video.

Sound output devices produce digitised sounds, ranging from beeps and chirps to music. To use sound output, you need appropriate software and a sound card. The sound card plugs into an expansion slot in your computer; on newer computers, it is integrated with the motherboard. Most computers have simple internal speakers. Many users hook up external speakers for high-quality sound. These are similar to the ones connected to a stereo but are smaller in size and have their own small amplifier.

Fig. 1.18. Speakers

Speakers receive the sound in form of constantly changing electric current from the sound card and then using a magnet convert it to sound format, which pushes the speaker core back and forth. Sound is created when pressure vibrations are generated.

LCD Projectors

Screen image projector is an output device used to project information from a computer on a large screen (such as a cloth, screen or wall) so that a group of people can view it simultaneously (See Figure 1.19). It is very useful for making presentations to a group of people with direct use of a computer.

Fig. 1.19. A screen image projector

A screen image projector can be plugged to a computer system directly, and a presenter can make a presentation to a group of people by projecting the presentation material one after the another on a large screen with the help of computer's keyboard or mouse.

Screen image projectors have become common presentation equipment today. These are used commonly with portable notebook computers to setup a modern presentation facility quickly at any place with great ease. Like monitors, screen image projectors provide a temporary softcopy output.

1.5 Memories

For a computer to work, it must contain memory where it can store data and programs until they are needed. So far we have described only the kinds of chips known as microprocessors. But other silicon chips called *memory chips* are attached to the motherboard. There are two types of storage, primary and secondary. Primary storage is temporary or working storage and is often called the *memory* or the *main memory;* secondary storage, usually called just *storage,* is relatively a permanent storage. *Memory* refers to storage media in the form of chips, and *storage* refers to media such as disks and tape. Computer memory exhibits perhaps the widest range of type, technology, organization, performance and cost of any feature of a computer.

Desirable Characteristics of Memory Unit

A memory unit consists of a large number of binary storage cells and information is stored semi-permanently in it during data processing. Besides the large number of storage cells, a memory has a few registers to facilitate storage and retrieval of information from memory and a set of control signals.

For a physical device to be usable as a binary storage cell in a memory unit, it must have the following desirable characteristics:

(*i*) *It must have two stable states.*

(*ii*) *Power consumption (if any) must be small.*

(*iii*) *It should be possible to switch between the two stable states an infinite number of times.*

(*iv*) *The information stored in a cell should not decay with the passage of time.*

(*v*) *The physical size should be small.*

(*vi*) *The cost of each cell must be low.*

(*vii*) *The time taken to read/write information from/to a group of cells must be small.*

Figure 1.20 illustrates the two types of memories.

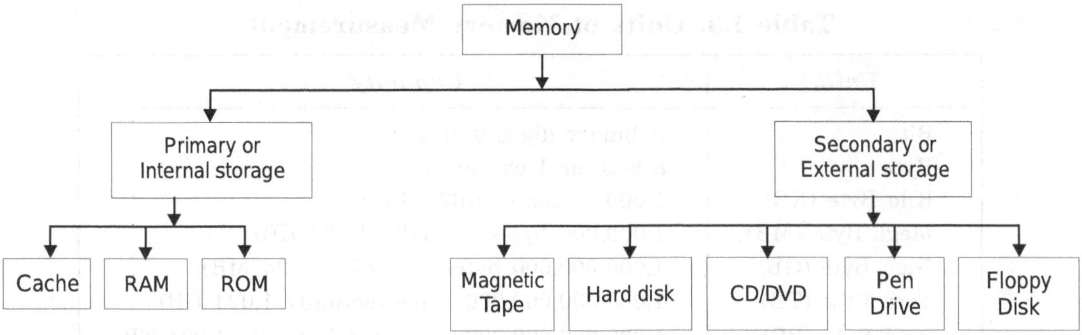

Fig. 1.20. Illustration of memory in a computer

Units

Memory capacity is denoted by **bits** and **bytes** and multiples thereof:

- **Bit:** In the binary system, each 0 or 1 is called a bit, which is short form of "binary digit".
- **Byte:** To represent letters, numbers, or special characters (such as * or?), bits are combined into groups. A group of 8 bits is called a byte, and a byte represents one character, digit or other value. The capacity of a computer's memory or of a floppy disk is expressed in number of bytes or multiples such as kilobytes and megabytes.
- **Kilo Byte:** A Kilo Byte (KB) is about 1,000 bytes. (Actually, it is precisely 1,024 bytes, but the figure is commonly rounded.) The Kilo Byte was a common unit of measure for memory or secondary storage capacity on older computers. 1 KB equals about one-half page of text.
- **Mega Byte:** A Mega Byte (MB) is about 1 million bytes (1,048,576 bytes). Measures of microcomputer primary-storage capacity these days are measured in Mega Bytes. 1 MB equals about 500 pages of text.
- **Giga Byte:** A Giga Byte (GB) is about 1 billion bytes (1,073,741,824 bytes). This measure was earlier used mainly with mainframe computers, but is typical of the secondary storage (hard disk) capacity of today's microcomputers. 1 GB equals about 500,000 pages of text.
- **Tera Byte:** A Tera Byte (TB) represents about 1 trillion bytes (1,009,511,627,776 bytes). 1 TB equals about 500,000,000 pages of text.
- **Peta Byte:** A Peta Byte (PB) represents about 1 quadrillion bytes (1,048,576 Giga Bytes).

Table 1.3 gives units of memory measurement:

Table 1.3. Units of Memory Measurement

Units	*Capacity*
Bit	A binary digit, 0 or 1
Byte	8 bits, or 1 character
Kilo Byte (KB)	1,000 (actually 1,024) bytes
Mega Byte (MB)	1,000,000 bytes (actually 1,024 KB)
Giga Byte (GB)	1,000,000,000 bytes (actually 1,024 MB)
Tera Byte (TB)	1,000,000,000,000 bytes (actually 1,024 GB)
Peta Byte (PB)	1,000,000,000,000,000 bytes (actually 1,024 TB)

Primary Memory

Primary memory is a semiconductor (MOS) memory used for storing program as well as data during program execution. It is directly accessible to the CPU. A given memory is divided into N words where each word is assigned an *address* in the memory. Each word consists of same number of bits and is known as it's **word length.**

The memory addresses are consecutive numbers, starting with the address 0, 1, 2, ... and running up to the largest address. Thus, at address 0, we have first word; at address 1, the second word; at address 2, the third word; and so on.

There is a difference between the *contents* of a memory address and the address itself. The size of primary or main memory is generally in the range of 64 MB to 2 GB. Thus, it is very large memory as compared to CPU registers but slower than CPU registers by a factor of 20 or so.

Cache

The CPU is an extremely fast device as compared to the main memory of the computer. The CPU on its own cannot work in isolation. In the system, it has to depend upon the main memory to supply the instructions and data as and when it needs. Because the CPU runs so much faster than the main system RAM, it ends up waiting for information, which is inefficient. To reduce this effect, we have **cache.**

Pronounced "cash", cache temporarily stores instructions and data that the processor is likely to use frequently (see Figure 1.21). Thus cache speeds up processing.

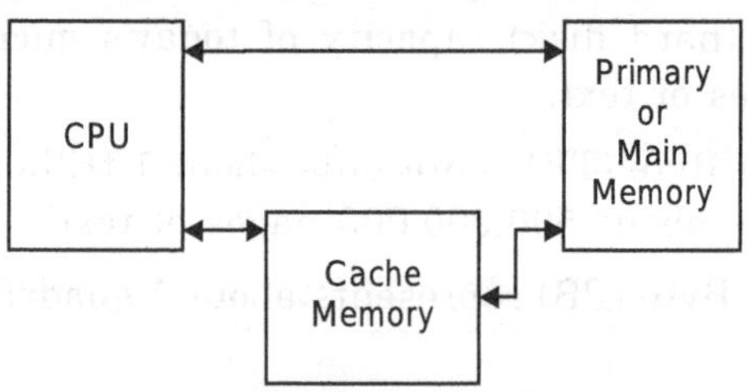

Fig. 1.21. Memory Organisation

There are two kinds of cache—Level 1 and Level 2:

- **Level 1 (L1) cache—part of the microprocessor chip**

  It is also called *internal cache* which is built into the processor chip. Ranging from 8 to 256 KB, its capacity is less than that of Level2 cache, although it operates faster.

In fact, when an instruction is fetched by the microprocessor from main memory, a block containing the required instruction is copied into the cache. The block may contain 128 or 256 or more instructions in all. Now the next instructions are fetched by the microprocessor from the cache which is a fast memory. When cache is exhausted, next block is brought into the cache and so on. The processing becomes even faster when the cache is built on the micro chip itself (see Figure 1.22).

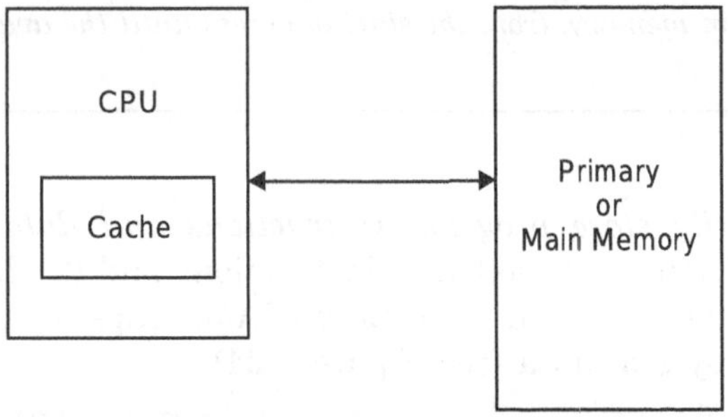

Fig. 1.22. Internal cache (Level1 or L1 cache)

If the CPU accesses the cache and the desired information (instruction or data) is found, we call it a **hit** and the information is transferred to the CPU. However, if the information is not found in the cache, it is known as a **miss.** In the case of a miss, the CPU accesses the main memory. The block containing the information needed by the CPU is also transferred to the cache. A block usually contains 4 to 16 words.

- **Level 2 (L2) cache—not part of the microprocessor chip**

  It is also called *external cache* which resides outside the processor chip and consists of SRAM (Static RAM) chips. Capacities range from 64 KB to 2 MB and is comparatively slower than L1. L2 cache is connected to the CPU by a *backside bus.* L2 cache is sometimes physically "on chip" (though running apart from CPU operations) and other times installed separately on the system's motherboard (in which case it is sometimes called L3 cache). On some powerful microprocessors (Intel Pentium III, IV), even L2 has been taken into the microprocessor.

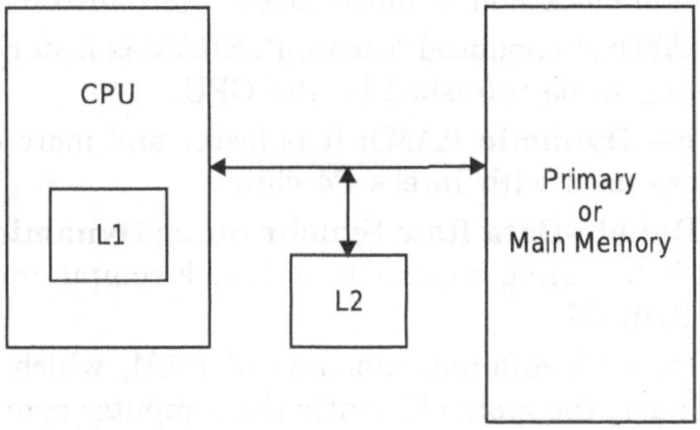

Fig. 1.23. External cache (Level2 or L2 cache)

L2 cache is generally quite a bit larger than L1 cache (most new systems have at least 512 KB of L2 cache) and is the most commonly cited of cache when measuring PC performance.

Cache is not upgradable; it is set by the type of the processor purchased with the system. Intel has produced another series of very power microprocessors called "Itanium". It has a Level 3 (L3) Cache of size 1.5 MB. It is being used for compute intensive applications, security applications, and dual processor systems. Intel Xeon 2.8 GHz also has L3 cache.

> ***Note:*** *The average access time of a cache memory is 0.25–25 ns. The amount of time taken to produce data required from memory, from the start of access until the availability of data, is called* ***Memory Access Time.***

RAM

RAM chips—to temporarily store program instructions and data: RAM (Random Access Memory) chips temporarily hold (1) software instructions and (2) data before and after it is processed by the CPU. You can think of memory (RAM) chips as a collection of boxes, each of which, holds a single byte of data (see Figure 1.24).

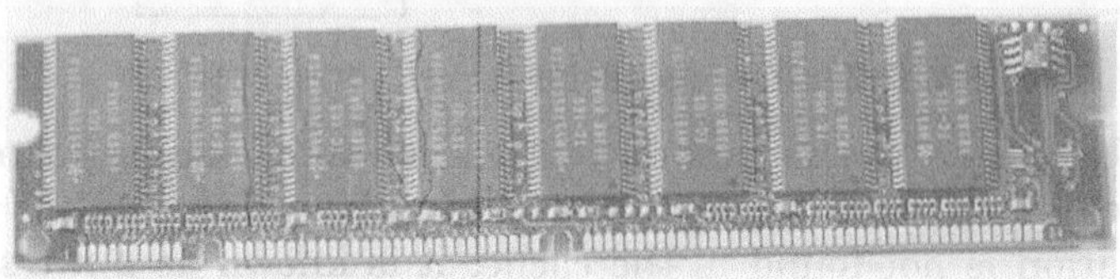

Fig. 1.24. Random Access Memory (RAM) chips

Because its contents are temporary, RAM is said to be *volatile—the contents are lost when the power goes off or is turned off.* This is why you should frequently—say, every 5 minutes, save your work to a secondary storage medium such as your hard disk, in case the electricity goes off while you are working.

RAM allows the stored data to be accessed in any order, that is, at *random.*

The various types of RAM chips used in PCs are given below:

1. DRAM (Dynamic RAM): Pronounced "dee-ram", DRAM must be constantly refreshed by the CPU or it will lose its contents.

2. SDRAM (Synchronous Dynamic RAM): It is used in most PCs today, which is synchronized by the system clock and is much faster than DRAM.

3. SRAM (Static RAM): Pronounced "ess-ram", SRAM is faster than DRAM and retains its contents without having to be refreshed by the CPU.

4. RDRAM (Rambus Dynamic RAM): It is faster and more expensive than SDRAM and is the type of memory used with Intel's P4 chip.

5. DDR–SDRAM (Double-Data Rate Synchronous Dynamic RAM): It is the newest type of RAM chip which is becoming popular in notebook computers and is considered to be the main competitor to RDRAM.

Microcomputers come with different amounts of RAM, which is usually measured in MB. The more RAM you have, the more efficiently the computer operates and the better your software performs. *Having enough RAM is a critical matter.*

If you are short on memory capacity, you can usually add more RAM chips by plugging RAM memory module into the motherboard. There are two types of such modules:

SIMM (Single Inline Memory Module)—has RAM chips on only one side.

DIMM (Dual Inline Memory Module)—has RAM chips on both sides.

For now, RAM is volatile, but researchers have recently developed new non-volatile forms of RAM that may soon be available.

ROM

ROM chips—to store fixed start-up instructions. Unlike RAM, to which data is constantly being added and removed, *ROM (read-only memory) cannot be written upon or erased by the computer user. ROM chips contain fixed start-up instructions.*

That is, ROM chips are loaded, at the factory, with programs containing special instructions for basic computer operations, such as those that start the computer (BIOS) or put characters on the screen. These chips are nonvolatile; their contents are not lost when power to the computer is turned off.

In computer terminology, *read* means to transfer data from an input source into the computer's memory or CPU. The opposite is *write*—to transfer data from the computer's CPU or memory to an output device. Thus, with a ROM chip, *read-only* means that the CPU can retrieve programs from the ROM chip but cannot modify or add to those programs.

The various types of ROM are given below:

1. PROM (Programmable Read Only Memory): It is a type of ROM which can be programmed even after its manufacture. The programming is possible with the help of special circuitry. Each bit in PROM can be individually programmed to a 1 or 0 by burning a fusible link. A link once fused is permanent and cannot be changed. The main disadvantage of a PROM is that it cannot be reprogrammed.

2. EPROM (Erasable Programmable Read Only Memory): This is a type of ROM better than PROM in the sense that it can be reprogrammed. To erase the data, EPROM is exposed to ultraviolet light. Once erased, EPROM can be reprogrammed with the help of electrical impulses. An electronic device called PROM programmer is needed for programming of EPROM. The EPROM requires 10 to 30 minutes for erasing.

3. EEPROM (Electrically Erasable Programmable Read Only Memory): It is also called Electrically Alterable ROM (EAROM). It can be repeatedly erased and programmed by electrical signals. These days it is being used as a back up to RAM memory. In case there is a power failure, the contents of RAM are lost. When power is returned, the contents of EEPROM are copied back into the RAM and the computer starts normal working as if nothing had taken place. The necessary circuitary is integrated in the computer itself so that the EEPROM does not have to be taken out from its socket for programming purpose. These days newer devices are coming with RAM and EEPROM memory in a single integrated circuit.

1.6 Secondary Storage Devices

Let us discuss more traditional forms of *secondary storage hardware*, devices that permanently hold data and information as well as programs.

Hard Disks

Hard disks are thin but rigid metal, glass or ceramic platters covered with a substance that allows data to be held in the form of magnetised spots. Most hard disk drives have at least two platters; the greater the number of platters, the larger the capacity of the drive. The platters in the drive are separated by spaces and are clamped to a rotating spindle that turns all the platters in unison. Hard disks are tightly scaled within an enclosed hard disk drive unit to prevent any foreign matter from getting inside. Data may be recorded on both sides of the disk platters (See Figure 1.25). In a microcomputer, the hard disk is enclosed within the system unit. Unlike a floppy disk, it is not accessible.

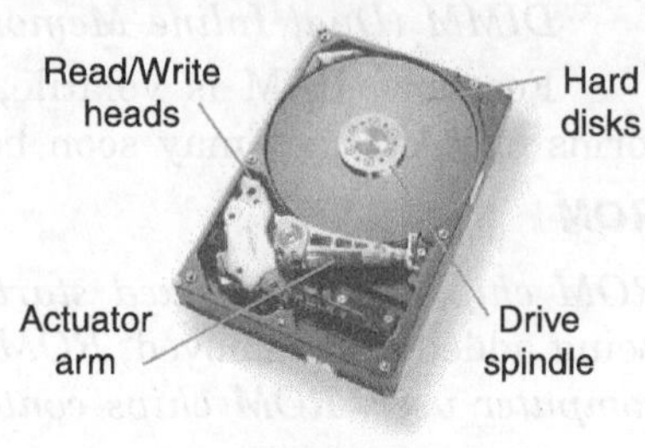

Fig. 1.25. Hard disk

Optical Disks

Everyone who has ever played an audio CD is familiar with optical disks. An *optical disk is a removable disk, usually 4.75 inches in diameter and less than one-twentieth of an inch thick, on which data is written and read through the use of laser beams.* An audio CD holds upto 74 minutes of high-fidelity stereo sound. Some optical disks are used strictly for digital data storage, but many are used to distribute multimedia programs that combine text, visuals and sound.

The storage density of optical disks is enormous, the storage cost is extremely low and the access time is relatively fast. An optical disk can hold over 4.7 gigabytes of data, the equivalent of 1 million typewritten pages.

Nearly every PC marketed today contains a CD or DVD drive, which can also read audio CDs. These, along with their recordable and rewritable variations, are the two principal types of optical-disk technology used with computers. Figure 1.26 shows how to use a CD/DVD disk.

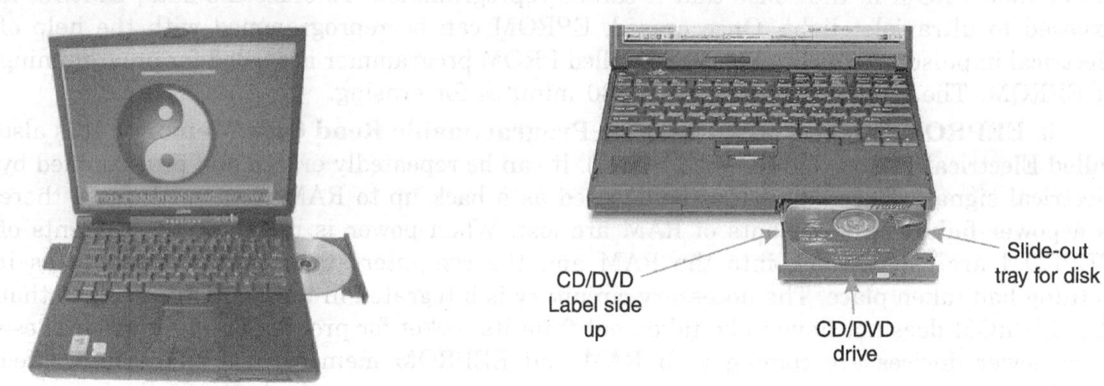

Fig. 1.26. How to use a CD/DVD disk

The types of optical disks are given below :

(*i*) CD-ROM — Compact Disk Read Only Memory

(*ii*) CD-R (Compact Disk Recordable)

(*iii*) CD-RW (Compact Disk Rewritable)

(*iv*) DVD-ROM (Digital Versatile or Digital Video Disk, with Read Only Memory)

(*i*) **CD-ROM—for reading only.** For PC users, the best known type of optical disk is the CD-ROM. *CD-ROM (Compact Disk Read Only Memory) is an optical-disk format that is used to hold prerecorded text, graphics and sound.*

(*ii*) **CD-R—for recording on once.** *CD-R (Compact Disk Recordable) disks can be written to only once but can be read many times.* You can view the disk on any personal computer with a CD-ROM drive and the right software. Many new computers come equipped with CD-R drives.

(*iii*) **CD-RW—for rewriting many times.** *A CD-RW (Compact Disk Rewritable) disk, also known as an erasable optical disk, allows users to record and erase data, so the disk can be used over and over again.* CD-RW drives are becoming more common on microcomputers. CD-RW disks are useful for archiving and backing up large amounts of data or work in multimedia production or desktop publishing. CD-RW disks cannot be read by CD-ROM drives. CD-RW disks have a capacity of 650–700 megabytes.

(*iv*) **DVD-ROM—the versatile video disk.** *A DVD-ROM (Digital Versatile Disk or Digital Video Disk, with Read Only Memory) is a CD-style disk with extremely high capacity, able to store 4.7 or more gigabytes.*

Many new computer systems now come with a DVD drive as standard equipment. A great advantage is that these drives can also take standard CD-ROM disks, so now you can watch DVD movies and play CD-ROMs using just one drive. DVDs have enormous potential to replace CDs for archival storage, mass distribution of software, and entertainment.

Like CDs, DVDs have their recordable and rewritable variants. *DVD-R (DVD-Recordable) disks allow one-time recording by the user*. Three types of reusable disks are DVD-RW (DVD-Rewritable), DVD-RAM (DVD-Random Access Memory), and DVD + RW (DVD + Rewritable), all of which can be recorded on and erased many times. DVD-R disks have a capacity of 4.7 (single-sided) – 9.6 (double-sided) Giga Bytes.

Not all the optical-disk drives and different types of optical media (read-only, rewritable, and so on) are mutually compatible. You should check product information before buying to make sure you get what you require.

Magnetic Tape

Magnetic tape is a secondary storage device which can hold large volumes of data on it. The tape is a sequential access media and data on it can be accessed sequentially. Large files are stored on them. Due to their sequential access nature, they are not suitable for storage of data that are accessed randomly.

Similar to the tape used on an audio tape recorder (but of higher density), *magnetic tape* is thin plastic tape coated with a substance that can be magnetised. Data is represented by magnetised spots (representing 1s) or non-magnetised spots (representing 0s). Today, "mag tape" is used mainly for backup and archiving—that is, for maintaining historical records—where there is no need for quick access.

On large computers, tapes are used on magnetic-tape units or reels and in special cartridges. These tapes store up to 160 gigabytes each. On microcomputers, tape is used in the form of *tape cartridges*, modules resembling audio cassettes that contain tape in rectangular, plastic housings (See Figure 1.27). An internal or external tape drive is required to use tape media.

Fig. 1.27. Magnetic tape cartridge and tape

Flash Drive (Pen Drive)

Flash drive is a compact device of the size of a pen, comes in various shapes and stylish designs (such as pen shape, wallet shape etc.), and may have different added features (such as with a camera, with a built-in MP3/WMA/FM Radio play back for music on the go, etc.). It enables easy transport of data from one computer to another.

Flash is a **'solid state'** memory *i.e.,* it has no moving parts unlike magnetic storage devices, nor does it make use of lasers—unlike optical drives.

Instead, it works in a similar way to RAM. The key difference is that data is retained in Flash memory even when the power is switched off.

Flash drive is a plug-and-play device that simply plugs into a USB (Universal Serial Bus) port of a computer. The computer detects it automatically as removable drive. A flash drive does not require any battery, cable, or software, and is compatible with most PCs, desktop, and laptop computers with USB port. All these features make it ideal external data storage for mobile people to carry or transfer data from one computer to another. It has the data retention capability of more than 10 years.

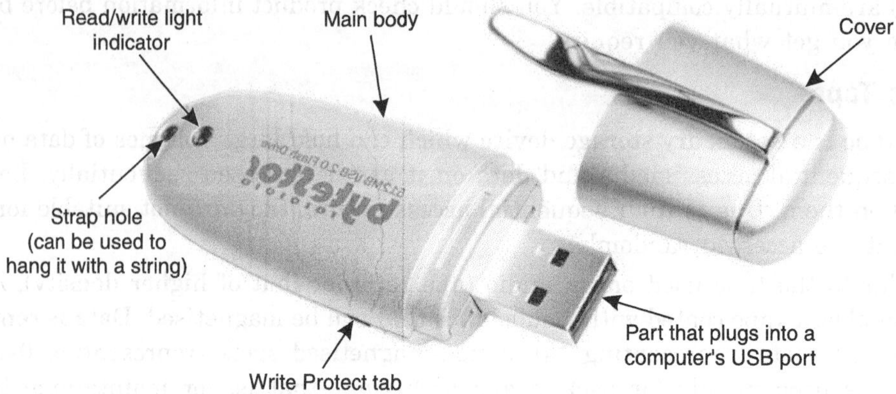

Fig. 1.28. A flash drive (pen drive)

Available storage capacities are 8MB, 16MB, 64MB, 128MB, 256MB, 512MB, 1GB, 2GB, 4GB, and 8GB. A pen drive of 16MB capacity has 5600 times more storage capacity than a 1.44MB floppy disk. These are very inexpense, costing from ₹ 600 or above.

Figure 1.28 shows a flash drive. It has a main body and usually a port connector cover. The cover is removed or port connector is pushed out when the drive is to be plugged into the USB port of a computer. The main body usually has a write protect tab, a read/write LED

(Light Emitting Diode) indicator, and a strap hole. Some manufacturers also provide software to be used with the drive.

> ***Note:*** *The Thumb drives/Pen drives, and cell phones of today use flash memories.*

Floppy Diskette

A floppy disk is a very popular direct access secondary storage medium for micro and mini computers. A floppy disk, often called a diskette or simply a disk, is a removable flat piece of mylar plastic packaged in a 3.5-inch plastic case. Data and programs are stored on the disk's coating by means of magnetised spots. The plastic case protects the mylar disk from being touched by human hands.

Floppy disks are inserted into a floppy-disk drive, a device that holds, spins, reads data from, and writes data to a floppy disk. *Read* means taking data from secondary storage (converted to electronic signals) to the computer's memory (RAM). *Write* means copying the electronic information processed by the computer to secondary storage.

On the diskette, data is recorded in concentric circles called **tracks.** On a formatted disk each track is divided into sectors, invisible wedge-shaped sections used for storage and reference purpose. The read/write head is used to transfer data between the computer and the disk. Figure 1.29 illustrates a 3½ inch floppy disk.

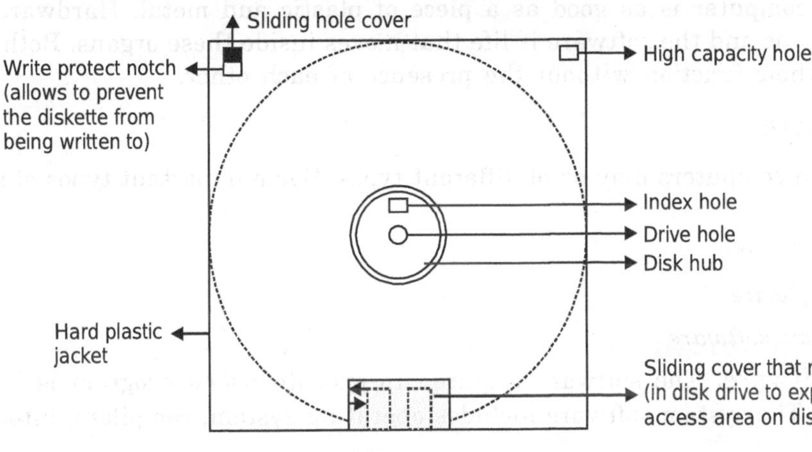

Fig. 1.29. 3½ inch floppy disk

The Floppy Drive is of a moving head variety and therefore, the floppy can be removed and replaced by another. The head actually contacts the surface during reading/writing, though in other times it is lifted up from the surface. The hole at the centre is to allow a spindle to lock the floppy so that it can rotate. The Index hole is used to recognise the starting sector of any track. The purpose of write permit notch is to protect valuable information recorded on the floppy from accidental damage. If this notch is covered, writing is not allowed on the floppy, only reading is possible. If the notch is not covered reading as well as writing is possible.

Floppies offer a number of advantages. They are exchangeable. The storage capacity is high as compared to its size and weight. These are portable. Floppies are inexpensive also as compared to hard disks. The most common uses of floppy disks are:

(*i*) Moving files between computers that are not connected through communication channel.

(*ii*) Loading new programs on to a system.

(*iii*) Backing up data or programs, the primary copy of which is stored on hard disk.

Useful Tip

Do not remove the disk when the access light is on or while working on a file open from that disk. Save and close the file before removing the disk.

1.7 Computer Software and Hardware

Software

Software is an internal set of programs that is designed to perform a well defined function. The software is created by grouping various related programs. A program is a sequence of instructions written to solve a particular problem. The programs are created in computer programming languages. These software are created by programmers and distributed by using disks or the Internet.

Software is the deriving force behind the working of computer. Without the presence of software, the computer is as good as a piece of plastic and metal. Hardware can be considered as organs and the software is life that moves inside these organs. Both of them cannot perform their function without the presence of each other.

Types of Software

Softwares used on computers may be of different types. Some important types of software are :

1. *System software*
2. *Utility software*
3. *Application software*

System Software. The software required to execute user's program is known as system software. The system software includes operating system, compilers, interpreters, assembler etc.

Utility Software. The softwares which are used for developing, writing, debugging and documenting programs are known as utility software. These help the users in the preparation of programs. There are two types of utilities :

- File management utilities
- Program development utilities.

The file management utilities are a part of operating system and help the user in copying, erasing (deleting), renaming and printing the files.

The program development utilities are used for writing and testing of programs. These include editor, compiler, assembler, linker, loader, debugger etc. A simple text editor is a part of operating system but an elaborate editor is stored separately. The compilers are stored separately. All the softwares are controlled by the operating system.

Application Software. A computer can perform different functions by changing programs. Many tasks that you work on with a computer are known as applications and the programs you use to perform them are known as *application software* or *application programs.* For example, an application is writing a letter, preparing a budget or creating a mailing list. The application programs you use for these applications are word processors, spreadsheets and database managers. The development and wide distribution of these inexpensive and useful application programs is what has made the computer an extremely useful tool for everyone throughout the world. The application program you use depends on the task you want to perform. New PCs are usually equipped not only with *system software* but also with some *application software.*

There are two main categories of application software: Prewritten and Customised Application Software.

> ***Note : Device drivers** are specialized software programs that allow input and output devices to communicate with the rest of the computer system. Newer operating systems recognize much new hardware on their own and automatically install the driver. If your OS does not recognize your new hardware, it will display a message and ask you to install the driver from the CD or floppy that came with your hardware.*

Hardware

The physical components of the computer that can be seen and touched are called as hardware. The term hardware is used to refer to all the components inside or outside the computer. In addition to this, components used to interconnect two or more components, for example, wires are also regarded as hardware. We have several hardware devices that are used at various phases of data processing cycle. The hardware that are used to supply input to computer are called as *input devices.* The hardware that are used to process the data, are called as *processing devices* and the devices that are used to present output of computer are called as *output devices.* Each of these categories has a broad variety of devices of various brands and qualities.

Review Questions and Exercises

1. Define a computer system.
2. Discuss the block diagram of a computer system and its working.
3. Discuss the peripherals of a computer system.
4. Write a short note on computer memories.
5. What are RAM and ROM?
6. What is the difference between RAM and ROM?
7. Discuss the commonly used input and output devices and their functions.
8. Write a short note on the following:

   (*i*) Keyboard (*ii*) Mouse
   (*iii*) Scanner (*iv*) Joystick
   (*v*) Trackball (*vi*) Bar Code Reader

9. Write a short note on the following:
   (*i*) Monitors (*ii*) Printers
   (*iii*) Speakers (*iv*) LCD projectors

10. What is the difference between impact and nonimpact printers?

11. Discuss the secondary storage devices.

12. Explain the various types of optical disks.

13. How is magnetic tape used?

14. Write a short note on the following:
   (*i*) CD (*ii*) DVD
   (*iii*) Magnetic Tape (*iv*) Pen drive
   (*v*) Floppy diskette

15. Write a short note on computer software and hardware.

❑❑❑

CHAPTER 2

Working Knowledge of Computer System

2.1 Introduction

We know that a computer system consists of hardware and software. Software, or programs, are instructions that tell the computer how to perform a task. System software enables the application software to interact with the computer and helps the computer manage its internal and external resources. Applications software is software that has been developed to solve a particular problem for users.

In this chapter, we will discuss about operating system and GUI based operating system Windows XP. A brief introduction to application software packages, MS-Word, PowerPoint, MS-Excel will be provided. The Internet is a worldwide computer network that connects hundreds of thousands of smaller networks. The evolution of Internet and its applications and services will also be covered.

2.2 Introduction to the Operating System

The Operating System (OS), also called the software platform, consists of the low-level, master system of programs that manage the basic operations of the computer. These programs provide resource management services of many kinds. In particular, they handle the control and use of hardware resources, including disk space, memory, CPU time allocation, and peripheral devices. Every general-purpose computer must have an operating system to run other programs. The operating system allows you to concentrate on your own tasks or applications rather than on the complexities of managing the computer. Each application program is written to run on top of a particular operating system.

Different sizes and makes of computers have their own operating systems. In general, an operating system written for one kind of hardware will not be able to run on another kind of machine. In other words, *different operating systems are mutually compatible.*

The two primary objectives of an operating system are :

1. Making a computer system easy to use.
2. Managing the resources of a computer system.

2.2.1 Need for Operating System

A computer must have, in addition to the hardware and high level language translators, many other routines which help a user to effectively use the system. An *operating system* provides these routines. The user of a computer does not only interact with the physical hardware or bare machine. He/she interacts with a bare machine + compilers + an operating system as shown in Figure 2.1.

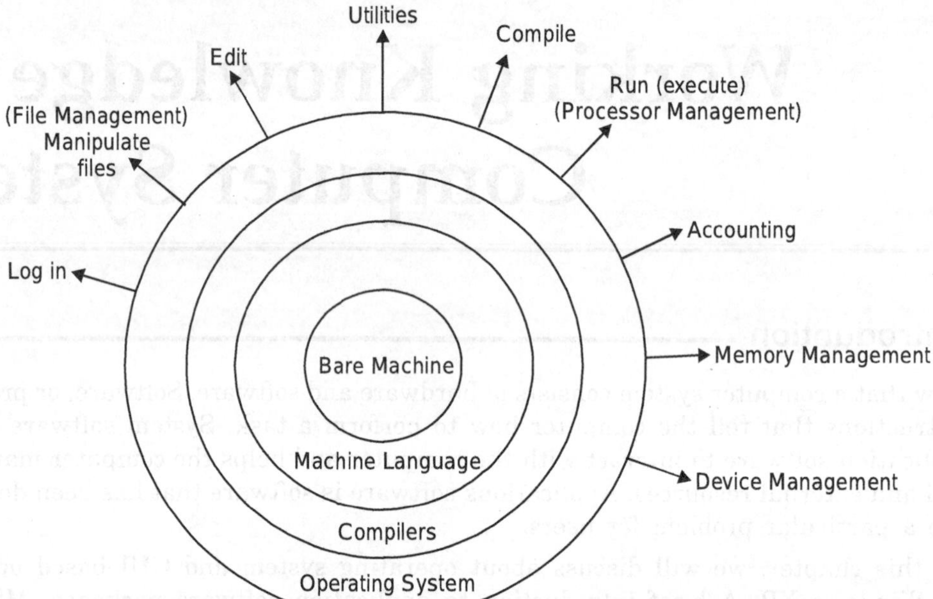

Fig. 2.1. Illustration of user's virtual (or non-existent) machine

When we switch on the computer, operating system or a part of it is loaded into the main memory of the computer system. Part of the operating system is stored in secondary memory on a floppy disk, hard disk, or magnetic tape, while part of it is stored permanently in ROM (Read Only Memory). When the computer is first started, it automatically starts to execute a program stored in the operating system portion of ROM. This program reads part of the operating system into RAM (Random Access Memory), and the computer begins to execute this part of the system. Now the computer system is controlled by the operating system program.

2.2.2 Functions of an Operating System

The operating systems perform the following functions :

1. Booting

(*i*) Uses diagnostic routines to test system for equipment failure.

(*ii*) Copies BIOS (Basic Input Output System) programs from ROM chips to main memory.

(*iii*) Loads operating system into computer's main memory.

2. Formatting

Formats (initializes) diskettes so they can store data and programs.

3. Managing Computer Resources

(*i*) Via the supervisor, *i.e.,* O.S., manages the CPU and directs other (nonresident) programs to perform tasks to support application programs.

(*ii*) Keeps track of locations in main memory where programs and data are stored (memory management).

(*iii*) Moves data and programs back and forth between main memory and secondary storage (swapping) via partitioning, using foreground and background areas, and using buffers and queues.

4. Managing Files

(*i*) Copies files/programs from one disk to another.

(*ii*) Backsup files/programs.

(*iii*) Erases (deletes) files/programs.

(*iv*) Renames files.

5. Managing Tasks

May be able to perform multitasking, multiprogramming, time-sharing or multiprocessing. Table 2.1 gives the comparison of task management. A *task* is an operation such as storing, printing, or calculating.

Table 2.1. Comparison of Task Management

Way of managing task	*Definition : Processing of Two or More Programs ...*	*Number of Users*	*Number of Processors*	*Order of Processing*
Multitasking	by one user concurrently on one processor	One	One	Concurrently
Multiprogramming	by multiple users concurrently on one processor	Multiple	One	Concurrently
Time sharing	by multiple users in round-robin fashion on one processor	Multiple	One	Round robin
Multiprocessing	by one or more users simultaneously on two or more processors	One or more	Two or more	Simultaneously

6. Managing Security

Controls computer access via user names and passwords.

2.2.3 Operating System as a Resource Manager

The operating system consists of programs that manage the various resources of the computer system, that is, Processor, Memory, File and Device. Since all the resource usage is chargeable, therefore all these must be managed efficiently and reliably.

As a resource manager, the operating system must perform the following functions for each resource :

(*i*) Keep track of the status of the resource.

(*ii*) Make a decision about the job and time for resource utilization, according to some policy.

(*iii*) Allocate the resource to the job as decided in (*ii*) above.

(*iv*) Make the resource free after the resource has been used for the allocated time.

Processor Management Functions

(*i*) Keep track of the processor by recording whether the processor is in use or not. If busy then who is using it.

(*ii*) Decide which job should use the processor and the time for it.

(*iii*) Allocate the processor to the job as decided in (*ii*) above.

(*iv*) Deallocate the processor (make it free) after the allowed time.

Memory Management Functions

(*i*) Keep track of the memory by recording what parts of the memory are used by which programs and the free portion of the memory.

(*ii*) Decide which job should get the memory and how much of it, in the case of multiprogramming.

(*iii*) Allocate the memory space to a job as decided in (*ii*) above.

(*iv*) Make the memory free, after it has been used, for the other users.

File Management Functions (Program and Data Management Functions)

(*i*) Keep track of files, that is, the files in use and the jobs using these and maintenance of directory of their locations.

(*ii*) Decide which job should use the file and for what purpose, that is, read, write or execute.

(*iii*) Allocate the file for use as decided in (*ii*) above.

(*iv*) Deallocate the file after its use, that is, close the file.

Device Management Functions

(*i*) Keep track of the status of the I/O devices and channels, that is, which devices and channels are in use and the jobs using them.

(*ii*) Decide which job should use which device and for how much duration.

(*iii*) Allocate the device to the job as decided in (*ii*) above.

(*iv*) Deallocate the device after it has been used.

2.2.4 Types of Operating System

The various types of operating systems are given below :

1. Interactive (GUI based)

An interactive operating system permits users to interact directly with a computer from a terminal. In effect, the user can interrupt a low priority batch job and cause the computer to perform his/her high priority work. Only multiprogramming and Real time systems can be interactive operating systems. The real time files must be updated immediately when the real world events occur. An **interrupt** (suspension of the program execution caused by an event external to the program) is handled and program execution is resumed later on. The interrupts may be caused by events like data input from an interactive terminal.

Initially, the user interface for nearly all the operating systems was command based, in which the user was required to memorize a predefined set of commands to carry out the desired task(s). But, this mode of communication was hard to adopt, especially for the non-programmer class of users, who found it extremely difficult and time-taking to go through such commands even when they need to use the computer restrictedly. Therein, to cope with their requirements, another, more user-friendly, interface was invented which is referred to as Graphical User Interface (GUI). With GUI, instead of memorizing commands to each stage, a user could select a command from a set of available commands according to his/her need.

Microsoft Windows is one such operating system which best fits the domain of GUI.

2. Time Sharing

Multiprogramming means the interleaved execution of two or more different and independent programs by the same computer. Multiprogramming operating system improved CPU utilization. But, sometimes a small job has to wait for a long time depending upon the execution time of other jobs. To avoid this problem, time sharing operating system were developed.

A time sharing operating system allow many users to share the computer on a time basis. Many programs reside in main memory. The CPU provides a fixed *time slice, time slot* or *quantum* in the range of 10 to 100 milliseconds to each job. When the quantum is over or the job needs to perform an Input/Output operation or it is finished, the operating system switches to the next job in the queue. Figure 2.2 illustrates the process state in a time-sharing system :

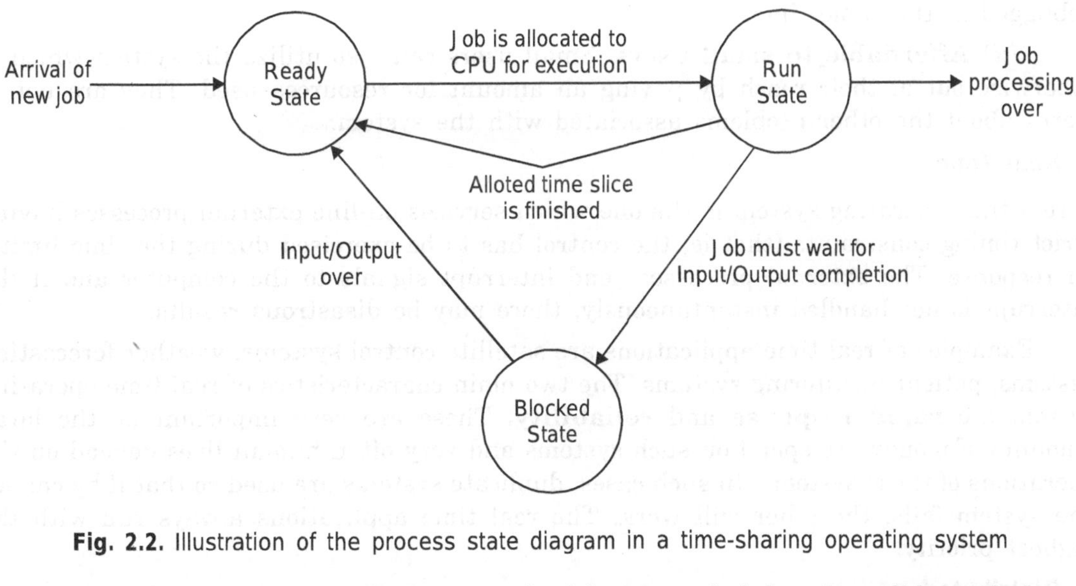

Fig. 2.2. Illustration of the process state diagram in a time-sharing operating system

As the CPU switches rapidly between the jobs, users feel that they all have their own computer, but really a single computer is shared by them.

Requirements of Time-sharing Operating Systems

The following are the additional requirements of time sharing systems :

(*i*) A large number of terminals for multiple users to use the system in interactive mode.

(*ii*) Large memory to support multiprogramming.

(*iii*) Memory protection mechanism so that different jobs may run without any interaction in the area allocated to other jobs in a multiprogramming environment.

(*iv*) Job status preservation mechanism for re-allocation of CPU to it next time.

(*v*) The CPU scheduling algorithm for allocation of CPU for user processes in a circular way.

(*vi*) CPU interrupt signal via alarm clock after each time slice.

Advantages of Time-sharing Operating Systems

The design of time-sharing operating systems is complex but there are several advantages also. These are given below :

(*i*) **Reduces CPU idle time.** The users work at a very slow speed in comparison to the processing speed of a computer *e.g.*, data entry during interactive usage of a system or thinking time is quite substantial. The time sharing system in the mean time assigns the CPU to other processes in the ready state and reduces the CPU idle time. The more busy the CPU, the maximum the throughput (the number of programs run per unit time).

(*ii*) **Quick response time.** A suitable CPU scheduling algorithm used by the time sharing operating systems helps in providing quick response time to all the users. It is quite useful in interactive programming and debugging which in turn effects the programmer's efficiency. Different problems or even parts of one problem can be written, tested and debugged at the same time.

(*iii*) **Affordable to small users.** Small users can also utilize the system which is otherwise out of their reach by paying an amount for resources used. They are not to worry about the other problems associated with the system.

3. Real Time

A real time operating system is the one which services on-line external processes having strict timing constraints (that is, the control has to be exercised during the time limits) on response. The external processes send interrupt signals to the computer and if the interrupt is not handled instantaneously, there may be disastrous results.

Examples of real time applications are satellite control systems, weather forecasting systems, patient monitoring systems. The two main characteristics of real time operating system are **rapid response** and **reliability.** These are very important as the large amounts of money are spend on such systems and very often human lives depend on the operations of these systems. In such cases, duplicate systems are used so that if by chance one system fails, the other will work. The real time applications always run with the highest priority.

4. Distributed

A distributed operating system handles many independent computer systems (which may be geographically at far distance) connected by a communication network, and in which messages, processing task, data, programs etc. are transmitted between cooperating computer systems. The individual computers are known as **nodes** in a distributed computing system.

The distributed operating systems are much more complex and difficult to write. The complexity is due to the following reasons :

(*i*) Effective use and management of very large number of distributive resources is required.

(*ii*) Smooth communication between various nodes, handling of loss of messages during transmission and prevention of overloading of network are required.

(*iii*) Security and privacy of resources is required.

The distributed operating systems are getting very popular. The main advantages are :

(*i*) **Inherently distributed applications.** Many applications can be implemented using a distributed computing system. For example, electronic mail facility, a computerized banking system, a computerized airline reservation system. The user can send mail, deposit/withdraw money, get reservation from any part of the world.

(*ii*) **Sharing of information.** The information can be easily shared by the users who are geographically far apart from one another, by exchanging the files or messages by electronic mail.

(*iii*) **Sharing of resources.** Not only information but the hardware (hard disks, printers and plotters), as well as software (software libraries and databases) resources can also be shared.

(*iv*) **Shorter response time.** In a distributed computing system the multiple processors can share the workload and give better throughput. Even a single complex problem can be run parallely.

(*v*) **More reliable.** A reliable system avoids loss of information in case any component fails. If any of the processors fails the distributed operating system assigns its workload to other processors and in case of failure of any storage device, the information can be used from the other storage device.

(*vi*) **Flexibility.** Using distributed computing system a user can utilize any one of the computers which is most suitable for his/her job, which is not possible in a centralized system. Even the power and functionality can be extended by simply adding the hardware and software resources (if required).

2.3 Working Knowledge of GUI based Operating System

Graphical User Interfaces (GUI-pronounced "goo-ee") were developed at Xerox PARC in the 70s and then first introduced in 1980 on a computer called the Xerox Star. These days we have many competing GUI interfaces available in the marketplace but the largest seller is *Microsoft's Windows.* All GUIs have a number of features in common :

- They display overlapping windows on the monitor (screen). Each window can contain an application program or a document. This allows a user to quickly switch back and forth between tasks.
- These are operated by pointing and clicking on a digital *"desktop"*. You execute commands by pointing to a command on the screen so you do not have to remember how to execute it.

- They have a *WYSIWYG* (What You See Is What You Get) display that shows a document on the screen much like it will look when it is printed (hard copy is taken out).
- Commands are consistent from program to program. For example, the way you delete (erase) something from a document is always the same whether it is a word, drawing, or database record that's being deleted. This makes it easier to learn new software because many of your existing skills are transferable.

From the fastest super computer and largest mainframe, right down to the smallest embedded microprocessor in your vehicle or watch, every computer uses an operating system. Over the years, a variety of operating systems have been developed and many remain in use. When the IBM (International Business Machines) PC set the standard for microcomputers, DOS (Disk Operating System) became the most widely used microcomputer operating system. Today, DOS has been replaced on many computers by more powerful operating systems such as Windows, UNIX, Windows NT, and OS/2. These more powerful operating systems make it possible to run tasks on less expensive PCs that were once performed on expensive mainframe and minicomputers. The most common operating system running on over 90 percent of all new computers sold is Windows. It has many versions, for example Windows XP, Windows Vista, Windows 7 etc.

User Interface : The first thing you look at when you call up any application software on the screen is the *user interface—the user-controllable display screen that allows you to communicate, or interact, with the computer.*

The three types of user interface are :

Command-driven

Menu-driven

Graphical (GUI)

The GUI (Graphical User Interface) is now most common. You must remember that *without user interfaces, no one could operate a computer system.*

Using the Keyboard

You can interact with the display screen using the keys on your keyboard. While using the keyboard you can use the following :

(*i*) The current menu box can be activated by tapping the ALT key.

(*ii*) For choosing an option from the menu option in the active menu, the underlined letter can be entered.

(*iii*) Use arrow keys to highlight menu options.

(*iv*) Use short cut keys (one key or key combination) to give commands within a specific application without activating a menu. For example, press the *Alt* and *F4* keys together to close an application)

Using the Mouse

You use your mouse more frequently. The mouse allows you to direct an on-screen pointer to perform any number of activities. *The pointer usually appears as an arrow, although it changes shape depending on the application.* The mouse is used to move the pointer to a particular place on the display screen or to point to little symbols, or icons. You can activate the function corresponding to the symbol by pressing ("clicking") buttons on the mouse.

Use your thumb and outside two fingers to move the mouse on your desk or mouse pad. Use your first two fingers to press the mouse buttons.

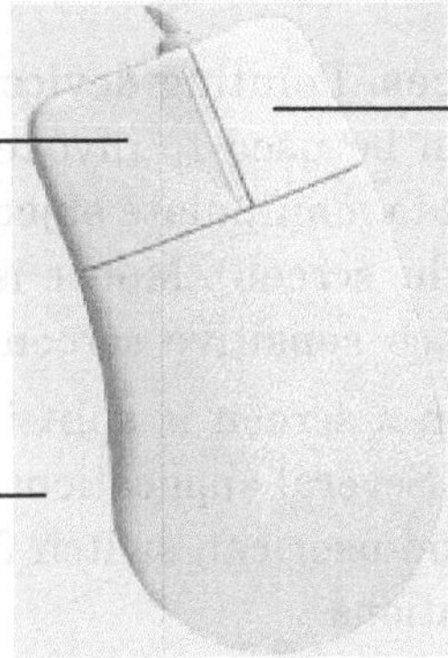

Fig. 2.3. Using the Mouse

Using the mouse, you can pick up and slide ("drag") an image from one side of the screen to the other side or change its size.

Table 2.2. Terms Associated with Mouse

S. No.	*Term*	*Action*	*Purpose*
1.	**Point** 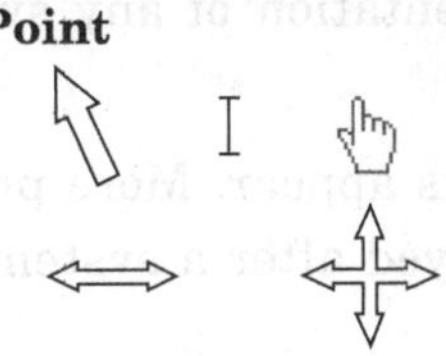	Move mouse across desk to guide pointer to desired spot on screen. The pointer assumes different shapes, such as arrow, hand, or I-beam, depending on the task you perform.	To execute commands, move objects, insert data, or similar actions on screen
2.	**Click** 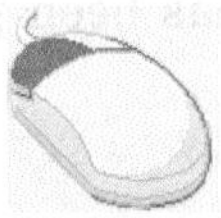	Press and quickly release left mouse button.	To select an item on the screen
3.	**Double-click** 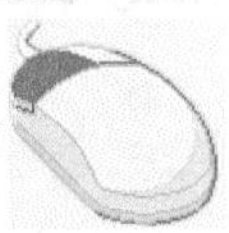	Quickly press and release left mouse button twice.	To open a document or start a program
4.	**Drag and drop** 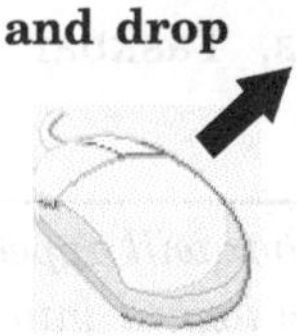	Position pointer over item on screen, press and hold down left mouse button while moving pointer to location in which you want to place item, then release.	To move an item on the screen
5.	**Right-click** 	Press and release right mouse button.	To display a shortcut list of commands, such as a popup menu of options

In this section, we are going to discuss a GUI based operating system—Windows XP.

Before switching to Windows XP, we briefly formalize some common terms associated with GUI :

- **Pointing devices.** Pointing devices allow users to point at different parts of a screen. They can be used to invoke a command from a list of commands. They can also be used to manipulate objects on the screen (like selecting and/or moving objects around the screen). Mouse is the most popular pointing device; light pen, joystick and touch sensitive screen being other members of the same set.
- **Windows.** When a screen is split into several independent regions, each one is called a window. Several applications can display results simultaneously in different windows. The end-user can switch from one application to another or share data between applications.
- **Menu.** A menu displays a list of commands available within an application. Each menu item can be either a word or/and an icon representing a command or a function. A menu item can be invoked by moving the cursor on the menu item and selecting the item by clicking the mouse.
- **Dialog Box.** Dialog boxes are used to collect information from the user or to present information to the user.
- **Icons.** Icons are used to provide a symbolic representation of any system/user defined object such as file, folder, applications etc.
- **Desktop.** It is the background on which the windows appear. More precisely, it is the total area of the VDU (monitor) that is displayed after a system boots up (with a GUI based operating system).

Now, that the primer for the operating system and GUI has been presented, we can comfortably switch you over to Windows XP.

2.3.1 Booting

If Windows XP is installed on your system, it will start automatically every time you switch on your PC. The steps involved, if put formally, are :

1. Switch on the PC.
2. Wait till a number of messages flash by (Booting).
3. The desktop will be displayed along with some icons, Taskbar and the Start menu.

> ***Note :*** *In case, your computer is connected to a network, a dialog-box will appear prompting you to enter a log in (user name) and password, so that you can be logged into the network.*

The large area on the screen that can be seen immediately after windows gets loaded in the memory is called the desktop.

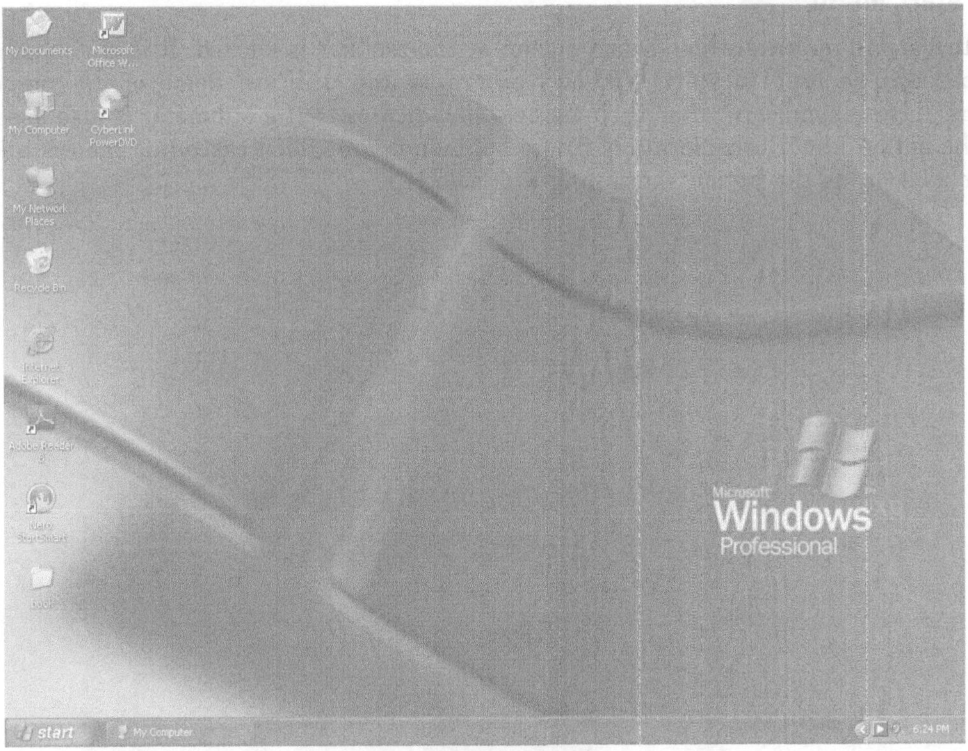

Fig. 2.4. The desktop

The small pictures on the desktop are called icons. These small images can represent a file, a folder or a program. The text below each icon is the icon name.

To open a file, folder or program on the desktop, you need to double-click on its icon. When the mouse is placed over the icon, a text appears identifying its contents. This is called the tool tip.

Fig. 2.5. The Recycle Bin icon

Fig. 2.6. The tool tip

The Task Bar

The narrow blue band at the bottom of the screen is called the task bar. The task bar has the Start menu at the left and the system tray on the right. The date and time are displayed on the system tray.

Fig. 2.7. Task Bar

2.3.2 Start Menu

The Start menu appears when 'Start' button at the taskbar is clicked. It is the most simple tool that can be used to start Windows programs and utilities. Some of its components (options) have a symbol '▸' after their names. It indicates that a submenu is also associated with the option under consideration. These submenus are called cascading menus and they appear as soon as the option containing ▸ is selected.

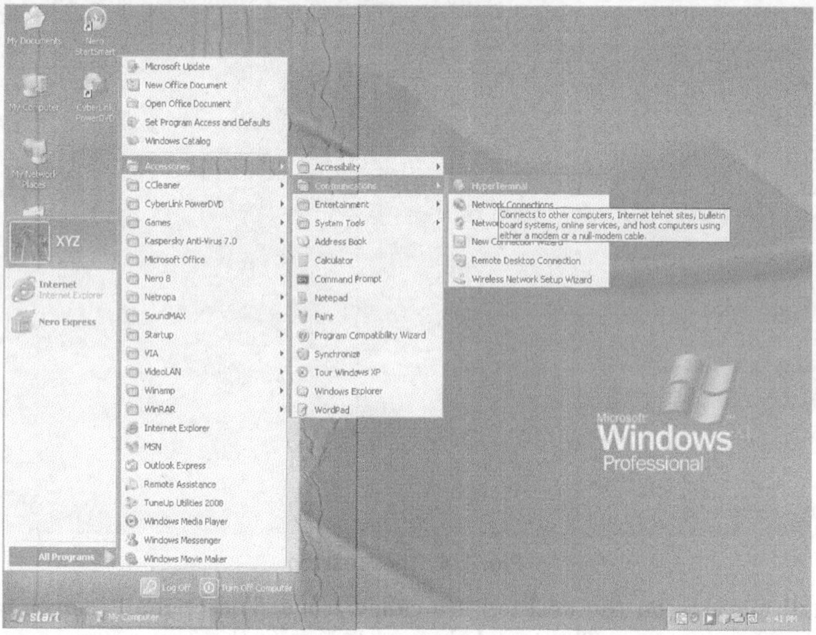

Fig. 2.8. Start Menu and Submenus

The Start menu has various menu options such as My Computer, My Documents, My Pictures and My Music and so on.

- **My Documents :** When a new document is created, it is saved in the My Documents folder by default.
- **My Recent Documents :** This option displays the list of files that have been opened recently. You can open a file in My Recent Documents by simply clicking its icon. This option acts as a shortcut to the recently-used files.
- **My Pictures :** By default, picture files are stored in this folder.
- **My Music :** By default, music files are stored in this folder.
- **My Computer :** It is a very important and frequently used option. It helps in accessing the files and folders in the computer.
- **My Network Places :** This option enables you to access other computers on the network. You can get information about files and folders on other machines. Using this option, you can also share files and folders in your machine so that others can access it from their machines.
- **Control Panel :** The Control Panel has a collection of tools that is used for setting various options in a system.

For example, using the Date and Time option in the Control Panel, the date and time can be set in the computer.

- **Printers and Faxes :** This option helps to add a printer to the machine or change the printer settings. Using this option, a fax machine can also be added to the system.
- **Help and Support :** This option guides and gives information about various topics. It can be used if any assistance is required. A topic can be chosen or typed in the Search text box and can search for it. The Help and Support option can be accessed by pressing the F1 key. In Windows XP there is an option called Help and Support that contains tutorials and demonstrations on how to use Windows XP.

  To access the Help and Support feature,

  1. Click the Start button.
  2. Click the Help and Support option.
- **The Search option :** This option is used for searching files and folders in the system. To find a file or folder, click the *All files and folders* option. Type the

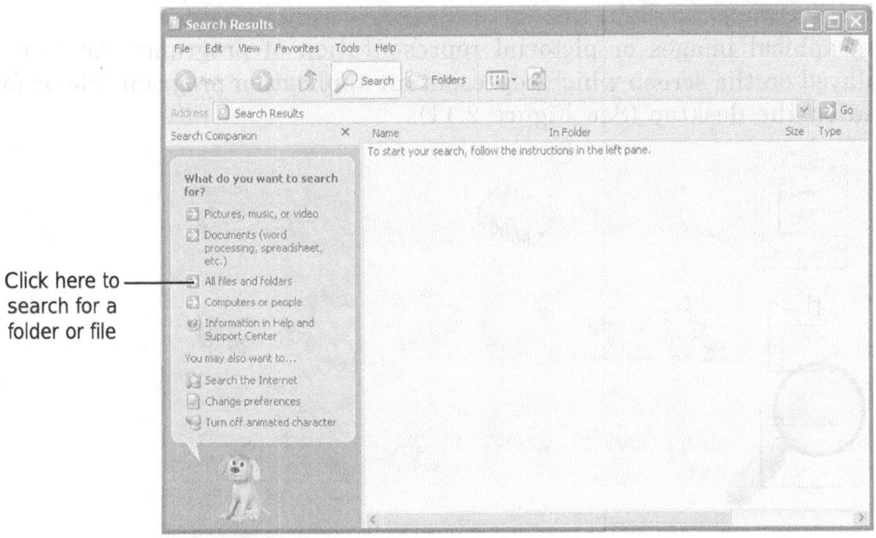

Fig. 2.9. The Search option for finding files and folders

filename or folder name in the textbox and click the Search button. The computer starts the search and lists all the files that match the specified criteria. The results are displayed in the right pane. You can also access the Search option by pressing the Ctrl and E keys simultaneously.

> ***Note :*** *While specifying the file names in **Name** box of **Find Files** dialog box, the wild cards * (asterisk) and ? (question mark) may be used. These are useful in searching files because they provide flexibility in specifying paths and files.*
>
> *? means any one or none character can occupy that position, * replaces any number of characters.*

- **Run** : The Run option enables you to open a program, folder or a website.

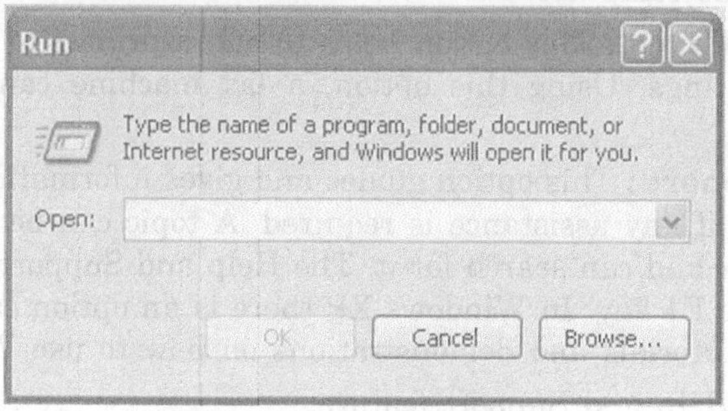

Fig. 2.10. The Run option

Type the name of the program, folder or a website in the Open combo box and click the OK button to run it. For example, to access the calculator, you can type **calc** in the Open combo box and click the OK button.

2.3.3 Icons

Icons are small graphical images or pictorial representation of programs. An icon is a small image displayed on the screen which represent an application program, file or folder and are displayed on the desktop (See Figure 2.11).

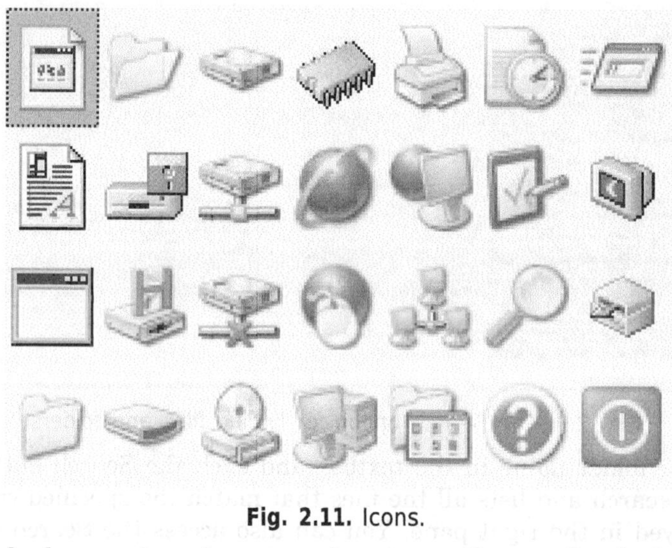

Fig. 2.11. Icons.

You can simply drag an icon from one place to another on the desktop by keeping the left button of the mouse pressed. To open the file/folder that an icon represents, place your mouse pointer over the top of it and double click (two clicks in quick succession) the left mouse button. This will activate the icon and either start a program or open file/ folder.

The icons on the desktop can be renamed by right clicking on them and select Rename, similarly they can be deleted by right clicking and selecting Delete. (See Figure 2.12)

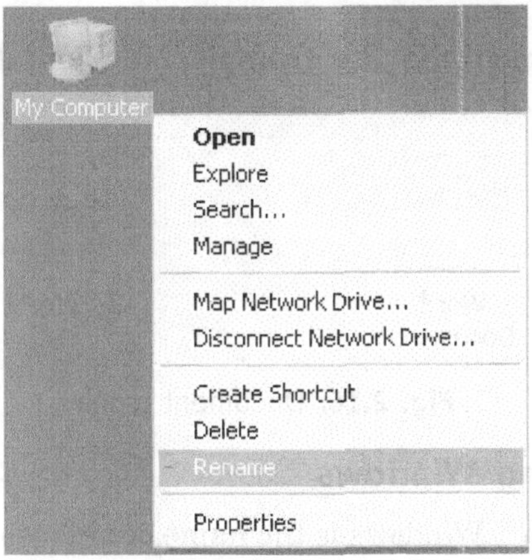

Fig. 2.12. Rename Icon

Types of Icons

The various types of icons are discussed below :

Disk Drive Icons

These types of icon represent the Drives of the computer. For example: Drive3½ Floppy A:, Hard Disk Drive, CD Drive, etc.

Fig. 2.13. Disk Drive Icons

Application Icons

Application icons mean the software package which are used to run various programs. For example, Calculator, Backup, MS-Paint, etc.

Fig. 2.14. Application Icons.

Shortcut Icons

Shortcut icons are used to quickly access the application. These icons are created by using the option Desktop/New/Shortcut. For example, Calculator, Disk Cleanup, Paint, etc.

Fig. 2.15. Shortcut Icons

Document Icons

These icons represent a document file. For example, MS-Word document, Notepad document, etc.

Fig. 2.16. Document Icons

2.3.4 Opening and Closing Windows

When spelled with a capital "W", Windows is the name of Microsoft's system software (Windows XP, Vista, 7 and so on). When spelled with a lowercase "w", *a window is a rectangular frame on the computer display screen. Through this frame, you can view a file of data—such as a document, spreadsheet, or database—or an application program.* To open a program window start the program. To open a content window, double-click the drive or folder icon from the desktop or select the folder from the **Start** menu. For instance, click **Start** and then **My Computer** to open this window (See Figure 2.17). The current window appears on top of any other open windows, and the title bar is brighter.

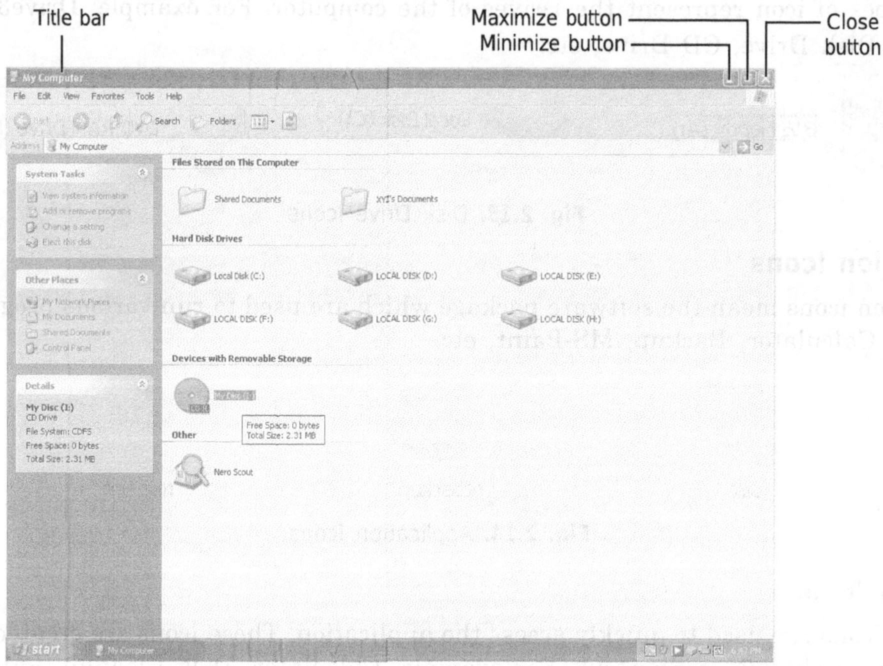

Fig. 2.17. All windows include common controls for working with that window

When a window is open, you see the controls for the window in the upper-right corner (from left to right : **Minimize, Maximize** and **Close**). For example, to close a window, click its **Close** button as shown in Figure 2.17.

The window closes and disappears from the taskbar and the desktop. If you close a program window, you also exit the program.

You can also use the mouse to move the window around the desktop, by clicking on and dragging the title bar.

Finally you can create *multiple windows* to show programs running concurrently. For example, one window might show the text of a paper you are working on, another might show the reference section for the paper, and a third might show something you are downloading from the Internet. If you have more that one window open, click on the *Maximize* button of the window you want to be the main window to *restore* it. You can close the window by clicking its *close* button.

2.3.5 Concept of Path and Path Name

The data in a computer is stored in files. Each file is characterized by its name. The name of a file comprises of two components, that is, a filename and an extension part. Files of same nature (that is, those belonging to the same application) have the same extension, whereas the filename is unique for each file. Thus, to identify a file, both its name and the extension plays an equally important role *e.g.,* a file containing the data of the employees of a company might be given the name *employee.doc.* Here, the filename is *employee* and the extension is *doc,* which is indicative of the fact that the file under consideration belongs to the application MS-WORD (extension for the MS-WORD documents is *'doc'* or *'docx'* in case you are using MS-WORD 2007). The extension of a file, somehow gives the idea of the nature of the data stored in the file and the purpose for which the file can be used.

The files stored in a computer actually resides on the disk in **folders** or **directories.** Folders are analogues to master files containing files and other folders. A file can be stored either directly on the disk (C :\), or within a folder (C :\XYZ) or within subfolder(s) (C :\XYZ\DATA).

A folder contained within a folder is called a **subfolder**. *The exact location of a file on the disk is called its* **path.** *The path of a file thus contains the list of all the folder(s) that it is into e.g.,* : If the file *employee.doc* is stored in the folder DATA a subfolder of XYZ on the disk, then the path name of this file is given as under :

C :\XYZ\DATA\EMPLOYEE.DOC

> ***Note** : In Windows XP, the file names can be upto 255 characters including spaces. However, file names cannot contain any of these characters :*
>
> \ / : * ? " < > |

Now the primer for files and folders has been provided, we switch over to some operations possible with files/folders.

2.3.6 Use of Operating System for Directory Listing

In operating system WINDOWS-XP we can list the directories or folders and files in two ways mainly :

(i) Using My Computer

'My Computer' is a system folder, placed at the desktop, which displays the contents of your computer. It is a file management tool that helps you in managing various drive(s), folders, files and devices in your PC.

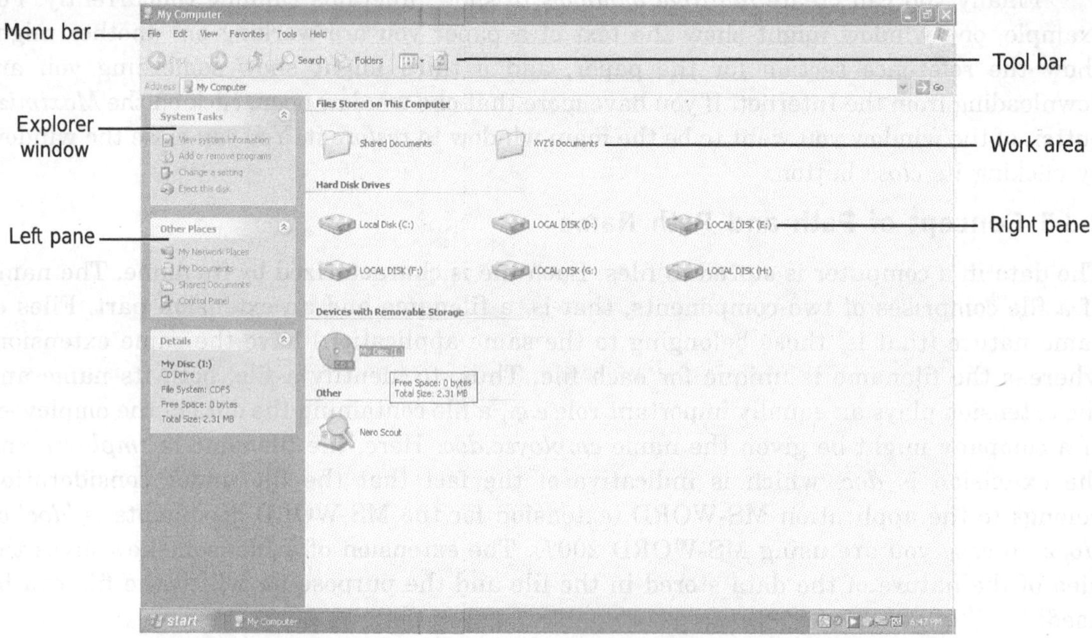

Fig. 2.18. Click any icon in My Computer to show the contents of the selected device

When you open up this folder by double clicking on it, a window opens up, displaying the contents of your PC, categorized according to drives and folders (usually system folders). You can select an item (drive/folder) to know about its brief description. When an item is selected, its description appears at the extreme left of the window. The description usually comprises of the general things about the item as the name of the selected item, its type (drive/folder), what for it can be used etc. In case, the item selected is a drive (C :\, D :\, A :\ etc.) then the total capacity of the drive, the used space in it and the unused/free space in it is also displayed. This is accompanied by a diagram also. In case, the selected item is a folder, a brief description about its intended purpose and use is provided. Almost all of the system resources can be easily accessed using 'My Computer'.

'My Computer' can be efficiently used as mentioned below :

1. Open up 'My Computer' by double clicking on its icon at the desktop.
2. In the window so displayed, you can open any folder/drive by double clicking on it, or optionally you can select an item to view its description.
3. You can navigate to a particular item (file/folder etc.) using 'My Computer'. To carry out this operation, simply follow the path of the item to be opened, that is, go through its path, opening up all folders/subfolders that are a part of its path *e.g.,* if a file is stored at a location C :\WINDOWS\DESKTOP\DETAILS.DOC, then in order to get to the file *details.doc* using 'My Computer', the sequence of the folders/files to be double clicked is : C :>WINDOWS>DESKTOP>DETAILS.DOC.

4. The file can also be manipulated using 'My Computer'. The basic file operations as copying and moving files can be carried out with the help of 'My Computer'.
5. You can view any other part of your computer by changing the contents of the Address Bar at the top of the window. Select the item, for which you wish to view details, from the drop down list provided in the field 'Address'. This will change the 'My Computer' window to the selected item window *e.g.,* if you selected the option 'Desktop' from the drop down list, then in place of displaying the contents of 'My Computer', the window displays the contents of the Desktop.
6. To close 'My Computer' window, select **File** menu and **Close.**

> ***Note :*** *Windows XP permits you to shift to Classic View of Windows OS. To shift to Classic View, you need to set it for Screen, Start menu, Taskbar and Control Panel.*
>
> *In Classic View, installed programs are used through **Start → Programs** rather than using Start → All Programs, which is the way in XP view.*

(ii) Using Windows Explorer

Windows explorer is yet another file management tool in the computer. It is almost the same (and can be used almost similarly) as 'My Computer' except the fact that it displays the contents of the computer in a window partitioned into two components; the parts being the left smaller subwindow named 'folder pane' and the larger right portion called 'working area'.

Within the folder pane portion of the Explorer, the **hierarchy** of the contents of the computer is displayed in the form of a tree. The items (drives/folders) that have a + sign displayed before them means that there are some other items (folders/files) associated with them (which belong to the item). The + sign, when clicked, shows the contents of the item concerned and the sign before it changes to a – which indicates that the item cannot be expanded for further details. The list of items can again be compacted by clicking the – sign to hide the detailed subtree of the item. The sign again changes to a +. When an item is selected within the Folders window, its contents are displayed in the right portion of the explorer. Within this portion, any item can be selected to view its description. The Windows Explorer can be used efficiently as under :

1. Click on the **Start** button and from the menu, select **All Programs** option.
2. From the cascading menu, select **Accessories** option and again from cascading menu select **Windows Explorer.**

   Alternatively,

   Click the **Start** button, point to **Run** and click it, and then type *Explorer* in the Run dialog box and click **OK** or press Enter key.

   Or

   Use the right mouse button to click the **My Computer** icon and then click **Explore.**

   Or

   Open **My Computer** and click on the **Folders** button in its tool bar.

It will display a window divided into two parts : left pane being called folder pane (containing a tree of drives/folder in the PC) and the right pane being called the working area (displaying the contents of the item selected in the left pane).

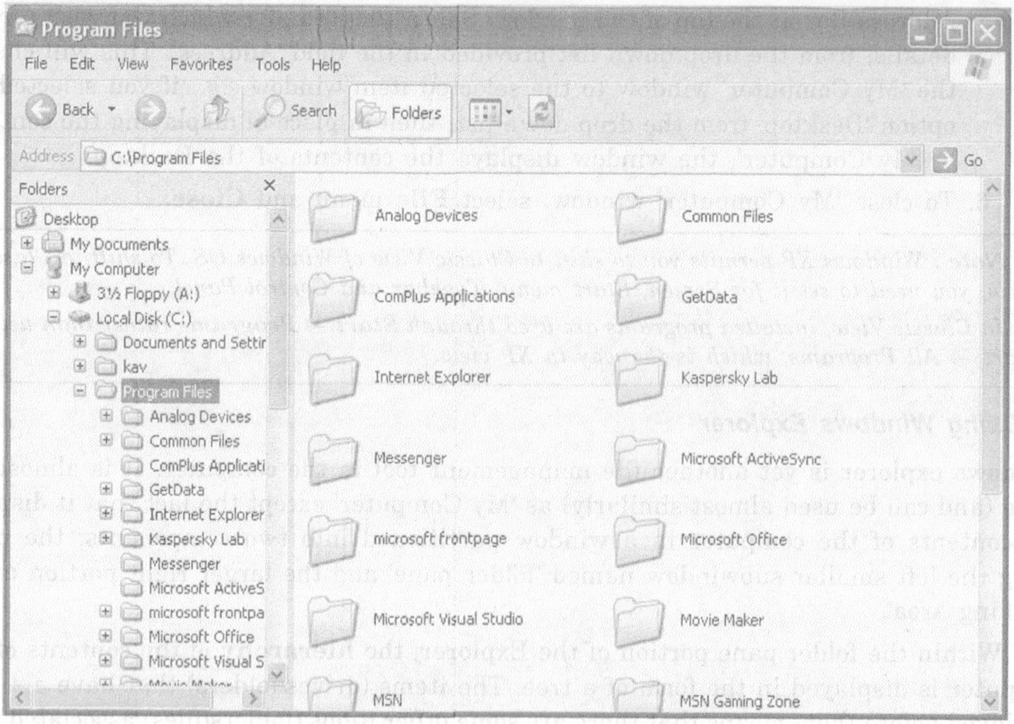

Fig. 2.19. The contents of any item highlighted in the folder pane of Windows Explorer are displayed in the working area.

3. Some of the items have a + sign preceding them (indicates that there is a detailed list/a subtree of items (folders/files) associated with it) and some of the items have a – sign preceding them (indicating that there is no such subtree associated with it or that the item cannot be expanded further).
4. Click the + sign to expand the item for detailed list (subfolders/files) or a – sign to contract the list.
5. Select an item in the left pane and its contents will be displayed in the right one. In turn an item can also be selected in the right pane in order to view its brief description.
6. A file/folder (in the right pane) can be operated upon for the operations like move/copy/rename/delete etc. as described later on.
7. To view the other parts of the PC using Windows Explorer, click the drop down list associated with Address bar at the top and select an option. The details of the option so selected are displayed.
8. To exit from the Windows Explorer, select **Close** from the **File** menu.

Note : *While using Windows Explorer, to show or hide folders on the left side of the window, click the + or – sign beside the folder.*

2.3.7 Hierarchical Directory Structure

It represents the files and folders in a tree like structure. To see the hierarchy of folders do the following :

Click the **Start** button, point to **All Programs,** point to **Accessories** and then click **Windows Explorer.**

The way of using Windows Explorer has been explained in the previous article.

2.3.8 Creating Folders or Directories

What are Files and Folders ?

File is a computerised document that contains information or data. A file name has two parts, the primary name and the extension, also called the secondary name. The primary name is used to identify the file. The extension is used to identify which application has been used to create the file. Every application has a specific extension attached to it. When you save a document, a default name is given to it and the secondary name is included automatically. Example: *Text.doc,* here *Text* is the primary part and *doc* is the extension. A dot is used to separate the primary name and the extension.Note that *doc* is the extension for Microsoft Word files or *docx* in case you are using MS WORD 2007. You can save your files at many places—on the hard disk, a floppy disk, a network drive (a drive shared through a network *i.e.,* interconnected computer) and so on.

Folder is like a container, which can store programs, files and also other folders.

Need to Organise Files and Folders

To keep files, folders, programs etc. in an ordered way in the computer, they have to be stored in a named location in the hard drive. This helps in finding the files and folders easily.

To organise files in a better way they can be put in a folder. A folder can contain another folder inside it. The folders can be named in such a way that would describe the nature of the files that it contains.

The tools provided by Windows to organise files and folders are My Computer and Windows Explorer, which have been discussed earlier.

A folder can either be created at the desktop and/or in some drive (C :\ or D :\ or E :\ etc.) or already existing folder(s).

(*i*) **To Create a Folder at the Desktop**

1. Right-click in an empty area of the desktop.
2. From the pop-up menu so displayed, select **New.**
3. From the cascading menu, select the option **Folder.** A folder icon appears with the name 'New Folder' highlighted.
4. Type a name for the newly created folder.

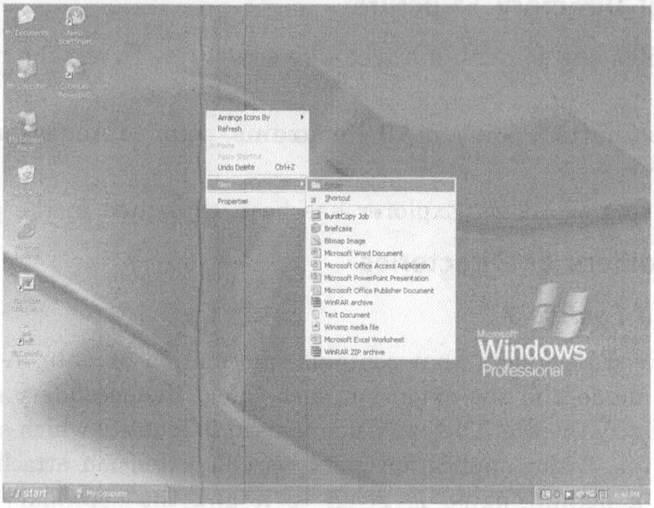

Fig. 2.20. Creating a folder at the desktop

(*ii*) To Create a Folder in a Drive/Folder

1. In 'My Computer' navigate to the item (drive/folder) in which you wish to create a new folder.
2. Double click on this item, so that a window exhibiting its contents is opened.
3. Right-click on an empty area in the window.
4. Select **New** from the pop-up menu displayed, and **Folder** from the cascading menu. A folder icon appears with the name 'New Folder' highlighted.
5. Type a name for the newly created folder.

Say, you create a new folder called Vansh in the Dixit folder. In this case, the Dixit folder is called the parent folder and the Vansh folder is called the subfolder.

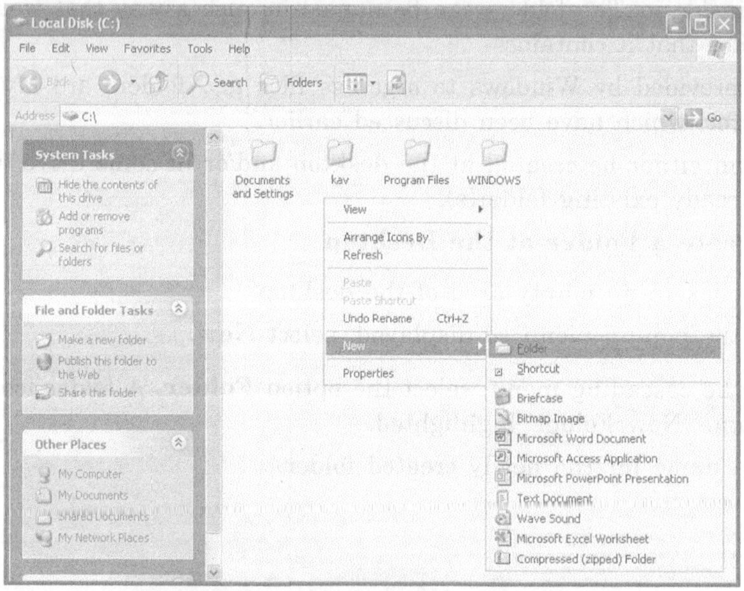

Fig. 2.21. Creating a folder in a drive/folder

2.3.9 File Operations

Files and folders can be copied, moved, deleted or renamed. For this you need to select files that are to be copied, moved or deleted. Selecting a file or a folder is simple, as you have to click that particular folder or file. The folder or file gets highlighted.

Renaming Files and Folders

A file or folder can be renamed immediately after it is created or later. To rename a file,

1. Select the file.
2. Click the Rename option in the File menu.

Alternatively,

1. Select the file.
2. Right-click the file.
3. Click the Rename option in the popup menu (See Figure 2.22).

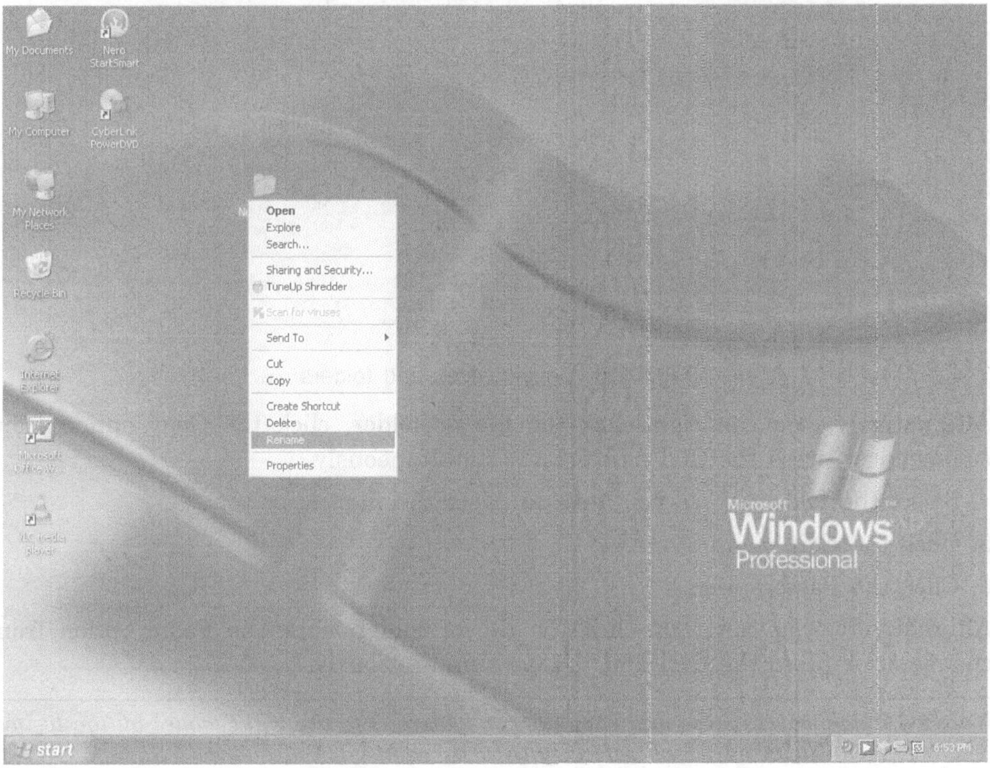

Fig. 2.22. Renaming files and folders

You can also select the file and press the F2 key to change the name.

The name of the file or folder is highlighted. Type the new name and press the Enter key.

Copying Files and Folders

To copy a file or a folder to another folder,

1. Select the file or folder.
2. Click the Edit menu.
3. Click the Copy option (See Figure 2.23).

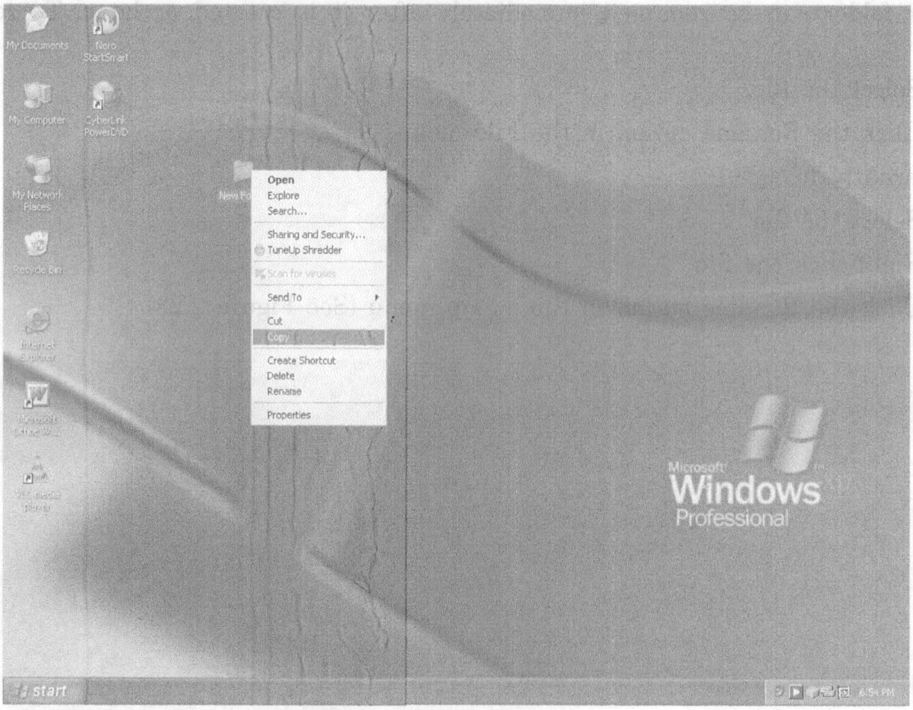

Fig. 2.23. Copying files and folders

Alternatively, you can right-click the file or folder, click the Copy option from the shortcut menu or press the Ctrl and C keys simultaneously.

4. Select the folder where you have to paste the file.
5. Click the Edit menu.
6. Click the Paste option.

Alternatively, you can right-click the file or folder, click the Paste option from the shortcut menu or press the Ctrl and V keys simultaneously.

> ***Note :*** *A quick way to move and copy files or folders is to use right mouse button to invoke the shortcut menu (a menu which gets displayed by right click of mouse).*

Moving Files and Folders

To move a file or a folder completely from one folder to another,

1. Select the file.
2. Click the Edit menu.

3. Click the Cut option (See Figure 2.24).

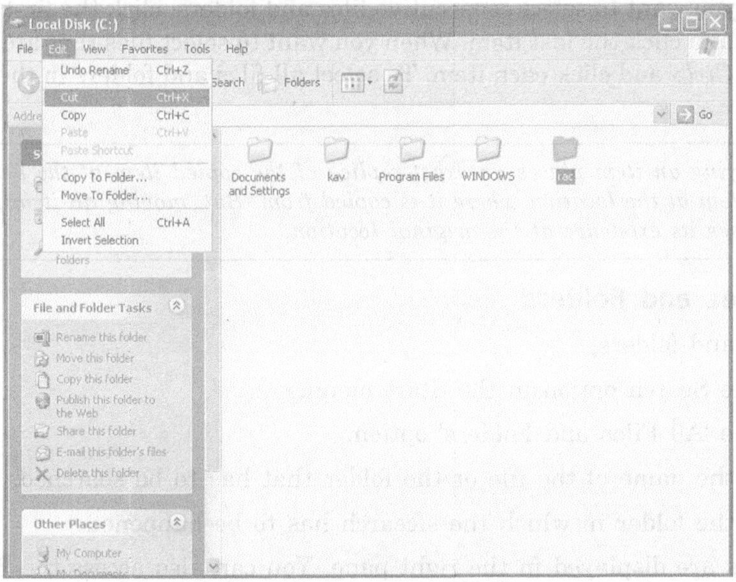

Fig. 2.24. Selecting the Cut option.

Alternatively, you can right-click the file or folder, select the *Cut* option from the shortcut menu or press the Ctrl and X keys simultaneously.

4. Select the folder where you have to paste the file.
5. Click the Edit menu.
6. Click the Paste option (See Figure 2.25).

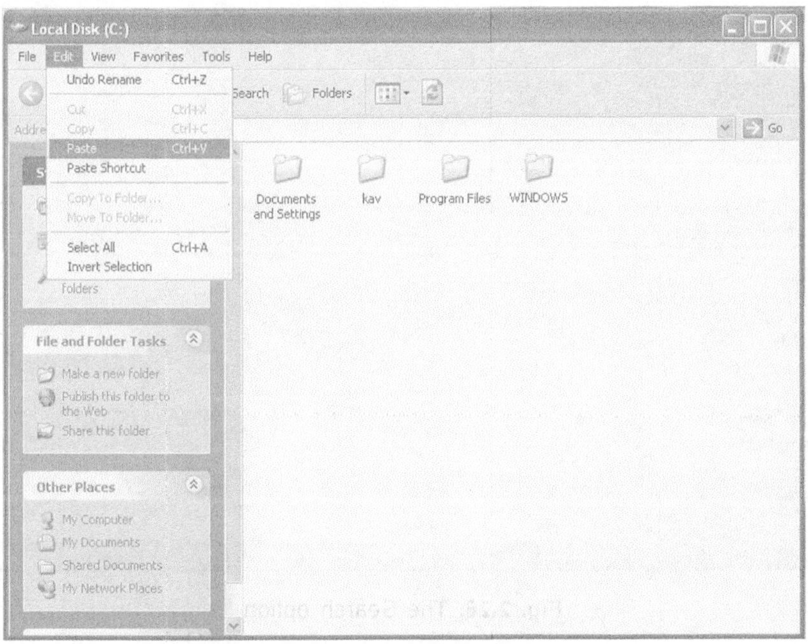

Fig. 2.25. Selecting the Paste option

If multiple files have to be copied or moved, it can be done using the Shift key or the Ctrl key. When you want to select consecutive files and folders, click the first item, hold down the <*Shift*> key and click the last item. When you want to select files that are not consecutive, hold down the <*Ctrl*> and click each item. To select all files and folders in the window, choose *Edit, Select All.*

> ***Note :*** *Copying an item places an exact replica of the copied item at the new location also retaining the item at the location where it is copied from. But, moving an item from a location to another erases its existence at the original location.*

Searching Files and Folders

To search files and folders,

1. Click the Search option in the Start menu.
2. Click the 'All Files and Folders' option.
3. Specify the name of the file or the folder that has to be searched.
4. Specify the folder in which the sfcearch has to be happened.

The results are displayed in the right pane. You can also access the Search option by pressing the Ctrl and E keys simultaneously.

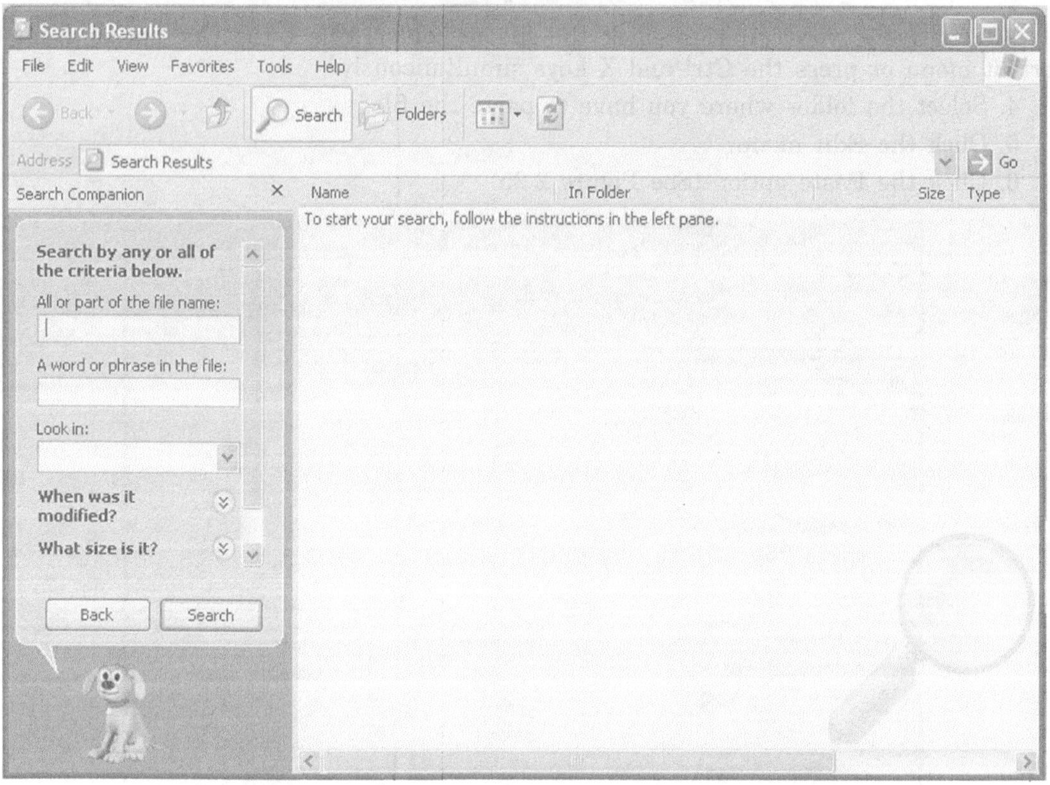

Fig. 2.26. The Search option

Deleting a File or Folder

To delete a file or folder,

1. Select the file or folder.
2. Press the Delete key.

Windows asks for confirmation before deleting a file or folder as shown in Figure 2.27. Click *Yes* to delete the file or folder. Click *No* to cancel the operation.

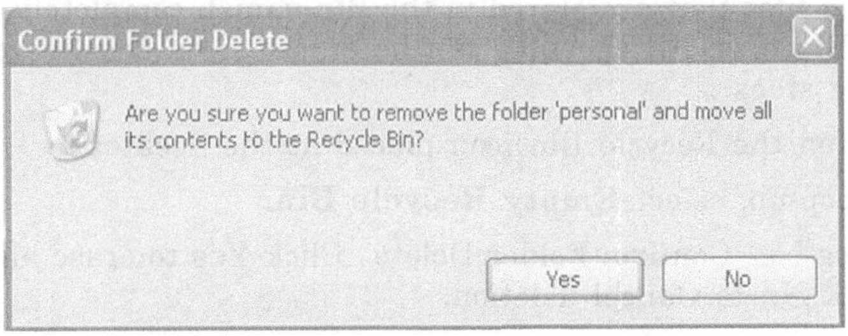

Fig. 2.27. Deleting a File or a Folder

Alternatively, you can right-click the file or folder and select the Delete option in the popup menu.

Deleted files and folders are stored in the Recycle Bin. If you delete the file by mistake, it can be restored by clicking the Restore option in the File menu. If any file or folder has to be deleted permanently from the machine, then right click on the Recycle Bin and select the *Empty Recycle Bin* option.

On clicking *Empty Recycle Bin* option the following message will be displayed. (See Figure 2.28).

Fig. 2.28. Confirm Multiple File Delete dialog box

Click yes to permanently delete the files and folders from Recycle Bin.

2.3.10 Recycle Bin Management

The deleted files are moved to the Recycle Bin. It is a folder which contains the deleted files of your PC. When a file is deleted, it is not abandoned completely. Instead of being washed away from the system, it is moved to Recycle Bin. If you need a deleted file back, it can be restored from the Recycle Bin to its original location (from where it was deleted).

The Recycle Bin takes up approximately 10 percent of the hard disk space at most. If you wish, you can minimize the size of this folder from time to time by erasing the files from it. The deleted files that are stored in the Bin vanish completely if they are deleted from the Recycle Bin also. All the files can be erased from the Recycle Bin at once by using the following steps :

1. Right-click on the Recycle Bin icon placed at the desktop.
2. From the pop-up, select **Empty Recycle Bin.**
3. In the dialog-box 'Confirm Folder Delete'. Click **Yes** to erase all the files from the Bin; or click **No** to Cancel deletion.

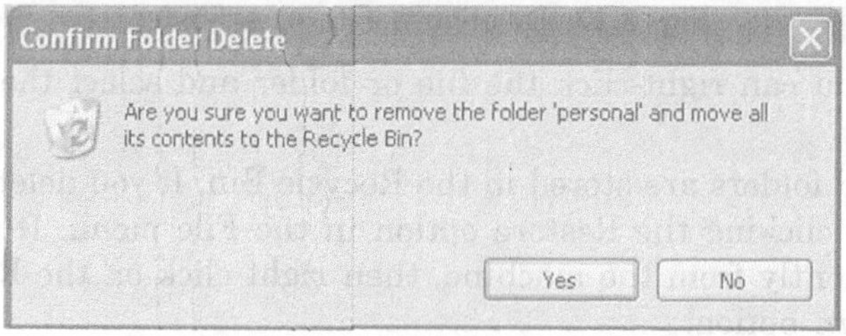

Fig. 2.29. Confirm Folder Delete dialog box

2.3.11 Restoring Deleted Files

The item(s) when deleted are moved to the Recycle Bin. They can, however be restored back to their original location as follows :

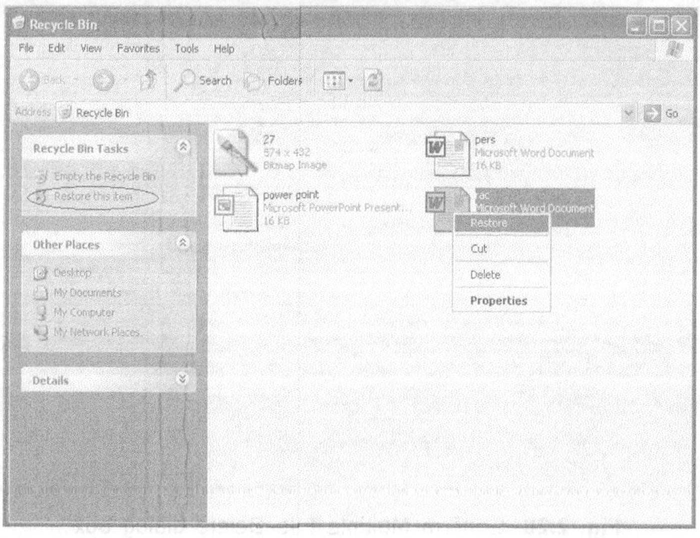

Fig. 2.30. You can restore a deleted file from the Recycle Bin

1. Double click on the Recycle Bin icon to open it up.
2. Select the item you want to put back to its original location.
3. Right-click on the item and from the pop-up, select **Restore.**

It will move the item back to its original location.

> ***Note :*** *If a file is deleted at the command prompt or from a floppy disk (A: or B: drive), it does not go into the Recycle Bin.*

2.3.12 Creating Shortcuts

Once you have created files and folders, you may place their shortcuts to another location. A shortcut is an icon that links to a file or folder. On double-clicking a shortcut, the original item opens.

For creating a shortcut to a file we follow the procedure given below :

1. In a window, select the file or folder for which you wish to create the shortcut. Here we have selected the file TC.EXE file located in the folder E:\tc. (See Figure 2.31).

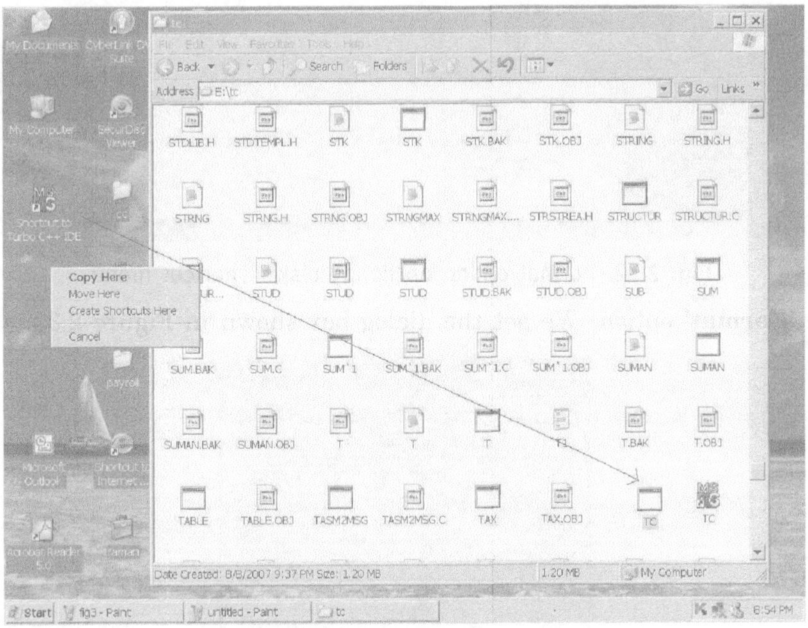

Fig. 2.31. Creating Shortcut

2. Drag the file by using the *right mouse button* to the location where you wish to place the shortcut. Here we wish to place the shortcut at the desktop, so the desired file icon will be dragged to the desktop.
3. Immediately on releasing the right mouse button, a menu will be displayed (See Figure 2.31).
4. Click on **'Create Shortcuts Here'** option in it.

> ***Note :*** *We can copy or move a shortcut which appears on the desktop to some other location also.*

2.3.13 Formatting Floppy

For formatting a floppy disk we follow the procedure given below :

1. Click on **'My Computer'.** It will open the 'My Computer' dialog box.
2. Select the **floppy icon** (3½ floppy [A:])
3. Right click the icon. It displays the shortcut menu shown in Figure 2.32.

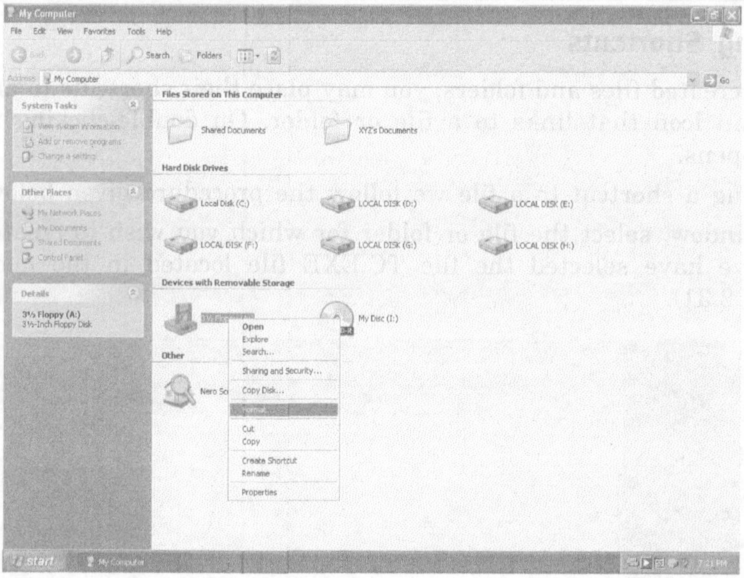

Fig. 2.32. Format option on floppy disk's shortcut menu

4. Click **'Format'** option. We get the dialog box shown in Figure 2.33.

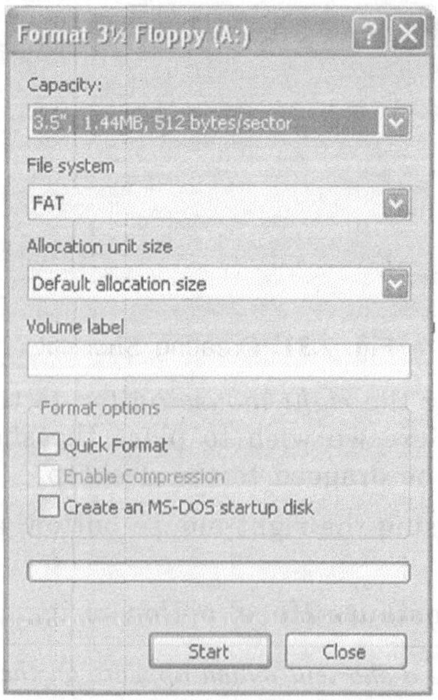

Fig. 2.33. Format dialog box

5. Select the options as per your requirement.
6. Click **'Start'** to start formatting.

After formatting the floppy a message is displayed. Now click on the OK button. We can format another floppy if we desire. Formatting a floppy deletes the existing contents (if any).

2.3.14 Switching between Tasks

Taskbar is the bar at the bottom of the screen in Windows XP. The Start button and the temporary buttons for the open applications (windows) appear at the taskbar. The taskbar can be manipulated in a number of ways :

Fig. 2.34. Taskbar

To switch between windows, just click the button for the window you want from the taskbar. When you close a window, its button disappears from the taskbar.

Depending on what task you are working on, other indicators can appear on the taskbar. To view or change settings, just double-click the clock or any of the indicators.

2.3.15 Control Panel

To start Control Panel,

1. Click the Start button.
2. Click the Control Panel option from the Start menu.

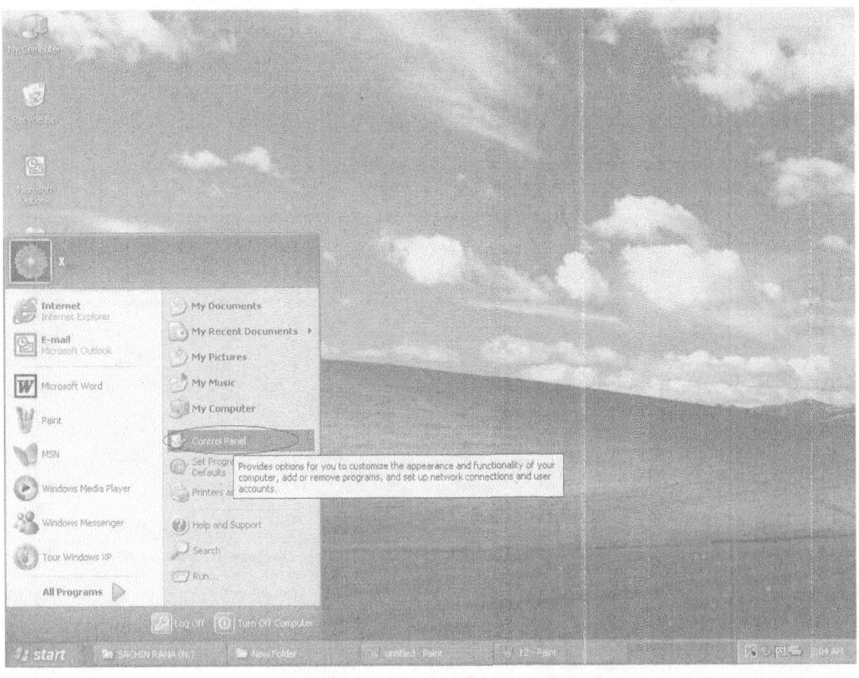

Fig. 2.35. The Control Panel Option

The Control Panel contains specialised tools to change the Visual settings and the system settings in the operating system. There are many options arranged in a category. This view is called the Category view. Sometimes all the options are not visible in the Category view. In such a case, one can switch to the Classic view. In the Classic view, each option is displayed separately.

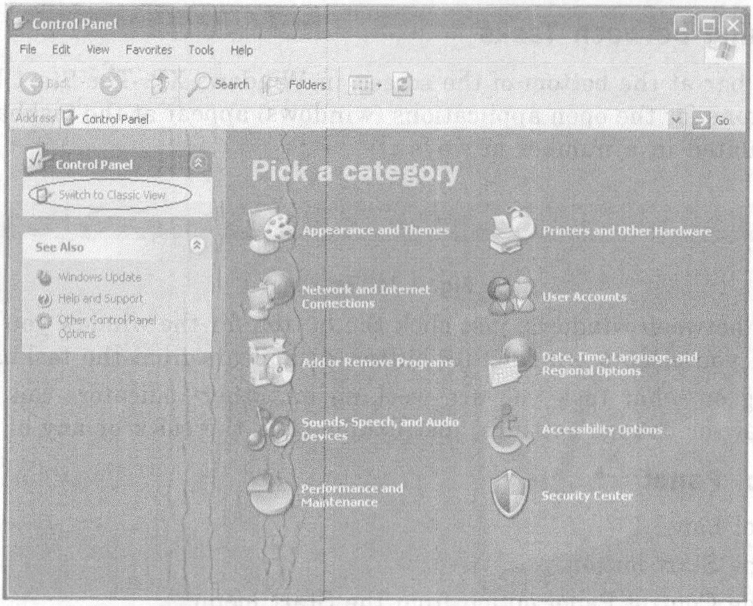

Fig. 2.36. The Categorical View of Control Panel

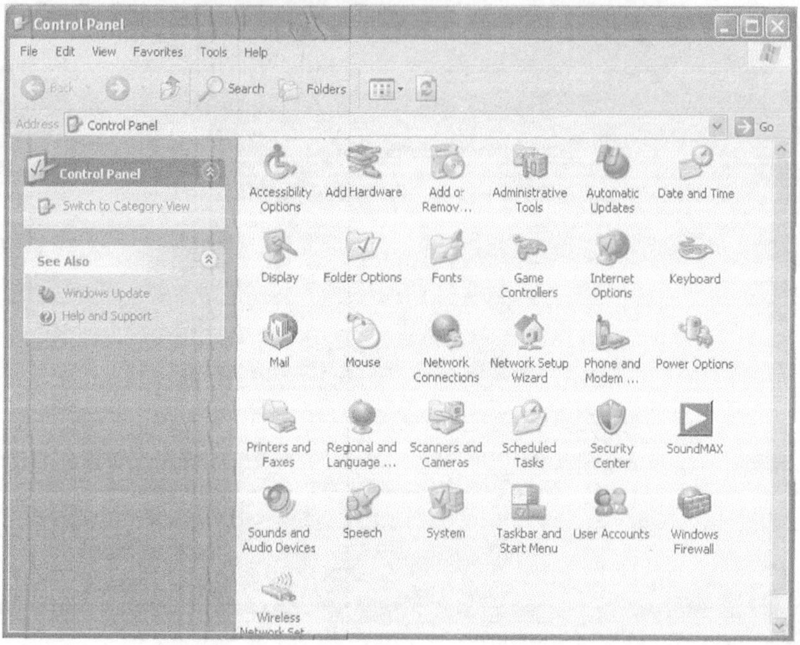

Fig. 2.37. The Classic view of Control Panel

Appearance and Themes

The appearance of the desktop can be changed using the *Appearance and Themes* option in the Control Panel. **Desktop** is the onscreen area where all the icons, windows and dialog boxes are displayed.

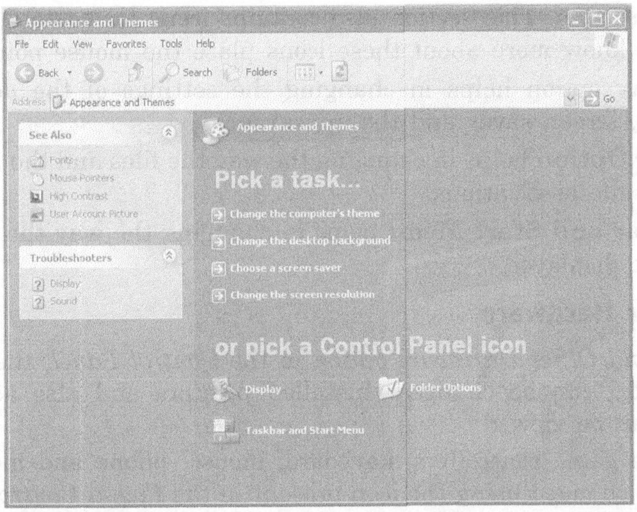

Fig. 2.38. The Appearance and Themes Option in the Control Panel

The Pick a Task section contains tasks that are used for customising the desktop. You can change the background picture, the screen saver and the theme of the desktop. You can also change the appearance and the resolution of the computer.

Theme is a predefined group of background, sounds, icons and other elements on the desktop.

To change the theme of the desktop,

1. Click on change the computer's theme from the *Appearance and Themes* window.
2. Click the Theme Combo Box drop down arrow.

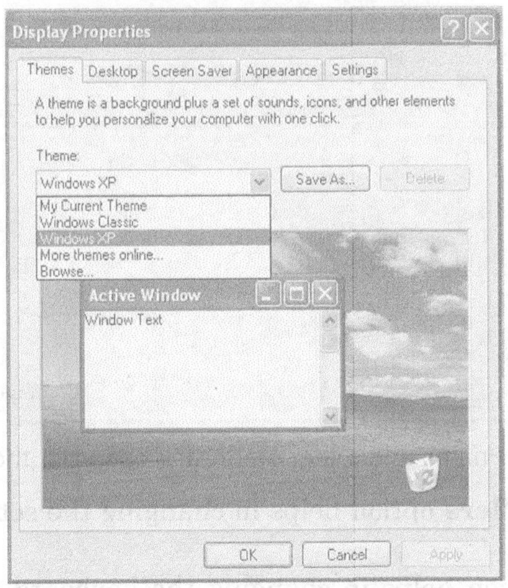

Fig. 2.39. The Display Properties window

3. Choose Windows XP.
4. Click the Apply button.
5. Click on the OK button.

The settings of the desktop can also be changed using the display icon in the Pick a Control Panel icon section. This section also contains icons for customising the folders and the Start menu. To know more about these icons place the mouse pointer over them.

- The **Display** option helps in changing the settings of the desktop, such as the background, screen saver and the appearance.
- The **Folder Option** helps in changing the way the files and the folders are displayed and change file associations.
- The **Taskbar and Start Menu** helps in changing the way the Start menu and the Taskbar are displayed.

Printer and Other Hardware

Using the *Printer and Other Hardware* option in the *Control Panel,* the settings of printer, keyboard, mouse etc., can be changed. Installed printers and also add a printer to the computer options can be viewed.

The settings of game controllers, keyboard, mouse, phone and modem, scanners and cameras can also be changed using the icon present in the *Pick a Control Panel icon* section.

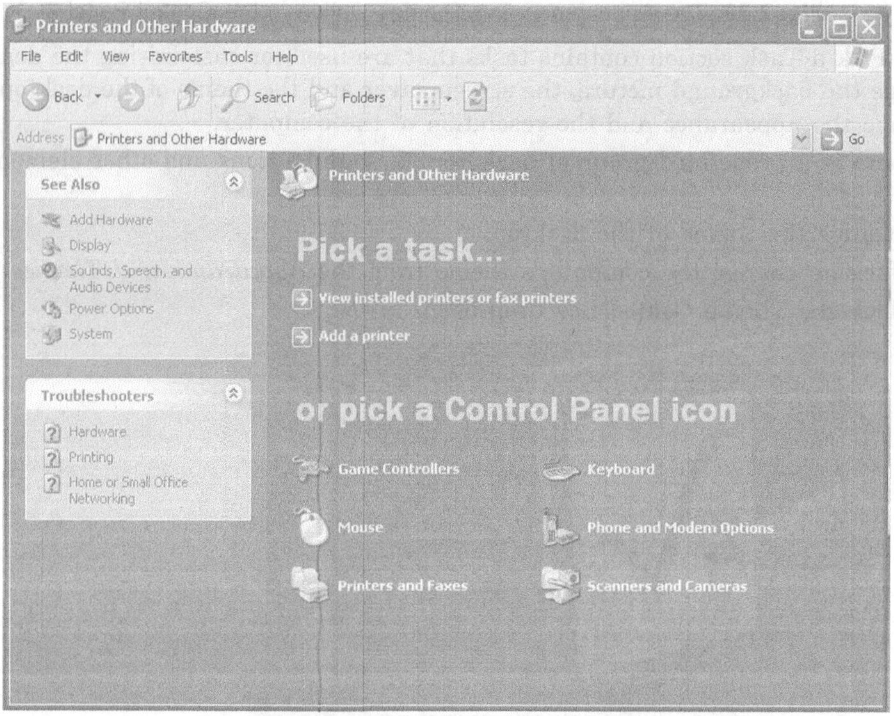

Fig. 2.40. The Printer and Other Hardware option in the Control Panel

- The **Game Controllers** option helps in changing the settings of the game controller hardware.
- The **Keyboard** option helps in changing the keyboard settings.

- The **Mouse** option helps in changing the mouse settings such as, mouse speed, pointers etc.
- The **Printers and Faxes** option helps in changing the display printers that are installed in the machine and also add and remove printers.
- The **Phone and Modem Options** option allows you to configure the telephone dialling rules and modem settings.
- The **Scanners and Camera** option helps in adding, removing and changing the scanner and camera settings.

Network and Internet Connections

The *Network and Internet Connections* option in the *Control Panel* allows creating a small office network and changing the settings of the network and Internet.

The Pick a Task section in the Network and Internet Connection window consists of tasks to change the settings of the Internet, connect to the workplace network from home and create a small office or home network.

Icons displayed in the Pick a Control Panel icon section are used for configuring the display and connection settings of the Internet and also to connect your computer to other networks and the Internet.

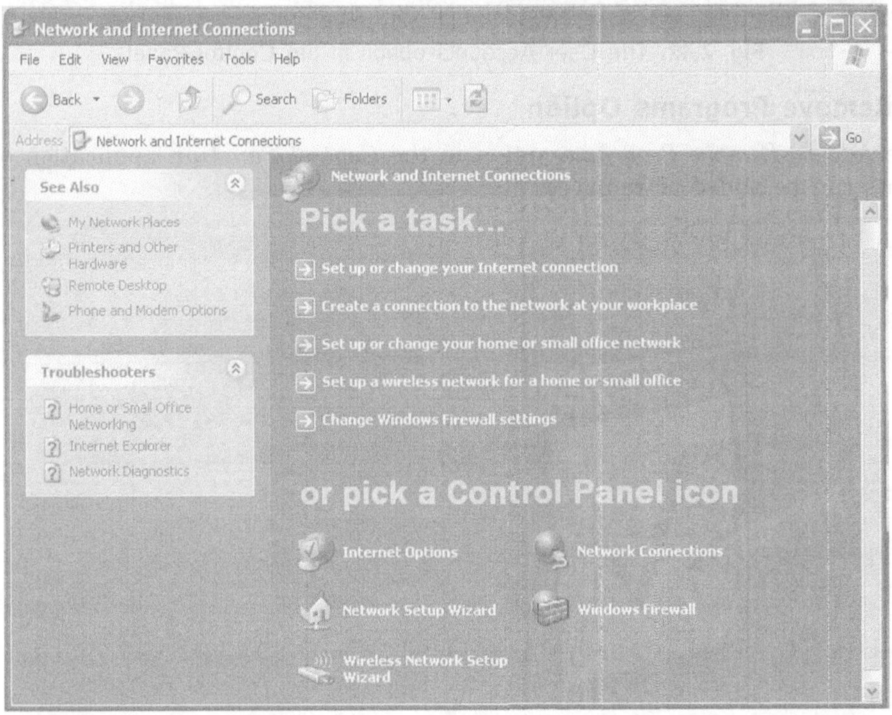

Fig. 2.41. The Network and Internet Connections Option in Control Panel

User Accounts Option

The *User Accounts* option in the *Control Panel* helps to control the rights and permissions, such as changing passwords and personal settings of a specific user. It also helps to create new accounts and change an account. It also helps to change the way users log on or off.

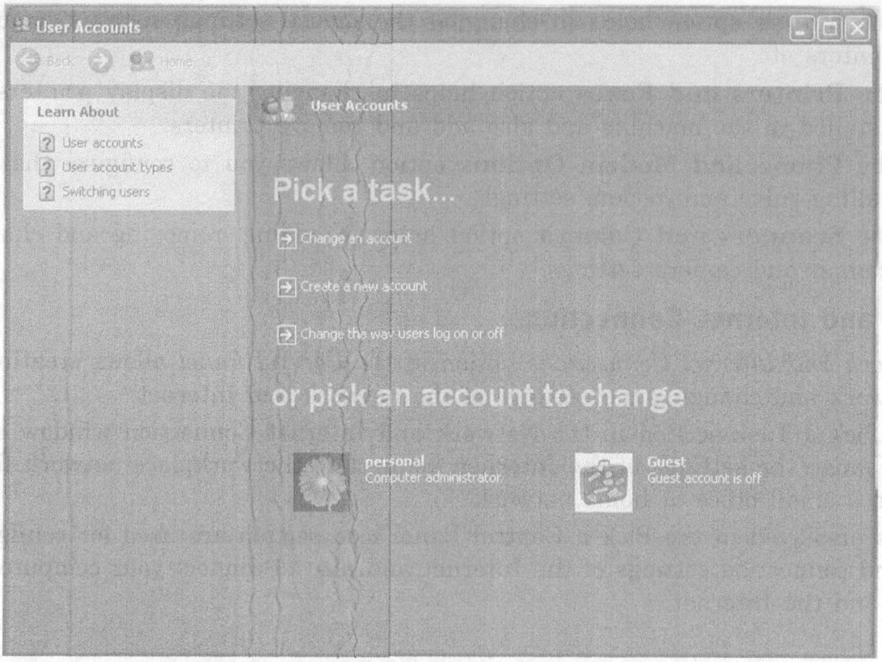

Fig. 2.42. The User Accounts option in the Control Panel

Add or Remove Programs Option

Using the *Add or Remove Programs* option in the *Control Panel* an application or window components can be added or removed.

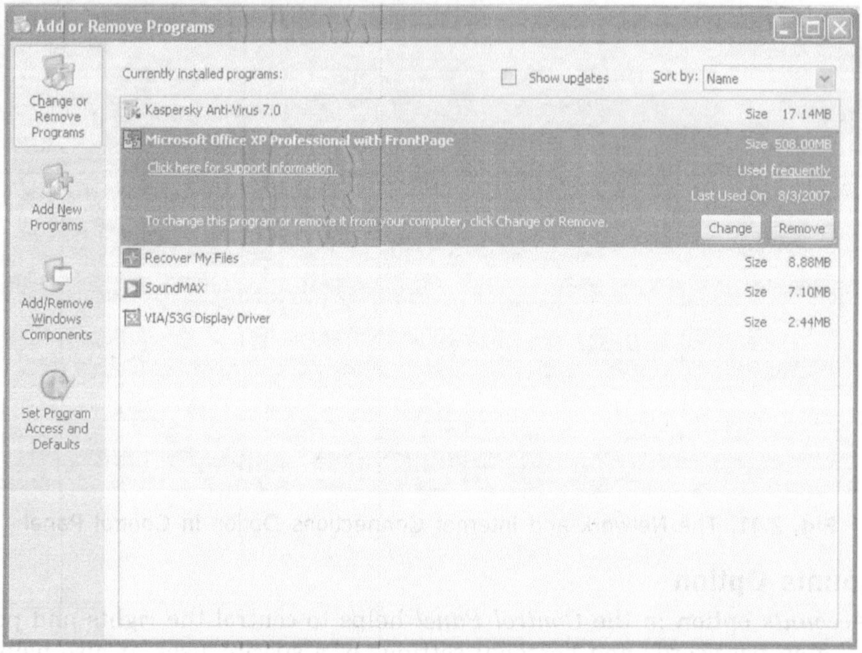

Fig. 2.43. The Add or Remove Programs option in Control Panel

Each item in the Control Panel, when clicked, opens up a dialog-box relative to the properties and settings of the control (item), which can then be adjusted according to requirement.

To open the *Control Panel* folder, following steps are to be followed :

1. Click on the **Start** button and select **Settings.**
2. From the cascading menu, select **Control Panel.**
3. Click on to **Add/Remove Programs** option. The dialog box shown in Figure 2.44 appears.

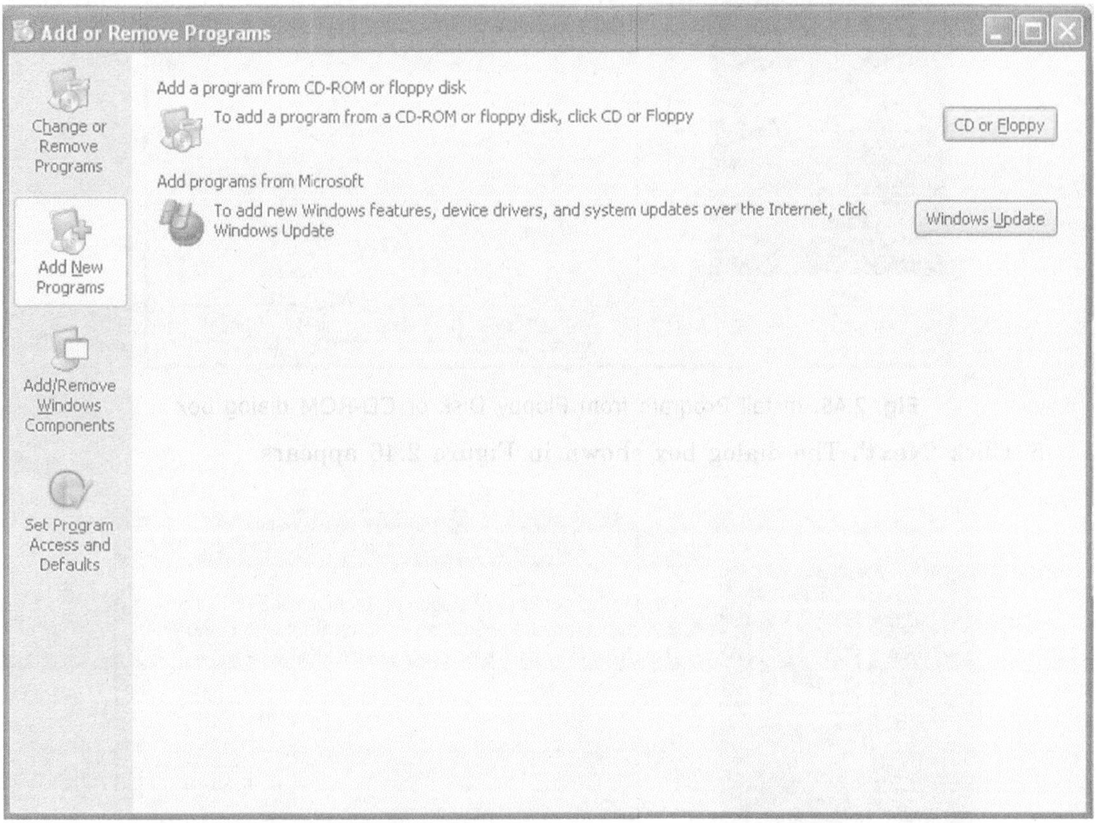

Fig. 2.44. Add or Remove Programs dialog box.

4. Click **'CD or Floppy'.** The dialog box shown in Figure 2.45 appears.

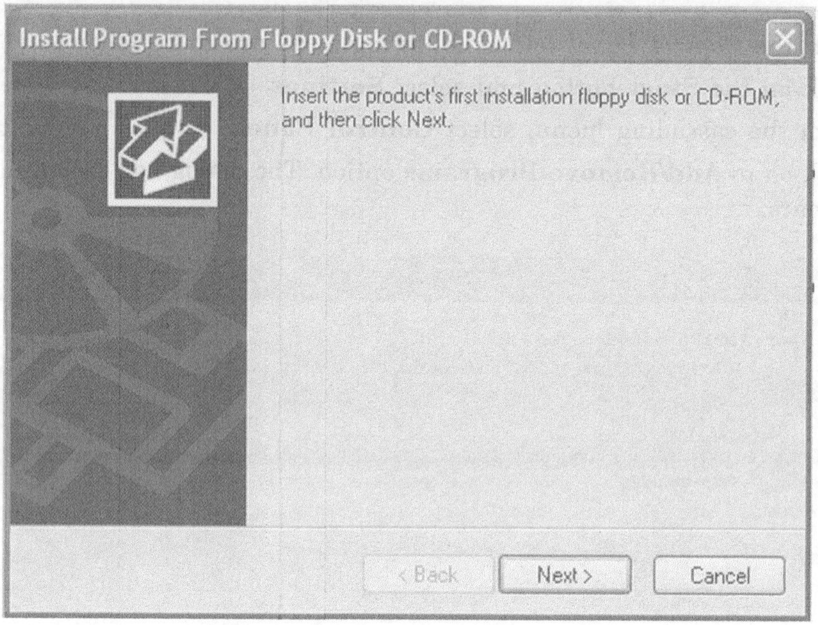

Fig. 2.45. Install Program from Floppy Disk or CD-ROM dialog box

5. Click **'Next'.** The dialog box shown in Figure 2.46 appears.

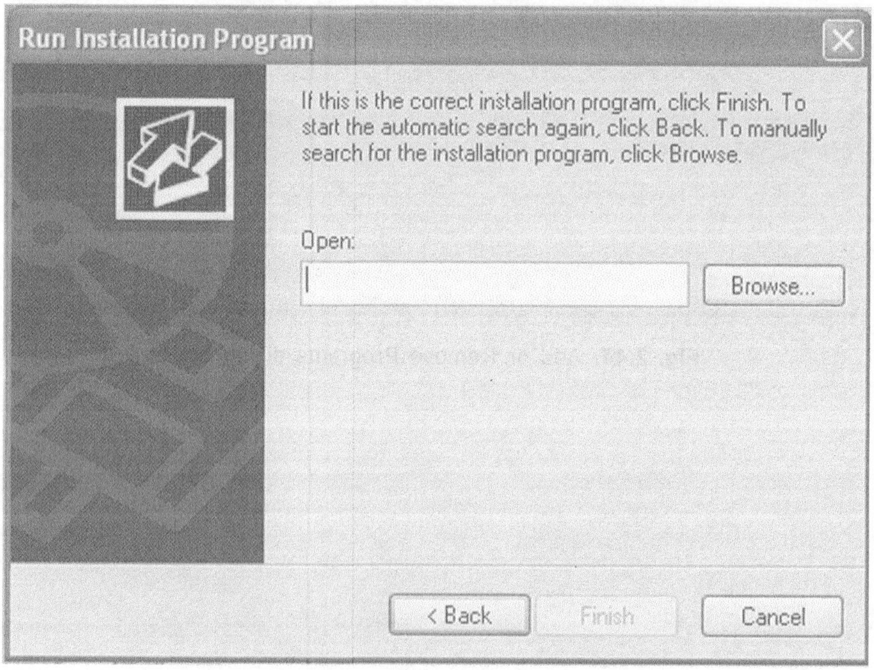

Fig. 2.46. Run Installation Program dialog box.

6. Browse the program which you want to install. In other words give the path name of the program which you want to install.
7. Click **'Finish'**.

Date and Time Option

You can change the date and time settings of your computer using the *Date, Time, Language, and Regional* options icon in the Control Panel. The *Pick a Task* section in this window consists of tasks, such as changing the date and time, changing the fonts of date and time and adding new languages.

To change the Date and Time,

1. Click the *Change Date and Time* icon.

To change the month,

1. Click the combo box where the months are listed.
2. Select the month.

To change the date,

1. Select the existing date and type the new date.
2. Change the date.
3. Click the Apply button.
4. Click the OK button.

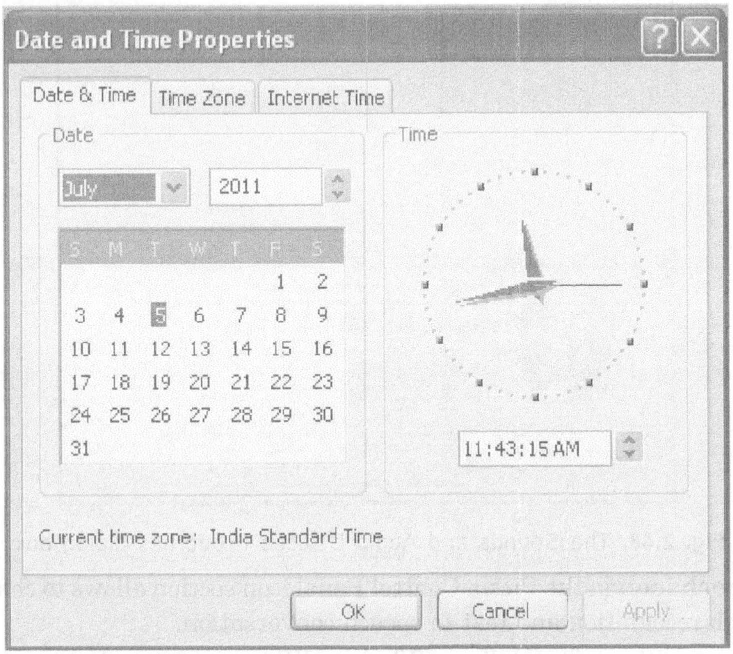

Fig. 2.47. The Date and Time Properties dialog box.

The Pick a Control Panel icon section contains icons to change the date and time and also to change the display the language, numbers, date, and time.

Sound, Speech and Audio Option

The *Sound, Speech and Audio* devices option in the *Control Panel* allows to customise the sound system and also to configure settings for the audio and recording devices.

The *Pick a Task* section in the Sound, Speech and Audio devices window contains tasks to change the system volume, sound scheme and speaker settings.

- **Adjust the system volume** helps in increasing or decreasing the volume associated with the system.
- **Change the sound scheme** helps to change the sound settings that are applied to events in Windows.
- **Change the speaker settings** helps to change the settings of individual speakers.
- The **Sounds and Audio Devices** icon in the Pick a Control Panel icon helps configure the settings of speakers and recording devices.

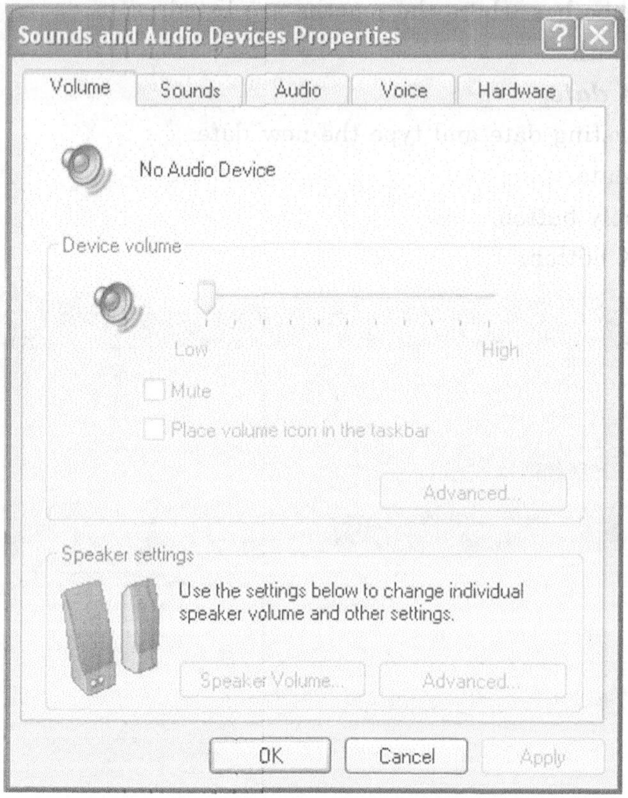

Fig. 2.48. The Sounds and Audio Devices Properties dialog box.

- The **Speech icon** in the Pick a Control Panel icon section allows to change the settings for speech recognition and text to speech conversation.
- Speech recognition is the ability of Windows XP to convert spoken words to written text.

Accessibility Options

The *Accessibility Option* in the *Control Panel* is used for customising the keyboard, display, and mouse functionality.

The *Pick a Task section* in the *Accessibility Options* consists of tasks to change the contrast for the screen elements, such as cursor and text and configure Windows to work for the users with disabilities. A Magnifier option is available in the **See Also** section of **Accessibility Options.** Using this Option, a portion of the screen can be increased.

Fig. 2.49. The Accessibility Options dialog box

Performance and Maintenance Option

The *Performance and Maintenance* option in the Control Panel allows to increase space on the hard disk, perform frequent checks on the computer, and configure settings to save power.

The Pick a Control Panel icon section contains icons to configure energy-saving settings and perform administrative settings for your computer.

- The *Administrative Tools* option helps in changing the administrative settings in the computer.
- The *Power Options* helps in changing the energy-saving settings in the computer.
- The *Scheduled Tasks* option helps in running the computer task automatically.
- The *System* option helps to change the hardware settings and also to see the information about the system.

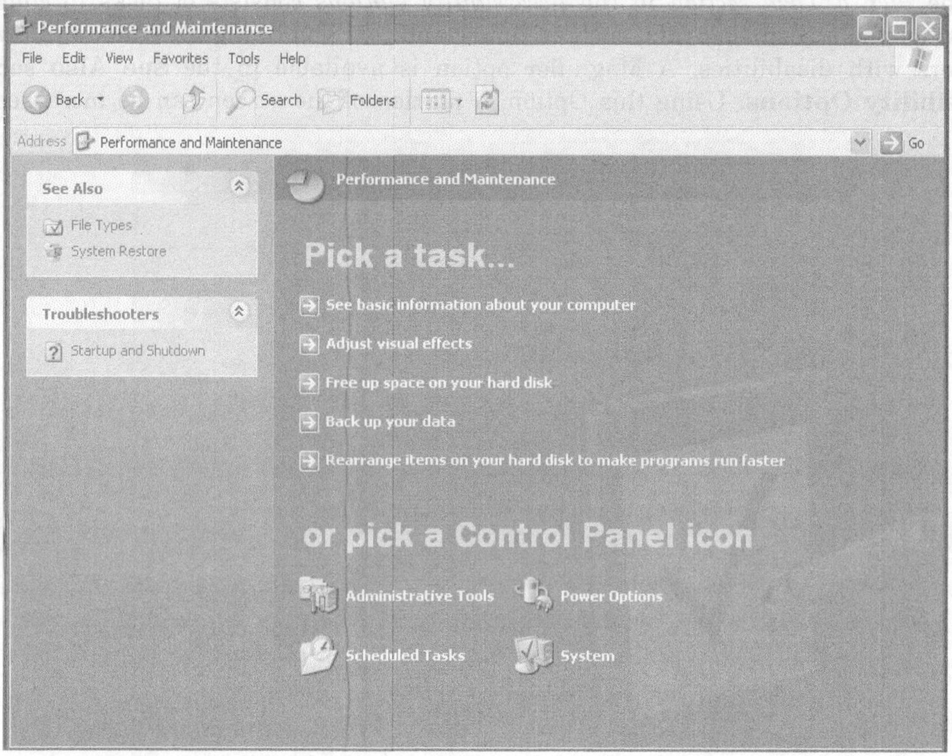

Fig. 2.50. The Performance and Maintenance option in the Control Panel

Useful Tip

To change the settings of the computer you can also go to the classic view of the Control Panel and click on the respective icon.

2.3.16 Arranging Icons on the Desktop

Icons can be arranged on the desktop. These can be dragged and placed anywhere on the screen. To automatically arrange these,

1. Right-click on the empty space on the desktop.

   A pop-up menu appears. A menu that appears when you click the right mouse button is called a context-sensitive menu.
2. Choose the *Arrange Icons By* option from the popup menu.
3. Click the *Auto Arrange* option.

   You can also arrange the icons by Name, Size, Type, etc.

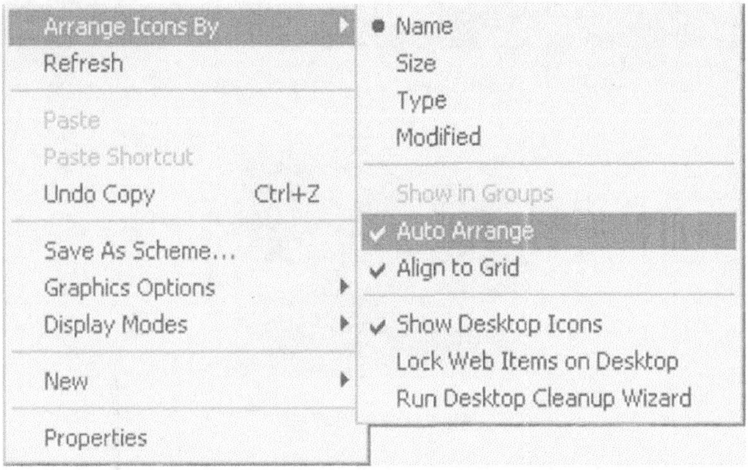

Fig. 2.51. Auto Arrange Icon option

Changing the Desktop

The appearance of a desktop can be changed. To change the appearance of the desktop,

1. Right-click on the empty space on the desktop.
2. Click the Properties option.
3. Click the Desktop tab.
4. Select any option from the list box. For example, Select Autumn as the background and click the Apply button.
5. Click the OK button to close the dialog box.

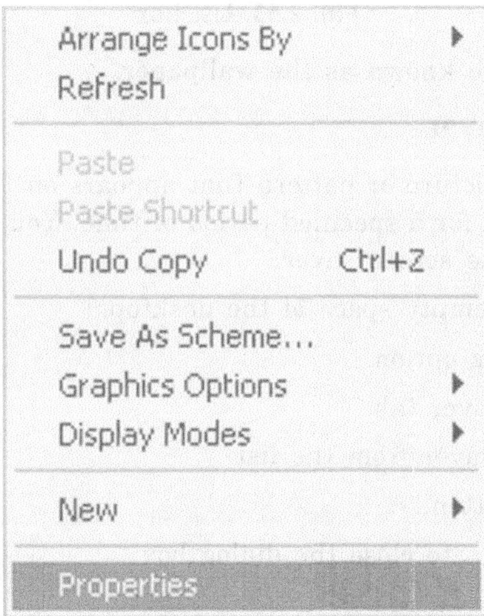

Fig. 2.52. Properties option

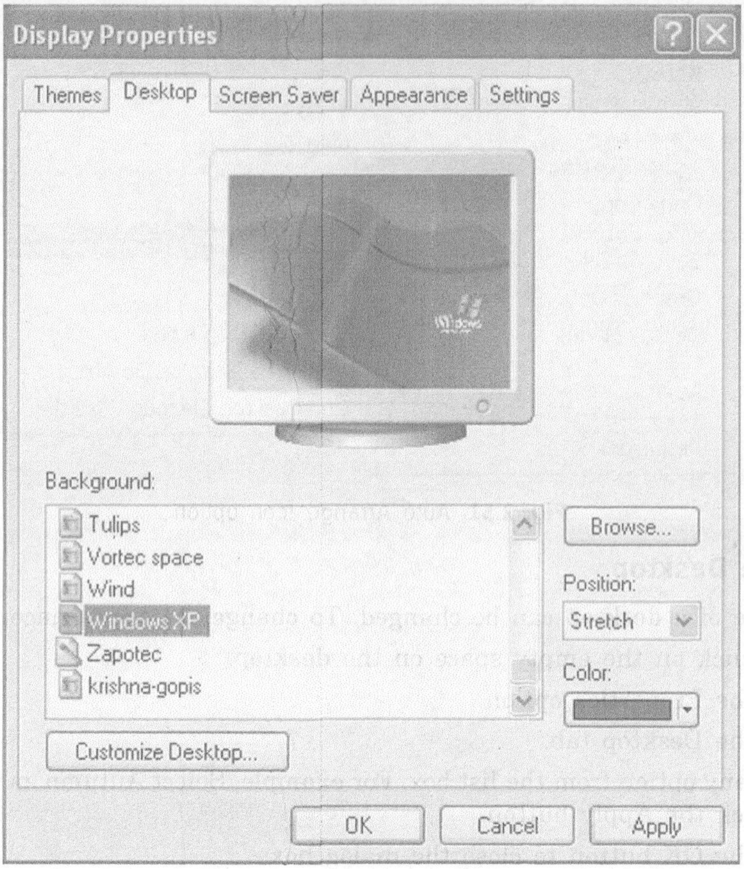

Fig. 2.53. List Box

The background is also known as the wallpaper.

Changing the Screen Saver

Screen saver is a moving picture or pattern that appears on the screen when the mouse or the keyboard is not used for a specified period of time. You can set the time using the Wait spin box. To select the screen saver.

1. Right-click on the empty space of the desktop.
2. Click the Properties option.
3. Click the Screen Saver tab.
4. Select any screen saver from the list.
5. Click the Apply button.
6. Click the OK button to close the dialog box.

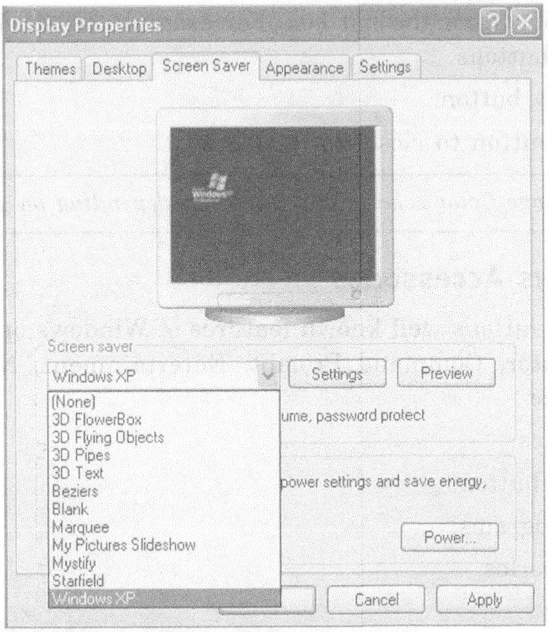

Fig. 2.54. Screen Saver

2.3.17 Changing the Appearance

The appearance of the desktop can be changed. To change the appearance of the desktop,

1. Right-click on the empty space of the desktop.
2. Click the properties option.
3. Click the Appearance tab.

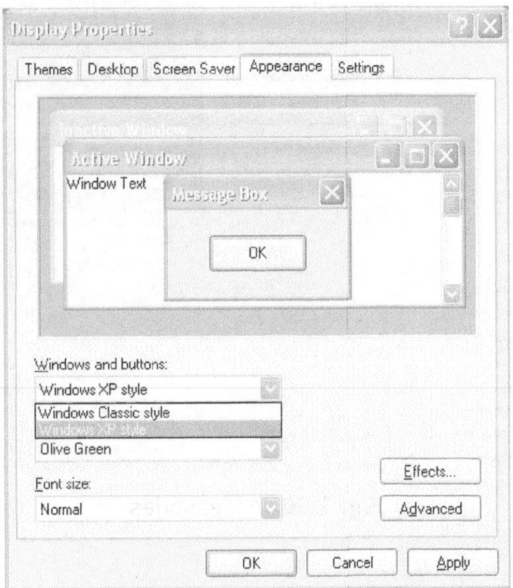

Fig. 2.55. Appearance

4. Select any option from the list box. For example, select Windows XP style from Windows and buttons.
5. Click the Apply button.
6. Click the OK button to close the dialog box.

Note : You can change Color scheme and Font size depending on your choice.

2.3.18 Using Windows Accessories

We can implement the various well known features of Windows operating system such as Address Book, Calculator, Command Prompt, Entertainment, Notepad, Paint, System Tools, and WordPad etc.

To open Accessories,

1. Click the Start button.
2. Click on All Programs.
3. Click on Accessories.

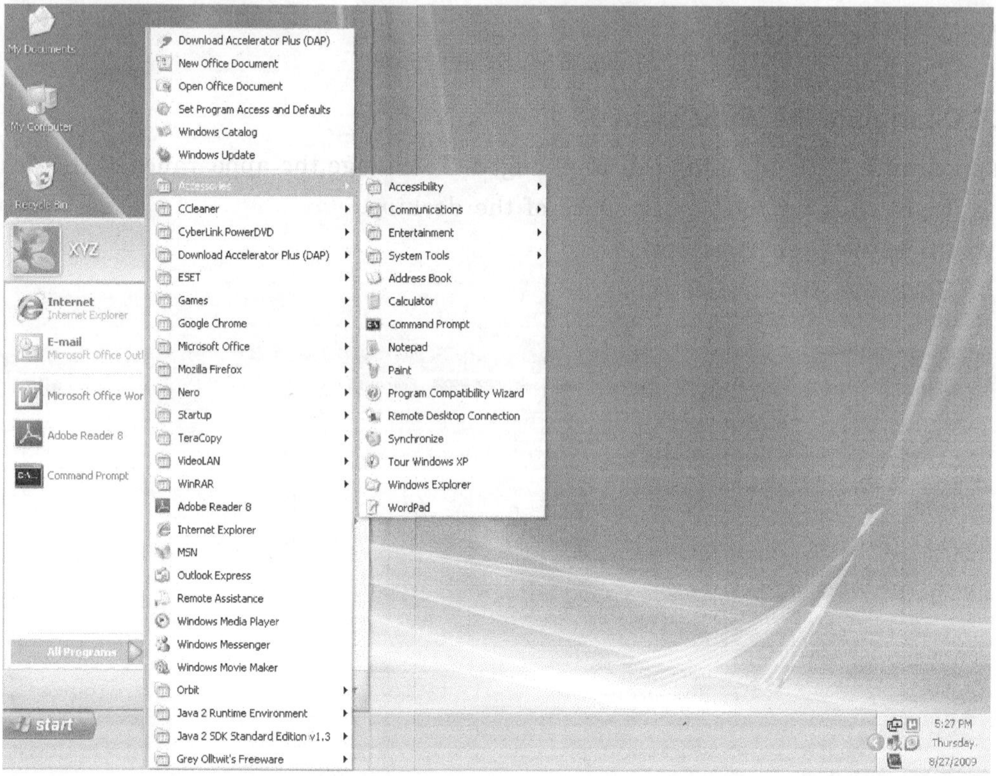

Fig. 2.56. Accessories

Address Book

It is used to manage contacts and find peoples and businesses using directory services.

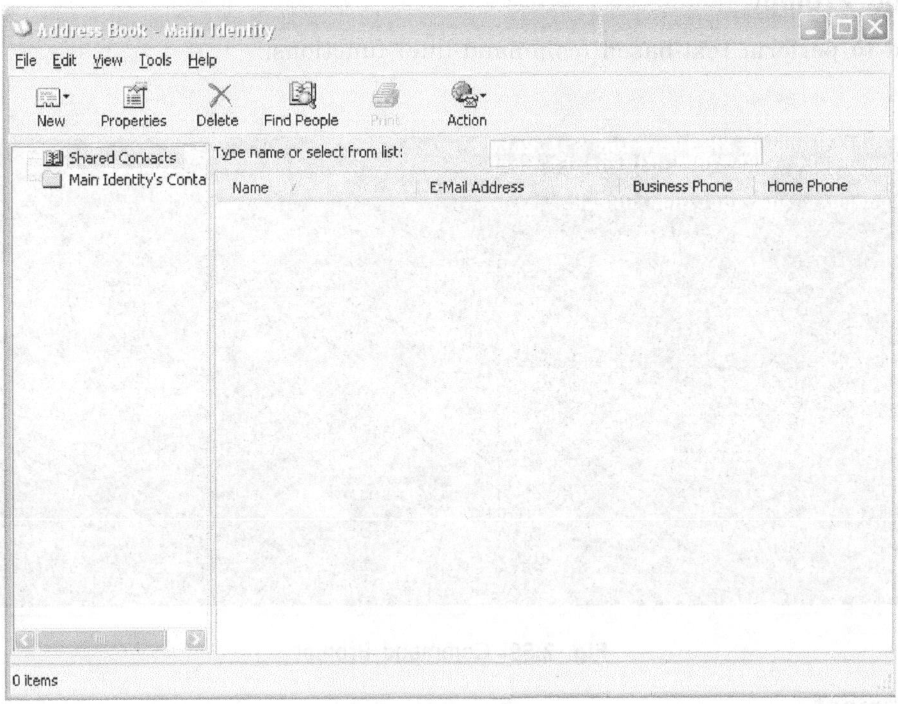

Fig. 2.57. Address Book

Calculator

It is used to perform basic arithmetic tasks with an on-screen calculator.

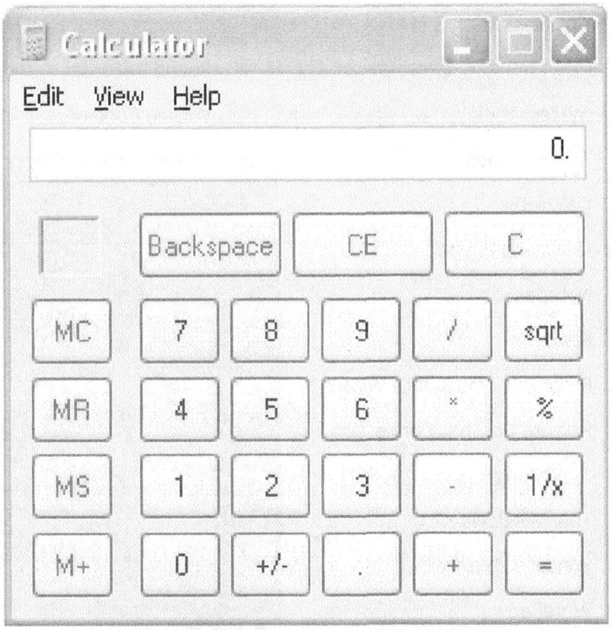

Fig. 2.58. Calculator

Command Prompt

It is used to perform text-based (command-line) functions.

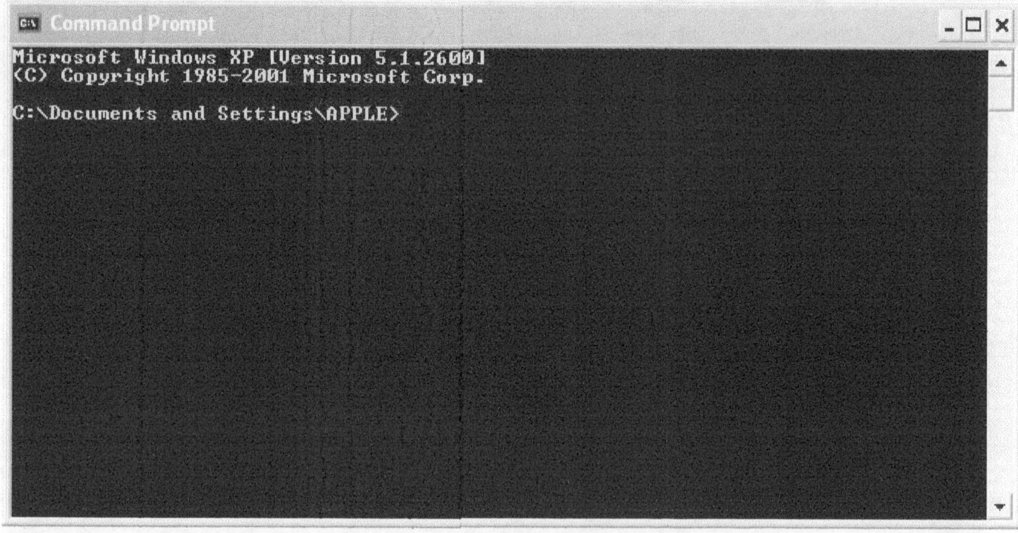

Fig. 2.59. Command Prompt

Entertainment

It has the option Sound Recorder, Volume Control, Windows Media Player for entertaining the user.

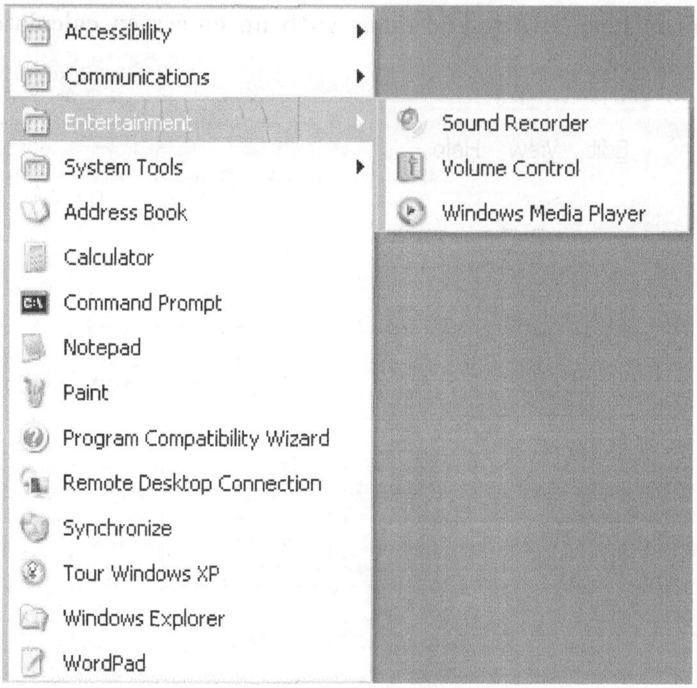

Fig. 2.60. Entertainment

- **Sound Recorder**

  It is used to record sound if a microphone or sound card is installed.
- **Volume Control**

  It is used to control volume level of recorded and play back sounds.
- **Windows Media Player**

  It plays your digital media including music, videos, CDs, DVDs, and Internet Radio.

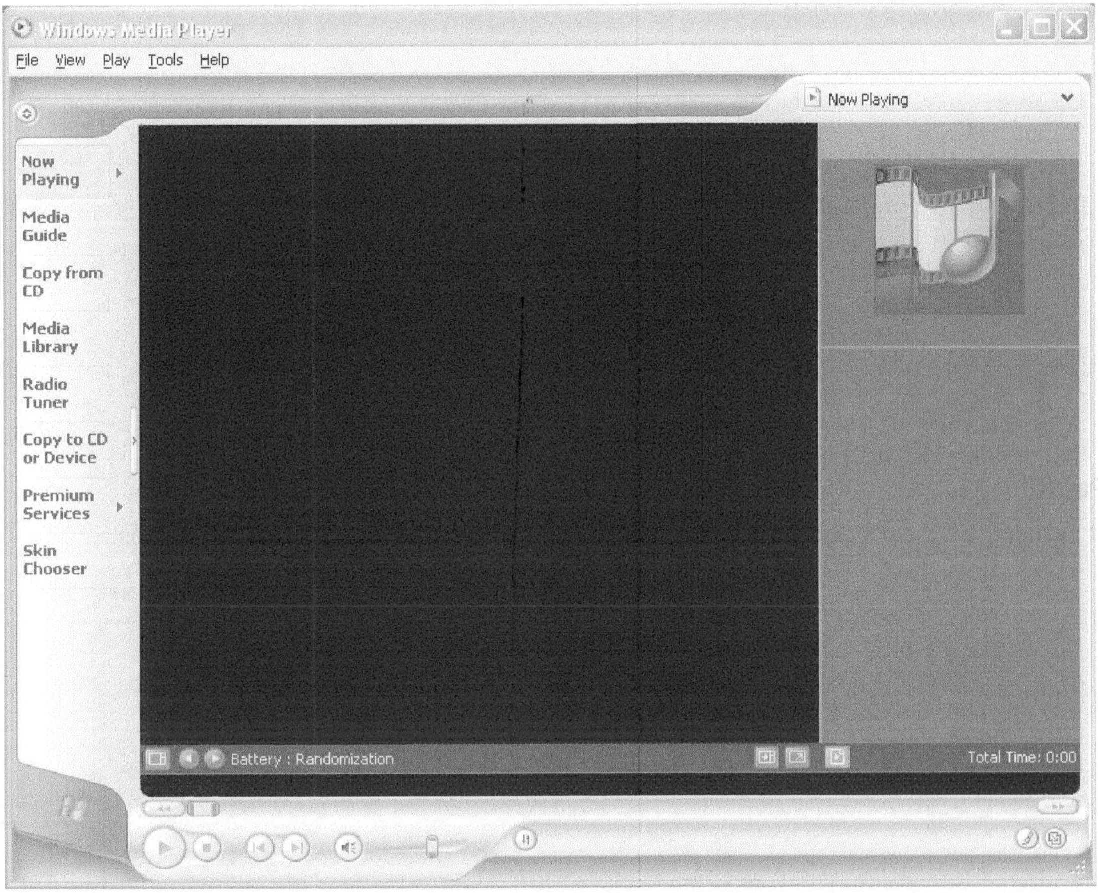

Fig. 2.61. Windows Media Player

Notepad

It is used to create and edit text files using basic text formatting.

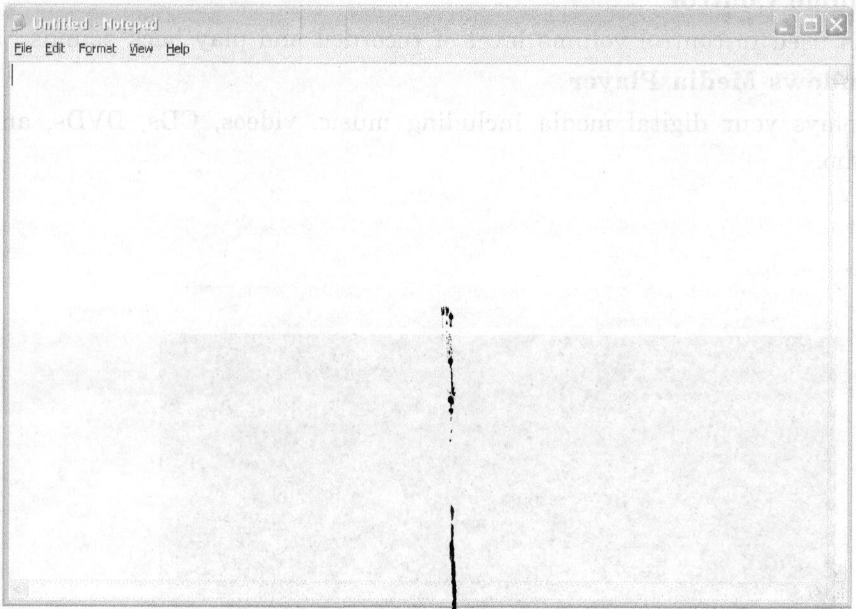

Fig. 2.62. Notepad

Paint

It is used to create and edit drawings and displays and edits scanned photos.

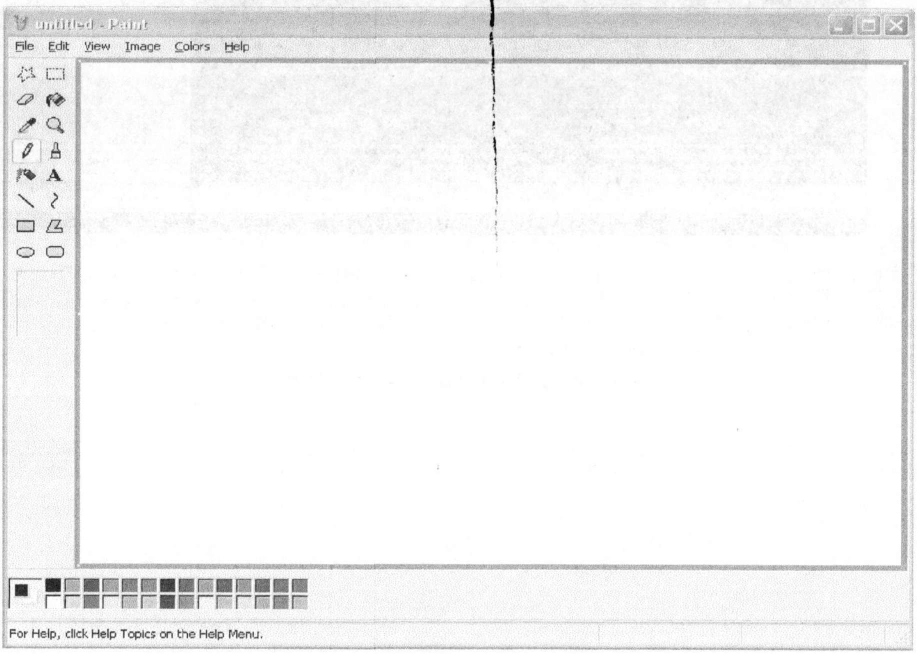

Fig. 2.63. Paint

System Tools

It has many options such as Backup, Disk Cleanup, Security Center, System Information and System Restore etc. which are very useful for managing the system.

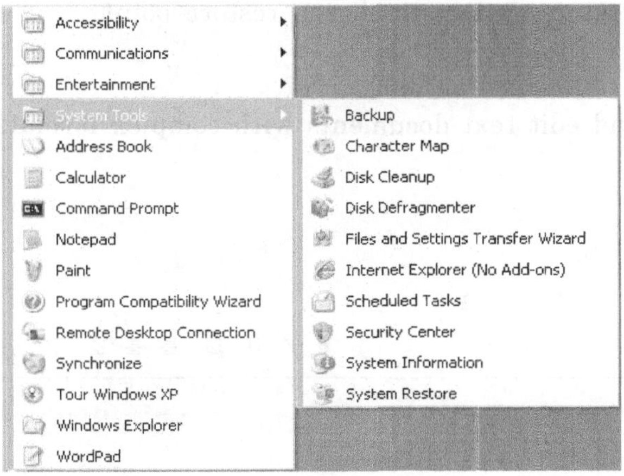

Fig. 2.64. System Tools

- **Backup**
  It archives data to protect it from accidental loss.
- **Disk Cleanup**
  It enables you to clear your disk of unnecessary files.
- **Security Center**
  It is used to view your current security status and access important settings like Firewall, Automatic Updates, and Virus Protection to help protect your PC.

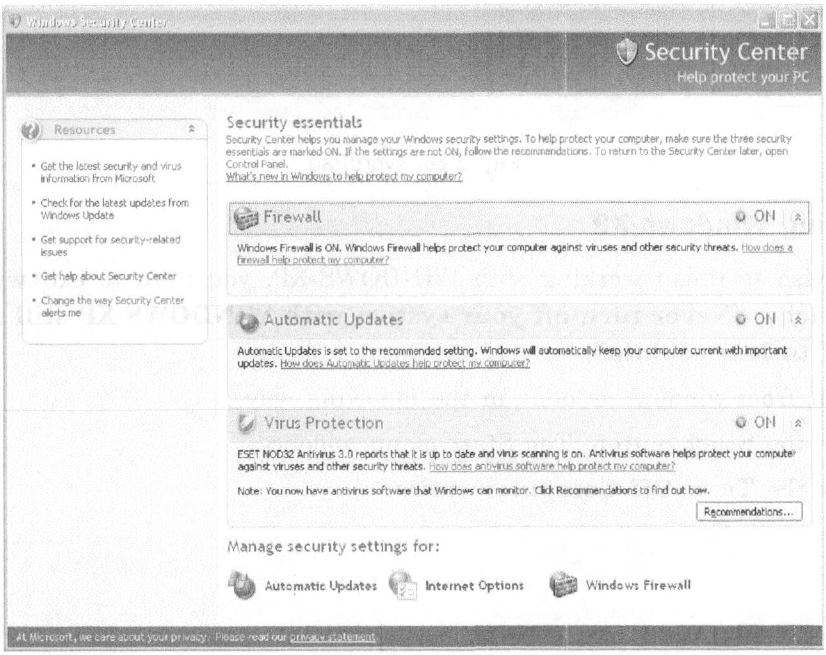

Fig. 2.65

- **System Information**

  It is used to display current System Information.
- **System Restore**

  It is used to restore system to chosen restore point.

WordPad

It is used to create and edit text documents with complex formatting.

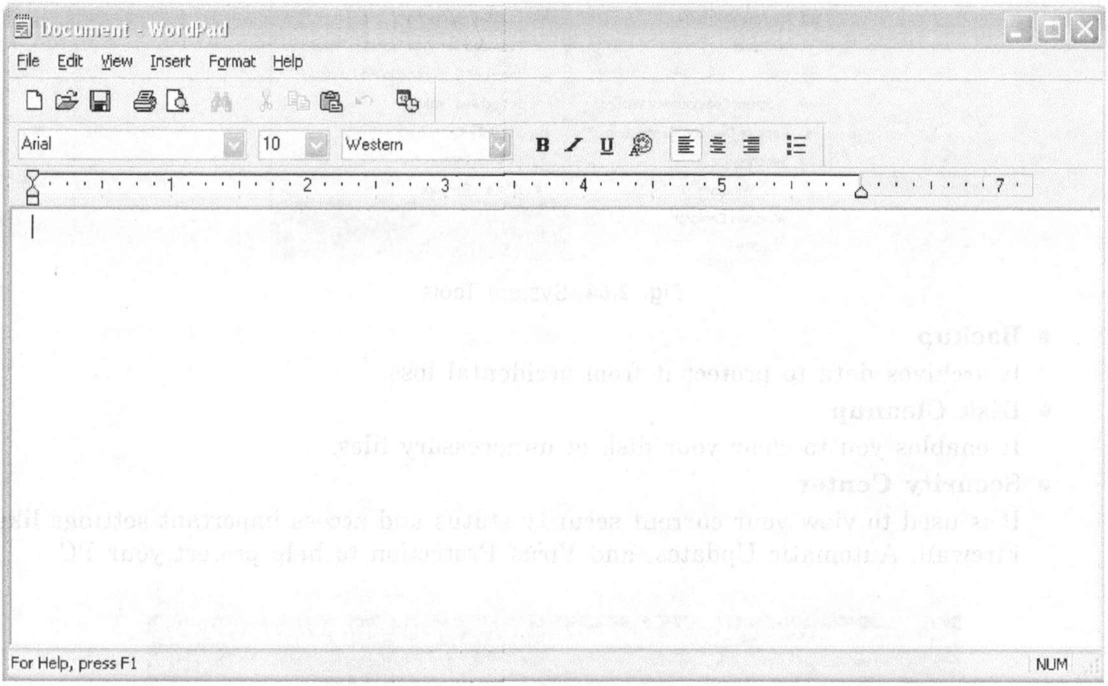

Fig. 2.66. WordPad

2.3.19 Exiting Windows-XP

When you wish to finish working with WINDOWS-XP, you need to exit windows. But always remember **"Never turn off your system with WINDOWS-XP still running as it can lead to loss of data".**

The exit from windows is done in the following way :

1. Click the **Start** button. The Start menu appears.
2. Click the **Turn Off Computer** option.

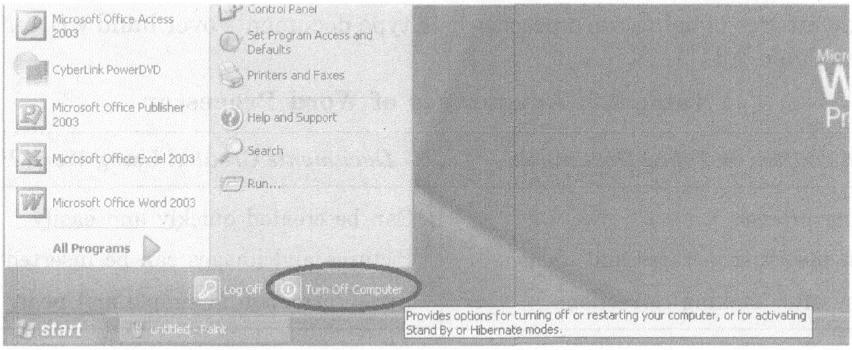

Fig. 2.67. The Turn Off Computer Button

3. In the Turn off computer dialog box, click the **Turn Off** option.

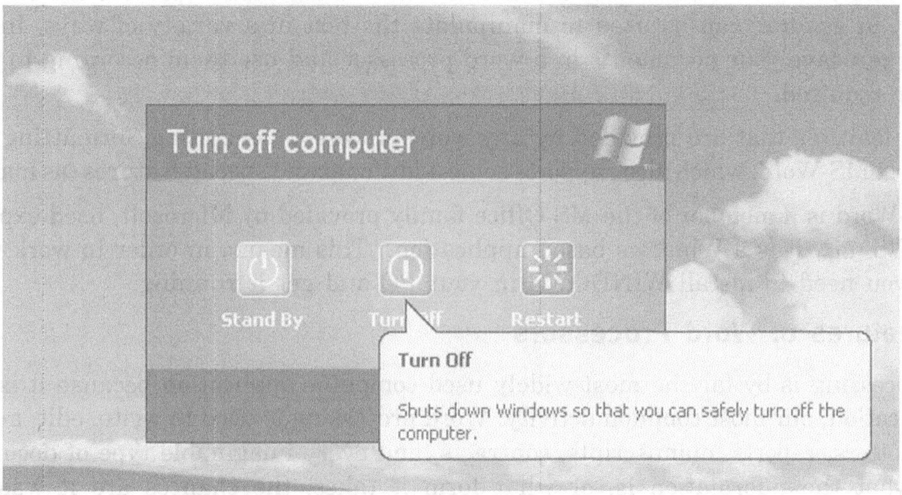

Fig. 2.68. The Turn Off Button

4. The computer shuts down.

2.4 Introduction to Word Processors and their Features

Word processing software allows you to create, edit, format, print, and store text material, among other things. Word processor is the most common application software. The well known word processing programs are :

- Microsoft Word
- Writer
- Wordpad
- Text Editor
- Star Word

Word processing software allows users to work through a document and *delete, insert* and *replace* text, the principal editing and correction activities. It also offers such additional features as *creating, formatting, printing* and *saving* documents such as letters memos, reports, manuscripts and contracts.

The advantages of using word processor to type documents over hand written documents are given in Table 2.3.

Table 2.3. Advantages of Word Processor

Hand Written or Typed Documents	*Documents Created Using Word Processors*
Slow creating process	Can be created quickly and easily
Difficulty in inserting pictures and images	Pictures and images can be inserted easily
Looks messy after making corrections	Error correction is simple and neat.

Microsoft Word—an Example of a Word Processing Package

Microsoft Word (MS-Word) is the most popularly used word processing application software that provides you with a number of useful and fabulous features to process the text. A word processor, in general, can be used to manipulate the text in a variety of ways. In addition to it, you can save your documents in a word processor and use them according to the need, whenever required.

The features that are provided by any word processor (as editing, formatting text) are available in MS-Word, which also supports some additional and special features (as mail merge).

MS-Word is a member of the MS-Office family provided by Microsoft, used explicitly for WINDOWS (*i.e.,* it is a Windows based application). This means, in order to work with MS-WORD, you need to install WINDOWS in your PC and get it running.

2.4.1 Features of Word Processors

Word processing is by far the most widely used computer application because it is used for communication, our most common activity. Word processing is used to write, edit, and format memos, letters, reports, manuscripts, contracts, and every imaginable type of document. No matter what the information is, or what form it takes, the chances are it was initially composed and written using a word processing program.

A word processor is software which provides a graphical user interface with better capabilities than a text editor does. The main advantage of a word processor is that it provides WYSIWYG (What You See Is What You Get) interface which helps you make changes quickly and easily. The main features of today's word-processing packages are :

Creating Documents

It means entering text using the keyboard. Word processing software has three features that affect this process—the *cursor, scrolling* and *word wrap.*

1. **Cursor** : The cursor is the movable symbol on the display screen (monitor) that shows us where we may next enter data or commands. It is often a blinking rectangle or an I-beam. We can move the cursor by using the keyboard's directional arrow keys or a mouse. The point where the cursor lies at a particular instant is known as the *insertion point.*
2. **Scrolling** : Scrolling means moving quickly upward, downward or sideways through the text or other screen display. A standard computer monitor displays only 20–22 lines of standard-size text at a time. Generally, the documents are longer

than that. Using the directional arrow keys, or the mouse and a scroll bar located at the side of the screen, we can move or "scroll" through the display screen and into the text above and below it.

3. **Word Wrap :** *Word wrap* automatically continues text on to the next line when we reach the right margin, *i.e.,* the text "wraps around" to the next line. We do not need to hit a "carriage return key" or Enter key, like in a typewriter.

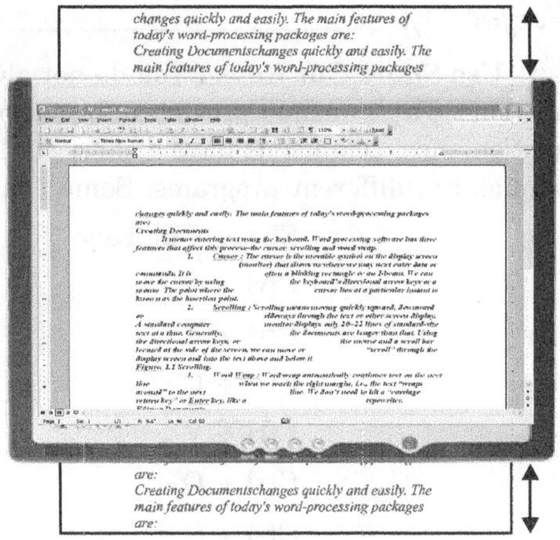

Fig. 2.69. Scrolling

Editing Documents

When editing a document to correct mistakes, we can move the insertion point where we wish to enter new text and then just type it in. To *delete* characters, we press *Backspace* or *Delete key*. Pressing Backspace key deletes characters to the left of the insertion point and pressing delete key deletes those to the right. We can also drag the mouse to highlight any section of the text and then *copy* it to another file, move it to some other place in the document being used, give it a new format, or delete it all at once.

The *Undo command* allows us to change our mind and restore text that we have just deleted. *Inserting* is the act of adding to the document. The *Insert key* plays an important role in the replacement of text and exiting from Insert mode.

In addition to the **insert and delete, cut/copy and paste** features of editing explained above, some other features of editing are :

1. **Find and replace** : The *Find* or *Search*, command allows us to find any word, phrase or number that exists in our document being edited. It can be replaced automatically with something else with the help of *Replace command.*
2. **Spelling checkers** : *Spelling checkers* compare all words in a document with a list of words in the program's dictionary. Words not available in the dictionary are highlighted and we can then decide whether to change them, leave them as such or add them to the dictionary. We must note that a highlighted word is not necessarily misspelled. It just means that the word is not available in the dictionary. Any word that is added into the program's dictionary is not highlighted again (if found next time).

   Spelling checkers help users prepare accurate documents.
3. **Grammar checkers** : Grammar checkers are programs that check the grammar wordiness, incomplete sentences and awkward phrases. The grammar checker does not fix things automatically, but it will flag (perhaps with a different colour of squiggly line) possible incorrect word usage and sentence structure.

   Grammar checkers help users produce better-written documents.
4. **Thesaurus** : Thesaurus is a word processing feature that presents the user with the appropriate word or alternative words.

   The thesaurus feature helps users prepare well-written documents.

Useful Tip

Use Short Cut Keys : You do not always need to use the mouse to pull down menus to perform functions. These menus provide information about which short cut keys serve the same mouse-click function. Most commands have a short cut key, and common functions usually have the same short cut command in different programs. Some examples of shortcut keys in MS-Word are:

Short Cut Key	Purpose
Ctrl + A	Select all the text
Ctrl + X	Cut the text
Ctrl + C	Copy the text
Ctrl + V	Paste the text
Ctrl + O	Open a file
Ctrl + S	Save a file

Formatting Documents with the Help of Templates and Wizards

Formats are used to make a document both more attractive and easier to read. All word processing programs have built-in format settings known as defaults, which are designed so we can easily override them.

Templates : These are preformatted documents that provide basic tools for shaping a final document—the text, layout and style for a letter, for example.

Wizards and helpers : These answer the user questions and uses the answers to lay out and format a document. In Word, we can use the Memo Wizard to create professional-looking memos or the Resumé Wizard to create a resumé.

Among the many aspects of formatting are the following :

1. *Margins* : These are the white spaces on all four sides of the text block. They set off the text and make it more attractive visually.
2. *Headers and footers* : These can be entered at the top or bottom of pages to identify sections or provide other useful information.
3. *Numbers* : These can be used to set off lists so when you insert or delete items, the numbers adjust automatically.
4. *Bullets* : We can use bullets to set off lists where the order is not important.
5. *Fonts* : These can be changed by selecting a new one from a list of those available on the system. We can then use *bold, italic, underline formats* to provide emphasis on the text.
6. *Tables* : These are used to present tabular materials.
7. *Indents* : These specify how much space the paragraph should be indented from the left and right margins.
8. *Page numbers* : These can be positioned almost anywhere on the page and printed in either Roman numerals (*i, ii, iii* etc.) or Arabic numbers (1, 2, 3 etc.).

Printing, Faxing or E-Mailing Documents

We have several options for printing in most of the word processing software. *For example*, we can print *several copies* of a document, *individual pages* or a range of pages can also be printed. We can even preview a document before taking its hard copy or print out. *Previewing* (*print previewing*) means viewing a document on the screen to see what it will look like in the printed form before printing it. Whole pages are shown in reduced size.

We can also send out a document off to someone else by fax or as an e-mail attachment, if the computer has the appropriate communication link.

Saving Documents

It means storing, or preserving, a document as an electronic file permanently—on floppy disk or hard disk (say). This feature is available in nearly all application softwares. The saved document can be retrieved and used when needed.

2.5 Creating Document

As mentioned earlier MS-Word is a member of the MS-Office family provided by Microsoft. It is a windows based application. Let us assume that your computer has MS-Word 2007 installed on it. Remember that there are differences in MS-Word 2003 and MS-Word 2007.

Starting Microsoft Word 2007

To start MS-Word or Word :

1. Click the *Start* button on the taskbar.
2. Choose the *All Programs* option in the *Start* menu (See Figure 2.70).
3. Click the *Microsoft Office* option from the *All Programs* menu.
4. Click the *Microsoft Office Word 2007* option.

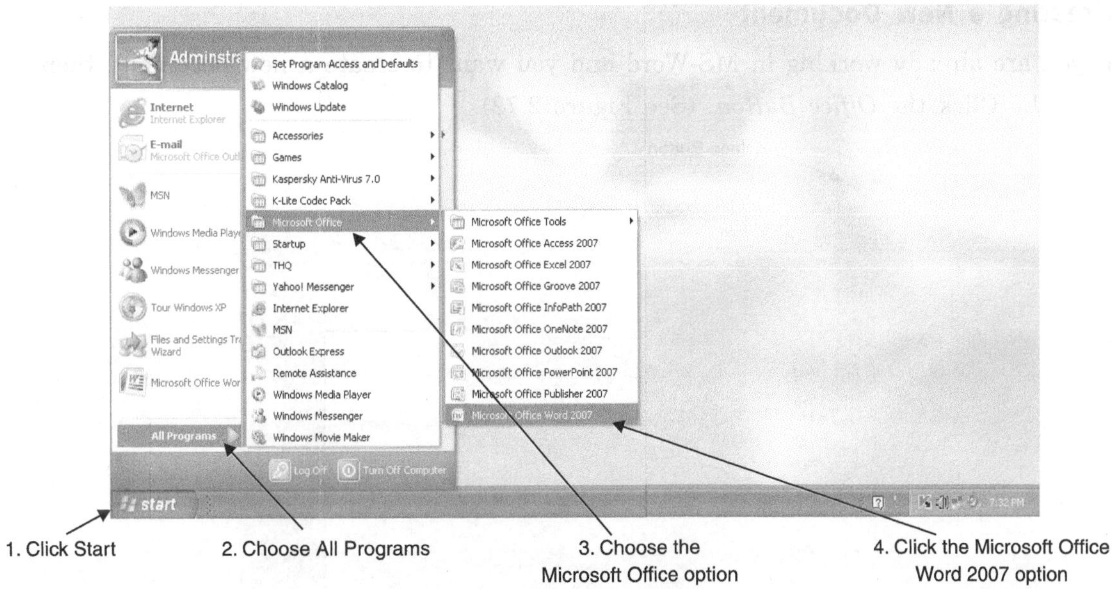

Fig. 2.70. Starting MS-Word 2007

This opens a blank new document. (See Figure 2.71)

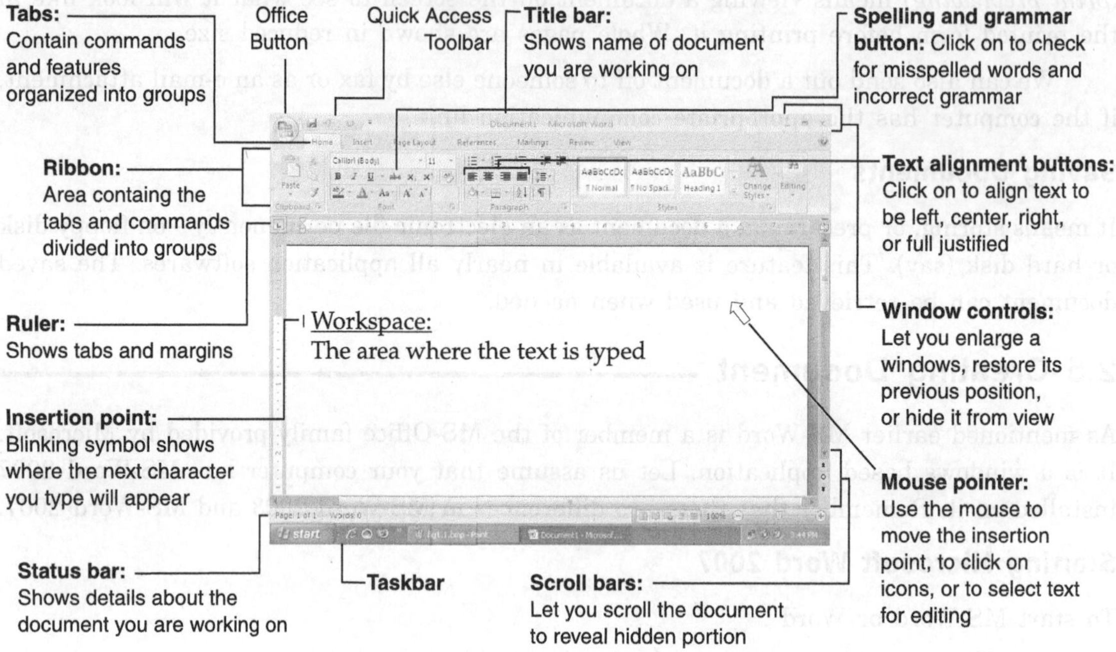

Fig. 2.71. Components of a Document Window

When you start MS-Word, a blank document window appears. MS-Word, by convention, names newly created documents as DOCUMENT1, DOCUMENT2, DOCUMENT3, ... and so on. Thus each new document, when created, is given a name DOCUMENT <serial number>.

Creating a New Document

If you are already working in MS-Word and you want to create a new document, then :

1. Click the *Office Button*. (See Figure 2.72)

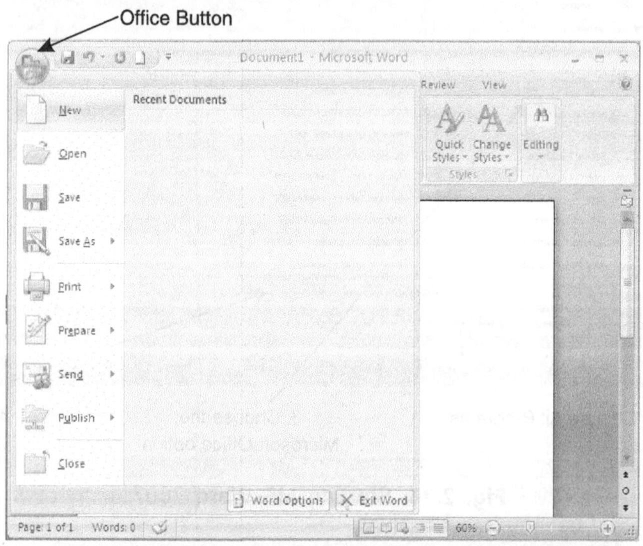

Fig. 2.72. Creating a new document

2. Click on the New option. It displays the following window. (See Figure 2.73)

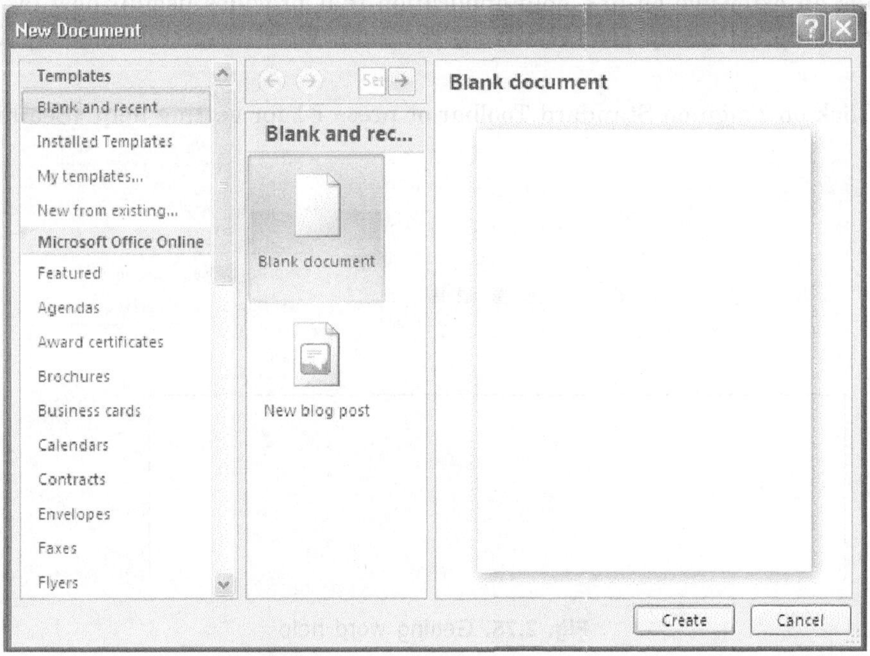

Fig. 2.73. On clicking the New option

3. Click on the *Create* button. It displays the newly created document. (See Figure 2.74)

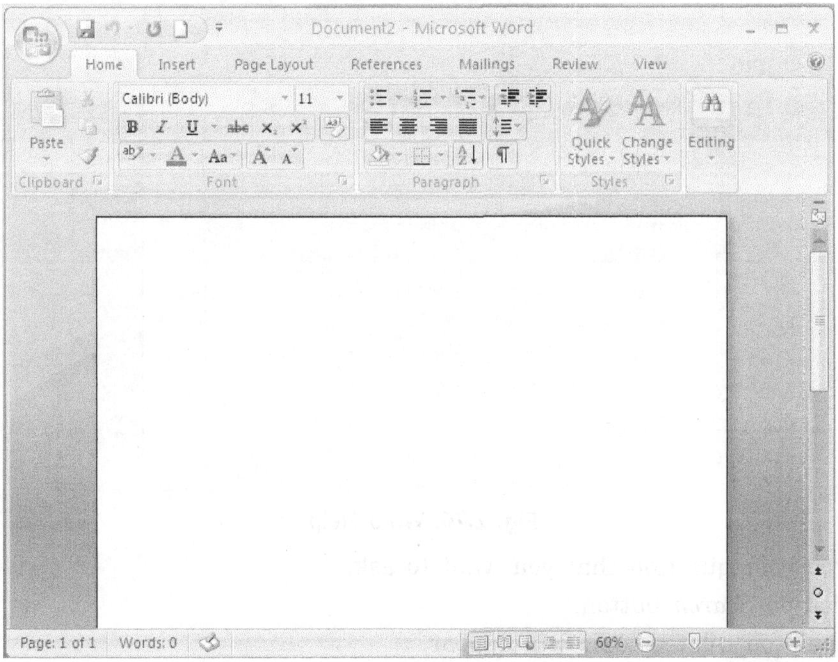

Fig. 2.74. Newly created word document

Microsoft Word Help

Word help is an extensive on-line help application that provides useful "how to" and "what is" information on every aspect of the Word program. Word help can be easily accessed as follows :

1. Click on ? sign on Standard Toolbar or press F1 for getting help. (See Figure 2.75)

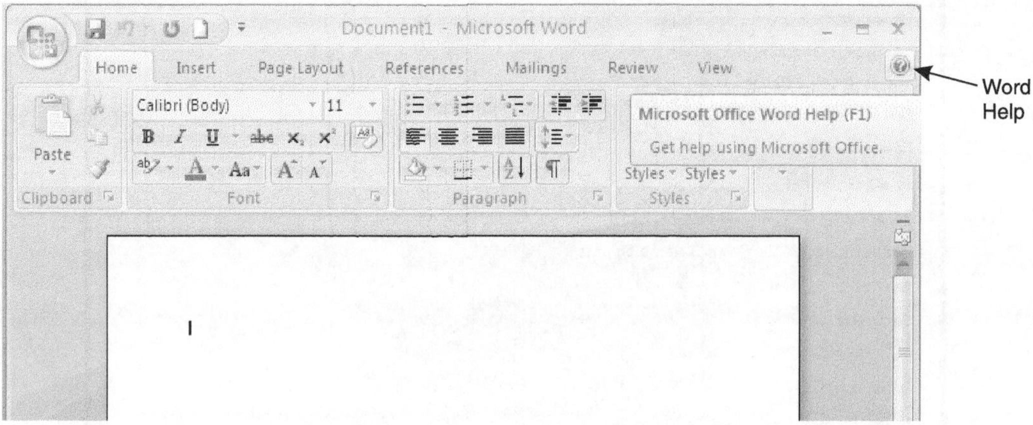

Fig. 2.75. Getting word help

2. On clicking, you will get the Word Help. (See Figure 2.76)

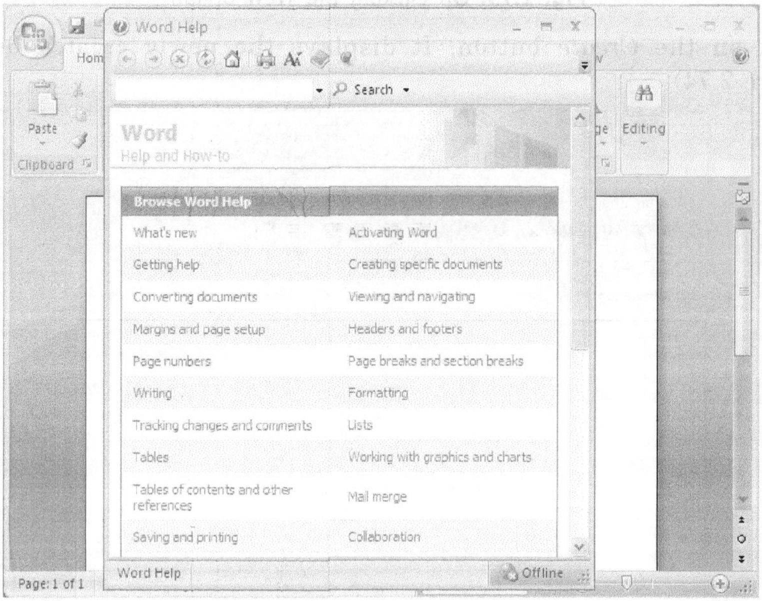

Fig. 2.76. Word Help

3. Type your question that you want to ask.
4. Click on *Search* button.
5. A help on related topic will appear.
6. For closing Word Help, click on ☒ in upper right corner of Word Help.

Typing a Passage Using MS-Word

To insert text in your document, place the cursor at the position where you want to enter the text and start typing.

To insert a paragraph you have to press the enter key and start typing.

When you type text in a document, MS-Word automatically inserts the text in the document area.

Figure 2.77 shows a typed passage in a document using MS-Word 2007.

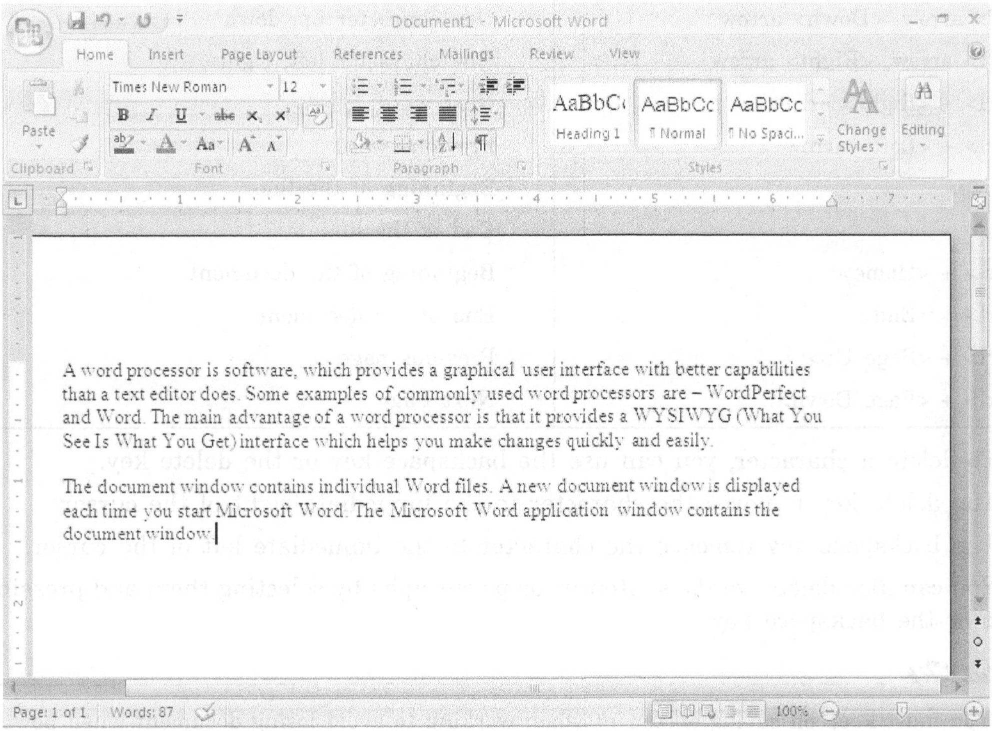

Fig. 2.77. Typing a passage in a Document using MS-Word

> ***Note :*** *1. In case, you need to add some text at a particular location, before an existing text sequence, the text sequence which follows the insertion point is shifted towards right as you type the characters.*
>
> *2. In case, you wish that the newly typed characters should replace the existing text, before starting typing the characters, press the key **'Insert'**. Now whatever you will type will overwrite the characters. To return to the normal mode of typing (i.e., to cancel the overtype feature) press the **'Insert'** key again.*

2.6 Editing Document

Editing is the act of altering your document. Some Edit features are *insert* and *delete, undelete, find and replace, cut/copy and paste, spelling checker, grammar checker,* and *thesaurus*. All of these commands are in the Home tab shown as icons.

When you edit text, you change text by either inserting text, deleting text or replacing text. To edit text, place the cursor at the required position and either insert, delete or replace text. Table 2.4 shows how to move around a document using the keyboard. You can also use the mouse to change the position of the cursor.

Table 2.4. Moving Around a Document Using the Keyboard

Keys	*Functions*
<UP> arrow, <Down> arrow	One character up, down
<Left> arrow, <Right> arrow	One character left, right
<Ctrl> + <Right> arrow	Next word
<Ctrl> + <Left> arrow	Previous word
<Home>	Beginning of the line
<End>	End of the line
<Ctrl> + <Home>	Beginning of the document
<Ctrl> + <End>	End of the document
<Ctrl> + <Page Up>	Previous page
<Ctrl> + <Page Down>	Next Page

To delete a character, you can use the backspace key or the delete key.

The delete key removes the character to the immediate right of the cursor.

The backspace key removes the character to the immediate left of the cursor.

You can also delete words, sentences or paragraphs by selecting them and pressing the delete or the backspace key.

Useful Tip

You must keep on saving document when working to avoid losing document when power goes off.

You can edit a Word document using the following editing tools :

- Spell check functions
- Copy/cut and paste facilities
- OVR
- Undo and redo keys
- Search and replace

Spell Check Functions

Spell checking is a very big plus point while talking about word processing. You can spell check your document for wrong spellings and even wrong grammar too.

Let us type some text in a document to use the above mentioned tools. (See Figure 2.78)

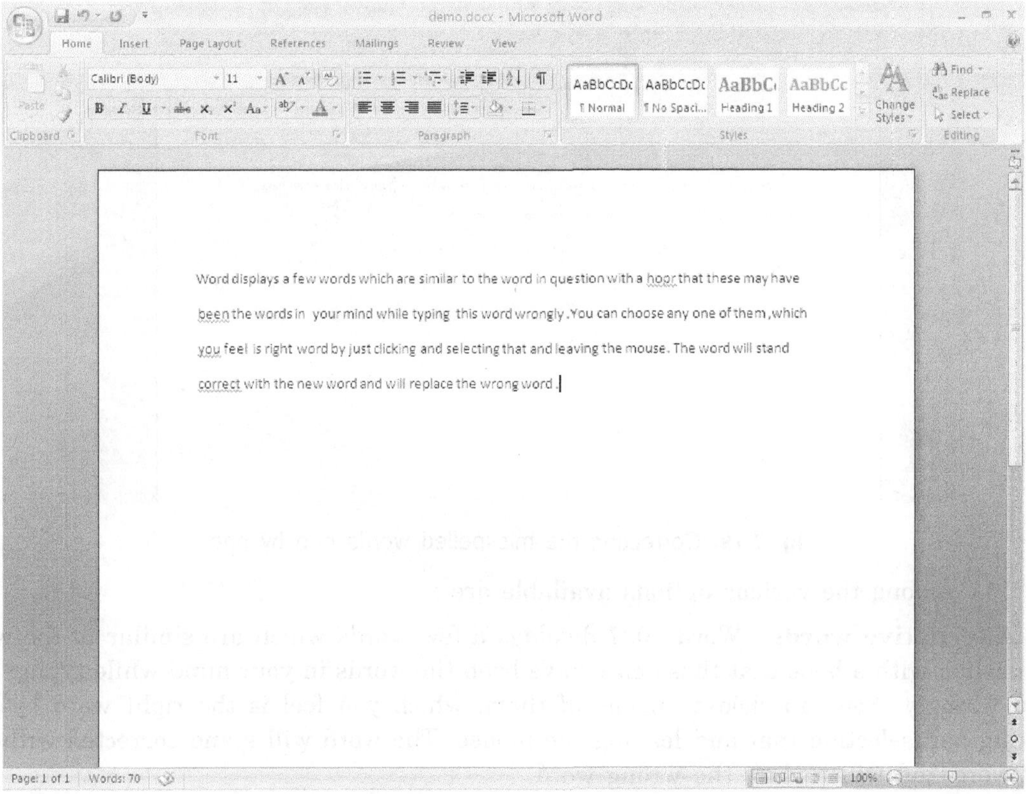

Fig. 2.78. A Word document

While typing the above document, you must have noticed that some words are underlined by wavy red lines and some with green lines. Well, the red lines show that the word is wrongly spelled whereas the grammatical mistakes are pointed out by the green lines.

There are two methods of correcting these errors. One method is to correct these errors one by one, picking them up. Secondly, you can spell check the whole document. First let us take up the option of correcting the misspelled words one by one.

For correcting the misspelled words one by one do the following :

1. Click with the mouse at any place within the word to be corrected, say "hopr".
2. Now right click the mouse button.
3. A pop-menu will pop-up as shown in Figure 2.79.

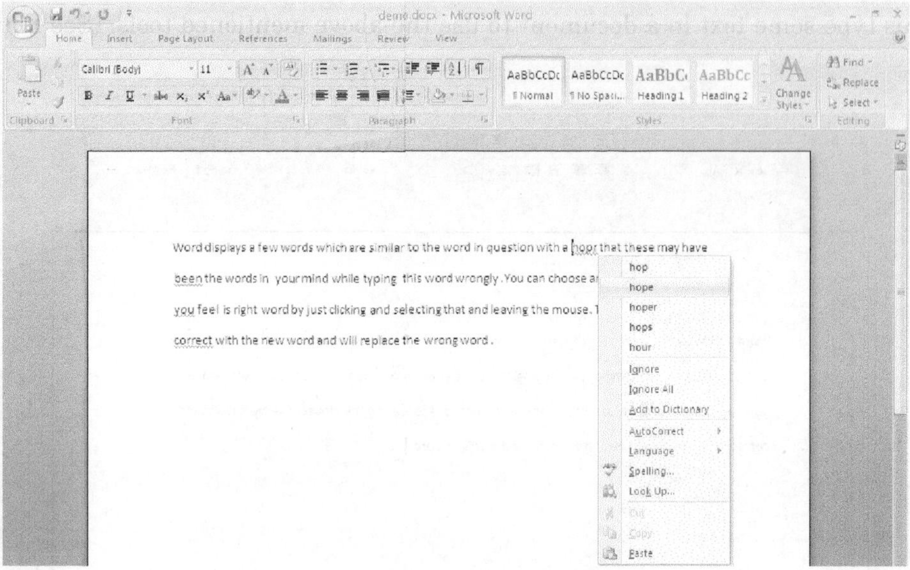

Fig. 2.79. Correcting the misspelled words one by one

4. Among the various options available are :

Alternative words : Word 2007 displays a few words which are similar to the word in question with a hope that these may have been the words in your mind while typing this word wrongly. You can choose anyone of them, which you feel is the right word by just clicking and selecting that and leaving the mouse. The word will stand corrected with the new word and will replace the wrong word.

In our case we select "hopr" and the word changes from "hopr" to "hope"–red line disappears.

Ignore : It is like over ruling the dictionary and saying that whatever you have typed is right and would like the dictionary to ignore this not only at this place but also at all other places within the document.

Ignore All : This will allow you to ignore this error throughout the document.

Add to Dictionary : If you feel that this word is right and would like this word to be added to the dictionary so that it is not shown as an error in the future.

Auto Correct : This is another option of Microsoft Word 2007 where you define the words which are most likely to be spelled wrong by you and their alternative words. These words when typed wrongly are corrected automatically.

Language : You feel that this particular word which has been pointed as wrong by the current dictionary would be available in other language dictionary. So mention here the name of the other dictionary where this word could be found. If you do not have a second dictionary loaded, just ignore this.

Spelling... : By clicking at this, you can start the spell checking of the whole document from this point onward.

Look Up... : It looks for an alternative word in the thesaurus.

Cut, Copy and Paste : These can be used for transferring the selected word to some other place in the document by cutting or copying it at this place and pasting it there.

For removing the wavy green lines, right click the mouse button. A pop-up menu appears. Select the appropriate option. Here we have selected *Ignore Once* option for the word 'been'. (See Figure 2.80)

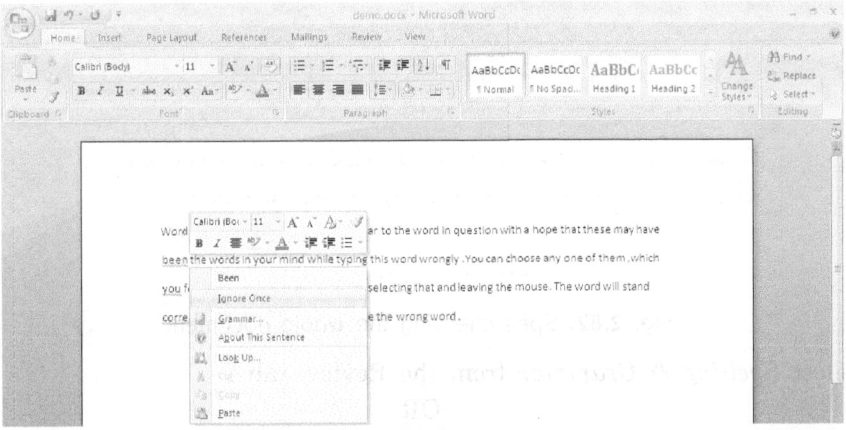

Fig. 2.80. Removing wavy green lines

Repeat the above process for the whole document.

5. After spell checking the document word by word, you will get the corrected document. (See Figure 2.81)

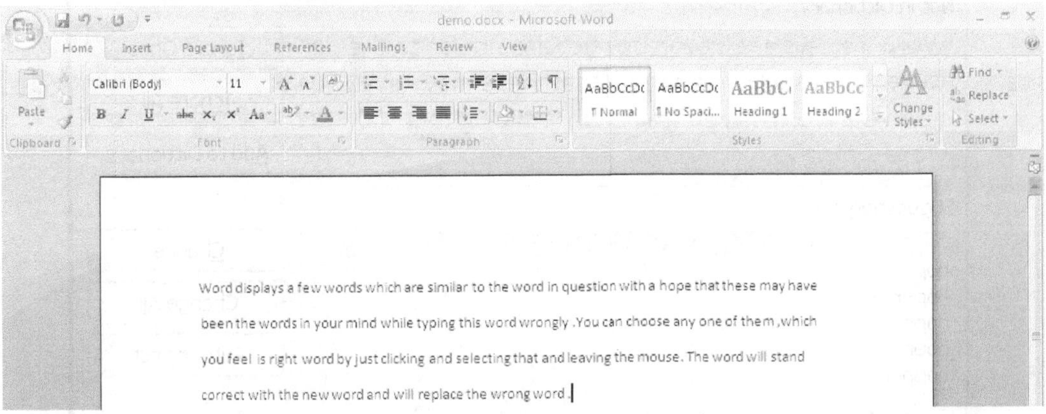

Fig. 2.81. Document after applying the corrections

6. Save and close the document.

For spell checking the whole document do the following :

As mentioned above you can correct all the misspelled words one by one. This method is little tedious since, you have to pick up word by word. On the other hand, if you have a long document, then the other method of spell checking is more appropriate. Let us discuss it.

1. Place the cursor at the beginning of the text in the document (See Figure 2.82)

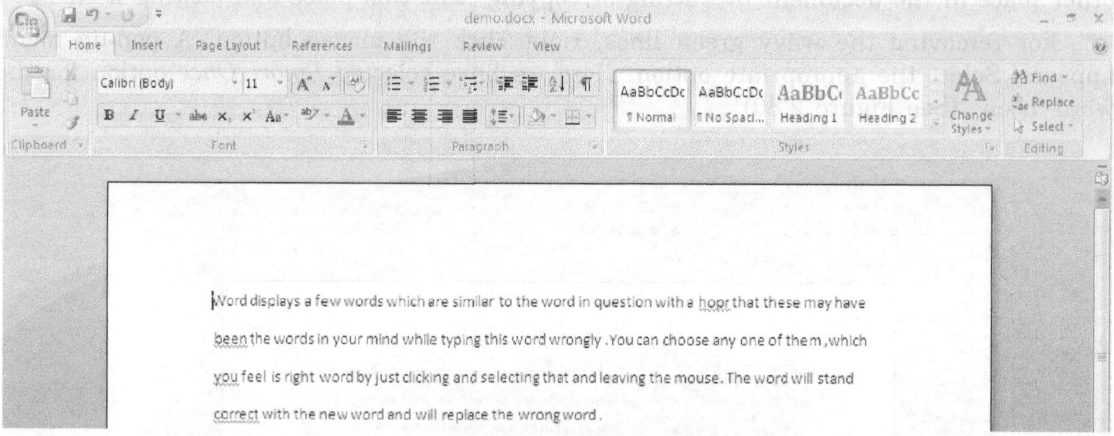

Fig. 2.82. Spell checking the whole document

2. Select *Spelling & Grammar* from the Review tab.

OR

Press F7

OR

Click at *Spelling* & *Grammar* in Proofing Panel of Review.

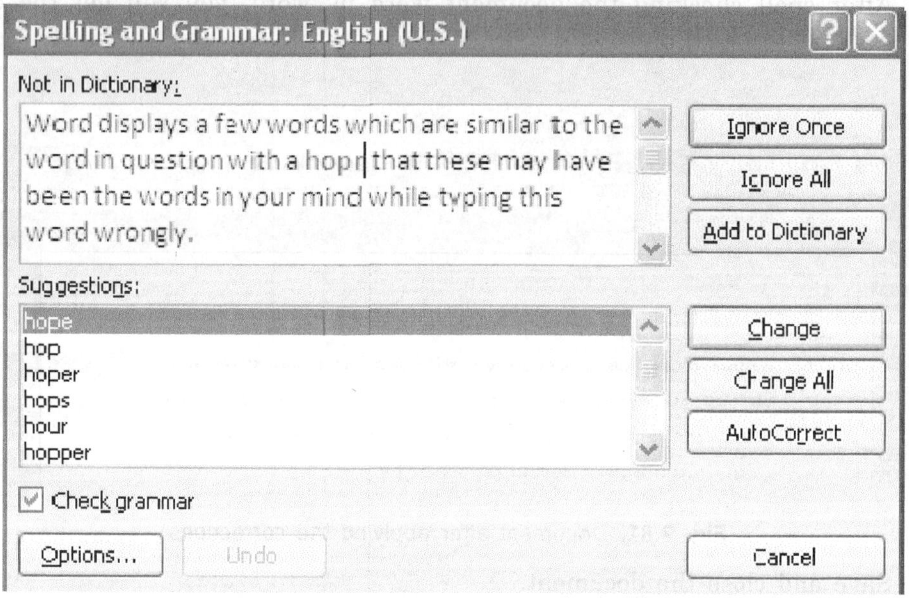

Fig. 2.83. Spelling and grammar check

This will initiate the spell checking process and will start the spell checking of the document with each word of the document being searched with the similar words available in the dictionary. If not found, it will point it out to you. Select the appropriate word from the suggestions box. Here we have selected 'hope'. For green wavy lines select *Ignore Once*.

3. After checking the spelling of the whole document, if there is no word left for checking, you will get the message shown in Figure 2.84.

Fig. 2.84. On completion of spelling and grammar check.

4. Click OK.
5. Save and Close the document.

Remember, you can spell check a portion of the text or a word by just highlighting it and then clicking at Spelling & Grammar icon.

Copy/Cut and Paste Facilities

You can copy text from one place in a document to another place.

When you copy text, you duplicate the text.

To copy text :

1. Open a document and select the text you want to copy. Here we have opened the demo. docx document.
2. Click the Home tab.
3. Click the Copy option from Clipboard panel. The copied text is placed in the Clipboard (See Figure 2.85).

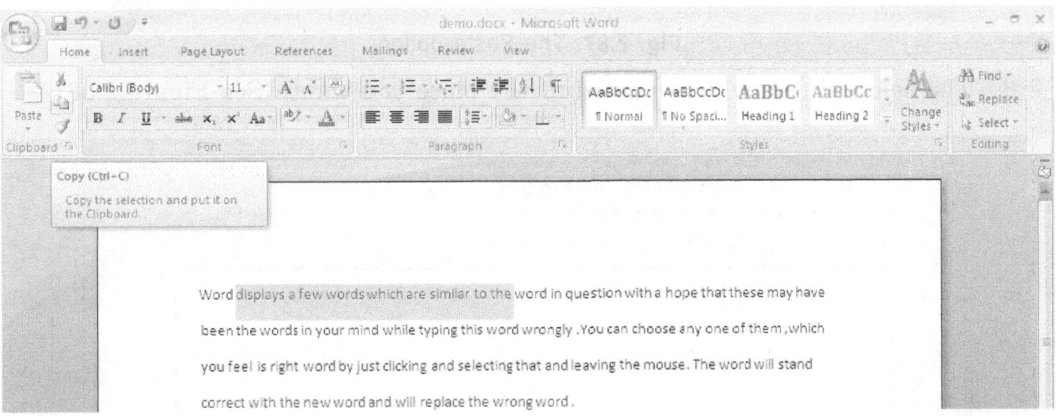

Fig. 2.85. The Copy option

4. Place the cursor at the place where you want to paste the text. (See Figure 2.86)

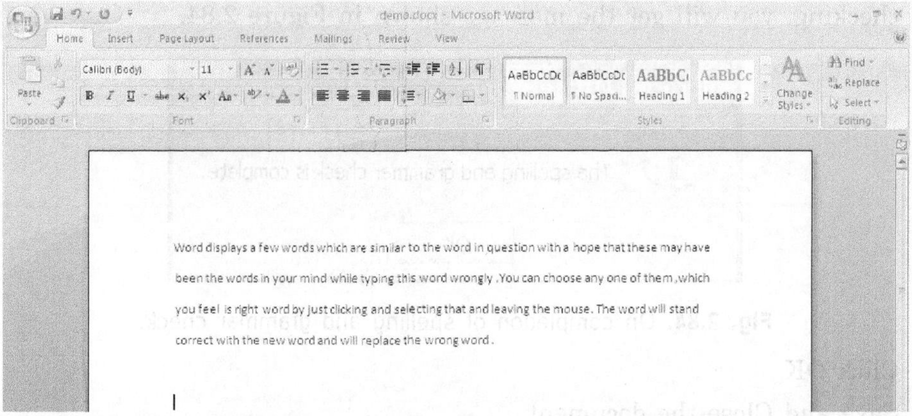

Fig. 2.86. Cursor position for pasting the text

5. Click the Paste option from the Clipboard panel. (See Figure 2.87)

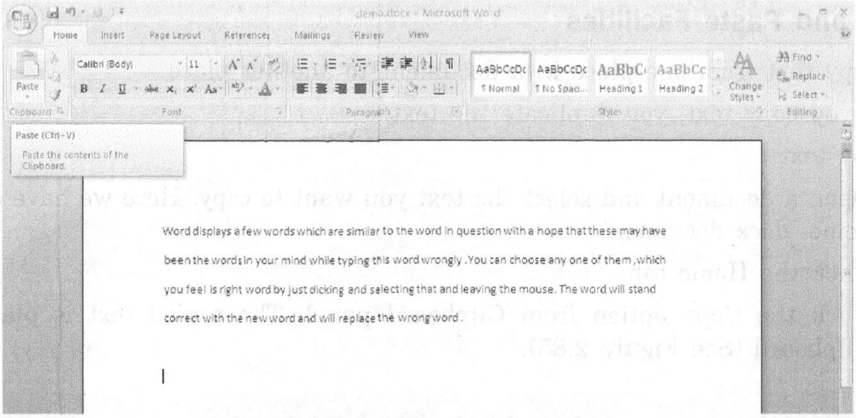

Fig. 2.87. The Paste option

6. The selected text will be pasted at the place you want. (See Figure 2.88)

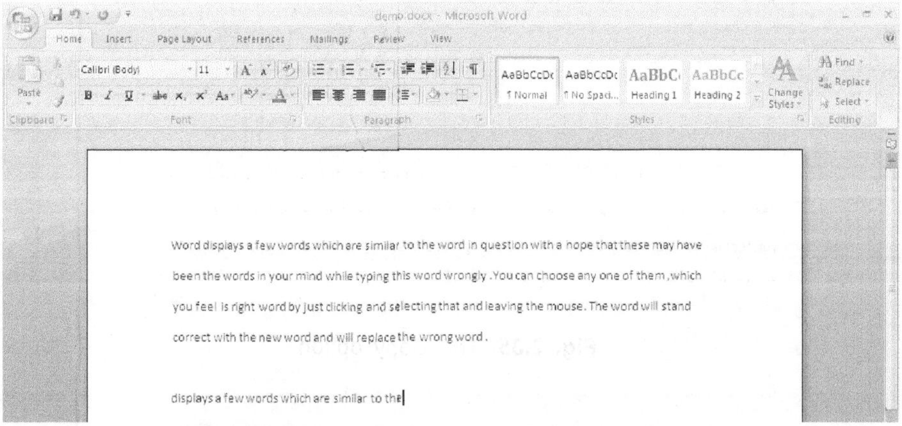

Fig. 2.88. Document after pasting of selected text

7. Save and close the document.

Useful Tip

1. You can use the <Ctrl> + C keys on the keyboard to Copy the text.
2. You can use the <Ctrl> + V keys on the keyboard to Paste text.

OVR (Overtype Mode)

Overtype mode is another utility, related to the editing of text in MS-Word. If you are working in overtype mode, typing of a character in the mid of two characters will replace the character to the right of the cursor. For example, if you want to add a word My before the line "Name is Sunny", place the cursore before N and type "My". The two characters typed by you, will replace the first two characters of the line and the output will be "Myme is Sunny". It is clear from the name and example, that in the overtype mode, characters are written over the presently typed characters.

You can activate the **OVR** mode by pressing the **Insert** key for once.

Useful Tip

In OVR *i.e.,* overtype mode, the typed characters replace the already typed characters instead of taking new space.

Undo and Redo Keys

In Word 2007, you can reverse or *undo* the last performed action(s) on the document.

To undo an action,

1. Open a document (Refer to Figure 2.88) and make changes in it (See Figure 2.89). First we delete the last line of the document and then change the word "hope" to "hopr" in the first line.
2. Click the Undo icon in the title bar (See Figure 2.89).

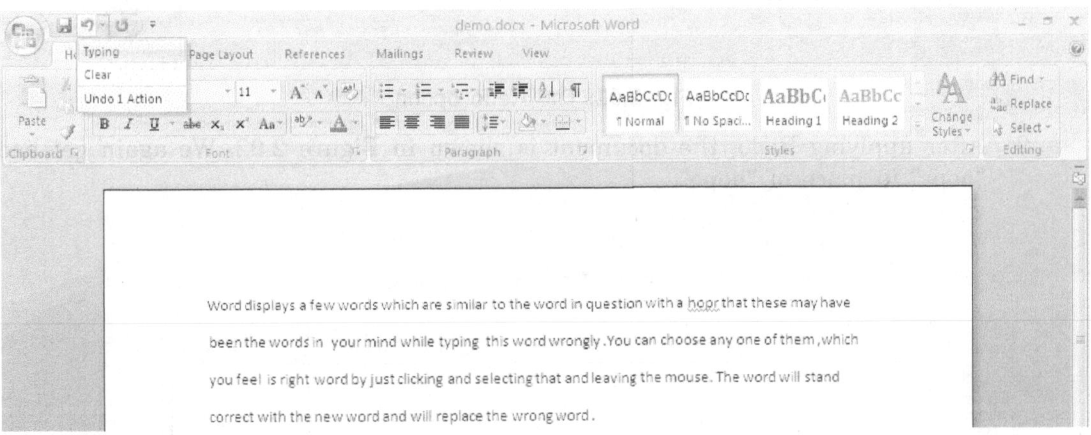

Fig. 2.89. The Undo option

3. After applying Undo, the document is shown in Figure 2.90.

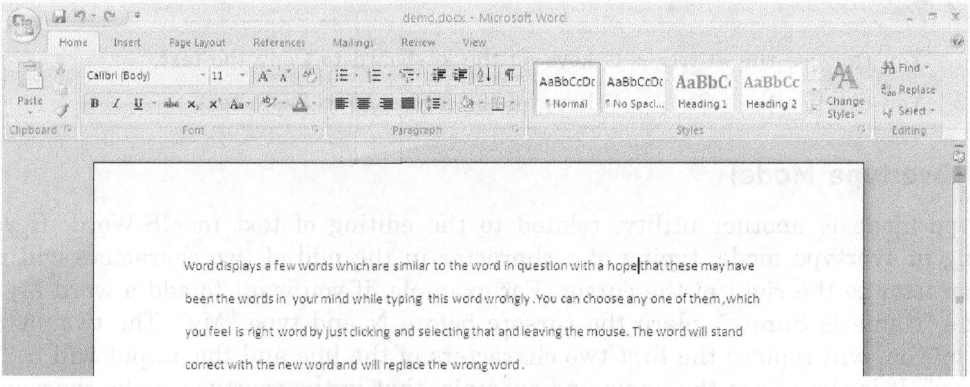

Fig. 2.90. After applying the undo option

You can undo the other action also if you wish to do so.

Similar to an *undo* action, you can perform a *redo* action. The Redo option is used to reverse the last Undo action on the document. Let us apply Redo option on the document demo.docx shown in Figure 2.90 after step 3 given above.

To redo an action,

1. Click the Redo icon in the Quick Access Toolbar. (See Figure 2.91)

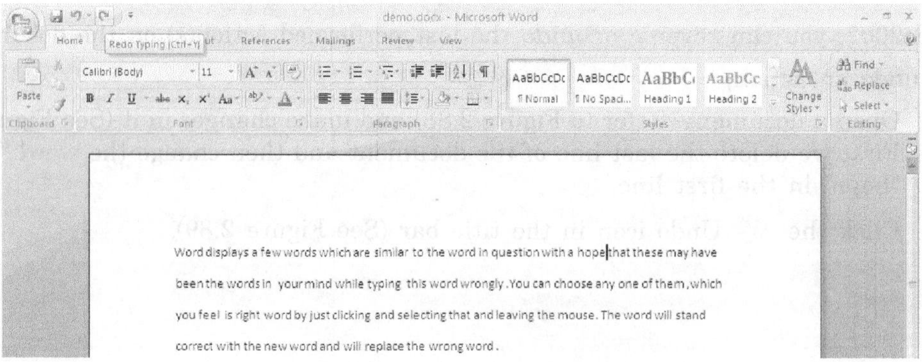

Fig. 2.91. The Redo option

2. After applying Redo, the document is shown in Figure 2.92. We again get back "hopr" in place of "hope".

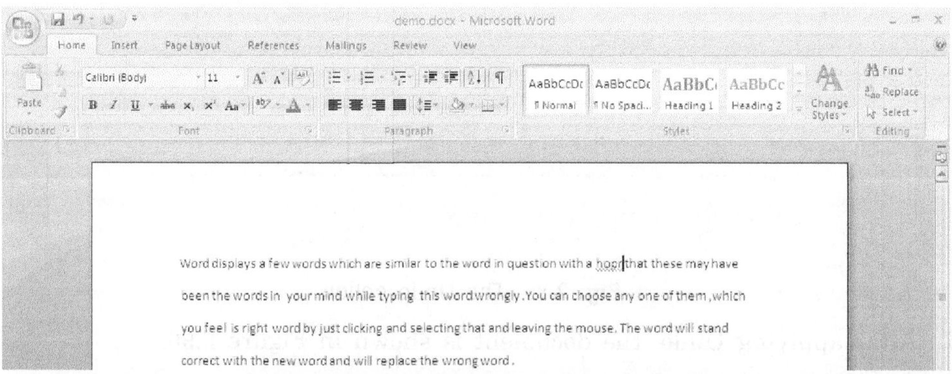

Fig. 2.92. After applying the Redo option

Useful Tip

1. You can use the <Ctrl> + Z keys on the keyboard to Undo action.
2. You can use the <Ctrl> + Y keys on the keyboard to Redo action.

Find and Replace

Word also has a feature that lets you look for a word and replace the word with another word. For example, if you want to replace every occurrence of the word "hopr" with "hope", you can use this command.

1. Place the cursor in the beginning of the document and click the Home tab.
2. Click the Replace option in Editing panel (See Figure 2.93).

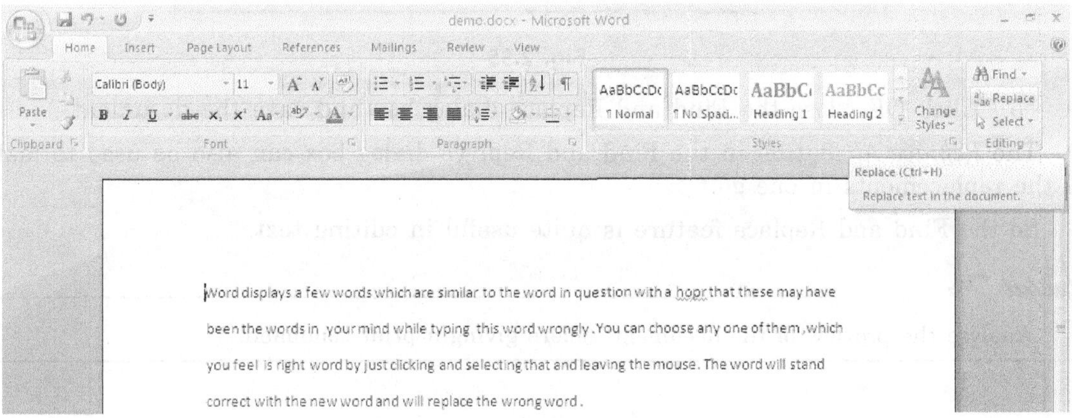

Fig. 2.93. The replace option

3. In Find and Replace dialog box, type the word "*hopr*" in the *Find what* : text box, and the word "hope" in the *Replace with* : text box. (See Figure 2.94)

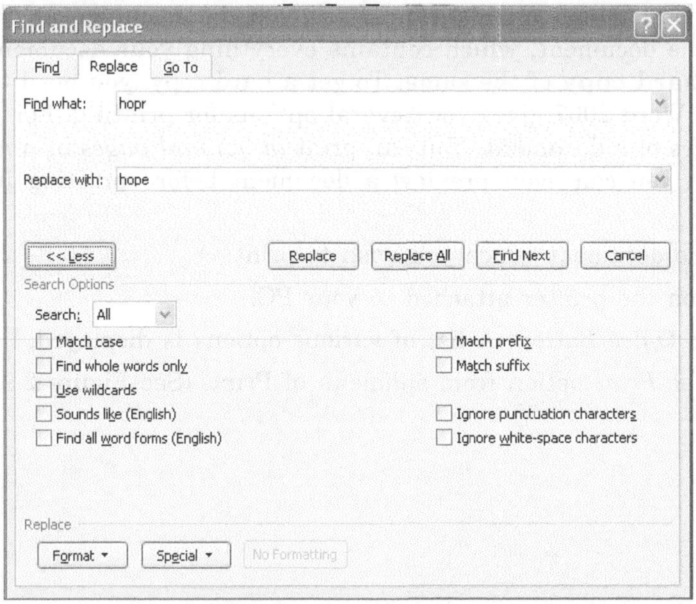

Fig. 2.94. The find and replace dialog box

4. Click the *Replace* button. The first word to be replaced (if present) is highlighted. Again press the replace button to replace it. In the same way Word replaces all the occurrence one by one and finally the following dialog box is displayed. (See Figure 2.95)

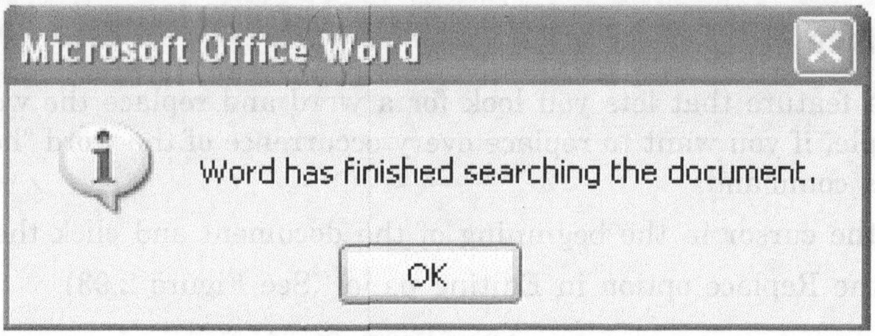

Fig. 2.95

5. Click OK, close the Find and Replace dialog box and save the document.

The *Replace All* button in the Find and Replace dialog box can also be used to make all the replacements in one go.

So the Find and Replace feature is quite useful in editing text.

Useful Tip

Analyse the preview of the document, before giving a print command.

2.7 Printing a Document

After typing in a document, you might need to hand over your work (say for assignment or managerial purposes) further to a teacher or an executive; or otherwise need it for your own records and use. This demands a handy copy of the document at your disposal. This 'handy copy' of the document, which contains everything your document has, in printed form is called a **hard copy** of the same. To get a hard copy, you need to take a printout of the document. Word 2007 gives you several options for printing. For example, you can print *several copies* of a document. You can print *individual pages* or a *range of pages*. As discussed earlier, you can even preview a document before printing it out. To print a document :

1. Open the document which you wish to print.
2. Switch on the printer attached to your PC.
3. Click on *Office Button*. A list of various options is displayed.
4. Select the *Print* option from submenu of Print. (See Figure 2.96)

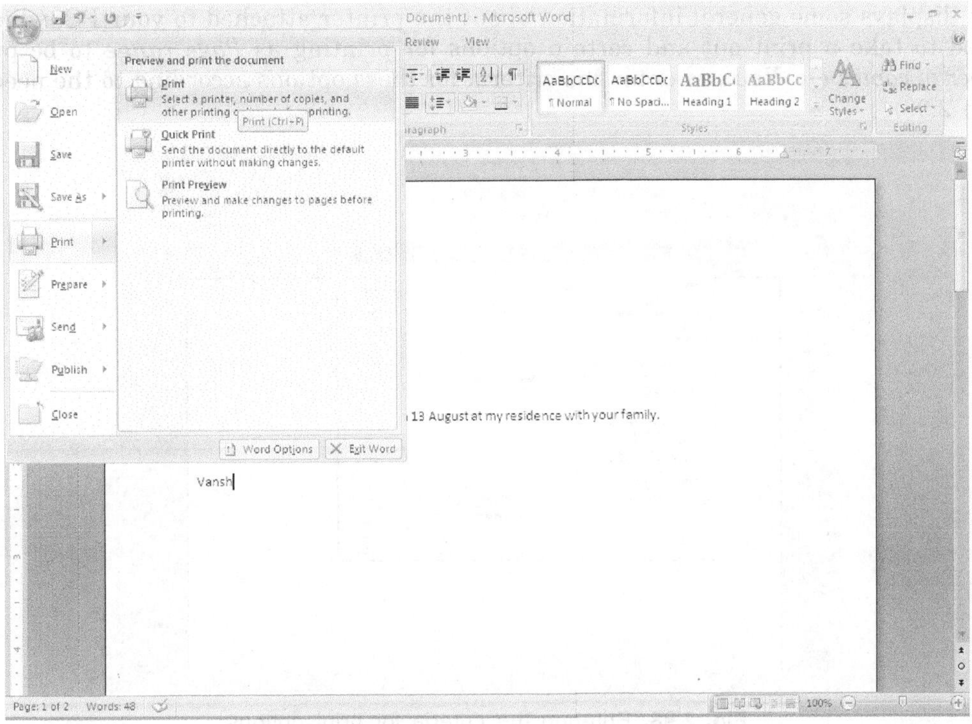

Fig. 2.96. Selecting the Print option

5. On clicking, a *Print* dialog box appears. (See Figure 2.97)

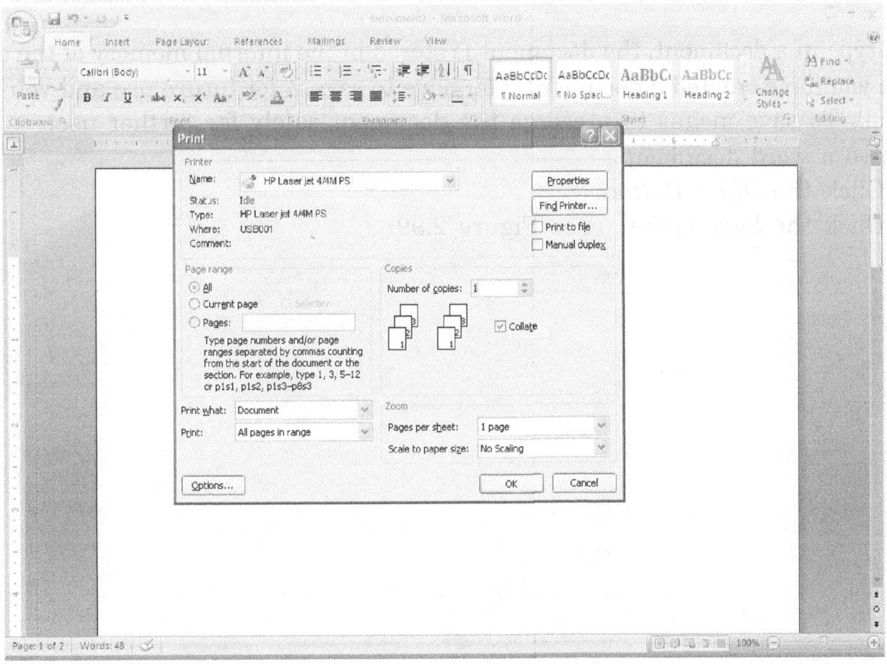

Fig. 2.97. Print dialog box

It displays some general information about the printer attached to your PC, which will be used to take a print out and certain options for printing as *Page range* to be printed, *Number of copies* etc. You can enter the criteria for these options according to the need. (See Figure 2.98)

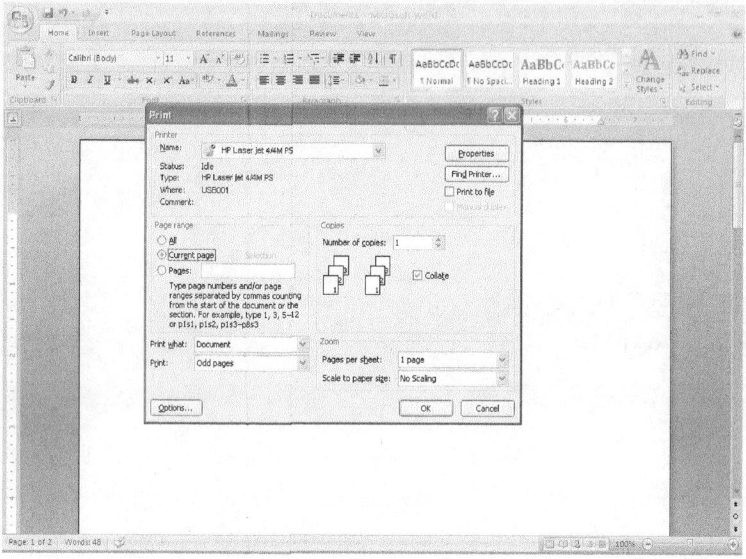

Fig. 2.98. Entering the criteria for print options

6. Click on OK button to start printing.

2.8 Saving Document

When you type in a document, the document is stored in the internal memory of the computer.

Once you have created a document, you have to save it for future use and you must save it on a disk. To save means to preserve the document safely for further use.

To save a word document :

1. Click the *Office Button*.
2. Click the *Save* option. (See Figure 2.99)

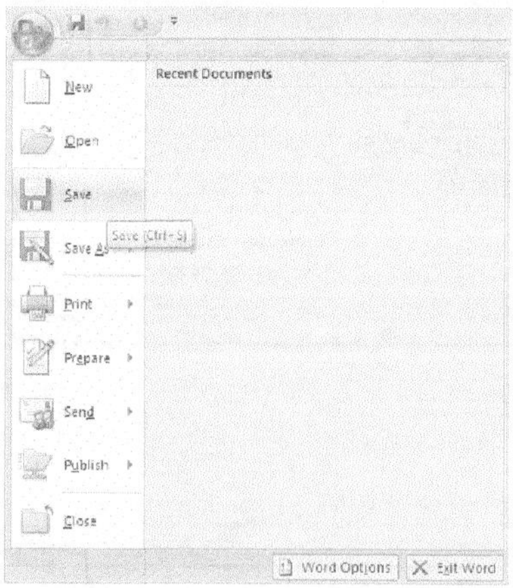

Fig. 2.99. Selecting the Save option

3. The 'Save As' dialog box is displayed as shown in Figure 2.100.

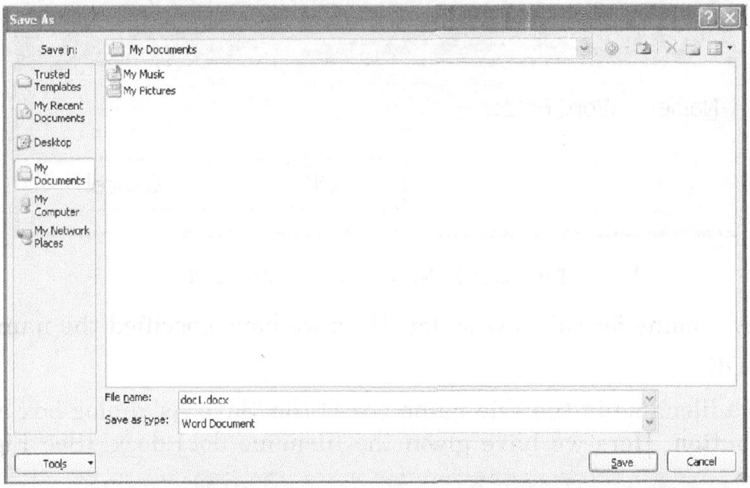

Fig. 2.100. The Save As dialog box

The Save As dialog box is displayed only under the following circumstances :

(*i*) When you have clicked 'Save As'.

(*ii*) If you have clicked Save and you are saving the document for the first time.

4. You must enter the name by which you want to save the document. Here we have given the name doc1.docx.
5. Click the *Save* button.

> ***Note** : MS-Word, by default, saves all the documents in the folder 'My Documents' with extensions.docx. However, you can save them elsewhere by selecting the desired location, from the **'Save in :'** drop-down list provided in the 'Save As' dialog box.*

Alternatively, you can click on the Save button on the Quick Access Toolbar or press the Ctrl and S keys to open the 'Save As' dialog box.

The steps to save a file in a new folder are :

1. Select the *Save* option after clicking the *Office Button*. The 'Save As' dialog box is displayed.
2. Click on the *Create New* Folder button (or press Alt+4). (See Figure 2.101)

Fig. 2.101. Creating New Folder for Saving a file

3. The New Folder dialog box is displayed. (See Figure 2.102)

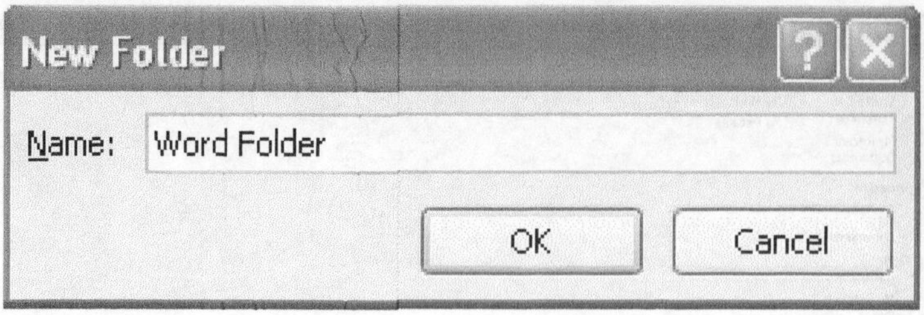

Fig. 2.102. New Folder dialog box

4. Specify a name for the new folder. Here we have specified the name Word Folder.
5. Click OK.
6. Enter a filename in the File name box of the 'Save As' dialog box and click on the *Save* button. Here we have given the filename doc1.docx. (See Figure 2.103)

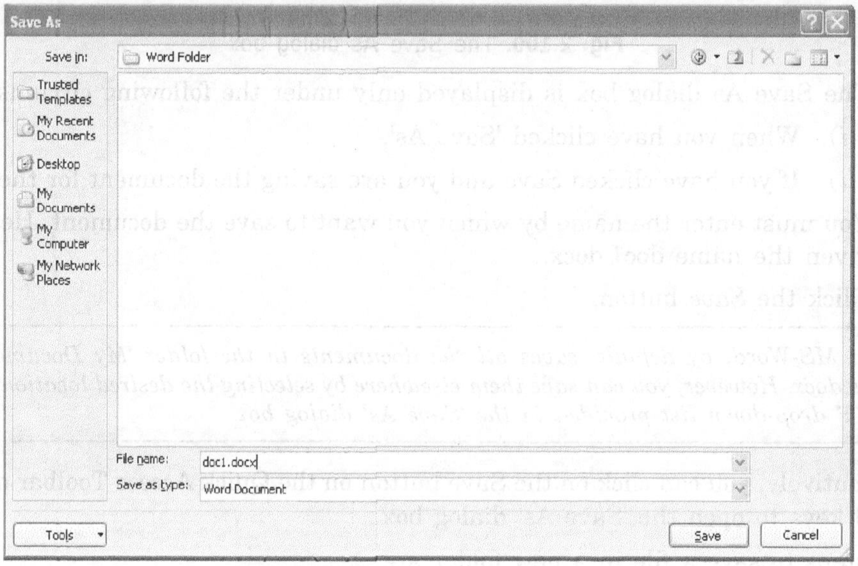

Fig. 2.103. Saving a document in a folder

Caution : When you are using the 'Save As' option, make sure that you do not overwrite the existing copy of the file.

Closing a Document

After your work is complete you need to close the document without exiting from the MS-Word.

To close a document without exiting the MS-Word,

1. Click the *Office Button*.
2. Click the *Close* option.

If you have not saved the document before closing, MS-Word gives you warning asking to save the document. (See Figure 2.104)

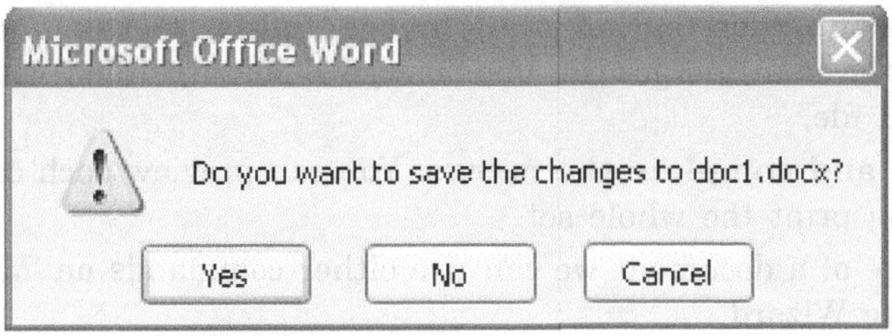

Fig. 2.104. The warning dialog box

From the dialog box shown in Figure 2.104 :

If you want to *Save* the document, click the *Yes* button.

If you do not want to *Save* the document, click the *No* button.

If you want to remove the message box, click the *Cancel* button.

Exiting Microsoft Word

When the Word Processing work is over, you must exit properly from MS-Word.

To exit MS-Word :

1. Click the *Office Button.*
2. Click the *Exit Word* button.

If you have not saved the document, Word prompts you to save changes before closing the application. (See Figure 2.104)

Useful Tip

You can close the document using Close button ⊠ available in the Title bar.

2.9 Mail Merge

Mail Merge is used to create a set of documents, such as a form, letter, that is sent to many customers or a sheet of address labels. Each letter or label has the same kind of information, yet the content is unique. For example, in letters to your customers, each letter can be personalized to address each customer by name. The uniqueness in each letter or label comes from entries in a data source. The mail merge process entails the following overall steps:

(*i*) **Setup the main document:** The main document contains the text and graphics that are the same for each version of the merged document. For example, the return address or salutation in a form letter.

(*ii*) **Connect the document to a data source:** A data source is a file that contains the information to be merged into a document. For example, the name and address of recipients of a letter.

(*iii*) **Refine the list of recipients or items:** Microsoft Office Word generates a copy of main document for each item, or record, in your data file. If your data file is a mailing list, these items are probably recipients of your mailing. If you want to generate copies for only certain items in your data file, you can choose which item (records) to include.

(*iv*) **Add placeholders, called mail merge fields, to the document:** When you perform the mail merge, the mail merge fields are filled with information from your data file.

(*v*) **Preview and complete the merge:** You can preview each copy of the document before you print the whole set.

For mail merge of a document we can use either commands on 'Mailings' tab or 'Step by Step Mail Merge Wizard.

For making you understand the working of Mail Merge, let us create a simple birthday invitation letter.

The steps involved in the process are:

1. Start Microsoft Office Word 2007.
2. On the panels menu select 'Mailings'. (See Figure 2.105)

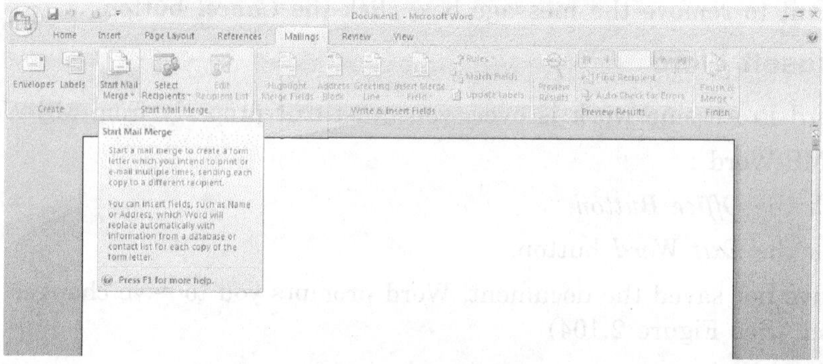

Fig. 2.105. Selecting Mailings

3. Click on 'Start Mail Merge' and then select 'Step by Step Mail Merge Wizard'. (See Figure 2.106)

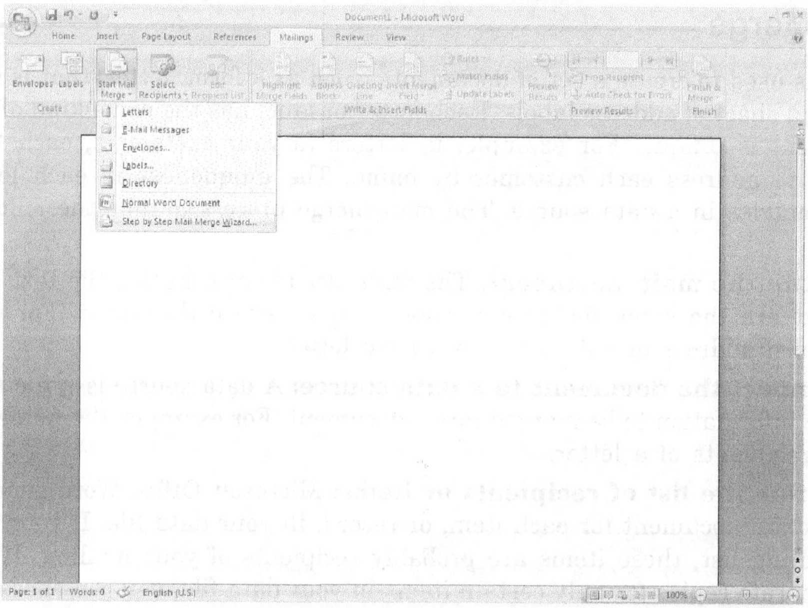

Fig. 2.106. Selecting Step by Step Mail Merge Wizard from Start Mail Merge

4. A Mail Merge window will appear. There are six steps involved in Mail Merge.

   Step–1

5. In Step 1, select type of document which you want to merge. Here I select 'Letters' type document. It is by default. you can also select other option like E-mail messages, Envelopes, Labels and Directory.
6. After selecting letters document type click on Next. (See Figure 2.107)

   Step–2

7. In this step, select the starting document which you want to merge whether it is current document, a template or any other existing document.
8. Select 'Use the current document' and then click on Next. (See Figure 2.108)

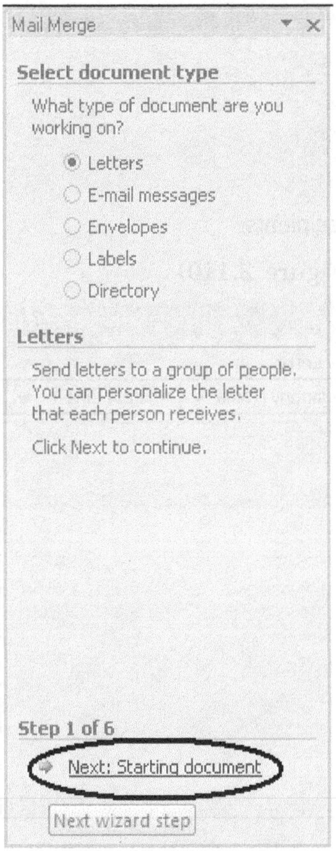

Fig. 2.107. Mail Merge window

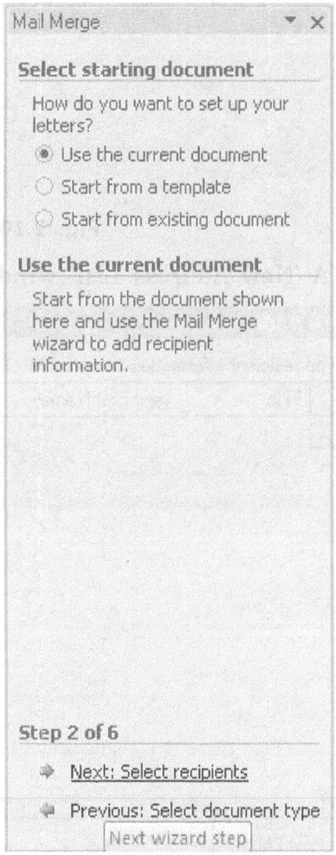

Fig. 2.108. Selecting Use the current document

Step–3

9. In this step, you have to select recipients. If you don't have any recipients list choose the 'Type a new list' and click on 'Create'. (See Figure 2.109)

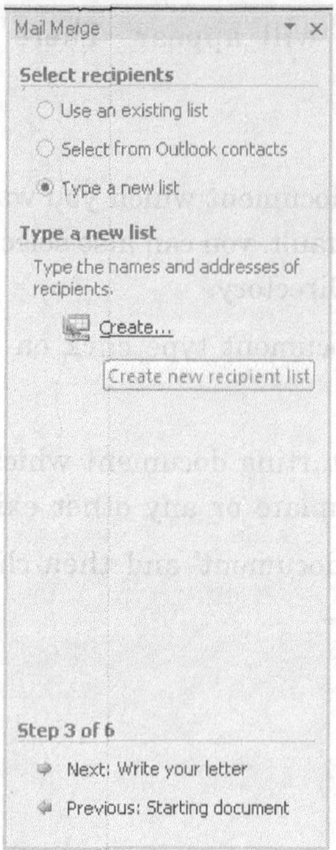

Fig. 2.109. Choosing Select recipients

10. A 'New Address List' window appears. (See Figure 2.110)

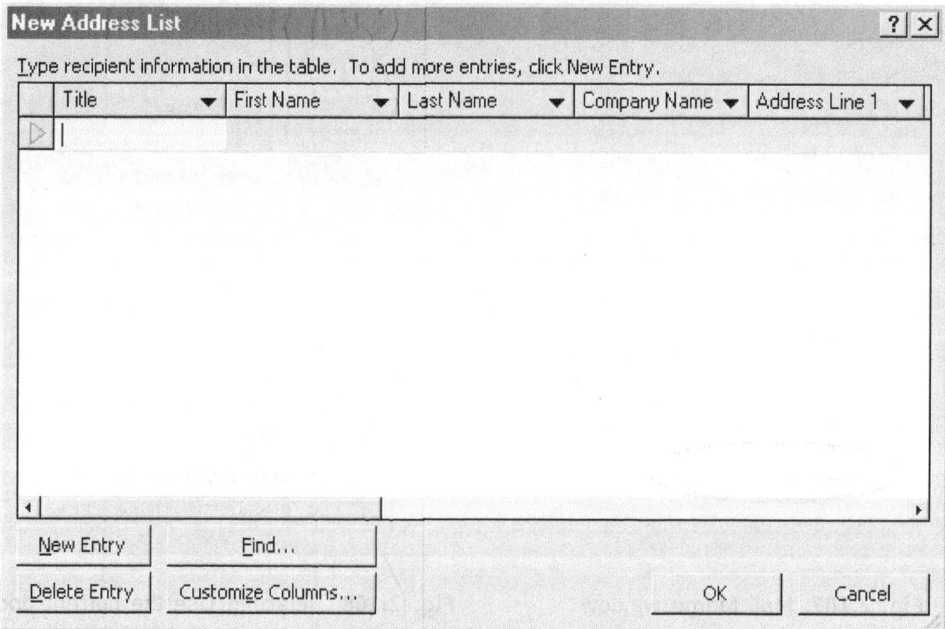

Fig. 2.110. New Address List window

11. You can create as many recipients information in your address list as you want.

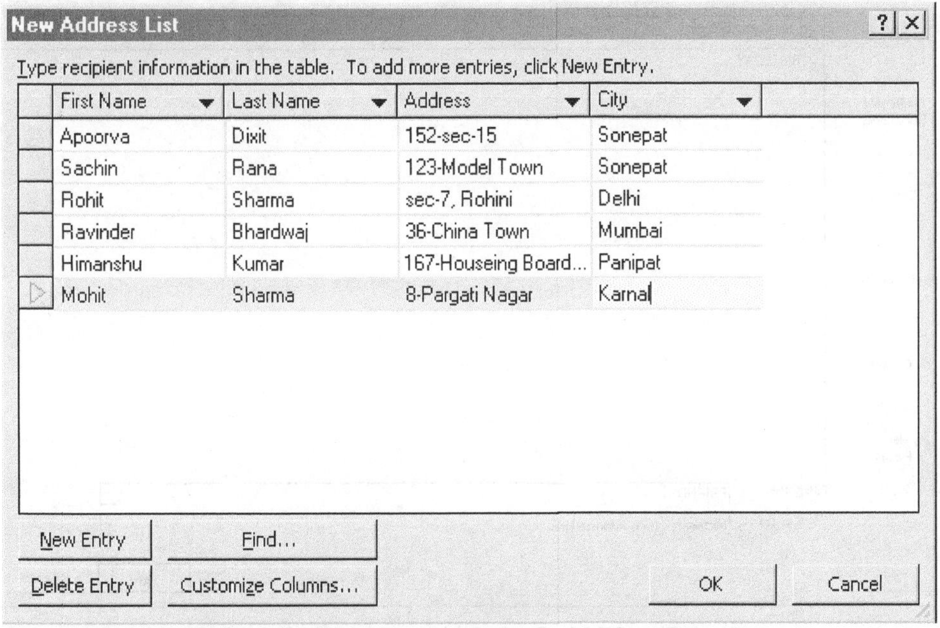

Fig. 2.111. Typing recipients information in the table

You can also add or delete fields name in your address list by using 'Customize Columns' option.

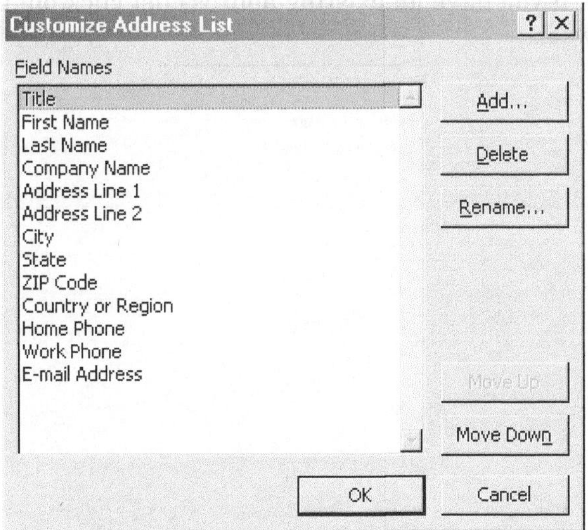

Fig. 2.112. Customize Address List window

12. After filling information of recipients according to fields name click on OK button.
13. It would ask you to save the address list with a name. Provide a name and click on 'Save' button.

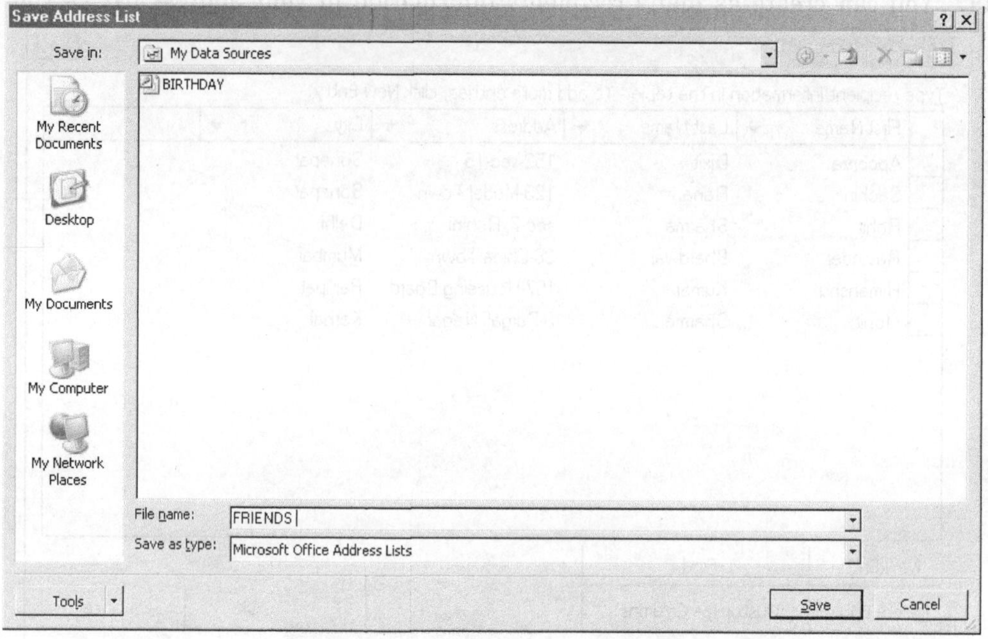

Fig. 2.113. Save Address List window

14. Now your created address list is your current address list.
15. Click on Next in Mail Merge window.

 Alternatively, if you have an existing address list click on 'Use an existing list' and click on Browse.

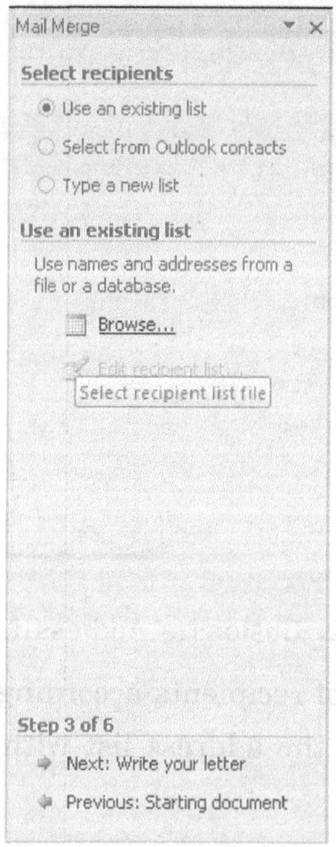

Fig. 2.114. Clicking Use an existing list

Select the address data source and click on Open.

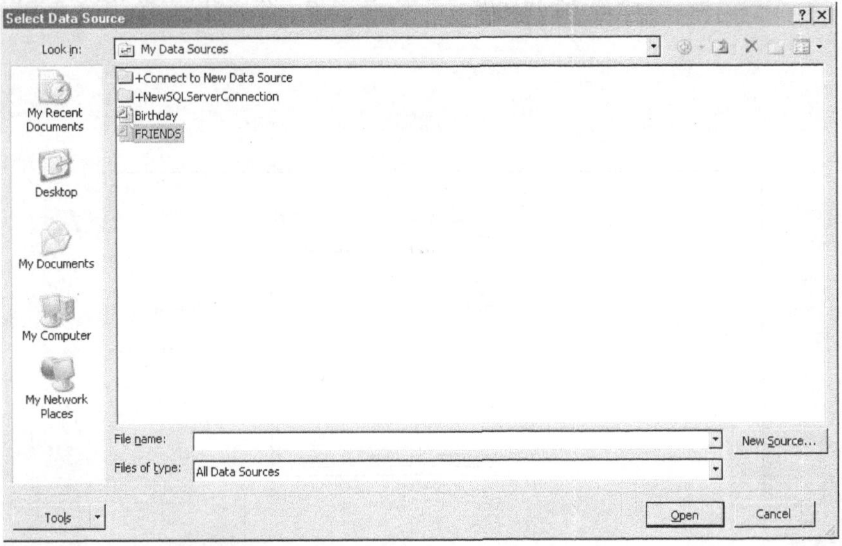

Fig. 2.115. Select Data Source window

Step–4

16. In this step you have to write the body of your letter into word text area.

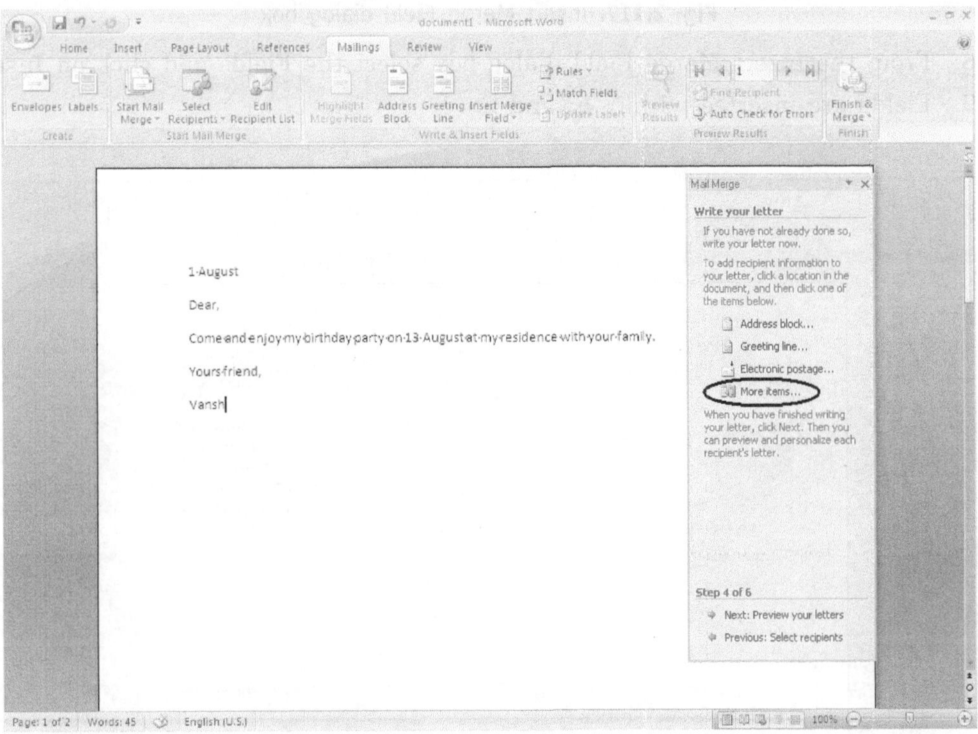

Fig. 2.116. Writing the body of your letter

17. After writing your letter, you have to insert recipients information by clicking on 'More items'. The 'Insert Merge Field' dialog box appears. (See Figure 2.117)

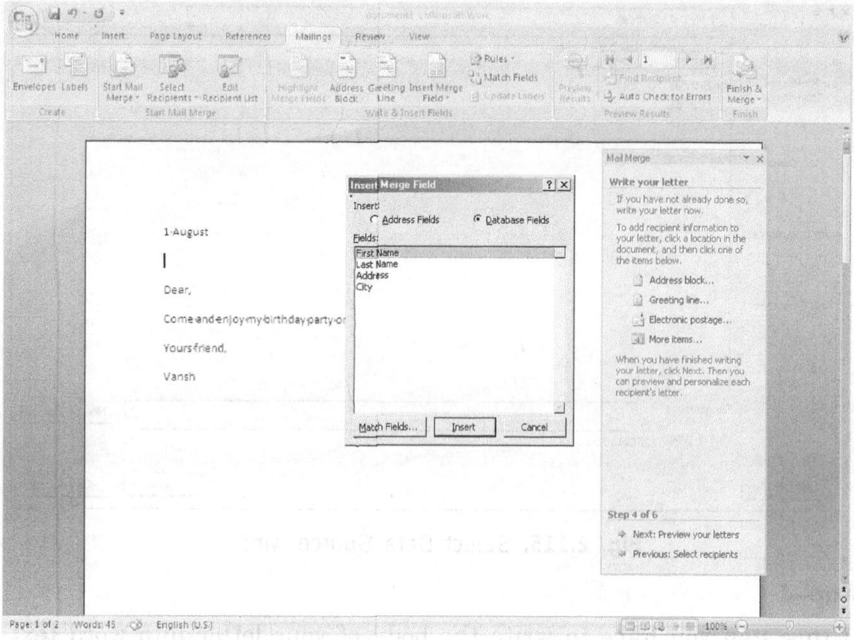

Fig. 2.117. Insert Merge Field dialog box

18. From the Insert Merge Field dialog box select the Fields and click on Insert.
19. Fields are inserted within << and >>.

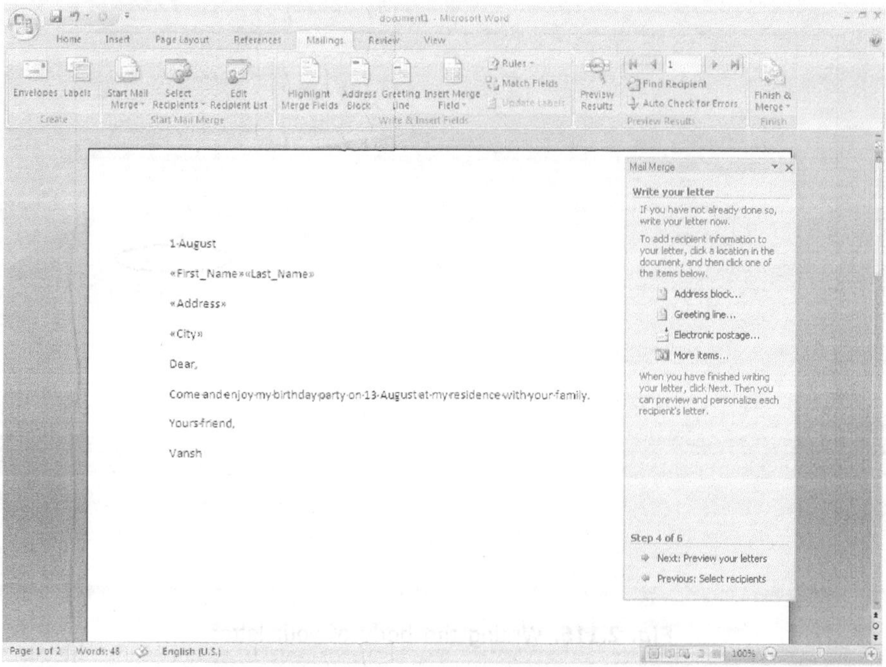

Fig. 2.118. Body of letter after inserting fields

> ***Note :*** *1. You have to adjust the position of curser on the letter to insert merge fields at their correct position. If you have already written your letter you can directly add merge fields from 'More items'.*
>
> 2. You can also insert Address block, Greeting line and Electronic postage according to your need.

20. Click on Next in the Mail Merge window.

Step–5

21. In this step you can see preview of your letters. Number of letters is according to your number of recipients information in the address list.

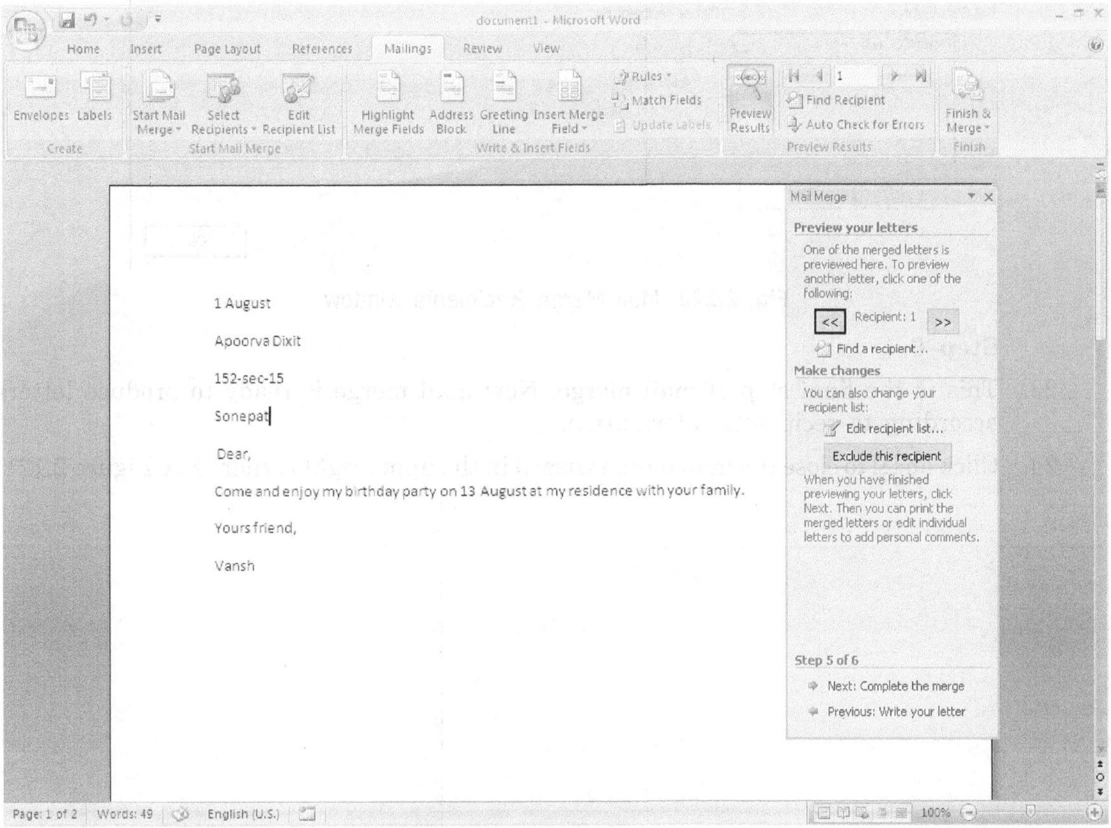

Fig. 2.119. Previewing your letters

22. Click on Next in the Mail Merge window.

> ***Note :*** *You can also edit your recipients list by clicking on 'Edit recipients list'.*

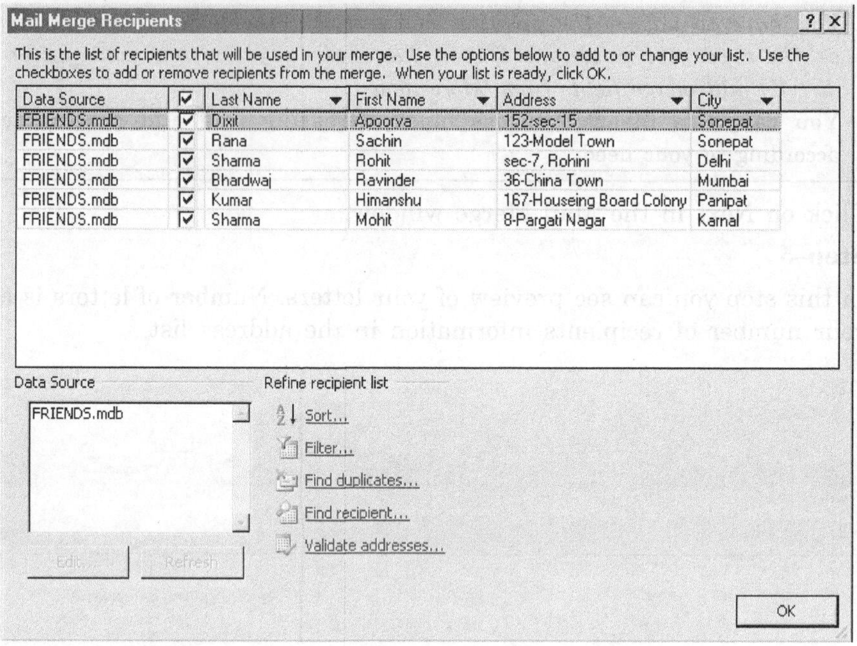

Fig. 2.120. Mail Merge Recipients window

Step–6

23. This is the final step of mail merge. Now mail merge is ready to produce letters according to recipients information.
24. Click on ☒ to close the mail merge wizard in the upper right corner. (See Figure 2.121)

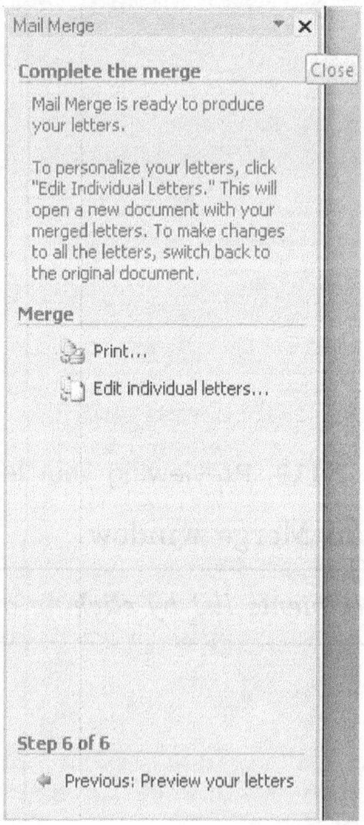

Fig. 2.121. Closing the Mail Merge window

> *Note : You can print and edit individual letters by clicking on 'Print' and 'Edit individual letters'.*

Now Mail Merge is complete.

2.10 Creating PowerPoint Presentations

Presentation is the process of presenting a topic to an audience, for example, presenting a lesson to students about global warming. Many people make use of presentation software to support them when they have to give a presentation to others.

Presentation software is a tool used to display information, normally in the form of a slide show. It generally includes three major functions: an editor that allows text to be inserted and formatted, a method for inserting and manipulating graphic images and a slide-show system to display the contents.

Microsoft PowerPoint is a presentation software that allows users to create presentations and slide shows using a variety of media, including images, video and music. The user compiles information regarding his/her topic presentation in any or all of these media formats and then applies effects to enhance the presentation. PowerPoint is often used for business presentations, but many students deliver presentations for class assignments. PowerPoint is simple to use, and with a little practice, you can create professional presentations that will effectively get your ideas across to others.

Features of Presentation Software

Following are some important key features of Presentation Software:

1. *Insert Slide Feature* allows you to insert slide anywhere in the presentation, at the beginning, middle or end.
2. *Deletion of Inserted slides*: Any slide of the presentation can be removed.
3. Allows copy/cut and paste slides in any order.
4. Allows animations and/or sounds manipulations on objects in the slide.
5. Simple Find and Replace, and text editor features.
6. *Good font specifications* allows you to change and use different font faces, styles, and effects.
7. Additional features for slide allows footnotes, cross references, advanced navigation system, headers, and footers.
8. *Good layout management system* presets or Customized layout designing.
9. Spell checkers and dictionary support.
10. Allows the slide show of the presentations.

In this section, we will discuss some of the basic concepts of Presentation Software.

Starting PowerPoint

PowerPoint is a presentation graphics program you can use to organize and present information. With PowerPoint, you can create visual aids for a presentation and then print copies of the aids as well as run the presentation.

A presentation in PowerPoint generally follows a presentation cycle. The general steps of this cycle include opening PowerPoint, creating and editing slides; saving, printing, running and closing the presentation; and then closing PowerPoint.

Suppose you are having MS-PowerPoint 2007 installed on your computer.

To start using PowerPoint:

Click **Start** → **All Programs** → **Microsoft Office** → **Microsoft Office PowerPoint 2007** (See Fig. 2.122).

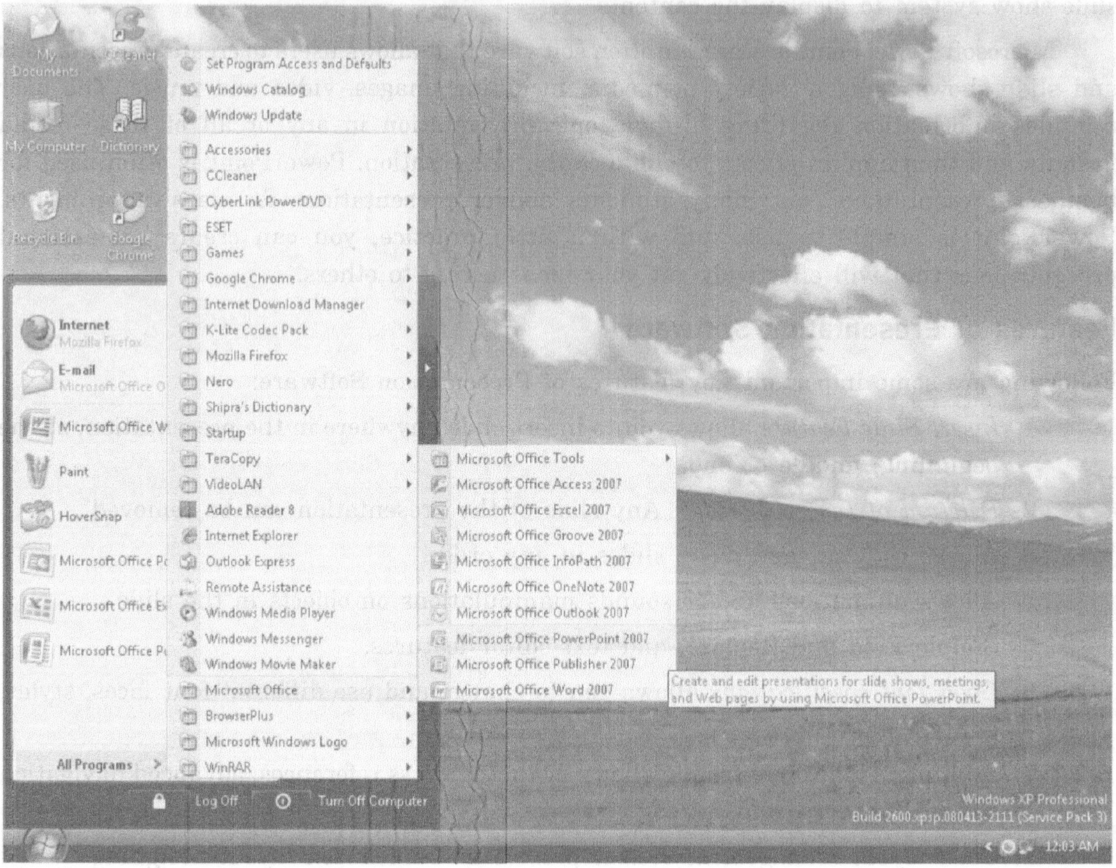

Fig. 2.122. Starting PowerPoint

> ***Note:*** *Depending on your system configuration, the steps you perform to start PowerPoint may vary.*

The PowerPoint window appears as shown in Fig. 2.123.

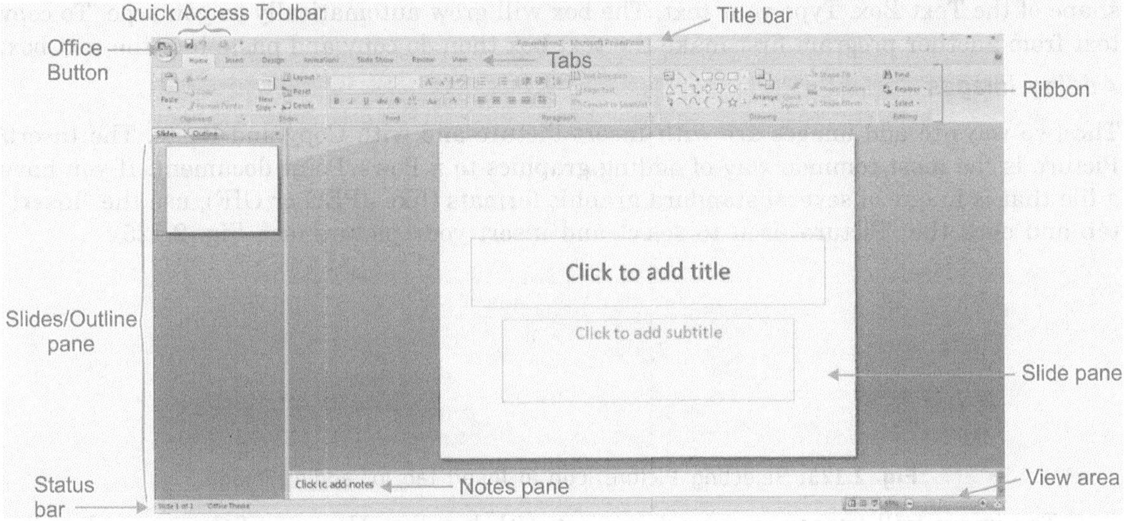

Fig. 2.123. PowerPoint window

Steps for Creating Presentation

A presentation may contain a number of slides (a slide is a page that may have various objects like title, subtitle, lists, cliparts, charts and organization charts), which are arranged in a sequence. Various effects are applied on the slide objects and slides to improve the presentations. Generally creating a presentation involves the following steps:

1. Creation of slides of required types.
2. Typing the required text in the slides.
3. Arranging the slides in a proper sequence.
4. Applying different effects to the slide objects, for example, text and sound effects.
5. Applying slide transitions to slides.
6. Setup the show.
7. Presenting the slide show.

Creating Slides Using Text and Images

You can create slides using text and images as explained below:

Adding Text

In order to add text, the text needs a "container" — a Text Box. Make a text box by clicking on the "Text Box" icon in the "Insert" tab (see Fig. 2.124). Choose horizontal or vertical as you wish.

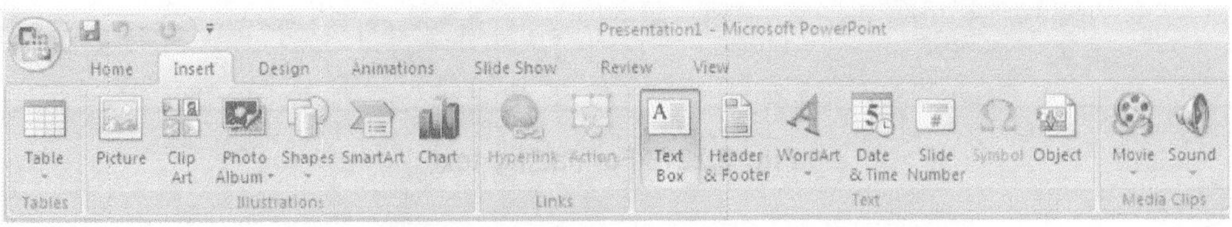

Fig. 2.124. Selecting Text Box for adding text

Click or click-and-drag where you want the text to be. You should see the rectangular shape of the Text Box. Type your text. The box will grow automatically as you type. To copy text from another program first make the text box then do copy and paste into the text box.

Adding Images

The two ways to add images are with Insert Picture and with Copy and Paste. The Insert/ Picture is the most common way of adding graphics to a PowerPoint document. If you have a file that is in one of several standard graphic formats (like JPEG or GIF), use the "Insert" tab and click the "Picture" icon to select and insert your picture (see Fig. 2.125).

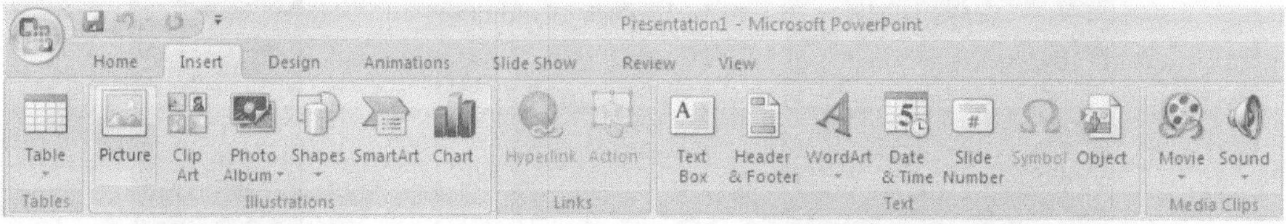

Fig. 2.125. Selecting Picture icon in Insert tab for adding image

The image will appear on your document with handles. Use one of the corner handles to re-size it. (The corner handles will keep the same aspect ratio; the side handles will not.) Click and drag in the middle of the graphic to move it. A Picture Tools tab automatically shows up when you insert the picture (see Fig. 2.126). You can edit the picture by clicking the icons for the numerous options in this tab.

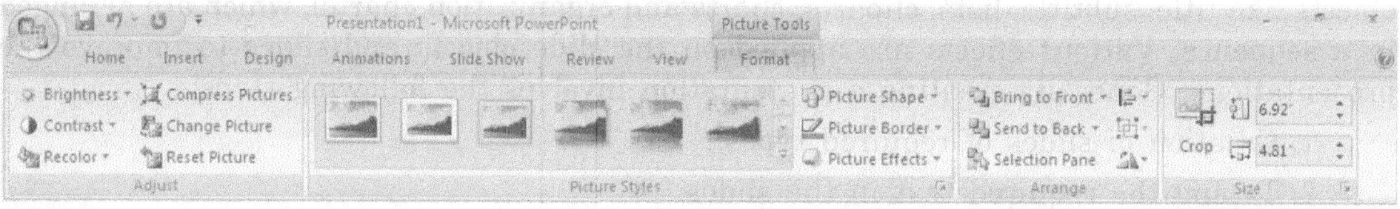

Fig. 2.126. Picture Tools tab for editing the picture

Formatting Text and Background

You can format text and background as explained below:

Text Format

As in many programs, you can change the font and size by highlighting the text to be changed and then making the changes within the "Home" tab (see Fig. 2.127). A 100-point font is about an inch high.

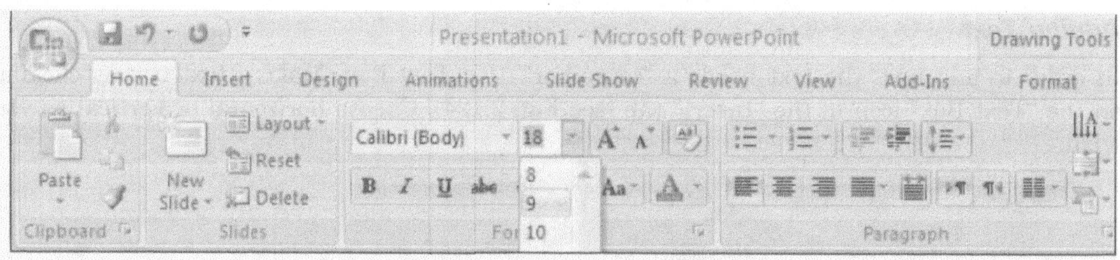

Fig. 2.127. Formatting text

If you do not see the size you want in the selection list, you can enter it in by hand. To move a Text Box, position your pointer over a part of the edge of the box that is not a handle. The pointer should become shaped like a plus sign with arrows. Click and drag the Text Box to the wanted position. You can change the color of the text, the edge, and the fill as well as other things with the options in the "Home" tab. Make a separate Text Box for each separate piece of text. "Separate text" means a portion of text that you want to be able to move independently from the others.

Backgrounds

You can select a background by clicking the "Background Styles" icon in the "Design" tab (see Fig. 2.128).

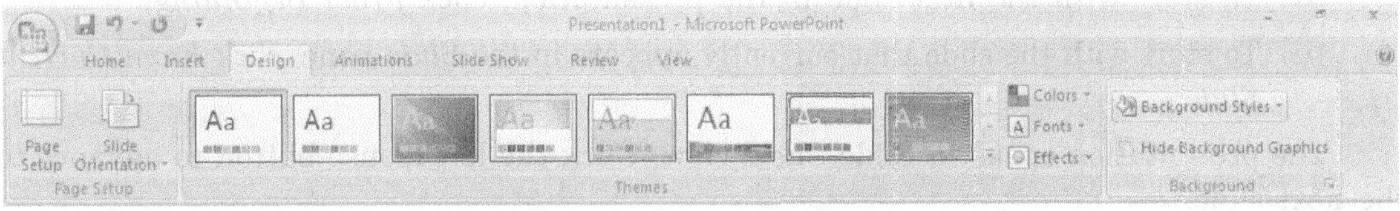

Fig. 2.128. Formatting background

Click on the Format Background option within the dropdown menu and you can choose from even more color choices. If you choose Fill effects you have a choice of tabs and one is Gradient. A gradient background is a smooth transition from one color to another. The best gradients are very dark or very light so that the text can easily be read on top of it. If you want a picture background click on the Picture tab, then Select Picture to browse to your picture. Be careful of using too big image—large files can become cumbersome to work with.

Inserting and Deleting Slides

You can insert and delete slides as explained below:

Inserting a New Slide

Click on the *New Slide* button on the *Home* tab of the ribbon to add a new slide to your presentation (see Fig. 2.129).

Fig. 2.129. Inserting a new slide

Deleting a Slide

On the *Slides* tab of the *Slides/Outline* task pane on the left of your screen, click on the thumbnail (a thumbnail describes a miniature version of a slide or picture) of the slide you wish to delete. Press the *Delete* key on your keyboard.

Presenting a Slide Show

You can present a slide show as explained below:

Press F5 or on the *Slide Show* tab, in the *Start Slide Show* group, do one of the following:

(*i*) To start with the first slide in the presentation, click *From Beginning*.

(*ii*) To start with the slide that currently appears in the *Slide* pane, click *From Current Slide*.

The presentation opens in Slide Show view. Click the left mouse button to advance to the next slide.

Press *Esc* key to return to Normal view at any time.

Creating a Slide Show using Animation and Sound

You can create the most effective visual presentations using PowerPoint because a series of slides that contains only bulleted lists is not the most dynamic choice. Lack of visual variety can cause your audience's attention to drift. And many kinds of information are not most clearly expressed in a paragraph or a bulleted list.

MS-Office PowerPoint 2007 makes it possible to add many other kinds of audio and visual content, including tables, SmartArt graphics, clip art, shapes, charts, music, movies, sounds, and animations. You can add transitions between slides.

Professionally designed slide shows contain all these properties to grasp the attention of the audience.

Changing Slide Layout

You can change the slide layout as follows:

Click the *Layout* button on the Home ribbon. This will show a contextual menu of the nine different slide layout choices in PowerPoint 2007 (see Fig. 2.130).

The current slide layout will be highlighted. Hover your mouse over the new slide layout of your choice and that slide type will also be highlighted. When you click the mouse this new slide layout will be applied to the current slide.

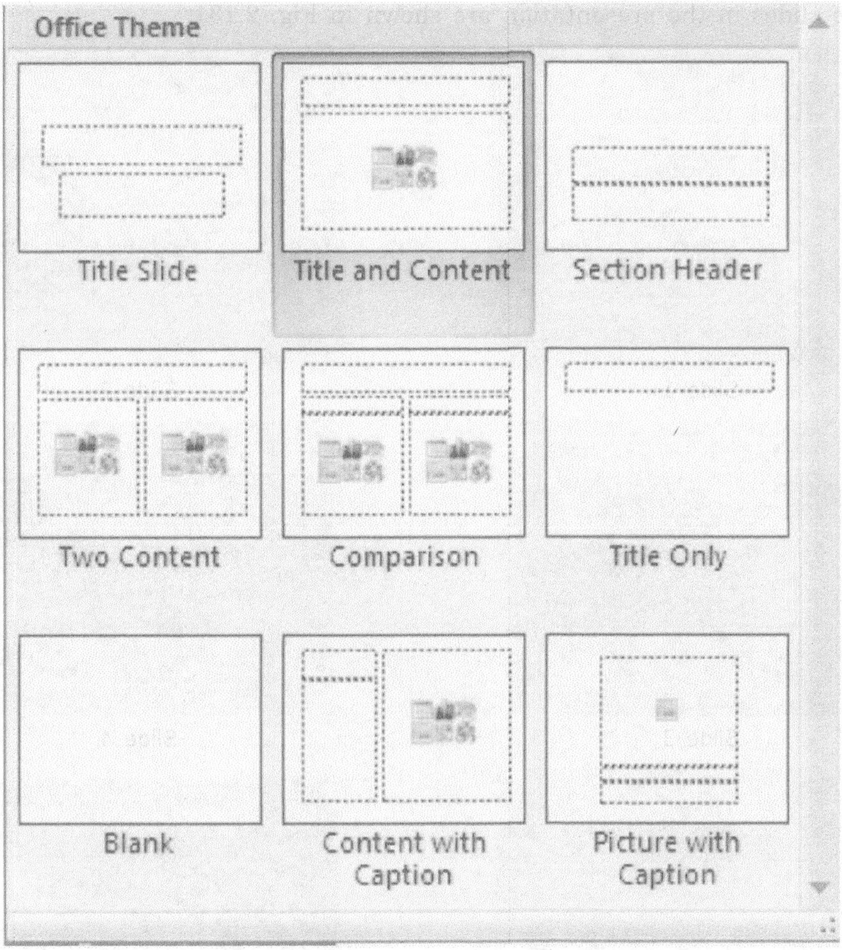

Fig. 2.130. Changing Slide Layout

Creating a Presentation and Presenting a Slide Show

Let us prepare a presentation on "Global Warming" and present a slide show.

Perform the following steps:

1. Click Start → All Programs → Microsoft Office → Microsoft Office PowerPoint 2007.
2. Click on *Office Button* and select *New*.
3. Prepare a presentation on Global Warming and save it in a file.
4. Select the appropriate file name and press Entery key or Double click on the file. The desired file will be opened.
5. Click the *Slide Show* tab.
6. Click the *From Beginning* icon in the *Start Slide Show* command group. PowerPoint displays the first slide of your presentation.
7. Click the left mouse button or press the SPACEBAR/ENTER key to view the next slide.

The slides in the presentation are shown in Fig. 2.131.

Slide 1

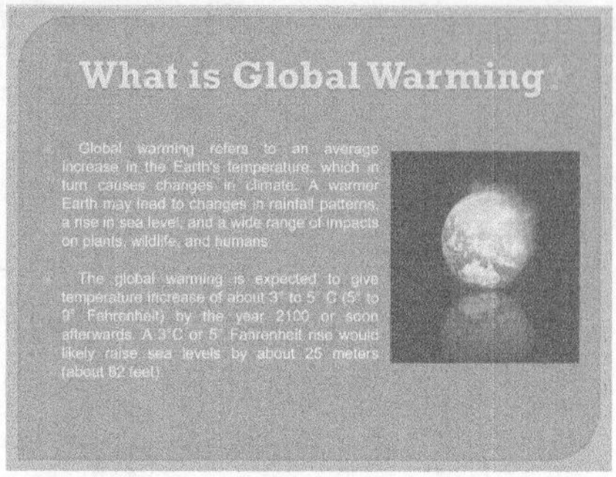

Slide 2

Slide 3

Slide 4

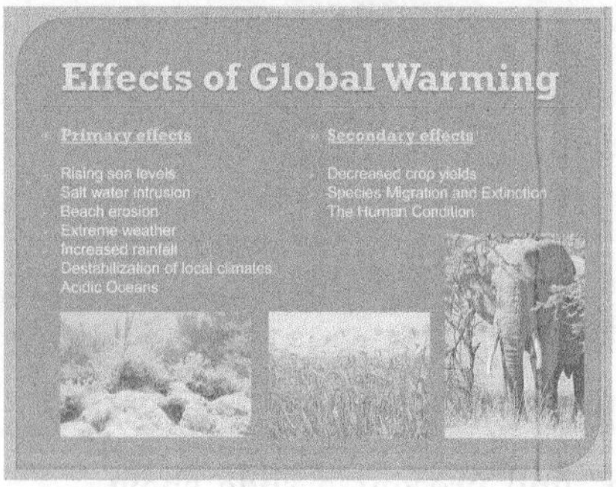

Slide 5

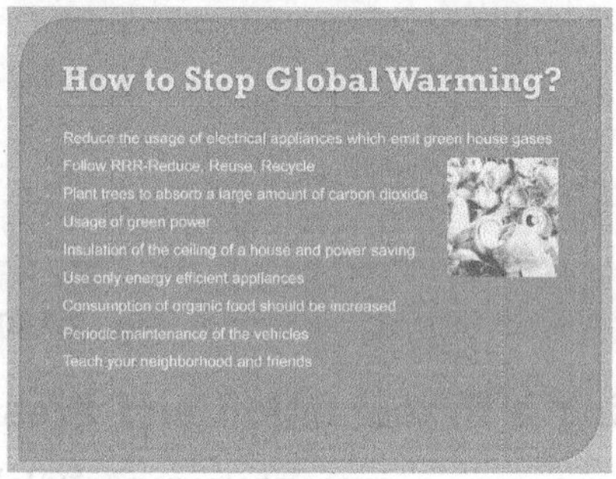

Slide 6

Slide 7

Fig. 2.131. Slide Show of presentation on Global Warming

8. Press *Esc* key to exit the slide show.

2.11 Creating Spreadsheets and Simple Graphs

The spreadsheets are one of the most widely used application software in the world. These are used everywhere from a small store to a large manufacturing house. These can be used for calculating accounts, managing inventory, managing payroll, managing and analysing the sales and marketing. These software are also used to manage household data like recording expenditures. As spreadsheets are much easier to learn than programming languages, these can be operated by any user having a moderate knowledge of programming. Miscrosoft Excel is a very popular spreadsheet package.

Starting Spreadsheets

MS-Excel 2007 is a GUI based spreadsheet package that is part of Microsoft Office 2007 suite of software. To start MS-Excel 2007, perform the following:

Double-click on the MS-Excel 2007 icon on the desktop.

Or

Click **Start → All Programs → Microsoft Office → Microsoft Office Excel 2007**

Screen Elements of Spreadsheets

On starting spreadsheet *i.e.*, MS-Excel 2007, a spreadsheet window appears. The screen elements of Excel spreadsheet are shown in Fig. 2.132.

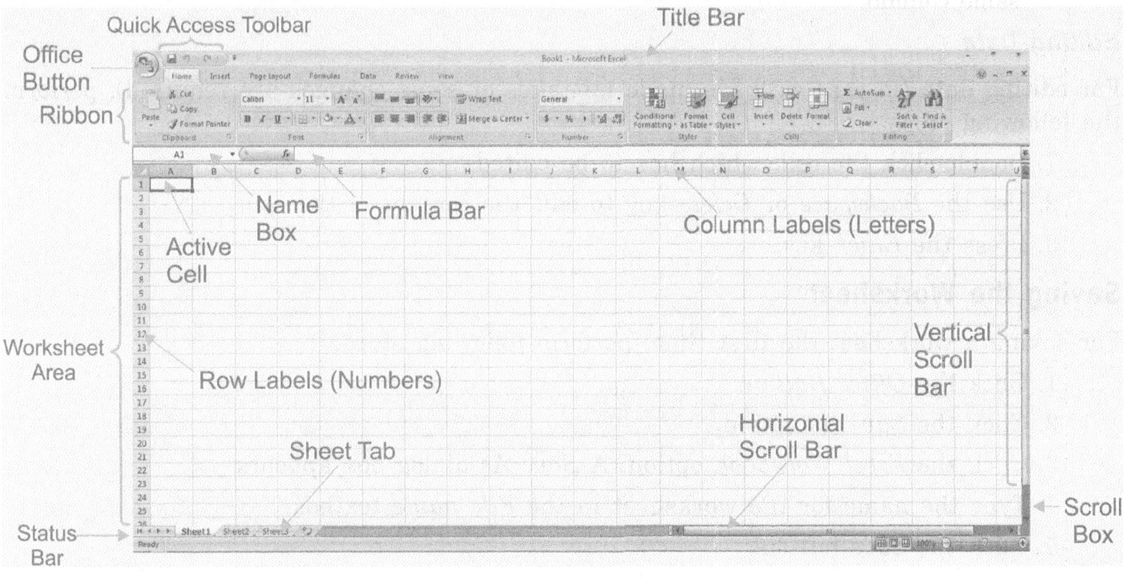

Fig. 2.132. Screen elements of Spreadsheet—Excel 2007

For exploring massive amounts of data, Excel 2007 grid is 1,048,576 rows by 16,384 columns. The columns now start from A and end at XFD.

> ***Note: Fill handle** is a small black square displayed at the bottom right corner of the active cell. The* fill handle *is used to fill adjacent cells with the same data or consecutive data. The entries that are automatically inserted in the adjacent cells are dependent on the contents of the active cell.*

Create and Use a Simple Spreadsheet

Creating a Worksheet

To create a worksheet, perform the following steps:

1. Click the *Office* Button.
2. Click the *New* option.
3. Double click the *Blank Workbook* or click on the *Create* button.

A new worksheet is created.

Using a Spreadsheet

After creating a worksheet, you can enter data (for example, words, a number, or a formula) in the active cell. The spreadsheet can be used as per your need.

Entering and Editing Text

Entering Data

For entering data, perform the following steps:

1. Select the cell where the data has to be entered.
2. Type the data. To enter data in active cell, type the characters. Either press *Tab* key to go to the next cell in the same row or press *Enter* key to go to the next cell in the same column.

Editing Data

For editing data (in case we have made mistakes or some changes are required), perform the following steps:

1. Double-click the cell, which has to be edited.
2. Use the *Backspace* or *Delete* key to edit the content of the cell.
3. Press the *Enter* key.

Saving the Worksheet

For saving a worksheet the first time, perform following steps:

1. Click the *Office Button*.
2. Click the *Save As* option.
3. Click the *Excel Workbook* option. A *Save As* dialog box appears.
4. Type the name for the worksheet in the *File name* textbox.
5. Click the *Save* button.

Using the Four Mathematical Operators on Data to Create Custom Formula

In MS-Excel, you can enter numbers and mathematical formulae into cells. When entering a mathematical formula, precede with an equal (=) sign. For example, = A2 + A3 can be typed in cell A5 (where cells A2 and A3 have data to be added).

> ***Note :*** *In MS-Excel, you can find the sum by dragging method and copy by using the fill handle.*

Definition of a Chart

A chart is a graphical representation of the figures in a spreadsheet.

Charts help in easy understanding of complex or detailed data. These reflect information in such a way that it can be easily understood just by having a look at the chart.

MS-Excel 2007 supports various types of charts to display data in meaningful ways. When you want to create a chart or change an existing chart, you can choose from a wide range of chart subtypes available for the different chart types. Figure 2.133 shows a pie chart.

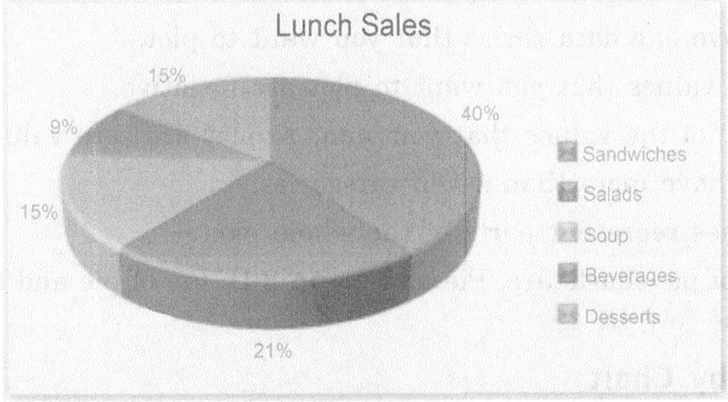

Fig. 2.133. Pie chart

Creating Charts

A picture is worth thousands of words. Popular feature of spreadsheet software is the ability to generate charts based on numeric data. In MS-Excel 2007, it is easy to create professional looking charts simply by choosing a chart type, a chart layout, and a chart style—all of which are available on the Ribbon. You can also take advantage of the powerful Excel charting functionality in other MS-Office 2007 programs, such as PowerPoint 2007 and Word 2007.

Column Chart

Data that is arranged in columns or rows on a worksheet can be plotted in a column chart. Column charts are useful for showing data changes over a period of time or for illustrating comparisons among items. In column charts, categories are typically organized along the horizontal axis and values along the vertical axis.

The subtypes of column charts are: Clustered column and clustered column in 3-D, Stacked column and stacked column in 3-D, 100% stacked column and 100% stacked column in 3-D, 3-D column, Cylinder, cone, and pyramid.

Bar Chart

Data that is arranged in columns or rows on a worksheet can be plotted in a bar chart. Bar charts illustrate comparisons among individual items. The bar charts are generally used when:

1. The axis labels are long.
2. The values that are shown are durations.

The subtypes of bar charts are: Clustered bar and clustered bar in 3-D, Stacked bar and stacked bar in 3-D, 100% stacked bar and 100% stacked bar in 3-D, Horizontal cylinder, cone, and pyramid.

Pie Chart

Data that is arranged in one column or row only on a worksheet can be plotted in a pie chart. Pie charts show the size of items in one data series, proportional to the sum of the items. The data points in a pie chart are displayed as a percentage of the whole pie (see Fig. 4.4). The pie charts are generally used when:

1. You only have one data series that you want to plot.
2. None of the values that you want to plot are negative.
3. Almost none of the values that you want to plot are zero values.
4. You do not have more than seven categories.
5. The categories represent parts of the whole pie.

The subtypes of pie charts are: Pie and pie in 3-D, Pie of pie and bar of pie, Exploded pie and exploded pie in 3-D.

Presenting Data by Chart

The *Chart Wizard* (which was composed of a series of dialog boxes that provided all the available options for creating a chart) of earlier versions is no longer available in Excel 2007. It has been replaced by chart options listed under the *Insert ribbon.*

MS-Excel 2007 has tools for creating effective, dynamic charts to visually represent the data. The new Office 2007 Ribbon makes accessing these charting functions even easier and more efficient.

To create a chart, perform the following steps:

1. Open Excel 2007 and either open an existing worksheet or use the default. Enter or create some data that supports the creation of a chart, for example Students Marks in ICT (see Fig. 2.134). This data should be in the form of a table, with the element values to be charted populating the left hand column and the data series, or information about the elements, in the cells across from each element. More than one series can be included for each element. Title the data series across the top of the table and do not leave any blank spaces in the table.

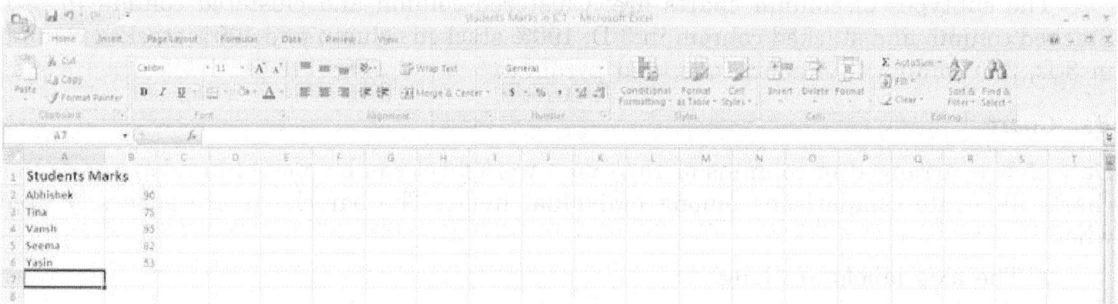

Fig. 2.134. Data in a worksheet to be charted

2. Select the data to be charted (see Fig. 2.135). Left-click and drag a box around the data to select it. Make sure to include both the data and the labels.

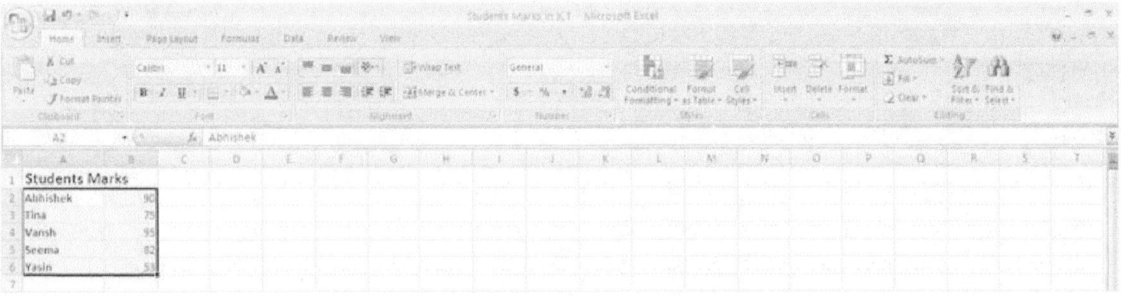

Fig. 2.135. Selecting data to be charted

3. Choose the chart type. Select *Insert* on the Excel 2007 ribbon and then choose from the chart types listed in the *Charts* section (see Fig. 2.136). For a chart type that's not visible, select the *Other Charts* icon. The chart will be placed on the worksheet near the table of data. By default, the series will be listed across the bottom, or "x-axis" and the elements will be listed to the side. The element values will be listed on the left, or "y-axis" of the chart.

Fig. 2.136. Selecting chart type

4. Position the chart. Left-click on any white space on the chart, and move it to the desired location (see Fig. 2.137).

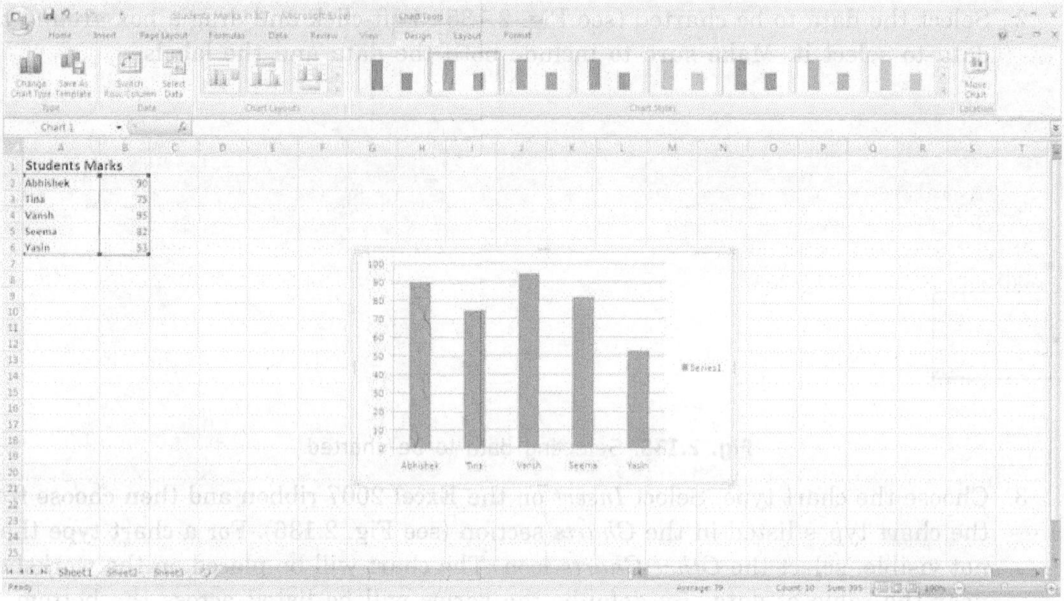

Fig. 2.137. Column chart ready to be placed in the desired location

5. Now you can format the chart. Right-click on the chart and a variety of options will appear in a dialog. Change the font displayed within the chart, change the chart type and select different chart data by selecting the relevant item from the list. To change the chart's appearance, select *Format Chart Area* and then select from the options to change the chart's *Fill*, *Border Color*, *Border Styles*, *Shadow* and *3-D Format*.

2.12 Evolution of Internet and its Application and Services

Internet is the network that is available to users across the globe (See Fig. 2.138). It is called "the mother of all networks".

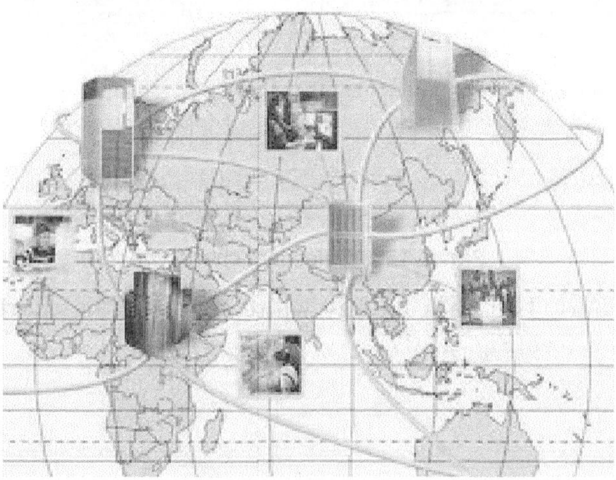

Fig. 2.138. The Internet

Or

Internet is the network that contains other networks of computers around the globe into one seamless network (See Fig. 2.138). These networks link educational, commercial, nonprofit and military entities, as well as individuals.

2.12.1 Evolution of Internet

The Internet was started in 1969 by the defense department of USA. Later, it was handed over to the Defense Advanced Research Projects Agency (DARPA). The DARPA launched the first Internet program. The DARPA established a network of 4 computers and named as ARPANet. The protocols (Software) that define the rules to exchange information between computers were created by DARPA.

The idea of computer networking soon became popular. Several universities and research organizations developed their own computer networks. They joined their networks to ARPANet. The ARPANet became the network of networks. This network of computer networks was named as Internet.

In 1986 the National Science Foundation (NSF), another federal agency of USA, established a network and named as NSFNet. It was established for academic purpose and was accessible to everyone. Later, it was expanded all over the country and large number of universities and research centers were connected to this network. The academic networks were established and all these were interconnected together to share the information. The way of connecting one network to another is termed as internetworking and "Internet" is also derived from internetworking. The NSF provided the connections for academic research centers only. After this many telecommunication companies established their own network backbones by using the same networking protocol as NSFNet used and also provided connections to private users. In 1995, NSF terminated its network on the Internet. Today, the Internet consists of many local, regional, national and international networks.

2.12.2 Applications and Services of Internet

Internet plays very important role in our society. It provides a lot of latest informative information about business, education etc. It becomes the main medium for advertisement, communication between users etc. Some applications and services provided by Internet are:

1. World Wide Web

The World Wide Web is simply referred to as Web. It is the latest addition to the Internet to exchange information. The Web is vast network of HTTP servers (Web servers) that store documents called Web pages and these are accessible on the Internet. It is abbreviated as WWW or 3W. It is the easiest way to search and to get information on the Internet.

2. Search Engines

A search engine is used to search for information on the internet. Search engine presents the search results in the form of a search results list. The search results can be web pages, images, videos, and other type of files. To gather and present the searched information, each search engines has their own algorithm, or combination of algorithmic and human input. *Google.com* is currently the most popular and frequently used search engine (See Fig. 2.139).

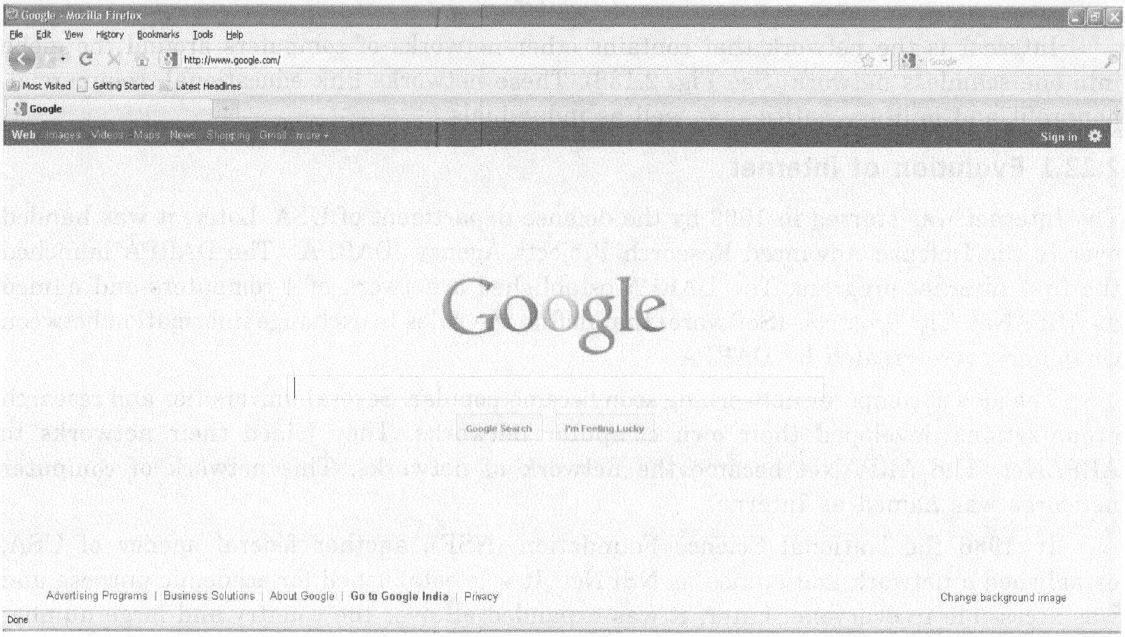

Fig. 2.139. Google.com search engine

3. Web Browsers

A Web Browser is a type of software that retrieves and presents information resources on the Internet. The information resource can be text, image, sound, video, or other type of content.

In a simple way, we can describe a web browser as a type of software that we use to 'surf' the Internet. Some examples of web browsers are:

- Microsoft Internet Explorer
- Mozilla Firefox
- Opera
- Safari
- Google Chrome

4. Newsgroups

The Newsgroups are the discussion forums that provide the services to Exchange messages on the Internet about a particular subject. This facility is provided on the Internet on special servers known as News servers. Different newsgroups are available for different purposes. For example, a newsgroup provides the services to exchange information about business and another provides the services about current affairs etc. You can become the member of any newsgroup on Internet for reading and posting messages on the newsgroup. Usually the news client program "Microsoft Internet News" is used to read and write articles in newsgroups.

5. FTP

FTP stands for File Transfer Protocol. It is a way to transfer files to others through Internet, The files are stored on a special type of server called the FTP server. The browsers can be used to transfer files from FTP server to the client computer but it is a slow process to transfer files. A lot of FTP client programs of different Software Companies are available through which files can be downloaded from FTP server into your local computer very easily and quickly. Similarly, the files from your computer can be uploaded to the FTP server. These special programs are WS_FTP and Cute FTP.

6. Chatting

Internet also provides the facility to Internet user to talk with people online all over the world. Different programs like MSN Messenger, Yahoo Messenger, ICQ, AOL online etc. are available for chatting on the Internet. You can add names of your friends or other people to these programs. These programs notify you when one or more people are online and then allow you to exchange messages or files with them or join a private chat room. The chat room allows the users to participate in a chat on the Internet. A chat room is an area on the web where you talk with people online. You send messages by typing with keyboard to the online people and receive messages from other end instantly. Some chat rooms support voice chats and video chats where you talk with people as well as see them.

7. E-Commerce

E-Commerce or Electronic Commerce is very important service provided by Internet through which financial transactions are carried out over the Internet. It is the modem way to carry out business on international basis. When business is conducted with the help of computer networks, this activity is usually termed as e-commerce or e-trade. Through e-commerce, goods can be purchased and sold from anywhere in the world. Credit cards are used for payments. It is estimated that the size of e-commerce is growing at a rate of 10% to 15% per month in the world. The examples of E-commerce are; online shopping, online advertising, online banking etc.

8. Telnet

Telnet is an Internet service (or tool) that is used to login and run commands or programs on a remote server on the Internet. Through this service, you can also access information on the Internet. You run the telnet client application on your computer. The telnet provides you a prompt on your screen and you can access the host computer by giving commands through this prompt. You will feel that you are sitting in front on the host computer and operating it. When you send commands to the host through this service, information are accessed from host and displayed on your own computer screen.

When telnet client program is run on your local computer, you have to give your account name (user name) and password to start the operating session. The expert users mostly use this service. In some remote servers, this service is not allowed.

9. Gopher

Gopher is an Internet service that organizes resources into multilevel menus to make finding information easier on the Internet. Before Gopher, it was difficult to find information on the Internet.

10. E-mail

E-mail stands for electronic mail. It is the most popular service or facility provided by the Internet through which we can electronically send and receive messages anywhere in the world. E-mail is a fast and efficient method of communication. It is almost free of cost. The e-mail reaches to the destination in a few seconds. You can also send documents, pictures, audio and video files via e-mail by attaching the file with e-mail. These days it is also possible to send or receive e-mail messages through a mobile phone.

11. Blog

A blog is a type of Internet website, usually maintained by an individual or a small company with frequent entries to descriptions of their interest, events, news, game, movies or to any person sharing his/her views. Material such as text, graphics, audio and video can also be shared using blog. Blog is normally a one way communication, where user gives his ideas or comments on that blog site. There are various types of blogs like science blog, social blog, movie blog, political blog, news channel blogs, etc.

To conclude, we can say that, today the world of the Internet permits services hardly imaginable 20 years ago. Table 2.5 provides the activities provided on the Internet.

Table 2.5. Activities provided on the Internet

Activity	*Purpose*
Auctions	Sell old stuff, acquire more stuff, with on-line auctions.
Career advancement	Search job listings, post resumes, interview online.
Distance learning	Attend online lectures, have discussions, research papers.
Download files	Get software, music and documents such as e-books.
E-business	Connect with coworkers, buy supplies, support customers.
E-mail and discussion groups	Stay in touch worldwide through electronic mail and online chat rooms.
Entertainment	Amuse yourself with Internet games, music and videos.
E-shopping	Price anything from tickets to cars; order anything from books to sofas.
Financial matters	Do investing, banking and bill paying online.
News	Stay current on politics, weather, entertainment, sports and financial news.
Research and information	Find information on any subject, using browsers and search tools.
Telephony and conferencing	Make inexpensive phone calls; have online meetings.

Review Questions and Exercises

1. What is an Operating System ? Give examples.
2. Why do we need an O.S. ? Discuss.
3. What are the functions of an O.S. ? Explain.
4. Explain briefly the functions performed by O.S. as a resource manager.
5. Give the various types of operating system.
6. Load Windows. List the various Windows Components like the Desktop, Recycle Bin, My Computer and Network Neighbourhood etc.
7. What is the significance of the following :

   (*i*) My Computer (*ii*) Network Neighbourhood (*iii*) Recycle Bin

   (*iv*) Start Menu (*v*) Task Bar (*vi*) Help
8. Discuss some of the advanced features of Windows XP.
9. What is the difference between a file and a folder?
10. How is a filename different from pathname? Give examples.
11. What is Windows Explorer ? Give some of its functions ?
12. What is the difference between copying and moving *files and folders* ?
13. When a folder is copied to another place do the subfolders in the folder also get copied ?
14. Write steps to create a new folder in Windows XP.
15. Open the My Computer window, and try out the following operations on My Computer window

    (*i*) Changing size (*ii*) Moving (*iii*) Maximize (*iv*) Minimize

    (*v*) Restore (*vi*) Scrolling (*vii*) Close
16. Start an application called MS-WORD and see the opening screen. Close the application using the Close button.
17. Create a folder and label it with your name *e.g.,* Vansh.
18. Create 3 sub-folders under the main folder and label them as follows :
    - Vansh
    - Studies
    - Sports
    - Entertainment
19. Create 3 files under the sub-folder 'Studies' and 2 files under the sub-folder 'Sports' and all these inside the parent folder Vansh.
    - Vansh
    - Studies
    - English
    - Hindi
    - Maths
    - Sports
    - Cricket
    - Football

20. How will you use Windows Accessories? Explain.

21. Write steps for closing down Windows XP.

22. What is a Word Processor? Give its features.

23. How will you create a document using a Word Processor? Explain.

24. Discuss the editing and saving of a Word document.

25. Give the steps to print a document using a Word Processor.

26. Explain spell check in MS-Word.

27. Write a short note on mail merge in MS-Word.

28. Write a short note on the following:

(*i*) Creating PowerPoint presentations.

(*ii*) Creating spreadsheets and simple graphs.

29. Write a short note on evolution of Internet.

30. What is Internet? Discuss its applications and services.

❑❑❑

CHAPTER 3

Problem Solving & Program Planning

3.1 Need for Problem Solving and Planning a Program

A **program** is a sequence of instructions written in a programming language. There are various programming languages, each having its own advantages for program development. Generally every program takes an input, manipulates it and provides an output as shown in Figure 3.1.

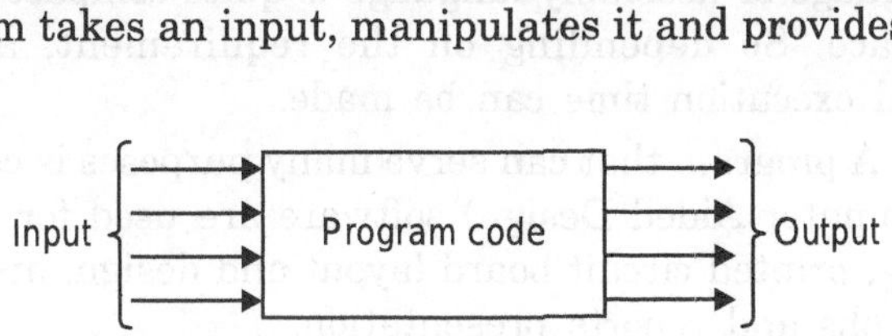

Fig. 3.1. A conceptual view of a program

For better designing of a program, a systematic planning must be done. Planning makes a program more **efficient** and more **effective.** A programmer should use planning tools before coding a program. By doing so, all the instructions are properly interrelated in the program code and the logical errors are minimized. Figure 3.2 explains the problem solving logic.

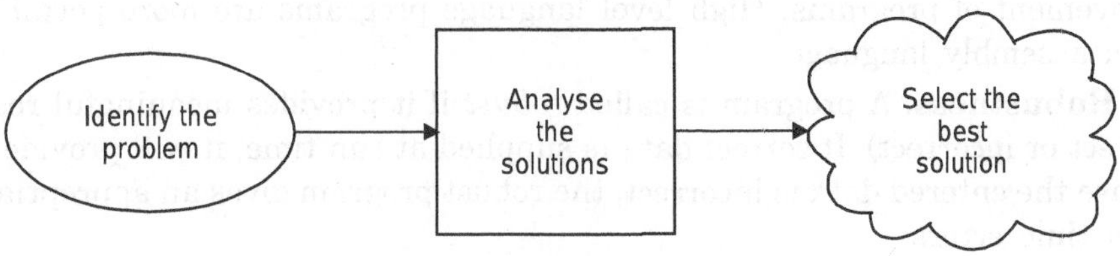

Fig. 3.2. Problem-solving Logic

We see from the above figure that before writing programs, it is a good practice to understand the complete problem, analyse the various solutions and arrive at the best solution.

There are various planning tools for mapping the program logic, such as **flowcharts, pseudocode** and **hierarchy charts** etc. A program that does the desired work and achieves the goal is called an effective program whereas the program that does the work at a faster rate is called an efficient program.

The software designing includes mainly two things—*program structure* and *program representation*. The program structure means how a program should be. The program structure is finalised using top-down approach or any other popular approach. The program structure is obtained by joining the subprograms. Each subprogram represents a logical subtask.

The program representation means its presentation style so that it is easily readable and presentable. A user friendly program (which is easy to understand) can be easily debugged and modified, if need arises. So the programming style should be easily understood by everyone to minimize the wastage of time, efforts and cost.

Change is a way of life, so is the case with software. The modification should be easily possible with minimum efforts to suit the current needs of the organization. This modification process is known as **program maintenance.**

3.2 Characteristics of a Good Program

The different aspects of evaluating a program are: efficiency, flexibility, reliability, portability and robustness etc. These characteristics are given below:

(*i*) **Efficiency.** It is of three types: programmer effort, execution time and memory space utilization. The high level languages are used for programmer efficiency. But, a program written in machine language or assembly language is quite compact and takes less machine time, and memory space. So depending on the requirement, a compromise between programmer's effort and execution time can be made.

(*ii*) **Flexibility.** A program that can serve many purposes is called a flexible program. For example, CAD (Computer Aided Design) software are used for different purposes such as: Engineering drafting, printed circuit board layout and design, architectural design. CAD can also be used in graphs and reports presentation.

(*iii*) **Reliability.** It is the ability of a program to work its intended function accurately even if there are temporary or permanent changes in the computer system. Programs having such ability are known as reliable.

(*iv*) **Portability.** It is desirable that a program written on a certain type of computer should run on different type of computer system. A program is called *portable* if it can be transferred from one system to another with ease. This feature helps a lot in research work for easy movement of programs. High level language programs are more portable than the programs in assembly language.

(*v*) **Robustness.** A program is called *robust* if it provides meaningful results for all inputs (correct or incorrect). If correct data is supplied at run time, it will provide the correct result. In case the entered data is incorrect, the robust program gives an appropriate message with no run time errors.

(*vi*) **User friendly.** A program that can be easily understood even by a novice is called user friendly. This characteristic makes the program easy to modify if the need arises. Appropriate messages for input data and with the display of result make the program easily understandable.

(*vii*) **Self-documenting code.** The source code which uses suitable names for the identifiers is called self-documenting code. A cryptic (difficult to understand) name for an identifier makes the program complex and difficult to debug later on (even the programmer may forget the purpose of the identifier). So a good program must have self-documenting code.

3.3 Problem Solving Methodology and Techniques

Computer problem-solving can be summed up in one word—*it is demanding!* It is a combination of many small parts put together in a complex way, and therefore difficult to understand. It requires much thought, careful planning, logical accuracy, continuous efforts, and attention to detail. Simultaneously it can be a challenging, exciting, and satisfying experience with a lot of room for personal creativity and expression. If computer problem-solving is approached in this spirit then the chances of success are very bright.

For creating efficient and effective programs, the programmer should adopt a proper problem solving methodology and use appropriate techniques. Let us discuss it.

Every type of software (pre-written software, or a customized software, or a public domain software) has to be developed by someone before we can use it. Software or program must be understood properly before its development and use. **A program is a list of instructions that the computer must follow in order to process data into information.** The instructions consist of statements used in a programming language, such as C or C++. Examples are programs that do word processing, desktop publishing, or railway reservation.

The decision whether to buy or develop a program forms part of Phase 4 in the systems development life cycle. Figure 3.3 illustrates this. Once the decision is made to develop a new system, the programmer starts his/her work.

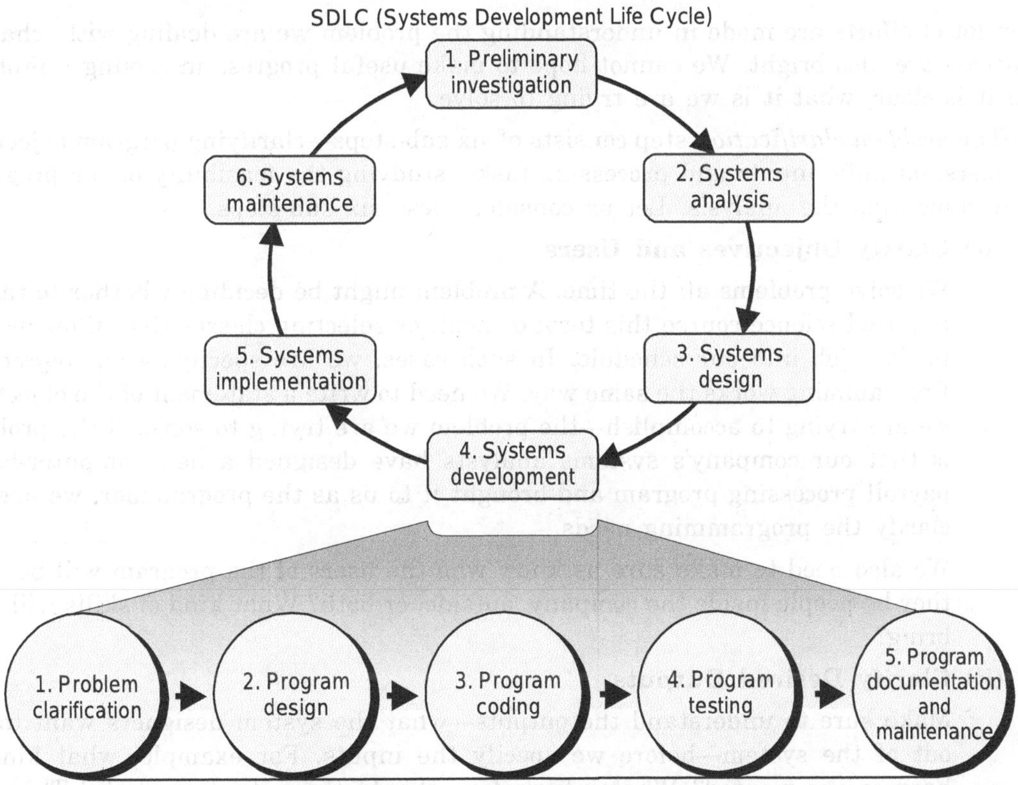

Fig. 3.3. Illustration of where programming fits in the SDLC

The Phase 4 of the six-phase SDLC includes a five-step procedure of its own as shown in the bottom of Figure 3.3. These five steps constitute the problem-solving or software development process known as programming. **Programming also known as software engineering, is a multistep process for creating that list of instructions** (that is, a program for the computer).

The five steps are given below:

1. Clarify the problem—include needed output, input, processing requirements.
2. Design a solution—use modeling tools to chart the program.
3. Code the program—use a programming language's syntax, or rules, to write the program.
4. Test the program—get rid of any logic errors, or "bugs", in the program ("debug" it).
5. Document and maintain the program—include written instructions for users, explanation of the program, and operating instructions.

Coding—sitting at the keyboard and typing words into a computer—is what many people imagine programming to be. As we see, however, it is only one of the five steps. Coding consists of translating the logic requirements into a programming language—the letters, numbers and symbols that make up the program.

3.3.1 Clarify the Problem

When lot of efforts are made in understanding the problem we are dealing with, chances of success are also bright. We cannot hope to make useful progress in solving a problem until it is clear, what it is we are trying to solve.

The *problem clarification* step consists of six sub-steps—clarifying program objectives and users, outputs, inputs and processing tasks; studying the feasibility of the program; and documenting the analysis. Let us consider these six sub-steps.

(*i*) **Clarify Objectives and Users**

We solve problems all the time. A problem might be deciding whether to take a required science course this term or next, or selecting classes that allow us also to fit a job into our schedule. In such cases, we are specifying our *objectives.* Programming works the same way. We need to write a statement of the objectives we are trying to accomplish—the problem we are trying to solve. If the problem is that our company's systems analysts have designed a new computer-based payroll processing program and brought it to us as the programmer, we need to clarify the programming needs.

We also need to make sure us know who the users of the program will be. Will they be people inside the company, outside, or both? What kind of skills will they bring?

(*ii*) **Clarify Desired Outputs**

Make sure to understand the outputs—what the system designers want to get out of the system—before we specify the inputs. For example, what kind of hardcopy is wanted? What information should the outputs include? This step may require several meetings with systems designers and users to make sure we are creating what they want.

(*iii*) **Clarify Desired Inputs**

Once we know the kind of outputs required, we can then think about input. What kind of input data is needed? What form should it appear in? What is its source?

The term input means identifying initial data for the problem or program. This data must be present before any operation can be performed on it. Many a times, no data is required for a program because initial data may be generated within the program. So, a problem may have no or many inputs.

The two ways to supply initial values to variables are by using internal and external data.

(*a*) ***Internal data*** means that values are generated within the problem.

(*b*) ***External data*** means that the required values of each element are to be inputted by the problem solver.

Therefore, the problem solver should understand the input data required for the program, and the output produced by the program. Many times the input data may be returned by some program module, that is, a function or any other program called by the program we are using or some built in function available in the library of the language used for coding the problem.

So, the problem must be understood thoroughly for the desired output which helps a lot in identification of minimum number of inputs.

(*iv*) **Clarify the Desired Processing**

There are many ways to solve most of the problems and also many solutions to most of the problems. This situation makes the job of problem-solving a difficult task. When we have many ways to solve a problem it is usually difficult to recognize quickly which paths are likely to be fruitless and which paths may be productive.

Here we make sure to understand the processing tasks that must occur in order for input data to be processed into output data.

(*v*) **Double-Check the Feasibility of Implementing the Program**

A block often occurs after the problem definition phase, because people become concerned with details of the implementation *before* they have completely understood or worked out an implementation-independent solution. The problem solver should not be too concerned about detail. That can be taken into account when the complexity of the problem as a whole has been brought under control. An old computer proverb states, **"the sooner you start coding your program the longer it is going to take".**

An approach that often allows us to make a start on a problem is to take a specific example of the general problem we wish to solve and try to work out the mechanism that will allow us to solve this particular problem (*e.g.,* if you want to find the top scorer in an examination, choose a particular set of marks and work out the mechanism for finding the highest marks in this set).

This approach of focusing on a particular problem can often give us a platform we need for making a start on the solution to the general problem. It is not always possible that the solution to a specific problem or a specific class of problems is also a solution to the general problem. We should specify our problem very carefully and try to establish whether or not the proposed algorithm (step by step procedure in a finite number of steps to solve a problem) can meet those requirements. If there are any similarities between the current problem and other problems that we have solved or we have seen solved, we should be aware of it. In trying to get a better solution to a problem, sometimes too much study of the existing solution or a similar problem forces us down the same reasoning path (which may not be the best) and to the same dead end. Therefore, a better and wiser way to get a better solution to a problem is, try to solve the problem *independently*.

Any problem we want to solve should be viewed from a variety of angles. When all aspects of the problem have been seen, one should start solving it. Sometimes, in some cases it is assumed that we have already solved the problem and then try to work backwards to the starting conditions. The most crucial thing of all in developing problem-solving skills is practice.

So, the main points in this sub step are:

Is the kind of program we are supposed to create feasible within the present budget? Will it require hiring a lot more staff? Will it take too long to accomplish?

Sometimes programmers decide they can buy an existing program and modify it rather than write it from scratch.

(*vi*) **Document the Analysis**

Throughout program clarification, programmers must document everything they do. This includes writing objective specifications of the entire process being described.

3.3.2. Design the Program

Assuming the decision is to make, or custom-write, the program, we then move on to design the solution specified by the systems analysts. **An algorithm is a formula or set of steps for solving a particular problem.** Inventing elegent algorithms is very important in programming.

Algorithms can be expressed in many ways. In the ***program design*** **step, the software is designed in two mini-steps. First, the program logic is determined through a top-down approach and modularization, using a hierarchy chart. Then it is designed in detail, either in narrative form, using pseudocode, or graphically, using flowcharts.**

Today most programmers use a design approach called structured programming. ***Structured programming*** **takes a top-down approach that breaks programs into modular forms.** It also uses standard logic tools called control structures (sequential, selection, case and iteration).

The two mini-steps of program design are:

1. Determine the Program Logic, Using a Top-Down Approach

The primary goal in computer problem-solving is an algorithm which helps in implementation of a correct and efficient computer program. Once we have defined the problem to be solved and have an idea of how to solve it, we can use the powerful techniques for designing algorithms. For successful design of an algorithm we must have proper understanding of the inherent complexity of the problem that require computer solution. A problem solver can properly focus on a very limited part of the logic or instructions. A technique which is very useful for algorithm design taking into account the limited part of it is known as **top-down design** or **stepwise refinement.**

The top-down design approach helps in bringing a vague outline solution to a precisely defined algorithm and program implementation. It provides us a way of handling the inherent logical complexity and detail, most commonly found in computer algorithms.

For solving any problem first of all we must have at least the broadest of outlines of a solution. Sometimes this might demand a lot more investigation into the problem while at other times the problem description may in itself give the necessary starting point for top-down design. The general outline may consist of a single statement or a set of statements.

Top-down design suggests that we take the general statements that we have about the solution, one at a time, and break them down into a set of more exactly defined subtasks. These subtasks should more accurately describe about reaching the final goal. When we split a task into subtasks, we must exactly define the way in which the subtasks will interact with each other. By doing so the overall structure of the solution to the problem can be preserved. The preservation of the overall structure in the solution to a problem makes the algorithm comprehensible and helps in proving the correctness of the solution.

The process of repeatedly breaking a task down into subtasks and then each subtask into still smaller subtasks must continue until we reach at the subtasks that can be coded as program statements. In most of the cases we need to go down to two or three levels but for large software projects this is not true. Figure 3.4 shows the schematic breakdown of a problem:

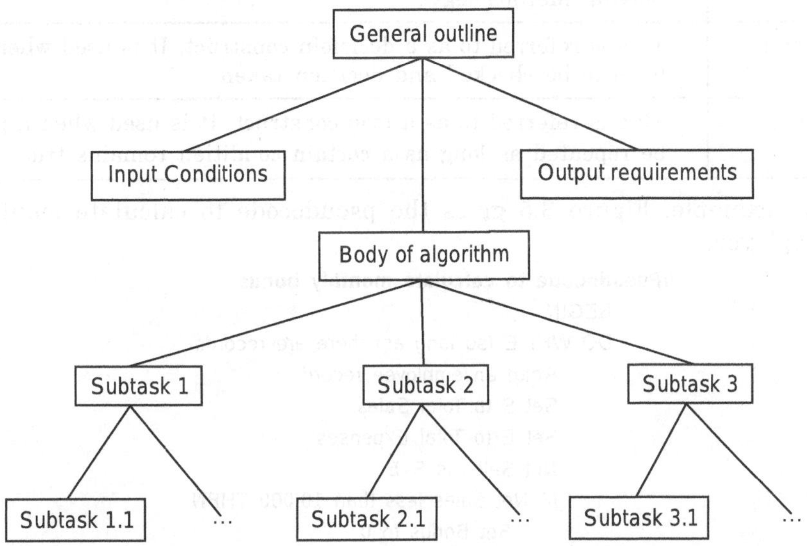

Fig. 3.4. Illustration of schematic breakdown of a problem into subtasks

The process of breaking down the solution to a problem into subtasks in the manner described gives an implementable set of subtasks which can be easily coded into languages like C, C++, VB etc. There can therefore be a smooth and natural interface between the stepwise refined algorithm and the actual program code—a highly desirable situation for keeping the implementation task very simple.

2. Design Details, Using Pseudocode and/or Using Flowcharts

After determining the essential logic of the program, through the use of top-down design and hierarchy charts, you can go to work on details.

There are two ways to show details—write them or draw them; that is, use pseudocode or use flowcharts. Most problems use both methods.

(*i*) **Pseudocode:** *Pseudocode is a method of designing a program using normal human-language statements (like English) to describe the logic and processing flow.* Pseudocode is like an outline or summary form of the program you will code. However, unlike the final code, pseudocode does not require exact syntax so the programmer is able to focus more on the logic.

Table 3.1 illustrates the conventions to be followed while writing a Pseudocode.

Table 3.1. Conventions to be followed while writing a Pseudocode

Keyword	*Usage*
//	This indicates that the line is a comment. A comment line is used to provide additional information about the steps in the pseudocode.
Begin – – End	Marks a block of code. The first statement in a pseudocode is a *begin* statement and the last statement is an *end* statement.
Accept	It is used to accept input. For example, to accept the name of a person we use "Accept Name".
Display	It is used to display output. For example, Display 'Welcome to Problem Solving Methodology'.
If-Else-Endif	This is referred to as a decisioin construct. It is used when conditions have to be checked and decision taken.
Do While – – End Do	This is referred to as a loop construct. It is used when a process may be repeated as long as a certain condition remains true.

For example, Figure 3.5 gives the pseudocode to calculate monthly bonus of employees.

```
//Pseudocode to calculate monthly bonus
    BEGIN
    DO WHILE (so long as) there are records
        Read an employee record
        Set S to Total Sales
        Set E to Total Expenses
        Net Sales is S–E
        IF Net Sales less than 10,000 THEN
            Set Bonus to 0
        ELSE
            Set Bonus to 5% of Net Sales
        ENDIF
        Display Bonus
    END DO
    END
```

Fig. 3.5. Pseudocode

(*ii*) **Program flowcharts:** *A program flowchart is a chart that graphically presents the detailed series of steps (algorithm, or logical flow) required to solve a programming problem.* The flowchart uses standard symbols—called *ANSI symbols,* after the American National Standards Institute, which developed them. These symbols are given in Table 3.2.

Table 3.2. Flowchart Symbols (ANSI symbols)

Symbol	*Name*	*Purpose*
	Terminal	Indicates the beginning and end of a program.
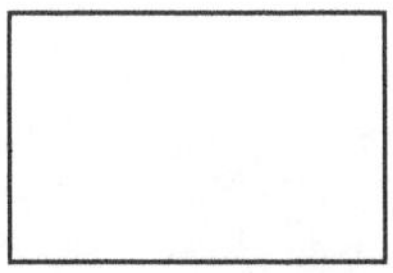	Process	A calculation or assigning of a value to a variable.
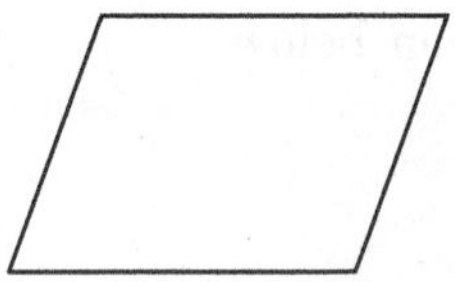	Input/Output (I/O)	Any statement that causes data to be input to a program (INPUT, READ) or output from the program, such as printing on the display screen or printer.
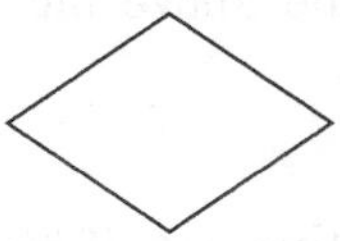	Decision	Program decisions. Allows alternate courses of action based on a condition. A decision indicates a question that can be answered *yes* or *no* (or *true* or *false*).
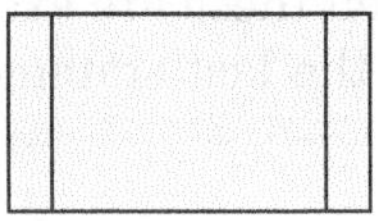	Predefined Process	A group of statements that together accomplish one task. Used extensively when programs are broken into modules.
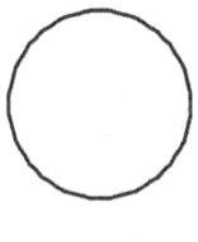	Connector	Can be used to eliminate lengthy flowlines. Its use indicates that one symbol is connected to another.
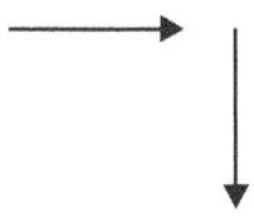	Flowlines and Arrowheads	Used to connect symbols and indicate the sequence of operations. The flow should go from top to bottom and from left to right. Arrowheads are only required when the flow violates the standard direction.
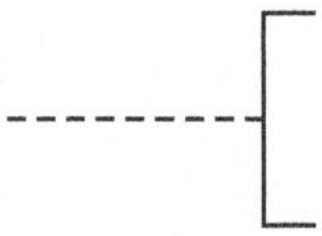	Annotation	Can be used to give explanatory comments.

For example, the flowchart in Figure 3.6 finds the product of two numbers.

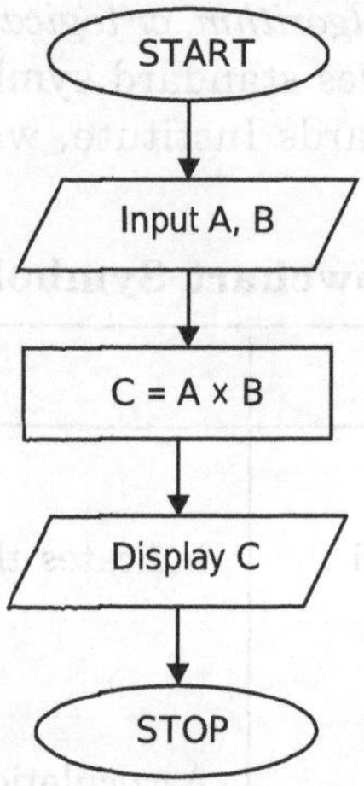

Fig. 3.6. Flowchart to find product of two numbers

• Using Control Structure

Any problem can be solved by using the three control structures given below:

(*i*) Sequence control structure

(*ii*) Conditional control

(*iii*) Looping

It depends on the nature of the problem whether to use all of the above mentioned control structures or some of these.

Sequence Control Structure

The sequence control structure selects all the steps, one followed by another *e.g.,* if there are n statements or steps say statement1, statement2, - - - -, statementn, then these are executed in the sequence —— statement1 followed by statement2 and so on till the last statement is executed. Figure 3.7 shows sequence control structure:

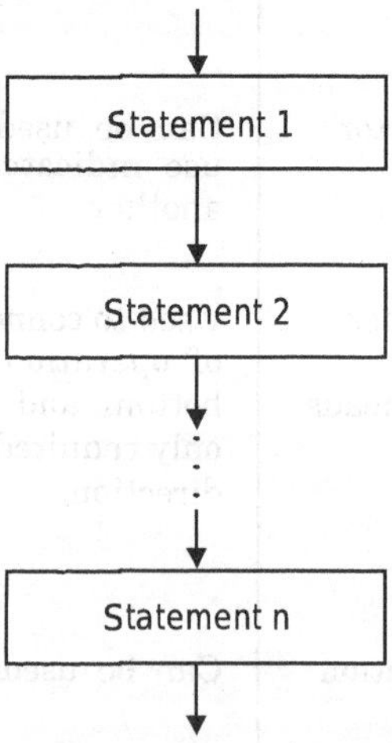

Fig. 3.7. Sequence control structure

Conditional Control

The conditional control structure selects one or more steps for execution depending upon a given condition being true or false. For example, consider the following binary decision structure (IF–THEN–ELSE):

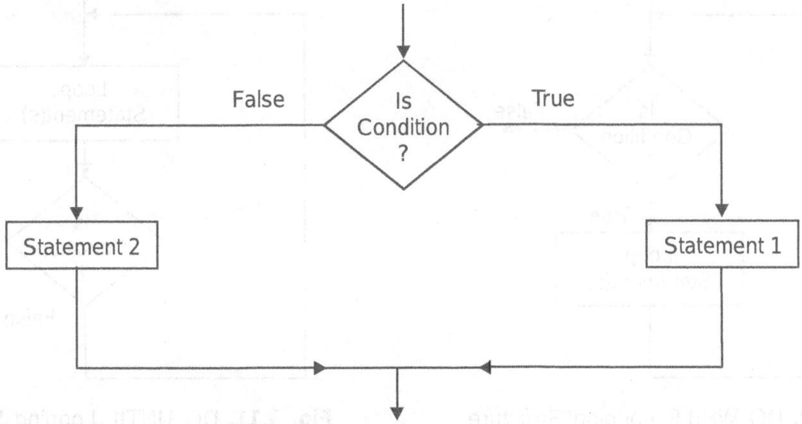

Fig. 3.8. Binary decision structure

This structure first evaluates a logical expression (an expression containing the relational symbols such as <, <=, =, ≠, >, >=). This logical expression is also known as a condition. If this condition happens to be true then Statement 1 is to be executed and if this condition is false then Statement 2 is to be executed.

For example, in C++ language **if-else**, Nested **if**, **switch...case...default**, Nested **switch...case** statements can be used to implement conditional control.

Case is an important version of selection (more than a single yes–or–no decision). The following figure illustrates **variation on selection: the case control structure.**

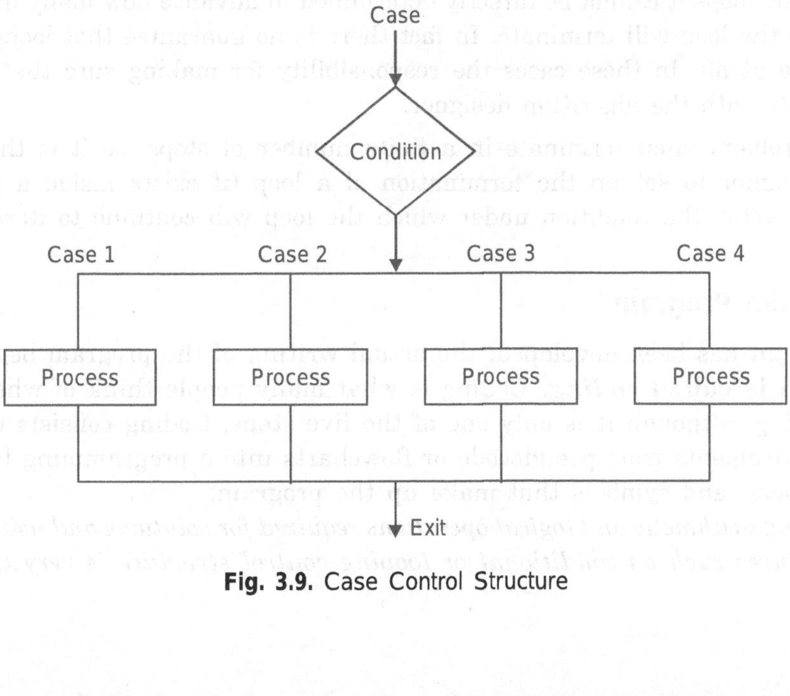

Fig. 3.9. Case Control Structure

Looping (finite and infinite)

The looping control structure executes a statement a number of times depending on the value of the boolean expression. Figures 3.10 and 3.11 show two types of looping structures:

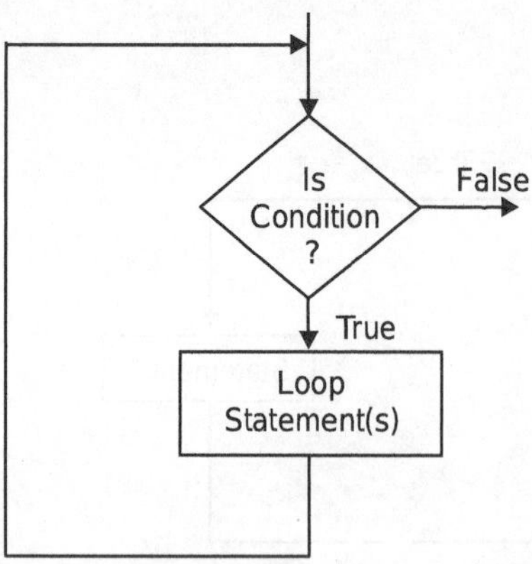

Fig. 3.10. DO WHILE Looping Structure

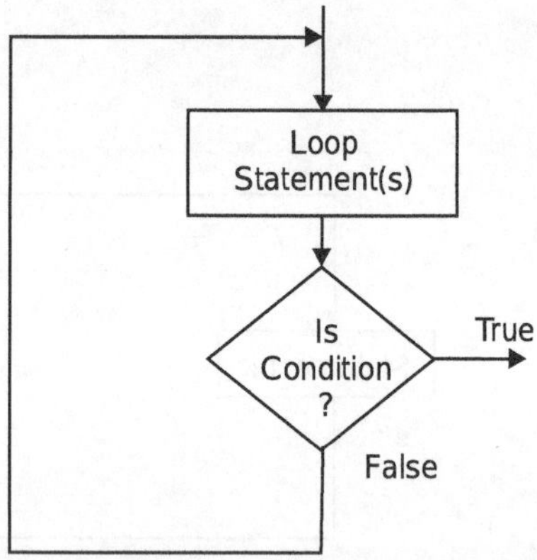

Fig. 3.11. DO UNTIL Looping Structure

In C++ language, **while, do...while, for** and nested loops can be used to implement looping. Looping is also known as Repetition or Iteration.

After refinement of a subtask we can get something that can be realized as an iterative construct. It can be easily implemented if we are aware of the basic structure of all loops. To construct any loop we must take into account three things:

(*i*) the initial conditions that need to apply *before* the loop starts to execute.

(*ii*) *the invariant relation* that must apply after each iteration of the loop.

(*iii*) the conditions under which the iterative process must *terminate.*

With some loops it cannot be directly determined in advance how many iterations there will be before the loop will terminate. In fact there is no guarantee that loops of this type will terminate at all. In these cases the responsibility for making sure that the loop will terminate rests with the algorithm designer.

Every problem must terminate in a finite number of steps, so it is the duty of the algorithm designer to set up the termination of a loop (if exists inside a problem). For example, by forcing the condition under which the loop will continue to iterate to become false.

3.3.3 Code the Program

Once the design has been developed, the actual writing of the program begins. **Writing the program is called *coding.*** Coding is what many people think of when they think of programming, although it is only one of the five steps. Coding consists of translating the logic requirements from pseudocode or flowcharts into a programming language—the letters, numbers, and symbols that make up the program.

Identifying arithmetic and logical operations required for solutions and using appropriate control structures such as conditional or looping control structure is very important.

(*i*) **Select the Appropriate Programming Language**

A ***programming language*** **is a set of rules that tells the computer what operations to do.** Examples of well-known programming languages are C, C++, COBOL, Visual Basic and JAVA. These are called "high-level languages". Not all languages are appropriate for all uses. Some, for example, have strengths in mathematical and statistical processing. Others are more appropriate for database management. Thus, in choosing the language, we need to consider what purpose the program is designed to serve and what languages are already being used in our organization or in our field.

(*ii*) **Follow the Syntax**

In order for a program to work, we have to follow the ***syntax,*** **the rules of the programming language.** Programming languages have their own grammar just as human languages do. But computers are probably a lot less forgiving if we use these rules incorrectly.

3.3.4 Test the Program

Program testing **involves running various tests and then running real-world data to make sure the program works.** Two principal activities are *desk-checking* and *debugging*. These steps are known as *alpha-testing*.

(*i*) **Perform Desk-Checking**

Desk-checking **is simply reading through, or checking, the program to make sure that it's free of errors and that the logic works.** In other words, desk-checking is like proofreading. This step could be taken before the program is actually run on a computer.

(*ii*) **Debug the Program**

Once the program has been desk-checked, further errors, or "bugs", will doubtless surface. To ***debug*** **means to detect, locate, and remove all errors in a computer program.** Mistakes may be syntax errors or logical errors. ***Syntax errors*** **are caused by typographical errors and incorrect use of the programming language.** ***Logic errors*** **are caused by incorrect use of control structures.** Programs called *diagnostics* exist to check program syntax and display syntax-error messages. Diagnostic programs thus help identify and solve problems.

(*iii*) **Run Real-World Data**

After desk-checking and debugging, the program may run fine—in the laboratory. However, it needs to be tested with real data; this is called *beta testing*. Indeed, it is even advisable to test the program with *bad data*—data that is faulty, incomplete, or in overwhelming quantities—to see if you can make the system crash. Many users, after all, may be far more heavy-handed, ignorant and careless than programmers have anticipated.

Several trials using different test data may be required before the programming team is satisfied that the program can be released. Even then, some bugs may persist, because there comes a point where the pursuit of errors is uneconomical. This is one reason why many users are nervous about using the first version (version 1.0) of a commercial software package.

3.3.5 Document and Maintain the Program

Writing the program documentation is the fifth step in programming. The resulting ***documentation*** **consists of written descriptions of what a program is and how to use it.** Documentation is not just an end-stage process of programming. It has been (or should have been) going on throughout all programming steps. Documentation is needed for people who will be using or be involved with the program in the future.

Documentation should be prepared for several different kinds of readers—users, operators and programmers.

(*i*) **Prepare User Documentation**

When we buy a commercial software package, such as a spreadsheet, we normally get a manual with it. This is *user documentation.*

(*ii*) **Prepare Operator Documentation**

The people who run large computers are called *computer operators.* Because they are not always programmers, they need to be told what to do when the program malfunctions. The *operator documentation* gives them this information.

(*iii*) **Write Programmer Documentation**

Long after the original programming team has disbanded, the program may still be in use. If, as is often the case, a fourth of the programming staff leaves every year, after 4 years there could be a whole new bunch of programmers who know nothing about the software. *Program documentation* helps train these newcomers and enables them to maintain the existing system.

(*iv*) **Maintain the Program**

Maintenance includes any activity designed to keep programs in working condition, error-free, and up to date—adjustments, replacements, repairs, measurements, tests and so on. The rapid changes in modern organizations—in products, marketing strategies, accounting systems, and so on—are bound to be reflected in their computer systems. Thus, maintenance is an important matter, and documentation must be available to help programmers make adjustments in existing systems.

3.4 Program Design Tools

There are various program design tools, such as algorithms, flowcharts and pseudocode etc. In this section, we will discuss these program design tools with illustrative examples.

3.4.1 Algorithms

Computers are basically used to solve complex problems in a systematic and easy manner. In order to solve a problem systematically, the solution should be written as a set of sequential steps. Each of these steps specify some simple actions that need to be performed. Thus, *an algorithm may be defined as a finite and ordered sequence of steps which when performed lead to the solution of the problem in a definite time.* Ordered sequence implies that the execution takes place in the same manner or order in which the statements are written *i.e.,* each step of the algorithm is written in such a way that the next instruction follows automatically. The ordering is provided by assigning positive integers to the steps. The words BEGIN and END normally refer to the beginning and end of the algorithm. An algorithm must possess following *characteristics :*

1. **Finiteness.** Finiteness implies that the algorithm must have finite number of steps. Also the time taken to execute all the steps of the algorithm should be finite and within a reasonable limit.
2. **Definiteness.** By definiteness it is implied that each step of the algorithm must specify a definite action *i.e.,* the steps should not be vague. Moreover, the steps should be such that it is possible to execute these manually in a finite length of time.
3. **Input.** The term input means supplying initial data for an algorithm. This data must be present before any operations can be performed on it. Sometimes no data is needed because initial data may be generated within the algorithm. Thus, the algorithm may have no or more inputs. Generally, the initial data, is supplied by a READ instruction or a variable can be given initial value using SET instruction.
4. **Output.** The term output refers to the results obtained when all the steps of the algorithm have been executed. An algorithm must have at least one output.
5. **Effectiveness.** Effectiveness implies that all the operations involved in an algorithm must be sufficiently basic in nature so that they can be carried out manually in finite interval of time.

Expressing Algorithms

The procedure for expressing algorithm is quite simple. The language used to write algorithms is similar to our day-to-day life language. In addition, some special symbols are also used which are described below :

(*i*) **Assignment symbol (←).** The assignment symbol (←) is used to assign values to various variables. For example, let A be any variable and B be another variable or constant or an expression. Then the statement

$$A \leftarrow B$$

is called assignment statement. The statement implies that A is assigned the value stored in B. If A contains any previous value then that value is destroyed and the new value is assigned.

(*ii*) **Relational symbols.** The commonly used relational symbols for algorithms are :

Symbol	*Meaning*	*Example*
<	Less than	A < B
<=	Less than or equal to	A <= B
=	Equal to	A = B
≠	Not equal to	A ≠ B
>	Greater than	A > B
>=	Greater than or equal to	A >= B

(*iii*) **Brackets ({}).** The pair of braces is used to write comments for the purpose of documentation.

For example,

(*i*) BEGIN {Start of the algorithm}

(ii) Set N ← N + 1 {Increase the value of N by 1}
(iii) END {End of the algorithm}.

Basic Control Structures

The basic control structures needed for writing good and efficient algorithms are :

(i) *Selection*
(ii) *Branching*
(iii) *Looping.*

(i) **Selection.** The selection structure is used when we have to perform a given set of instructions if the given condition is TRUE and an alternative set of instructions if the condition is FALSE. The basic statement available for selection is IF-THEN-ELSE.

The syntax is :

```
IF (condition is true) THEN
{
        s1
        s2
        .
        .
        .
        sn
}
ELSE
{
        f1
        f2
        .
        .
        .
        fn
}
```

For example, consider the following algorithm which finds greater among 2 numbers.

```
            BEGIN
STEP 1      Read NUM1, NUM2
STEP 2      IF NUM1 > NUM2 THEN
                 Write (NUM1, "is greater")
            ELSE
                 Write (NUM2, "is greater")
            END
```

(*ii*) **Branching.** The branching statement is required when we want to transfer the control of execution from one part or step of the algorithm to another part or step. The statement available for branching is GOTO and its syntax is :

GOTO *n*

where *n* is a positive integer and specifies the step number where the control of execution is to be transferred.

(*iii*) **Looping.** The looping structure is used when a statement or a set of statements is to be executed a number of times. The following two loop control structures are commonly used in algorithms :

(*a*) WHILE-DO

(*b*) REPEAT-UNTIL

(*a*) **WHILE-DO :** The syntax is :

```
STEP 1      WHILE (Condition) DO
STEP 2      S1
STEP 3      S2
.
.
.
STEP N+1    SN
STEP N+2    END-WHILE {End of While-Do loop}
```

This control loop structure implies that as long as the condition remains true, all the steps listed between WHILE-DO and END-WHILE are executed again and again. As soon as the condition becomes false, the execution of the loop stops and control is transferred to next statement following END-WHILE.

For example, consider the following algorithm

```
            BEGIN
STEP 1      Set N ← 1
STEP 2      WHILE (N <= 10) DO
STEP 3      Write N
STEP 4      Set N ← N + 1
STEP 5      END-WHILE
            END
```

This algorithm initially sets the value of N to 1. The while statement then checks if the value of N <= 10. If the condition is true it executes steps 3 and 4. When the value of N exceeds 10 the condition becomes false and the control goes to the statement following END-WHILE which is END statement marking the END of algorithm.

(*b*) **REPEAT-UNTIL :** This is similar to WHILE-DO except the fact that the loop is executed till the condition remains false or condition becomes true. The syntax is :

```
STEP 1      REPEAT
```

STEP 2 S1
STEP 3 S2
.
.
.
STEP N + 1 SN
STEP N + 2 UNTIL (Condition)

This control loop structure implies that as long as the condition remains false, all the steps listed between REPEAT and UNTIL are executed again and again. As soon as the condition becomes true, the execution of the loop stops and control is transferred to next statement following UNTIL (condition). *For example,* consider the following algorithm :

```
            BEGIN
STEP 1      Set N ← 1
STEP 2      REPEAT
STEP 3      Write N
STEP 4      Set N ← N + 1 {Increment N by 1}
STEP 5      UNTIL (N > 10)
            END
```

Initially, the value of N is set to 1. The loop executes till the value of N exceeds 10. After this, the control goes to the next statement following UNTIL (N > 10).

Advantages of Algorithms

The main advantages of algorithm are given below :

(*i*) It is simple to understand step by step solution of the problem.

(*ii*) It is easy to debug *i.e.,* errors can be easily pointed out.

(*iii*) It is independent of programming languages.

(*iv*) It is compatible to computers in the sense that each step of an algorithm can be easily coded into its equivalent in high-level language.

Development of Algorithms for Simple Problems

ALGORITHM : Exchanging Values of Two Variables

Given two variables A and B. We have to exchange these variables. TEMP is used for exchanging the variables.

```
1.  INPUT A, B
2.  TEMP ← A
        A ← B
        B ← TEMP
3.  Write "Exchanged values are ", A, B
4.  End.
```

ALGORITHM : Biggest of Three Numbers

Given the three numbers A, B, C. We have to find the biggest of these.

```
1.  INPUT A, B, C
2.  IF (A > B) THEN
    Begin
        IF (A > C) THEN
            Write "Biggest number is ", A
        ELSE
            Write "Biggest number is ", C
    End
    ELSE
    Begin
        IF (B > C) THEN
            Write "Biggest number is ", B
        ELSE
            Write "Biggest number is ", C
    End
3.  END.
```

ALGORITHM : Area of a Triangle

Given three sides A, B, C of a triangle. We have to find the area (if possible). S denotes the semi-perimeter.

```
1.  INPUT A, B, C
2.  IF (((A+B) > C) AND ((B+C) > A) AND ((C+A) > B)) THEN
    Begin
        S ← (A + B + C)/2
        Area ← √(S × (S − A) × (S − B) × (S − C))
        Write "Area of triangle is ", Area, " sq. units"
    End
    ELSE
        Write "Triangle is not possible"
3.  END.
```

ALGORITHM : Roots of a Quadratic Equation ($Ax^2 + Bx + C = 0$)

```
1.  INPUT A, B, C
2.  IF A = 0 THEN
    Begin
        IF B = 0 THEN
        Begin
            Write "Equation is degenerate"
            goto step 5
```

```
            End
            ELSE
            Begin
                    Write "Linear equation has single root"
                    x1 = –C/B
                    Write "Root = ", x1
                    goto step 5
            End
        End
3.      D = B × B – 4.0 × A × C
4.      IF D > 0 THEN
        Begin
            Write "Real and distinct roots"
            x1 = (–B + √D ) / (2.0 × A)
            x2 = (–B – √D ) / (2.0 × A)
            Write "First root = ", x1
            Write "Second root = ", x2
        End
        ELSE
        Begin
            IF (D = 0) THEN
            Begin
                    Write "Real and equal roots"
                    x1 = –B / (2.0 × A)
                    x2 = x1
                    Write "First root = ", x1
                    Write "Second root = ", x2
            End
            ELSE
            Begin
                    Write "Imaginary roots"
                    x1 = –B / (2.0 × A)
                    x2 = x1
                    y1 = √–D  / (2.0 × A)
                    y2 = –y1
                    Write "First root "
                    Write "Real part ", x1, " Img. part ", y1
                    Write "Second root "
```

```
            Write "Real part ", x2, " Img. part ", y2
        End
    End
5.  END.
```

ALGORITHM : Sum of Series 1 + 5 + 9 + 13 + ... 20 Terms

Given the series 1 + 5 + 9 + 13 + ... We have to find the sum of 20 terms. NUM is a temporary variable for storing a term. SUM denotes the sum of terms. Variable COUNT is used as loop computer.

```
1.  SUM ← 0
2.  NUM ← 1
3.  Repeat for COUNT = 1, 2, ........, 20
    Begin
        SUM ← SUM + NUM
        NUM ← NUM + 4
    End
4.  Write "Sum of 20 terms is", SUM
5.  End.
```

ALGORITHM : Summation of a Set of Numbers

Given N numbers. We have to find the sum of these numbers. NUM is a temporary variable for storing a number. SUM denotes the sum of numbers. Variable COUNT is used as loop counter.

```
1.  Read N
2.  SUM ← 0
3.  Repeat for COUNT = 1, 2, ........, N
    Begin
        Read NUM
        SUM ← SUM + NUM
    End
4.  Write "Sum of inputted numbers is ", SUM
5.  End.
```

ALGORITHM : Reversing Digits of an Integer

Given an integer NUM. We have to reverse digits of this integer. Variables Q and R denote quotient and remainder respectively.

```
1.  Read NUM
2.  Write "Reversed number is "
3.  While (NUM ≠ 0) DO
    Begin
        Q ← Integral part of (NUM/10)
```

```
        R ← NUM – (Q × 10)
        Write R
        NUM ← Q
    End
4.  End.
```

ALGORITHM : Traversal in an Array

Given an array A of N elements. We have to traverse the array elements one by one. I denotes the array index. Let **CHANGE** denote the desired operation to be performed.

```
1.  I ← 1
2.  While (I ≤ N) DO
    Begin
        Apply CHANGE on A[I]
              I ← I + 1
    End
3.  END
              OR
1.  Repeat for I = 1, 2, ..........., N
        Apply CHANGE on A[I]
2.  END.
```

ALGORITHM : Reverse Order of Elements of an Array

Given an array A of N elements. This algorithm reverses the order of array elements. I, MID denote array indices. TEMP is used for swapping of elements.

```
1.  MID ← Integral part of (N/2)
2.  I ← 1
3.  Repeat for I = 1, 2, ........., MID
    Begin
        TEMP ← A[I]
        A[I] ← A[N – I + 1]
        A[N – I + 1] ← TEMP
    End
4.  END.
```

ALGORITHM : Concatenation of Two Arrays

Given two arrays A and B of size M and N, respectively. This algorithm concatenates the arrays in C having size M + N. I denotes array index. Let us assume that A is housed first in C and then B.

```
1.  Repeat for I = 1, 2, ............., M
        C[I] ← A[I]
2.  Repeat for I = 1, 2, .............., N
        C[M+I] ← B[I]
3.  END.
```

ALGORITHM : Find Largest of N Numbers in an Array

Given an array A having N elements. This algorithm finds the LARGEST of the elements. I denotes array index.

```
1.  LARGEST ← A[1]
2.  Repeat for I = 2, 3, ................, N
    Begin
        IF (A[I] > LARGEST) THEN
                LARGEST ← A[I]
    End
3.  Write "Largest number is ", LARGEST
4.  END.
```

ALGORITHM : Sum and Average of N Numbers in an Array

Given an array A of N elements. This algorithm finds the sum and average of all the numbers. I denotes array index.

```
1.  SUM ← 0
2.  Repeat for I = 1, 2, ................, N
        SUM ← SUM + A[I]
3.  AVG ← SUM/N
4.  Write SUM, AVG
5.  END.
```

ALGORITHM : Linear Search or Sequential Search

Given an array A of N elements. This algorithm searches for an element DATA in the array. I denotes the array index. This algorithm gives the first location where DATA is found.

```
1.  I ← 1
2.  While (I ⩽ N) DO upto step 3
3.  IF (A[I] = DATA) THEN
    Begin
        Write "Successful search"
        Write DATA, " found at position ", I
        goto step 5
    End
    ELSE
    Begin
        I ← I + 1
    End
4.  Write "Unsuccessful search"
5.  END.
```

ALGORITHM : Binary Search (Always Applicable on Sorted Data)

Given an array A of N elements in ascending order. This algorithm searches for an element DATA. LOW, HIGH, MID denote the lowest, highest and middle position of a search interval respectively.

```
1.  LOW ← 1
    HIGH ← N
2.  While (LOW ⩽ HIGH) DO upto step 4
3.  MID ← Integral part of ((LOW + HIGH)/2)
4.  IF (DATA = A[MID]) THEN
    Begin
        Write "Successful search"
        Write DATA, " found at position ", MID
        goto step 6
    End
    ELSE
    Begin
        IF (DATA > A[MID]) THEN
            LOW ← MID + 1
        ELSE
            HIGH ← MID – 1
    End
5.  Write "Unsuccessful search"
6.  END.
```

ALGORITHM : Organize Numbers in Ascending Order

Given an array A of N elements. This algorithm arranges the elements in ascending order. I and J denote array indices. Variable TEMP is used for swapping.

```
1.  Repeat for I = 1, 2, ......., N–1
    Begin
        Repeat for J = I + 1, I + 2, ........., N
        Begin
            IF (A[J] < A[I]) THEN
            Begin
                TEMP ← A[I]
                A[I] ← A[J]
                A[J] ← TEMP
            End
        End
    End
2.  END.
```

ALGORITHM : Insertion Sort

Given an array A of N elements. This algorithm arranges the elements in ascending order. CURRENT denotes the value of the element to be placed at proper position during a pass. POS is used for finding the appropriate position of CURRENT among the elements above it (if possible). I, J denote the array indices. Assuming the array index begins at 1.

```
1.  Repeat for I = 2, 3, ..., N upto step 5
2.  CURRENT = A[I]
3.  POS = 1
4.  Repeat while (POS < I) AND (A[POS] ≤ CURRENT))
          POS = POS + 1
5.  IF (POS ≠ I) THEN
    Begin
          Repeat for J = I–1, I–2, ..., POS
          Begin
                A[J+1] = A[J]
          End
          A[POS] = CURRENT
    End
6.  End
```

ALGORITHM : Selection Sort

Given an array A of N elements. This algorithm arranges the elements in ascending order. PASS denotes the pass counter and MIN_INDEX the position of the smallest element during a pass. N–1 passes are required in this sorting technique as each pass places one element properly. Variable TEMP is used for swapping (interchanging) two elements. I denotes array index. Assume the array index begins at 1.

```
1.  Repeat for PASS = 1, 2, ..., N – 1
    Begin
          MIN_INDEX = PASS
          Repeat for I = PASS + 1, PASS + 2, ..., N
          Begin
                IF (A[I] < A[MIN_INDEX]) THEN
                      MIN_INDEX = I
          End
          IF (Pass ≠ MIN_INDEX) THEN
          Begin
                TEMP = A[PASS]
                A[PASS] = A[MIN_INDEX]
                A[MIN_INDEX] = TEMP
          End
    End
2.  End
```

ALGORITHM : Bubble Sort

Given an array A of N elements. This algorithm arranges the elements in ascending order. PASS denotes the pass counter and LAST the position of the last unsorted element during a pass. In the worst case N – 1 passes are applied for sorting N elements. Only one pass is needed if the given array is already sorted. EXCHS denote the number of exchanges during a pass. Variable TEMP is used for swapping of elements. I denotes array index. Assume the array index begins at 1.

```
1.  LAST = N
2.  Repeat for PASS = 1, 2, ..., N – 1 upto step 5
3.  EXCHS = 0
4.  Repeat for I = 1, 2, ..., LAST – 1
    Begin
          IF (A[I] > A[I + 1]) THEN
          Begin
                TEMP = A[I]
                A[I] = A[I + 1]
                A[I + 1] = TEMP
                EXCHS = EXCHS + 1
          End
    End
5.  IF (EXCHS = 0) THEN
          goto step 6
    ELSE
          LAST = LAST – 1
6.  End
```

ALGORITHM : Merging of Two Arrays

Given two arrays A and B of size M and N respectively in ascending order of elements. This algorithm merges the two arrays in C of size M + N, in ascending order. I, J, K denote array indices.

```
1.  I ← 1
    J ← 1
    K ← 1
2.  Repeat While ((I ≤ M) AND (J ≤ N))
    Begin
          IF (A[I] ≤ B[J]) THEN
          Begin
                C[K] ← A[I]
                I ← I + 1
          End
          ELSE
          Begin
                C[K] ← B[J]
                J ← J + 1
          End
          K ← K + 1
    End
```

```
3.  IF (I > M) THEN
    Begin
          Repeat While (J ≤ N)
          Begin
                C[K] ← B[J]
                J ← J + 1
                K ← K + 1
          End
    End
    ELSE
    Begin
          Repeat While (I ≤ M)
          Begin
                C[K] ← A[I]
                I ← I + 1
                K ← K + 1
          End
    End
4.  END
```

ALGORITHM : Matrix Multiplication

Given two matrices A and B of orders m×n and p×q respectively. This algorithm multiplies the two matrices (if possible) and stores the result in matrix C (of order m×q). I, J, K denote array indices.

```
1.  IF n ≠ p THEN
    Begin
          Write "Matrix multiplication not possible"
          goto step 3
    End
2.  Repeat for I = 1, 2, ................., m
    Begin
          Repeat for J = 1, 2, ..............., q
          Begin
                C[I,J] ← 0
                Repeat for K = 1, 2, ............., n
                      C[I,J] ← C[I,J] + (A[I,K] × B[K,J])
          End
    End
3.  END.
```

3.4.2 Flowcharts

A flowchart is a pictorial representation of the sequence of operations necessary to solve a problem with a computer. The technique of drawing *flowcharts* is known as flowcharting. The first formal flowchart is attributed to *John Von Neumann* in 1945. The flowcharts are read from left to right and top to bottom. Program flowcharts show the sequence of instructions in a program or a subroutine. The symbols used in constructing a flowchart are simple and easy to learn. These are very important planning and working tools in programming. The purposes of the flowcharts are given below :

1. Provide better communication

These are an excellent means of communication. The programmers, teachers, students, computer operators and users can quickly and clearly get ideas and descriptions of algorithms.

2. Provide an overview

A clear overview of the complete problem and its algorithm is provided by the flowchart. Main elements and their relationships can be easily seen without leaving important details.

3. Help in algorithm design

The program flow can be shown easily with the help of a flowchart. A flowchart can be easily drawn in comparison to writing a program and testing it. Different algorithms (for the same problem) can be easily experimented with flowcharts.

4. Check the program logic

All the major portions of a program are shown by the flowchart, precisely. So, the accuracy in logic flow is maintained.

5. Help in coding

A program can be easily coded in a programming language with the help of a flowchart. All the steps are coded without leaving any part so that no error lies in the code.

6. Modification becomes easy

A flowchart helps in modification of an already existing program without disrupting the program flow.

7. Better documentation provided

A flowchart gives a permanent storage of program logic pictorially. It documents all the steps carried out in an algorithm. A comprehensive, carefully drawn flowchart is always an indispensable part for the program's documentation.

Flowchart Symbols

Flowcharts have only a few symbols of different sizes and shapes for showing necessary operations. Each symbol has specific meaning and function in a flowchart. These symbols have been standardized by the *American National Standards Institute (ANSI)*. The basic rules that a user must keep in mind while using the symbols are :

1. Use the symbols for their specific purposes.
2. Be consistent in the use of symbols.

3. Be clear in drawing the flowchart and the entries in the symbols.
4. Use the annotation symbol when beginning a procedure.
5. Enter and exit the symbols in the same way.

The flowchart symbols alongwith their purposes are given in Table 3.2.

Program Control Structures

A *control structure,* or logic structure, is a structure that controls the logical sequence in which computer program instructions are executed. In structured program design, three control structures are used to form the logic of a program : *sequence, selection* and *iteration* (or *loop*). These are also used for drawing flowcharts.

The three control structures have been discussed earlier in this chapter.

Types of Flowcharts

The systems designer and programmer use the following types of flowcharts in developing algorithms :

1. System flowcharts
2. Modular program flowcharts
3. Detail program flowcharts or application flowcharts

1. System flowchart

It plays a vital role in the system analysis. A system is a group of interrelated components tied together according to a plan to achieve a predefined objective. The elements and characteristics of a system are graphically shown and its structure and relationship are also represented by flowchart symbols. The system analysts use the system flowcharts for analysing or designing various systems. The different stages of a system are :

(*i*) Problem recognition
(*ii*) Feasibility
(*iii*) System analysis
(*iv*) System design
(*v*) Implementation
(*vi*) Evaluation

All the above stages use the system flowchart for convenience. Any alternative solution for the existing system or the entirely new system can be systematically represented. The working system is well documented by a precisely drawn system flowchart.

2. Modular program flowchart

A system flowchart indicates the hardware, identifies the various files and represents the general data flow. A modular program flowchart on the other hand defines the logical steps for the input, output and processing of the information of a specific program. In structured or modular programs, the independent modules or units are written for different procedures. This module is useful in performing the specified operation in other programs too. The exact operation in detail is not performed but only the relationship and order in which processes are to be performed are included.

It is also called as block diagram. Its main advantage lies in the fact that the programmer can concentrate more on flow of logic and temporarily computer level details are ignored. Alternate algorithms without much time consumption or effort can also be tried using it. These help a lot in communicating the main logic of the program.

3. Detail program flowchart

These are the most comprehensive and elemental charts in developing the programs. The symbols represented by it are quite useful for coding the program in any computer language. Each computer language has its own syntax, so there may be some difference in performing the operations to be followed for coding a program. A detail program flowchart represents each minute operation in its proper sequence, reduced to its simplest parts.

Rules for Drawing Flowcharts

The following rules and guidelines are recommended by ANSI for flowcharting :

1. First consider the main logic, then incorporate the details.
2. Maintain a consistent level of detail for a flowchart.
3. Do not include all details in a flowchart.
4. Use meaningful descriptions in the flowchart symbols. These should be easy to understand.
5. Be consistent in using variables and names in the flowchart.
6. The flow of the flowchart should be from top to bottom and from left to right.
7. For a complex flowchart, use connectors to reduce the number of flow lines. The crossing of lines should be avoided as far as possible.
8. If a flowchart is not drawn on a single page, it is recommended to break it at an input or output point and properly labelled connectors should be used for linking the portions of the flowchart on separate pages.
9. Avoid duplication so far as possible.

Levels of Flowcharts

There are two levels of flowcharts :

(*i*) Macro flowchart

(*ii*) Micro flowchart

(*i*) **Macro flowchart.** It shows the main segment of a program and shows lesser details.

(*ii*) **Micro flowchart.** It shows more details of any part of the flowchart.

***Note :** A flowchart is independent of all computer languages.*

Examples of Flowcharts

The following figure depicts the flowchart for converting celsius temperature to fahrenheit using the formula $°F = \frac{9}{5} \times °C + 32.0$.

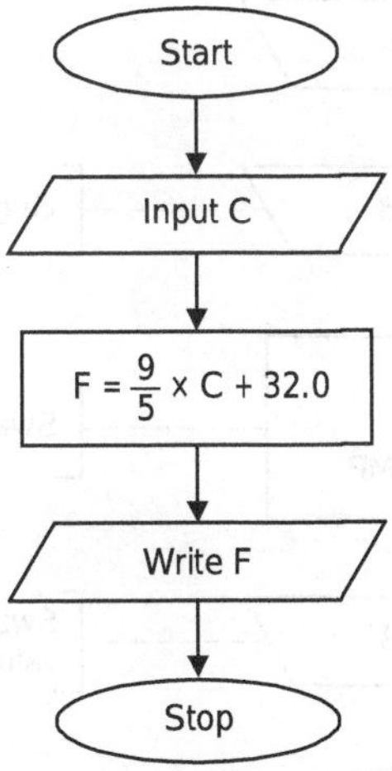

Fig. 3.12

The following figure depicts the flowchart for finding the area and circumference of a circle, whose radius *r* is given.

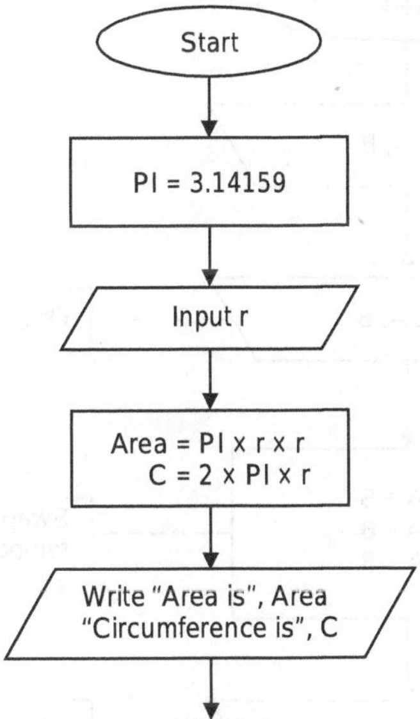

Fig. 3.13

The following figure depicts the flowchart for swapping (interchanging) two numbers using a temporary variable.

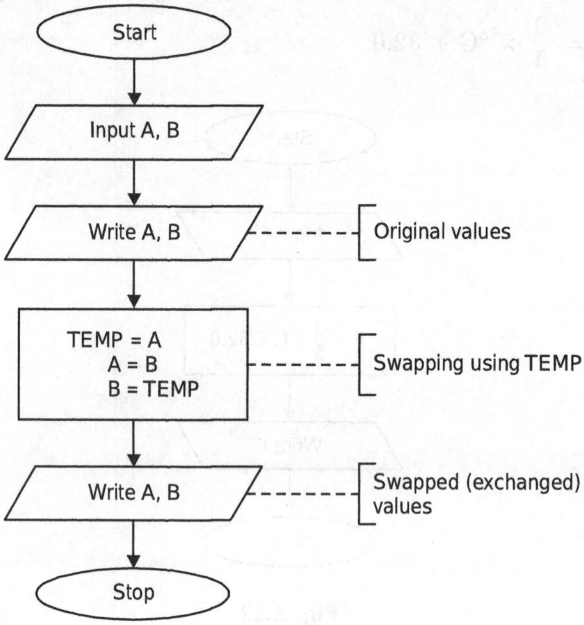

Fig. 3.14

The following figure depicts the flowchart for swapping two numbers without using a temporary variable.

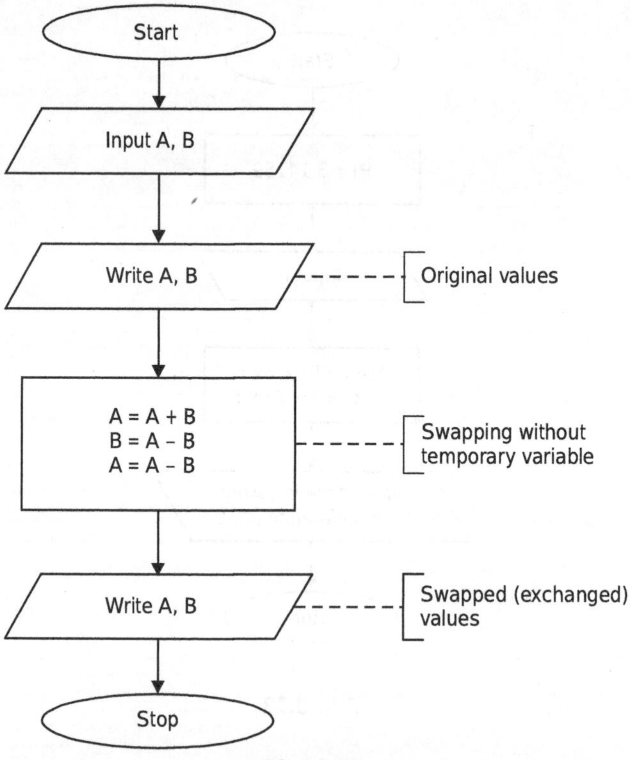

Fig. 3.15

The following figure depicts the flowchart for checking a year for leap year. (If a year is divisible by 4 and not divisible by 100, or, if the year is divisible by 400, it is a leap year). Here **mod** is used for finding remainder.

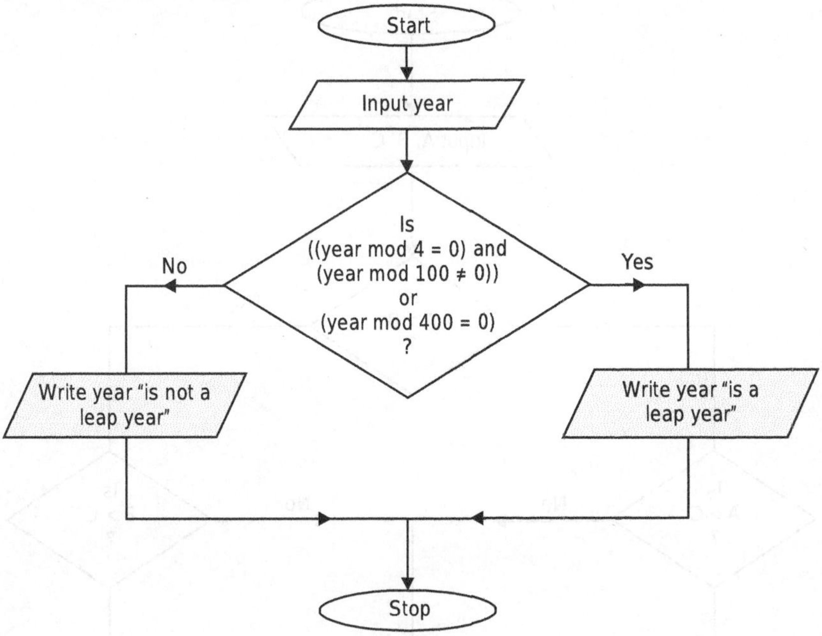

Fig. 3.16

The following figure depicts the flowchart to find out the biggest of three numbers.

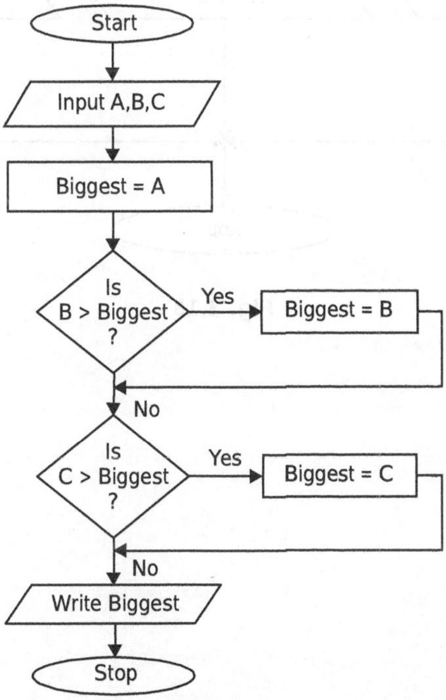

Fig. 3.17

The flowchart for finding the biggest of three numbers can also be drawn as given below :

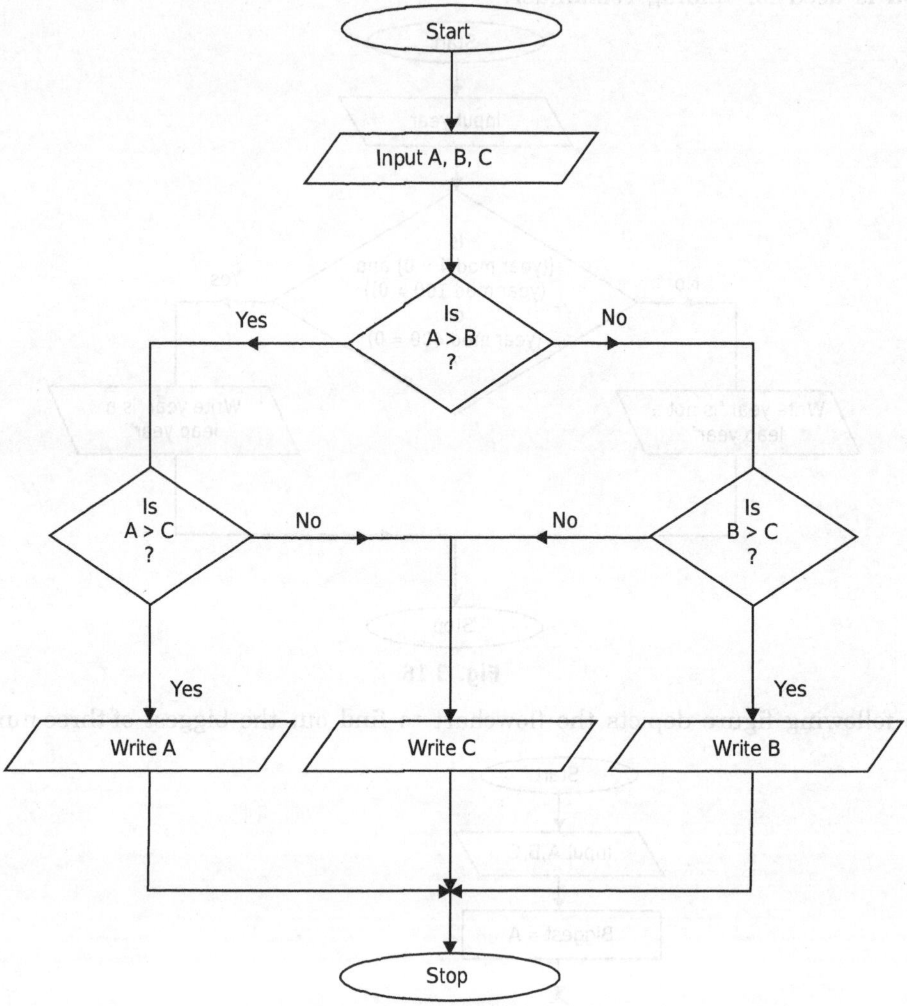

Fig. 3.18

The following figure depicts the flowchart for solving a given quadratic equation.

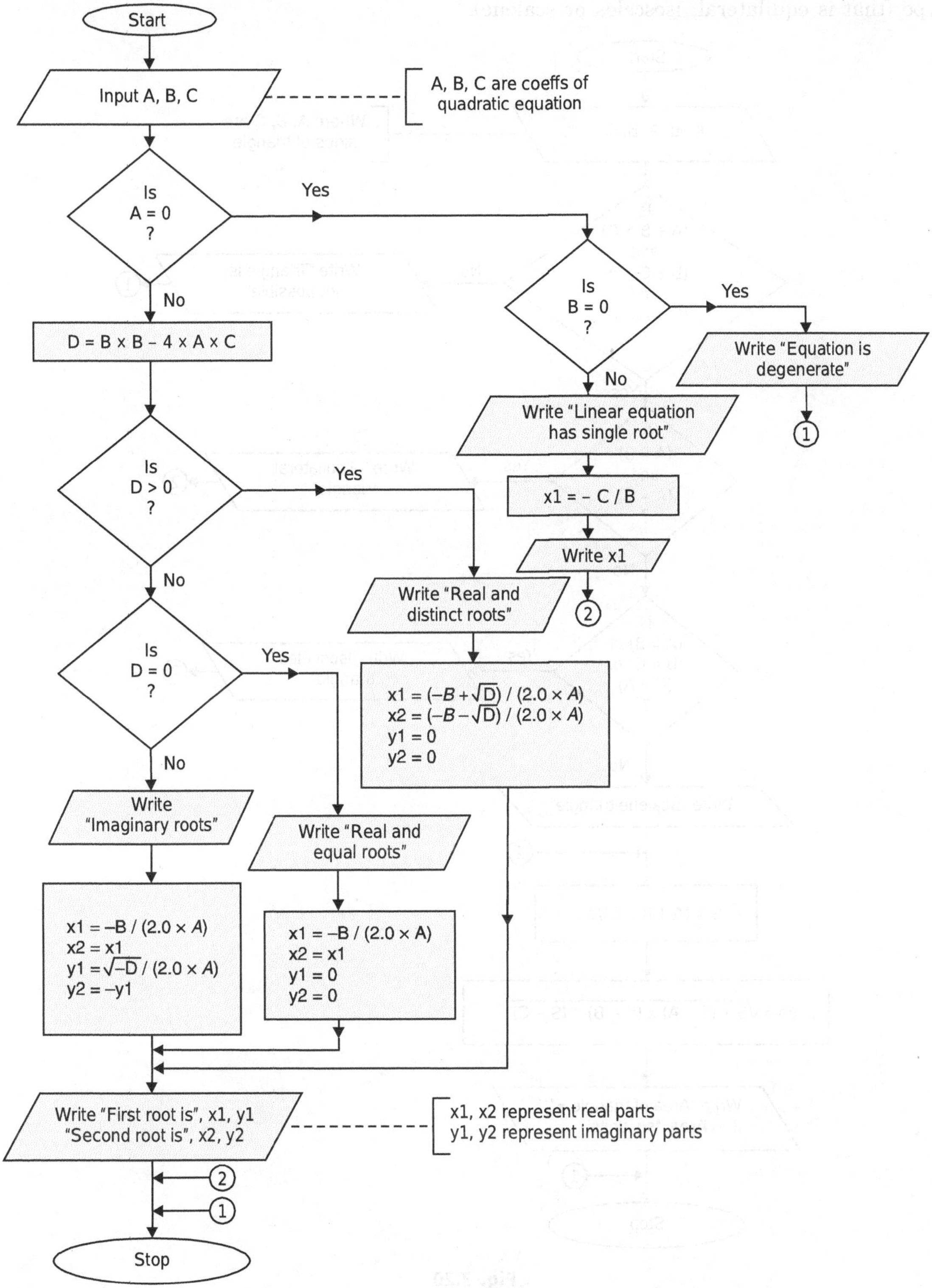

Fig. 3.19

The following figure illustrates the flowchart for finding the area of a triangle and its type (that is equilateral, isosceles or scalene).

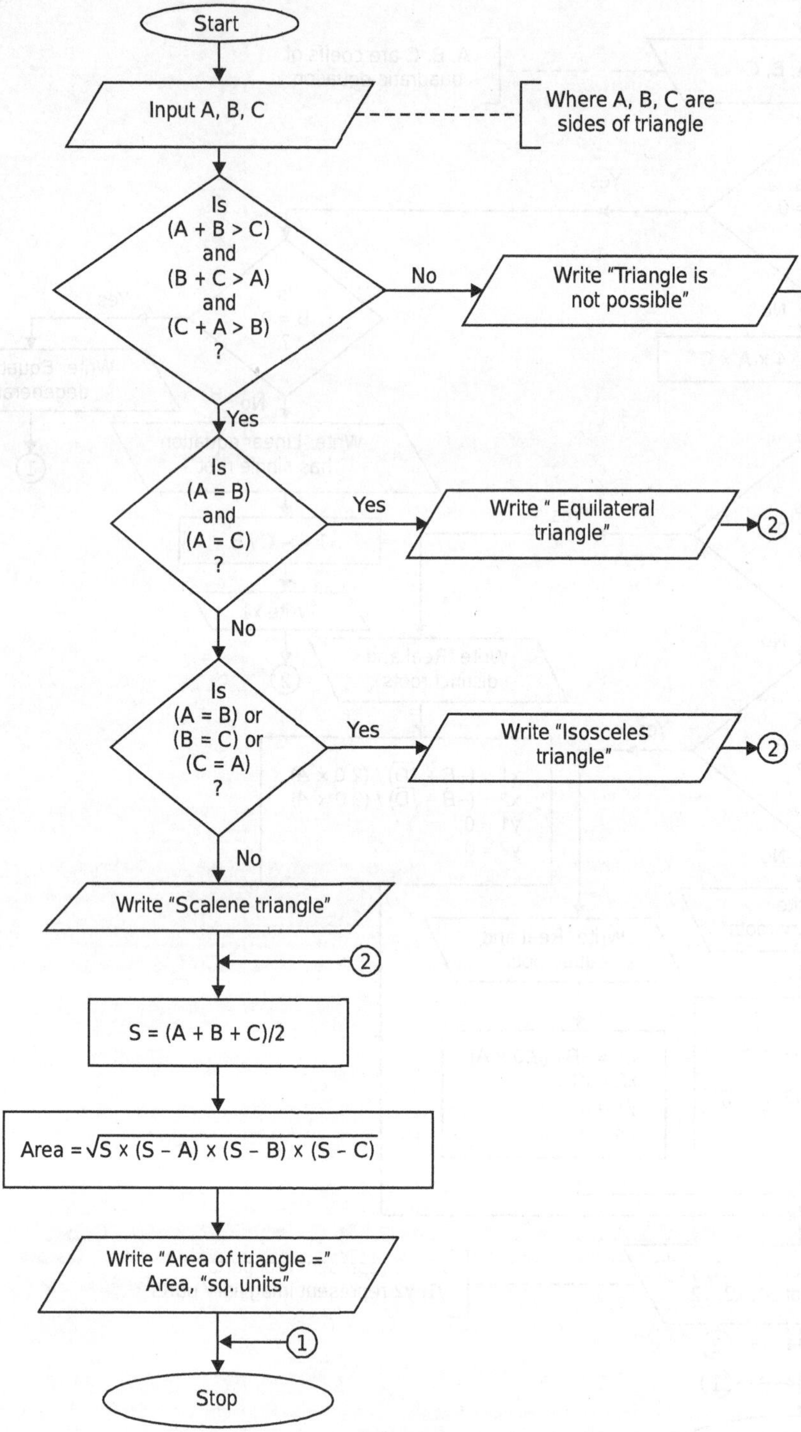

Fig. 3.20

The following figure depicts the flowchart for simulating a simple calculator (that is performing +, –, ×, /)

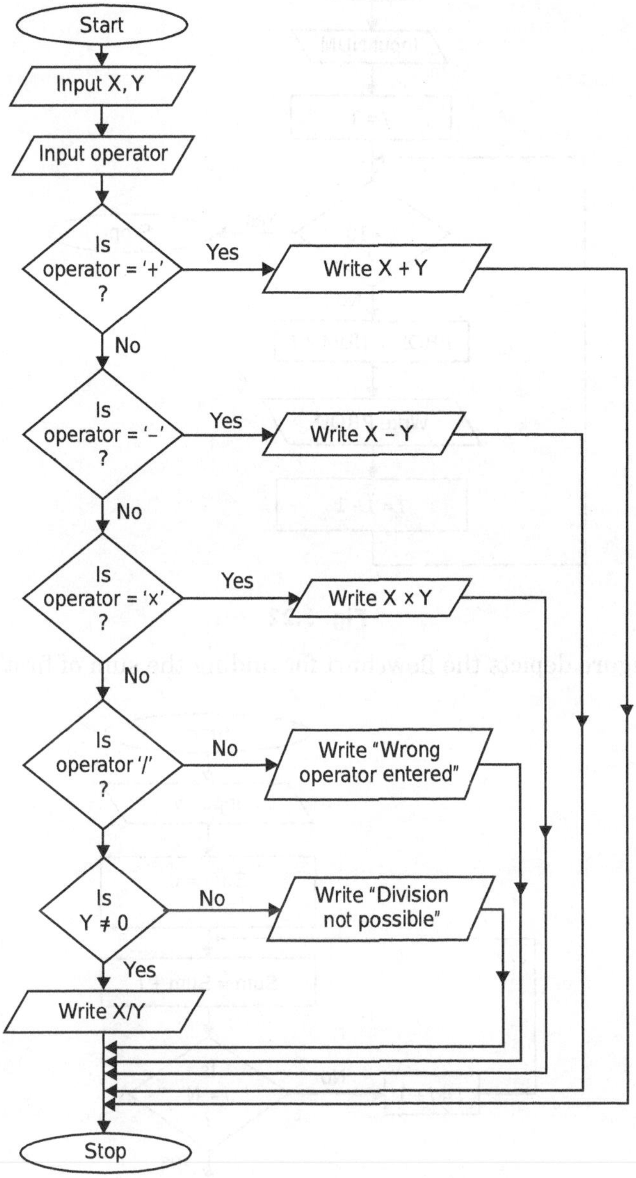

Fig. 3.21

The following figure depicts the flowchart for printing the multiplication table of an integer.

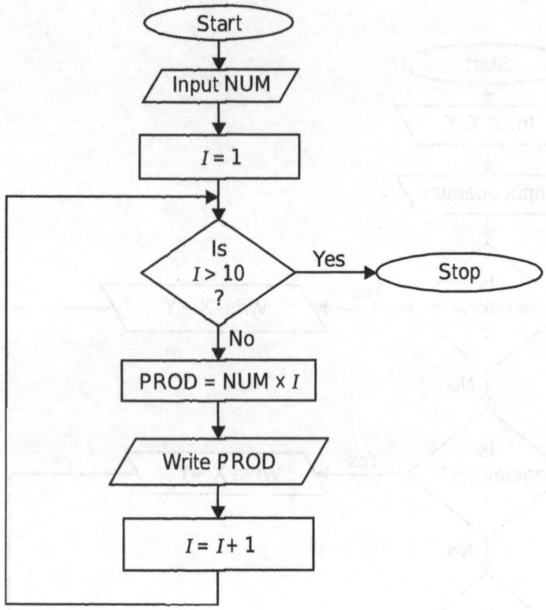

Fig. 3.22

The following figure depicts the flowchart for finding the sum of first N natural Numbers.

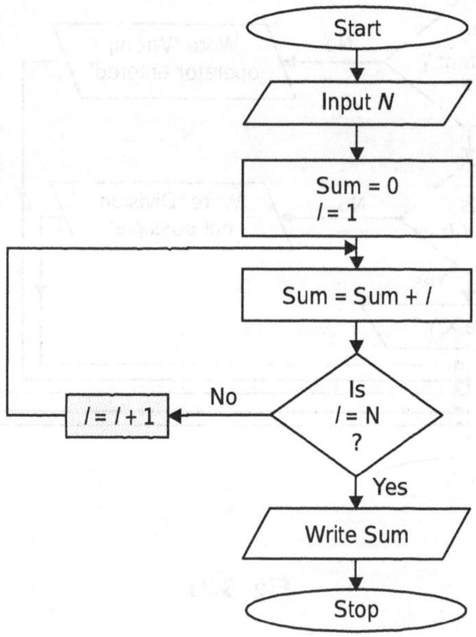

Fig. 3.23

The following figure depicts the flowchart for finding the factorial of a given number.

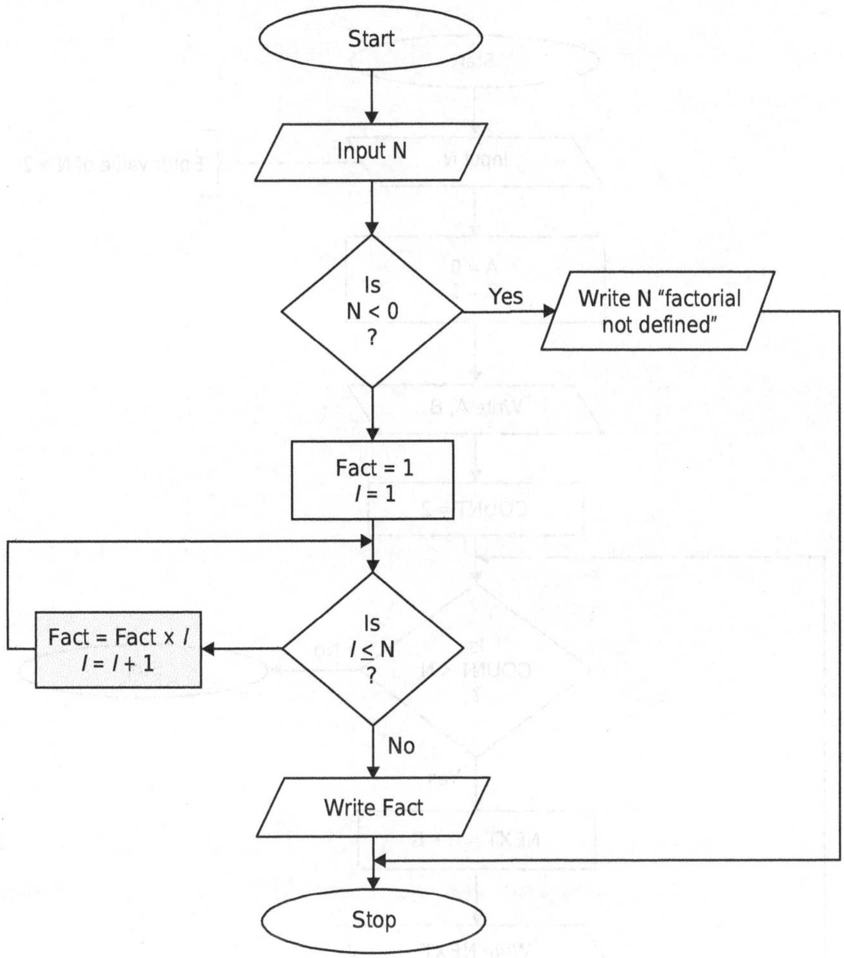

Fig. 3.24

The following figure depicts the flowchart for generating first n (n ⩾ 2) fibonacci terms (Fibonacci terms are 0, 1, 1, 2, 3, 5, 8, 13, 21 ......).

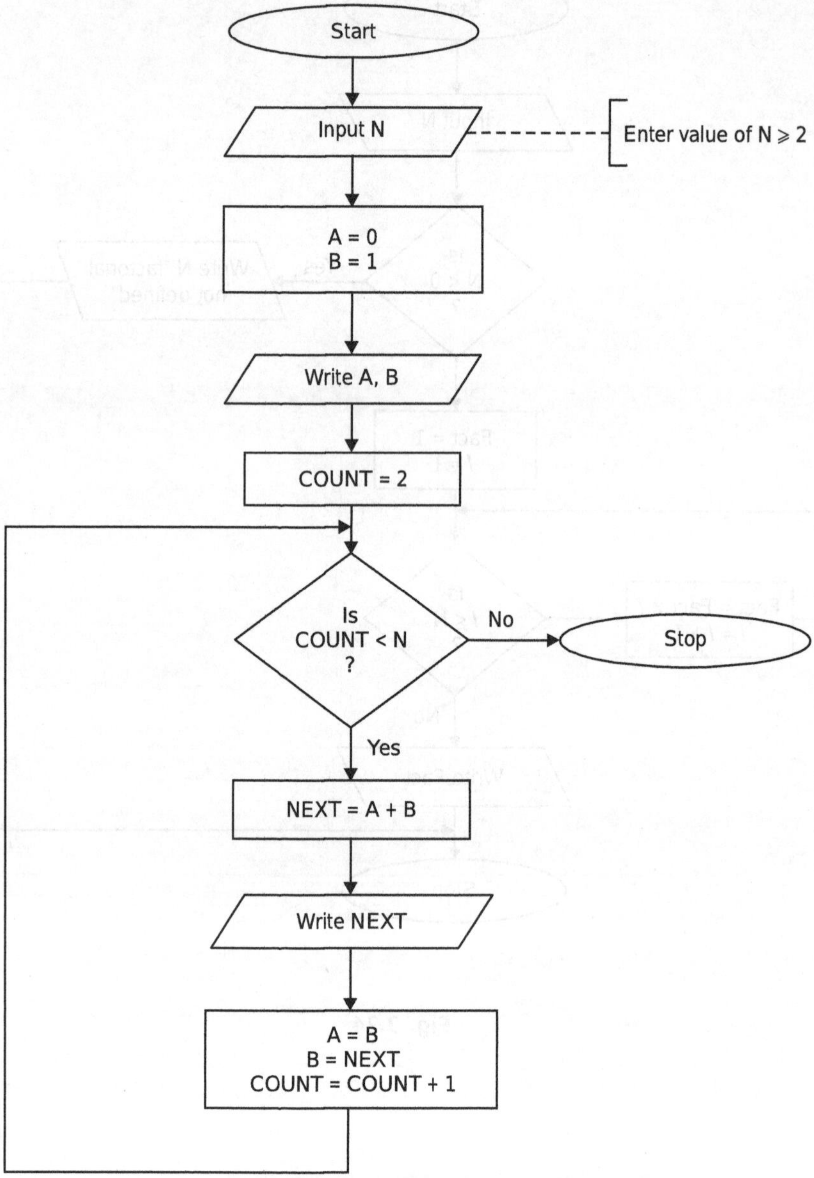

Fig. 3.25

The following figure depicts the flowchart for checking an integer for prime number (A number p > 1 whose only divisors are 1 and itself is a prime number).

> ***Note :*** *A number is prime if it is not divisible by any integer greater than 1 and less than or equal to the integral part of its square root.*

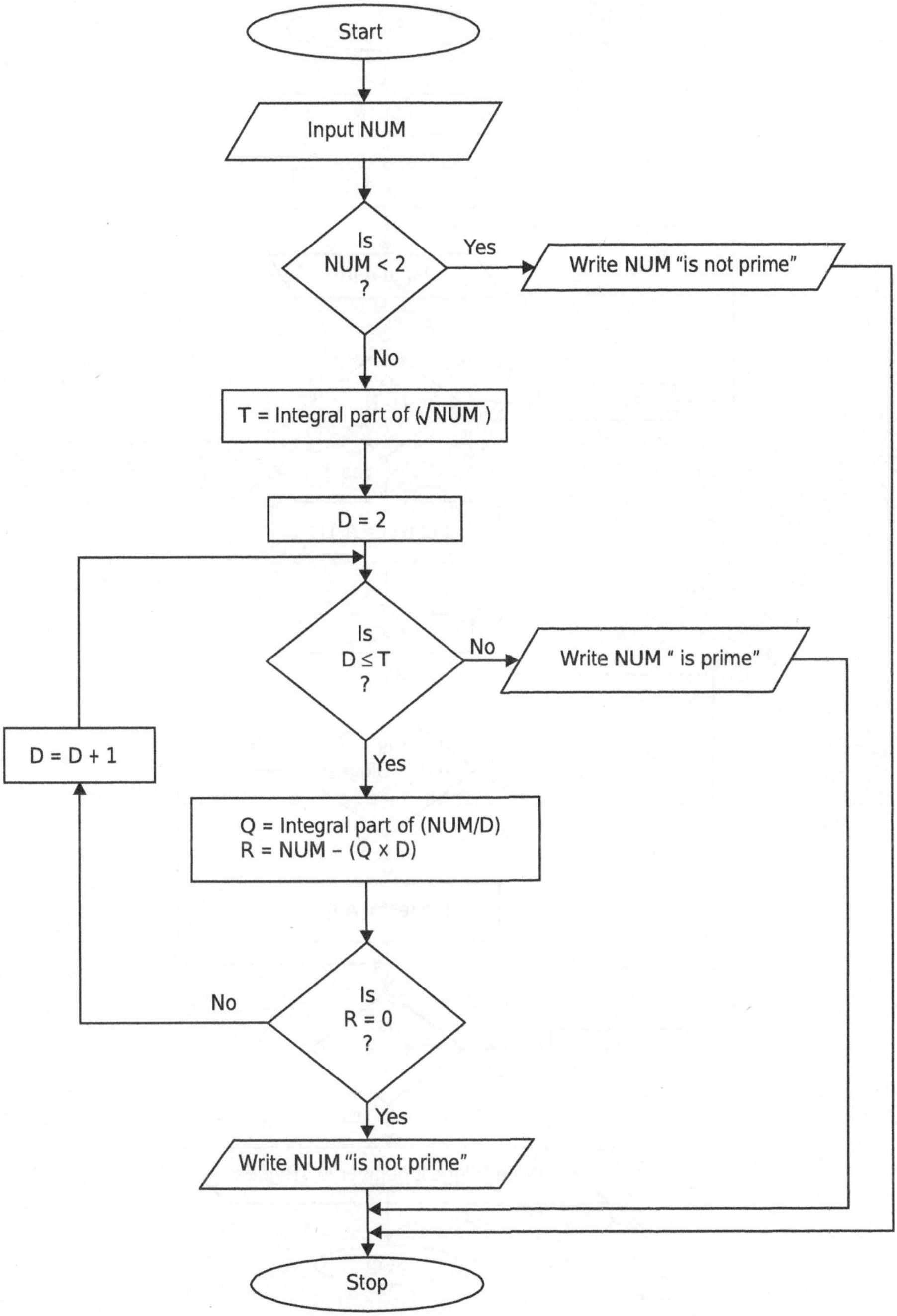

Fig. 3.26

The following figure depicts the flowchart for finding the biggest of given set of numbers in an array.

> ***Note :*** *The subscript is started from 1, it may be the same or start from 0 in some of the computer languages when you code the program.*

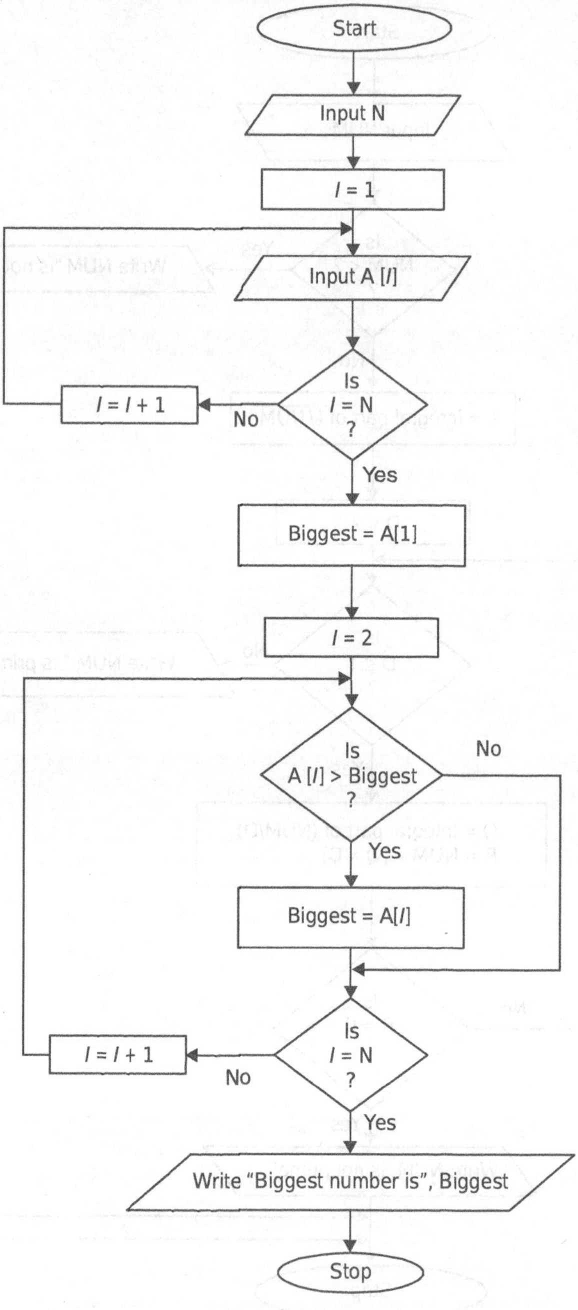

Fig. 3.27

The following figure depicts the flowchart for searching an element from an array using linear search or sequential search method (only first occurrence will be searched).

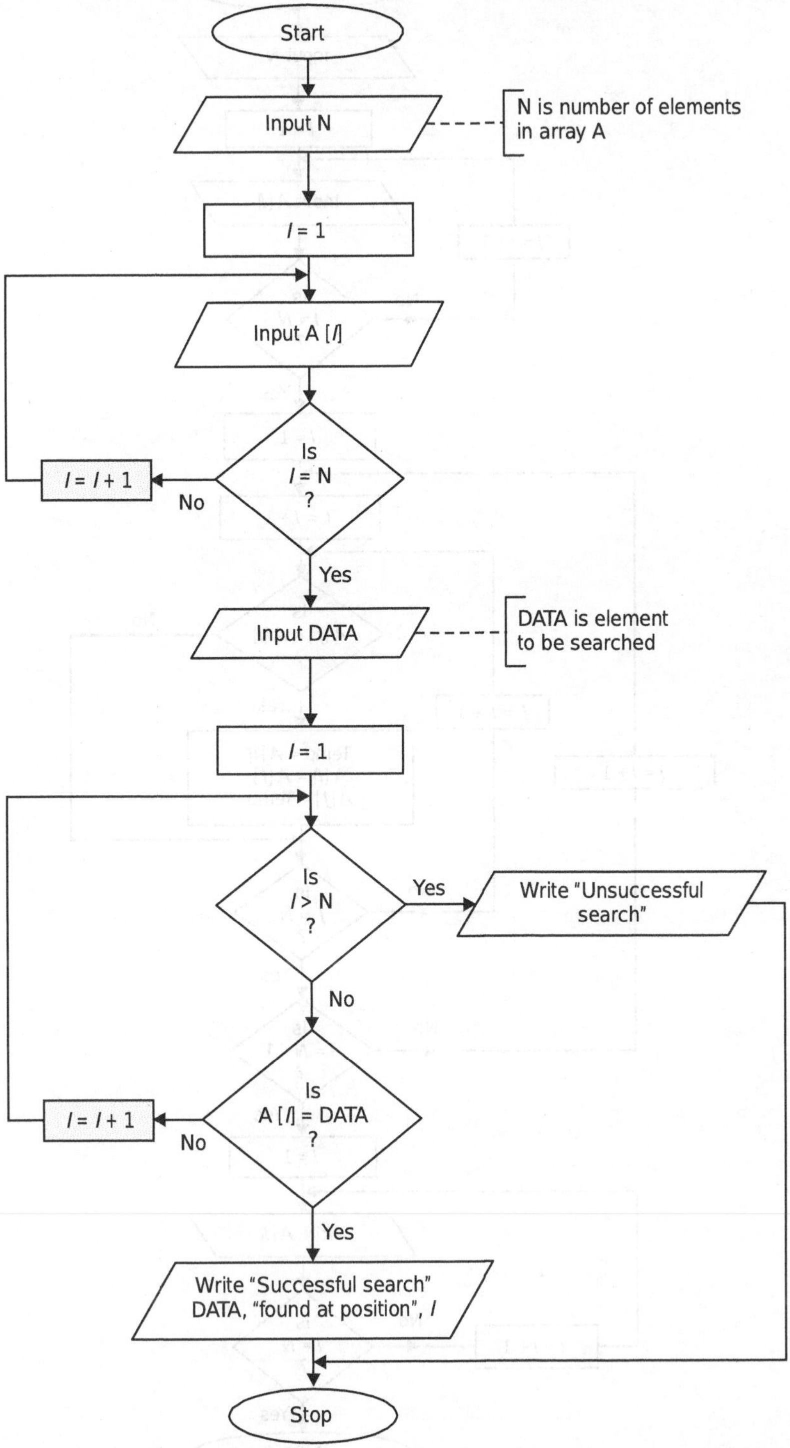

Fig. 3.28

The following figure depicts the flowchart of organizing numbers in ascending order.

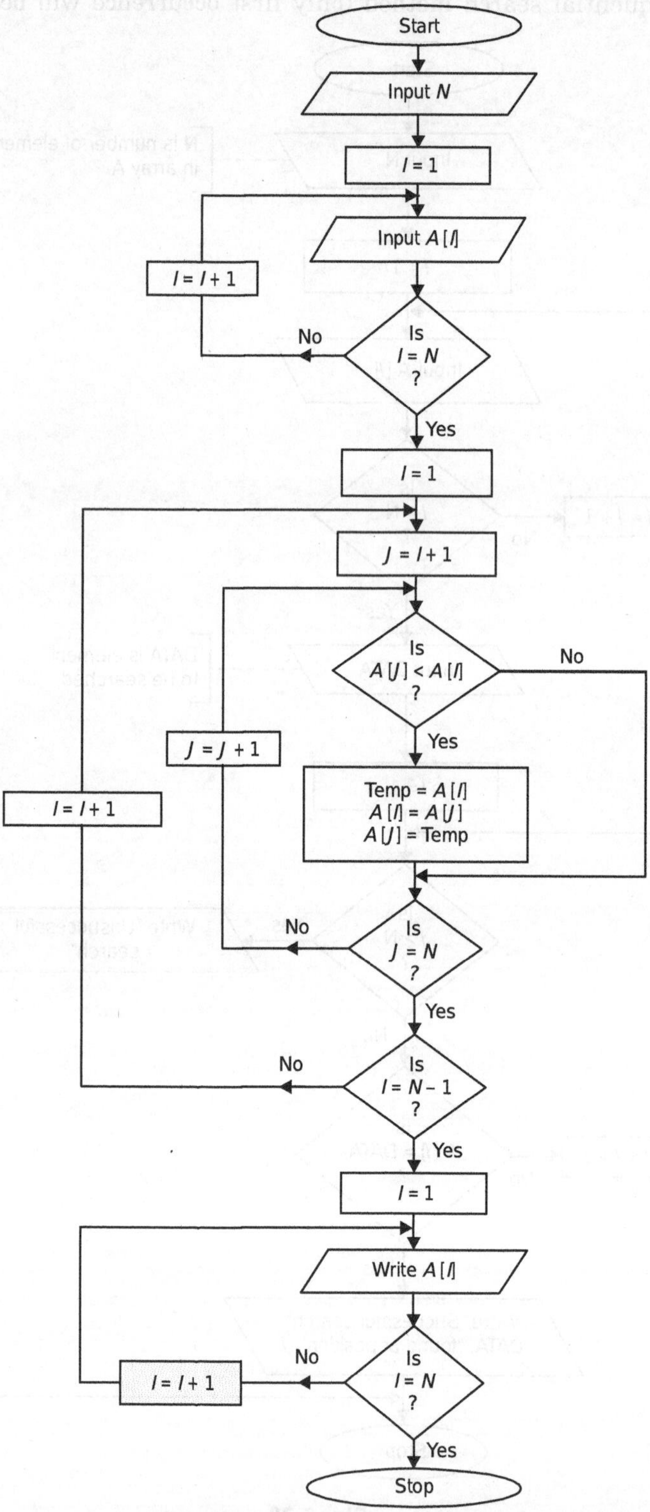

Fig. 3.29

The following figure depicts the flowchart for multiplication of two matrices.

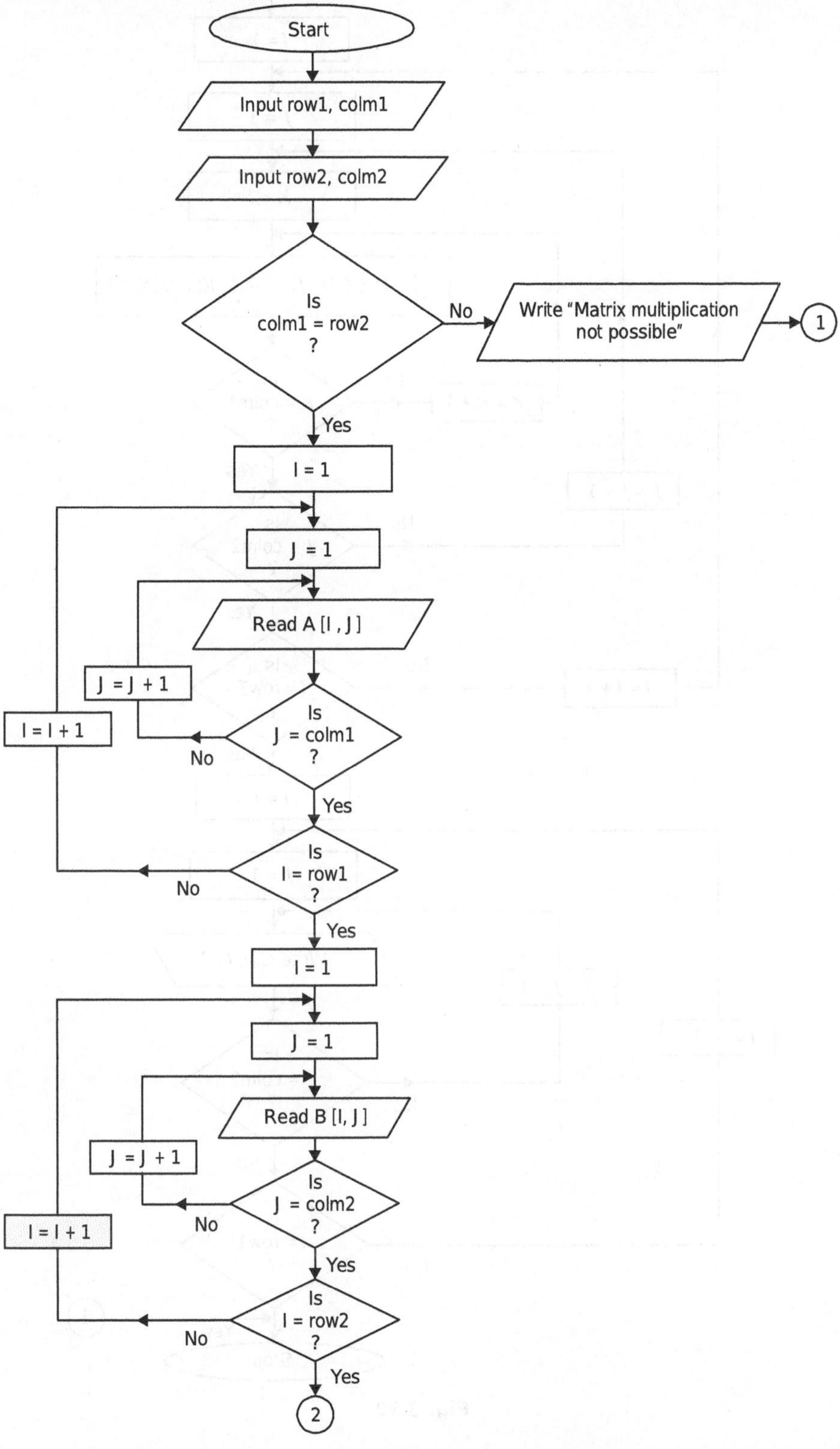

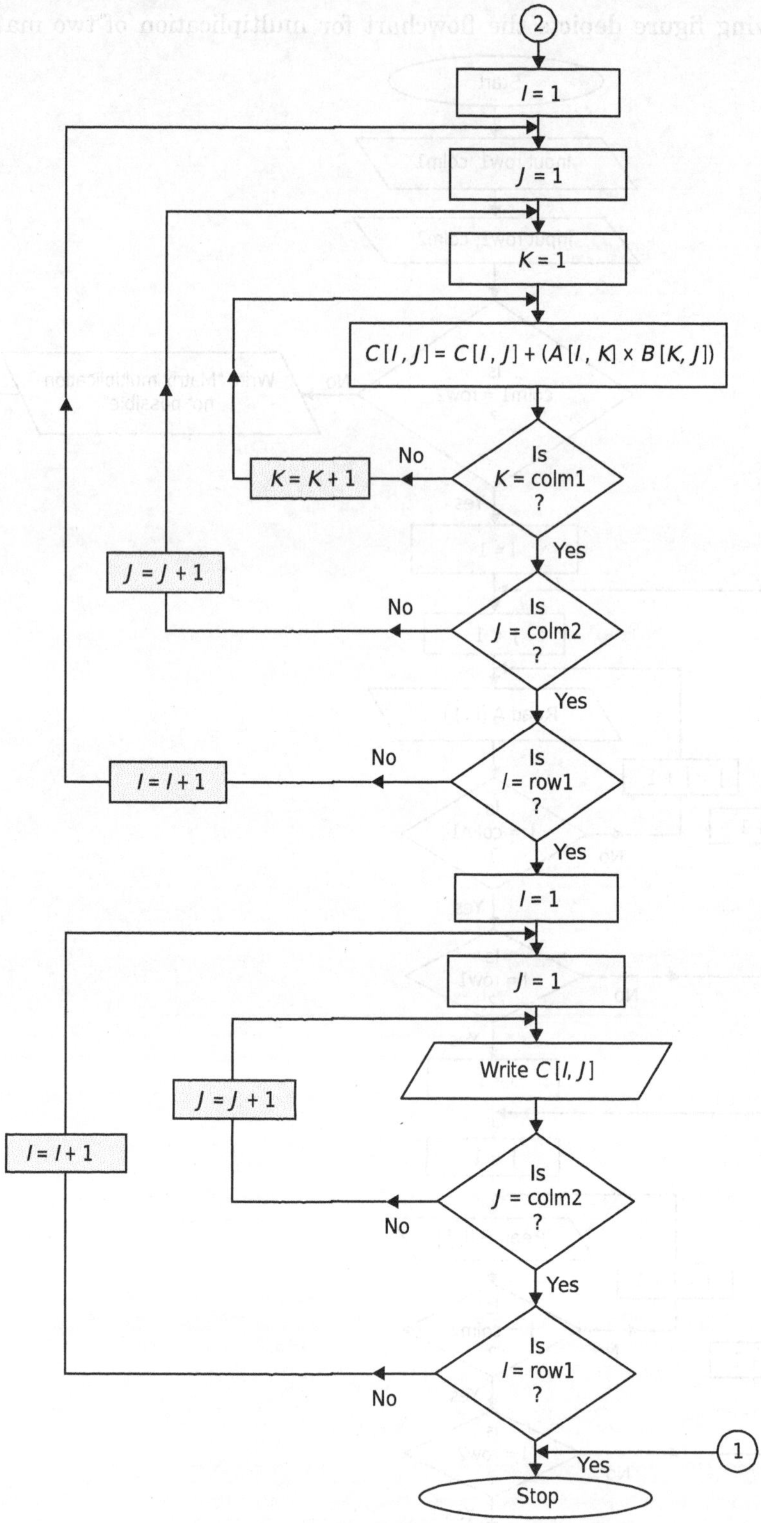
2
I = 1
J = 1
K = 1
C [I, J] = C [I, J] + (A [I, K] × B [K, J])
Is
K = colm1
?
No
K = K + 1
Yes
J = J + 1
Is
J = colm2
?
No
Yes
Is
I = row1
?
No
I = I + 1
Yes
I = 1
J = 1
Write C [I, J]
J = J + 1
I = I + 1
Is
J = colm2
?
No
Yes
Is
I = row1
?
No
Yes
1
Stop

Fig. 3.30

Flowcharts Having Functions

Problems can be broken up into sections so complex tasks are completed through a sequence of simpler steps. One way of doing this is by using functions. Functions can be written once and then used over and over again as the need arises. For example, the following flowchart converts fahrenheit temperature to centigrade using the formula $°C = \frac{5}{9} \times (°F - 32)$.

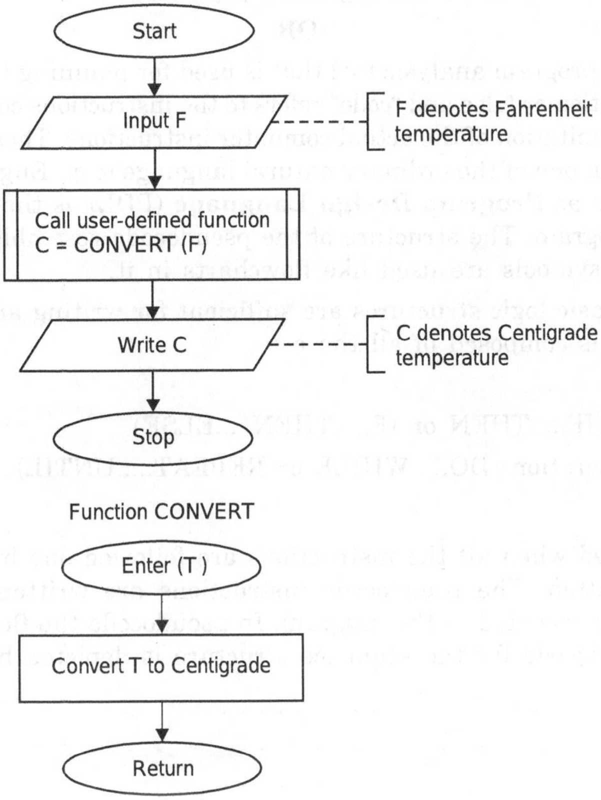

Fig. 3.31. Flowchart for converting fahrenheit temperature to centigrade temperature

Limitations of Flowcharts

Flowcharts have some limitations also. These are given below :

Time consuming

These take a lot of time and are laborious to draw with proper symbols and spacing, especially for large complex programs.

Difficult to modify

Any change or modification in the logic of the program generally requires a completely new flowchart for it. Redrawing a flowchart is tedious and many organizations either do not modify it or draw the flowchart using a computer program.

No standard available

There are no standards provided all over the world for the details to be included in drawing a flowchart. So different people draw flowchart with different views.

3.4.3 Pseudocode

Pseudocode is a method of designing a program using normal human-language (an English language) statements to describe the logic and processing flow.

OR

Pseudocode is a program analysis tool that is used for planning the logic of a program. "Pseudo" means imitation or false and "code" refers to the instructions coded in a programming language. So it is an imitation of the actual computer instructions. These pseudo instructions are phrases written in one of the ordinary natural language (*e.g.*, English, German, French etc.). It is also known as **Program Design Language** (PDL) as the main emphasis is on the design of the program. The structure of the pseudocode resembles with the computer instructions and no symbols are used like flowcharts in it.

The following basic logic structures are sufficient for writing any computer program and the pseudocode is composed of all these :

1. Sequence
2. Selection (IF.....THEN or IF.....THEN.....ELSE)
3. Loop or Iteration (DO.....WHILE or REPEAT.....UNTIL)

1. Sequence

Sequence logic is used when all the instructions are followed one by one in the order in which these are written. The pseudocode instructions are written in the sequence in which these are to be executed in the program. In pseudocode the flow of logic is from top to bottom. The pseudocode for the sequence structure is depicted below :

```
. . . . . . . . .
. . . . . . . . .
. . . . . . . . .
Procedure–1
Procedure–2
Procedure–3
. . . . . . . . .
. . . . . . . . .
. . . . . . . . .
```

(Pseudocode for sequence structure)

2. Selection

Selection logic or decision logic, is used for making decisions using simple or compound conditions. It is used for selecting one proper path out of the two or more alternative paths at our disposal in the program logic. It is depicted in one of the two following forms :

IF......THEN

IF.....THEN.....ELSE

Pseudocode for IF......THEN.....ELSE

```
...........
...........
IF CONDITION THEN
      Procedure–1
      Procedure–2
      Procedure–3
ELSE
      Procedure–1
      Procedure–3
      Procedure–2
ENDIF
...........
...........
```

Here, if the CONDITION is true then the following procedures are performed : Procedure–1, Precedure–2, Procedure–3 else the precedures Procedure–1, Procedure–3, Procedure–2 are performed.

Pseudocode for IF......THEN

```
...........
...........
IF CONDITION THEN
      Procedure–1
      Procedure–2
      Procedure–3
ENDIF
...........
...........
```

Here, if the CONDITION is true then Procedure–1, Procedure–2, Procedure–3 are performed otherwise the instrcutions written after ENDIF are performed without performing any of these procedures. The instructions will also be followed after ENDIF when the condition is true but after performing the three precedures. ENDIF indicates the end of the decision structure.

3. Loop or Iteration

Iteration logic is used when the instructions are to be executed many times depending on some condition (s). The two structures used for it are :

DO.....WHILE
REPEAT.....UNTIL

Pseudocode for DO.....WHILE

```
...........
...........
DO WHILE CONDITION
        Procedure–1
        Procedure–2
        Procedure–3
        .
        .
        .
        Procedure–n
ENDDO
...........
...........
```

Here, the looping will continue as long as the CONDITION remains true and the control comes out of the loop when the CONDITION becomes false. The loop may not execute even once if the CONDITION is false initially. These must be a loop terminating condition to avoid infinite looping.

Pseudocode for REPEAT.....UNTIL

```
...........
...........
REPEAT
        Procedure–1
        Procedure–2
        ....................
        ....................
        ....................
        Procedure–n
UNTIL   CONDITION
...........
...........
```

Here, the looping will be executed at least once as the CONDITION is tested in the end of the loop. The loop is executed till the CONDITION remains false and the control comes out of the loop when the CONDITION becomes true. The loop must contain a loop terminating condition to avoid infinite looping.

Examples of Pseudocodes

Example 1. *A company gives the commission to its sales person on the following basis :*

Commission is 1% on the sales less than 1,000

Commission is 5% on the sales greater than or equal to 1,000 but less than 10,000.

Commission is 10% on the sales greater than or above 10,000.

Write the pseudocode for the above commission policy.

Solution : Input SALES

```
IF SALES < 1000 THEN
        COMMISSION = 1% of SALES
ELSE
        IF SALES < 10000 THEN
                COMMISSION = 5% of SALES
        ELSE
                COMMISSION = 10% of SALES
        ENDIF
ENDIF
Print COMMISSION
```

Example 2. *Write the pseudocode for simulating a simple calculator for performing +, –, *, /.*

Solution :

```
Input two numbers X, Y
Display the menu as
        '+' Add
        '–' Subtract
        '*' Multiply
        '/' Divide
Input the operator (+, –, *, /) as op
IF op = '+' THEN
        Add the two numbers (X + Y) and store the result in SUM
        Print SUM
ENDIF
IF op = '–' THEN
        Subtract the two numbers (X – Y) and store the result in DIFF
        Print DIFF
ENDIF
IF op = '*' THEN
        Multiply the two numbers (X * Y) and store the result in MUL
        Print MUL
ENDIF
IF op = '/' THEN
        IF Y = 0 THEN
                Print "Division by zero not possible"
        ELSE
                Divide the two numbers (X/Y) and store the result in QUO
                Print QUO
        ENDIF
ENDIF
```

Example 3. *Given two dimensional square matrics A and B, each having N rows and columns. Write the pseudocode for storing the product of the matrices in matric C.*

Solution :

```
Input A, B and N
I = 1
DOWHILE I <= N
    J = 1
    DOWHILE J <= N
        SUM = 0
        K = 1
        DOWHILE K <= N
            SUM = SUM + A[I,K] * B[K,J]
            Increment the value of K by 1
        ENDDO
        C[I,J] = SUM
        Increment the value of J by 1
    ENDDO
    Increment the value of I by 1
ENDDO
I = 1
DOWHILE I <= N
    J = 1
    DOWHILE J <= N
        PRINT C[I,J]
        Increment the value of J by 1
    ENDDO
    Increment the value of I by 1
ENDDO
```

Here the variables I, J and K are integer variables denoting the array indices. The variable SUM is a dummay variable for storing the intermediate elements of the product matrix C. N denotes the order of the square matrices A and B and that of the resultant matrix C.

Example 4. *Thirty candidates in an engineering examination are required to take 5 single subject papers. For passing the examination, a candidate must score at least 35 marks in each subject and obtain an average of at least 40. The details of each candidate's result is stored in the form of records in a file as given below :*

RollNo Name M1 M2 M3 M4 M5

Write pseudocode to process the file and print the list of successful candidates with their RollNo, Name and total marks.

Solution :
```
Open file
Read a record
DOWHILE (NOT END OF FILE)
    Set total = 0
    Set i = 1
    Set failed = false
    DOWHILE (i <= 5 and not failed)
        IF (M_i < 35) THEN
            failed = true
        ELSE
            total = total + M_i
        ENDIF
        Increment the value of i by 1
    ENDDO
    IF failed = false and total >= 200 THEN
        PRINT ROLLNO, NAME, total
    ENDIF
    Read a record
ENDDO
Close file
```

Advantages of Pseudocodes

There are three main advantages of pseudocodes are :

1. The conversion of a pseudocode to a program (in any programming language) is much easier than a flow chart or a decision table.
2. Pseudocode are much easier to modify (when required) as compared to a flowchart.
3. Less time and effort is involved while writing a pseudocode in comparison to draw a flowchart. A programmer can concentrate more on the logic of the program because only fewer rules are to be followed in writing pseudocodes than writing a program in any computer language.

Limitations of Pseudocodes

The limitations of pseudocodes are :

1. For a beginner, it is easier to draw a flowchart to follow the logic of the program in comparison to write the pseudocode for it.
2. A graphical representation of the program logic is not available when we write pseudocode.
3. No standard rules are available in using pseudocode.So, Communication problems exist due to lack of standardization as different programmers follow different styles.

REVIEW QUESTIONS AND EXERCISES

1. Write a short note on problem solving and planning a program.
2. Write a short note on program design tools.
3. What is an algorithm ? Explain its need.
4. What are the characteristics necessary for a sequence of instructions to qualify as an algorithm ?
5. What is step-wise refinement ? Explain by giving a suitable example.
6. Explain the use of program control structures in problem solving with suitable examples.
7. What is a flowchart ? List the flowcharting rules.
8. Write an algorithm and draw a flowchart to check an integer for even or odd.
9. Draw a flowchart and write the algorithm for finding the smallest of three numbers.
10. Draw a flowchart to accept marks of students having *n* subjects, find their average and calculate the highest marks in the class.
11. Draw a flowchart and write the algorithm to find the smallest of N numbers.
12. Draw a flowchart and write the algorithm to find the GCD (Greatest Common Divisor) of two numbers.
13. Draw a flowchart and write the algorithm for factorial computation.
14. Draw a flowchart and write an algorithm for checking a number of palindrome.
15. Draw a flowchart and write the algorithm for printing the fibonacci terms upto a specific limit.
16. Draw a flowchart and write the algorithm for printing first N prime numbers.
17. Draw a flowchart for searching an element from a sorted array (ascending order) having N elements using binary search method.
18. Draw a flowchart for finding the transpose of a matrix A of order N × N.
19. Write an algorithm and draw a flowchart for addition of two matrices.
20. Write an algorithm and draw a flowchart to print elements of upper triangular matrix.
21. Draw a flowchart and write the algorithm for checking a square matrix for symmetry.
22. Is it feasible to have more than one flowchart for a given problem ? Give reasons for your zxanswer.
23. Differentiate between a macroflowchart and a microflowchart. Give examples.
24. What are the various guidelines to be followed while drawing a flowchart ? Discuss the advantages and limitations of flowcharting.
25. What is a pseudocode ? Why is it so called ? Give another name for pseudocode.
26. What is indentation ? What is its importance in writing pseudocodes ?
27. Write the pseudocode to produce a printed listing of all students over the age 18 in a class. The input records contain the name and age of the students. Assume a sentinel value of 111 for the age field of the trailer record.
28. Each paper in a set of examination papers includes a grade of A, B, C, D or E. A count is to be made of how many papers have the grade of B and how many have the grade of D ? The total count of both types have to be printed at the end. Prepare a flowchart to perform this task. Assume a suitable sentinel value for the trailer record. Write the pseudocode also.
29. Write the pseudocode to find the sum of all the odd numbers between 0 and 200. Before ending, print the result of the calculation.
30. Write the pseudocode for checking the type of a triangle. Assume that the angles of the triangle are given as input. Print the answer as yes or no.
31. Discuss the advantages and limitations of pseudocode.
32. Give the characteristics of a good program.
33. Write a short note on problem solving methodology and techniques.

❑❑❑

Part

B

BASICS OF PROGRAMMING USING C++

CHAPTER 4

Overview of C++ Language

4.1 Introduction to C++ Language

Object Oriented Programming (OOP) is a way of organizing programs. *C++ is an object-oriented programming language.* It was developed by Bjarne Stroustrup in 1983 at the AT&T Bell Laboratories, New Jersey, USA. He found 'C' lacking for simulations and decided to extend the language by using additional features from his favourite language, *Simula 67*. Simula 67 was one of the earliest object-oriented languages. Bjarne Stroustrup called it "C with Classes" originally. Strictly speaking, C++ is a superset of C: Almost every correct statement in C is also a correct statement in C++, although the reverse is not true. The name C++ (C plus plus) was given by *Rick Mascitti* where "++" is the C increment operator. The version 1.0 became available commercially in 1985, version 2 in 1989 and versions 3 in 1992. C++ evolved to cope with problems encountered by users, and through discussions at AT&T. In fact, the maturation of the C++ language was attested to by the *two* events given below:

(*i*) The formation of an ANSI (American National Standard Institute) C++ committee and

(*ii*) The publication of *The Annotated C++ Reference Manual* by Ellis and Stroustrup.

The ANSI/ISO issued the latest C++ standards document in year 2003.

C++ has the following characteristics:

(*i*) Reduces complexity while solving problems.

(*ii*) Correctness of results is ensured.

(*iii*) Affordable in terms of hardware and other resources.

(*iv*) Easier and cheaper for integrating existing software facilities and libraries.

(*v*) Portable, that is, can be used on different types of computers with little or no change in the programs.

An object-oriented program is a collection of discrete objects, which are self-contained collections of both data structures and functions that interact with other objects.

C++ adds **classes, inheritance, function overloading** and **operator overloading.** With the help of these one can create abstract data types, inherit properties from existing data types and use polymorphism. Thus we can say that C++ is an advancement of C, providing an additional set of object-oriented facilities. However, C++ has many other new features as well, including an improved approach to I/O and a new way to write comments. Figure 4.1 shows the relationship of C and C++.

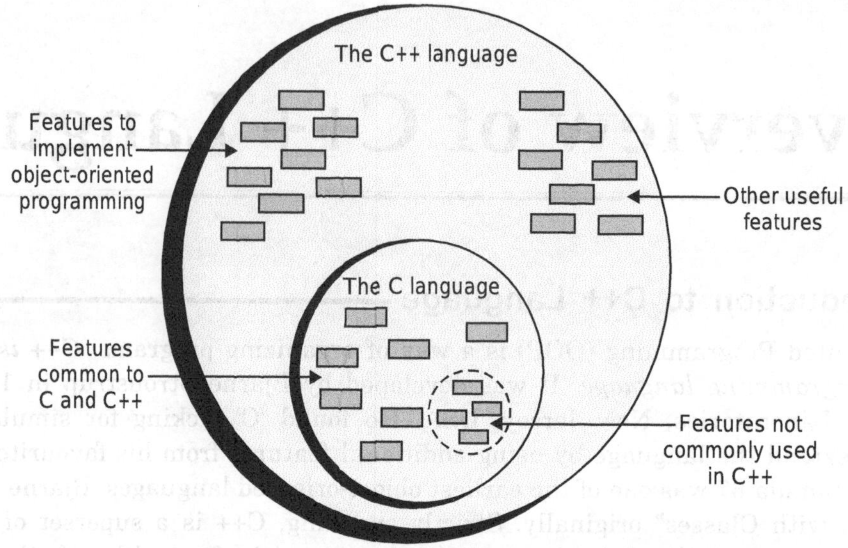

Fig. 4.1. The relationship between C and C++

In fact, the practical differences between C and C++ are larger than you might think. Although you *can* write a program in C++ that looks like a program in C, hardly anyone does. C++ programmers not only make use of the new features of C++; they also emphasize the traditional C features in different proportions than do C programmers. Table 4.1 gives the differences between C and C++.

Table 4.1. Differences between C and C++

S. No.	C	C++
1.	It is a procedure oriented language.	It is an object-oriented language.
2.	It employes top to bottom approach.	It employes bottom to top approach.
3.	It does not support classes and methods.	It supports classes and methods.
4.	It does not support inheritance and polymorphism.	It supports inheritance and polymorphism.
5.	It does not support abstract and virtual classes.	It supports abstract and virtual classes.
6.	It does not support operator and function overloading.	It supports operator and function overloading.
7.	It is not so flexible on various platforms.	It is comparatively more flexible than C on various platforms.

If you are familiar with C language, you will have a head start in learning C++ (although you may also have some bad habits to unlearn), but much of the matter will be new. Our main goal is to help you begin writing OOP programs as soon as possible.

> ***Note:*** *With the help of C++, one can develop editors, compilers, communication systems, databases and any other real life application system.*

4.2 Structure of a C++ Program

A C++ program is a collection of functions. The program also contains the list of library file(s) included for adding the contents to the program.

For example, the following program illustrates the structure of a C++ program:

Program 4.1

```
//Printing a message
#include<iostream.h>     //header file (use of Preprocessor directive)
#include<conio.h>        //header file
void main( )
{
   clrscr( );  //library function to clear the screen
   cout<<"Welcome to the world of C++ programming";
}
```

The above example contains two functions, main() and clrscr().

Every C++ program must have a function main() as the program execution always begins with main(). It is a free form language.

// represents a comment and it may start anywhere

// represents a single line comment and do not require closing symbol

// a comment is ignored by the compiler, *i.e.,* compiler does not execute comments.

The library file **<iostream.h>** is used for keyword **cout** and **<conio.h>** for function **clrscr( ),** which are examples of use of preprocessor directives.

The function type tells us about the kind of return value, if any, here **void** means that the function does not return a value.

The opening brace ({) marks the beginning of the block of code and closing brace (}) marks the end of the block.

clrscr( ) function clears the screen. It is a library function.

The statement

cout<<"Welcome to the world of C++ programming";

displays the string in quotation marks on the screen.

Every executable statement in C++ must be terminated with a semicolon (;). Notice that # instructions are not executable.

> ***Note:*** *1. You can write #include<iostream> in place of #include<iostream.h> if you are using a new compiler. If you omit it, each reference to cin and cout will be flagged as a type of error by the C++ compiler.*
>
> *2. Programs in C++ are written in lowercase. C++ distinguishes between lower and uppercase letters, i.e., case sensitive language.*
>
> *3. The clrscr( ) library function works only on Turbo C++ version. For other versions of C++, you can use system("cls") command to clear the screen; but for this include stdlib.h in place of conio.h header file.*

The structure of a C++ program is given below:

```
#include<header file>
void main( )
{
    .....
    .....   // statement(s)
    .....
}
```

4.3 Use of Editor (Creating Source File)

Turbo C++ and Borland C++ provide an IDE *(Integrated Development Environment)* for developing and editing a program. On the DOS system **edlin** or any other editor present or a word processor system in non-document mode can be used. On UNIX, you can use **vi** or **ed** text editor for creating and editing the source code. *You must consult the operating system manual which you are having on your system.*

There should be a proper file name extension for a C++ program. Turbo C++ and Borland C++ use extension **.cpp** (c plus plus) for a C++ program. Zortech C++ uses extension *.cxx* and UNIX AT&T versions use *.c* and *.cc* extensions for the programs.

For writing and executing programs in Turbo C++, the Turbo C++ software must be stored on the hard disk of your computer. After booting your computer there are two ways of getting to the IDE of Turbo C++. Obtain the DOS prompt on the screen. Change to the required directory (say TURBOC3 on the C:\> drive of your hard disk) as shown below :

C:\TURBOC3>

Now type TC and press Enter key *i.e.,* C:\TURBOC3>TC ↵

It will take you to the IDE of Turbo C++.

OR

Double click on the Turbo C++ icon on the desktop of your computer to start the IDE of Turbo C++.

Figure 4.2 shows the IDE screen of Turbo C++. The message window may be opened if required.

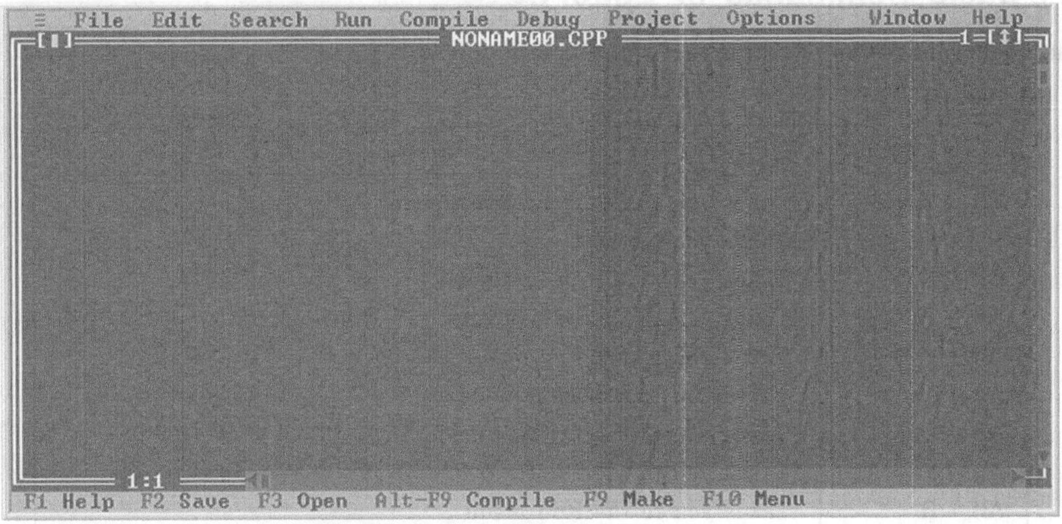

Fig. 4.2. Turbo C++ IDE Opening Screen

The following steps should be followed for creating a source file:

1. *You must have developed the program (source code) that you want to store in the file.*
2. *A suitable file name (of your choice) should be selected for storing the program.*
3. *Enter the program in the computer and save it in the file you have selected, known as source code file.*

Suppose we select the filename TRY.CPP for saving the source file then after creating it the editor screen looks as shown in Figure 4.3.

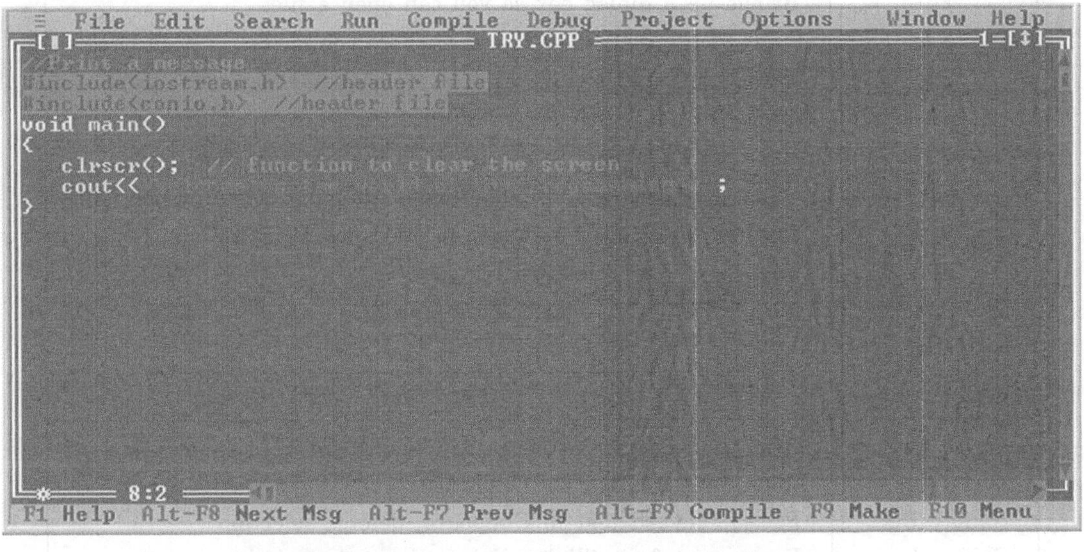

Fig. 4.3. Turbo C++ IDE after creating a C++ program

4.4 Basic Commands of Editor

The basic commands of editor are given below:

- **Menu Bar**

Hot Key	*Function*
Alt + Spacebar	Takes you to the ≡ (System) menu
Alt + C	Takes you to the Compile menu
Alt + D	Takes you to the Debug menu
Alt + E	Takes you to the Edit menu
Alt + F	Takes you to the File menu
Alt + H	Takes you to the Help menu
Alt + O	Takes you to the Options menu
Alt + P	Takes you to the Project menu
Alt + R	Takes you to the Run menu
Alt + S	Takes you to the Search menu
Alt + W	Takes you to the Window menu
Alt + X	Exits Turbo C++

- **General IDE (Integrated Development Environment)**

Hot Key	*Function*
F1	Displays a help screen.
F2	Saves the file that's in the active edit window.
F3	Brings up a dialog box so you can open a file.
F4	Runs your program to the line where the cursor is positioned.
F5	Zooms the active window.
F6	Cycles through all open windows.
F7	Runs your program in debug mode, tracing into functions.
F8	Runs your program in debug mode, stepping over function calls.
F9	Invokes the Project Manager to make an .EXE file.
F10	Takes you to the menu bar.

- **Editing**

Hot Key	*Function*
Ctrl + Del	Removes selected text from window; doesn't put it in Clipboard
Ctrl + Ins	Copies selected text to Clipboard
Shift + Del	Places selected text in Clipboard, deletes selection
Shift + Ins	Pastes text from Clipboard into the active window
Alt + Bkspc	Restores text in active window to previous state

- **Window Management**

Hot Key	*Function*
Alt + #	Displays a window, where # is the number of the window you want to view
Alt + O	Displays a list of open windows
Ctrl + F4	Closes the active window
Shift + F5	Tiles all open windows
Alt + F5	Opens an Inspector window
Shift + F5	Displays User Screen
	Zooms/unzooms the active window
Ctrl + F6	Switches the active window
	Changes size or position of active window

- **Online Help**

Hot Key	*Function*
F1	Opens a context-sensitive help screen
F1F1	Brings up Help on Help. (Just press F1 when you're already in the help system.)
Shift + F1	Brings up Help index
Alt + F1	Displays previous Help screen
Ctrl + F1	Calls up language-specific help in the active edit window

- **Debugging/Running**

Hot Key	*Function*
Alt + F5	Opens an Inspector window
Alt + F7	Takes you to previous error
Alt + F8	Takes you to next error
Alt + F9	Compiles to .OBJ
Ctrl + F2	Resets running program
Ctrl + F5	Adds a watch expression
F5	Sets or clears conditional breakpoint
Ctrl + F9	Runs program
F7	Executes tracing into functions
F8	Executes skipping function calls
F9	Makes (compiles/links) program

- **Block Commands**

Hot Key	***Function***
Ctrl + Q B	Move to beginning of block
Ctrl + Q K	Move to end of block
Ctrl + K B	Set beginning of block
Ctrl + K K	Set end of block
Ctrl + K D	Exit to menu bar
Ctrl + K H	Hide/Show block
Ctrl + K L	Mark line
Ctrl + K P	Print selected block
Ctrl + K T	Mark word
Ctrl + K Y	Delete block
Ctrl + K C	Copy block
Ctrl + K V	Move block
Ctrl + Ins	Copy to Clipboard
Shift + Del	Cut to Clipboard
Ctrl + Del	Delete block
Ctrl + K I	Indent block
Shift + Ins	Paste from Clipboard
Ctrl + K R	Read block from disk
Ctrl + K U	Unindent block
Ctrl + K W	Write block to disk

4.5 Compiling and Linking

It depends upon the operating system being used. In Turbo C++ we compile the program under the option *Compile*, as shown in Figure 4.4:

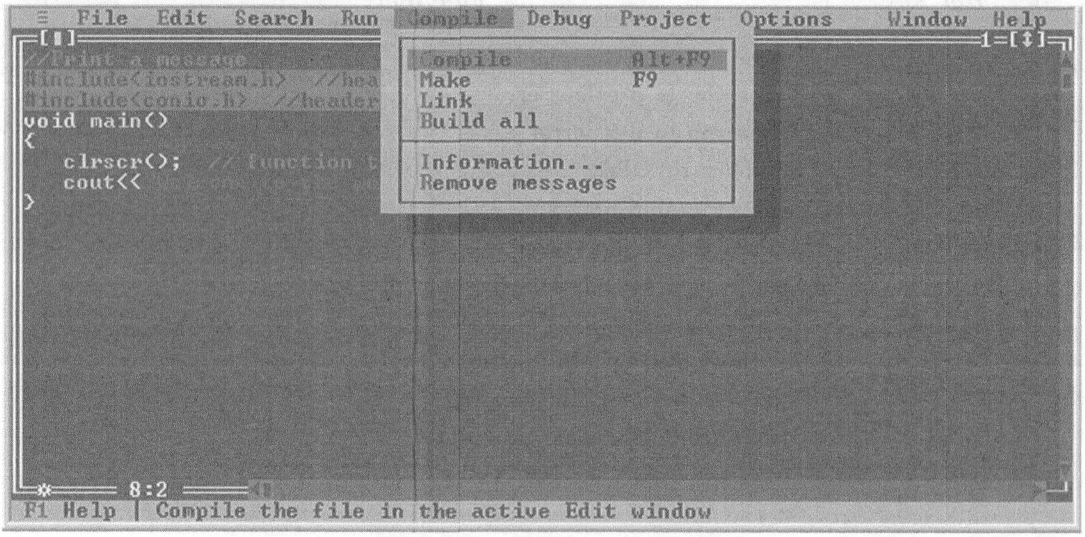

Fig. 4.4. The Compile Submenu

The following steps are followed while compiling the source code file:

1. *The source code is compiled and the translated code (the compiler does it) is known as object code.If some errors are there, debug them and compile again. Any program having syntax (grammatical) errors cannot be compiled successfully.*

2. *The object code is linked with other library code which are needed for execution of the program. The resulting code is known as executable code. If some error(s) occur during linking, debug them and compile the program again.*

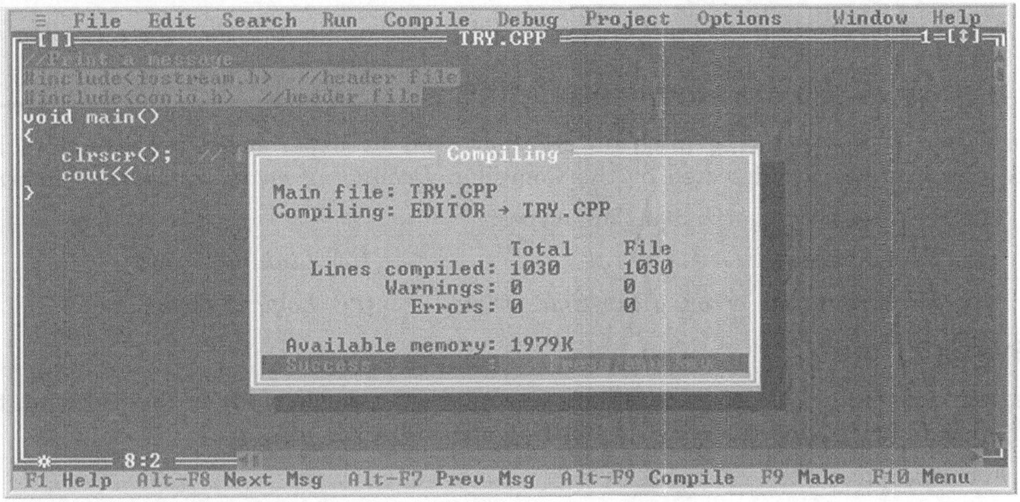

Fig. 4.5. Program Compilation

We will get a file TRY.OBJ after successful compilation and after the linking TRY.OBJ will be linked and a file named as TRY.EXE will be created (which is an executable file).

4.6 Execution of the Program (Running the Program)

Now select the *Run* option for getting the result as shown in Figure 4.6:

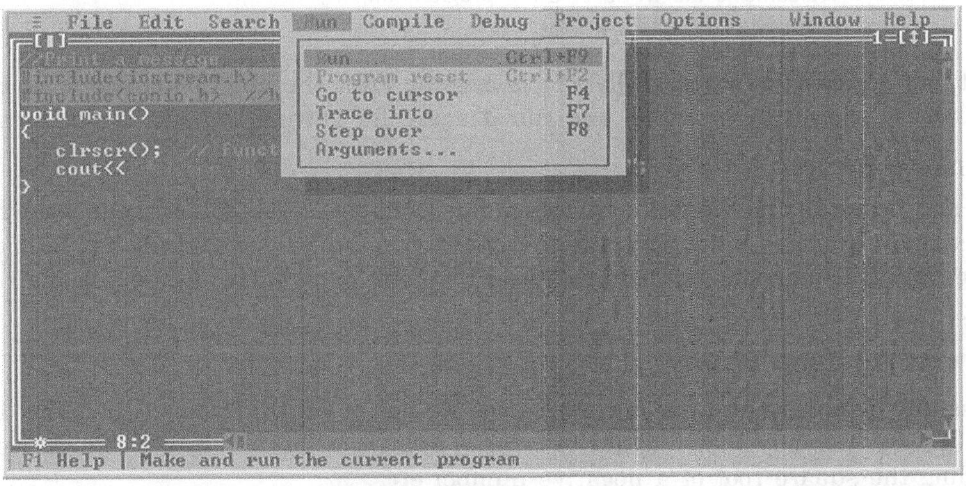

Fig. 4.6. The Run Submenu

After execution of the program the output goes to the user screen. Select <Alt + F5> to see the user screen, which displays the following message:

Welcome to the world of C++ programming

Now press any key to return to editor screen. For exiting from it press <Alt + X>.

The following steps are followed while executing the executable file:

1. *Execute the* ***exe*** *file and result is obtained (if no errors present).*
2. *The program is debugged in case there is some error.*
3. *In case of errors the compilation step is repeated again and then the execution step.*

4.7 Types of Errors and Debugging

Errors may be made during program creation even by experienced programmers also. Such type of errors are detected by the Compiler. *Debugging means removing the errors.*

The errors are categorized in four types:

(*i*) *Syntax errors* (*ii*) *Linking errors*
(*iii*) *Execution-time errors (Run-time errors)* (*iv*) *Logical errors.*

(*i*) Syntax Errors

These are detected by the compiler. If any grammatical error is made in the program, then during compilation step the compiler will display an error message.

For example,

```
//Print a message
#include<iostream.h>
#include<conio.h>
void main( )
{
   clrscr( ) //function to clear the screen
   cout<<"Welcome to the world of C++ programming\n";
}
```

It will not compile successfully as ; is missing after the function clrscr( ). So change it to clrscr ( ) ; and then compile and run it again for getting the output on the screen.

(*ii*) Linking Errors

These may occur during the linking process. For example, if you do not include the header file **iostream.h** or any other such file the program compiles successfully but fails during linking. An error message will be displayed in the linking window. Correct it and then go ahead.

(*iii*) Execution-time Errors

Successfully compiling and linking a program do not mean that you will get the desired result. The results may be wrong due to error(s) in logic or division by zero, stack overflow, in finding the square root of a negative number etc.

(*iv*) Logical Errors

Logical errors are most difficult to debug, which give wrong result on account of mistakes made by the programmer in logic.

You should check out for such errors from your teacher or consult the user manual for debugging.

4.8 Basic Terminology

Let us understand the basic terminology in C++.

4.8.1 Character Set

Character set is a set of valid characters that a language can recognize. A character represents any letter, digit or any other sign. We have two character sets in C++. These are:

(*i*) *Source characters*

(*ii*) *Escape sequences / Execution characters.*

(i) Source Characters

The source text is created with the help of source characters. Following are the source characters:

Alphabets	A to Z, a to z and _ (underscore)
Digits	0 to 9
Special characters	Space + – * / ^ ~ % = ! & ¦ ( ) { } [ ]? " ;: \ # ' < > · <= >= @

(ii) Escape Sequences/Execution Characters

These characters are interpreted at run time (execution time). The values of escape sequence characters are implementation defined.

C++ has characters which cannot be printed or displayed directly, for example, line feed, form feed, tab etc.

These escape sequence characters are represented by a backslash (\) followed by a character. Two characters together in an escape sequence are treated as a single character.

For example,

'\n'	Newline	'\b'	Backspace	\\	Backslash
'\t'	Horizontal tab	'\f'	Form feed	\?	Question mark
'\a'	Bell (beep)	'\r'	Carriage return	\N	Octal constant (where N is an octal constant)
'\0'	Null	'\"'	Double quote	\xN	Hexadecimal constant (where N is a hexadecimal constant)
'\v'	Vertical tab	'\''	Single quote		

4.8.2 Tokens or Lexical Units

The smallest individual units in a program are called tokens or lexical units or lexical elements. C++ has the following tokens:

1. *Keywords*
2. *Identifiers*
3. *Constants (literals)*
4. *Punctuators (Separators)*
5. *Operators.*

All the C++ programs are written using these tokens, white spaces and the syntax (grammer) of the language. Most of the C++ tokens are similar to those of C tokens except few additions and minor changes.

> ***Note:*** *The smallest individual unit in a C++ program is called a token or a lexical unit.*

1. Keywords/Reserved Words

These words are reserved to do specific tasks and must not be used as normal identifier names. Table 4.2 illustrates the Turbo C++ Keywords.

Table 4.2. Turbo C++ Keywords

asm	auto	break	case	cdecl	char
class	const	continue	_cs	default	delete
do	double	_ds	else	enum	_es
extern	_export	far	_fastcall	float	for
friend	goto	huge	if	inline	int
interrupt	_loadds	long	near	new	operator
pascal	private	protected	public	register	return
_saveregs	_seg	short	signed	sizeof	_ss
static	struct	switch	template	this	typedef
union	unsigned	virtual	void	volatile	while

Additional keywords have been added to the keywords in order to enhance its features. These are given below:

using namespace bool static_cast const_cast dynamic_cast true false

Some implementations and standard libraries contain a double underscore (––) as a reserved word and so it should be avoided in C++ programs.

2. Identifiers

These are the fundamental building blocks of a program and are used to give names to variables, functions, arrays, objects, classes etc.

An identifier in C++ must follow the rules given below:

(*i*) *It is a collection of letters, digits and underscores.*

(*ii*) *The first character must be a letter (underscore _ counts as a letter).*

(*iii*) *Uppercase and lowercase letters are different, i.e.,* C++ is **case sensitive.**

(*iv*) *All the characters are significant.* Some operating systems impose a restriction on the length of an identifier, *i.e.,* it varies from one version to another.

(*v*) *Reserved words cannot be used as names of identifiers/variables.*

Examples of acceptable identifiers are:

num, sum, average, total_salary, big, SIZE, Value

Examples of unacceptable identifiers are:
continue (reserved word)
Ma rks (blank not allowed)
B, pay (special character ',' used)
It may be noted that **SUM** and **sum** are two different identifier names.

> ***Note:*** *An underscore may be used in declaration of variable names to separate parts of the variable name, such as avg_marks, or you may go for "Capital style" notation, such as avgMarks, i.e., capitalizing first letter of the next word in it.*

3. Constants (Literals)

These are the items which cannot be changed during the program execution. Every constant used in a C++ program has a type that is determined by its form and a value. Its value is set when the program is coded (written), and it retains this value throughout the program's existence. The C++ language has three different types of constants according to their form and value. These are given below:

(*i*) *Numeric constants (Integer constants and Floating point constants).*
(*ii*) *Character constants.*
(*iii*) *String constants.*

More about these constants later on.

4. Punctuators (Separators)

The following characters are used as separators in C++:

( ) { } [ ] , ; : * ... = #

Parentheses ( ) These are used for function calls and function parameters. These are group expressions and separate conditional statements.

Braces { } These are used for blocking of code having simple or compound (more than one) executable statement(s).

Brackets [ ] These are used for enclosing subscripts in case of single and multidimensional arrays.

Comma , It is used for separating argument (parameter) list in a function.

Semicolon ; It is used as a statement terminator in the case of an executable statement.

Colon : It is used in the case of a labelled statement.

Asterisk * It is used for a pointer declaration or as a multiplication operator.

Ellipsis ... These are used in the formal parameter lists of function declaration (prototype) to have a variable number of parameters (arguments).

Equal to sign = It is used for assignment and initialization of variables.

Pound sign # It is used for preprocessor directives.

5. Operators

These are tokens that do some computation when applied to variables and other objects in an expression. C++ has a rich set of operators. It includes all the C operators and some additional operators. Unary operators are those operators which require one operand to operate upon. Binary operators are those operators which require two operands to operate upon. The ternary operator (conditional operator) operates on three values. For example,

– (Unary minus)

++ (Increment operator)

– – (Decrement operator)

sizeof

these are unary operators. The following are some of the binary operators:

+, –, *, /, %

The ternary operator (conditional operator) is ? :

> ***Note:*** *Exponentiation operator is missing in C++.*

More about operators later on in Chapter 5.

4.8.3 Concept of Data Types

The kind of data a variable may hold in a programming language is called it's data type. The two basic reasons for differentiating between data types are:

(*a*) *use of proper internal representation by the compiler.*

(*b*) *use of proper operators for each type by the programmer.*

Figure 4.7 shows the various categories of the data types:

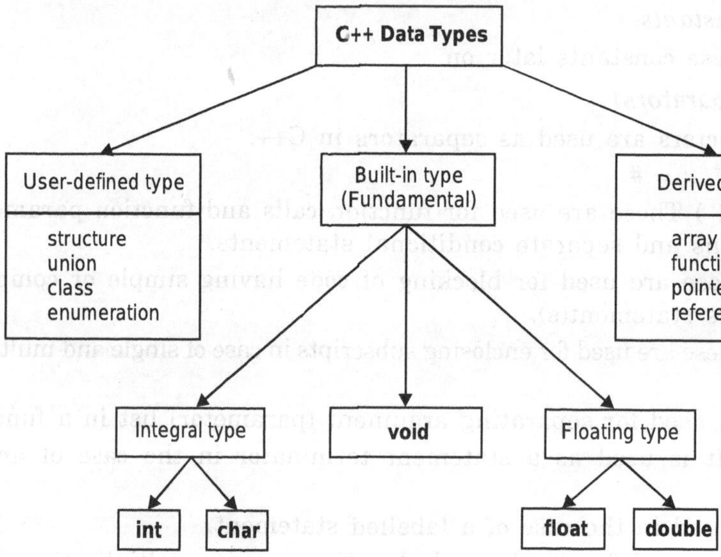

Fig. 4.7. Illustration of data types in C++

Here, we will discuss about fundamental data types.

Fundamental Data Types

The fundamental data types available in C++ are:

1. *Integral type*
2. *Floating type*
3. *void*

These are also called built-in data types. The size and range of these data types vary from computer to computer. The fundamental data types are the data types at the lowest level, that is, those which are used for actual data representation in memory.

1. Integral Type

It can be further classified into:

(*i*) int

(*ii*) char

(*i*) **int Data Type.** *An integer is an integral whole number without a decimal point.* Integers are numbers used for counting purpose. An integer can be positive or negative but it depends on the modifiers, which will be discussed later on in this chapter.

Examples of valid integers are:

1024

3313

336

– 67

15498

32767

– 32768

(*ii*) **char Data Type.** *A character is a non-numeric data type consisting of single alphanumeric character enclosed between two apostrophies, that is, single quotation marks.*

Examples of valid character type are:

'A'

'a'

'7'

'&'

You must note that 7 and '7' are of different data types. The former is of type *int* and the later of type *char*.

char type is often said to be an integer type. It is due to the fact that the alphabets, symbols etc., are stored in computer memory by ASCII codes. It must be clear that the ASCII code of 'A' is 65, 'a' is 97 and '0' is 48.

2. Floating Type

A floating point number is represented in two ways:

decimal form and **exponent form.** It can be further classified into:

(*i*) float (*ii*) double

(*i*) **float Data Type**

Decimal form. The floating point number in this form has a decimal point in it. A decimal point must be present even if the number has an integral value. These numbers are used for measurement, *e.g.*, height, area, distance etc.

Examples of valid floating point numbers in decimal form are:

1345.89

–4917.37

336.0

0.006

192.

Examples of invalid floating point numbers in decimal form are:

5,237.58	(Comma not allowed)
– 54	(No decimal point)

Exponent form. Another way of representing a floating point number in C++ is **exponent form.** In this form the number is broken into two parts: **mantissa** and **exponent.** The **mantissa** is a floating point number in decimal form. The *exponent* starts with a letter 'e' followed by an integer (signed or unsigned). For example, floating point number 9325.5 can be written as 9.3255×10^3. In exponent form, the base 10 of decimal number system is replaced by the character **e** or **E.** So 9.3255×10^3 will be written as **9.3255 e 3.**

Examples of valid floating point numbers in exponent form are:

594.15 e 07

6.017 e –15

– 15.65 e 23

76.00825 e + 8

Examples of invalid floating point numbers in exponent form are:

5.047 e 1.5	(exponent has decimal point)
– 73.19 e	(exponent has no digit)

The main advantages of floating-point numbers over integers are:

(*i*) *These can represent values between the integers.*

(*ii*) *These can represent a much greater range of values both positive and negative.*

The main disadvantage of using floating-point numbers is that the operations on these numbers are slower than integer operations. So the computational time is more in case of floating-point numbers.

(*ii*) **double Data Type.** The word *double* stands for double precision floating point. The meaning of precision is the number of digits after the decimal point. It is also used for handling floating-point numbers. It is capable of representing floating-point numbers with much larger range. It occupies twice as much memory as type **float.** It is used when type float is too small or insufficiently precise.

The **double** data type is larger and slower than **float** data type. So one must always use the smallest variable type for storing values in a C++ program to make it efficient.

3. void Data Type

The **void** data type specifies an empty set of values. The void data type has two important purposes:

(*i*) Indicates that a function does not return a value.

(*ii*) Declares a generic pointer.

No object of type **void** may be declared.

For example, we may define a function in C++ as:

```
#include<iostream.h>
void main( )
{
   ........
```

```
        ........ // body of function
        ........
    }
```

This indicates that the function **main( )** does not return any useful value.

4.8.4 Constants (Literals)

These are the data items that never change their value during the program execution. In C++ there are several types of literals:

(*i*) *Integer constants*

(*ii*) *Character constants*

(*iii*) *Floating Point constants*

(*iv*) *String constants.*

(i) Integer Constants

These are whole numbers without any fractional part. The following rules are followed for constructing integer constants.

(*a*) *It must have at least one digit*

(*b*) *It must not contain a decimal point*

(*c*) *It may either have + or –sign*

(*d*) *When no sign is present it is assumed to be positive*

(*e*) *Commas and blanks are not permitted in it*

In C++ there can be three types of integer constants:

- Decimal (base or radix 10)
- Octal (base or radix 8)
- Hexadecimal (base or radix 16)

Decimal integer constants. These consist of a sequence of digits unless it begins with 0 (digit zero). For example: 1024, 3313, + 275, – 12 etc.

Range of integer constants. The computer memory consists of a number of cells called words. The number of bits in a word is called word length. Generally the PC's have word length of 16 bits (some may have 32 or more). Let us take **n** as the word length. The integer range is given by -2^{n-1} to $2^{n-1} - 1$.

If $n = 16$, the integer range is -2^{16-1} to $2^{16-1} - 1$

that is, –32768 to 32767

If you will give an integer less than –32768 an underflow error will occur and if the integer is more than 32767 an overflow error will occur.

Octal integer constants. These are preceded by 0 (digit zero).

For example, decimal integer 14 will be written as 016 as octal integer (as $14_{10} = 16_8$).

Hexadecimal integer constants. These are preceded by 0x or OX. For example, decimal integer 14 will be written as 0XE as hexadecimal integer (as $14_{10} = E_{16}$).

The suffix l or L, u or U forces any constant to be represented as *long* and *unsigned* respectively.

(ii) Character Constants

A character constant is one character enclosed in single quotes. For example, 'A', ' ', '\n' etc. The rule for writing a character constant in C++ is:

A C++ character constant must have one character and it must be enclosed in single quotation marks.

The character constants have their data type as *char,* which is the data type for characters in C++. The value of a single character constant is the numeric value of the character in the computer's character set. For example, the value of 'A' will be 65 (ASCII value of 'A'), value of 'a' will be 97 and value of '0' will be 48. Multi-character constants have type *int,* a C++ data type for integer values. The value of a multicharacter constant is implementation dependent.

Backslash character constants. *These are interpreted at execution time.* The values of these characters are implementation-defined.

C++ uses some characters such as line feed, formfeed, tab etc., through execution characters, that is, which cannot be printed or displayed directly.

Each of these characters has a unique implementation-defined value which can be assigned to a single character. *Every escape sequence character starts with a backslash (\) followed by a character but both are considered as a single character.*

Table 4.3 shows some of the escape sequence characters:

Table 4.3. Escape sequence characters

Escape	*Meaning*	*Execution time Result*
\0	End of string	Null
\n	End of line	Takes the Control to next line
\r	Carriage return	Takes the Control to next paragraph
\f	Form feed	Takes the Control to next logical page
\t	Horizontal tab	Takes the Control to next horizontal tabulation position
\v	Vertical tab	Takes the Control to next vertical tabulation position
\b	Backspace	Takes the Control to the previous position in the current line
\\	Backslash	Presents with a backslash
\a	Alert	Provides an audible alert
\'	Single quote	Presents with a single quote '
\"	Double quote	Presents with a double quote "
\?	Question mark	Presents with a question mark?
\On	Octal number	Represents the number in octal
\xHn	Hexadecimal number	Represents the number in hexadecimal

Also if a character is put after backslash (\) in output statement, we will have the same character appearing in the output.

For example, cout <<'\J'; will result in display of J.

Here the identifier cout (pronounced as 'see-out') is a predefined object, is used for standard output stream (screen) in C++. The operator << called *insertion* or put to operator sends (or inserts) the contents on its right to the object on its left.

> ***Note:*** *An escape sequence represents a single character and hence takes one byte in ASCII representation.*

(iii) Floating Point Constants (Real Constants)

These have fractional parts. These may be written in either *fractional form* or *exponent form.* The following rules are followed for constructing real constants in fractional form:

(*a*) *A floating constant in fractional form must have at least one digit before and after the decimal point.*

(*b*) *It may either have + or – sign.*

(*c*) *When no sign is present it is assumed to be positive.*

(*d*) *Commas and blanks are not permitted in it.*

For example, 12.5, –18.3, –0.0025

The exponent form consists of two parts: **mantissa** and **exponent.** These are usually used when the constant is either too small or too big. But there is no restriction for us to use exponential form of representation for other floating constants.

In exponent form the part before **'e'** is called mantissa and the part after **'e'** is called exponent. The following rules are followed for constructing real constants in exponent form:

(*a*) *The mantissa and exponent are separated by 'e'.*

(*b*) *The mantissa must be either an integer or a proper real constant.*

(*c*) *The mantissa may have either + or – sign.*

(*d*) *When no sign is present it is assumed to be positive.*

(*e*) *The exponent must be at least one digit integer (either positive or negative). Default sign is +.*

For example, 2.4e–5, –3.5e–5, –0.6e+5

The range of floating-point constants in exponent form for a 16 bit PC is –3.4 e 38 to 3.4 e 38. It occupies 4 bytes of memory.

(iv) String Constants

The 'Multi character' constants are treated as string constants. These represent a sequence of zero or more characters enclosed by double quotes. For example, the string given below:

"JBD" will occupy 4 bytes because it will be added with a special character '\0', which marks the end of a string. Note that '\0' is a single character. Thus "JBD" will be actually represented as "JBD\0" in memory, that is, the terminator character is stored in the end.

> ***Note:*** *The multicharacter character constants are treated as integers (type* ***int****) and the value of these constants depends upon the implementation (version). Whereas an array of* ***char*** *type is used to store string literals. An array is a collection of homogeneous elements which is static, this will be more clear in the Chapter 9 on Arrays and Strings.*

4.8.5 Symbolic Constants

A symbolic constant is a constant that is represented by a name, just as a variable is represented. Unlike a variable, however, after a constant is initialized, its value cannot be changed. In C++, you can create symbolic constants in two ways:

1. Using the qualifier const

In C++, we can use **const** in a constant expression. For example,

```
const int SIZE =20;
char string[SIZE];
```

If we use the **const** modifier alone, it defaults to **int**. For example,

```
const SIZE =20;
```

means

```
const int SIZE = 20;
```

This method has several advantages in making your code easier to maintain and in preventing bugs. The biggest difference is that this constant has a type, and the compiler can enforce that it is used according to its type.

> ***Note:*** *Symbolic constants cannot be changed while the program is running. If you need to change SIZE, for example, you need to change the code and recompile.*

2. Defining a set of integer constants using enum keyword

In C++, you can name integer constants by using enumeration. For example,

```
enum {red, blue, green, white, black};
```

This statement defines red, blue, green, white, and black as integer constants with values 0,1,2,3 and 4 respectively. This is equivalent to:

```
const red = 0;
const blue = 1;
const green = 2;
const white = 3;
const black = 4;
```

Every enumerated constant has an integer value. If you do not specify otherwise, the first constant will have the value 0, and the rest will count up from there. Any one of the constants can be initialized with a particular value, however, and those that are not initialized will count upward from the ones before them. For example,

```
enum {red=100, blue, green=500, white, black=700};
```

Using this declaration, red will have the value 100; blue, the value 101; green, the value 500; white, the value 501; and black, the value 700.

4.8.6 Declaration/Initialization of Variables

A variable is a named location in memory that is used to hold a value that can be modified by the program. These are fundamental to any language. All C++ variables must be declared before their use. Values can be assigned to variables, which can be changed during program execution. Variable names should be user friendly. For example, if the sum of two numbers is to be calculated, the variable can be named as 'sum' rather than 'Zangura' or some other cryptic (difficult to understand) name.

The value assigned or inputted to a variable is stored in the memory allocated to it. We can create variables using the keyword **char, int** and **float.**

The definition of a variable has the *data type followed by the name of the variable.* For example,

```
char ch;          // ch is a character variable
int sum;          // sum is an integer variable
float salary;     // salary is a floating point variable
```

The storage scheme of **char** data type variable has been shown earlier. Figure 4.8 illustrates the storage of **int** and **float** type variables in memory:

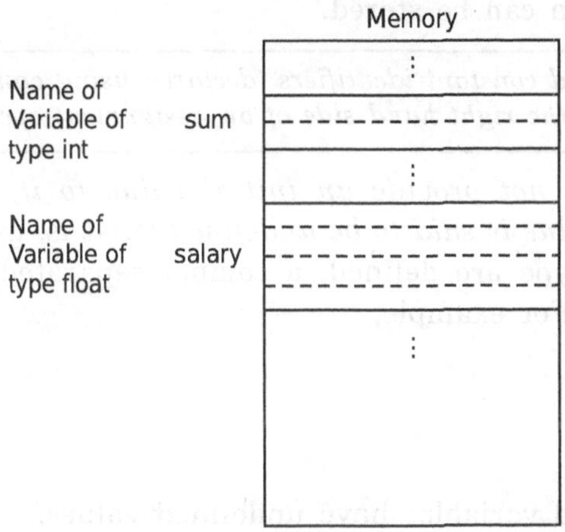

Fig. 4.8. Variables of type **int** and **float** in memory

The two values associated with a symbolic variable are:

(*i*) Data value, stored at some location in memory. It is also known as variable's **rvalue** (pronounced "are-value").

(*ii*) Location value; that is, the memory address of data value. It is also known as variable's **lvalue** (pronounced "el-value").

Figure 4.9 illustrates the concept of *rvalue* and *lvalue* of variables:

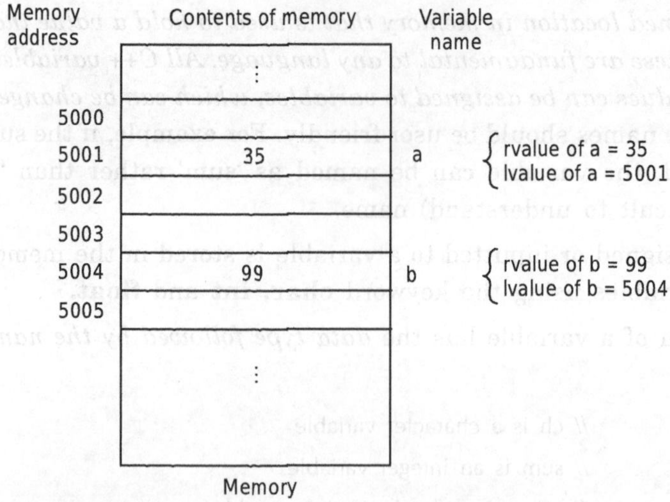

Fig. 4.9. Illustration of rvalue and lvalue of variables

An **lvalue** is a C++ expression which can be assigned a value. The left hand side of an assignment (=) operator must be an lvalue, that is, it must provide an accessible memory address where the data can be stored.

> ***Note:*** *The constant values and constant identifiers (declared using* ***const*** *keyword) are not lvalues and can only appear on the right hand side of an assignment operator.*

A variable definition does not provide an initial value to it, that is, variable is initialized and the variable's value is said to be undefined (that is, garbage value). When more than one variable of a type are defined, a comma separated list of variables is followed by the type specifier. For example,

```
int i, j, k;
float x, y;
double d1, d2, d3;
```

Here, all the above defined variables have undefined values.

> ***Note:*** *A variable contains a garbage (or junk) value if no value is assigned or inputted. This garbage value may be the value left over from the program that used this memory location last time.*

Initialization of a variable means providing an initial value when it is declared. C++ permits two types of initialization at the time of variable definition. For example,

```
int i = 40;
```

and

```
int i(40);
```

Here, both the statements initialize **i** with value 40. Few more examples of variable initialization are:

```
float salary = 20000.0;
char ch1 = 'A', ch2 = 'a';
double amount = 570.15;
```

In C++, the variables can be initialized at run time also. It is known as *dynamic initialization.* A variable can be initialized at run time (execution time) by using expressions at the place of declaration. For example,

```
int total = amount + deposit;
```

Here, total will be initialized using the values of amount and deposit provided at run time.

> ***Note:*** *You can declare a variable anywhere in a C++ program but before its first reference.*

4.8.7 Assignment Statement

An assignment statement is used to assign values to a variable or a constant.

For example,

```
int x = 50;
float a = 30.6;
const float PI = 3.14159;
const char ch = 'A';
```

The equal sign =, causes the value on the right hand side of the variable or constant to be assigned to the variable or constant on the left. The general format of an assignment statement is shown below:

```
lvalue = rvalue;
```

Here, the symbol '=' is called the *assignment operator.* In C++, the assignments can be chained together, that is, it can be used serially. It is useful when the same value is to be assigned to a number of items. For example,

```
int i, j, k;
i = j = k = 0; or (i = (j = (k = 0)));
```

Here, first of all 0 is assigned to **k**, then the value of **k** is assigned to **j**, then value of **j** is assigned to **i.** Always remember that a chained statement cannot be used to initialize variables at the time of declaration. But we may write,

```
int i = 0, j= 0, k = 0;
```

The TURBO C++ version 3.0 permits to chain maximum 70 assignments. All the variables used in the multiple assignment statement must be declared before.

In case we try to chain more than 70 variables in TURBO C++ version 3.0, through a single assignment statement, the following error message will be displayed:

Out of memory

Another way of assignment in C++ is known as **embedded assignment.** For example,

```
int i, j;
i = (j=20) * 4;
```

Here, (j = 20) represents embedded assignment. First of all the value 20 is assigned to **j** and then the result 20 * 4 = 80 is assigned to **i**. This statement is identical to the following two statements:

```
j = 20;
i = j * 4;
```

> ***Note:*** *Never use commas in numerical values when you assign these values to variables.*

4.8.8 Type Modifier

In C++, the basic data types (except *void*) can be modified according to our requirements. The keywords **signed, unsigned, long** etc., can be used to define the type. Data type representation is machine dependent in C++. Table 4.4 shows the **data types** and their **modifiers** for a 16–bit word computer.

Table 4.4. Data types and their modifiers

Type	*Range*		*Bytes*	*Represents*
	From	*To*		
char	– 128	127	1	characters
signed char	– 128	127	1	characters
unsigned char	0	255	1	characters
int	– 32,768	32,767	2	whole numbers
unsigned int	0	65,535	2	whole numbers
long int	–2,147,483,648	2,147,483,647	4	whole numbers
unsigned long int	0	4,294,967,295	4	whole numbers
float	–3.4 e 38	3.4 e 38	4	fractional numbers
double	–1.7 e 308	1.7 e 308	8	fractional numbers
long double	–3.4 e 4932	3.4 e 4932	10	fractional numbers

The type modifier **signed** is applicable on **char** and **int** data types. It has the same effect as that of type without it's presence. The data type **int** is **signed int** by default.

The type modifier **unsigned** is applicable on **char** and **int** data types. It makes these data types to hold only positive values. The **unsigned** type modifier is used to increment the range of the variable and representing the quantities that are never negative, for example, number of students, number of goals or runs in sports etc.

Some implementations may allow you to apply **unsigned** on the floating point types (as in unsigned double). However, this reduces the portability of your program and is generally avoided.

The type modifier **long** is applicable on **char, int** and **double** data types. It also increases the range of the values associated with a variable.

The type modifiers can be used together also. The following examples will give you an idea of type modifiers:

```
unsigned int no_of_students;
unsigned long int factorial;
long double x;
```

REVIEW QUESTIONS AND EXERCISES

1. What is C++? Who has developed it?
2. Write a short note on the evolution of C++ as a programming language.
3. Write a short note on C++ character set.
4. What are tokens? Explain in brief the C++ tokens.
5. Describe with an example the structure of a C++ program.
6. What is the purpose of a header file in a program?
7. Write two advantages of using include compiler directive.
8. Why main function is special? Give two reasons.
9. Define the terms: (*i*) Keyword (*ii*) Identifier (*iii*) Constant (*iv*) Operator
10. What is the difference between an identifier and a keyword?
11. What are error messages? Explain.
12. How can a C++ editor be used? Explain.
13. Explain the basic commands of editor.
14. Write short notes on the following:
    (*i*) Compilation (*ii*) Linking and execution.
15. Differentiate between Run Time Error and Syntax error. Also give suitable examples of each in C++.
16. Differentiate between a Logical Error and Syntax Error. Also give suitable examples of each in C++.
17. Write a short note on fundamental data types in C++ with the help of examples.
18. What are the applications of void data type in C++?
19. What is a constant? Describe various types of constants available in C++ by giving suitable examples.
20. What is the difference between 'A' and "A" in C++?
21. What is the significance of \n and \t character constants in C++? Give examples.
22. What is an access modifier? Give one example.
23. Write a short note on variables of built-in data types in C++. Give suitable examples.
24. Describe declaration/initialization of variables in C++ giving suitable examples.
25. What is the purpose of an assignment statement in C++?
26. What do you mean by dynamic initialization of a variable? Give examples.
27. What is a type modifier?
28. Why does C++ have type modifiers?
29. Explain with the help of suitable examples the following type modifiers: signed, unsigned, long.
30. A variable can be declared anywhere in a C++ program. Explain the significance of this feature.
31. Describe the rule(s), if any, that should be followed while declaring a C++ variable. How many values are associated with a variable?
32. What is the impact of type modifiers on built in data types? Give examples.

❑❑❑

CHAPTER 5

Operators and Expressions

5.1 Operators

The C++ language provides a number of operators. These operators are used in different combinations to form expressions. For example, the symbol '–' is a subtract operator that subtracts two data items called **operands.** An **operator** *can be defined as a symbol that specifies an operation to be performed. The data items on which the operators act upon are called operands.* Some operators require a single operand while others might require two operands to act upon. The order in which the operations are performed by the operators is known as the *order of precedence.* Let us get ourselves familiar with these different categories of operators available in C++ language.

5.1.1 Arithmetic Operators

Arithmetic operators are used to form arithmetic expressions. The valid arithmetic operators used in the C++ language are given in Table 5.1:

Table 5.1. Arithmetic operators

Symbol	*Meaning*	*Example*
–	Subtraction	a – b
+	Addition	a + b
*	Multiplication	a * b
/	Division	a / b
%	Modulus or Remainder	a % b

For example,

Let **a** and **b** be the two integer variables having the value 15 and 7 respectively. The following table gives the result of different operations:

Expression	*Result*
a – b	8
a + b	22
a * b	105
a / b	2
a % b	1

Remember the following points while using the arithmetic operators:

(*i*) *The division of an integer by another integer always give an integer result.* For example, 25/4 is 6 (the decimal point is dropped).

(*ii*) *If both or one of the operands in a division operation happens to be a floating point value, the result is always a floating point number.* For example, 25/2.0 is 12.5.

(*iii*) *The modulus or remainder operator % provides remainder on an* **integer division.** For example, 33% 7 is 5. *We can't use this operator on floating point numbers.*

(*iv*) *The remainder operator % requires that both operands be integers and the second operand be non-zero.*

(*v*) *The division operator / requires that the second operand be non-zero, though the operands need not be integers.*

In C++, the operands can have an integer value, floating point number or characters. The character constants are represented as integer values, as determined by the ASCII character set.

Let *cvar1* and *cvar2* be two character type variables having the characters **a** and **A** respectively. Several arithmetic expressions formed by using these variables and the results are given below:

Expression	*Result*
cvar1	97
cvar2	65
cvar1 – cvar2	32
cvar1 + cvar2 – 5	157
cvar1 + cvar2 + '5'	215

Note that **a** is encoded as 97, **A** is encoded as 65, and **5** is encoded as 53 in the ASCII character set.

If any of the operands has negative value, then the usual rules of algebra apply to them for performing any arithmetic operation. Integer division will give the result truncated toward zero, *i.e.*, the result will always be smaller in magnitude than the true quotient.

The natural precedence of operators can be changed by using parentheses. We can use *nested* parentheses also, that is, one pair within another. In such cases the innermost operations are performed first, then the next innermost, and so on. Sometimes it is a good idea to use parentheses for clarity of an expression, even though we don't require the parentheses.

The operations carried out in the arithmetic expression follow an order of precedence. Operations having higher precedence are carried out first. The multiplication, division and remainder operations have higher precedence than addition and subtraction. More about precedence later on in this chapter.

> ***Note:*** *There is no exponentiation operator in C++ like C. However, the library function* ***pow()*** *performs exponentiation, which is in header file* ***math.h.***

5.1.2 Unary Operator: Minus (-)

An operator that requires only one operand or data item is known as unary operator. C++ supports the unary minus (–), ++ (increment) and – – (decrement) operators on arithmetic operands. As compared to binary operators, the unary operators are right associative in the sense that these are evaluated from right to left.

The unary minus precedes a numerical value, variable or an expression. For example, (*i*) –13 (*ii*) –336 (*iii*) –a (*iv*) –(x * y) (*v*) 5 * (– (x * y))

The result of the unary minus on an operand (constant or variable or expression) is the negation of its operand.

For example,

```
int result,i,j;
i = 10;
j = 25;
result = –(i+j)/5;
cout<<"Result = "<<result;
```

The output will be **Result = –7.** The unary minus does so.

5.1.3 Increment and Decrement Operators

In C++, the other unary operators are ++ (Increment operator) and – – (Decrement operator). These operate only on one operand (constant or variable).

Increment operator (++). *It increases the value of a variable by 1.*

For example,

```
int i,j;
i = 10;
j = i++;
cout<<i<<" "<<j;
```

Here the output would be 11 10. First **i** is assigned to **j** and then **i** is incremented by 1, that is, post-increment takes place. This is shown in Figure 5.1.

Postfix:

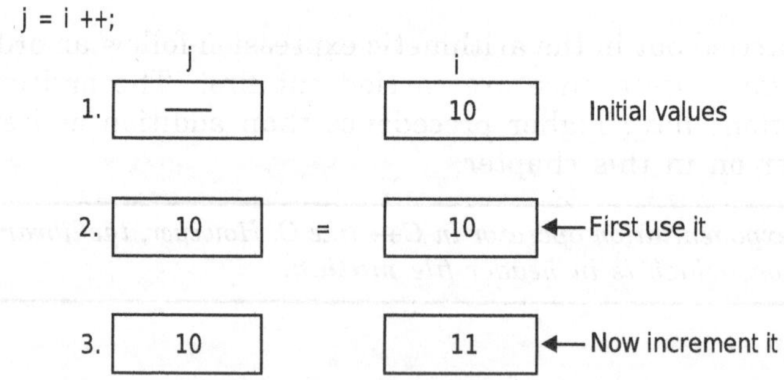

Fig. 5.1. The increment operator with postfix notation

If we have

```
int i,j;
i = 20;
j = ++i;
cout<<i<<" "<<j;
```

The output would be 21 21. First **i** is incremented by 1 and then assignment takes place, that is, pre-increment of **i.** This is shown in Figure 5.2.

Prefix:

```
j = ++ i;
```

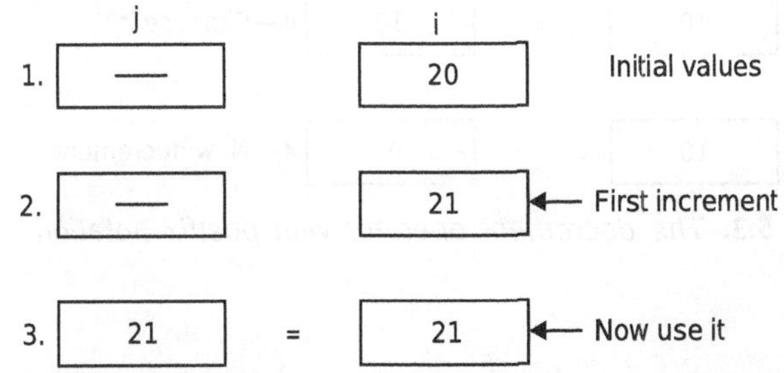

Fig. 5.2. The increment operator with prefix notation

The following three statements are equivalent:

```
i = i+1;
i++;
++i;
```

Example 1. *What is the output of the following program?*

```
#include<iostream.h>
void main( )
{
    int x=5,y;
    y=x++ + ++x;
    cout<<y;
}
```

Solution. The output of the program is

12

In Turbo C++, first of all ++*x* evaluates to 6 making the value of **x** as 6. This value is used for all **x's** in the expression and addition takes places making **y** 12. Now postfix x++ takes place making the value of x as 7. Finally *y* is printed as 12.

Decrement operator (– –). *It decreases the value of a variable by 1.*

For example,

```
int i,j;
i = 10;
```

```
j = i– –;
cout<<i<<" "<<j;
```

Here the output will be 9 10. First **i** is assigned to **j** and then **i** is decremented by 1, that is, post-decrement takes place. This is shown in Figure 5.3.

Postfix:

```
j = i - -;
```

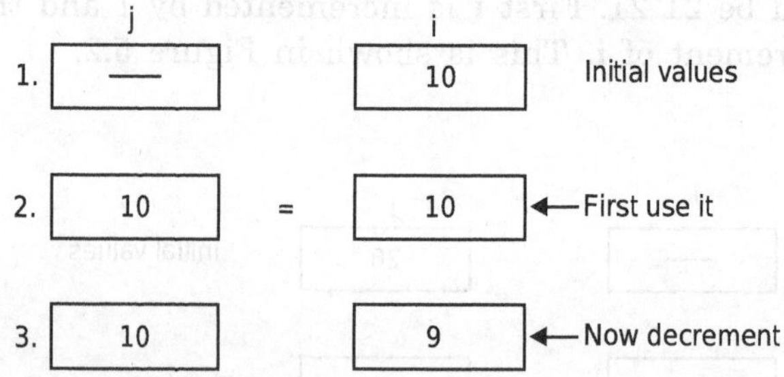

Fig. 5.3. *The decrement operator with postfix notation.*

If we have

```
int i,j;
i = 20;
j = – – i;
cout<<i<<" "<<j;
```

The output would be 19 19. First **i** is decremented by 1 and then assignment takes place, that is, pre-decrement of **i.** This is shown in Figure 5.4.

Prefix:

```
j = - - i;
```

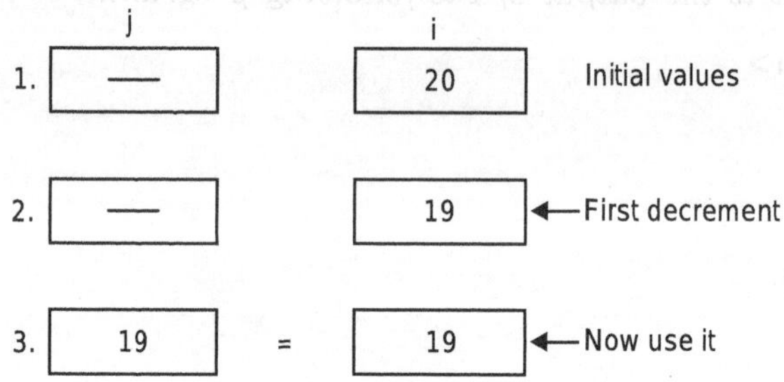

Fig. 5.4. *The decrement operator with prefix notation.*

The following three statements are equivalent:

```
i = i–1;
i– –;
– –i;
```

From the above discussion we observe that there is a difference between the prefix and postfix forms of the ++ and –– operators. When an increment or decrement operator precedes its operand, the increment or decrement operation is performed before obtaining the value of the operand for use in the expression. If the operator follows its operand, the value of the operand is obtained before incrementing or decrementing it.

> *Note: 1. Most C++ compilers produce very fast, efficient object code for increment and decrement operations—code that is better than that generated by using the equivalent assignment statement. For this reason, you should use the increment and decrement operators when you can.*
>
> *2. Bjarne Stroustrup, the developer of C++, has mentioned in his book—The C++ Programming Language that the postfix operator has higher precedence than prefix. But Turbo C++ implements it other way round i.e., prefix operator has higher precedence than postfix.*

Example 2. *Find the output of the following program?*

```
#include<iostream.h>
void main( )
{
    int x=5, y=5;
    cout<<x++;
    cout<<",";
    cout<<++x;
    cout<<",";
    cout<<y++<<","<<++y;
}
```

Solution. The output of the program is

5, 7, 6, 6

Example 3. *Write the output of the following program?*

```
#include<iostream.h>
void main( )
{
    int x=5,y=5;
    cout<<x--;
    cout<<",";
    cout<<--x;
    cout<<",";
    cout<<y--<<","<<--y;
}
```

Solution. The output of the program is

5, 3, 4, 4

5.1.4 Relational Operators

In C++, the *relational operators are used to compare two values*. The result of the comparison is either true (1) or false (0). Table 5.2 gives the list of relational operators:

Table 5.2. Relational operators

Operator	*Meaning*	*Example*
>	greater than	a > b
>=	greater than or equal to	a >= b
<	less than	a < b
<=	less than or equal to	a <= b
= =	equal to	a = = b
!=	not equal to	a != b

Note: *The equal to (= =) operator is not the same as the assignment operator (=).*

For example, let the two variables **a** and **b** have initial values 20 and 25 respectively. The following table illustrates the usage of the relational operators:

Expression	*Result*
a > 10	True
a + b >= 50	False
a < b	True
a <= b	True
a + 5 = = b	True
a != 10	True

As the floating point numbers are not exactly stored, so **avoid the equality and inequality comparisons on these.**

Always avoid comparisons of signed and unsigned values. When a signed value is compared with an unsigned value, the signed value will be treated as unsigned. In case the signed value is negative, it will be treated as an unsigned integer having the same bit pattern as the signed value, and the result of the comparison will be arbitrary.

Note: *Always avoid comparisons of signed and unsigned values.*

If the comparison of signed and unsigned numbers is really needed, we should type cast (explicitly convert the data type) anyone of the two values so that both are either signed or unsigned. More on type casting later on in this chapter.

5.1.5 Logical Operators

These are used to combine two or more test expressions.

C++ provides the **!** (NOT), the **&&** (AND) and ¦¦ (OR) logical operators.

! operator. *! is a unary operator as it takes only one operand. It reverses the logical value of the operand. Remember that the unary negation operator ! is useful as a test for zero.* For example,

```
int num;
cout<<"Enter an integer\n";
```

```
cin>>num; //input a value from keyboard
if(! num)
    cout<<"You have entered 0"<<endl;
else
    cout<<"You have entered non zero"<<endl;
```

> ***Note:*** *C++ considers 0 as a false value and any non-zero value as a true value. The values 0 (false) and 1 (true) are the truth values of expressions.*

&& operator. *It combines two or more logical expressions and evaluates to true if all the conditions are true.* For example,

```
int num;
cout<<"Enter an integer"<<endl;
cin>>num; //input a value from keyboard
if((num != 0) && ((num % 2)==0))
    cout<<"Even integer entered"<<endl;
else
    cout<<"Odd integer or zero entered"<<endl;
```

|| operator. *It combines two or more logical expressions and evaluates to true if any one of the condition is true.* For example,

```
int num;
cout<<"Enter the number 100 or 200\n";
cin>>num; //input a number from keyboard
if((num == 100) || (num == 200))
    cout<<"You are a good follower\n";
else
    cout<<"You don't follow others\n";
```

The following points must be remembered while using the logical operators:

(*i*) The precedence order of logical operators is:

!	Highest
&&	Middle
||	Lowest

(*ii*) The logical **!** operator has a higher precedence over any relational or arithmetic operator, so always negate an expression by using the parenthesis if the expression involves these operators.

(*iii*) The logical || and logical && operator have a lower precedence than relational operators.

5.1.6 Conditional Operator (?:) or Ternary Operator

C++ contains a very powerful and convenient operator that replaces certain statements of the if-then-else form. *The conditional operator consists of both the question mark (?) and the colon (:).* It is also known as **ternary** operator as it operates on three values. The syntax of conditional operator is as given below:

<condition> ? <if true> : <else>;

or expression1 ? expression2 : expression3;

Here, expression1 is evaluated. If it is true, the conditional expression takes on the value of expression2, and if false, expression3 becomes the values of the conditional expression. Figure 5.5 illustrates this:

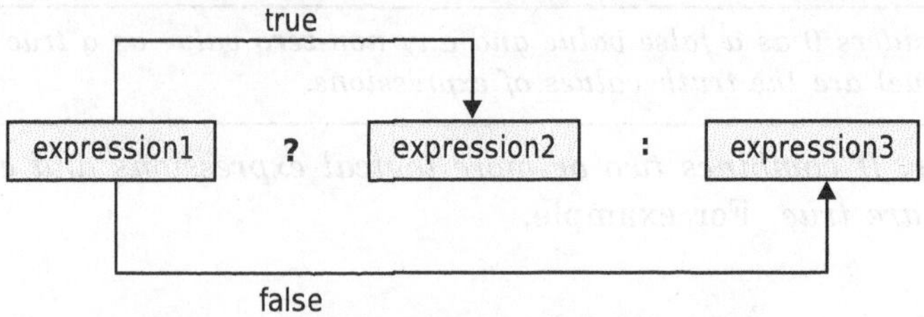

Fig. 5.5. *Illustration of conditional operator.*

For example,

```
int x,y,max;
cout<<"Enter two integers\n";
cin>>x>>y;
max = (x>y)? x: y;
```

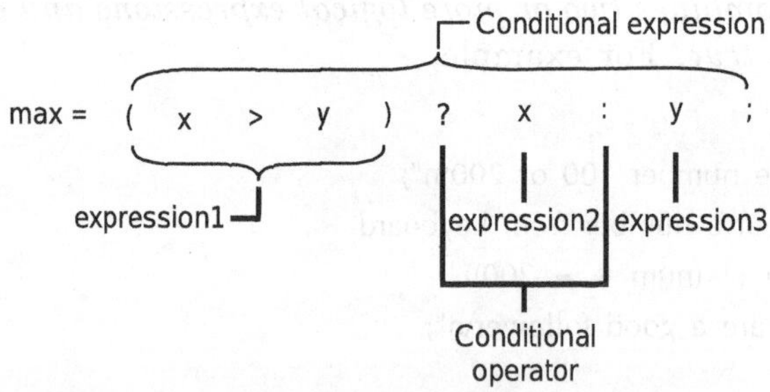

Fig. 5.6. *Syntax of the conditional operator.*

The expression x > y is evaluated. If x is greater than y, then x is assigned to max, otherwise y. *The only limitation of using a conditional operator is that you can use only one statement after the? or after the colon (:).* For example,

```
int age;
cout<<"Enter your age\n";
cin>>age;
(age>=18)? cout<<"\nYou must vote\n": cout<<"\nYou can't vote\n";
```

Remember that the conditional operator has a lower precedence than most other operators and it may produce unexpected results in some cases. For example,

```
int a,b,c;
cout<<"Enter two integers\n";
cin>>a>>b;
c = a-b > 0? 10:5;
```

In this code we are trying to subtract from *a* the value 10 or 5 depending upon whether *b > 0* is true or false. But it will not work in the desired way. It will be interpreted as:

c = (a – b) > 0 ? 10 : 5;

because the arithmetic operator '–' has higher precedence over > and ? : .

Therefore, we should code it as:

c = a – (b > 0 ? 10 : 5);

The conditional operator can be nested also, as given below:

largest = (*x* > *y* ? (*x* > *z* ? *x* : *z*): (*y* > *z* ? *y* : *z*));

Here if the condition *x* > *y* is true than the statement *(x > z ? x : z)* is evaluated; otherwise the statement *(y > z ? y : z)* is evaluated.

The code written above shows that the conditional operators can either be in the true part *i.e.,* before colon : or / and in the false part *i.e.,* after : .

The conditional operator is allowed even on the left side of an expression. The result of the conditional operator?: is an *lvalue,* provided both the alternatives (true part alternative and false part alternative) are values of the same type. As mentioned earlier, *an lvalue is an expression that can be assigned a value.* There must exist an *lvalue* on the left side of an assignment operator = . It means a value can be assigned to a conditional expression. For example,

```
int a,b;
float num;
cout<<"Enter a number\n";
cin>>num;
num<100? a:b = 25;
```

Here, the variable *a* or *b* will be initialized depending upon the condition *num < 100.* If *num* is less than 100, *a* will have 25 otherwise y will have 25.

As mentioned earlier, constant values and constant identifiers are not lvalues and can appear only on the right side of an assignment operator = . So the following code will not work at all.

```
int a;
const int b=10;     // notice that b is not lvalue
float num;
cout<<"Enter a number\n";
cin>>num;
num<100? a:b = 25; // incorrect as b lies on left of =
```

5.1.7 Some other Operators

Let us discuss few more useful operators:

The Compile-Time Operator sizeof

sizeof is unary compile-time operator that returns the length, in bytes, of the variable or parenthesized type-specifier that it precedes. For example, assuming that integers are 2 bytes and **doubles** are 8 bytes.

```
int i;
cout<<"The size of int variable i is "<< sizeof i;
cout<<"\nThe size of double variables is "<< sizeof(double);
```

The output of above code will be 2 and 8 in separate lines. Using *sizeof* the type name must be enclosed in parentheses but it is not mandatory (necessary) for variable names.

sizeof primarily helps to generate portable code that depends upon the size of built-in data types.

Remember that *sizeof* is evaluated at compile time, and the value it produces is treated as a constant within your program.

> ***Note:*** *The sizeof operator has the same precedence as prefix increment/decrement operators have.*

The Comma Operator

The comma operator strings together several expressions. The left side of the comma operator is always evaluated as **void**. It means that the expression on the right side becomes the value of the total comma-separated expression. For example,

```
y = (x = 5, x + 2);
```

First assigns x the value 5 and then assigns y the value 7. The parenthesis are necessary because the comma operator has a lower precedence than the assignment operator.

> ***Note:*** *The comma operator (,) has the lowest precedence among all the C++ operators.*

5.1.8 Precedence and Associativity of Operators

The Turbo C++ operators are divided into 16 categories as shown in Table 5.3.

These are ordered from the highest precedence to the lowest precedence.

The operators within each category have equal precedence. In C++, the operators having the equal precedence are evaluated either from left to right or from right to left, depending on the level. It is known as the **associativity** property of an operator.

The Unary, Conditional and Assignment operators associate right-to-left and all other operators associate left-to-right.

Table 5.3. Turbo C++ operators

Category	***Operator***	***What it does?***
1. Highest	( )	Function call
	[ ]	Array subscript
	->	C++ indirect component selector
	::	C++ scope access/resolution
	.	C++ direct component selector
2. Unary	!	Logical negation (NOT)
	~	Bitwise (1's) complement
	+	Unary Plus

	–	Unary minus
	++	Pre-increment or post-increment
	– –	Pre-decrement or post-decrement
	&	Address
	*	Indirection
	sizeof	(returns size of operand, in bytes)
	new	(dynamically allocates C++ storage)
	delete	(dynamically deallocates C++ storage)
3. Multiplicative	*	Multiply
	/	Divide
	%	Remainder (modulus)
4. Member access	.*	C++ dereference
	–>*	C++ dereference
5. Additive	+	Binary plus
	–	Binary minus
6. Shift	<<	Shift left
	>>	Shift right
7. Relational	<	Less than
	<=	Less than or equal to
	>	Greater than
	>=	Greater than or equal to
8. Equality	= =	Equal to
	! =	Not equal to
9.	&	Bitwise AND
10.	^	Bitwise XOR
11.	¦	Bitwise OR
12.	&&	Logical AND
13.	¦¦	Logical OR
14. Conditional	?:	(exp? x: y means "if exp then x, else y")
15. Assignment	=	Simple assignment
	*=	Assign product
	/=	Assign quotient
	%=	Assign remainder (modulus)
	+=	Assign sum
	–=	Assign difference
	&=	Assign bitwise AND
	^=	Assign bitwise XOR
	¦=	Assign bitwise OR
	<<=	Assign left shift
	>>=	Assign right shift
16. Comma	,	Evaluate

Table 5.3 shows all the operators available in C++. We have discussed only the arithmetic operators (–, +, *, /, %), unary operator (–), Increment and Decrement operators (++, – –), Relational operators (>, >=, <, <=, = =, !=), Logical operators (!, &&, ¦ ¦) and the conditional operator (?:) so far in this Chapter. So check for the precedence of various operators carefully.

5.2 Expressions

An operand or a combination of operands and operators that, when evaluated, gives a single value is known as an expression. In C++, the expressions can be of the following types:

(*i*) *Arithmetic expression*

(*ii*) *Logical (or relational expression)*

(*iii*) *Mixed expression (or compound expression)*

(*i*) Arithmetic Expression

It can either be an *integer expression* or a *real expression.* The combination of real and integer expression forms a *mixed expression.*

Integer expressions are formed by connecting integer constants and/or integer variables using integer arithmetic operators. The result of an integer expression is always an integer. For example,

```
int a=13,b=5,q;
q=a/b;
```

The value of **q** will be 2 (due to integer division).

Real expressions are formed by connecting real constants and/or real variables using real arithmetic operators (you must note that % is not a real arithmetic operator). The result of a real expression is always real. For example,

```
float x=13.0,y=5.0,q;
q=x/y;
```

The value of **q** will be 2.6 (due to floating point number division).

An arithmetic expression may even consist of C++ mathematical functions in addition to variables, constants and arithmetic operators. These functions are part of C++ standard library and are contained in the header file *math.h.* Therefore, the header file *math.h* must be included in your program for using these built-in mathematical functions. More about mathematical functions later on.

(*ii*) Logical Expression

It may contain just one signed or unsigned variable or a constant, or it may have two or more variables or/and constants, or two or more expressions connected by valid relational and/or logical operators. For example,

```
int a,b,c;
```

Now the valid logical expressions are

```
a<b, (a–c)>=b, –c
```

(iii) Mixed Expression

It is the combination of real and integer expressions. For example,

```
int a=13,b=5,c;
float x=4.0,y;
c=a*x;
y=b/x;
```

After the execution of the above statements **c** will have value 52 and **y** will be 1.25 due to mixed mode variables used.

The rules of formation of an expression in C++ language are:

1. *A signed or unsigned constant or variable is an expression.*
2. *An expression connected by a valid C++ operator or a constant is an expression.*
3. *Two or more expressions form another expression when connected by an operator or operators.*
4. *Two or more operators cannot occur in succession.*

The expressions are evaluated from left to right on the basis of the priority of the operators. However, the precedence of operators can be overridden with the use of parentheses. Thus, in an expression the sub-expressions enclosed within parentheses will be evaluated first. *It must be noted that the operators having same priority like *, /, % are performed from left to right but the unary operators like –, ++ etc., are evaluated from right to left in an expression.*

5.2.1 Expression Evaluation

The operators within C++ are grouped hierarchically according to their precedence. Operations with a higher precedence are carried out before operations having a lower precedence. *The natural order of evaluation can be altered by the use of parentheses.*

Another important consideration is the order in which consecutive operations having same precedence are carried out. It is known as **associativity.**

In C++ an expression is first divided into component sub-expressions upto the level of two operands and an operator. The conversion rules are applied to the sub-expression (if needed). Using the results of sub-expressions, the next higher level of expression is evaluated and its type is decided. This process continues till the final result of the expression is obtained. For example, consider the arithmetic expression:

```
int i   =  12, j=20, k=7, result;
result  =  6* ((i%5) * (9 + (j-3) / (k + 1)));
```

The above expression would be evaluated as:

result = 6 * ((12%5) * (9 + (20 – 3) / (7 + 1)))
 = 6 * (2 * (9 + (17/8)))
 = 6 * (2 * (9 + 2))
 = 6 * (2 * 11)
 = 6 * 22
 = 132

It is generally better to break this long arithmetic expression up into several shorter expressions, such as:

```
int a      = i%5;
int b      = 9 + (j – 3) / (k + 1);
int result = 6* (a * b);
```

These equivalent expressions are much more likely to be written correctly than the original lengthy expression.

5.3 Automatic Type Conversion in Expressions

Type conversion is the process of converting one predefined type into another. The automatic type conversion is performed by the compiler automatically. It is generally applied when a mixed mode expression is evaluated so that there is no loss of information. The C++ compiler converts all operands upto the type of the largest operand, also known as **type promotion.**

Data types are considered "higher" or "lower" based on the order given in Table 5.4:

Table 5.4. Illustration of Order of Data Types

Data type	*Order*
long double	Highest ↑
double	
float	
unsigned long int	
long int	
unsigned	
int	
char	Lowest

For example,

```
int n=25;
float avg_height=160.5;
double tot_height;
tot_height=avg_height*n;
cout<<"\n\nTotal height = "<<tot_height;
```

In the above code a variable of type **int** is multiplied by a variable of type **float** to give a result of type **double.** The data conversion is shown in Figure 5.7.

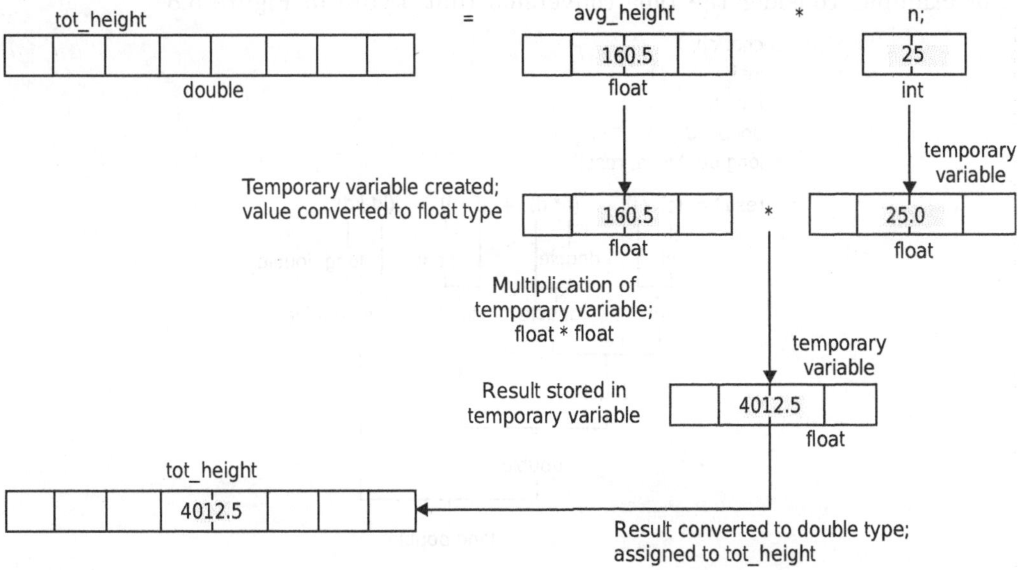

Fig. 5.7. *Illustration of automatic type conversion.*

Not all languages have this relaxation. Some do not allow mixed expressions and give an error in the statement that performs the arithmetic in mixed mode. C++, however, assume that you must have a good understanding of such type of mixing *i.e.*, intensions are clear. *This is one reason that makes C++ so popular as it provides freedom.*

Table 5.5 summarizes the assignment type conversions on a 16-bit machines.

Table 5.5 The Outcome of Common Type Conversions

Target Type	*Expression Type*	*Possible Info Loss*
signed char	char	If value > 127, target is negative
char	short int	High-order 8 bits
char	int	High-order 8 bits
short int	int	None
int	long int	High-order 16 bits
int	float	Fractional part and possibly more
float	double	Precision, result rounded
double	long double	Precision, result rounded

You should remember that the conversion of an **int** to **float** or a **float** to a **double** does not add any precision or accuracy. These kind of conversions only change the form in which the value is represented. For making a conversion not shown here, simply convert one type at a time until you finish. For example, to convert from **double** to **int**, first convert from **double** to **float** and then from **float** to **int**.

For example, consider the type conversion that occurs in Figure 5.8.

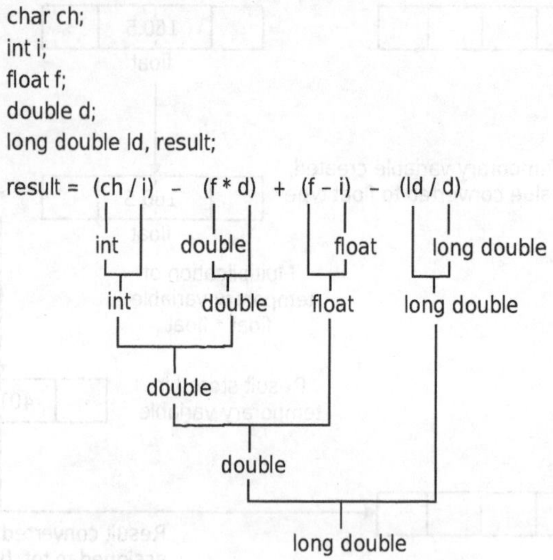

Fig. 5.8. *A type conversion example.*

> ***Note:*** *The automatic type conversion is performed by the compiler only on built-in data types.*

5.4 Type Casting

Sometimes a programmer needs to convert a value from one type to another in a situation where the compiler will not do it automatically.

C++ provides a facility to convert variables to a specific type before being evaluated in an expression through the type cast facility. This is also known as **explicit type conversion.** In C++ type casting is done as shown below:

(type) expression

Here, type is a valid C++ data type to which conversion is required. For example,

```
int sum,n;
float avg;
.......................
.......................
avg = (float)sum/n;
```

Here, the variable **sum** is used as a float variable and the value of **age** will be float type as per declaration. *You must note that type casting does not change the value of the variable or expression permanently, but it is converted to the specific type only at the place of type cast.* If type casting is not applied in the above shown statement, then the assignment will be without the fractional portion, that is, **avg** will be assigned the quotient of the division of the two integers **sum** and **n.**

We can use another syntax for casts. For example,

```
int num=30000;              //range of signed: -32768 to 32767
num = (long(num) * 5) /10;  //cast to long
cout<<"num = "<<num<<endl;
```

One way of getting the above result is by redefining the data type of the variable **num** to be **long.** But for keeping the program small (as long takes more memory for storage) the above shown solution is preferred. This is sometimes called **coersion;** the data is *coerced* into becoming another type. The expression

long(num)

casts **num** to type **long.** It generates a temporary variable of type **long** with the same value as **num.** This approach in C++ is known as **"functional notation",** due to the similarity with writing of functions. You should prefer it while type casting.

> ***Note:*** *In C++, the "functional notation" is preferred for type casting, because it is similar to the way other parts of C++, such as functions, are written.*

5.5 C++ Shorthands

C++ offers several ways to shorten and clarify the coding. One of these is the arithmetic assignment operator. For example,

```
int sum=50;
sum=sum+20;
```

can be written as:

```
sum += 20; //adds 20 to sum
```

The arithmetic assignment operator eliminates the repeated operand. *The arithmetic assignment operator is the combination of an arithmetic operator and an assignment operator.* The general form of the C++ shorthand is given as:

variable = variable operator **expression** **//simple assignment**

or **variable** operator = **expression** **//arithmetic assignment**

Figure 5.9 illustrates the arithmetic assignment operator:

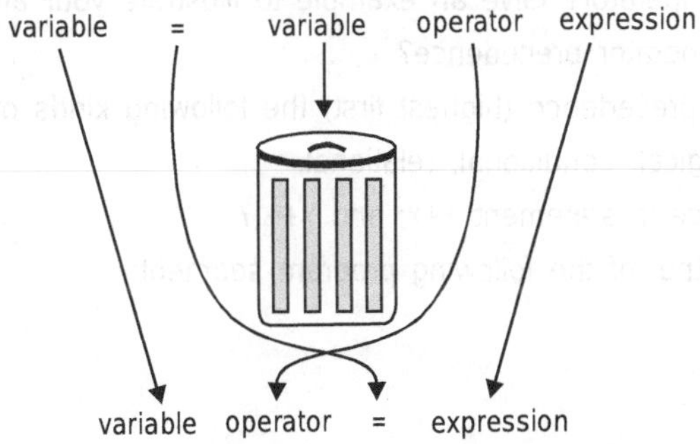

Fig. 5.9. Arithmetic assignment operator

For example,

```
int x, y;
x = 55;
y = 10;
```

then

x += y;	is same as	x = x + y;	results x = 65
x −= y;	is same as	x = x − y;	results x = 55
x *= y;	is same as	x = x * y;	results x = 550
x /= y;	is same as	x = x / y;	results x = 55
x %= y;	is same as	x = x % y;	results x = 5

Here, the result of each statement has been used in next one for all the above five statements.

You do not need to use arithmetic assignment operators in your code, but they are a common feature of C++; as you will see throughout this book.

> ***Note:*** *Shorthand assignment also called* compound assignment *is widely used in professionally written C++ programs.*

Review Questions and Exercises

1. What is an operator? Describe several different types of operators included in C++.
2. What is an operand? What is the relationship between operators and operands?
3. Describe the five arithmetic operators in C++. Give their examples.
4. What are unary operators? How many operands are associated with a unary operator?
5. Describe the relational operators included in C++. With what type of operands can these be used? What type of expression is obtained?
6. Describe the logical operators included in C++. What is the purpose of each? With what type of operands can they be used? What type of expression is obtained?
7. What is conditional operator? Give an example to illustrate your answer.
8. What is meant by operator precedence?
9. Arrange in order of precedence (highest first) the following kinds of operators:

   arithmetic, unary, logical, conditional, relational.
10. What is the difference in statement ++x; and x++;?
11. What will be the output of the following program segment:

```
int i = 10;
i++;
i += 1;
cout<<"i = "<<i--;
```

12. What is an expression? What are its components?
13. Write C++ expressions for the following:

    (*i*) Volume of a sphere given it's radius $\left(V = \frac{4}{3}\pi r^3\right)$ (*ii*) $(a^2 + b^2)\frac{x+y}{x-y}$

    (*iii*) $(a + b + c)^4$
14. What do you understand by type casting? Give examples of explicit and implicit type casting.
15. What is the purpose of type conversion?
16. What is the difference between automatic type conversion and type casting? Also, give a suitable C++ code to illustrate both.
17. What will be the output of the following codes? Justify:

    (*i*)
```
int a=20, b=7, c;
float d;
----
----
c=a/b;
d=a/b;
cout<<c<<','<<d;
```

    (*ii*)
```
char y='A';
int z;
z = 'y' + y;
cout<<z;
```

18. What are C++ shorthands? What are their advantages? Explain with the help of suitable examples.
19. Explain the usage of compound assignment operators with the help of suitable examples.
20. What would be the output of the following code:

```
#include<iostream.h>
void main( )
{
    int i=30;
    cout<<i--<<endl;
    cout<<++i<<endl;
}
```

21. What would be the output of the following code:

```
#include<iostream.h>
void main( )
{
    int j=25;
    j = ++j == 26;
    cout<<j;
}
```

22. An arithmetic assignment operator combines the effect of which two operators?

23. What would be the output of the following code:

```
#include<iostream.h>
void main( )
{
    int k=5<7? 500: 700;
    cout<<k;
}
```

24. Suppose i, j and k are integer variables that have been assigned values i = 10, j = 8 and c = –3. Determine the value of each of the following arithmetic expressions:

(*i*) i + j – k (*ii*) 5 * j + 6 * (i + k) (*iii*) i/j (*iv*) i%j (*v*) i/k

(*vi*) i%k (*vii*) i*j/k (*viii*) i*(j/k) (*ix*) (i*k)%j (*x*) i*(k%j)

25. Suppose a, b and c are floating point variables that have been assigned the values a = 15.8, b = 10.5 and c = –2.2. Determine the value of each of the following arithmetic expressions:

(*i*) a + b – c (*ii*) 5 * b + 6 * (a + c) (*iii*) a/b (*iv*) a%b (*v*) a/(b+c)

(*vi*) (a/b) + c (*vii*) 6*a/5 * b (*viii*) 6*a/(5*b).

❑❑❑

CHAPTER 6

Beginning with C++ Program

6.1 Introduction

All the input and output operations are supported by the *istream* (input stream) and *ostream* (output stream) classes.

The identifier **cout** (pronounced "see-out") is a predefined object in C++ that corresponds to the standard output stream (A stream is simply a sequence of bytes).

The identifier **cin** (pronounced "see-in") is a predefined object in C++ that corresponds to the standard input stream.

In this chapter, we will discuss about input/output using extraction (>>) and insertion (<<) operators and write simple C++ programs.

6.2 Input/Output using Extraction (>>) and Insertion (<<) Operators

Input Operator ">>"

The input operator >> is known as **extraction** or **get from** operator. The extraction operator takes the value from the stream object on its left and places it in the variable on its right, which will be stored in the RAM (**R**andom **A**ccess **M**emory).

Figure 6.1 shows its use:

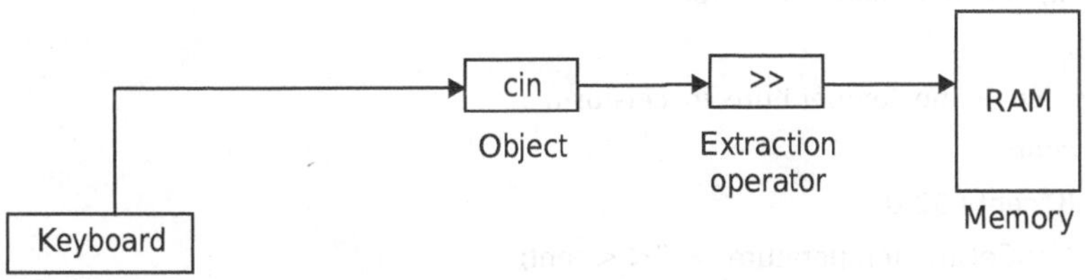

Fig. 6.1. Standard input **cin**.

For example,

```
int x;
cin > > x;        //input the value of x
```

Output Operator "<<"

The output operator << is known as **insertion** or **put to** operator. It outputs the contents of the variable on its right to the object on its left.

Figure 6.2 shows its use:

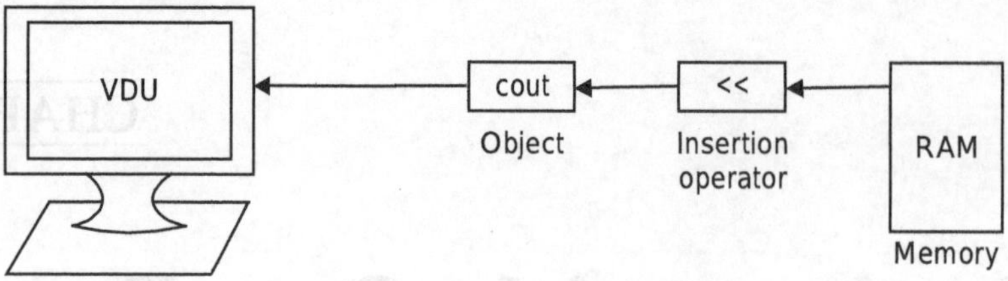

Fig. 6.2. Standard Output **cout.**

For example,

cout<<"India is great";

cout<<"\nWe love our country";

The above statements will give the following output:

India is great

We love our country

Here the newline character (\n) used in the second statement causes the output to be directed to the next line; otherwise the output is displayed at the next column after the previous output.

For example, the following program illustrates the use of cout and cin:

Program 6.1

```
//demonstrates the use of cout and cin
//conversion of celsius temperature to fahrenheit
#include<iostream.h> //for cin and cout
#include<conio.h> //for clrscr( )
void main( )
{
    float cent,fahr; //variables declared
    clrscr( );
    cout<<"Enter the temperature in celsius\n";
    cin>>cent;
    fahr=1.8*cent+32.0;
    cout<<"\nCelsius temperature = "<<cent;
    cout<<"\nFahrenheit temperature = "<<fahr;
}
```

Output

```
Enter the temperature in celsius
37
Celsius temperature = 37
Fahrenheit temperature = 98.599998
```

In the above program the first statement of the function **main( )**

```
float cent, fahr;
```

declares two variables in the program.

A variable refers to a storage (memory) area whose contents can change during program execution.

The statement cin>>cent; reads the value entered by the user and stores it in variable *cent.* The result is displayed after computing the *fahr* temperature.

6.2.1 USE OF endl AND setw ( )

These are operators used with the insertion operator << to modify or manipulate the output. Some useful manipulators are given below:

The endl manipulator

It is a manipulator that inserts a linefeed into the stream. It has the same effect as the newline character ('\n'). For example,

```
cout<<endl;
```

The above statement takes the control to the next line.

The setw manipulator

It is a manipulator that specifies the width for the variables as per our choice. The file **iomanip.h** must be included for it in the program. It causes the number (or string) to be printed within the specified width. For example,

```
int x;
cout<<setw(8)<<x;
```

The above statement prints the value of x in width of 8 and right-justifies the value.

The setprecision( ) manipulator

It is a manipulator that sets the precision of a float value to the right of the decimal place, with the number of digits as an argument. The file **iomanip.h** must be included for it in the program. For example,

```
float x = 79.5;
cout<<setprecision(2) << x;
```

The above statement prints the value of **x** as 79.50.

Following program illustrates the use of manipulators:

Program 6.2

```
//illustrating use of endl and setw( )
#include<iostream.h>
#include<conio.h>        //for clrscr( )
#include<iomanip.h>      //for setw( )
void main( )
{
    int x,y,z; //variables declared
```

```
    clrscr( );
    cout<<"Enter the value of x";
    cout<<endl;
    cin>>x;
    cout<<"Enter the value of y";
    cout<<endl;
    cin>>y;
    cout<<"Enter the value of z";
    cout<<endl;
    cin>>z;
    cout<<endl;
    //print the values with setw( )
    cout<<"The entered numbers printed using setw( ) are";
    cout<<endl;
    cout<<setw(8)<<x;
    cout<<endl;
    cout<<setw(8)<<y;
    cout<<endl;
    cout<<setw(8)<<z;
}
```

Output

```
Enter the value of x
1024
Enter the value of y
3313
Enter the value of z
336
The entered numbers printed using setw( ) are:
    1024
    3313
     336
```

6.2.2 Cascading of I/O Operators

We have used the insertion operator << and the extraction operator >> for output and input operations respectively. C++ allows repeated use of these operators for writing and reading data.

The repeated use of input (>>) or output (<<) operators in one statement is known as cascading of I/O operators.

Following program illustrates this concept:

Program 6.3

```
//illustrating cascading of I/O operators
#include<iostream.h>
#include<conio.h>    //for clrscr( )
void main( )
{
    int x,y,z; //variables declared
    clrscr( );
    cout<<"Enter the value of x,y,z"<<endl;
    cin>>x>>y>>z;
    cout<<endl;
    cout<<"The entered numbers are: "<<endl<<endl;
    cout<<"x = "<<x<<" y = "<<y<<" z = "<<z;
}
```

Output

```
Enter the value of x, y, z
37 84 19
The entered numbers are:
x = 37 y = 84 z = 19
```

In the above program the three values entered by the user are correctly read into *x*, *y* and *z* respectively. The input operator >> discards all white spaces (*e.g.*, blanks, tabs, newlines etc., between two successive input values.

The above program illustrates the *cascading of output operator* as well as the *cascading of input operator.*

The last statement can also be written as:

```
cout <<"x = "<<x
     <<" y = "<<y
     <<" z = "<<z;
```

for the purpose of increasing the readability.

The cascading of input (>>) operator eliminates the opportunity to prompt the user between inputs, so it may not be liked by some programmers.

6.3 Writing Simple C++ Programs

Let us write some simple C++ programs.

Program 6.4

```
// Illustration of ASCII code of characters and vice versa
#include<iostream.h>
#include<conio.h>
void main( )
{
    // assign ASCII code of 'b' to ch1 and '7' to ch2
    char ch1='b', ch2='7';
    int acode1=ch1,acode2=ch2; // store these codes in int type
    clrscr( );
    cout<<"\nASCII code of "<<ch1<<" is "<<acode1<<endl;
    cout<<"\nASCII code of "<<ch2<<" is "<<acode2<<endl<<endl;
    cout<<"After subtracting 1 from the character codes:"<<endl;
    ch1 = ch1 - 1;
    acode1 = ch1;
    ch2 = ch2 - 1;
    acode2 = ch2;
    cout<<"\nASCII code of "<<ch1<<" is "<<acode1<<endl;
    cout<<"\nASCII code of "<<ch2<<" is "<<acode2<<endl;
    getch( ); // freeze the monitor
}
```

Output

```
ASCII code of b is 98
ASCII code of 7 is 55
After subtracting 1 from the character codes:
ASCII code of a is 97
ASCII code of 6 is 54
```

Program 6.5

```
// find average of three numbers
#include<iostream.h>
#include<conio.h>    // for clrscr( )
void main( )
```

```
{
    float a,b,c,sum=0.0,avg;
    clrscr( );
    cout<<"Enter three numbers\n";
    cin>>a>>b>>c;
    // echo the data
    cout<<"\na = "<<a<<" b = "<<b<<" c = "<<c<<endl;
    sum = a+b+c;
    avg = sum/3.0;
    cout<<"\nAverage = "<<avg;
}
```

Output

```
Enter three numbers
5   3   10
a = 5  b = 3  c = 10
Average = 6
```

Program 6.6

```
//Illustration of access modifier (const)
#include<iostream.h>
#include<conio.h>
void main( )
{
    const float PI = 3.14159; // type const float
    float radius,area,perimeter;
    clrscr( );
    cout<<"Enter radius of circle"<<endl<<endl;
    cin>>radius;
    area=PI*radius*radius;
    perimeter=2.0*PI*radius;
    cout<<endl;
    cout<<"Area = "<<area<<" square units"<<endl<<endl;
    cout<<"Perimeter = "<<perimeter<<" units"<<endl;
}
```

Output

```
Enter radius of circle
4.7
Area = 69.39772 square units
Perimeter = 29.530947 units
```

Program 6.7

```
//Illustration of arithmetic operators
#include<iostream.h>
#include<conio.h>
void main( )
{
    int a=15, b=7;
    float x=25, y=2.0;
    char cvar1='a', cvar2='A';
    clrscr( );
    cout<<"Result of integer arithmetic is: "<<endl;
    cout<<endl<<a<<" - "<<b<<" = "<<a-b
        <<endl<<a<<" + "<<b<<" = "<<a+b
        <<endl<<a<<" * "<<b<<" = "<<a*b
        <<endl<<a<<" / "<<b<<" = "<<a/b
        <<endl<<a<<" % "<<b<<" = "<<a%b<<endl<<endl;
    cout<<"Result of floating point arithmetic is: "<<endl;
    cout<<endl<<x<<" - "<<y<<" = "<<x-y
        <<endl<<x<<" + "<<y<<" = "<<x+y
        <<endl<<x<<" * "<<y<<" = "<<x*y
        <<endl<<x<<" / "<<y<<" = "<<x/y<<endl<<endl;
    cout<<"Result of character arithmetic is: "<<endl;
    cout<<endl<<cvar1<<" - "<<cvar2<<" = "<<cvar1-cvar2
         <<endl<<cvar1<<" + "<<cvar2<<" = "<<cvar1+cvar2
        <<endl<<cvar1<<" + "<<cvar2<<" + '5' = "<<cvar1+cvar2+'5';
}
```

Output

```
Result of integer arithmetic is:
15 - 7 = 8
15 + 7 = 22
15 * 7 = 105
15 / 7 = 2
15 % 7 = 1
Result of floating point arithmetic is:
25 - 2 = 23
25 + 2 = 27
25 * 2 = 50
25 / 2 = 12.5
```

Result of character arithmetic is:

a – A = 32

a + A = 162

a + A + '5' = 215

Program 6.8

```
//Illustration of increment (++) and decrement (--) operators
#include<iostream.h>
#include<conio.h>
void main( )
{
    int i=10,j=20;
    clrscr( );
    cout<<"Result of increment (++) operator: "<<endl<<endl;
    cout<<"i = "<<i++<<endl; //displays     10 (postfix)
    cout<<"i = "<<++i<<endl; //displays     12 (prefix)
    cout<<"i = "<<i<<endl; //displays       12
    cout<<"i = "<<++i<<endl; //displays     13 (prefix)
    cout<<"i = "<<i++<<endl; //displays     13 (postfix)
    cout<<"i = "<<i<<endl; //displays       14
    cout<<endl;
    cout<<"Result of decrement (--) operator : "<<endl<<endl;
    cout<<"j = "<<--j<<endl; //displays     19 (prefix)
    cout<<"j = "<<j--<<endl; //displays     19 (postfix)
    cout<<"j = "<<j<<endl; //displays       18
    cout<<"j = "<<j--<<endl; //displays     18 (postfix)
    cout<<"j = "<<--j<<endl; //displays     16 (prefix)
    cout<<"j = "<<j--<<endl; //displays     16 (postfix)
}
```

Output

Result of increment (++) operator:

i = 10

i = 12

i = 12

i = 13

i = 13

i = 14

Result of decrement (– –) operator:

j = 19

j = 19

j = 18

j = 18

j = 16

j = 16

Program 6.9

```
//Illustration of relational operators
#include<iostream.h>
#include<conio.h>
void main( )
{
    int a=20,b=25;
    clrscr( );
    cout<<"Result of relational operators: "<<endl<<endl;
    cout<<"a >  b is "<<(a>b)<<endl;
    cout<<"a >= b is "<<(a>=b)<<endl;
    cout<<"a <  b is "<<(a<b)<<endl;
    cout<<"a <= b is "<<(a<=b)<<endl;
    cout<<"a == b is "<<(a==b)<<endl;
    cout<<"a != b is "<<(a!=b)<<endl;
}
```

Output

```
Result of relational operators:
a  >    b  is  0
a  >=   b  is  0
a  <    b  is  1
a  <=   b  is  1
a  ==   b  is  0
a  !=   b  is  1
```

Program 6.10

```
//Illustration of the use of && operator
#include<iostream.h>
#include<conio.h>
```

```
void main( )
{
    int num;
    clrscr( );
    cout<<"Enter an integer"<<endl;
    cin>>num; //input a value from keyboard
    if((num != 0) && ((num % 2)==0))
        cout<<"Even integer entered"<<endl;
    else
        cout<<"Odd integer or zero entered"<<endl;
}
```

Output

```
Enter an integer
50
Even integer entered
Enter an integer
13
Odd integer or zero entered
```

Program 6.11

```
//demonstrate the use of || operator
#include<iostream.h>
#include<conio.h>
void main( )
{
    int num;
    clrscr( );
    cout<<"Enter the number 100 or 200\n";
    cin>>num; //input a number from keyboard
    if((num == 100) || (num == 200))
        cout<<"You are a good follower\n";
    else
        cout<<"You don't follow others\n";
}
```

Output

```
Enter the number 100 or 200
200
```

You are a good follower
Enter the number 100 or 200
2011
You don't follow others

Program 6.12

```
//Illustration of conditional or ternary operator (? :)
#include<iostream.h>
#include<conio.h>
void main( )
{
    int num;
    clrscr( );
    cout<<"Enter the positive integer"<<endl<<end1;
    cin>>num;
    cout<<endl;
    (num%2==0)? cout<<num<<" is even number\n" :
                cout<<num<<" is odd number\n";
}
```

Output

Enter the positive integer
50
50 is even number

Enter the positive integer
77
77 is odd number

Program 6.13

```
//Illustration of automatic type conversion
#include<iostream.h>
#include<conio.h>
void main( )
{
    int n=25;
    float avg_height=160.5;
```

```
    double tot_height;
    clrscr( );
    tot_height=avg_height*n;
    cout<<"\n\nTotal height = "<<tot_height;
}
```

Output

```
Total height = 4012.5
```

Program 6.14

```
//Illustration of type casting (explicit type conversion)
#include<iostream.h>
#include<conio.h>
void main( )
{
    int i,j,num,num1,num2;
    float d;
    clrscr( );
    cout<<"Enter the positive integers i and j"<<endl;
    cin>>i>>j;
    d=(float)i/j; //type casting
    cout<<"\nResult of division = "<<d<<endl<<endl;
    num=30000; //range of signed: -32768 to 32767
    cout<<"num = "<<num<<endl<<endl;
    num1= (num*5)/10;
    cout<<"num1 = "<<num1<<endl<<endl; //wrong answer here
    //type casting functional approach
    num2= (long(num)*5)/10;
    cout<<"num2 = "<<num2<<endl; //correct answer here
    getch( ); //freeze the monitor
}
```

Output

```
Enter the positive integers i and j
1275 10
Result of division = 127.5
num = 30000
num1 = 1892
num2 = 15000
```

Program 6.15

```
//Illustration of C++ shorthands (arithmetic assignment operators)
#include<iostream.h>
#include<conio.h>
void main( )
{
    int i=50,j=25;
    clrscr( );
    cout<<"\nResults of arithmetic assignment operations are: "<<endl<<endl;
    i += 10; //same as: i = i + 10;
    j *= 3; //same as: j = j * 3;
    cout<<"i = "<<i<<" j = "<<j<<endl<<endl;
    i /= 6; //same as: i = i/6;
    j -= 20; //same as: j = j - 20;
    cout<<"i = "<<i<<" j = "<<j<<endl<<endl;
    i %= 8; //same as: i = i % 8;
    j %= 4; //same as: j = j % 4;
    cout<<"i = "<<i<<" j = "<<j<<endl<<endl;
    getch( ); //freeze the monitor
}
```

Output

```
Results of arithmetic assignment operations are:
i = 60 j = 75
i = 10 j = 55
i = 2 j = 3
```

Program 6.16

```
//Smallest of three integers using conditional operator
#include<iostream.h>
#include<conio.h>
void main( )
{
    int a,b,c,small;
    clrscr( );
    cout<<"Enter the three integers"<<endl;
    cin>>a>>b>>c;
    small = a<b? (a<c? a:c): (b<c? b:c);
    cout<<"Smallest integer is "<<small<<endl;
}
```

Output

```
Enter the three integers
5 9 3
Smallest integer is 3
```

6.4 Comments in C++

In C++, the comments start with // (double slash) and terminate at the end of the line. For example,

```
//illustration of a comment
```

A comment may start anywhere in the line, and whatever follows till the end of the line is ignored by the C++ compiler. Note that there is no closing symbol.

The // (double slash) comment is basically a single line comment. We can write multiline comments as given below:

```
//illustration of a
//multiline comment
```

The C comment symbols /*, */ are also allowed in C++ and are more suitable for multiline comments. For example

```
/* illustation of a
   multiline comment */
```

We can use either or both styles in our C++ programs. Remember that we cannot insert a // style comment within the text of a program statement. For example, the double slash comment cannot be used in the following way:

```
for(int i=0; i<n; /* loops n times */ i++)
```

6.5 Stages of Program Execution

Executing/running a computer program written in any high-level language requires several steps, as given below:

(*i*) Develop the source code (program).

(*ii*) Select a suitable filename to store the program.

(*iii*) Create the program (type the program) and save it under the filename decided in step (*ii*). This file is known as *source code file.*

(*iv*) Compile the source code. The file having the translated code is known as *object code file.* If any error(s) occur, debug and compile the program again.

(*v*) Link the object code with other library code that are needed for execution. The resulting code is called the *executable code.* If any error found during linking, correct them and compile the program again.

(*vi*) Run the executable code and get the results, if there are no errors then stop.

(*vii*) Debug the program, if error(s) is/are found in the result.

(*viii*) Go to step (*iv*) and repeat the steps again.

These steps are illustrated with the help of flowchart in Figure 6.3. The exact steps depend upon the program environment and the compiler in use. But, they will resemble with the above explained steps.

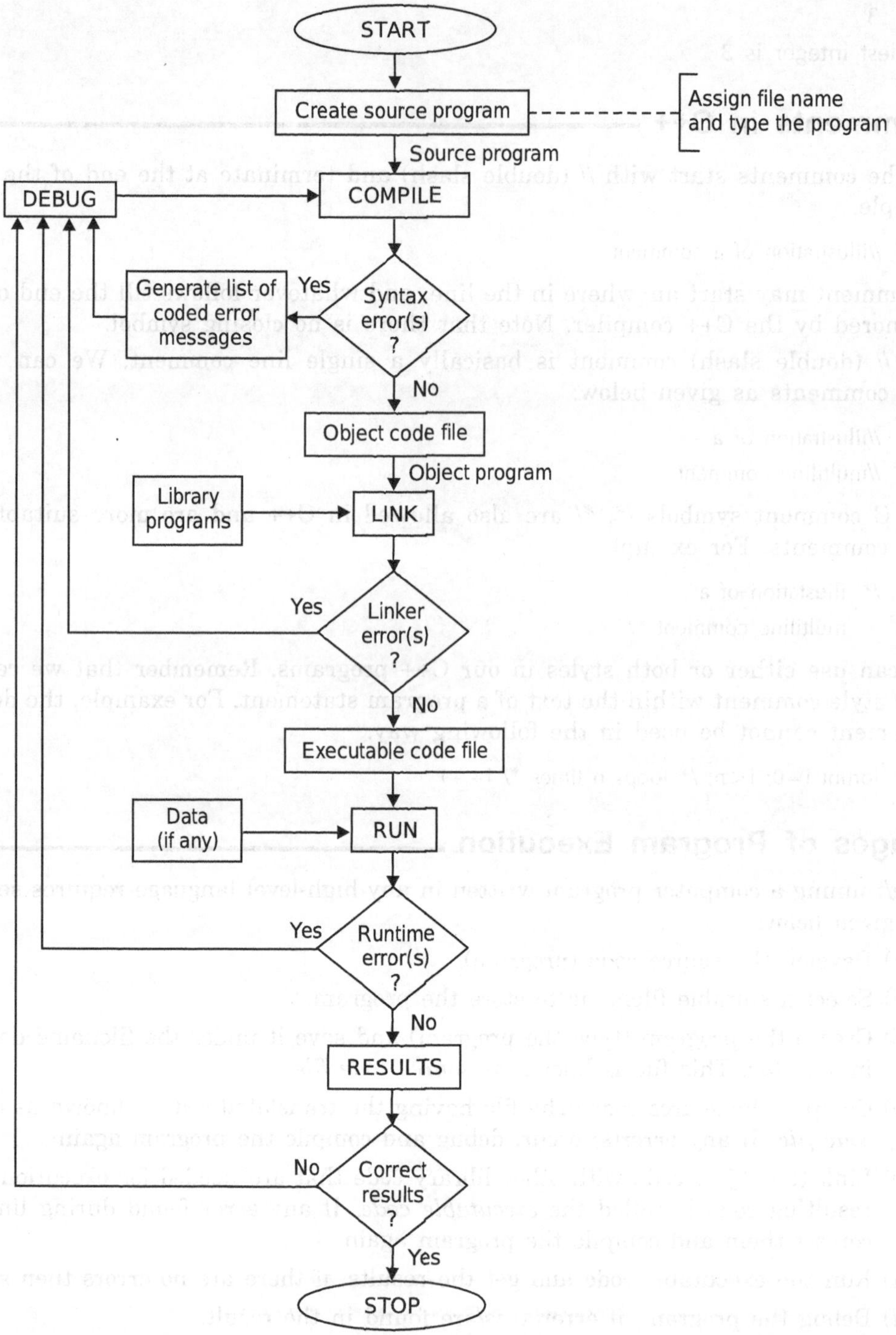

Fig. 6.3. Flowchart illustrating development and running of a high level language program.

The execution of a C++ program has been done using Turbo C++ compiler in Chapter 5.

REVIEW QUESTIONS AND EXERCISES

1. What is the use of I/O operators (>> and <<) in a C++ program?
2. What is the use of endl and setw( ) in a C++ program? Explain by giving a suitable example.
3. What do you mean by cascading of I/O operators? Explain with examples.
4. Differentiate between the following:
   (*i*) cin and cout   (*ii*) >> and << operators.
5. Write a C++ program to find the area of a rectangle.
6. What do you think is the main advantage of the comment // in C++ as compared to the old C type comment?
7. Write a C++ program to read two numbers from the keyboard and display the larger value on the screen.
8. Write a C++ program to convert the Fahrenheit temperature into Celsius.
9. Write a C++ program to swap two integers without using a temporary variable.
10. Discuss the stages of program execution.

CHAPTER **7**

Control Structures

7.1 Introduction

Every C++ program must have at least one function called **main( ).** When you run a C++ program, the first statement executed will be at the beginning of function **main( )** and the last statement at the end of function **main( ).** Therefore, the **main( )** function is also known as driver function as it drives the program. If there is no function called **main( )** in your program, the linker will signal an error.

In most C++ programs, as we will see later, **main( )** calls other functions. The parentheses following the word **main** are the distinguishing feature of a function. Without the parentheses the compiler would treat **main** as a variable or some other program element.

The *Von-Neumann architecture* of computers supports only sequential processing. The normal flow of execution of statements in a high-level language program is also in the sequential order, that is, each statement is executed in its order of occurrence in the program. For example, the following C++ program statements will be executed in the sequential order:

```
....
....
a = 50;
b = 10;
q = a/b;
....
....
```

First of all the statement $a = 50$ will be executed, followed by the statement $b = 10$ and then the statement $q = a/b$, **strictly** in the sequential order. Here all the statements are executed only once in the specified manner.

Some problems oftenly require that the normal flow of control be altered depending on the requirements. It means that we may wish **selective** and/or **repetitive** execution of any portion of the program. C++ supports a number of *control structures* to perform the processing.

7.2 Control Structures

A function is a set of statement(s) to perform a specific task. For solving a specific task, we may have many algorithms, some simple and other complex. The program should be written in a user friendly way so that it may be modified later on by anyone who wishes to change it, if the need arises. Debugging and maintenance would be easy if the program is coded with a proper format. For attaining the objective of a good program, we use one or any combination of the following three control structures:

1. *Sequence control structure*
2. *Selection control structure (branching)*
3. *Looping control structure (repetition or iteration)*

These control structures have been discussed earlier in Chapter 3 (Problem Solving and Program Planning).

We can code any program using these three structures. Any program coded using the above shown control structures is called a **structured program** and the approach is known as **structured programming.** The main objectives of structured programming are readability and clarity of program, maintenance and reduced testing problems. Structured programming eliminates the use of goto (unconditional control).

C++ supports all the three control structures as shown in Figure 7.1.

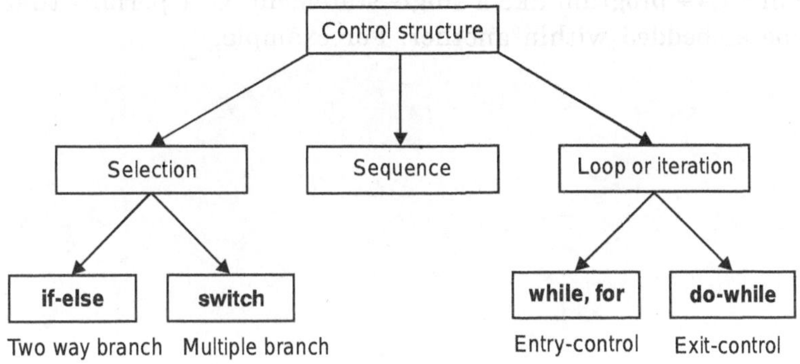

Fig. 7.1. Various control structures in C++

C++ implements the above three control structures and uses the following language constructs:

(*i*) *all straight line statements such as assignment statement, input and output statements.*

(*ii*) *function calls*

(*iii*) *if, if-else (two way branching) and switch (multiple branching) statements*

(*iv*) *while, for (entry control loops) and do..while (exit control loop)*

(*v*) *a restricted use of goto statement.*

So, you may get an idea that C++ combines the features of **structured programming** with **OOP** (Object Oriented Programming) features.

7.3 Statements

These are the instructions given to the computer to perform some action and form the smallest executable unit within a C++ program. A semicolon (;) terminates a statement. The *empty* or *null statement* is written as,

```
; //a null statement
```

It is useful in the situations where the syntax of language needs the presence of a statement but the program logic does not. It will be used in loops and their bodies.

A **simple** statement is a single statement terminated by a semicolon.

A **compound** statement is formed by two or more statements enclosed by a pair of braces ({ }), also known as a *block*.

For example,

```
{
    statement1;
    statement2;
        :
    statementn;
}
```

represents a compound statement.

A *compound statement* or a *block statement* is considered as a single unit. It may be used anywhere in a C++ program like a single statement. C++ permits that one compound statement can be embedded within another. For example,

```
{
    ...
    ...
    {
        ...
        ...
    }
    ...
    ...
}
```

Here, the braces are known as delimiters.

7.4 Decision Making or Conditional Statements (Selection)

There are situations when we wish to execute some part of the program based on some condition(s) being *true* or *false*. As mentioned earlier, *in C++, any non-zero value is true including negative numbers. A 0 (zero) is always false.* In C++, **if** and **switch** statements are used for selective execution of a program segment. The conditional operator (**?:**) is used in specialized situations as an alterate to **if ... else** statement.

7.4.1 if Statement

It tests a condition. The statement(s) associated with if is (are) executed only when the condition is true, otherwise the statement(s) is (are) not executed at all. The syntax of if statement is as shown below:

```
if (condition)
    statement;
```

Here *statement* may consist of a *single statement, a compound statement* or *nothing* (in case of empty statement). *Remember that a semicolon (;) is not required after the test condition.* If you do so, the block or statements following this line will not be taken as part of **if.**

It can be shown with the help of flow chart given in Figure 7.2:

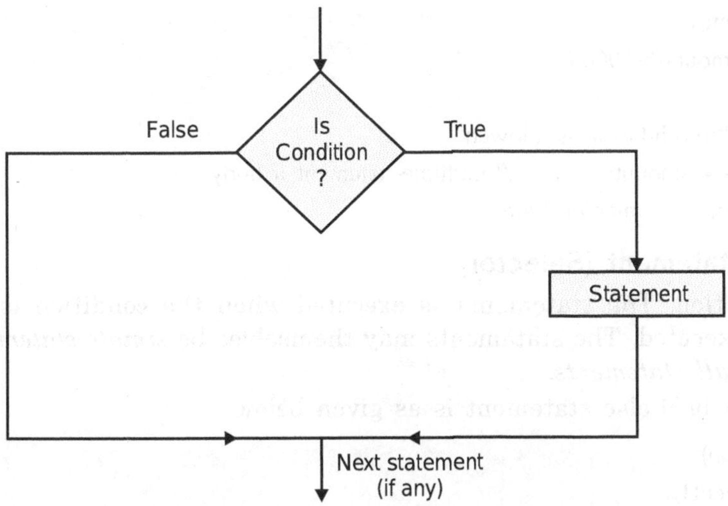

Fig. 7.2. Flow chart of **if** statement

For example, the following program illustrates the use of if statement:

Program 7.1

```
//illustration of use of if statement
#include<iostream.h>
#include<conio.h>
void main( )
{
    int x,y;
    clrscr( );
    cout<<"Enter the two integers\n";
    cin>>x>>y;
    if(x>y)         // no semicolon required here
       cout<<x;   // single-statement if body
}
```

Output

```
Enter the two integers
8   5
8
```

If the specified condition after *if* is not true then statement is not executed and control is transferred to the next statement. The statement itself may be a conditional statement. For example,

```
float amount,balance;
cout<<"Enter the amount to be withdrawn"<<endl;
cin>>amount;
if((balance–amount)>1000.0)
{
    cout<<"\nWithdrawal is allowed";
    balance –= amount;          // multiple-statement if body
}     // Note: no semicolon here
```

7.4.2 if-else Statement (Selector)

It tests a condition. The statement1 is executed when the condition is *true* otherwise statement2 is executed. The statements may themselves be *simple statements, compound statements* or *null statements.*

The syntax of if-else statement is as given below:

```
if(condition)
    statement1;
else
    statement2;
```

> ***Note:** The **if-else** statement is used when we want to do one thing if a condition is true, do something else if it is false but not both.*

The **if-else** statement can be shown with the help of flow chart given in Figure 7.3.

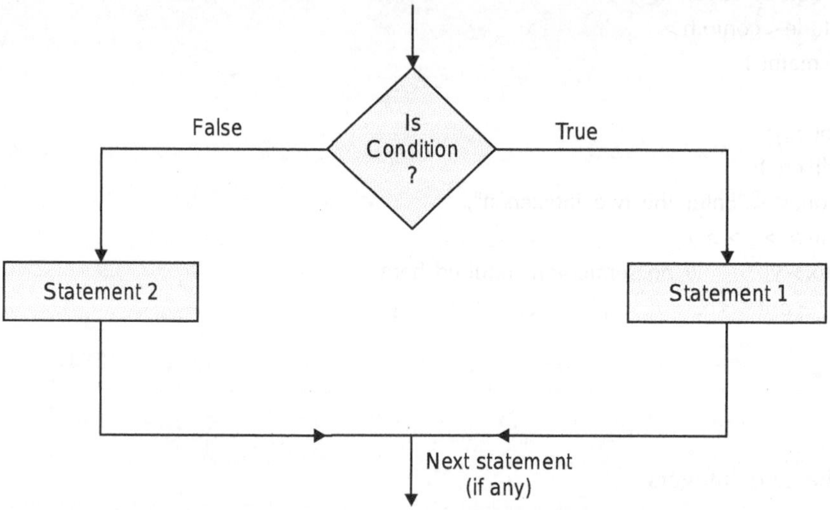

Fig. 7.3. Flow chart of if-else statement

For example, the following program illustrates the use of if-else statement:

Program 7.2

```
//illustration of use of if-else statement
#include<iostream.h>
#include<conio.h>
void main( )
{
   int num;
   clrscr( );
   cout<<"Enter an integer\n";
   cin>>num;
   if(num)       // check the truth value of an integer variable num
   {
      cout<<num<<" is non-zero\n";  // single-statement if body
   }
   else
   {
      cout<<num<<" is zero\n";      // single-statement else body
   }
}
```

Output

```
Enter an integer
7
7 is non-zero
Enter an integer
0
0 is zero
```

Remember that the braces ({ }) are not required if only single statement follows if or else, however, it is a good idea to enclose the executable code of if/else in { }.

> ***Note:** An item declared in a conditional statement cannot be accessed outside it.*

Example 1. *Draw the flow chart and write a C++ program to find the largest of three numbers.*

Solution. The flow chart for finding the largest of three numbers is given as:

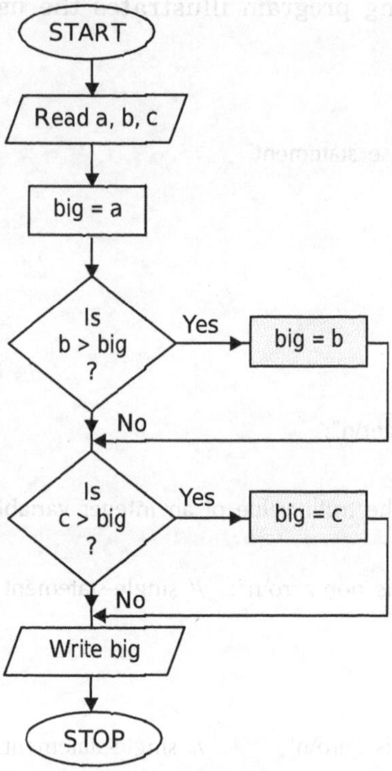

Fig. 7.4. Flow chart for finding largest of three numbers

The program for finding the largest of three numbers is given below:

```
//Find largest of three numbers
#include<iostream.h>
#include<conio.h>
void main( )
{
   int a,b,c,big;
   clrscr( );
   cout<<"Enter the three numbers"<<endl;
   cin>>a>>b>>c;
   big=a; //assuming 'a' as the largest number
   if(b>big)
      big=b;
   if(c>big)
      big=c;
   cout<<"\nLargest number is: "<<big;
}
```

Output

Enter the three numbers

45 28 69

Largest number is: 69

Example 2. *Write a C++ program to check a year for leap year.*

Solution.

```
//Leap year checking
#include<iostream.h>
#include<conio.h>
void main( )
{
    int year;
    clrscr( );
    cout<<"Enter the year"<<endl;
    cin>>year;
    cout<<endl;
    if( ((year%4==0) && (year%100!=0)) || (year%400==0) )
        cout<<year<<" is a leap year\n";
    else
        cout<<year<<" is not a leap year\n";
}
```

Output

Enter the year

2012

2012 is a leap year

Enter the year

2013

2013 is not a leap year

7.4.3 Nested if

One or more if statement(s) **embedded within the if statement (*i.e.*, either in its if's body or in its else's body) are called nested ifs.** The following if-else statement is a nested if statement nested to level three.

```
if(condition1)
{
    if(condition2)
    {
        if(condition3)
            statement3;
        else
```

```
            statement2;
        }
    else
            statement1;
    }
else
    statement0;
```

The logic of execution is shown in Figure 7.5. If the *condition1* is false, the statement0 will be executed; otherwise it continues to perform the second test. If the *condition2* is false, the statement1 will be executed; otherwise it continues to perform the third test. If the *condition3* is true, the statement3 will be evaluated; otherwise the statement2 will be evaluated and then the control is transferred to the statement following the statement0 (if any). Such a nested group of **if ... else** statement is called a *decision tree.*

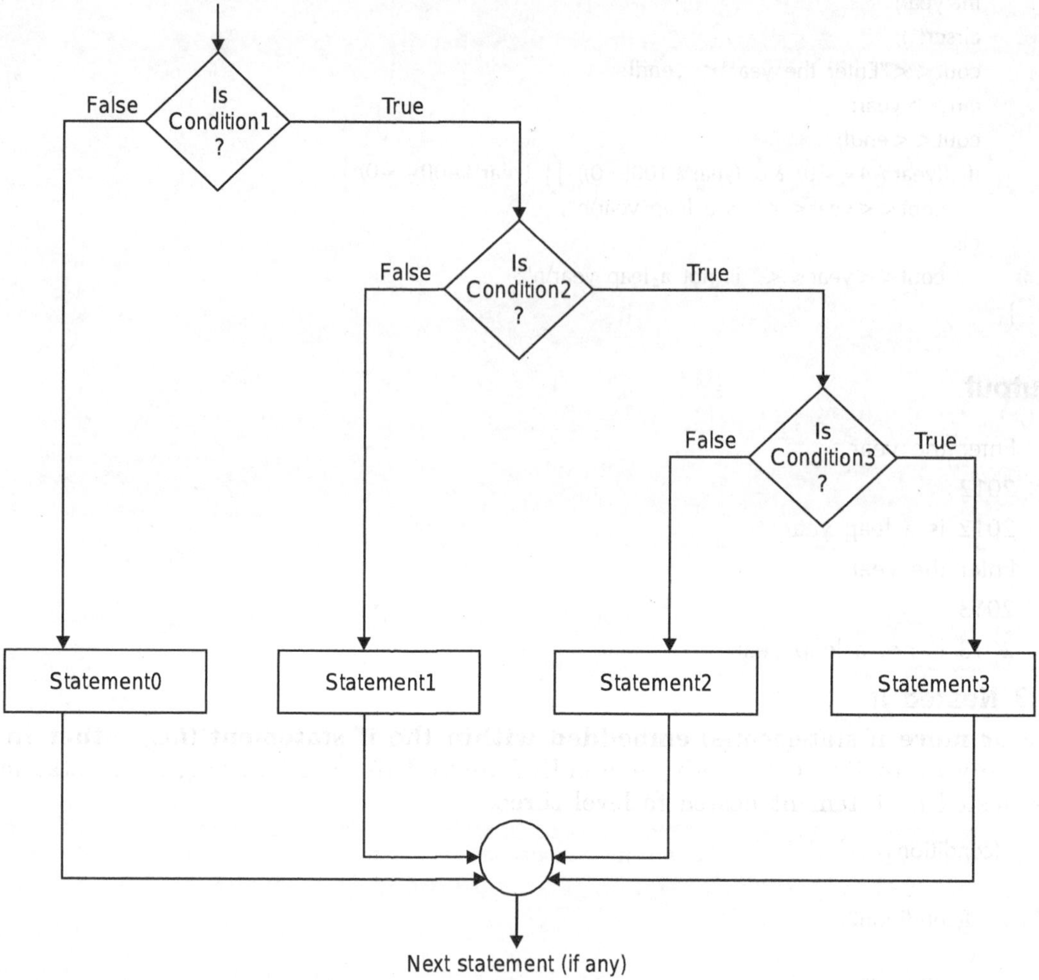

Fig. 7.5. Flow chart of nested **if ... else** statements

The nested **if** statements should be written with proper indentation. It becomes very difficult for the user to understand, if nested **ifs** are not written properly. Use braces { } generously if you are in doubt. For example,

Consider the following statements:

```
int a,b,x,y;
----------
----------
if(a>=b)
if(x>y)
   x=x+1;
else
   y=y+1;
```

There is a possibility of interpreting this statement in two different ways:

(*i*) if $a < b$ then nothing happens.

(*ii*) if $a < b$ then $y = y + 1$.

Which interpretation is correct cannot be easily told by a novice. This is called a **"dangling else"** problem. C++ makes the (*i*) interpretation. C++ always associates the innermost **else** with the innermost **if.** To make things clear one must use { } as shown below:

```
int a,b,x,y;
----------
----------
if(a>=b)
{
   if(x>y)
      x=x+1;
   else
      y=y+1;
}
```

For the sake of readability of the if-else statements, the reserved words should be properly indented so as to make their meaning clear. *Indentation means horizontal spacing.*

Following program illustrates the use of nested ifs:

Program 7.3

```
//accept a character as input from keyboard and convert it
//into capital letter if it is a small letter and vice_versa

#include<iostream.h>
#include<conio.h>
void main( )
```

```
{
    char ch1,ch2;
    clrscr( ); //clears the screen
    cout<<"Enter a character\n\n";
    cin>>ch1;
    //echo the data
    cout<<"\nEntered character is: "<<ch1<<end1;
    if( (ch1 >='A' && ch1 <='Z') || (ch1 >='a' && ch1 <='z') )
    {
        cout<<"\nCase converted character is: ";
        if(ch1 >='A' && ch1 <= 'Z') //if upper case
            ch2=ch1+32;
        else
            ch2=ch1-32;
        cout<<ch2; //display the converted character
    }
    else
        cout<<"\nEntered character is not an alphabet\n";
    getch( ); //freeze the monitor
}
```

Output

```
Enter a character
d
Entered character is: d
Case converted character is: D
Enter a character
A
Entered character is: A
Case converted character is: a
Enter a character
7
Entered character is: 7
Entered character is not an alphabet
```

> ***Note:*** *Every else goes with its nearest unmatched preceding if. You can override the default dangling-else matching by using braces { }.*

Example 3. *Draw a flow chart to find the roots of a quadratic equation. Also write a C++ program to solve this problem.*

Solution.

Flow Chart for Finding the Roots of a Quadratic Equation is given below:

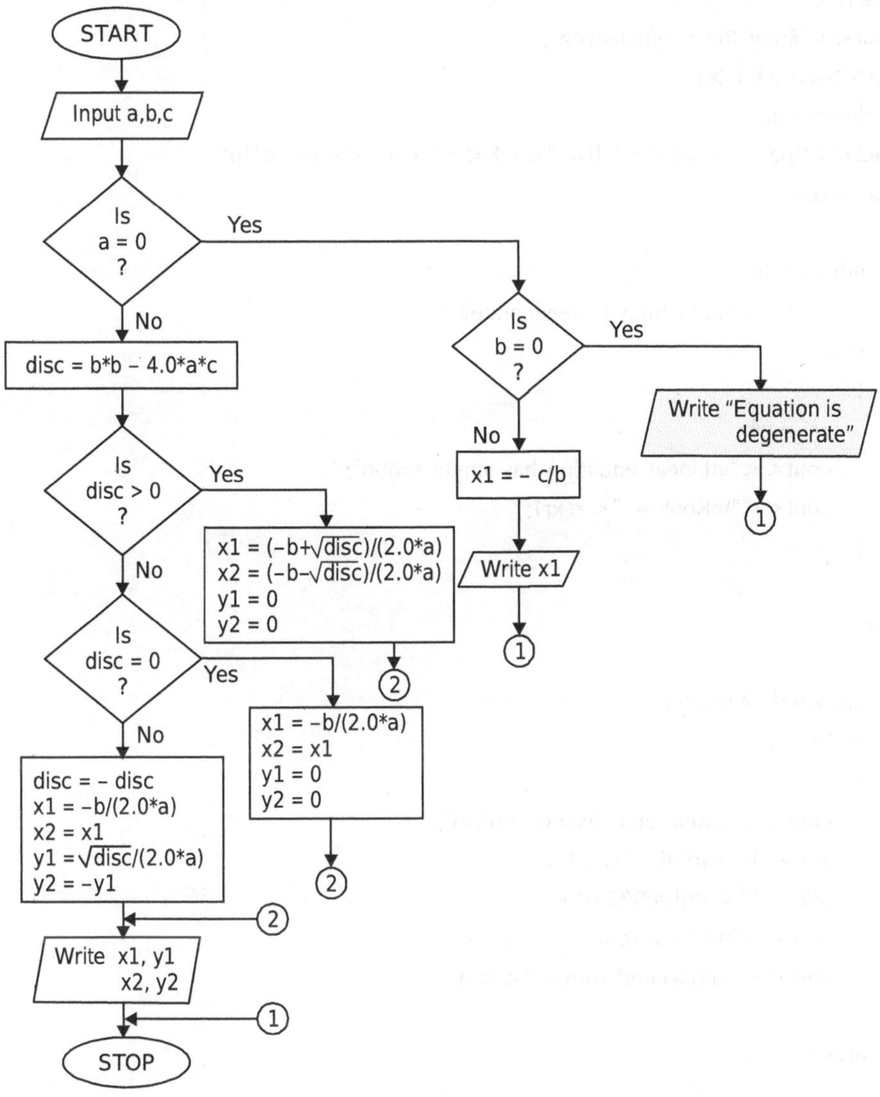

Fig. 7.6. Flow chart for finding the roots of a quadratic equation

The program for finding the roots of a quadratic equation is given below:

```
//Find the roots of a quadratic equation
//Illustration of use of nested if statements
#include<iostream.h>
#include<conio.h>
#include<math.h> //for sqrt( )
void main( )
```

```
{
    float a,b,c,disc,xr1,xr2,img1,img2;
    clrscr( );
    cout<<"Enter the coefficients\n";
    cin>>a>>b>>c;
    //echo the data
    cout<<"\na= "<<a<<" b= "<<b<<" c= "<<c<<"\n";
    if(a==0.0)
    {
        if(b==0.0)
            cout<<"\nEquation is degenerate\n";
        else
        {
            xr1=c/b;
            cout<<"\nLinear equation has single root\n";
            cout<<"\nRoot = "<<xr1;
        }
    }
    else
    {
        disc=b*b-4.0*a*c;
        if(disc>0.0)
        {
            cout<<"\nReal and distinct roots\n";
            xr1=(-b+sqrt(disc))/(2.0*a);
            xr2=(-b-sqrt(disc))/(2.0*a);
            cout<<"\n\nFirst root = "<<xr1;
            cout<<"\n\nSecond root= "<<xr2;
        }
        else
        {
            if(disc==0.0)
            {
                cout<<"\nReal and equal roots\n";
                xr1= -b/(2.0*a);
                xr2= xr1;
                cout<<"\n\nFirst root = "<<xr1;
                cout<<"\n\nSecond root= "<<xr2;
            }
```

```
        else
        {
            cout<<"\nComplex conjugate roots\n";
            xr1=-b/(2.0*a);
            img1=sqrt(-disc)/(2.0*a);  //square root of a negative number
                                       //can't be computed on the system
            xr2=xr1;
            img2= -img1;
            cout<<"\nFirst root is:\n";
            cout<<"\nReal part= "<<xr1;
            cout<<"\nImg. part= "<<img1;
            cout<<"\n\nSecond root is:\n";
            cout<<"\nReal part= "<<xr2;
            cout<<"\nImg. part= "<<img2;
        }
      }
    }
}
```

Output

```
Enter the coefficients
1 - 5 6
a= 1 b= - 5 c= 6
Real and distinct roots
First root = 3
Second root = 2
Enter the coefficients
1 4 4
a =1 b= 4 c= 4
Real and equal roots
First root = - 2
Second root = - 2
Enter the coefficients
3 - 1 5
a= 3 b= - 1 c= 5
Complex conjugate roots
First root is:
Real part= 0.166667
```

```
Img. part= 1.280191
Second root is:
Real part= 0.166667
Img. part= - 1.280191
Enter the coefficients
0 2 4
a= 0 b= 2 c= 4
Linear equation has single root
Root = - 2
Enter the coefficients
0 0 7
a= 0 b= 0 c= 7
Equation is degenerate
```

7.4.4 The if-else-if ladder

The nested **if ... else** statements sometime look clumsy (*i.e.,* awkward and ungraceful in shape) and can be hard-for humans-to interpret, especially if they are nested more deeply. However there is another way of writing these statements. The conditions and the statements can be associated in the following form:

```
if(condition1)
    statement-1;
else    if(condition2)
    statement-2;
else    if(condition3)
    statement-3;
    .
    .
    .
else if(condition n)
    statement-n;
else
    default-statement;
```

The different conditions are evaluated from the start and when a condition is evaluated as true, the following statement(s) are executed and the rest of the statement(s) are skipped. The above shown construct is known as **if-else-if ladder** or *if-else-if staircase* because of its appearance. When all the n conditions become false, then the final **else** having the *default-statement* will be executed. This format is clearer and easier to follow than the **if...else** approach. Figure 7.7 shows the logic of execution of **if-else-if ladder:**

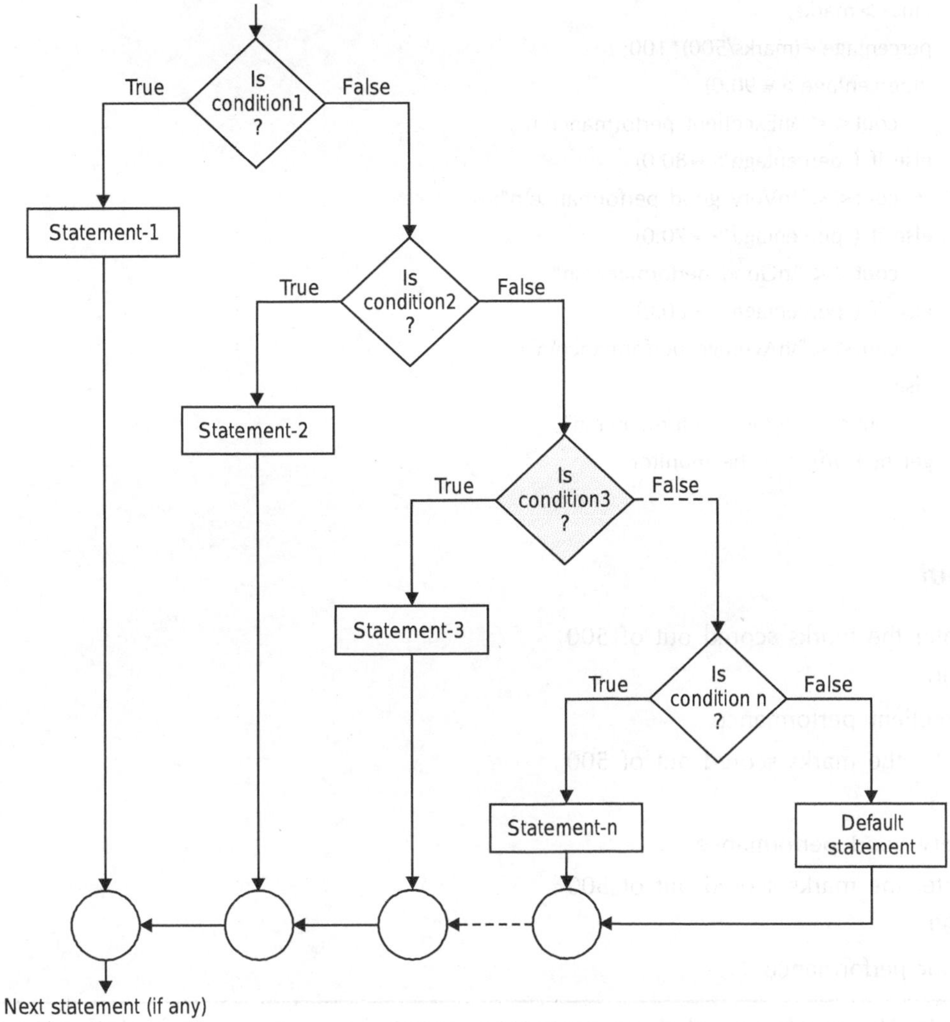

Fig. 7.7. Flow chart of **if-else-if ladder**

Following program illustrates this concept:

Program 7.4

```
//Evaluate the performance of a student
//Illustration of if-else-if ladder
#include<iostream.h>
#include<conio.h>
void main( )
{
    float marks,percentage;
    clrscr( );
    cout<<"Enter the marks scored out of 500\n\n";
```

```
        cin>>marks;
        percentage=(marks/500)*100;
        if(percentage>=90.0)
            cout<<"\nExcellent performance\n";
        else if ( percentage>=80.0)
            cout<<"\nVery good performance\n";
        else if ( percentage>=70.0)
            cout<<"\nGood performance\n";
        else if ( percentage>=60.0)
            cout<<"\nAverage performance\n";
        else
            cout<<"\nPoor performance\n";
        getch( ); //freeze the monitor
    }
```

Output

```
Enter the marks scored out of 500
490
Excellent performance
Enter the marks scored out of 500
425
Very good performance
Enter the marks scored out of 500
299
Poor performance
```

> ***Note:*** *Always take care when you compare for equality i.e., use = = to check whether two values are equal as = sign means assignment.*

7.4.5 switch ... case ... default (multiselector)

If you have a large decision tree, and all the decisions depend on the value of the same variable, you will probably wish to consider a **switch** statement instead of a series of **if ... else** or **if ... else ... if** ladder. The switch statement *tests a control expression (condition). The control is transferred to one of several alternatives, i.e.,* to a case constant which matches the value of the expression. *The value of the expression may be of type* ***int*** *or* ***char*** *but not of type float or double.* It is generally used for menu driven options.

The syntax of switch statement is as follows:

```
switch(control expression)              // no semicolon here
{
    case constant1     :   statement(s);    // first-case body
                           break;           // causes exit from switch
```

```
case constant2      :  statement(s)      // second-case body
                       break;
  .
  .
  .
case constantn      :  statement(s)      // nth-case body
                       break;
            default  :  statement(s);     // default body
                       break;
} // no semicolon here
```

The *switch* statement can have *at least* 16,384 **case** statements. In practice, you will want to limit the number of *case* statements to a smaller amount for efficiency. Although *case* is a label statement, it cannot exist by itself, outside of a *switch*.

It can be shown with the help of flow chart given in Figure 7.8:

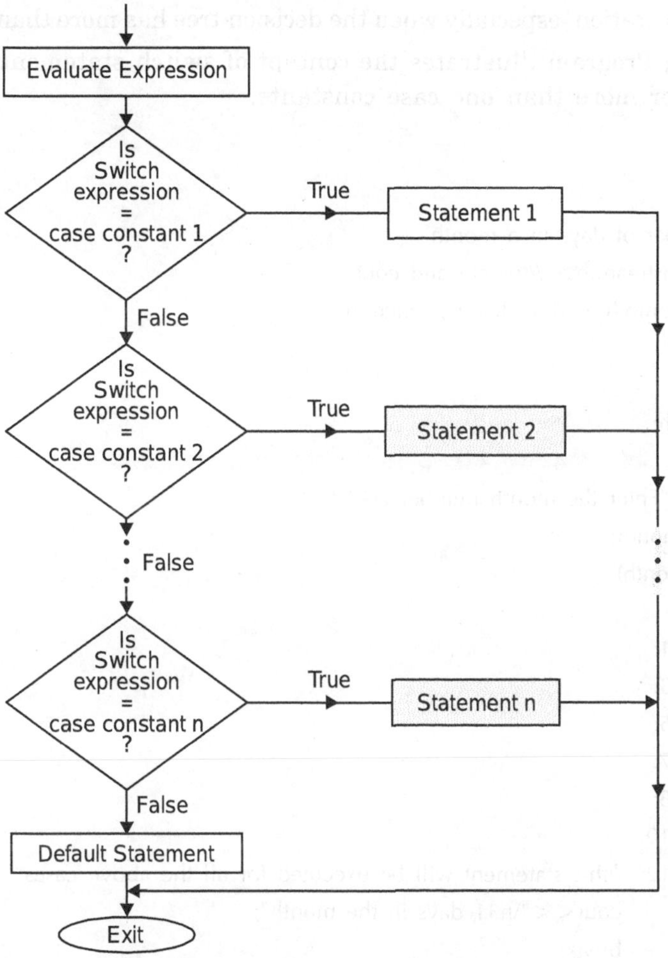

Fig. 7.8. Working of switch statement

The following points must be remembered when switch statement is used:

1. The *switch* differs from the if in that *switch* can only test for equality, whereas *if* can evaluate any type of relational or logical expression.
2. Two case constants in a switch statement cannot have the same value, but the same statement(s) can be executed for two or more different case constants. Of course, a *switch* statement enclosed by an outer *switch* may have case constants that are the same.
3. The data type of the case constants should match that of the switch control expression or variable.
4. If character constants are used in *switch* statement, they are automatically converted to integers (that is, equivalent ASCII codes).
5. Always put a *break* statement after the last *case* statement in a *switch* as you may have to add another *case* statement at the end of the *switch.*
6. The *switch* statement is more efficient than *if* in situations that support the nature of *switch* operation, especially when the decision tree has more than a few possibilities.

The following Program illustrates the concept of switch statement that executes the same statement for more than one case constants.

Program 7.5

```
//Print number of days in a month
#include<iostream.h> //for cin and cout
#include<conio.h> //for clrscr( ) function
void main( )
{
    int month;
    clrscr( );
    cout<<"Enter the month number (1-12): ";
    cin>>month;
    switch(month)
    {
        case 1:
        case 3:
        case 5:
        case 7:
        case 8:
        case 10:
        case 12: //this statement will be executed for all the above cases
                 cout<<"\n31 days in the month";
                 break;
        case 2:  cout<<"\n28 or 29 days in the month";
                 break;
```

```
        case 4:
        case 6:
        case 9:
        case 11: //this statement will be executed for all the above cases
                 cout<<"\n30 days in the month";
                 break;
        default: cout<<"\nWrong choice\n";
                 break;
    } //switch statement ends here
    getch( ); //freeze the monitor
}
```

Output

```
Enter the month number (1–12): 5
31 days in the month
Enter the month number (1–12): 9
30 days in the month
Enter the month number (1–12): 15
Wrong choice
```

> ***Note:*** *Always have space between the keyword case and integral value being tested in a switch statement otherwise it can cause a logical error. For example, writing cases 1: instead of case 1: will create an unused label and it will not perform the required actions when the switch control expression has value of 1.*

7.4.6 break Statement (to be used in switch...case only)

The *break* keyword causes an exit from the switch body. Control goes to the first statement following the end of the switch statement. If the break statement is not used, the control passes down (or *"falls through"*) to the next case constant, and the remaining statements in the *switch* construct will also be executed. The *break* keyword is also used to escape from loops; as discussed later on in this chapter.

7.4.7 default Keyword

The *default* keyword (if present) in the switch construct gives a way to take action if the value of the switch expression does not match with any of the case constants. The *default* statement is optional and, if it is not written, no action takes place if all matches with case constants fail. No *break* is necessary after *default,* since it is generally written at the end of *switch* statement.

Example 4. *Draw a flow chart for simulating a simple calculator (that is, performs +, –, * and /). Write a C++ program to implement the simulation.*

Solution.

Flow Chart for Simulating a Simple Calculator is given below:

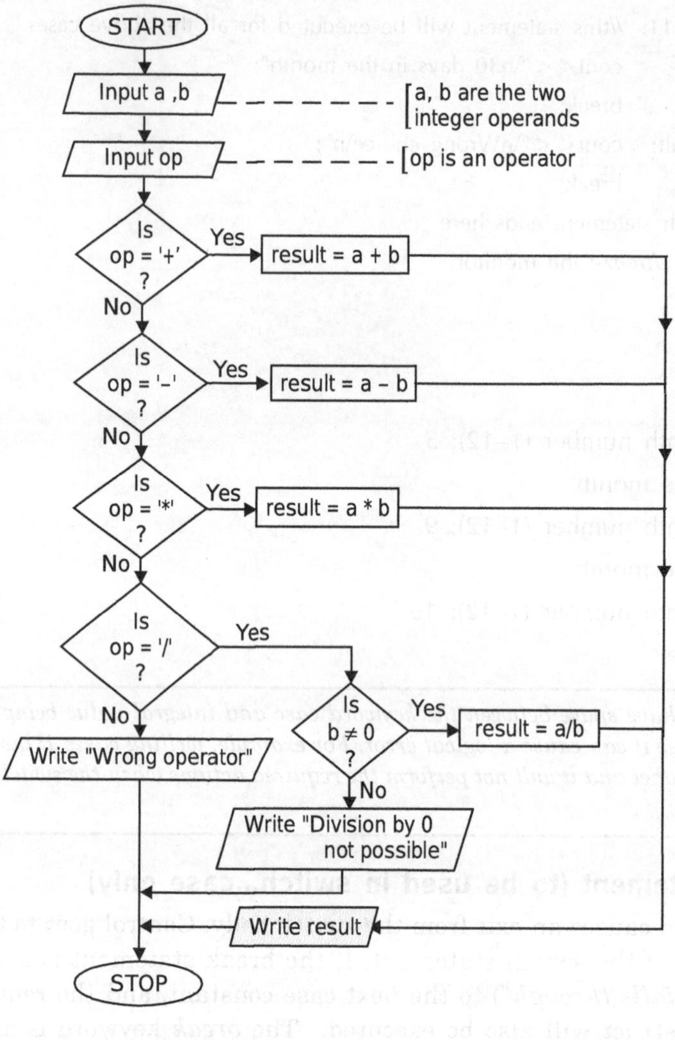

Fig. 7.9. Flow chart for simulating a simple calculator

The program for Simulating a Simple Calculator is given below:

```
//Simulation of a simple calculator
#include<iostream.h>
#include<conio.h>
void main( )
{
    int a,b;
    char op;
    clrscr( );
    cout<<"Enter the two operands: ";
```

```
    cin>>a>>b;
    cout<<"\nEnter the operator (+,–,*,/): ";
    cin>>op;
    switch(op)
    {
        case '+' :  cout<<endl<<a<<'+'<<b<<" = "<<a+b;
                    break;
        case '–' :  cout<<endl<<a<<'–'<<b<<" = "<<a–b;
                    break;
        case '*' :  cout<<endl<<a<<'*'<<b<<" = "<<a*b;
                    break;
        case '/' :  if(b)
                        cout<<endl<<a<<'/'<<b<<" = "<<a/b;
                    else
                        cout<<"\nDivision by zero not possible";
                    break;
        default  :  cout<<"\nWrong Choice\n";
                    break;
    }
    getch( ); //freeze the monitor
}
```

Output

```
Enter the two operands: 50 2
Enter the operator (+, –, *, /): /
50/2 = 25
Enter the two operands: 40 60
Enter the operator (+, –, *, /): *
40*60 = 2400
Enter the two operands: 25 0
Enter the operator (+, –, *, /): /
Division by zero not possible
```

> ***Note:*** *The optimization of code, in switch statements, can be done by writing the most common cases in the body of switch at its beginning. This avoids unnecessary comparisons and in turn saves a lot of CPU time.*

7.4.8 Nested switch...case

A switch...case statement embedded within another switch statement(s) is known as a nested switch...case. The syntax of nested switch...case in C++ is shown as:

```
switch(control expression)
{
    case constant1:
                    switch(control expression)
                    {
                        case constant1:
                                         statement(s);
                                         break;
                        case constant2:
                                         statement(s);
                                         break;
                                .
                                .
                                .
                        case constantn:
                                         statement(s);
                                         break;
                        default:
                                         statement(s);
                                         break;
                    }
                    break;
    case constant2: statement(s);
                    break;
            .
            .
            .
    case constantn:
                    statement(s);
                    break;
    default:
                    statement(s);
                    break;
}
```

> ***Note:** In case of nested **switch...case** statements the **case** constants of the outer and the inner **switch...case** can have same values.*

Following program illustrates the above concept:

Program 7.6

```
//Illustration of nested switch...case
#include<iostream.h>
#include<conio.h>
```

```
#define PI 3.14159
void main( )
{
   int choice,option
   float radius,side,length,breadth,area,perimeter;
   clrscr( );
   cout<<"Enter: 1 for Circle, 2 for Square, 3 for Rectangle"<<endl;
   cout<<endl;
   cout<<"Enter your choice (1 or 2 or 3): ";
   cin>>choice;
   cout<<endl;
   switch(choice)
   {
      case 1   :  cout<<"Enter the radius: ";
                  cin>>radius;
                  cout<<endl;
                  cout<<"Enter: 1 for area, 2 for perimeter"<<endl;
                  cout<<endl;
                  cout<<"Enter your choice (1 or 2): ";
                  cin>>option;
                  switch(option)
                  {
                     case 1:
                              area=PI*radius*radius;
                              cout<<"\nArea = "<<area<<" sq. units\n";
                              break;
                     case 2:
                              perimeter=2*PI*radius;
                              cout<<"\nPerimeter = "<<perimeter<<" units\n";
                              break;
                     default:
                              cout<<"\nWrong choice\n";
                              break;
                  }
                  break;
      case 2   :  cout<<"Enter the side: ";
                  cin>>side;
                  cout<<endl;
                  cout<<"Enter: 1 for area, 2 for perimeter"<<endl;
                  cout<<endl;
                  cout<<"Enter your choice (1 or 2): ";
                  cin>>option;
```

```
            switch(option)
            {
              case 1:
                        area=side*side;
                        cout<<"\nArea = "<<area<<" sq. units\n";
                        break;
              case 2:
                        perimeter=4*side;
                        cout<<"\nPerimeter = "<<perimeter<<" units\n";
                        break;
              default:
                        cout<<"\nWrong choice\n";
                        break;
            }
            break;
    case 3  : cout<<"Enter the length and breadth: ";
            cin>>length>>breadth;
            cout<<endl;
            cout<<"Enter: 1 for area, 2 for perimeter"<<endl;
            cout<<endl;
            cout<<"Enter your choice (1 or 2): ";
            cin>>option;
            switch(option)
            {
              case 1:
                        area=length*breadth;
                        cout<<"\nArea = "<<area<<" sq. units\n";
                        break;
              case 2:
                        perimeter=2*(length+breadth);
                        cout<<"\nPerimeter = "<<perimeter<<" units\n";
                        break;
              default:
                        cout<<"\nWrong choice\n";
                        break;
            }
            break;
  default:
            cout<<"\nWrong choice\n";
            break;
  }
  getch( ); //freeze the monitor
}
```

Output

```
Enter: 1 for Circle, 2 for Square, 3 for Rectangle
Enter your choice (1 or 2 or 3): 1
Enter the radius:10.0
Enter: 1 for area, 2 for perimeter
Enter your choice (1 or 2): 1
Area = 314.158997 sq. units
Enter: 1 for Circle, 2 for Square, 3 for Rectangle
Enter your choice (1 or 2 or 3): 2
Enter the side: 9
Enter: 1 for area, 2 for perimeter
Enter your choice (1 or 2): 2
Perimeter = 36 units
Enter: 1 for Circle, 2 for Square, 3 for Rectangle
Enter your choice (1 or 2 or 3): 3
Enter the length and breadth: 8 6
Enter: 1 for area, 2 for perimeter
Enter your choice (1 or 2): 1
Area = 48 sq. units
Enter: 1 for Circle, 2 for Square, 3 for Rectangle
Enter your choice (1 or 2 or 3): 5
Wrong choice
```

7.5 Loops or Repetitions or Iterations

C++ provides three statements which allow a set of instructions to be executed repeatedly until a certain condition is reached. This condition may be predefined (as in the **for** loop), or open-ended (as in the **while** and **do-while** loops). *Always remember that a true condition is any non-zero value and a false condition is zero value.* The three kinds of loops in C++ are **while, do-while** and **for.**

7.5.1 while Loop

The *while* loop is an *entry-controlled* loop. The syntax of the while statement is as follows:

```
while(condition)    // no semicolon here
{
    body of loop
}  // no semicolon here
```

The *condition* may be any expression, and true is any non-zero value. The body of loop may have a simple, a compound statement or an empty statement.

It can be shown with the help of the flow chart given in Figure 7.10:

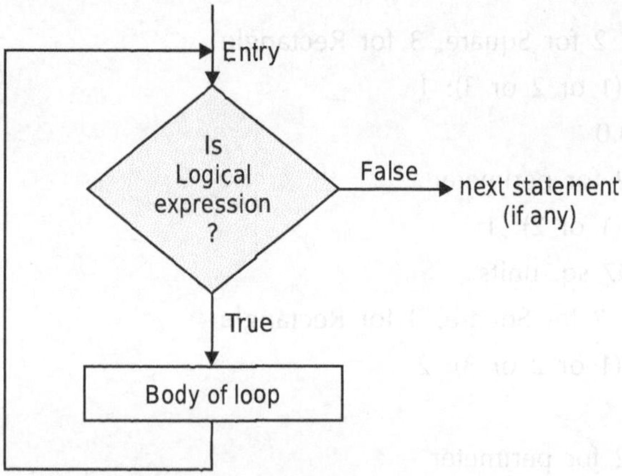

Fig. 7.10. Working of while loop

The following points should be remembered while using the **while** loop:

(i) *It may not be executed even once if the condition is false initially.*

(ii) *It is executed till the condition remains true (or non-zero if the condition evaluates to a number) and the control comes out of the loop when the condition becomes false (or zero if the condition evaluates to a number).*

(iii) *There must be some loop terminating condition inside the body of the loop to avoid infinite looping.*

The loop control variable must be *initialized* before the loop begins as an uninitialized variable can be used in an expression. The loop body must update the loop variable inside it so that it may not be an *infinite* loop.

Sometimes the *while* loop can be an *empty loop i.e.,* it does not have any statement in its body except the null statement (only a ;). For example,

```
unsigned long delay=0;
while(++delay < 400000)  // time delay loop
        ;                // null statement
```

The above shown loop works as a *timedelay loop* which helps in pausing the program at run time for sometime. It can be quite useful in situations when you wish to flash an important message on the screen for reading, before it goes off. For example,

```
unsigned long delay=0;
while(++delay < 400000) // time delay loop
   cout<<"Wait a while, processing going on\n";
```

Let us take an example for finding the area of circle. The program should terminate when 0 (zero) as radius is entered. The following program illustrates the use of the while construct:

Program 7.7

```
//Calculate the area of the circle until radius entered is zero
#include<iostream.h>
#include<conio.h>
#include<math.h> //for pow( ) function
#define PI 3.14159
void main( )
{
    float radius,area;
    clrscr( );
    cout<<"Enter the radius(to terminate enter 0): ";
    cin>>radius;
    while(radius)          //the radius is non-zero
    {
        if(radius>0.0)
        {
            area=PI*pow(radius, 2);
            cout<<"\nArea is: "<<area<<" sq.units\n";
        }
        else
            cout<<"\nArea is not possible\n";
        getch( );          //freeze the monitor
        clrscr( );
        cout<<"Enter the radius(to terminate enter 0): ";
        cin>>radius;   //update the loop control variable inside loop
    }
}
```

Output

```
Enter the radius (to terminate enter 0): 5
Area is: 78.539749 sq. units
Enter the radius (to terminate enter 0): 0
```

Example 5. *Draw a flow chart and also write a C++ program to print first n natural numbers and their sum (use while loop).*

Solution. The flow chart for printing the first *n* natural numbers and their sum is given in Figure 7.11.

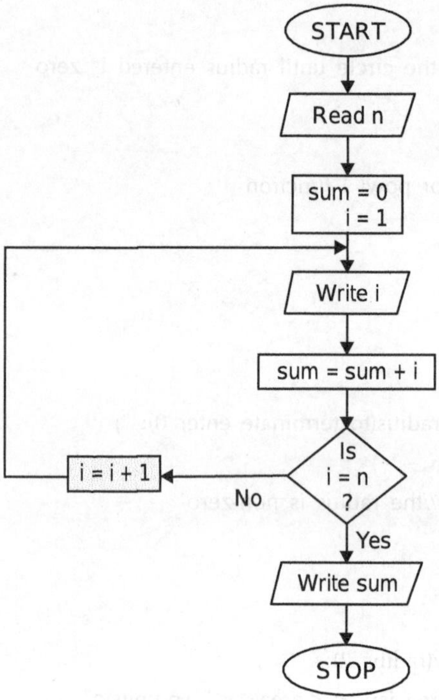

Fig. 7.11. Flow chart to print n natural numbers and their sum

The program for printing the first *n* natural numbers and their sum is given below:

```
//Print first n natural numbers and their sum using while loop
#include<iostream.h>
#include<conio.h>
void main( )
{
    int n,i=1,sum=0;
    clrscr( );
    cout<<"Enter the value of n: ";
    cin>>n;
    cout<<"\nFirst "<<n<<" natural numbers are: \n\n";
    while(i<=n)
    {
        cout<<i<<' ';
        sum += i;
        i++;
    }
    cout<<"\n\nSum = "<<sum;
}
```

Output

```
Enter the value of n: 10
First 10 natural numbers are:
1 2 3 4 5 6 7 8 9 10
Sum = 55
```

Example 6. *In the following program:*

(i) How many times will the while loop run?

(ii) What will be the last value of A displayed out?

```
#include<iostream.h>
void main( )
{
    int A=10;
    while(++A<15)
    {
        cout<<A++;
    }
}
```

Solution. (*i*) The while loop will run two times.

(*ii*) The last value of A displayed will be 13.

7.5.2 do-while Loop

It is an **exit-controlled** loop, that is, the condition is tested at the bottom of the loop after execution of loop statement(s). This means that a **do-while** loop always executes at least once.

The syntax of the do-while statement is as follows:

```
do                          // no semicolon here
{
    body of loop
} while(condition);         // semicolon here
```

The braces are not required when there is only single statement in the loop, they are usually used to avoid confusion (to you, not the compiler) with the *while*.

Perhaps the most common use of the do-while loop is in a menu selection function, when the menu is shown at least once. Then depending on the user's choice the menu will be repeated or terminated.

The **do-while** loop can be shown using the flow chart given in Figure 7.12:

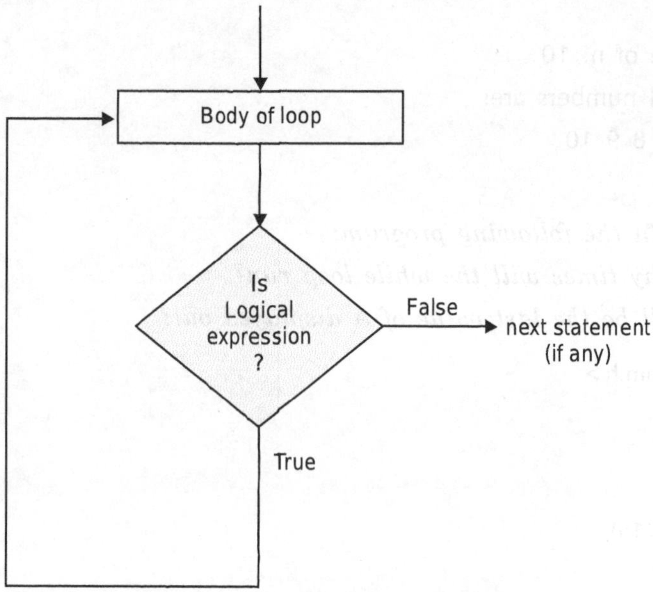

Fig. 7.12. Working of do-while loop

The following points should be remembered while using the **do-while** loop:

(i) *It is executed at least once.*

(ii) *It is executed till the condition remains true (or non-zero if the condition evaluates to a number) and the control comes out of the loop when the condition becomes false (or zero if the condition evaluates to a number).*

(iii) *There must be some loop terminating condition inside the body of the loop to avoid infinite looping.*

Let us take an example for checking a number for an armstrong number. A number is called armstrong if it equals the sum of cubes of its digits.

For example; 1, 153, 370, 371, 407 etc.

Here 153 = $1^3 + 5^3 + 3^3$ and similarly others.

The following program illustrates the use of the **do-while** loop:

Program 7.8

```
//Check a number for Armstrong
//Illustrating use of do-while loop
#include<iostream.h>
#include<conio.h>
void main( )
{
    int num,n,sum,r;
```

```
    clrscr( );
    cout<<"Enter the number"<<endl;
    cin>>num;
    n=num;
    sum=0;
    do
    {
        r=n%10;             //obtain the remainder
        sum += (r*r*r);
        n /=10;
    }while(n);
    cout<<endl;
    if(sum==num)
        cout<<num<<" is an armstrong number";
    else
        cout<<num<<" is not an armstrong number";
    getch( );  //freeze the monitor
}
```

Output

```
Enter the number
153
153 is an armstrong number
Enter the number
55
55 is not an armstrong number
```

In the above program first of all the number is read in variable **num** and then assigned to a dummy variable **n.** The do-while loop adds the sum of cubes of the individual digits of the value in **n.** The loop terminates when **n** becomes 0. The value of **sum** is compared with the value of **num,** if these are equal the number **num** is an armstrong number otherwise not an armstrong number.

The following program prints the first **n** natural numbers and their sum using a **do-while** loop:

Program 7.9

```
//Print first n natural numbers and their sum using do-while loop
#include<iostream.h>
#include<conio.h>
void main( )
```

```
{
    int n,i=1,sum=0;
    clrscr( );
    cout<<"Enter the value of n: ";
    cin>>n;
    cout<<"\nFirst "<<n<<" natural numbers are:\n\n";
    do
    {
        cout<<i<<' ';
        sum +=i;
        i++;
    }while(i<=n);
    cout<<"\n\nSum = "<<sum;
    getch( ); //freeze the monitor
}
```

Output

```
Enter the value of n: 10
First 10 natural numbers are:
1 2 3 4 5 6 7 8 9 10
Sum= 55
```

7.5.3 for Loop

The while and do...while loops are generally used when the number of iterations (that is, the number of times the body of the loop is executed) is not known. *The for loop is usually (although not always) used when number of iterations is known in advance.* The *for* loop is (for many people, anyway) the easiest to understand of the C++ loops.

The syntax of the for loop is as follows:

```
for(initialization; test expression; re-initialization) // no semicolon
{
    body of the loop
} // no semicolon here
```

It can be shown with the help of the flow chart given in Figure 7.13:

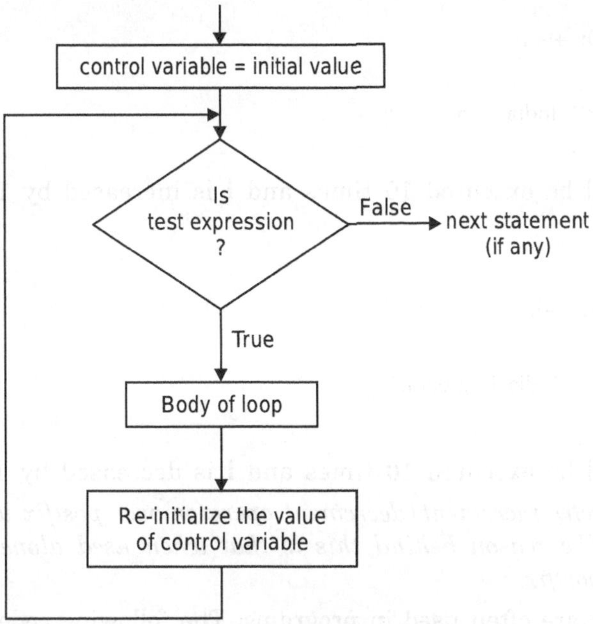

Fig. 7.13. Working of for loop

Initialization Expression. It is executed only once when the loop first starts. It provides the loop variable (control variable) an initial value.

Test Expression. It involves relational operators. It is executed every time through the loop before the body of the loop is executed. If the test expression is true, the body of the loop is executed, and if false, the control comes out of the loop.

Increment/Decrement (re-initialization) Expression. It is always executed at the end of the loop, after the body of the loop.

In a **for** loop, initialization expression, test expression and re-initialization expression are optional *i.e.,* you can skip any or all of these expressions.

For example, the following **for** loop is an infinite loop in C++:

```
for(; ;)
    cout<<"Infinite for loop\n";
```

The body of a **for** loop enclosed by braces is not executed at all if a semicolon is there after the **for** statement. For example,

```
int i;
for(i=1; i<=10; ++i);        //notice the semicolon here
{
    cout<<i<<" India is great\n";
}
```

In the above statement the body of **for** loop is not executed for the value of i from 1 to 10 due to the presence of semicolon mentioned above.

But if we write the above statement as:

```
int i;
for(i=1; i<=10; ++i)
{
    cout<<i<<" India is great\n";
}
```

then the for loop will be executed 10 times and **i** is increased by 1 every time.

When we write:

```
int i;
for(i=10; i>=1; --i)
{
    cout<<i<<" India is great\n";
}
```

then the for loop will be executed 10 times and **i** is decreased by 1 every time.

Always prefer prefix increment/decrement operator over postfix when to be used alone (e.g., ++ i or -- i). The reason behind this is that when used alone, prefix operators are executed faster than postfix.

Time delay loops are often used in programs. The following code shows how to create one by using **for** loop:

```
for (int t = 0; t < SOME_VALUE; t ++);
```

> ***Note:*** *The re-initialization expression can be both increment or decrement expression not only 1 but some other value also.*

The following program finds the factorial of a number and illustrates the working of a **for** loop:

Program 7.10

```
//Factorial of a number
#include<<iostream.h>
#include<conio.h>
void main( )
{
    int num;
    long factorial=1;
    clrscr( );
    cout<<"Enter the number: ";
    cin>>num;
    if(num<0)
        cout<<"\n"<<num<<" factorial not defined";
    else
    {
```

```
        for (int i=1; i<=num; ++i)
            factorial *=i;
        cout<<"\nFactorial of "<<num<<" is "<<factorial;
    }
    getch( ); //freeze the monitor
}
```

Output

```
Enter the number: 8
Factorial of 8 is 40320
Enter the number: - 4
- 4 factorial not defined
```

The following program prints first **n** natural numbers and their sum using a **for** loop:

Program 7.11

```
//Print first n natural numbers and their sum using for loop
#include<iostream.h>
#include<conio.h>
void main( )
{
    int n,sum=0,i;
    clrscr( );
    cout<<"Enter the value of n: ";
    cin>>n;
    cout<<"\nFirst "<<n<<" natural numbers are: \n\n";
    for(i=1; i<=n; ++i)
    {
        cout<<i<<' ';
        sum+=i;
    }
    cout<<"\n\nSum = "<<sum;
}
```

Output

```
Enter the value of n: 10
First 10 natural numbers are:
1 2 3 4 5 6 7 8 9 10
Sum = 55
```

In C++, one important aspect of a block is that *a variable defined inside the block is not visible outside it.* One advantage of restricting the visibility of variables is that the same variable name can be used within different blocks in the same program.

> ***Note:** An item declared in a loop, cannot be accessed after the loop is over. But it would be implemented in newer compilers based on ANSI/ISO specifications.*

You can have more than one expression in the initialization part of the **for** statement, separating the different expressions by commas. You can also have more than one re-initialization expression, although you can have only one test expression. For example,

```
int i,j,k;
----------
----------
for(i=0,j=20; i<10; ++i,--k)
{
    // body of loop
}
```

This example has a normal loop variable **i**, but it also initializes another variable **j**, and re-initializes a third variable, **k**. The variables **j** and **k** do not need to have anything to do with each other, or with **i**. Multiple initialization expressions and multiple re-initialization expressions are separated by commas.

You should avoid using such multiple expressions. While this approach can make the code more concise, it also tends to decrease its readability. It is always possible to use stand-alone statements to get the same effect.

7.5.4 Nested Loops

Nesting of loops means one or more loop(s) within a loop. But remember that in a nested loop, the inner loop must terminate before the outer loop. For example,

```
int i,num,sum;
for(i=1; i<=5; ++i)        // outer loop
{
    cout<<'1';
    sum=1;
    for(num=2; num<=i; ++num) // inner loop
    {
        cout<<'+'<<num;
        sum +=num;
    }
    cout<<"="<<sum<<endl;
}
```

Here the inner *for* loop is executed for value of i > = 2. The inner loop is executed once for i = 2 according to condition num = i (*i.e.,* 2 < = 2 means once), twice for i = 3, thrice for i = 4 and four times for i = 5.

An important thing to remember while working with nested loops is that the value of outer loop control variable will change only after the inner loop has been completely executed.

Try to find the output of the above program segment.

Now let us write a program to generate the pattern of **n** lines given below using nested loops:

```
      A
     ABC
    ABCDE
   ABCDEFG
      :
   n lines
```

The following program illustrates the use of nested loops to generate the above shown pattern of characters:

Program 7.12

```
//Print design
#include<iostream.h>
#include<conio.h>
void main( )
{
    int n,i,j,space;
    char ch;
    clrscr( );
    cout<<"Enter the value of n <=13\n\n";
    cin>>n;
    cout<<"\nDesired Pattern is\n\n";
    for(i=1;i<=n;++i)
    {
        for(space=1;space<=n-i;++space)
            cout<<' ';
        ch='A';
        for(j=1;j<=2*i-1;++j)
        {
            cout<<ch;
            ch++;
        }
        cout<<endl;
    }
    getch( ); //freeze the monitor
}
```

Output

```
Enter the value of n <= 13
9
Desired Pattern is
                A
               ABC
              ABCDE
             ABCDEFG
            ABCDEFGHI
           ABCDEFGHIJK
          ABCDEFGHIJKLM
         ABCDEFGHIJKLMNO
        ABCDEFGHIJKLMNOPQ
```

7.5.5 Comparison of Loops

The criteria of selecting a loop in C++ are somewhat arbitrary. Which loop type to use is more a matter of style than of hard-and-fast rules. You can actually make any of the loop types work in almost any situation. You should select the type that makes your program clearest and easiest to follow. Table 7.1 compares the loops in C++.

Table 7.1. Comparison of the loop control structures in C++

S.No.	*for loop*	*while loop*	*do-while loop*

1.	A **for** loop is used to execute and repeat a statement block depending on a condition which is evaluated at the beginning of the loop.
	Example:
	int i;
	for(i=1; i<=5; ++i)
	{
	sum = sum + i;
	}
		A **while** loop is used to execute and repeat a statement block depending on a condition which is evaluated at the beginning of the loop.
		Example:
		int i = 1;
		while(i <= 5)
		{
		sum = sum + i;
		++i;
		}
			A **do-while** loop is used to execute and repeat a statement block depending on a condition which is evaluated at the end of the loop.
			Example:
			int i = 1;
			do
			{
			sum = sum + i;
			++i;
			} while(i <= 5);

2.	A variable value is initialized at the *beginning* of the loop and is used in the condition.	A variable value is initialized at the *beginning* or *before* the loop and is used in the condition.	A variable value is initialized *before* the loop or *assigned inside* the loop and is used in the condition.
3.	A statement to change the value of the condition or to increment the value of the variable is given at the *beginning* of the loop.	A statement to change the value of the condition or to increment the value of the variable is given *inside* the loop.	A statement to change the value of the condition or to increment the value of the variable is given *inside* the loop.

4.	The statement block will not be executed when the value of the condition is **false.**	The statement block will not be executed when the value of the condition is **false.**	The statement block will not be executed when the value of the condition is **false,** but the block is executed at least once irrespective of the value of the condition.
5.	A **for** loop is commonly used by many programmers.	A **while** loop is also widely used by many programmers.	A **do-while** loop is used in some cases where the condition need to be checked at the end of the loop.

7.6 Jump Statements

C++ has four statements that perform an unconditional branch: **return, goto, break,** and **continue.** The *return* and *goto* statements can be used anywhere in a program. The *break* and *continue* statements can be used in conjuction with any of the loop statements. As mentioned earlier, you can also use *break* with *switch* statement. Just as you can break out of a loop, you can break out of a program by using the standard library function **exit( ).** Let us discuss the jump statements: **break, continue** and **goto** alongwith the library function **exit( ).**

7.6.1 break Statement

It transfers control out of a loop, bypassing the normal loop condition test. So it is a **jump** statement. We have already used the break statement for separating case labels in switch statements. When a *break* is encountered inside a loop, the loop is terminated and the control passes to the statement following the body of the loop. If a *break* statement appears in a nested-loop structure, then it causes an exit from only that loop in which it appears.

It can be shown with the help of the flow chart given in Figure 7.14:

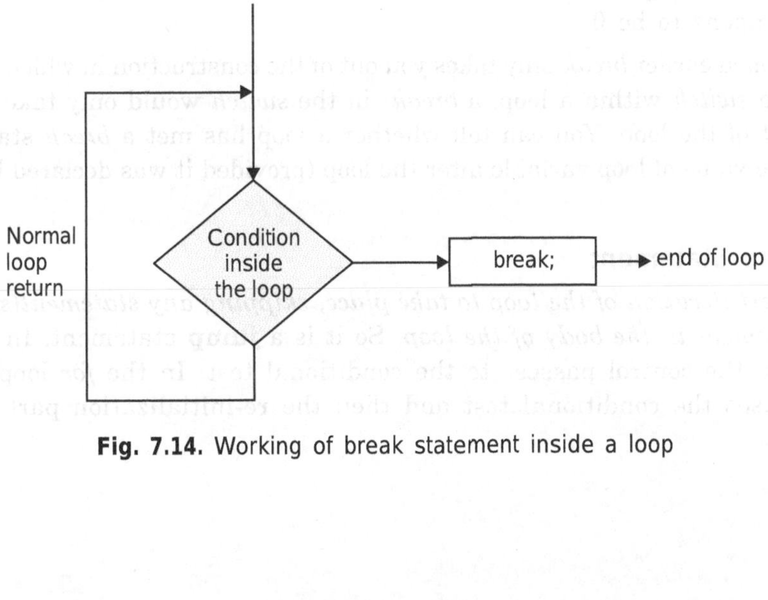

Fig. 7.14. Working of break statement inside a loop

For example, the following program illustrates the use of **break** statement:

Program 7.13

```
//illustration of break statement
#include<iostream.h>
#include<conio.h>
void main( )
{
    int num1,num2;
    do
    {
    clrscr( );
    cout<<"Enter two integers\n";
    cin>>num1>>num2;
    if(num2==0)
        break;
    else
        cout<<"\nWe can divide "<<num1<<" by "<<num2<<endl;
    cout<<"\nPress any key to continue......\n";
    getch( ); //freeze the monitor
    }while (num2);
}
```

In Program 7.13, if the user enters the second number as 0 then, as division by 0 will hang the system, the break statement causes immediate termination of the loop. We are not actually performing division here but if we do so then break can rescue us, in case the divisor happens to be 0.

As mentioned earlier *break* only takes you out of the construction in which it is embedded. If there were a *switch* within a loop, a *break* in the *switch* would only take you out of the *switch,* not out of the loop. You can tell whether a loop has met a *break* statement simply by checking the value of loop variable after the loop (provided it was declared before entering it).

7.6.2 continue Statement

It forces the next iteration of the loop to take place, skipping any statement(s) following the ***continue*** *statement in the body of the loop.* So it is a **jump** statement. In the *while* and *do-while* loops, the control passes to the conditional test. In the *for* loop, the *continue* statement causes the conditional test and then the re-initialization part of the loop is executed.

The flow chart in Figure 7.15 shows the operation of the continue statement:

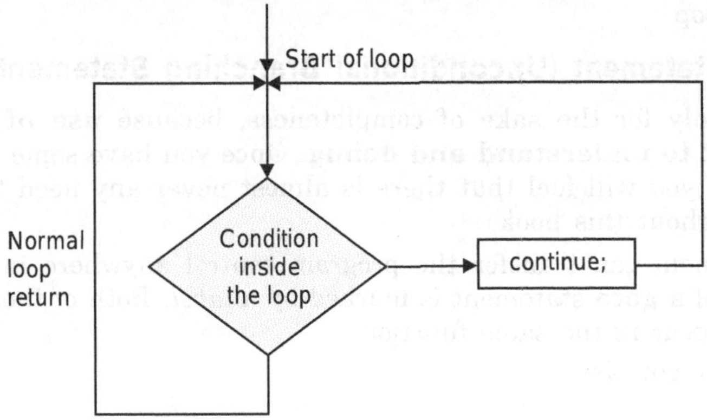

Fig. 7.15. Working of continue statement

For example, the following program illustrates the use of **continue** statement:

Program 7.14

```
//illustration of continue statement
#include<iostream.h>
#include<conio.h>
void main( )
{
    int i,j;
    clrscr( );
    for(i=1;i<=3;++i)
    {
        for(j=1;j<=3;++j)
        {
            if(i != j)
                continue;            // goto top of inner loop
            cout<<"\n"<<i<<" "<<j;
        }
    }
}
```

Output

```
1 1
2 2
3 3
```

In the above program when the value of **i** is not equal to that of **j**, the **continue** statement forces the output statement bypassed and the control passes to the conditional test of inner for loop.

7.6.3 The goto Statement (Unconditional Branching Statement)

It is given here only for the sake of completeness, because **use of a goto makes a program difficult to understand and debug.** Once you have some experience of writing C++ programs, you will feel that there is almost never any need to use goto, as you will observe throughout this book.

A **goto** statement can transfer the program control anywhere in the program. The target destination of a **goto** statement is marked by a *label.* Both of these (*i.e.,* target *label* and **goto**) must appear in the same function.

The syntax for goto is:

```
goto label;
```

The label is a valid C++ identifier followed by colon. You may have any statement after the label in the form:

```
label: statement;
```

For example,

```
int num;
for(num=1;num<=20;++num)
{
    if(num%2==0)
        goto target;
    cout<<num<<" ";
    target: ;           // control will begin here following goto
}
```

The above code fragment will print odd numbers in the range 1 to 20.

In C++, a label can not immediately precede a closing right brace. To handle this constraint, a null statement may be used that follows the label. For example,

```
----------
----------
{
    --------
    goto target;
    --------
    --------
    target: ; // null statement follows the label
}
```

A **goto** statement may not jump forward over a variable declaration. It is possible only when the variable is occuring in a block and you jump over the entire block. But the reverse of the above constraint works fine *i.e.,* you can make a backward jump over an initialized variable.

> ***Note:*** *If a label appears just before a closing brace, a null statement must follow the label.*

7.6.4 The exit( ) Function

Although **exit( )** is not a program control statement, a short discussion that discusses it is relevant here. *It is a run time library routine that causes a program to end, returning the control to the operating system.* Zero argument to exit() means that program ends normally. Non-zero arguments indicate abnormal termination.

For example, the following program uses **exit( )** to quit the program and return to the operating system.

Program 7.15

```
//Compute the square root of a number
#include<iostream.h>
#include<conio.h>
#include<math.h>        //for sqrt( )
#include<process.h>     //for exit( )
void main( )
{
    float num;
    clrscr( );
    cout<<"Enter the number\n";
    cin>>num;
    if(num>=0.0)
    {
        cout<<"\nSquare root of "<<num<<" is "<<sqrt(num);
        exit(0);        // return to operating system
    }
    cout<<"\nSquare root of a negative number cannot be found\n";
}
```

The above program finds the square root of positive numbers only and terminates normally when **exit(0)** is encountered. In case you enter negative number the message

"Square root of a negative number cannot be found"

is printed.

Solved Problems

Problem 1. *Give differences between the following:*

(i) while and do-while statement.

(ii) break and continue statement.

(iii) break and exit( ) function.

Solution. (*i*) The differences between while and do-while statement are given below:

S. No.	*while statement*	*do-while statement*
1.	The statement block in **while** statement is executed when the values of the condition is **true.**	The statement block is executed at least once irrespective of the value of the condition.
2.	The condition is evaluated at the beginning of the loop. The statement block is executed if the value of the condition is **true.**	The condition is evaluated at the end of the loop. The statement block is executed again if the value of the condition is **true.**

(*ii*) The differences between the **break** and **continue** statement are given below:

S. No.	*break statement*	*continue statement*
1.	A **break** statement is used to terminate the execution of a statement block. The next statement which follows this statement block will be executed. The keyword is **break;**	A **continue** statement is used to transfer the control to the beginning of a statement block. The keyword is **continue;**
2.	When a **break** statement is executed in a loop, the repetition of the loop will be terminated.	When a **continue** statement is executed in a loop, the execution is transferred to the beginning of the loop.

(*iii*) The differences between **break** and **exit( )** function are given below:

S. No.	*break statement*	*exit( ) statement*
1.	A **break** statement is used to terminate the execution of a statement block. The next statement which follows this statement block will be executed.	An **exit( )** function is used to terminate the execution of a C++ program permanently.
2.	It is used in a program as **break;**	It is built-in function and is used/called with necessary argument as **exit(0);**

Problem 2. *Write a C++ program to compute the simple interest.*
Solution.

```
//Compute the simple interest
#include<iostream.h>
#include<conio.h>
void main( )
{
    float principal,rate,time,interest;
    clrscr( );
    cout<<"Enter the principal: ";
    cin>>principal;
    cout<<"\nEnter the rate of interest: ";
```

```
    cin>>rate;
    cout<<"\nEnter the time in years: ";
    cin>>time;
    interest=(principal*rate*time)/100.0;
    cout<<"\n\nSimple Interest is: "<<interest;
}
```

Problem 3. *Write a C++ program to calculate the sum and average of five numbers.*
Solution.

```
//calculate the sum and average of five numbers
#include<iostream.h> //for 'cout' and 'cin'
#include<conio.h> //for clrscr( ) function
void main( )
{
    float a,b,c,d,e,sum,avg;
    clrscr( );
    cout<<"Enter the five numbers\n";
    cin>>a>>b>>c>>d>>e;
    sum=a+b+c+d+e;
    avg=sum/5.0;
    cout<<"\nSum=  "<<sum<<endl;
    cout<<"\nAverage=  "<<avg;
}
```

Problem 4. *Write a C++ program to swap (interchange) two numbers without using a third variable.*
Solution.

```
//Swapping of two numbers without using a temporary variable
#include<iostream.h>
#include<conio.h>
void main( )
{
    int a,b;
    clrscr( );
    cout<<"Enter the two numbers: ";
    cin>>a>>b;
    cout<<"\n\nInputted numbers are:\n";
    cout<<"A="<<a;
    cout<<"\nB="<<b;
    //swapping
    a=a+b;
    b=a-b;
    a=a-b;
    cout<<"\n\nNumbers after swapping are:\n";
    cout<<"A="<<a;
    cout<<"\nB="<<b;
    getch( ); //freeze the monitor
}
```

Problem 5. *Write a C++ program to find the smallest of three numbers.*

Solution.

```
//find smallest of three numbers
#include<iostream.h>
#include<conio.h>
void main( )
{
    int a,b,c;
    clrscr( );
    cout<<"Enter the three numbers\n";
    cin>>a>>b>>c;
    if(a<b)
    {
        if(a<c)
            cout<<"\nSmallest number is "<<a;
        else
            cout<<"\nSmallest number is "<<c;
    }
    else
    {
        if(b<c)
            cout<<"Smallest number is "<<b;
        else
            cout<<"Smallest number is "<<c;
    }
}
```

Problem 6. *Write a C++ program to print day of the week corresponding to the number (1–7) entered using* ***switch ... case*** *statement.*

Solution.

```
//Illustration of switch..case control structure
//Input a number from 1-7 and write corresponding day of week
#include<iostream.h>
#include<conio.h>
void main( )
{
    int day;
    clrscr( );
    cout<<"Enter the number of weekday (1-7)"<<endl<<endl;
    cin>>day;
    cout<<endl;
    switch(day)
    {
        case 1:  cout<<"Weekday is Sunday";
                 break;
```

```
        case 2:  cout<<"Weekday is Monday";
                 break;
        case 3:  cout<<"Weekday is Tuesday";
                 break;
        case 4:  cout<<"Weekday is Wednesday";
                 break;
        case 5:  cout<<"Weekday is Thursday";
                 break;
        case 6:  cout<<"Weekday is Friday";
                 break;
        case 7:  cout<<"Weekday is Saturday";
                 break;
        default:
                 cout<<"Wrong choice";
                 break;
    }
}
```

Problem 7. *Write a C++ program to find the area of a triangle and show its type.*
Solution.

```
//Find area of a triangle and its type
#include<iostream.h>
#include<conio.h>
#include<math.h> //for sqrt( ) function
void main( )
{
    float a,b,c,s,area;
    clrscr( );
    cout<<"Enter the three sides of the triangle\n";
    cin>>a>>b>>c;
    cout<<"\na= "<<a<<" b= "<<b<<" c= "<<c<<endl;
    if( ((a+b)>c) && ((b+c)>a) && ((c+a)>b) )
    {
        if((a==b) && (a==c))
            cout<<"\nEquilateral triangle\n";
        else
        {
            if((a==b) || (b==c) || (c==a))
                cout<<"\nIsosceles triangle\n";
            else
                cout<<"\nScalene triangle\n";
        }
        s=(a+b+c)/2.0;
        area=sqrt(s*(s-a)*(s-b)*(s-c));
        cout<<"\nArea= "<<area<<" sq.units";
    }
```

```
    else
        cout<<"\nTriangle not possible\n";
}
```

Problem 8. *Draw a flow chart and write a C++ program to generate first n fibonacci terms. The fibonacci terms are 0,1,1,2,3,5,8,13,.........*

Solution.

Flow Chart for Generating First n Fibonacci Terms

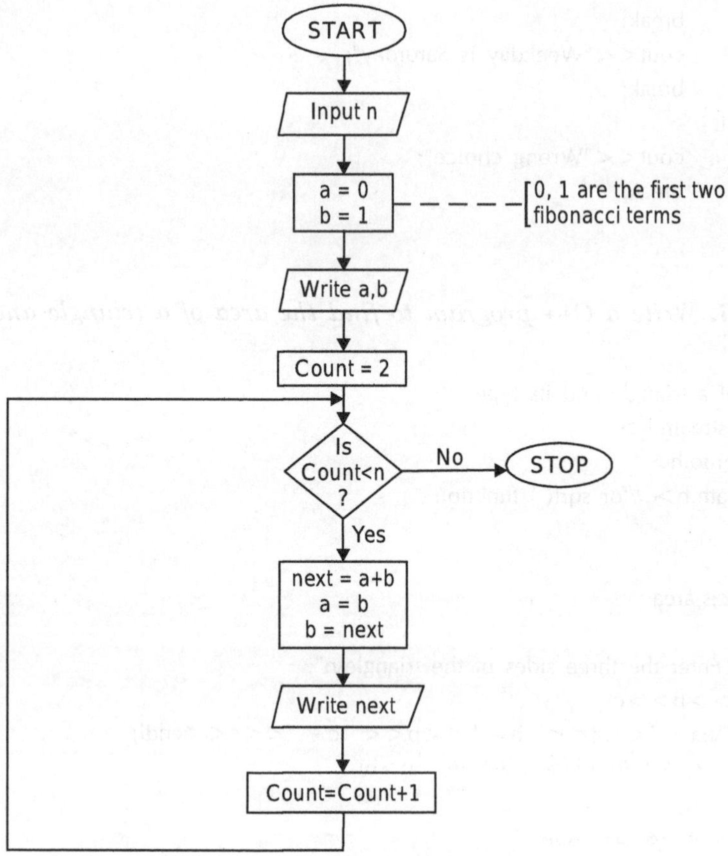

Fig. 7.16. Flow chart for generating first n Fibonacci terms

Following program generates first n fibonacci terms:

```
//Generate first n fibonacci terms
#include<iostream.h>
#include<conio.h>
void main( )
{
    int a,b,next,n,count;
    clrscr( );
    cout<<"How many fibonacci terms required >=2 and <= 24?\n";
```

```
    cin>>n;
    a=0;
    b=1;
    cout<<"\nFirst "<<n<<" fibonacci terms are:\n\n";
    cout<<a<<' '<<b;
    count=2;
    while(count<n)
    {
        next=a+b;
        cout<<' '<<next;
        count++;
        a=b;
        b=next;
    }
    getch( ); //freeze the screen until some key is pressed
}
```

Problem 9. *Write a for loop for the following sequences of statements without effecting the output.*

```
int Lvalue=9;
cout<<Lvalue<<endl;
Lvalue=Lvalue-3;
cout<<Lvalue+1<<endl<<Lvalue-1<<endl;
Lvalue=Lvalue-3;
cout<<Lvalue<<endl;
```

Solution. The output of the given sequence of statement is

9

7

5

3

So the for loop for these statements will be

```
for(int Lvalue = 9; Lvalue >= 3; Lvalue -= 2)
    cout<<Lvalue<<endl;
```

Problem 10. *What values will be assigned to the variables **ua, ub, uc** and **fail** after the execution of the following program segment:*

```
void main( )
{
    int i=0, ua=0, ub=0, uc=0, fail=0;
    while(i<=5)
    {
        switch(i++)
```

```
        {
            case 1:
            case 2:    ++ua;
            case 3:
            case 4:    ++ub;
            case 5:    ++uc;
            default:   ++fail;
        }
    }
    cout<<ua<<endl;
    cout<<ub<<endl;
    cout<<uc<<endl;
    cout<<fail<<endl;
}
```

Solution. The values assigned to ua, ub, uc and fail will be 2, 4, 5 and 6 respectively as given below:

Step No.	***Value of i***	***Match with constant***	***Executed statements***	***Value after the step is over***			
				ua	***ub***	***uc***	***fail***
1.	0	default	++ fail	0	0	0	1
2.	1	case 1	++ua, ++ub, ++uc, ++fail	1	1	1	2
3.	2	case 2	++ua, ++ub, ++uc, ++fail	2	2	2	3
4.	3	case 3	++ub, ++uc, ++fail	2	3	3	4
5.	4	case 4	++ub, ++uc, ++fail	2	4	4	5
6.	5	case 5	++uc, ++fail	**2**	**4**	**5**	**6**
7.	6	—	Loop terminates	—	—	—	—

Problem 11. *What will be the output of the following C++ program segment:*

```
for(int i=1;i<=5;++i)
{
    cout<<"\n";
    for(int j=1;j<=i;++j)
        cout<<"*";
}
```

Solution. The output will be

```
*
**
***
****
*****
```

Problem 12. *Write a C++ program to compute the LCM and GCD of two positive integers.*

Solution.

```
//Calculate LCM and GCD of two positive integers
#include<iostream.h>
#include<conio.h>
void main( )
{
    int num1,num2,m,n,rem,lcm,gcd,prod;
    do
    {
        clrscr( );
        cout<<"Enter the two positive integers: ";
        cin>>num1>>num2;
    }
    while(num1<=0 || num2<=0); //loop continues until correct values are entered
    m=num1;
    n=num2;
    prod=num1*num2;
    while(n)
    {
        if  (m%n==0)
            break;
        else
        {
            rem=m%n;
            m=n;
            n=rem;
        }
    }
    gcd=n;
    lcm=prod/gcd;
    cout<<"\nLCM of "<<num1<<" and "<<num2<<" is "<<lcm<<endl;
    cout<<"\nGCD of "<<num1<<" and "<<num2<<" is "<<gcd;
    getch( ); //freeze the monitor
}
```

Problem 13. *Write a C++ program to check a number for prime. A number p>1 is prime if it's only divisors are 1 and itself.*

Solution. A number p>1 is prime if it is **not divisible** by any number in the range 2 to integral part of it's square root.

```
//Check a number for prime
#include<iostream.h>
```

```
#include<conio.h>
#include<math.h> //for sqrt( ) function
void main( )
{
    int num,d,t;
    clrscr( );
    cout<<"Enter the number"<<endl;
    cin>>num;
    cout<<endl;
    if(num<2)
        cout<<num<<" is not prime";
    else
    {
        t=sqrt(num); //t stores the integral part of square root of num
        d=2;
        while(d<=t)
        {
            if(num%d==0)
                break;
            d++;
        }
        if(d>t)
            cout<<num<<" is prime";
        else
            cout<<num<<" is not prime";
    }
    getch( ); //freeze the monitor
}
```

Problem 14. *Write a C++ program to print the prime factors of a positive integer.*

Solution.

```
//Print the prime factors of a positive integer
#include<iostream.h>
#include<conio.h>
#include<math.h> //for sqrt( )
void main( )
{
    int num,mid,t,d;
    do
    {
        clrscr( );
        cout<<"Enter the positive integer: ";
```

```
    cin>>num;
  }
  while(num<=0); //loop continues until positive value is entered
  t=sqrt(num); //store square root of num in 't'
  d=2;
  while(d<=t)
  {
    if(num%d==0)
      break;
    d++;
  }
  if(d>t)
    cout<<'\n'<<num<<" is prime so no prime factors";
  else
  {
    cout<<"\nPrime factors of "<<num<<" are:\n\n";
    d=2; //take d as the divisor
    mid=num/2;
    while( (num != 1) && (d<=mid) )
    {
      while(num%d==0)
      {
        cout<<d<<' ';
        num /= d;
      }
      d++;
    }
  }
  getch( ); //freeze the monitor
}
```

Problem 15. *Write a C++ program to check a number for palindrome. A number is palindrome if it is equal to its reverse number.*

Solution.

```
//Check a number for palindrome
#include<iostream.h>
#include<conio.h>
void main( )
{
  unsigned long num,n,revnum=0;
  int r;
  clrscr( );
  cout<<"Enter the number\n\n";
```

```
        cin>>num;
        cout<<endl;
        n=num; //store num in a dummy variable n
        while(n)
        {
            r = n%10;
            revnum = revnum*10 + r;
            n /= 10;
        }
        if(revnum==num)
            cout<<num<<"is a palindrome";
        else
            cout<<num<<"is not a palindrome";
        getch( );   //freeze the monitor
}
```

Problem 16. *Write a C++ program to generate the pattern. For example, for n = 4 the pattern should be as given below:*

```
      4
    4 3 4
  4 3 2 3 4
4 3 2 1 2 3 4
  4 3 2 3 4
    4 3 4
      4
```

Solution.

```
//generate the desired pattern
#include<iostream.h>
#include<conio.h>
#include<iomanip.h> //for setw( )
void main( )
{
    int n,i,j;
    clrscr( );
    cout<<"Enter a number <=11 for generating the pattern\n";
    cin>>n;
    cout<<"Desired pattern is\n";
    for(i=1;i<=n;i++)
    {
        cout<<"\t";
        for(j=1;j<=n-i;j++)       //for blanks in upper portion
            cout<<"    ";
        for(j=n;j>=n+1-i;j--)  //for left half
```

```
            cout<<setw(3)<<j;
        for(j=n+2-i;j<=n;j++) //for right half
            cout<<setw(3)<<j;
        cout<<endl;
    }
    for(i=1;i<n;i++)
    {
        cout<<"\t";
        for(j=1;j<=i;j++)           //for blanks in lower portion
            cout<<"   ";
        for(j=n;j>=i+1;j--)         //for left half
            cout<<setw(3)<<j;
        for(j=i+2;j<=n;j++)         //for right half
            cout<<setw(3)<<j;
        cout<<endl;
    }
    getch( );
}
```

Problem 17. *Write a C++ program to generate the following pyramid:*

```
    *
   * *
  * * *
 * * * *
* * * * *
```

Solution.

```
//display the pattern of asterisk (*)

#include<iostream.h>
#include<conio.h>
void main( )
{
    int i,j;
    clrscr( ); //clears the screen
    cout<<"Desired pattern is\n\n";
    for(i=1;i<=5;i++)
    {
        //for blanks on left side
        for(j=1;j<=5-i;j++)
            cout<<' ';
        //for * of pyramid
        for(j=1;j<=i;j++)
            cout<<"* ";
        cout<<'\n';
    }
    getch( ); //freeze the monitor
}
```

REVIEW QUESTIONS AND EXERCISES

1. What is a compound statement? What is selection statement? Which selection statements does C++ provide?
2. What is a "Dangling else" problem? When does it arise? What is the default "Dangling else" matching and how it can be overridden?
3. Write a program to check whether the inputted character is an alphabet, digit or special character.
4. In a control structure switch-case, explain the purpose of using default.
5. In any C++ program, using switch statement, if all break statements are removed from all cases of switch statement, how does it affect the functionality of switch statement? Give example.
6. Write a program to print the multiplication table of a number.
7. Write a C++ program to print the largest of *n* numbers.
8. Write a program to find the area of a circle, rectangle or triangle depending upon the user's choice.
9. What are iteration statements? Explain the iteration statements provided by C++.
10. What is the difference between a while and a do...while loop?
11. What is the effect of continue in a loop?
12. Write a program to generate armstrong numbers upto a specific limit.

> ***Note.*** *A number is armstrong if it equals the sum of cubes of it's digits. For example,* $153 = 1^3 + 5^3 + 3^3$.

13. Write a program to generate prime numbers upto a specific limit.
14. Write a C++ program to compute cosine series, that is, $\cos(x) = 1 - \frac{x^2}{2!} + \frac{x^4}{4!} - \frac{x^6}{6!} + \ldots\ldots$ upto *n* terms accuracy.
15. Write a C++ program to generate fibonacci terms upto a specific limit.
16. Write a C++ program to check a given number for fibonacci term.
17. Write a program to generate the pattern given below:

```
1
1 2
1 2 3
1 2 3 4
1 2 3 4 5
```

18. Write a program to generate the pattern given below:

```
1 2 3 4 5
1 2 3 4
1 2 3
1 2
1
```

19. Write a C++ program to find the sum of geometric series:

$$a + ar + ar^2 + \dots\dots\dots + ar^{n-1}$$

20. Write a program to generate the following pattern:

```
1 = 1
1 + 2 = 3
1 + 2 + 3 = 6
1 + 2 + 3 + 4 = 10
.....................................
.....................................
1 + 2 + 3 + 4 + 5 + 6 + 7 + 8 + 9 + 10 = 55
```

21. Write a program in C++ to accept three digits (0–9) and print all possible combinations from these digits. (For example, if the three digits are 2, 3 and 5 then all possible combinations are 235, 253, 325, 352, 523 and 532).

22. Write a program to count the number of occurrences of positive numbers, negative numbers and zeros in a stream of data terminated by some specific value.

23. Write a program to determine all Pythagorean triplets in the range 100 to 1000. (A Pythagorean triplet is a set of three integers i, j, k, such that $i^2 + j^2 = k^2$).

24. Write a C++ program to print the sum of first n even natural numbers.

25. Write a C++ program to generate the following pyramid of digits:

```
                  1
                2 3 2
              3 4 5 4 3
            4 5 6 7 6 5 4
          5 6 7 8 9 8 7 6 5
        6 7 8 9 0 1 0 9 8 7 6
      7 8 9 0 1 2 3 2 1 0 9 8 7
    8 9 0 1 2 3 4 5 4 3 2 1 0 9 8
  9 0 1 2 3 4 5 6 7 6 5 4 3 2 1 0 9
0 1 2 3 4 5 6 7 8 9 8 7 6 5 4 3 2 1 0
```

> ***Note:*** *Use nested loops for the pyramid generation.*

26. Write a program to sum the series $x + x^2 + x^3 + x^4 + x^5 + \dots\dots + x^n$.

27. Write an infinite loop in C++ language, which does not use any variable or constant.

28. Write a C++ program to print a number in reverse order, *e.g.,* 435 should be printed as 534.

29. Write a C++ program using loops and switch statement to print word equivalent of a number of 1-3 digits, *e.g.,* 365 should be printed as—three hundred sixty five.

30. Use of goto statement should be avoided in a C++ program. Why?

31. Write a C++ program to check a number for perfect number.

> ***Note:*** *A number is perfect if it equals the sum of it's proper divisors, i.e., the divisors excluding the number itself. For e.g., 28 = 1 + 2 + 4 + 7 + 14.*

32. Write a C++ program to generate pyramid of digits for $n \leq 9$ as shown below (for n = 9):

```
                1
              1 2 1
            1 2 3 2 1
          1 2 3 4 3 2 1
        1 2 3 4 5 4 3 2 1
      1 2 3 4 5 6 5 4 3 2 1
    1 2 3 4 5 6 7 6 5 4 3 2 1
  1 2 3 4 5 6 7 8 7 6 5 4 3 2 1
1 2 3 4 5 6 7 8 9 8 7 6 5 4 3 2 1
```

33.
```
for(i=1; i<=10; i=i+1)
        cout<<i<<" ";
```

In the above for loop, if i = i+1 is changed to

(*i*) i++

(*ii*) ++i

What will be the output of this loop? Justify your answer.

(*iii*) If a semicolon is put after for loop *i.e.*,

```
for(i=1; i<=10; i=i+1);
    cout<<i<<"  ";
```

What will be the output? Justify your answer.

34. Find syntax errors in following program and write equivalent corrected code:

```
include<iostream.h>
main( )
{
   int x; y=10;
   20=x;
   int z;
   z=x+y
   cout>>'The sum='<<z;
}
```

35. Write a C++ program to generate the following pattern:

```
* * * * * * * * * *
* * * *     * * * *
* * *         * * *
* *             * *
*                 *
```

36. Write a C++ program to get the following output using nested loops. Here number of iterations are important.

```
z y x w v w x y z
  z y x w x y z
    z y x y z
      z y z
        z
```

❑❑❑

• Suggested Readings •

1. Mastering C++ Programs *by J.B. Dixit*

— **Published by Firewal Media (An Imprint of Laxmi Publications Pvt. Ltd.)**

2. Object Oriented Programming Using C++ *by J.B. Dixit*

— **Published by University Science Press (An Imprint of Laxmi Publications Pvt. Ltd.)**

CHAPTER 8

Functions

8.1 Introduction

A **function** *groups a number of program statements into a single unit and gives it a name.* This unit can be called (invoked) from other parts of the program. Functions are the building blocks of C++ programs where all the program activity occurs.

All C++ compilers come with a standard library functions that perform most commonly needed tasks. Turbo C++ has a set of functions. More about library functions later on.

Let us learn to code functions as per our need *i.e.,* User Defined Functions Figure 8.1 shows an outline of using the user defined functions.

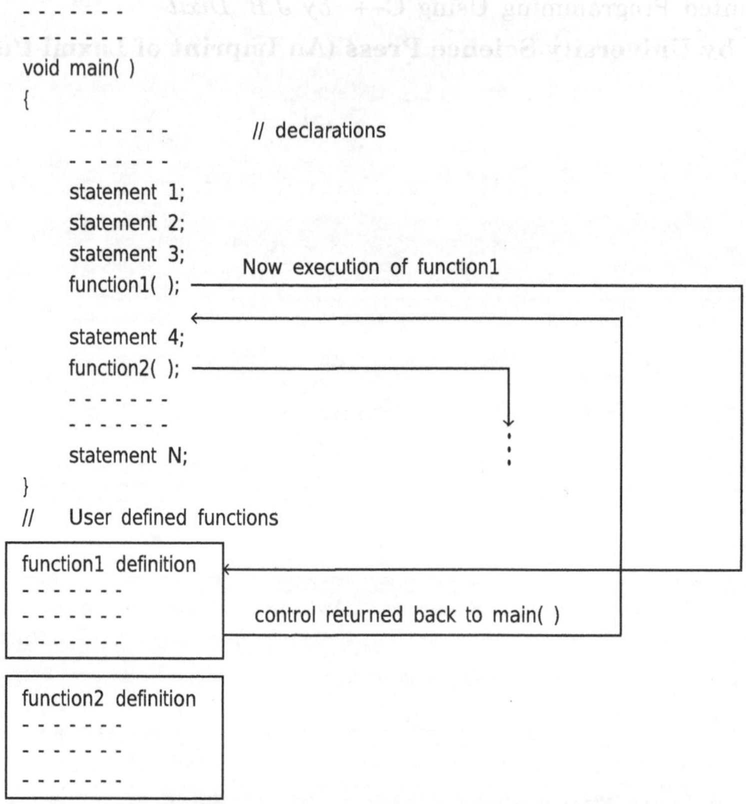

Fig. 8.1. Illustration of user defined functions.

Need for a Function

Monolithic program (a large single list of instructions) becomes difficult to understand. For this reason functions are used. *A function has a clearly defined objective (purpose) and a clearly defined interface with other functions in the program. A function is also called a subprogram and it is easy to understand, debug and test. It avoids ambiguity. A group of functions together is called a module.*

Reduction in program size is another reason for using functions. Any sequence of statements that is repeated in a program can be combined together to form a function. The function code is stored in only one place in memory, even though it may be executed as many times as a user needs thus saving both time and space.

We can use a function (already tested) in many programs and thus only the additional coding is required.

8.1.1 Advantages of Using Functions in C++

Some advantages of using functions in C++ are listed below:

(*i*) *A complex program can be divided into small subtasks and function subprograms can be written for each.*

(*ii*) *These are easy to write, understand and debug.*

(*iii*) *A function can be utilised in many programs by separately compiling it and loading them together.*

(*iv*) *C++ has the facility of defining a function in terms of itself i.e.,* **recursion.** *Recursion suits to some processes but not to all.*

(*v*) *Many functions such as* **cin, cout, sqrt** *etc. are kept in C++ library and the compiler of C++ is written for calling any such function.*

Following program illustrates the use of a function:

Program 8.1

```
//display general message using function
#include<iostream.h>
#include<conio.h>
void main( )
{
    void display_message( );   //function prototype
    clrscr( ); //clears the screen
    display_message( ); //function call
    getch( );   //freeze the monitor
}
//function definition display_message( )
void display_message( )
{
    cout<<"Welcome to the world of programming\n";
    cout<<"Programming is nothing but logic implementation";
}
```

Output

```
Welcome to the world of programming
Programming is nothing but logic implementation
```

In Program 8.1, the function **clrscr ()** clears the screen (it is a library function) then the function **display_message ()** is invoked from **main ()**. The control passes to the function **display_message ()**, and the body of the function executed, that is, the two output statements display the messages as shown in the output. The control then returns to **main ()** and the remaining code gets executed. The function **getch ()** waits for any key to be pressed. It is a library function.

In Program 8.1, the function **main ()**, which invokes **display_message( )**, function is called the **calling function**, and the function **display_message( )** is the **called function.**

Now, let us understand the above concepts one by one in detail.

8.2 Defining a Function

In C++, a function must be defined prior to it's use in the program. The function definition contains the code for the function. The definition for display_message ( ) function in program 8.1 is given below the main ( ) function. The general syntax of a function definition in C++ is shown below:

```
ret–type Name_of_the_function(argument list) //No semicolon required here
{
    //body of the function
}
```

Here, the ret-type specifies the type of the value to be returned by the function.

It may be any valid C++ data type. *When no type is given, then the compiler returns an integer value from the function.*

Name_of_the_function is a valid C++ identifier (no reserved word allowed) defined by the user and it can be used by other functions for calling this function.

Argument list is a comma separated list of variables of a function through which the function may receive data or send data when called from other function. When no parameters, the argument list is empty as you have already seen in Program 8.1. However, even if there are no parameters, the parentheses are still required.

In variable declarations, you can declare many variables to be of a common type by using a comma-seperated list of variable names. In contrast, all function parameters must be declared individually, each having both the type and name. That is, the parameter declaration list for a function has the following general form:

```
Name_of_the_function(type varl, type var2, ..., type varN)
```

For example, here are correct and incorrect parameter declarations:

```
Name_of_the_function(int a, int b, int c) // Correct
Name_of_the_function(int a, b, float c) // Incorrect
```

Now let us discuss the concept of function definition.

8.2.1 Different Styles of Coding Functions

In C++, you have the following four styles of coding functions:

Style I: void function without arguments

This style of function simply performs an independent task. It does not send or receive any parameters and it does not return any value. It's form is as given below:

```
void Name_of_the_function( )
{
    - - - - - - - - -    //  statement(s) inside the function
    - - - - - - - - -
}
```

Or

```
void Name_of_the_function(void)
{
    - - - - - - - -    //  statement(s) inside the function
    - - - - - - - -
}
```

For example, the following function illustrates the above mentioned style:

```
//  function definition add( )
void add( )
{
    int a, b, sum = 0;      //local variables
    cout<<"\nEnter two integers\n";
    cin>>a>>b;
    sum = a + b;
    cout<<"\nSum of two integers is: "<<sum<<endl;
    return;        //  only control returns, no value is returned
}
```

Style II: void function having argument(s)

This style of function does receive some arguments (parameter) but does not return a value. It's form is as given below:

```
void Name_of_the_function(argument list)
{
    - - - - - - - -  //  statements(s) in side the function
    - - - - - - - -
}
```

For example, the following function illustrates the above mentioned style:

```
//  function definition add( )
void add(int a, int b)       //variable names are must in definition
{
```

```
    int sum = 0;    //local variable
    sum = a + b;
    cout<<"\nSum of two passed integers is: "<<sum<<endl;
    return;         // notice no value is returned
}
```

Style III: Non-void function without arguments

This style of function takes no arguments but does return a value. It's form is as given below:

```
ret–type Name_of_the_function( )
{
    - - - - - - - -     // statement(s) inside the function
    - - - - - - - -
    return(value);  // this value is of type ret–type
}
```

For example, the following function illustrates the above mentioned style:

```
//function definition add( )
int add( )
{
    int a, b, sum = 0;  //local variables
    cout<<"\nEnter two integers\n";
    cin>>a>>b;
    sum = a + b;
    return sum;
}
```

The return-value can be a constant, a variable or an expression but must have the type as that of ret-type.

Style IV: Non-void function having argument(s)

This style of function takes some arguments and does return a value. It's form is as given below:

```
ret–type Name_of_the_function(argument list)
{
    - - - - - - - - -       //statement(s) inside the function
    - - - - - - - - -
    return(value) ;  //this value is of type ret–type
}
```

For example, the following function illustrates the above mentioned style:

```
//function definition add( )
int add(int a, int b)
{
    int sum = 0;    //local variable
```

```
sum = a + b;
return sum;
}
```

The return-value can be a constant, a variable or an expression but must have the type as that of ret-type. More about **return** statement later on in this chapter.

In C++ you can define a function that has a variable number of parameters. To tell the compiler that an unknown number of arguments may be passed to a function, you must end the definition of its parameters using three periods. For example,

```
ret-type Name_of_the_function(type arg1, ...);
```

Any function that uses a variable number of parameters must have atleast one actual parameter. For example, this is incorect:

```
void func(...);    //illegal
```

> ***Note:*** *In C++, you cannot define a function within a function. This is why C++ is technically not a block-structured language.*

8.3 Function Prototype (Declaration)

Like any variable in a C++ program it is necessary to prototype or declare a function before it's use. It informs the compiler that the function would be referenced at a later stage in the program.

For example, in Program 8.1, the statement

```
void display_message( );
```

is a function prototype or declaration. Here **void** specifies that this function does not return any value, and the empty parentheses indicates that it takes no parameters (arguments).

Need for Prototypes

Prototypes have always been **required** by C++. Prototypes enable C++ to provide stronger type checking. When you use prototypes, the compiler can find and report an illegal type conversions between the type of arguments used to call a function and the type definition of its parameters. The compiler will also catch differences between the number of arguments used to call a function and the number of parameters in the function.

The general syntax of a function prototype is given below:

```
ret-type Name_of_the_function(argument list); //Semicolon required here
```

> ***Note:*** *In C++, the function prototype is essential and is always terminated with a semicolon.*

In a function declaration, the names of the parameters are optional. For example,

```
void add(int,int); //variable names are optional in prototype
```

However, they enable the compiler to identify any type mismatches by name, when an error occurs, so it is a good idea to include them.

Use of void inside an empty parameter list

You know that **void** data type means an empty set of values and it is used as the return type for functions that do not return a value. Thus a function that does not require any argument or parameter can be declared as given below:

```
ret–type Name_of_the_function(void);
```

For example,

```
int func(void);
```

This tells the compiler that the function has no parameters, and any call to that function that has parameters is an error. In C++, the use of **void** inside an empty parameter list is redundant.

> *Note: In C++, **func( )** and **func(void)** are equivalent.*

The type must be declared for the functions that return non-integer values. For example,

```
float largest(float,float,float);  //prototype
```

Function prototypes help you trap bugs before they occur. In addition, they help verify your program is working correctly by not allowing functions to be called with mismatched arguments. So every function in a C++ program must be fully prototyped.

> ***Note:** The function **prototype** and function **definition** must match on the return type, function name, and number and type of argument list.*

8.3.1 Eliminating the Prototyping

If the called function definition appears before the calling function's definition then the called function's prototype may be avoided. For example, Program 8.1 can be modified to avoid function prototype as given below:

Program 8.2

```
//display general message using a function
#include<iostream.h>
#include<conio.h>
//function definition display_message( )
void display_message( )
{
    cout<<"Welcome to the world of programming\n";
    cout<<"Programming is nothing but logic implementation";
}
void main( )
{
    clrscr( ); //clears the screen
    display_message( ); //function call
    getch( ); //freeze the monitor
}
```

The output of Program 8.2 will be same as that of Program 8.1.

The above approach removes the prototyping but it is less **flexible,** because you will have to write all the functions before **main ()** and most of the time you are not sure of the fact that which function will be invoked by which one.

Since execution of the program starts with main ( ), some programmers always prefer to arrange **main ()** in first place. Now it's upto you to decide which approach you will prefer. Perhaps the first one, as in Program 8.1.

8.4 Invoking/Calling a Function

A function is *invoked* (*called* or *executed*) by providing it's name, followed by the arguments or parameters being sent enclosed in parentheses. For example, to invoke a function whose declaration is given below:

```
float largest(float,float,float); //prototype
```

the function call statement may be:

```
largest(a,b,c); //function call
```

Here, a, b, c are **float** type arguments. So the syntax of invoking a function is:

```
Name_of_the_function(argument list);
```

where the argument list is optional.

When a function is called from another function or itself, the control passes to the called function, and the body of the function gets executed. The control then returns to the statement of it's call or next statement as the case may be.

The concept of function prototyping, function definition and function invoking/calling has been already used in Program 8.1.

In C++, some functions may be used in expressions. But remember that it is allowed with only those functions that return a value. More about it later on. As mentioned earlier the program execution always begins with **main ( ).** Which in turn may call other function(s). The called function(s) in turn may call other function(s) and so on. When a function has done its thing the control returns back to the calling function, which in turn returns back the control to the calling function and so on. The program execution terminates when main ( ) function statement(s) are over. Following program illustrates this concept:

Program 8.3

```
//Illustration of invoking/calling functions
#include<iostream.h>
#include<conio.h>
void main( )
{
    void func1( );        //function prototype
    clrscr( );
    cout<<"You are in function main( )\n";
    cout<<"\nCalling function func1( )\n";
    func1( ); //function call
```

```
    cout<<"\nA return from function func1( )\n";
    cout<<"\nFinally you are back in main( )\n";
    getch( ); //freeze the monitor
}
//function definition func1( )
void func1( )
{
    void func2( ); //function prototype
    cout<<"\nYou are in function func1( )\n";
    cout<<"\nCalling function func2( )\n";
    func2( ); //function call
    cout<<"\nA return from function func2( )\n";
}
//function definition func2( )
void func2( )
{
    void func3( ); //function prototype
    cout<<"\nYou are in function func2( )\n";
    cout<<"\nCalling function func3( )\n";
    func3( ); //function call
    cout<<"\nA return from function func3( )\n";
}
//function definition func3( )
void func3( )
{
    cout<<"\nYou are in function func3( )\n";
    cout<<"\nHope now you are comfortable with function calls !\n";
}
```

Output

```
You are in function main()
Calling function func1()
You are in function func1()
Calling function func2()
You are in function func2()
Calling function func3()
You are in function func3()
Hope now you are comfortable with function calls !
A return from function func3()
```

A return from function func2( )

A return from function func1( )

Finally you are back in main( )

> ***Note:** The function(s) is/are invoked/called in the order of appearance of it's/their name(s) in the invoking/calling function.*

8.4.1 Passing Arguments to a Function

Argument(s) of a function is (are) the data that the function receives when called/invoked from another function. It is not always necessary for a function to have arguments or parameters.

Following example illustrates the concept of passing arguments to a function SUMFUN ( ):

```
//demonstration of passing arguments to a function
#include<iostream.h>
void main( )
{
    float x,result; //local variables
    int N;                                 } formal parameters
                                               Semicolon here
    float SUMFUN(float x,int N); //function declaration
      Return type
    ......................
    ......................
    result=SUMFUN(x,N); //function call
                                } actual parameters
}
//function definition SUMFUN( )
                                   No semicolon here
float SUMFUN(float x,int N)  //function declaration
{
    ......................
    ......................   Body of the function
    ......................
}
   No semicolon here
```

Actual parameter(s)—is/are the argument(s) provided in the function call.

Formal parameter(s)—is/are the argument(s) provided in the function definition.

> ***Note:** If the function is called with different actual argument(s) more than once in a program, the same set of statements within the function are executed. Without using function, the same set of statements would have to be coded the required number of times in the function main ( ).*

Following program shows the concept of argument passing to a function SUMFUN ( ) for finding the sum of the series $1 - \frac{x^2}{2} + \frac{x^3}{3} - \frac{x^4}{4} + \frac{x^5}{5} - \frac{x^6}{6} + ... + \frac{x^N}{N}$.

Program 8.4

```
//Sum of the series
#include<iostream.h>
#include<conio.h>
#include<math.h> //for pow( ) function
void main( )
{
    void SUMFUN(float,int);  //function prototype
    float x;
    int N;
    cout<<"Enter x and N\n";
    cin>>x>>N;
    SUMFUN(x,N);  //function call
    getch( );   //freeze the monitor
}
//function definition SUMFUN( )
void SUMFUN(float x,int N)
{
    float sum=1.0,sign=1,term;
    int i;
    for(i=2;i<=N;i++)
    {
        sign *= -1;
        term = sign * pow(x,i)/i;
        sum += term;
    }
    cout<<"\nResult = "<<sum<<endl;
}
```

Output

```
Enter x and N
1 4
Result = 0.583333
```

8.4.2 Specifying Argument Data Types

C++ is a strongly data typed language. The C++ compiler checks for the type of argument list and its return type. If you make a data type mismatch between actual and formal arguments an implicit data conversion takes place if possible. If the number of arguments is not equal or an implicit conversion is not feasible then a compile time error is signalled. The function prototype gives the compiler the necessary information at the compile time. So a function must be declared before calling it. For example,

```
void add(int, int); //argument data types specified
void divide(int, int); //argument data types specified
void SUMFUN(float, int); //argument data types specified
```

8.4.3 Default Arguments

C++ allows a function to assign a parameter the default value in case no argument for that parameter is specified in the function call. The default value (s) is/are specified in the function declaration. For example, the following program illustrates the use of default arguments:

Program 8.5

```
//demonstration of default arguments function
#include<iostream.h>
int Calc(int U)
{
    if(U % 2 == 0)
        return U+10;
    else
        return U*2;
}
void Pattern(char M,int B=2)
{
    for(int CNT=0;CNT<B;CNT++)
        cout<<Calc(CNT)<<M;
    cout<<endl;
}
void main( )
{
    Pattern('*');
    Pattern('#',4);
    Pattern('@',3);
}
```

Output

```
10*2*
10#2#12#6#
10@2@12@
```

In the above program if **Pattern ( )** is called with a single argument then 2 is taken as default.

One reason that default arguments are included in C++ is because they provide another method for the programmer to manage greater complexity. To handle the widest variety of situations, quite frequently a function contains more parameters than are needed for its most common usage. Thus, when the default arguments apply, you need specify only the arguments that are meaningful to the exact situation, not all those needed by the most general case. For example, many of the C++ I/O functions make use of default arguments for just this reason. For example,

```
clrscr( ); //clears 25 lines on monitor(by default)
```

When the default value is appropriate to the situation, no argument need be specified when **clrscr ( )** is called. However, it is still possible to override the default and give **size** a different value when needed.

When you are writing functions that have default arguments, it is important to remember that the default values must be specified only once, and this must be the first time the function is declared within the file.

All parameters that take default values must appear to the right of those that do not. For example, it is incorrect to define a function as:

```
// wrong !
void input(int x=10, int y);
```

Once you begin to define parameters that take default values, you cannot specify a nondefaulting parameter. That is, a declaration like this is also wrong and will not compile:

```
int func (float a, char ch, int x = 10, int y); //incorrect
```

Because **x** has been given a default value, **y** must be given one too.

> **Note:** *The default value of an argument is used only when it has no matching argument (value) in the function call statement.*

Using Default Arguments Correctly

No doubt, the default arguments can be a very powerful tool when used correctly but they can also be misused. The point of default arguments is to allow a function to perform its job in an efficient, easy-to-use manner while still allowing considerable flexibility. Toward this end, all default arguments should reflect the way a function is generally used, or a reasonable alternate usage. When there is no single value that can be meaningfully associated with an argument/parameter, there is no reason to declare a default argument. In fact, declaring default arguments when there is insufficient basis for doing so destructures your code, because they are liable to mislead and confuse anyone reading your program.

Another important point that should be kept in mind when using default arguments is this: No default argument should cause a harmful or destructive action. That is, the accidental use of a default argument should not cause a catastrophe.

Example 1. *Rewrite the following program after removing the syntactical error(s) if any. Underline each correction.*

```
#include<iostream.h>
void main( )
{
    First = 10, Second = 20;
    Jumpto(First; Second);
    Jumpto(Second);
}
void Jumpto(int N1, int N2=20)
{
    N1 = N1 + N2;
    cout<<N1>>N2;
}
```

Solution. The program after removing the syntactical error(s) and underlining is given below:

```
#include<iostream.h>
void main( )
{
    int First = 10, Second = 20;
    void Jumpto (int N1, int N2=20);
    Jumpto(First, Second)
    Jumpto(Second);
}
void Jumpto (int N1, int N2)
{
    N1 = N1+N2;
    cout<<N1<<N2;
}
```

8.4.4 Constant Arguments

A C++ function may have constant argument(s). These argument(s) is/are treated as constant(s). These values cannot be modified by the function. For example,

Observe carefully the function call given below:

```
manipulate ("String");   //constant argument
```

This function call cannot modify its argument **"String"** as it is a constant value *i.e.*, a string constant. But it can be modified if it is not a constant.

For making the argument(s) constant to a function, we should use the keyword **const** as given below in the function prototype:

```
void max(const float x,const float y,const float z);
```

Here, the qualifier **const** informs the compiler that the argument(s) having **const** should not be modified by the function **max ( )**. These are quite useful when call by reference method is used for passing arguments.

8.4.5 Call by Value

In C++ programs, functions with arguments can be invoked by:

- *Value*
- *Reference.*

You have already seen the call by value method in Program 8.4. *In this method the values of the actual parameters (appearing in the function call) are copied into the formal parameters (appearing in the function definition), i.e., the function creates its own copy of argument values and operates on them.* Following program illustrates this concept:

Program 8.6

```
//Calculation of simple interest using a function
#include<iostream.h>
#include<conio.h>
void main( )
{
    float principal,rate,time; //local variables
    void calculate(float, float, float); //function prototype
    clrscr( );
    cout<<"Enter the following values:\n";
    cout<<"\nPrincipal:";
    cin>>principal;
    cout<<"\nRate of interest:";
    cin>>rate;
    cout<<"\nTime period (in years): ";
    cin>>time;
    calculate(principal,rate,time); //function call
    getch( );    //freeze the monitor
}
//function definition calculate( )
void calculate(float p, float r, float t)
{
    float interest; //local variable
    interest = (p*r*t)/100.0;
    cout<<"\nSimple interest is: "<<interest;
}
```

Output

```
Enter the following values:
Principal: 1000
Rate of interest: 5
```

Time period (in years): 2

Simple interest is: 100

In Program 8.6 values entered for the variables **principal, rate** and **time** are passed to the function **calculate ( ).** When the function **calculate ( )** is invoked, these values get copied into the memory locations of the arguments **p, r** and **t** respectively.

This is shown in Figure 8.2:

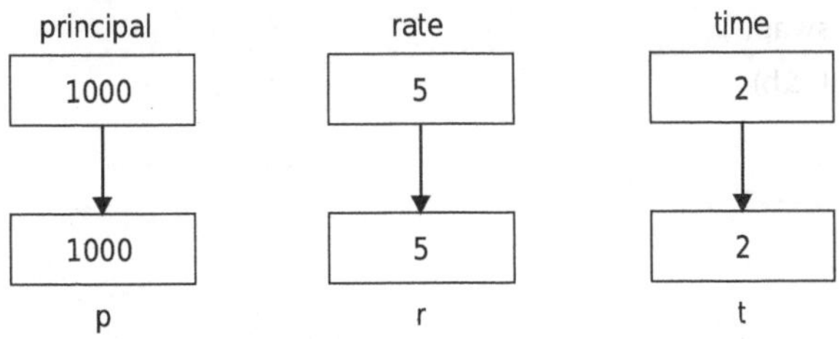

Fig. 8.2. Illustration of call by value method

So, we observe that the variables in the calling function main ( ) are different from the variables in the called function calculate ( ) because they use different memory locations.

> ***Note:*** *The values of the actual arguments in the calling function do not get modified when the arguments are passed by value even though the name of formal arguments may be same (these are considered different).*

8.4.6 Call by Reference

A reference provides an alias—an alternate name—for the variable, that is, the same variable's value can be used by two different names: the original name and the alias name.

In call by reference method, a reference to the actual argument(s) in the calling program is passed (only variables). So the called function does not create its own copy of original value(s) but works with the original value(s) with different name. Any change in the original data in the called function gets reflected back to the calling function.

It is useful when you want to change the original variables in the calling function by the called function. Following program illustrates this concept:

Program 8.7

```
//Swapping of two numbers using function call by reference
#include<iostream.h>
#include<conio.h>
void main( )
{
    clrscr( );
    int num1, num2;
    void swap(int &, int &); //function prototype
    cout<<"Enter two numbers: ";
    cin>>num1>>num2;
    cout<<"\nBefore swapping the numbers are\n\n";
```

```
    cout<<num1<<" "<<num2<<endl;
    swap(num1,num2); //function call
    cout<<"\nAfter swapping the numbers are\n\n";
    cout<<num1<<" "<<num2<<endl;
    getch( );    //freeze the monitor
}
//function definition swap( )
void swap(int &a, int &b)
{
    int temp=a;
    a=b;
    b=temp;
}
```

Output

```
Enter two numbers: 47 29
Before swapping the numbers are
47    29
After swapping the numbers are
29    47
```

Reference arguments are indicated by an ampersand (&) before them (as shown in Program 8.7):

```
void swap (int &a, int &b); // function prototype
```

You may omit the names of the variables in the prototype as:

```
void swap (int &, int &);
```

Also note that no ampersand sign is required in function call:

```
swap(num1,num2); // function call
```

In Program 8.7, the values in the variables **num1** and **num2** in the calling program are interchanged. This is shown in Figure 8.3:

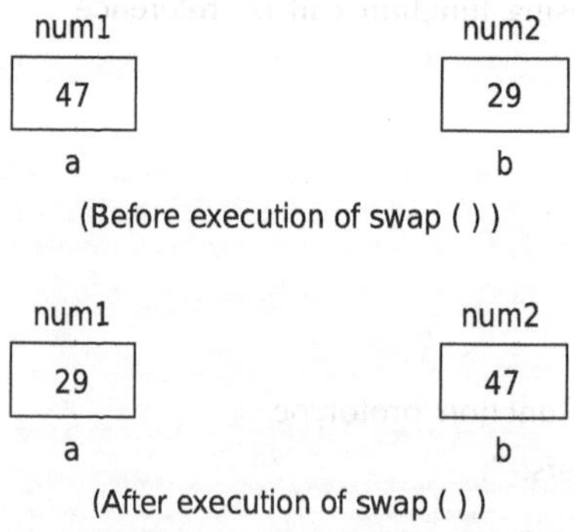

Fig. 8.3. Illustration of call by reference method

> **Note:** *Only the variables can be passed by reference and not the constants or expressions.*

8.4.7 Comparison of Call by Value and Call by Reference

The comparison of call by value and call by reference is given below:

S.No.	*Call by Value*	*Call by Reference*
1.	It is the usual method to call a function in which only the value of the variable is passed as an argument or parameter.	In this method, the address of the variable is passed as an argument or parameter.
2.	Any change in the value of the argument passed is local to the function and is not reflected back in the calling program.	Any change in the value of the argument passed is reflected back in the calling program (since alternation is made indirectly in the memory location using the pointer).
3.	Memory location occupied by formal and actual arguments is different.	Memory location occupied by formal and actual arguments is same and there is a saving of memory.
4.	Since a new location is created, this method is slow.	Since the existing memory location is used through its address, this method is fast.
5.	There is no possibility of wrong data manipulation since the arguments are directly used in an expression.	There is a possibility of wrong data manipulation since the addresses are used in an expression. A good skill of programming is needed here.

Example 2. *Write the output of the following program:*

```
#include<iostream.h>
int func(int &x,int y=10)
{
    if(x%y == 0) return ++x; else return y--;
}
void main( )
{
    int p=20,q=23;
    q=func(p,q);
    cout<<p<<','<<q<<endl;
    p=func(q);
    cout<<p<<','<<q<<endl;
    q=func(p);
    cout<<p<<','<<q<<endl;
}
```

Solution. The output of program will be:

20, 23

10, 23

11, 11

8.5 Returning Values from a Function

A function can return a single value to the calling function when it completes its execution. When a function returns a value, the data type of the value must be specified in the prototype.

8.5.1 The return Statement

The **return** statement is used to return from a function. It is categorized as a jump statement because it causes execution to return (jump back) to the point at which the call to the function was made. A **return** may or may not have a value associated with it. If **return** has a value associated with it, that value becomes the return value of the function.

The general form of the **return** statement is: return **expression;**

The expression is present only if the function is declared as returning a value. In this case, the value of *expression* will become the return value of the function.

You can use as many **return** statements as you like within a function. However, the function will stop executing as soon as it encounters the first **return.** The } that ends a function also causes the function to return. It is the same as a **return** without any specified value. If it occurs within a non-**void** function, then the return value of the function is undefined.

A function declared as **void** may not contain a **return** statement that specifies a value. Since a **void** function has no return value, it makes sense that no **return** statement with a **void** function can return a value. So the return statement has two important uses:

1. It causes an immediate exit from the function that it is in. That is, it causes program execution to return to the calling code.
2. It may be used to return a value.

For example, in the following program, the type **double** is placed before the function SUMFUN( ) and it returns a value to main( ).

Program 8.8

```
//Compute sum of the series X + X^2/3! + X^3/5!+ ..... + X^n/(2n-1)!
#include<iostream.h>
#include<conio.h>
#include<math.h> //for pow( )
void main( )
{
    double SUMFUN(double,int); //function prototype
    double X;
    int n;
    clrscr( );
    cout<<"Enter the value of X and n: ";
    cin>>X>>n;
    cout<<"\n\nSum of the series is "<<SUMFUN(X,n)<<endl;
    getch( ); //freeze the monitor
}
```

```
//function definition SUMFUN( )
double SUMFUN(double X,int n)
{
    double fact,sum=X;
    int i,j;
    for(i=2,i<=n;i++)
    {
        fact=1;
        for(j=1;j<=2*i-1;j++)
            fact *=j;
        sum += pow(x,i)/fact;
    }
    return sum;
}
```

Output

```
Enter the value of X and n: 1 4
Sum of the series is 1.175198
```

> ***Note:*** *If some value is returned by the function then either it can be directly outputted using* ***cout*** *where the function is invoked or it can be stored in some variable of the same type as the return type of the function.*
>
> *Always remember that a return statement always returns one value. When return is used without parenthesis, no value is returned to the calling program. When no return is specified the function returns an integer value.*

8.5.2 Returning by Reference

A reference can also be returned by a function. For example, the following program illustrates this concept:

Program 8.9

```
//illustration of function returning reference
#include<iostream.h>
#include<conio.h>
void main( )
{
    float &max(float &a, float &b, float &c)  //function prototype
    float x,y,z;
    clrscr( );
    cout<<"Enter the three numbers\n\n";
    cin>>x>>y>>z;
    //echo the data
```

```
    cout<<"\n\nx = "<<x<<" y = "<<y<<" z = "<<z<<endl;
    max(x,y,z) = 32767; //function call on left of assignment statement
    cout<<"\n\nx = "<<x<<" y = "<<y<<" z = "<<z<<endl;
    getch( ); //freeze the monitor
}
//function definition max( )
float &max (float &a, float &b, float &c)
{
    if(a>b)
    {
        if(a>c)
            return a;
        else
            return c;
    }
    else
    {
        if(b>c)
            return b;
        else
            return c;
    }
}
```

Output

```
Enter the three numbers
4 8 1
x = 4  y = 8  z = 1
x = 4  y = 32767  z = 1
```

As the return type of the function **max ()** is **float &,** that is, the function **max()** returns a reference (that is, an alias) to a, b or c. It does not return a value. The function call **max (x, y, z)** will return a reference to either a, b or c whichever is largest. It means that in the case of such a function, the function call can appear on the left-hand side of an assignment statement.

For example,

max(x, y, z) = 32767;

The above statement is a legal one and assigns 32767 to the largest of the three numbers x, y or z.

> ***Note:*** *Any function which returns a reference can appear on the left-hand side of an assignment statement.*

8.5.3 What Does main Return?

The **main( )** function returns an integer value to the calling process, which is generally the operating system in use. Returning a value from **main ( )** is the equivalent of calling **exit ( )** with the same value. If **main( )** does not return a value, the value passed to the calling process is technically undefined. In practice, most C++ compilers automatically return 0, but do not rely on this if probability is a concern.

8.6 Inbuilt Functions or Library Functions

A **library** is a collection of functions or programs that can be used by other programs. C++ provides function libraries having **built-in functions** or **library functions,** so that these can be called in any program. Many of the functions, like finding the square root of a number, sine value of a number, clearing the screen etc., are frequently used by the programmers in their programs. Writing programs for such functions in the programs that require these, is an unnecessary and complex job. These built-in functions when used in a program are combined with the program code by the linker at the time of linking. *The main advantages of library functions are given below:*

(*i*) **Reusability of code.** Every program involves the three main activities: *coding of program, testing* and *debugging*. An already tested function (either by self or someone else) available in the standard library can be easily included in a program that needs it. So, once written and tested function code can be utilised as and when needed.

(*ii*) **Faster program development.** Since a lot of useful functions are available to the programmer, the coding of the program can be done very fast and in this way the **productivity** increases.

(*iii*) **Easy maintenance.** Since a function stored in the library is utilized by many users, the alterations or changes in it can be done at only one place, that is, in the library. So, the software maintenance is quite easy.

(*iv*) **Saving of disk space.** Due to availability of only a single copy for each function, a lot of *disk space* is saved.

8.6.1 String Functions

String functions are available in header file **string.h.** Most commonly used string functions are given in Table 8.1.

Table 8.1. Commonly used String Functions

S. No.	*Function*	*Library file*	*Purposes: (Example)*
(*i*)	strcpy(target, source)	<string.h>	Copies the contents of string **source** into **target** ; strcpy (target, "NEW DELHI") would copy the string NEW DELHI to string **target,** provided size of target is greater than or equal to size of source string, that is, "NEW DELHI".
(*ii*)	strcat(target, source)	<string.h>	Concatenates a copy of **source** to **target** and terminates with a NULL. The **target** string should be large enough to store both its original contents and those of **source:** strcat (target, "FUNNY") will concatenate string FUNNY with the string in **target.**

(*iii*)	strlen(str)	<string.h>	Returns the length of the null terminated string pointed to by **str.** It does not count the trailing NULL: strlen ("DIXIT") would give 5.
(*iv*)	strcmp(source, target)	<string.h>	Compares the strings **source** and **target** character by character and returns an **int** value as follows: < 0 if source < target = 0 if source == target > 0 if source > target.
(*v*)	strcmpi(source, target)	<string.h>	Compares the strings **source** and **target** character by character ignoring the case and returns an int value as follows: < 0 if source < target = 0 if source == target > 0 if source > target.

More about strings later on.

8.6.2 Character Functions

Character functions are available in header file **ctype.h.** Most commonly used character functions are given in Table 8.2.

Table 8.2. Commonly used Character Functions

S. No.	*Function*	*Library file*	*Purposes: (Example)*
(*i*)	isalnum(ch)	<ctype.h>	Returns nonzero if its argument is a letter or a digit. Returns zero if its argument is not an alphanumeric: if **ch** is 'A', isalnum(ch) is nonzero.
(*ii*)	isalpha(ch)	<ctype.h>	Returns nonzero if **ch** is an alphabet, otherwise it returns zero: if ch is 'A', isalpha(ch) is nonzero.
(*iii*)	isdigit(ch)	<ctype.h>	Returns nonzero if **ch** is a digit (*i.e.,* 0–9), otherwise returns zero: if ch is '5', isdigit(ch) is nonzero.
(*iv*)	islower(ch)	<ctype.h>	Returns nonzero if **ch** is a lowercase letter, otherwise returns zero: if ch is 'a', islower(ch) is nonzero.
(*v*)	isupper(ch)	<ctype.h>	Returns nonzero if **ch** is an uppercase letter, otherwise returns zero: if ch is 'A', isupper(ch) is nonzero.

(vi)	tolower(ch)	<ctype.h>	Returns lowercase equivalent of **ch** if **ch** is a letter, otherwise **ch** is returned unchanged : if ch = 'A', tolower(ch) will be 'a'.
(vii)	toupper(ch)	<ctype.h>	Returns uppercase equivalent of **ch** if **ch** is a letter, otherwise **ch** is returned unchanged : if ch = 'a', toupper(ch) will be 'A'.

> ***Note:*** *The argument type of all the functions is* ***int*** *as internally the characters are processed numerically (using their ASCII codes).*

Let us implement the character functions:

isalnum( )—checks a character for alphanumeric. Following program illustrates the use of **isalnum( )** function:

Program 8.10

```
//Program to illustrate the use of function isalnum( )
#include<iostream.h>
#include<ctype.h>
#include<conio.h>
void main( )
{
    int ch;
    clrscr( );
    cout<<"Enter a character\n";
    ch=getche( );
    if(isalnum(ch))        //isalnum( ) takes argument of type int
        cout<<"\nYou have entered an alphanumeric character";
    else
        cout<<"\nYou have not entered an alphanumeric character";
    getch( ); //freeze the screen
}
```

Output

```
Enter a character
r
You have entered an alphanumeric character
Enter a character
?
You have not entered an alphanumeric character
```

isalpha( )—checks a character for an alphabet. Following program illustrates the use of **isalpha( )** function:

Program 8.11

```
//Program to illustrate the use of function isalpha( )
#include<iostream.h>
#include<ctype.h>
#include<conio.h>
void main( )
{
   int ch;
   clrscr( );
   cout<<"Enter a character\n";
   ch=getche( );
   if(isalpha(ch))    //isalpha( ) takes argument of type int
      cout<<"\nYou have entered an alphabet";
   else
      cout<<"\nYou have not entered an alphabet";
   getch( ); //freeze the monitor
}
```

Output

```
Enter a character
r
You have entered an alphabet
Enter a character
5
You have not entered an alphabet
```

isdigit( )—checks a character for a digit. Following program illustrates the use of **isdigit( )** function:

Program 8.12

```
//Program to illustrate the use of function isdigit( )
#include<iostream.h>
#include<ctype.h>
#include<conio.h>
void main( )
{
   int ch;
   clrscr( );
   cout<<"Enter a character\n";
```

```
    ch=getche( );
    if(isdigit(ch))        //isdigit( ) takes argument of type int
        cout<<"\nYou have entered a digit";
    else
        cout<<"\nYou have not entered a digit";
    getch( ); //freeze the monitor
}
```

Output

```
Enter a character
8
You have entered a digit
Enter a character
j
You have not entered a digit
```

islower( )—checks a character for lower case. Following program illustrates the use of islower( ) function:

Program 8.13

```
//Program to illustrate the use of function islower( )
#include<iostream.h>
#include<ctype.h>
#include<conio.h>
void main( )
{
    char ch;
    clrscr( );
    cout<<"Enter a character\n";
    ch=getche( );
    if(islower(ch))
        cout<<"\nThe entered character is a lower case letter";
    else
        cout<<"\nThe entered character is not a lower case letter";
    getch( ); //freeze the monitor
}
```

Output

```
Enter a character
d
```

The entered character is a lower case letter

Enter a character

G

The entered character is not a lower case letter

isupper( )—checks a character for upper case. Following program illustrates the use of **isupper( )** function:

Program 8.14

```
//Program to illustrate the use of function isupper( )
#include<iostream.h>
#include<ctype.h>
#include<conio.h>
void main( )
{
    char ch;
    clrscr( );
    cout<<"Enter a character\n";
    ch=getche( );
    if(isupper(ch))
        cout<<"\nThe entered character is an upper case letter";
    else
        cout<<"\nThe entered character is not an upper case letter";
    getch( );  //freeze the monitor
}
```

Output

Enter a character

R

The entered character is an upper case letter

Enter a character

f

The entered character is not an upper case letter

tolower( )—converts an alphabet to lowercase. Following program illustrates the use of **tolower( )** function:

Program 8.15

```
//Program to illustrate the use of function tolower( )
#include<iostream.h>
#include<ctype.h>
```

```
#include<conio.h>
void main( )
{
    char ch;
    clrscr( );
    cout<<"Enter an alphabet\n";
    ch=getche( );
    cout<<"The alphabet in lower case is\n\n";
    cout<<tolower(ch);
    getch( ); //freeze the monitor
}
```

Output

```
Enter an alphabet
A
The alphabet in lower case is
a
```

toupper( )—converts an alphabet to upper case. Following program illustrates the use of **toupper( )** function:

Program 8.16

```
//Program to illustrate the use of function toupper( )
#include<iostream.h>
#include<ctype.h>
#include<conio.h>
void main( )
{
    char ch;
    clrscr( );
    cout<<"Enter an alphabet\n";
    ch=getche( );
    cout<<"The alphabet in upper case is\n\n";
    cout<<toupper(ch);
    getch( );  //freeze the monitor
}
```

Output

```
Enter an alphabet
b
The alphabet in upper case is
B
```

8.6.3 Mathematical Functions

C++ provides many mathematical functions which help in mathematical calculations. The header files **math.h** and **stdlib.h** have various mathematical functions. For example, **fabs( ), log( ), log10( ), pow( ), sqrt( ), sin( ), cos( ), abs( )** etc.

Let us implement these mathematical functions:

fabs( )

This function has a prototype in **math.h** header file. The argument to this function is a float or double number. It calculates the absolute value of the argument or parameter. Following program illustrates the use of **fabs( )** function:

Program 8.17

```
//Program to illustrate the use of fabs( ) function
#include<iostream.h>
#include<math.h>
#include<conio.h>
void main( )
{
    float x;
    clrscr( );
    cout<<"Enter a floating point value\n\n";
    cin>>x;
    //fabs( ) takes argument of type float or double
    cout<<"\nAbsolute value of "<<x<<" is "<<fabs(x);
    getch( ); //freeze the monitor
}
```

Output

```
Enter a floating point value
- 87.5
Absolute value of - 87.5 is 87.5
Enter a floating point value
32.5
Absolute value of 32.5 is 32.5
```

log( )

This function has a prototype in **math.h** header file. The argument to this function is a double number. It calculates the natural logarithm of the argument or parameter. Following program illustrates the use of **log( )** function:

Program 8.18

```
//Program to illustrate the use of log( ) function
#include<iostream.h>
#include<math.h>
#include<conio.h>
void main( )
{
    double x,nlog;
    clrscr( );
    cout<<"Enter a value of type double\n\n";
    cin>>x;
    //log( ) takes argument of type double
    nlog=log(x);
    cout<<"\nNatural logarithm of "<<x<<" is "<<nlog;
    getch( ); //freeze the monitor
}
```

Output

```
Enter a value of type double
150.6
Natural logarithm of 150.6 is 5.014627
```

log10( )

This function has a prototype in **math.h** header file. The argument to this function is a double number. It calculates the base 10 logarithm of the argument or parameter. Following program illustrates the use of **log10( )** function:

Program 8.19

```
//Program to illustrate the use of log10( ) function
#include<iostream.h>
#include<math.h>
#include<conio.h>
void main( )
{
    double x,result;
    clrscr( );
    cout<<"Enter a value of type double\n\n";
    cin>>x;
    // log10( ) takes argument of type double
    result=log10(x);
```

```
    cout<<"\nLogarithm to the base 10 of "<<x<<" is "<<result;
    getch( ); //freeze the monitor
}
```

Output

```
Enter a value of type double
1000.0
Logarithm to the base 10 of 1000 is 3
```

pow( )

This function has a prototype in **math.h** header file. The arguments to this function are of type double (say b and p). It returns b^p. Results of excessively large magnitude can cause **pow( )** to give result out of range. Following program illustrates the use of **pow( )** function:

Program 8.20

```
//Program to illustrate the use of function pow( )
#include<iostream.h>
#include<math.h>
#include<conio.h>
void main( )
{
    double b,p,result;
    clrscr( );
    cout<<"Enter the value of base\n\n";
    cin>>b;
    cout<<"\nEnter the value of exponent\n\n";
    cin>>p;
    result=pow(b,p);
    cout<<endl<<b<<" raise to the power "<<p<<" is "<<result;
    getch( ); //freeze the monitor
}
```

Output

```
Enter the value of base
2.5
Enter the value of exponent
3
2.5 raise to the power 3 is 15.625
```

sqrt( )

This function has a prototype in **math.h** header file. The argument to this function is of type double. It calculates the **positive square root** of the input value *i.e.*, the argument or parameter. Following program illustrates the use of **sqrt( )** function:

Program 8.21

```
//Program to illustrate the use of function sqrt( )
#include<iostream.h>
#include<math.h>
#include<conio.h>
void main( )
{
    double x,sqroot;
    clrscr( );
    cout<<"Enter a number\n\n";
    cin>>x;
    sqroot=sqrt(x);
    cout<<"\nSquare root of "<<x<<" is "<<sqroot;
    getch( ); //freeze the monitor
}
```

Output

```
Enter a number
625
Square root of 625 is 25
```

sin( )

This function has a prototype in **math.h** header file. The argument to this function is of type double. It computes the sine of the input value *i.e.*, the argument or parameter. **Angles are specified in radians.** The results are in the range –1 to 1. Following program illustrates the use of **sin( )** function:

Program 8.22

```
//Program to illustrate the use of function sin( )
#include<iostream.h>
#include<math.h>
#include<conio.h>
void main( )
{
    double angle,sine;
    clrscr( );
```

```
    cout<<"Enter the angle in radians whose sine is to be calculated\n\n";
    cin>>angle;
    sine=sin(angle);
    cout<<"\nSine of "<<angle<<" radian is "<<sine;
    getch( ); //freeze the monitor
}
```

Output

```
Enter the angle in radians whose sine is to be calculated
0
Sine of 0 radian is 0
Enter the angle in radians whose sine is to be calculated
0.5238
Sine of 0.5238 radian is 0.500174
```

cos( )

This function has a prototype in **math.h** header file. The argument to this function is of type double. It computes the cosine of the input value *i.e.*, the argument or parameter. **Angles are specified in radians.** The results are in the range –1 to 1. Following program illustrates the use of **cos( )** function:

Program 8.23

```
//Program to illustrate the use of function cos( )
#include<iostream.h>
#include<math.h>
#include<conio.h>
void main( )
{
    double angle,cosine;
    clrscr( );
    cout<<"Enter the angle in radians whose cosine is to be calculated\n\n";
    cin>>angle;
    cosine=cos(angle);
    cout<<"\nCosine of "<<angle<<" radian is "<<cosine;
    getch( ); //freeze the monitor
}
```

Output

```
Enter the angle in radians whose cosine is to be calculated
0
Cosine of 0 radian is 1
```

```
Enter the angle in radian whose cosine is to be calculated
0.5238
Cosine of 0.5238 radian is 0.865925
```

abs( )

This function/macro has a prototype in **math.h/stdlib.h** header files. If **abs( )** is called when **stdlib.h** has been included, it is treated as a macro that expands to inline code.

If you want to use the **abs( )** function instead of the macro, include **#undef abs** in your program, after the **#include<stdlib.h>.**

It returns the absolute value of the argument or parameter. The argument is always an integer and the returned value is an integer in the range 0 to 32,767. Following program illustrates the use of **abs( )** function:

Program 8.24

```
//Program to illustrate the use of abs( ) function
#include<iostream.h>
#include<math.h>
#include<conio.h>
void main( )
{
    int x;
    clrscr( );
    cout<<"Enter an integer\n\n";
    //abs( ) only takes integeral argument
    cin>>x;
    cout<<"\nAbsolute value of "<<x<<" is "<<abs(x);
    getch( ); //freeze the monitor
}
```

Output

```
Enter an integer
- 85
Absolute value of - 85 is 85
Enter an integer
73
Absolute value of 73 is 73
```

8.6.4 Other Functions

In addition to the various functions discussed so far in this chapter, there are some miscellaneous and useful functions present in header file **stdlib.h.** For example, **randomize( ), random( ), itoa( )** and **atoi( ).**

Let us discuss these four functions:

randomize( )

This macro has a prototype in **stdlib.h** header file. It takes no argument. It's declaration is given below:

void randomize(void);

It initializes the random number generator with a random number. Because **randomize( )** is implemented as a macro that calls the **time( )** function prototyped in the header file **time.h**, you should include **time.h** when you use this routine. It does not return any value. Following program illustrates the use of **randomize( )** macro:

Program 8.25

```
//Program to illustrate the use of randomize( )
#include<iostream.h>
#include<stdlib.h>
#include<conio.h>
#include<time.h>
void main( )
{
    void randomize(void); //prototype
    int x,i;
    randomize( );
    clrscr( );
    cout<<"Enter a number\n\n";
    cin>>x;
    cout<<"\n10 random number between 0 and "<<x<<" are:\n\n";
    for(i=0;i<10;i++)
        cout<<random(x)<<" ";
    getch( ); //freeze the monitor
}
```

Output

```
Enter a number
500
10 random numbers between 0 and 500 are:
455  82  131  394  124  133  317  328  105  58
```

random( )

This macro has a prototype in **stdlib.h** header file. It returns an integer. It's declaration is given below:

- Macro: random(x);
- Function: int random(int x);

It returns a random number between 0 and (x–1).

Following program illustrates the use of **random( )** macro:

Program 8.26

```
//Program to illustrate the use of random( )
#include<iostream.h>
#include<stdlib.h>
#include<conio.h>
void main( )
{
    int x,y;
    clrscr( );
    cout<<"Enter a number\n\n";
    cin>>x;
    y=random(x);
    cout<<"\nA random number between 0 and "<<x<<" is "<<y;
    getch( ); //freeze the monitor
}
```

Output

```
Enter a number
750
A random number between 0 and 750 is 7
Enter a number
30000
A random number between 0 and 30000 is 316
```

itoa( )

The *itoa( )* function converts an integer to a string. The header file *<stdlib.h>* is required for using this function.

The space allocated for string must be large enough to hold the returned string, including the terminating null character (\0). The *itoa( )* function can return upto 17 bytes.

Following program illustrates the use of **itoa( )** function:

Program 8.27

```
//Program to illustrate the use of itoa( )
#include<iostream.h>
#include<stdlib.h>
#include<conio.h>
```

```
void main( )
{
    int number = 12345;
    char string[25];
    clrscr( );
    itoa(number, string,10);
    cout<<"Integer = "<<number;
    cout<<"\n\nString = "<<string;
    getch( ); //freeze the monitor
}
```

Output

```
Integer = 12345
String = 12345
```

atoi( )

The *atoi( )* macro converts a string to an integer. The header file <*stdlib.h*> is required for using it. In *atoi( )*, the first unrecognized character ends the conversion. If the string cannot be converted, returns 0.

Following program illustrates the use of atoi( ):

Program 8.28

```
//Program to illustrate the use of atoi( )
#include<iostream.h>
#include<stdlib.h>
#include<conio.h>
void main( )
{
    int number;
    char string[ ] = "12345.67";
    clrscr( );
    number = atoi(string);
    cout<<"String = "<<string;
    cout<<"\n\nInteger = "<<number;
    getch( ); //freeze the monitor
}
```

Output

```
String = 12345.67
Integer = 12345
```

8.7 Recursion

In C++, a function can invoke itself, this is called recursion. A function is said to be recursive if there exists a statement in its body for the function call itself. For example,

The factorial of a positive integer n can be defined recursively as,

$$0! = 1$$

$$n! = n \times (n-1)\,!$$

While coding recursive function, we must take care that there exists a reachable termination condition inside the function so that function may not be invoked endlessly.

Let us compute the factorial of a positive integer recursively:

Program 8.29

```
//Compute factorial of a number recursively
#include<iostream.h>
#include<conio.h>
//Recursive function definition factorial( )
unsigned long factorial(int n)
{
    if(n= =0) //base case
        return 1;
    else
        return(n*factorial(n–1));
}
void main( )
{
    int num;
    clrscr( );
    cout<<"Enter the number for finding factorial\n\n";
    cin>>num;
    if(num<0)
        cout<<"\n"<<num<<" factorial not defined\n";
    else
        cout<<"\n"<<num<<" factorial  =  "<<factorial(num)<<endl;
    getch( ); //freeze the monitor
}
```

Output

```
Enter the number for finding factorial
10
10 factorial = 3628800
```

Enter the number for finding factorial

-7

-7 factorial not defined

Let us understand the working of function factorial( ) when factorial of 4 is to be computed:

1. It calls itself, but with a parameter one less than the current parameter, that is, *factorial(4)* calls *factorial(3)* while *factorial(3)* calls *factorial(2)* and so on.
2. The recursive calling (*factorial(4)* calling *factorial(3)* and so on) ends when *factorial(1)* calls *factorial(0)—factorial(0)* which returns 1.

During program execution, as the function calls itself, a stack (pile) of pointers (addresses of instructions of the caller function to which control must return after the called function is executed) is created in memory. This stack is shown in Figure 8.4, assuming that factorial of 4 is to be found.

factorial(0) 1 (factorial(0) is not put in stack because it does not invoke any other function)

		Return Valu(	
factorial(1)	return	1	(1 x 0!)
factorial(2)	return	2	(2 x 1!)
factorial(3)	return	6	(3 x 2!)
factorial(4)	return	24	(4 x 3!)

Fig. 8.4. Stack for **factorial( )** evaluation

Once the stopping condition is true, the control returns to the address of the instruction stored at the top of the stack in order to complete the execution of the previous call of the function. Then control returns to the next address stored in the stack, and it continues till the end of stack, thus completing execution of all the previous calls to the function. *Note that everytime the function is called, it gets loaded in a different portion of memory.*

Since each function returns the factorial of the integer one less than what was passed to it, the stack has pointers to the *return* statement for each of the functions except *factorial(0)* which returns the value 1. When the return statement of *factorial(4)* is executed, the stack becomes empty.

The fibonacci terms are 0, 1, 1, 2, 3, 5, 8, ... In this sequence each term (except the first two) is obtained by adding the sum of its two immediate predecessor terms. The recursive definition of this sequence is:

$$\text{fib}(n) = \begin{cases} 0 \text{ if } n = 1 \\ 1 \text{ if } n = 2 \\ \text{fib}(n-1) + \text{fib}(n-2) \text{ if } n > 2 \end{cases}$$

Following function illustrates the use of recursion (through we can code it iteratively also):

```
//function definition fib( )
long fib(int n)
{
```

```
    if(n==1)
        return(0);
    else
    {
        if(n==2)
            return(1);
        else
            return(fib(n-1)+fib(n-2)); //recursive call to fib( )
    }
}
```

During each call of a recursive function, a different set of local variables is created. The names of these local variables are same, but all of them are different. They store different set of values during each call of the subprogram.

Another good example of recursive function is binomial coefficient definition:

$^{n}C_{r} = {}^{n-1}C_{r} + {}^{n-1}C_{r-1} \quad (0 <= r <= n)$

Following function implements the above recursive definition:

```
//function definition bin( )
int bin(int n,int r)
{
    if (r==0)
        return(1);
    else
    {
        if(n<r)
            return(0);
        else
            return(bin(n-1,r)+bin(n-1,r-1));
    }
}
```

8.8 Scope Rules of Functions and Variables

The *scope rules* of a langauge are the rules that govern whether a piece of code knows about or has access to another piece of code or data.

The scope of an identifier is that part of the C++ program in which it is accessible. Generally, users understand that the name of an identifier must be unique. It does not mean that a name can't be reused. We can reuse the name in a program provided that there is some scope by which it can be distinguished between different cases or instances.

In C++ there are four kinds of scope as given below:

1. *Local Scope*
2. *Function Scope*
3. *File Scope*
4. *Class Scope.*

1. Local Scope

A block in C++ is enclosed by a pair of curly braces, that is, '{' and '}'. The variables declared within the body of the block are called **local variables** and can be used only within the block. These come into existence when the control enters the block and get destroyed when the control leaves the closing brace. You should note that the variable(s) is/are available to all the enclosed blocks within a block.

For example,

```
int x=100;
{
    cout<<x<<endl;
    int x=200;
    {
        cout<<x<<endl;
        int x=300;
        {
            cout<<x<<endl;
        }
    }
    cout<<x<<endl;
}
```

The output of above program segment will be:

100
200
300
200

All the variables declared in a function have a local scope and same is the case of formal arguments.

2. Function Scope

Each function is a discrete block of code. A function's code is private to that function and cannot be accessed by any statement in any other function except through a call to that function (For instance, you cannot use **goto** to jump into the middle of another function). The code that forms the body of a function is hidden from the rest of the program and, unless it uses global variables or data, it can neither affect nor be affected by other parts of the program.

For example,

```
//function definition add1( )
void add1(int x,int y,int z)
{
    int sum = 0;
    sum = x+y+z;
    cout<<sum;
}
```

```
//function definition add2( )
void add2(float x,float y,float z)
{
    float sum = 0.0;
    sum = x+y+z;
    cout<<sum;
}
```

Here, the formal arguments **x, y, z** and local variable **sum** in two different functions **add1( )** and **add2( )** are declared and used locally.

3. File Scope

If the declaration of an identifier appears outside all functions, it is available to all the functions in the program and its scope becomes file scope. For example,

```
int x;      // global variable declaration
// global function definition square( )
void square(int n)
{
    cout<<n*n;
}
void main( )
{
    int num;
    - - - - - - - - - - - -
    cout<<x<<endl;
    cin>>num;
    square(num);
    - - - - - - - - - - - -
}
```

Here, the declarations of variable **x** and function **square ( )** are outside all the functions so these can be accessed from any place inside the program. Such variables/ functions are called global.

4. Class Scope

In C++, every class maintains its own associated scope. The class members are said to have local scope within the class. If the name of a variable is reused by a class member, which already has a file scope, then the variable will be hidden inside the class. Member functions also have class scope. More about classes later on in chapter 11.

8.9 Local and Global Variables

The variables which are defined within a function and hidden from other functions are called **local** variables. These can have the same name as that of the variables outside the function. In such cases the outside variables cannot be used directly. A local variable comes into existence when the function is entered and is destroyed upon exit. That is, local variables cannot hold their value between function calls. The only exception to this rule is when the variable is declared with the **static** storage class specifier. This causes the compiler to treat the variable as if it were a global variable for storage purposes, but limits its scope to within the function.

On the other hand, the variables that are declared outside of any function and which are accessible to all functions are called **global** variables. Global variables have their life throughout the program execution. Global variables can be corrupted by functions that have no business changing these.

In C++, the **scope resolution operator** (::) can be used to uncover the hidden variable (global variable) from the local variable.

Scope Resolution Operator (::)

C++ is a block structured language. A block is a group of statements enclosed within braces *i.e.,* { }. We know that the same variable name can be used for different purposes in two or more different blocks. A local variable has a local scope. For example,

```
---------
---------
  {
     float a=12.5;
     -------
     -------
  }
  --------
  --------
  {
     float a=30.7;
     -------
     -------
  }
```

The two declarations of **a** in two different blocks have different values *i.e.,* the values of **a** cannot be used interchangeably.

We may also have nested blocks in C++. For example,

```
  -------
  -------
  {
       float a = 12.5;
       -------
       -------
       {
          float a = 30.7;                    outer block
                                 inner block
          -------
          -------
       }
  }
```

Here the variable **a** declared inside the inner block can't be used in outer block. The following program illustrates the use of **scope resolution operator:**

Program 8.30

```
//illustration of the use of:: (scope resolution operator)
#include<iostream.h>
#include<conio.h>
int x=100; //global variable x
void main( )
{
    int x=200; //x local to main( )
    clrscr( );
    {
        int y=x;
        int x=300; //x local to inner block
        cout<<"You are in inner block\n";
        cout<<"x = "<<x<<endl;
        cout<<"y = "<<y<<endl;
        cout<<"::x = "<<::x<<endl;
    }
    cout<<"\nYou are in outer block\n";
    cout<<"x = "<<x<<endl;
    cout<<"::x = "<<::x<<endl;
}
```

Output

```
You are in inner block
x = 300
y = 200
:: x = 100
You are in outer block
x = 200
:: x = 100
```

> ***Note:*** *::x refers to global variable everywhere in Program 8.30.*

8.10 Data Storage Types

Data storage types determine about the storage of a variable. Its syntax is:

```
storage_specifier type variable_name;
```

There are four storage class specifiers in C++:

- auto
- register
- static
- extern.

A variable is completely defined with the above specification. *A variable can be stored either in the memory or the CPU registers.* So, to completely know about the variable's whereabouts *i.e.*,

(*i*) Storage place
(*ii*) Default initial value
(*iii*) Scope
(*iv*) Lifetime.

a storage specifier is needed.

- **auto.** A variable is declared automatic as given below:

```
auto type variable_name;
```

By default, all the variables are auto unless we specify some other storage specifier. So, with an auto storage specifier a variable has:

(*i*) Storage place: Memory
(*ii*) Default initial value: Garbage Value
(*iii*) Scope: Local to the function
(*iv*) Lifetime: Till the parent function is running.

The following program illustrates the above concept:

Program 8.31

```
#include<iostream.h>
#include<conio.h>
void main( )
{
    void show( ); //function prototype
    clrscr( );
    show( );  //function call
    show( );  //function call
}
//function definition show( )
void show( )
{
    auto int num=10;
    cout<<num*num<<endl;
    num +=5;
}
```

Output

100
100

Here, the value of **num** in function **show()** is initialized to 10 for each call. When the function terminates, **num** vanishes and its new value 15 is lost.

- **register.** A variable is declared register as given below:

```
register type variable_name;
```

All the variables can't be defined of register storage type for two reasons:

(*a*) Limited number of CPU registers (14 in a PC usually)

(*b*) Size of the CPU registers (16 bits in a PC usually)

But a register variable provides a fast access than those in memory. So, the time taken to read a variable from memory is saved in this case. A variable with a register storage specifier has:

(*i*) Storage place: CPU registers (if possible)

(*ii*) Default initial value: Garbage Value

(*iii*) Scope: Local to the function

(*iv*) Lifetime: Till the parent function is running.

The following program illustrates the above concept:

Program 8.32

```
#include<iostream.h>
#include<conio.h>
void main( )
{
    register int count;
    clrscr( );
    for(count=1;count<=5;count++)
        cout<<count<<" ";
}
```

Output

1 2 3 4 5

Here we are not sure that variable **count** would be stored in a CPU register.

- **static.** There are static local and static global variables. A variable is declared static as given below:

```
static type variable_name;
```

A static global variable is available for the entire file in which it is declared. From other files of the program, it is hidden.

A static local variable is initialized only once when the function is called first time (in which it is declared). It holds (retains) its value even when the control leaves the function and the value last time around will be used when the control enters next time in the function. It can be accessed only with the function it is declared but has the lifetime of a global variable.

A variable with a static storage specifier has:

(*i*) Storage place: Memory
(*ii*) Default initial value: 0 (zero)
(*iii*) Scope: Local to the function or file scope
(*iv*) Lifetime: Entire program execution.

The following program illustrates this concept:

Program 8.33

```
#include<iostream.h>
#include<conio.h>
void main( )
{
    void show( ); //function prototype
    clrscr( );
    show( );  //function call
    show( );  //function call
}
//function definition show( )
void show( )
{
    static int num=10;
    cout<<num*num<<endl;
    num +=5;
}
```

Output

```
100
225
```

Here, variable **num** in function **show()** is initialized to 10 only once. It is never initialized again. During the first call to **show()**, num is increment to 15. Because **num** is **static,** this value is retained for the next call.

- **extern.** A variable is declared extern as given below:

```
extern type variable_name;
```

When a program is divided into two or more files, then a global variable should not be declared separately for each file. In this case the global variable is preceded by the keyword **extern.** It tells the compiler that the variable name after **extern** has been declared somewhere else and no separate memory is allocated to it.

A variable with an extern storage specifier has:

(*i*) Storage place: Memory
(*ii*) Default initial value: 0 (zero)
(*iii*) Scope: File scope
(*iv*) Lifetime: Entire program execution.

8.11 Storage Class Specifiers and Functions

In C++, static and extern storage class specifiers can be used with functions.

Static function. When the keyword **static** is used before a function, it can be accessed only in the file in which it is declared. This function can't be accessed outside its own file. But, the same name can be used by some other file.

Extern function. It is similar to an extern variable. When the keyword **extern** is used before a function, it means that this function exists in some other file. For dividing a large program into multiple files it is quite useful.

Solved Problems

Problem 1. *What are the three things in using a function?*

Solution. Three things required for using a function in C++ are:

1. Function declaration (*i.e.,* prototype) to specify the function's interface to the program.
2. Function definition to tell the program about what and how a function is doing.
3. Function call to invoke the function.

Problem 2. *Find the output of the following program:*

```
#include<iostream.h>
void Withdef(int HisNum = 30)
{
    for(int I = 20; I <= HisNum; I += 5)
        cout<<I<<",";
    cout<<endl;
}
void Control(int &MyNum)
{
    MyNum += 10;
    Withdef(MyNum);
}
void main( )
{
    int YourNum = 20;
```

```
    Control(YourNum);
    Withdef( );
    cout<<"Number="<<YourNum<<endl;
}
```

Solution. The output of program will be:

20,25,30,

20,25,30,

Number = 30

Problem 3. *Write definition for a function SumSeries( ) in C++ with two arguments/ parameters—double x and int n. The function should return a value of type double and it should perform sum of the following series:*

$$x - x^2/3! + x^3/5! - x^4/7! + x^5/9! - \ldots \text{ upto n terms.}$$

*(**Note:** The symbol ! represents Factorial of a number i.e.,*

$$5! = 5 \times 4 \times 3 \times 2 \times 1)$$

Solution.

```
//function definition SumSeries( )
double SumSeries(double x, int n)
{
    double fact,sum=x;
    int i,j,sign=-1;
    for(i=2,i<=n;i++)
    {
        fact=1;
        for(j=1;j<=(2*i-1);j++)
            fact *=j;
        sum += sign*pow(x,i)/fact;
        sign *= -1;
    }
    return sum;
}
```

Problem 4. *Write definition for a function SumSequence( ) in C++ with two arguments/ parameters—double x and int n. The function should return a value of type double and it should perform sum of the following series:*

$$1/x - 3!/x^2 + 5!/x^3 - 7!/x^4 + 9!/x^5 - \ldots \text{ upto n terms.}$$

*(**Note:** The symbol ! represents Factorial of a number i.e.,*

$$5! = 5 \times 4 \times 3 \times 2 \times 1)$$

Solution.

```
//function definition SumSequence( )
double SumSequence(double x, int n)
{
    double fact,sum=1.0/x;
```

```
    int i,j,sign=-1;
    for(i=2;i<=n;i++)
    {
        fact=1;
        for(j=1;j<=(2*i-1);j++)
            fact *=j;
        sum += sign*(fact/pow(x,i));
        sign *= -1;
    }
    return sum;
}
```

Problem 5. *Write the output of the following program:*

```
#include<iostream.h>
int Execute(int M)
{
    if(M % 3 == 0)
        return M*3;
    else
        return M+10;
}
void Output(int B=2)
{
    for(int T=0;T<B;T++)
        cout<<Execute(T)<<"*";
    cout<<endl;
}
void main( )
{
    Output(4);
    Output( );
    Output(3);
}
```

Solution. The output of program will be:

```
0*11*12*9*
0*11*
0*11*12*
```

Problem 6. *Write a C++ function SUMFUN() having two parameters Y (of type double) and m (of type integer) with a result type as double to find the sum of the following series:*

$$Y + \frac{Y^3}{2!} + \frac{Y^5}{3!} + \ldots\ldots + \frac{Y^{2m-1}}{m!}$$

using this function write the complete C++ program to find the desired sum.

Solution.

```
//Compute sum of series Y + Y^3/2! + Y^5/3! + ....... + Y^(2m–1) /m!
#include<iostream.h>
#include<conio.h>
#include<math.h> //for pow( )
//function definition SUMFUN( )
double SUMFUN(double Y,int m)
{
    double fact,sum=Y;
    int i,j;
    for(i=2;i<=m;i++)
    {
        fact=1;
        for(j=1;j<=i;j++)
            fact *=j;
        sum += pow(Y,2*i–1)/fact;
    }
    return sum;
}
void main( )
{
    double Y;
    int m;
    clrscr( );
    cout<<"Enter the value of Y and m: ";
    cin>>Y>>m;
    cout<<"\n\nSum of the series is "<<SUMFUN(Y,m)<<endl;
    getch( ); //freeze the monitor
}
```

Problem 7. *Write a function zero_Small() that has two integer arguments being passed by reference and sets the smaller of the two numbers to 0. Write the main program to access this function.*

Solution.

```
#include<iostream.h>
#include<conio.h>
void zero_Small(int &x , int &y)
{
    if(x<y)
        x=0;
```

```
    else
        y=0;
}
void main( )
{
    int num1,num2;
    clrscr( );
    cout<<"Enter two integers\n\n";
    cin>>num1>>num2;
    //echo the data
    cout<<"\nEntered integers are: "<<num1<<" "<<num2<<endl;
    zero_Small(num1,num2); //function call
    cout<<"\nAfter function call the integers are: ";
    cout<<num1<<" "<<num2<<endl;
    getch( ); //freeze the monitor
}
```

Problem 8. *Raising a number n to a power p is the same as multiplying n by itself p times. Write a function called power that takes two arguments, a double value for n and an int value for p, and returns the result as double value. Use default argument of 2 for p, so that if this argument is omitted that number will be squared. Write the main function that gets value from the user to test power function.*

Solution.

```
#include<iostream.h>
#include<conio.h>
//function definition power( )
double power(double n,int p=2) //default argument is p=2
{
    double result=1;
    int i;
    for(i=1;i<=p;i++)
        result *=n;
    return result;
}
void main( )
{
    double num;
    int p;
    clrscr( );
    cout<<"Enter the number and power\n";
    cin>>num>>p;
    cout<<"\nResult="<<power(num,p)<<endl; //function call
```

```
    cout<<"\nEnter the number\n";
    cin>>num;
    cout<<"\nResult="<<power(num)<<endl; //function call
    getch( );
}
```

REVIEW QUESTIONS AND EXERCISES

1. What is a function? How will you define a function in C++?
2. What do you understand by function prototyping? What are the advantages of function prototyping in C++?
3. How is function definition different from function prototype?
4. What is meant by invoking/calling a function? Explain with the help of a suitable example of your choice.
5. Write a short note on passing arguments to function. Give suitable example also.
6. How are the argument data types specified for a C++ function? Explain with suitable example.
7. When do we use default argument(s) in a function? Give example.
8. What is the purpose of using constant argument(s) in a C++ function? Explain with the help of an example.
9. What do you mean by default arguments and constant arguments? Write a short note on their usefulness.
10. What is the difference between call by value and call by reference? Also, give a suitable C++ code to illustrate both.
11. What is the main advantage of passing arguments by reference?
12. What types of functions are available in C++? Explain.
13. Write a program in C++ to convert a decimal whole number to any other base *i.e.*, binary, octal or hexadecimal depending on the user's choice.
14. Write a program to find the area and perimeter of a circle (use call by reference method).
15. Write a program to sum the series:

$$1 + \frac{1}{1!} + \frac{1}{2!} + \frac{1}{3!} + \frac{1}{4!} + \ldots\ldots\ldots\ldots + \frac{1}{n!}$$

16. Write a function sum( ) in C++ with two arguments, double x and int n. The function should return a value of type double and it should find the sum of the following series:

$$1 + \frac{x}{1!} + \frac{x^3}{2!} + \frac{x^5}{3!} + \frac{x^7}{4!} + \ldots\ldots\ldots\ldots + \frac{x^{2n-1}}{n!}$$

17. What are the main advantages of library functions in C++?
18. What is the use of **math.h** header file? Explain the usage of any three functions contained in it with the help of suitable examples.
19. What is the use of **stdlib.h** header file? Explain the usage of any two functions contained in it with the help of suitable examples.

20. Explain the usage of the following mathematical functions with the help of suitable examples:

(*i*) fabs ( ) (*ii*) log ( ) (*iii*) log10 ( )

(*iv*) pow ( ) (*v*) sqrt ( ) (*vi*) abs ( )

21. Explain the usage of the following trigonometric functions with the help of suitable examples:

(*i*) sin ( ) (*ii*) cos ( )

22. Explain the usage of the following with the help of suitable examples:

(*i*) randomize ( ) (*ii*) random ( ) (*iii*) itoa( )

(*iv*) atoi( )

23. Write a C++ program to compute cosine series *i.e.*,

$\cos(x) = 1 - \frac{x^2}{2!} + \frac{x^4}{4!} - \frac{x^6}{6!} + \ldots$ upto accuracy of 8 terms without using built-in function **cos ( ).**

24. Computers are playing an important role in education. Write a C++ program that will help an elementary school students learn multiplication. Use *random* function to produce two positive one-digit integers. It should then type a question such as:

How much is 6 times 7?

The student then types the answer. Your program checks the students's answer. If it is correct, print "Very Good !" and then ask another multiplication question. If the answer is wrong, print, "No, Please try again." And then let the student try the same question again repeatedly until the student finally gets it right.

25. Name the header files to which the following belong:

(*i*) abs( ) (*ii*) strcmp( )

(*iii*) puts( ) (*iv*) isalnum( )

(*v*) strcat( ) (*vi*) atoi( )

(*vii*) abs( ) (*viii*) isupper( )

(*ix*) pow( ) (*x*) random( )

(*xi*) puts( ) (*xii*) sin( )

(*xiii*) setw( ) (*xiv*) sqrt( )

26. What is recursion? While writing any recursive function what thing(s) must be taken care of?

27. Write a recursive function in C++ to find the sum of digits of a number.

28. Write a recursive function to find HCF of two positive integers. Write the main function that gets values from the user to test it.

29. Write a recursive function in C++ to add two positive integers.

30. Explain various storage types available in C++.

31. Write a short note on returning values from a function. Give suitable example also.

32. What is the difference between global variables and local variables? Give an example to illustrate the same.

33. Write a C++ function which accepts an integer as its argument and displays it in reverse form *e.g.*, 4375 should be displayed as 5734.

34. Write a C++ program to find the average of prime numbers between 10 and 50 using functional approach.

35. Write a C++ function to generate and print first n prime numbers.

36. Write a C++ function to evaluate the following investment equation:

$$V = P(1 + r)^n.$$

37. Distinguish between the following:

(*i*) Actual and Formal parameters (*ii*) Automatic and Static variables.

38. Write a C++ function to find the factorial of a number non-recursively.

39. Write a C++ program which reads 2 integer numbers and finds their sum, difference, multiplication and division using a separate function for each of these operations.

40. Write a C++ function that reads a number in binary form and converts it into hexadecimal form. Hexadecimal value must be stored also.

41. Write a recursive function in C++ that will generate and print first *n* fibonacci numbers.

42. Write a function in C++ that will calculate and display the real roots of a quadratic equation $ax^2 + bx + c = 0$, using the well known quadratic formula:

$$x = \left(-b \pm \sqrt{b^2 - 4ac}\right) / 2a$$

use the function in the program.

43. What is the difference between Actual Parameter and Formal Parameter? Give an example in C++ to illustrate both types of parameters.

❑❑❑

CHAPTER 9

Arrays and Strings

9.1 Introduction

So far we have used C++ basic data types. C++ provides the *derived* data types also, which are built from the basic integer and floating data types. An array is a C++ *derived* type that can store several values of one type. *An array is a collection of homogeneous (same type) elements that are referred by a common name.* It is also called a **subscripted variable** as the array elements are used by the name of an array and an index or subscript.

In C++, all arrays consist of *contiguous memory locations*. The lowest address corresponds to the first element and the highest address to the last element. Arrays can store data items of simple types like **int** or **float** or even of user-defined types like structures and objects.

Need for Arrays

Why do we need arrays? Consider the following example:

```
#include<iostream.h>
void main( )
{
    int a = 10;       // ordinary variable a
    a = 20;
    cout << a;        // output will be 20
}
```

In the above example the value of *a* printed is 20. As shown above 10 is assigned to *a* before assigning 20 to it. When we assign 20 to *a* then the value 10 stored in *a* is replaced with the new value 20. Hence ordinary variables are capable of storing one value at a time. This fact is same for all the data types. But in application the variables must be assigned to more than one value. It can be achieved with the help of arrays. *Array variables are used to store and process more than one elements of the same (data) type at a time.*

Arrays are of two types:

(*i*) *One-dimensional array*

(*ii*) *Multi-dimensional array (2 or more).*

The exact limit (of dimensions), if any, is determined by the compiler you will use. This chapter focuses on arrays and strings.

9.2 One-Dimensional Array

The simplest type of an array is one-dimensional array. Let us focus on one-dimensional arrays.

9.2.1 Declaration/Initialisation of One-dimensional Array

Like other variables, arrays must be explicitly declared so that the compiler may allocate space for them in memory. The syntax of declaring a one-dimensional array in C++ is as given below:

```
type arr_name[size];
```

Here, *type* declares the **base type** of the array, which is the type of each element of the array. The **arr_name** specifies the array name by which the array will be referenced and **size** defines the number of elements the array will store. For example,

```
int a[5]; // array 'a' declared having size 5
```

In C++, *the array index always begins with 0.* So, a [2] would refer to the third element in the array **a** where 2 is the array index or subscript. The entire array can be shown as in Figure 9.1:

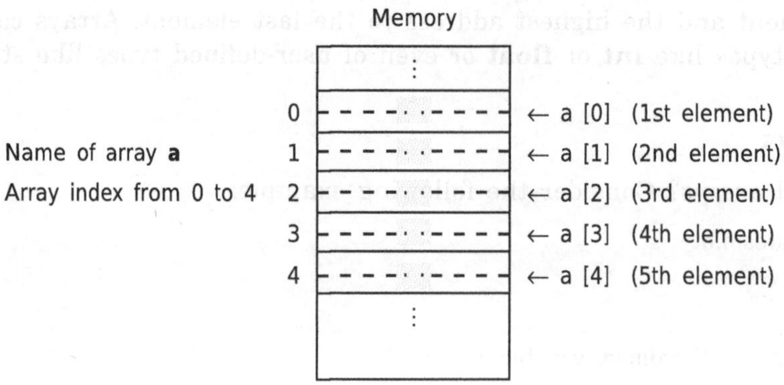

Fig. 9.1. Schematic representation of an array **a[5]** having 5 elements

Since each element in **a** is an integer, it occupies two bytes. Notice that the first element has the index 0. Thus, since there are five elements, the last one is number 4.

The amount of storage required to store an array in memory is directly related to its type and size. For a one-dimensional array, the total size in bytes is computed as shown below:

Total bytes = sizeof (base type) × size of array

The **sizeof** operator returns the size of a data type in bytes on a system.

You can initialize array (that is, give value to each array element) when the array is first defined. For example,

```
int a[5]={55,90,17,88,36};
```

The values to which **a** is initialized are enclosed in braces and separated by commas. They are connected to the array expression by = sign.

Assuming the integer size as 2 bytes, the array **a** shown in Figure 9.1 will be stored in memory as shown in Figure 9.2. (Assume the *base address* or starting address of **a** is 2000).

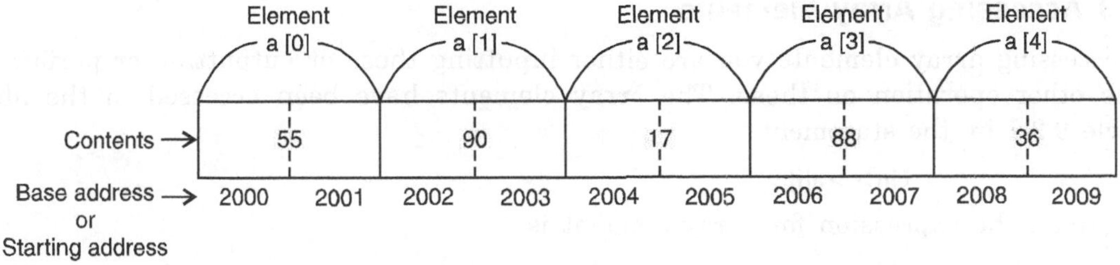

Fig. 9.2. A five element integer array **a** beginning at location 2000

Note that the array contents are actully stored in memory in binary form. For the above shown array, the total bytes needed are 2 × 5 = 10 bytes.

In case we provide all the array elements during initialization the specification of array size is not essential. The compiler will automatically count the number of elements for reserving the space in memory for the array. Thus we can write

```
int a[ ]={55,90,17,88,36};  //Ragged array
```

In case you use an explicit array size, but it is not having the number of elements equal to size of array, the missing elements will be set to 0. If the number of elements is greater than the specified size, an error message will be displayed. Consider few more examples of array initialization:

```
      float marks[ ]  =  {80.5,90.6,78.3,59.7,100.0,62.0};
long int salary[4]  =  {50000,18000,25000};
```

Note that the element salary[3] will be initialized to 0 in the last example.

> ***Note:*** *In C++, all arrays have 0 as the index of their first element.*

9.2.2 Inputting Array Elements

For reading the array elements (input operation) you must declare the array first along with the index to be used on the array. Then the array elements can be inputted as given below:

```
int a[5],i;
cout<<"Enter the five integers\n";
for(i=0;i<5;++i)
    cin>>a[i];
```

It is the duty of the programmer or user to check that the number of elements entered must not exceed the size of the array. The array index may be declared in the loop also as C++ permits the declaration of a variable anywhere prior to it's use.

You could overwrite either end of an array and write into some other variable's data or even into the program's code. For example, the following code will compile without error, but is incorrect because the **for** loop will cause the array **marks** to be overrun.

```
float marks[10];
for(int i=0; i<20; i++) // this causes marks to be overrun
    marks[i]=0.0;
```

9.2.3 Accessing Array Elements

By accessing array elements you are either inputting these or outputting or performing some other operation on these. The array elements have been accessed in the above article 9.2.2 by the statement

```
cin>>a[i];
```

Here, the expression for array element is

```
a[i]
```

Since **i** is the loop variable in the **for** loop, it starts at 0 and is incremented until it reaches 4, thereby accessing each element of array **a.**

For writing the elements (output operation) from the array use the following method :

```
for(i=0;i<5;++i)
    cout<<a[i]<<' ';
```

A **vector** is a mathematical term used for the collection of numbers which are analogous, that is, one-dimensional (linear) array. So, in C++ a **vector** can represent only integers and floating point numbers.

> ***Note:** In memory the array name refers to the starting position or the address of the area which gets allocated for storage of elements of the array.*

Following program finds the average male and female height using arrays:

Program 9.1

```
//Find average male and female height
#include<iostream.h>
#include<conio.h>
const int SIZE=10;
void main( )
{
    float maleht[SIZE],femaleht[SIZE],totmaleht=0.0,totfemaleht=0.0;
    int sexcode,mcount=0,fcount=0;
    clrscr( );
    cout<<"Maximum "<<SIZE<<" males and females (each) are allowed\n";
    cout<<"\nEnter 0 as sexcode for termination\n";
    cout<<"\nEnter sexcode: 1(for male) or 2(for female): ";
    cin>>sexcode:
    while(sexcode != 0)
    {
        if(sexcode == 1)
```

```
        {
            cout<<"\nEnter male height\n";
            cin>>maleht[mcount];
            totmaleht += maleht[mcount];
            mcount++;
        }
        if(sexcode == 2)
        {
            cout<<"\nEnter female height\n";
            cin>>femaleht[fcount];
            totfemaleht += femaleht[fcount];
            fcount++;
        }
        clrscr( );
        cout<<"\nEnter sexcode: ";
        cin>>sexcode;
    }
    clrscr( );
    if(mcount>0) //if male candidate(s) exist
        cout<<"\nAverage male height = "<<totmaleht/mcount<<endl;
    else
        cout<<"\nNo male candidate\n";
    if(fcount>0) //if female candidate(s) exist
        cout<<"\nAverage female height = "<<totfemaleht/fcount<<endl;
    else
        cout<<"\nNo female candidate\n";
    getch( ); //freeze the monitor
}
```

Output

```
Maximum 10 males and females (each) are allowed
Enter 0 as sexcode for termination
Enter sexcode: 1 (for male) or 2 (for female): 1
Enter male height
180
Enter sexcode: 1
Enter male height
174
Enter sexcode: 2
Enter female height
160
```

```
Enter sexcode: 1
Enter male height
184
Enter sexcode: 2
Enter female height
140
Enter sexcode: 0
Average male height = 179.333328
Average female height = 150
```

> ***Note:*** *Using a variable makes it easier to change the array size e.g.,* ***SIZE*** *in above Program.*

9.2.4 Passing Arrays as Arguments to a Function

Arrays are always passed to functions by address. The name of an array is actually the address of the first element it stores (that is, a pointer). A pointer is a variable that stores the address of some element. When a function has an array as a parameter the corresponding parameters in both the calling and the called function must be compatible.

We have three ways to declare the receiving parameter, which stores the array pointer.

First way. *Formal parameter may be declared as an array.* For example,

Program 9.2

```
//Find the largest of n numbers
#include<iostream.h>
#include<conio.h>
void main( )
{
    int arr[20],i,n; //array arr declared
    void largest(int a[20],int n); //function prototype
    clrscr( );
    cout<<"Enter number of elements <=20\n";
    cin>>n;
    cout<<"Enter "<<n<<" elements\n";
    for(i=0;i<n;++i)
        cin>>arr[i];
    largest(arr,n); //function call
}
//function definition largest( )
void largest(int a[20], int n)
```

```
{
    int big, i; //local variables declared
    big = a[0];
    for(i=1;i<n;++i)
    {
        if(a[i] > big)
            big = a[i];
    }
    cout<<"\nLargest number is "<<big<<endl;
}
```

Output

```
Enter number of elements <= 20
7
Enter 7 elements
200 45 40 15 600 3 150
Largest number is 600
```

Second way. *Formal parameter may be declared as an unsized array.* For example,

Program 9.3

```
//Find the largest of n numbers
#include<iostream.h>
#include<conio.h>
void main( )
{
    int arr[20],i,n; //array arr declared
    void largest(int a[ ], int n);    // function prototype (no array size given)
    clrscr( );
    cout<<"Enter number of elements<=20\n";
    cin>>n;
    cout<<"Enter "<<n<<" elements\n";
    for(i=0;i<n;++i)
        cin>>arr[i];
    largest(arr,n); //function call
}
//function definition largest( )
void largest(int a[ ], int n)
{
    int big, i; //local variables declared
```

```
    big = a[0];
    for(i=1;i<n;++i)
    {
        if (a[i] > big)
        big = a[i];
    }
    cout<<"\nLargest number is "<<big<<endl;
}
```

The output of Program 9.3 will be same as that of Program 9.2.

> ***Note:*** *When an argument is a multi-dimensional array the size must be specified but the size of first dimension is optional.*

Third way. Formal parameter may be declared as a pointer. For example,

Program 9.4

```
//Find the largest of n numbers
#include<iostream.h>
#include<conio.h>
void main( )
{
    int arr[20],i,n; //array arr declared
    void largest(int *a, int n); //function prototype (a declared as an int pointer)
    clrscr( );
    cout<<"Enter number of elements <=20\n";
    cin>>n;
    cout<<"Enter "<<n<<" elements\n";
    for(i=0;i<n;++i)
        cin>>arr[i];
    largest(arr,n); //function call
}
//function definition largest( )
void largest(int *a, int n)
{
    int big,i; //local variables declared
    big = a[0];
    for(i=1;i<n;++i)
    {
        if(a[i] > big)
        big = a[i];
    }
```

```
        cout<<"\nLargest number is "<<big<<endl;
    }
```

The output of Program 9.4 will be same as that of Program 9.2.

9.3 Null-Terminated Strings

By far the most common use of one-dimensional arrays in C++ is the string.

Let us focus on the strings in C++.

9.3.1 Declaration/Initialisation of a String

A string is defined as a character array being terminated by a NULL character, that is, '\0'. (A NULL is zero.) So the character arrays must be declared one character longer than the size of the string you wish to store. The last byte stores the string terminator '\0'. The syntax of declaration of a string is:

```
char arr_name[SIZE];
```

For example, if an array name is used to store a 7 character string, the declaration must be:

```
char name[8];
```

This makes room for the NULL at the end of the string. Figure 9.3 shows how array **name** appears in memory if it starts at memory location 3000 (A character size is 1byte):

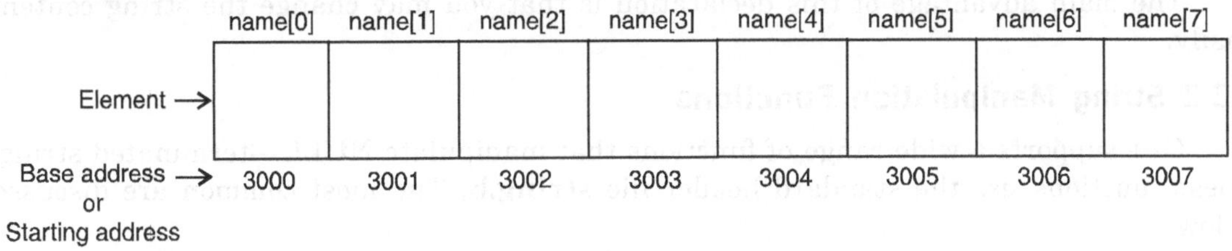

Fig. 9.3. An eight element character array **name** beginning at address 3000

Total bytes = sizeof (base type) × size of array.

So the total bytes needed for storage of array **name** are 1 × 8 = 8 bytes.

The individual characters of the string are accessed using a subscript. The end of the string can be checked by comparing the character with NULL character.

Initializing Strings

A string can be initialized while declaring it by specifying value of some or all of its elements. We can directly initialize the array in two ways:

```
char name[8] = {'A', 'p', 'o', 'o', 'r', 'v', 'a', '\0'};
char name[8] = {"Apoorva"};
```

When individual array elements are moved then the terminator must be explicitly specified. But in the case of string assignment, the terminator is automatically attached.

Following program illustrates the above concept:

Program 9.5

```
//illustration of array initialization during declaration
#include<iostream.h>
#include<conio.h>
char book_name[40] = {"Mastering C++ Programs by J.B.Dixit"};
void main( )
{
    clrscr( );
    cout<<"I hope you have enjoyed: "<<book_name<<endl;
}
```

Output

```
I hope you have enjoyed: Mastering C++ Programs by J.B. Dixit
```

C++ permits you to skip the *size* of the array in an array initialization statement. It is called an *unsized array*. C++ compiler automatically calculates the dimensions of unsized arrays. For example,

```
char str[ ]="Abhinav Bindra Won a Gold Medal in Beijing Olympics 2008";
```

The main advantage of this declaration is that you may change the string contents easily.

9.3.2 String Manipulation Functions

C++ supports a wide range of functions that manipulate NULL—terminated strings. These functions use the standard header file **string.h.** The most common are discussed below:

strcpy( )

The syntax of strcpy( ) function is given below:

```
strcpy(dest,source);
```

Copies source into dest.

The following program illustrates the use of strcpy( ) function:

Program 9.6

```
//Program to illustrate the use of strcpy( ) function
#include<iostream.h>
#include<string.h>
#include<conio.h>
const int SIZE=50;
void main( )
{
    char source[SIZE],dest[SIZE];
```

```
    clrscr( );
    cout<<"Enter a string of length <= "<<SIZE-1<<endl;
    cin.getline(source,SIZE);        // reads a multiword string
    strcpy(dest,source);
    cout<<"\nThe string is copied in destination string and is\n\n";
    cout<<dest;
    getch( ); //freeze the monitor
}
```

Output

```
Enter a string of length <= 49
COMPUTER SCIENCE
The string is copied in destination string and is
COMPUTER SCIENCE
```

strcat( )

The syntax of strcat( ) function is given below:

```
strcat(source,dest);
```

Concatenates dest onto the end of source.

The following program illustrates the use of strcat( ) function:

Program 9.7

```
//Program to illustrate the use of strcat( ) function
#include<iostream.h>
#include<string.h>
#include<conio.h>
void main( )
{
    char source[ ]="brave",dest[ ]="heart";
    clrscr( );
    strcat(source,dest);
    cout<<"The string after concatenation is \n\n";
    cout<<source;
    getch( );   //freeze the monitor
}
```

Output

```
The string after concatenation is
braveheart
```

strlen( )

The syntax of strlen( ) function is given below:

```
strlen(source);
```

Returns the length of source.

The following program illustrates the use of strlen( ) function:

Program 9.8

```
//Program to illustrate the use of strlen( ) function
#include<iostream.h>
#include<string.h>
#include<conio.h>
void main( )
{
    char source[50];
    int len;
    clrscr( );
    cout<<"Enter a string\n";
    cin.getline(source,50);      // reads a multiword string
    len=strlen(source);
    cout<<"The length of the entered string is "<<len;
    getch( ); //freeze the monitor
}
```

Output

```
Enter a string
The gateway of India
The length of the entered string is 20
```

strcmp( )

The syntax of strcmp( ) function is given below:

```
strcmp(str1,str2);
```

Compares str1 and str2 character by character. Returns 0 if str1 and str2 are the same; less than 0 if str1 < str2; greater than 0 if str1 > str2.

The following program illustrates the use of strcmp( ) function:

Program 9.9

```
//Program to illustrate the use of strcmp( ) function
#include<iostream.h>
#include<string.h>
#include<conio.h>
```

```
void main( )
{
    char str1[50],str2[50];
    clrscr( );
    cout<<"Enter a string of length <50\n";
    cin.getline(str1,50);      // reads a multiword string
    cout<<"Enter another string of length <50\n";
    cin.getline(str2,50);      // reads a multiword string
    int flag=strcmp(str1,str2);
    if(flag)
        cout<<"\nEntered strings are unequal ";
    else
        cout<<"\nEntered strings are equal ";
    getch( ); //freeze the monitor
}
```

Output

```
Enter a string of length < 50
MOHAN
Enter another string of length < 50
MOHANAN
Entered strings are unequal
Enter a string of length < 50
GOOD LUCK
Enter another string of length < 50
GOOD LUCK
Entered strings are equal
```

strcmpi( )

The syntax of strcmpi( ) function is given below:

```
strcmpi(str1,str2);
```

Compares str1 and str2 by ignoring the case. Returns 0 if str1 and str2 are the same; less than 0 if str1 < str2; greater than 0 if str1 > str2.

The following program illustrates the use of strcmpi( ) function:

Program 9.10

```
//Program to illustrate the use of strcmpi( ) function
#include<iostream.h>
#include<string.h>
#include<conio.h>
```

```
const int SIZE=50;
void main( )
{
    char str1[SIZE],str2[SIZE];
    clrscr( );
    cout<<"Enter a string of length < "<<SIZE<<"\n\n";
    cin.getline(str1,SIZE);        // reads a multiword string
    cout<<"Enter another string of length < "<<SIZE<<"\n\n";
    cin.getline(str2,SIZE);        // reads a multiword string
    int flag=strcmpi(str1,str2);
    if(flag)
        cout<<"\nEntered strings are unequal ";
    else
        cout<<"\nEntered strings are equal ";
    getch( );   //freeze the monitor
}
```

Output

```
Enter a string of length < 50
Good lUCk
Enter another string of length < 50
gOOd LUCK
Entered strings are equal
Enter a string of length < 50
GOGA
Enter another string of length < 50
kapoor
Entered strings are unequal
```

9.3.3 Passing Strings to a Function

In C++, we can pass strings to a function and perform the desired and permissible operation on its elements. For example,

(i) *Counting vowels / consonants / digits / special characters*

(ii) *Case conversion, that is, uppercase to lowercase and vice versa*

(iii) *Reversing a string*

(iv) *Reversing each word of a string etc.*

(i) Counting Vowels/Consonants/Digits/Special Characters

Individual characters of a string are accessed from start and their comparison is done with the related category characters. The related count variable is incremented. This process is continued till we reach the end of the string. Finally all the results are printed.

Following program illustrates the above concept:

Program 9.11

```
//Counting vowels/consonants/digits/special characters in a string
#include<iostream.h>
#include<conio.h>
#include<stdio.h> //for gets( ) and puts( )
const int SIZE=80;
void main( )
{
    char str[SIZE];
    void pass_string(char string[ ]); //function prototype
    clrscr( );
    cout<<"Enter the string of length <= "<<SIZE-1<<"\n\n";
    gets(str); //for storing multiword string
    cout<<"\n\nEntered string is\n\n";
    puts(str);
    pass_string(str);        //function call
}
//function definition pass_string( )
void pass_string(char string[ ])
{
    int i,vowel_count,consonant_count,digit_count,spl_count;
    vowel_count=consonant_count=digit_count=spl_count=0;
    //count different characters
    i=0;
    while(string[i] != '\0')
    {
        if ( string[i]=='a'     ||  string[i]=='A'  ||  string[i]  ==  'e'
          ||  string[i]=='E'    ||  string[i]=='i'  ||  string[i]  ==  'I'
          ||  string[i]=='o'    ||  string[i]=='O'  ||  string[i]  ==  'u'
          ||  string[i]=='U')
            vowel_count++;
        else if( (string[i] >='a' && string[i] <='z') || (string[i] >= 'A' && string[i] <= 'Z') )
            consonant_count++;
        else if(string[i] >= '0' && string[i] <= '9')
            digit_count++;
        else
            spl_count++;
        i++;
    }
```

```
    cout<<"\n\nThe character count is";
    cout<<"\n\nNumber of vowels: "<<vowel_count;
    cout<<"\nNumber of consonants: "<<consonant_count;
    cout<<"\nNumber of digits: "<<digit_count;
    cout<<"\nNumber of special characters: "<<spl_count;
}
```

Output

```
Enter the string of length <=79
LAXMI PUBLICATIONS (P) LTD. 113, Golden House, Daryaganj, New Delhi–110002
Entered string is
LAXMI PUBLICATIONS (P) LTD. 113, Golden House, Daryaganj, New Delhi–110002
The character count is
Number of vowels: 18
Number of consonants: 31
Number of digits: 9
Number of special characters : 15
```

(ii) Case Conversion

As mentioned earlier the C++ character set is implemented using **ASCII** code. The ASCII code of 'A' is 65 and that of 'a' is 97. So the difference between the two is 32. Therefore, for converting an uppercase character to lowercase, 32 is added and for converting the lowercase character to uppercase 32 is subtracted from its ASCII code value. Following program implements the above concept:

Program 9.12

```
//Case conversion of a string
#include<iostream.h>
#include<conio.h>
#include<stdio.h> //for gets( ) and puts( )
void main( )
{
    char str[80];
    void convert(char string[ ]);       //function prototype
    clrscr( );
    cout<<"Enter the string of length < 80\n\n";
    gets(str);
    cout<<"\nEntered string is\n\n";
    puts(str);
    convert(str);     //function call
}
```

```
//function definition convert( )
void convert(char string[ ])
{
    int i=0;
    //case conversion
    while(string[i] != '\0')
    {
        if(string[i] >= 'A' && string[i]<='Z')
                string[i]=string[i]+32;
        else
          {
                if(string[i]>='a' && string[i]<='z')
                    string[i]=string[i]-32;
          }
        i++;
    }
    cout<<"\nCase converted string is\n\n";
    puts(string);
}
```

Output

```
Enter the string of length < 80
Case Conversion
Entered string is
Case Conversion
Case converted string is
cASE cONVERSION
Enter the string of length < 80
nEW aPPROACH
Entered string is
nEW aPPROACH
Case converted string is
New Approach
```

(iii) Reversing a String

Reversing a string means interchanging the characters from both ends of it. First of all find the length of the string by traversing through it. Compute the value of **mid**, that is, the middle position of the string and then starting from position 0, swap (interchange) the characters till position mid–1. Following program illustrates the above concept:

Program 9.13

```
//Reversing a string
#include<iostream.h>
#include<conio.h>
#include<stdio.h> //for gets( ) and puts( )
const int SIZE=80;
void main( )
{
    char str[SIZE];
    void reverse(char string[ ]);    //function prototype
    clrscr( );
    cout<<"Enter a string of length <= "<<SIZE-1<<"\n\n";
    gets(str);
    cout<<"\n\nEntered string is\n\n";
    puts(str);
    reverse(str);       //function call
}
//function definition reverse( )
void reverse(char string[ ])
{
    char tempch;
    int length, mid, i=0;
    while(string[i] != '\0')
        i++;
    length=i;
    mid=length/2;
    i=0;
    //reverse the string
    while(i<mid)
    {
        tempch = string[i];
        string[i] = string[length-1-i];
        string[length-1-i] = tempch;
        i++;
    }
    cout<<"\n\nReversed string is\n\n";
    puts(string);
}
```

Output

```
Enter a string of length <= 79
taerg si aidnI
Entered string is
taerg si aidnI
Reversed string is
India is great
Enter a string of length <= 79
The Times of India
Entered string is
The Times of India
Reversed string is
aidnI fo semiT ehT
```

(iv) Reversing Each Word of a String

We start from the beginning of the string and find the initial and final position of each individual word using the variables **beg** and **end** respectively either by checking for a blank character or string terminator. The string's individual words so found are reversed. Finally the string after reversing each word is displayed. Following program implements the above concept:

Program 9.14

```
//Reversing each word of a string
#include<iostream.h>
#include<conio.h>
#include<stdio.h>  //for gets( ) and puts( )
const int SIZE=80;
void main( )
{
    char str[SIZE];
    void reverse_words(char string[ ]);   //function prototype
    int i=0,beg=0,end;
    clrscr( );
    cout<<"Enter a string of length <= "<<SIZE-1<<"\n\n";
    gets(str);
    cout<<"\nEntered string is\n\n";
    puts(str);
    reverse_words(str);     //function call
}
```

```
//function definition reverse_words( )
void reverse_words(char string[ ])
{
    char tempch;
    int i=0, beg=0, end;
    do
    {
        while( (string[i] != ' ') && (string[i] != '\0') )
            i++;
        end=i-1;
        while(beg<end)
        {
            tempch=string[end];
            string[end]=string[beg];
            string[beg]=tempch;
            beg++;
            end--;
        }
        if(string[i] == '\0')
            break;
        beg=++i;
    } while(1);
    cout<<"\n\nAfter reversing each word the string is\n\n";
    puts(string);
    getch( ); //freeze the monitor
}
```

Output

```
Enter a string of length <= 79
Computer Science
Entered string is
Computer Science
After reversing each word the string is
retupmoC ecneicS
```

9.4 Two-Dimensional Arrays

C++ supports multidimensional arrays. The simplest form of the multidimensional array is the two-dimensional array. A two-dimensional array is, essentially, an array of one-dimensional arrays. Let us focus on two-dimensional arrays.

9.4.1 Declaration/Initialisation of a Two-Dimensional Array

A two-dimensional array is a grid having rows and columns in which each element is specified by two subscripts. It is the simplest of multi-dimensional arrays. For example,

An array **a[m][n]** is an **m** by **n** table having m rows and n columns containing m × n elements (see Figure 9.4). The number of elements is obtained by calculating m × n.

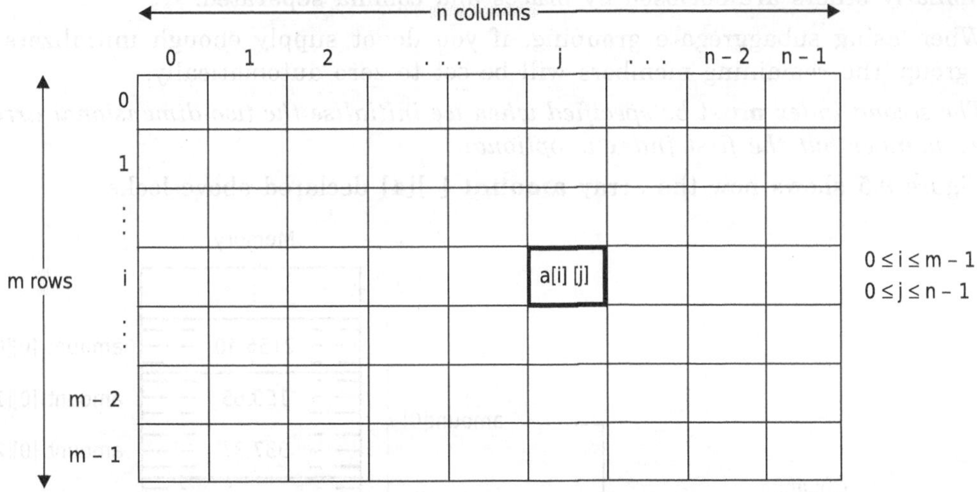

Fig. 9.4. Two-dimensional array a[m][n]

Here, a[i][j] denotes the element in the ith row and jth column. The syntax of declaring a two-dimensional array in C++ is as follows:

```
type variable_name[number of rows][number of columns];
```

Pay careful attention to the declaration. Some other computer languages use commas to separate the array dimensions; C++, in contrast, places each dimension in its own set of brackets. For example,

```
int a[5][5];
```

Here 'a' is the name of the array of type **int** of size 5 by 5.

The array elements are a[0][0], a[0][1], ..., a[4][4].

In case of a two-dimensional array, the following formula yields the total number of bytes of memory needed to store it.

Total bytes = size of 1st dimension × size of 2nd dimension × size of (base type)

Therefore, assuming 2-byte integers, the array **a** declared above, would have

5 × 5 × 2

or 50 bytes allocated.

You can initialize a two-dimensional array, like a one-dimensional array, when the array is first defined. For example,

```
float amount[ ][4] = {
                        {2155.40, 159.65, 937.37, 10918.66},
                        {517.00, 17936.35, 5009.39, 88.75},
                        {7500.60, 7039.55, 4085.25, 837.00}
                     };
```

Remember that a two-dimensional array is really an array of arrays. The format for initializing such an array is based on this fact. The initializing values for each sub-array are enclosed in braces (called *subaggregate grouping*) and separated by commas:

{2155.40, 159.65, 937.37, 10918.66}

and similarly others are enclosed by braces and comma separated.

When using subaggregate grouping, if you donot supply enough initializers for a given group, the remaining members will be set to zero automatically.

The second index **must** *be specified when we initialise the two-dimensional arrays in unsized manner but the first index is optional.*

Figure 9.5 shows how the array **amount [ ][4]** declared above looks:

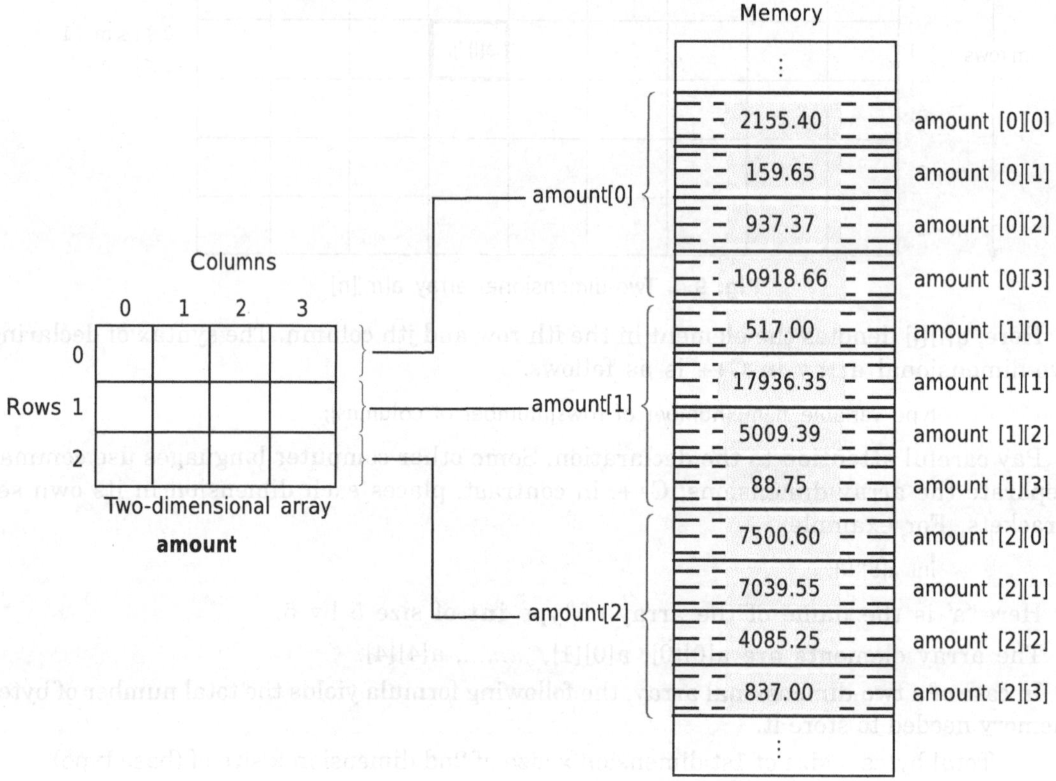

Fig. 9.5. Illustration of storage of array amount [ ][4]

If the number of rows in the above array amount[ ][4] are increased or decreased in the initialisation, the array will also grow or shrink accordingly.

> ***Note:*** *The size of first index (first dimension) is optional in array initialization.*

9.4.2 Inputting Array Elements

For reading the two-dimensional array elements (input operation) you must declare the array first along with the indices to be used on the array. Then the array elements can be inputted as given below:

```
const int S = 5;
int a[S][S],i,j,m,n;
```

```
cout<<"Enter the size of two-dimensional array <= "<<S<<" * "<<S<<endl;
cin>>m>>n;
cout<<"\nEnter the array of size "<<m<<" * "<<n<<endl;
for(i=0;i<m;i++)
{
    for(j=0;j<n;j++)
        cin>>a[i][j];
}
```

9.4.3 Accessing Array Elements

By accessing array elements you are either inputting these or outputting or performing some other operation on these. The array elements have been accessed in the above article 9.4.2 by the statement

```
cin>>a[i][j];
```

Here, the expression for array element is

```
a[i][j]
```

Since **i** and **j** are the loop variables, **i** is set to **0** and **j** is incremented until it reaches **n**, then **i** is incremented to **1** and **j** again varies from 0 to n–1, that is, the inner **for** loop is again executed **n** times.

This process continues until **i** reaches **m** and the loop terminates. It means the array elements have been accessed.

For writing the elements (output operation) from the array use the following method:

```
for(i=0;i<m;i++)
{
    for(j=0;j<n;j++)
        cout<<a[i][j]<<' ';
    cout<<endl;
}
```

Following program implements the above concept:

Program 9.15

```
//Accessing array elements
#include<iostream.h>
#include<conio.h>
const int SIZE=5;
void main( )
{
    int a[SIZE][SIZE],m,n,i,j;
    clrscr( );
    cout<<"Enter size of two-dimensional array <= "<<SIZE<<" * "<<SIZE<<"\n";
    cin>>m>>n;
```

```
    cout<<"\nEnter the array of size "<<m<<" * "<<n<<"\n\n";
    //row wise reading
    for(i=0;i<m;i++)
    {
        for(j=0;j<n;j++)
            cin>>a[i][j];
    }
    //echo the data
    cout<<"\nEntered array is\n\n";
    for(i=0;i<m;i++)
    {
        for(j=0;j<n;j++)
            cout<<a[i][j]<<'\t';
        cout<<endl;
    }
}
```

Output

```
Enter size of two-dimensional array <= 5 * 5
3 4
Enter the array of size 3 * 4
1 2 3 4
6 5 2 8
9 7 3 6
Entered array is
1       2       3       4
6       5       2       8
9       7       3       6
```

Let us write a C++ program to find the sum of elements on both the diagonals of a two-dimensional array of size N×N. For example:

```
   5    8                    1    2    3
   2    4                    4    5    6
Sum of diagonal              7    8    9
elements = 19             Sum of diagonal
                           elements = 25
```

In the 3 by 3 array the element 5 on both diagonals have been added only once.

As mentioned earlier the array indices for two-dimensional arrays start with 0 in C++. Following program implements the above concept:

Program 9.16

```
//Find sum of both diagonal's elements
#include<iostream.h>
#include<conio.h>
const int SIZE=5;
void main( )
{
    int a[SIZE][SIZE],m,n,i,j,sum=0;
    do
    {
        clrscr( );
        cout<<"Enter size of two-dimensional array <= "<<SIZE<<" * "<<SIZE<<"\n";
        cin>>m>>n;
    }
    while( (m != n) || (m <= 0) ); //get ranged values only
    cout<<"\nEnter the array of size "<<n<<" * "<<n<<"\n\n";
    //row wise reading
    for(i=0;i<n;i++)
    {
        for(j=0;j<n;j++)
        cin>>a[i][j];
    }
    //echo the data
    cout<<"\nEntered array is \n\n";
    for(i=0;i<n;i++)
    {
        for(j=0;j<n;j++)
            cout<<a[i][j]<<'\t';
        cout<<endl;
    }
    //sum of both diagonal elements
    for(i=0;i<n;i++)
    {
        for(j=0;j<n;j++)
        {
            if( (i==j) || (i+j == n-1) )
```

```
            sum+ =a[i][j];
        }
    }
    cout<<"\nSum of both diagonals elements is: "<<sum;
}
```

Output

```
Enter size of two-dimensional array <= 5 * 5
3 3
Enter the array of size 3 * 3
1 2 3
4 5 6
7 8 9
Entered array is

1       2       3
4       5       6
7       8       9

Sum of both diagonals elements is: 25
```

9.4.4 Array of Strings

It is not uncommon in programming to use an array of strings. An array of strings is a two-dimensional character array. The row size determines the number of strings and the column size specifies the maximum length of each string.

The following code declares an array of 12 strings, each with a maximum length of 9 characters, plus the NULL character.

```
char monthnames[12][10]; //declare array of 12 strings
```

It is easy to access an individual string *i.e.,* you can do it by specifying only the row number.

A two-dimensional array can be initialized in the same way as that of a one-dimensional array. For example,

```
char monthnames[12][10]={ "January","February","March","April","May",
                          "June","July","August","September",
                          "October","November","December"};
```

Here, monthnames[0] refers to "January" and monthnames[3][2] refers to the character **r** of the string "April".

Figure 9.6 illustrates the storage of array **monthnames** in memory:

|← 10 →|

	0	1	2	3	4	5	6	7	8	9	
0	J	a	n	u	a	r	y	\0			monthnames[0]
1	F	e	b	r	u	a	r	y	\0		monthnames[1]
2	M	a	r	c	h	\0					monthnames[2]
3	A	p	r	i	l	\0					monthnames[3]
4	M	a	y	\0							monthnames[4]
5	J	u	n	e	\0						monthnames[5]
6	J	u	l	y	\0						monthnames[6]
7	A	u	g	u	s	t	\0				monthnames[7]
8	S	e	p	t	e	m	b	e	r	\0	monthnames[8]
9	O	c	t	o	b	e	r	\0			monthnames[9]
10	N	o	v	e	m	b	e	r	\0		monthnames[10]
11	D	e	c	e	m	b	e	r	\0		monthnames[11]

Fig. 9.6. Illustration of array **monthnames** of strings

The following program illustrates the use of an array of strings.

Program 9.17

```
//Accept a month number and display the month name
#include<iostream.h>
#include<conio.h>
void main( )
{
    char monthnames[12][10]={ "January","February","March","April","May",
                              "June","July","August","September",
                              "October","November","December"};

    int month;
    clrscr( );
    cout<<"Enter the month number (1-12)\n";
    cin>>month;
    if(month<1 || month>12)
        cout<<"\nWrong month number entered\n";
    else
        cout<<"\nMonth name is: "<<monthnames[month-1]<<"\n";
    getch( ); //freeze the monitor
}
```

Output

```
Enter the month number (1–12)
4
Month name is: April
Enter the month number (1–12)
13
Wrong month number entered
```

9.5 Multidimensional Arrays

C++ allows arrays of more than two dimensions. The exact limit, if any, is determined by the compiler in use. The syntax of a multidimensional array declaration is given below:

```
type array_name[Size1] [Size2] [Size3] ... [SizeN];
```

The general form of array initialization is similar to that of other variables, as given below:

```
type array_name[Size1] [Size2] [Size3] ... [SizeN] = {value_list};
```

The *value–list* is a comma-seperated list of values whose type is compatible with *type*. The first value is placed in the first position of the array, the second value in the second position, and so on. Note that a semicolon follows the **}**.

Arrays of more than three dimensions are not generally used because of the amount of memory they require.

In multidimensional arrays, it takes the computer time to compute each index. This means that accessing an element in a multidimensional array can be slower than accessing an element in a one-dimensional array.

When passing multidimensional arrays into functions, you must declare all but the left most dimension. For example, if you declare array **arr** as

```
int arr[3][5][4][6];
```

a function **func1( )**, that receives **arr**, would look as given below:

```
void func1(int arr[ ][5][4][6])
{
    - - - - - - - -
    - - - - - - - -      // body of function
}
```

Of course, you can include the first dimension if you wish. In C++, pointers and arrays are closely related. An array name without an index is a pointer to the first element in the array.

Solved Problems

Problem 1. *Write a C++ program to check a string for palindrome. (A string is a palindrome if it reads same from both ends e.g., MADAM, NITIN, MALAYALAM etc.)*

Solution.

```
//Check a string for palindrome
#include<iostream.h>
#include<conio.h>
#include<stdio.h>          //for gets( )
#include<string.h>         //for strlen( )
const int SIZE=80;
void main( )
{
    char arr[SIZE];
    int i,len,mid;
    clrscr( );
    cout<<"Enter the string of length <= "<<SIZE-1<<"\n\n";
    gets(arr);
    //find length of string
    len=strlen(arr);
    mid=len/2;
    //checking for palindrome
    i=0;
    while(i<mid)
    {
        if(arr[i] != arr[len-1-i])
            break;
        i++;
    }
    if(i==mid)
        cout<<"\nString is a palindrome\n";
    else
        cout<<"\nString is not a palindrome";
}
```

Problem 2. *Write a C++ program that accepts an integer from the keyboard and give the sum of the digits of the number, for example if the integer is 123, the output should be 1 + 2 + 3 = 6.*

Solution.

```
//input an integer from the keyboard and give
//the sum of the digits of the number, for example
//if the integer is 123, the output should be
//1+2+3=6
```

```
#include<iostream.h>
#include<math.h>
#include<string.h>
#include<stdlib.h>        //for itoa( ) converts integer to a string
#include<conio.h>
void main( )
{
    int num,temp,len,digit,sum=0;
    char string[6]; //for storing integer as string
    clrscr( ); //clears the screen
    cout<<"Enter the integer\n\n";
    cin>>num;
    cout<<"\nEntered integer is: "<<num<<endl;
    if(num<=9)
        cout<<endl<<num<<'='<<num<<endl;
    else
    {
        temp=num;
        itoa(num,string,10); //convert integer to string
        //find number of digits in the string
        len=strlen(string);
        cout<<endl<<endl;
        while(len-1) //execute the loop len-1 times
        {
            digit = temp / pow(10,len-1);
            sum += digit;
            cout<<digit<<'+';
            temp = temp - digit * (pow(10,len-1));
            len--;
        }
        sum += temp;
        cout<<temp<<'='<<sum<<endl;
    }
    getch( ); //freeze the monitor
}
```

Problem 3. *Write a C++ program to delete all occurrences of an integer number from an array. Shift all the non-deleted members to left and fill the unused space by 0 (zero).*

Solution.

```
//Delete all occurrences of an integer number
//Shift all the non deleted numbers to left
//and fill the unused space by 0(zero)
```

```
#include<iostream.h>
#include<conio.h>
const int S=10;
void main( )
{
        void enter(int [ ],int); //function prototype
        void display(int [ ],int);
        void del(int [ ],int,int);
        int n,data,flag,a[S];
        clrscr( );
        cout<<"Enter number of elements<= "<<S<<"\n";
        cin>>n;
        cout<<"\nEnter "<<n<<" elements\n";
        enter(a,n); //function call
        //echo the data
        cout<<"\nGiven array is\n";
        display(a,n); //function call
        cout<<"\nEnter the element to be deleted\n";
        cin>>data;
        cout<<"\n\nElement whose all occurrences are to be deleted is "<<data<<"\n";
        //deletion
        flag=del(a,data,n); //function call
        if (flag != 0) //function call
        {
           cout<<"\nArray after deletion is\n\n";
           display(a,n);  //function call
        }
        else
           cout<<"\nDeletion not possible\n";
}
//function definition enter( )
void enter(int a[S], int n)
{
    for(int i=0;i<n;i++)
        cin>>a[i];
}
//definition of the function display( )
void display(int a[S], int n)
{
    for(int i=0;i<n;i++)
    cout<<a[i]<<" ";
}
```

```
//function definition del( )
int del(int a[S], int data, int n)
{
    int i,j,last,count; //local variables declared
    last=n-1;
    i=0;
    count=0;
    while(i<=last)
    {
        if(a[i]==data)
        {
            count++;
            for(j=i+1;j<=last;j++)
                a[j-1]=a[j]; //shifting
            last--;
        }
        else
            i++;
    }
    for(j=last+1;j<n;j++)
        a[j]=0;
    return(count);
}
```

Problem 4. *Write a C++ program to calculate the frequency of all characters in a string.*

Solution.

```
//Calculate the frequency of all characters in a string
#include<iostream.h>
#include<conio.h>
#include<string.h>
#include<stdio.h>
const int SIZE=80;
void main( )
{
    char arr[SIZE];
    int i,j,count,occurred,len=0,total=0;
    clrscr( );
    cout<<"Enter the string of length <= "<<SIZE-1<<"\n\n";
    gets(arr);
    //echo the data
    cout<<"\nInputted stream of characters is:\n\n";
```

```
	puts(arr);
	//find length of string
	len=strlen(arr);
	cout<<"\nTotal characters inputted: "<<len<<"\n";
	cout<<"\nCharacter                    Frequency\n\n";
	for(i=0;i<len;i++)
	{
		occurred=0;
		count=1;
		//check in array whether the character has already
		//been counted from the current position to the first
		//character in reverse direction
		for(j=i-1;j>=0;j--)
		{
			if(arr[j]==arr[i])
			{
				occurred=1;  //set occurred=1 if character has been counted
				break;
			}
		}
		if( ! occurred)   //if character not found earlier
		{
			total++;
			//count for the character in the forward direction
			for(j=i+1;j<len;j++)
			{
				if(arr[j]==arr[i])
				{
					count++;
					total++;
				}
			}
			cout<<" "<<arr[i]<<"\t\t\t"<<count<<'\n';
		}
		if(total==len)    //if all characters have been counted
			break;
	}
	getch( ); //freeze the monitor
}
```

Problem 5. *Write a C++ program to reverse all strings stored in a two-dimensional array of characters.*

Solution.

```
//Reverse all strings stored in an array
#include<iostream.h>
#include<conio.h>
#include<string.h>
#include<stdio.h>
const int SIZE=80;
void main( )
{
    char a[10][SIZE],temp;
    int n,i,j,mid,length;
    clrscr( );
    cout<<"Enter the number of strings in the array <=10\n";
    cin>>n;
    cout<<"\nEnter "<<n<<" strings\n\n";
    for(i=0;i<n;i++)
        gets(a[i]);
    clrscr( );
    cout<<"Inputted strings are\n";
    for(i=0;i<n;i++)
        puts(a[i]);
    //reversal of strings
    for(i=0;i<n;i++)
    {
        length=strlen(a[i]);
        mid=length/2;
        for(j=0;j<mid;j++)
        {
            temp=a[i][j];
            a[i][j]=a[i][length-j-1];
            a[i][length-j-1]=temp;
        }
    }
    cout<<"\nReversed strings are\n";
    for(i=0;i<n;i++)
        puts(a[i]);
    getch( ); //freeze the monitor
}
```

Problem 6. *Write a C++ program to generate a magic square. A magic square is a two-dimensional array of odd order in which integers starting from 1 to n^2 (where n is the order of array of size n × n) appear only once such that the sum of any row or any column or either diagonal is equal. For example, a magic square of order 3 is given below:*

8	1	6
3	5	7
4	9	2

The logic for generating an n × n magic square for an odd integer n is given below:

1. *Place 1 in the middle of the top row.*
2. *After writing an integer i in a box, move up one row and one column to the right and write integer i+1 unless one of the following occurs:*
   (i) *If by moving one row up, you reach above the top row in the jth column, then move to the bottom of jth column and write the integer i+1 and continue step 2.*
   (ii) *If by moving one row up and moving to the right column takes you outside the square on right, then move to the left most place in the same row and write integer i+1 and continue with step 2.*
   (iii) *If by moving one row up and moving to right column, you reach a place which is already filled, then write i+1 below i, and continue with step 2.*

Solution.

```
//Program to generate a magic square of odd order
#include<iostream.h>
#include<conio.h>
#include<iomanip.h>
const int SIZE=10;
void main( )
{
    int magic[SIZE][SIZE],n,i,row,colm,newrow,newcolm;
    do
    {
        clrscr( );
        cout<<"Enter the order of the magic square to be created\n";
        cout<<"Enter only odd order < "<<SIZE<<endl;
        cin>>n;
    } while(n%2==0);
    //initialize magic square elements with 0
    for(row=0;row<n;row++)
    {
        for(colm=0;colm<n;colm++)
            magic[row][colm]=0;
    }
```

```
    row=0;
    colm=n/2;
    for(i=1;i<=n*n;i++)
    {
        magic[row][colm]=i;
        newrow=row--;
        newcolm=colm++;
        if(row<0)
            row=n-1;
        if(colm>n-1)
            colm=0;
        if(magic[row][colm] != 0)
        {
            row=newrow+1;
            colm=newcolm;
        }
    }
    cout<<"Required magic square is\n";
    for(i=1;i<=6*n;i++)
        cout<<"_";
    cout<<endl;
    for(row=0;row<n;row++)
    {
        cout<<"|";
        for(colm=0;colm<n;colm++)
            cout<<setw(4)<<magic[row][colm]<<" |";
        cout<<endl;
        for(i=1;i<=6*n;i++)
            cout<<"_";
        cout<<endl;
    }
    getch( ); //freeze the monitor
}
```

Problem 7. *Write a C++ program to multiply two matrices using functional approach.*

Solution.

```
//Multiplication of two matrices
#include<iostream.h>
#include<conio.h>
#define SIZE 5
```

```
//function definition enter( )

void enter(int x[SIZE][SIZE], int row, int colm)
{
    int i,j;
    for(i=0;i<row;i++)
    {
      for(j=0;j<colm;j++)
          cin>>x[i][j];
    }

}
//function definition display( )
void display(int x[SIZE][SIZE], int row, int colm)
{
    int i,j;
    for(i=0;i<row;i++)
    {
      for(j=0;j<colm;j++)
          cout<<x[i][j]<<'\t';
      cout<<endl;
    }
}

//function definition mat_multiply( )

void mat_multiply(int x[SIZE][SIZE], int y[SIZE][SIZE], int z[SIZE][SIZE], int row1, int colm1, int colm2)
{
    int i,j,k;
    //matrix multiplication
    for(i=0;i<row1;i++)
    {
      for(j=0;j<colm2;j++)
      {
          z[i][j]=0;
          for(k=0;k<colm1;k++)
              z[i][j] +=x[i][k]*y[k][j];
      }
    }
}
```

```
void main( )
{
    int a[SIZE][SIZE],b[SIZE][SIZE],c[SIZE][SIZE],row1,colm1,row2,colm2;
    clrscr( );
    cout<<"Enter the order of first matrix <= "<<SIZE<<" * "<<SIZE<<"\n";
    cin>>row1>>colm1;
    cout<<"\nEnter the order of second matrix <= "<<SIZE<<" * "<<SIZE<<"\n";
    cin>>row2>>colm2;
    if(colm1==row2)
    {
        cout<<"\nEnter the first matrix of order "<<row1<<" * "<<colm1<<endl;
        enter(a,row1,colm1); //function call
        cout<<"\nEnter the second matrix of order "<<row2<<" * "<<colm2<<endl;
        enter(b,row2,colm2);
        clrscr( );
        //echo the data
        cout<<"\nFirst matrix is\n\n";
        display(a,row1,colm1); //function call
        cout<<"\nSecond matrix is\n\n";
        display(b,row2,colm2);
        //matrix multiplication
        mat_multiply(a,b,c,row1,colm1,colm2); //function call
        cout<<"\nResultant matrix is\n\n";
        display(c,row1,colm2);
    }
    else
        cout<<"\nMatrix multiplication is not possible";

        getch( ); //freeze the monitor
}
```

Review Questions and Exercises

1. What is an array? What is the need of arrays?
2. What do you understand by two-dimensional arrays? State some situations that can be easily represented by these.
3. If an array is initialized at the time of declaration; what thing one must keep in mind?
4. What is meant by unsized array initialisation in C++?

5. Write short notes on the following:
   (*i*) Declaration/Initialisation of one-dimensional array.
   (*ii*) Inputting array elements.
   (*iii*) Accessing array elements.
   (*iv*) Manipulation of array elements.
6. What is a string?
7. Write a short note on the declaration/initialisation of a string.
8. What do you understand by string manipulation? Explain with the help of a suitable program of your choice.
9. Write a program in C++ that reads a string and counts the number of vowels, words and white spaces in it.
10. Write a program that counts the frequency of a character in a string.
11. Write a C++ program to calculate the length of a string without using library functions.
12. Write a C++ program to compare two strings.
13. Write a short note on string and character related library functions (three each).
14. Write short notes on the following:
    (*i*) Declaration/initialisation of a two-dimensional array.
    (*ii*) Inputting array elements.
    (*iii*) Accessing array elements.
    (*iv*) Manipulation of array elements.
15. Write a C++ program to convert an integer number to its binary equivalent.
16. Write a C++ program to find the sum of all the non-diagonal elements sum of a two-dimensional N x N array A.
17. Write a C++ program to find the product of elements on diagonal of an array A of size N x N.
18. Write a C++ program to print the maximum/minimum values in a two-dimensional array and their squares.
19. Write a C++ program to exchange the non-diagonal elements of a two-dimensional array A of size N x N without using any other array, that is, each A[I] [J] with A[J] [I] where I ^{1} J.
20. Write a C++ program to read in an array of strings and print out its contents backwards. For example, the array of three strings:

    hello

    programming

    world

    would be displayed as:

    world programming hello.
21. Write a C++ program that reads the marks of N students and provides grade as follows:

Marks	*Grade*
80 and above	A
70 and above	B
60 and above	C
40 and above	D
below 40	E

22. Write a C++ program which will read a string text and count the number of words in it.

23. Write a C++ program to find the sum of all elements of a two-dimensional array A of order M x N.
24. Write a C++ program to list those numbers which are not divisible by 2 in an array of N integers.
25. Write a C++ program to read ten numbers from keyboard in an array and print the sum of even and odd numbers.
26. Write a C++ program to search an item in an ordered array of size N (array is given in ascending order) using linear search method.
27. Write a C++ program to display all consonants in a given line, without using any if statement.
28. Write a C++ program to produce the following output:

```
          1
        1   1
      1   2   1
    1   3   3   1
  1   4   6   4   1
1   5   10  10  5   1
```

29. A magic square is a square array of positive integers such that the sum of each row, column, and diagonal is the same constant. For example:

16	3	2	13
5	10	11	8
9	6	7	12
4	15	14	1

is a magic square whose constant is 34.
Write a C++ program to determine whether or not the given square is a magic square.
30. Write a C++ program to cycle string frequently. For example,

shukla
ashukl
lashuk
klashu
uklash
huklas

❑❑❑

CHAPTER **10**

Concepts of Object Oriented Programming

10.1 Introduction to Object-Oriented Programming

Object-Oriented Programming (OOP) was developed because limitations were discovered in earlier approaches to programming. A recent trend in programming methodology is OOP where the real world is represented by objects. An object is a combination of data structures and procedures that operate upon or extract information from these data structures. Imagine you are programming in a traditional third-generation language, such as BASIC, creating your coded instructions one line at a time. As you work on some segment of the program (such as how to compute overtime pay), you may think, "I will bet some other programmer has already written something like this. Wish I had it. It would save a lot of time". Fortunately, a kind of recycling technique now exists. This is object-oriented programming.

The main advantage of object-oriented programs is their reliability and manageability, especially in situations where many programmers work on the same project.

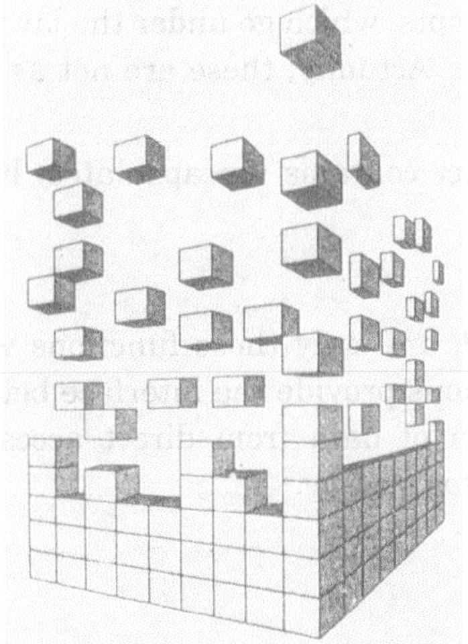

Fig. 10.1. Conventional Programs

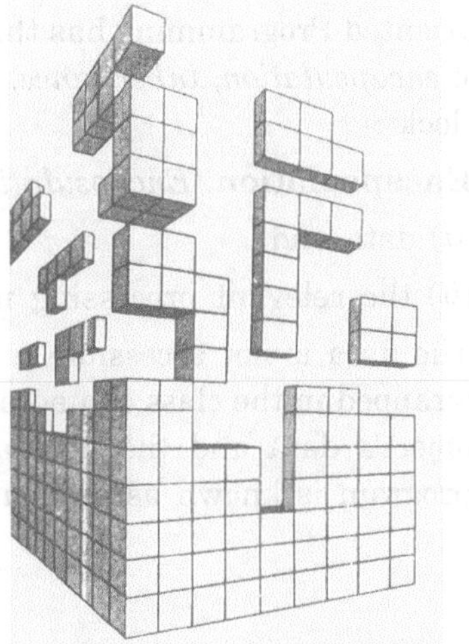

Fig. 10.2. Object-Oriented Programs

1. **What OOP is?** In ***Object-Oriented Programming*** **(OOP, pronounced "oop"), data and the instructions for processing that data are combined into a self-sufficient "object" that can be used in other programs.** The important thing here is the object.
2. **What an "object" is?** An *object* is a self-contained module consisting of preassembled programming code. The module contains, or encapsulates, both:

   (*i*) a chunk of data and

   (*ii*) the processing instructions that may be performed on that data.
3. **When an object's data is to be processed—sending the "message".** Once the object becomes part of a program, the processing instructions may or may not be activated. A particular set of instructions is activated only when the corresponding "message" is sent. A *message* is an alert sent to the object when an operation involving that object needs to be performed.
4. **How the object's data is processed—the "methods".** The message need only identify the operation. How it is actually to be performed is embedded within the processing instructions that are part of the object. These processing instructions within the object are called the *methods.*

Once you have written a block of program code (that computes overtime pay, for example), it can be reused in any number of programs. Thus, with OOP, unlike traditional programming, you do not have to start from scratch—that is, reinvent the wheel—each time.

Object-oriented programming takes longer to learn than traditional programming because it means training oneself to a new way of thinking. However, the beauty of OOP is that an object can be used repeatedly in different applications and by different programmers, speeding up development time and lowering costs.

10.2 Three Important Concepts of OOP

Object-Oriented Programming has three important concepts, which go under the jaw-breaking names of *encapsulation, inheritance,* and *polymorphism.* Actually, these are not as fearsome as they look:

1. **Encapsulation.** *Encapsulation* means an object contains (encapsulates) both

   (*i*) data and

   (*ii*) the relevant processing instructions.

   The data is not accessible to the outside world, and only those functions which are wrapped in the class can access it. These functions provide the interface between the object's data and the program. The insulation of data from direct access by the program is known as *data hiding* or *information hiding.*

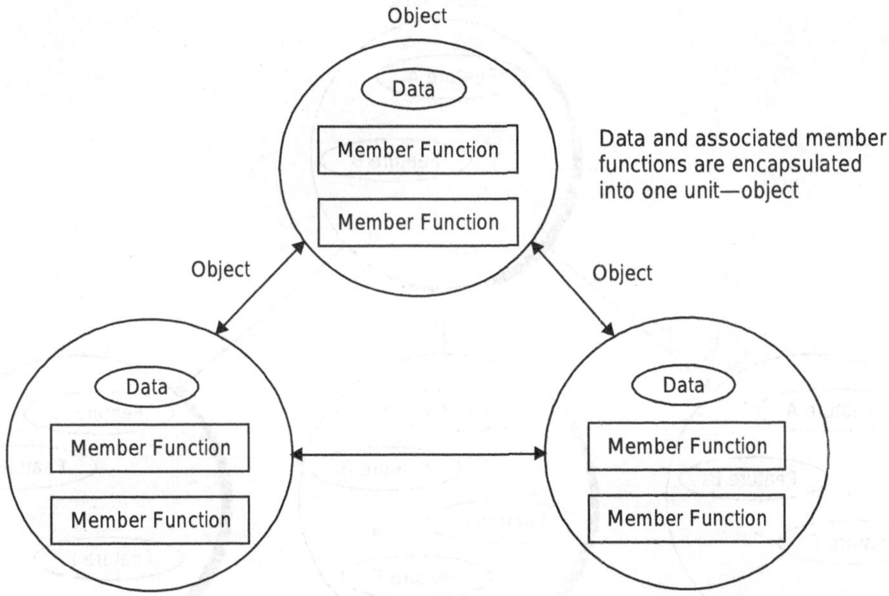

Fig. 10.3. The Object-Oriented Programming approach (Data abstraction and encapsulation)

Once an object has been created, it can be reused in other programs. An object's uses can also be extended through concepts of *class* and *inheritance.* Figure 10.4 illustrates two classes *Student* and *Course.*

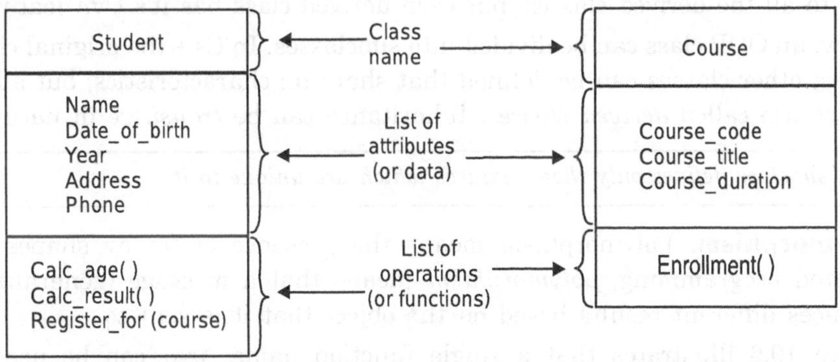

Fig. 10.4. Illustration of two classes Student and Course

Since the classes use the concept of data abstraction, these are known as *Abstract Data Types* (ADT). 'Data types' because these can be used to create objects of its own type.

2. **Inheritance.** Once you have created an object, you can use it as the foundation for similar objects that have the same behaviour and characteristics. All objects that are derived from or related to one another are said to form a *class.* Each class contains specific instructions (methods) that are unique to that group.

   Classes can be arranged in hierarchies—classes and subclasses. *Inheritance* is the method of passing down traits of an object from classes to subclasses in the hierarchy. Thus, new objects can be created by *inheriting* traits from existing classes.

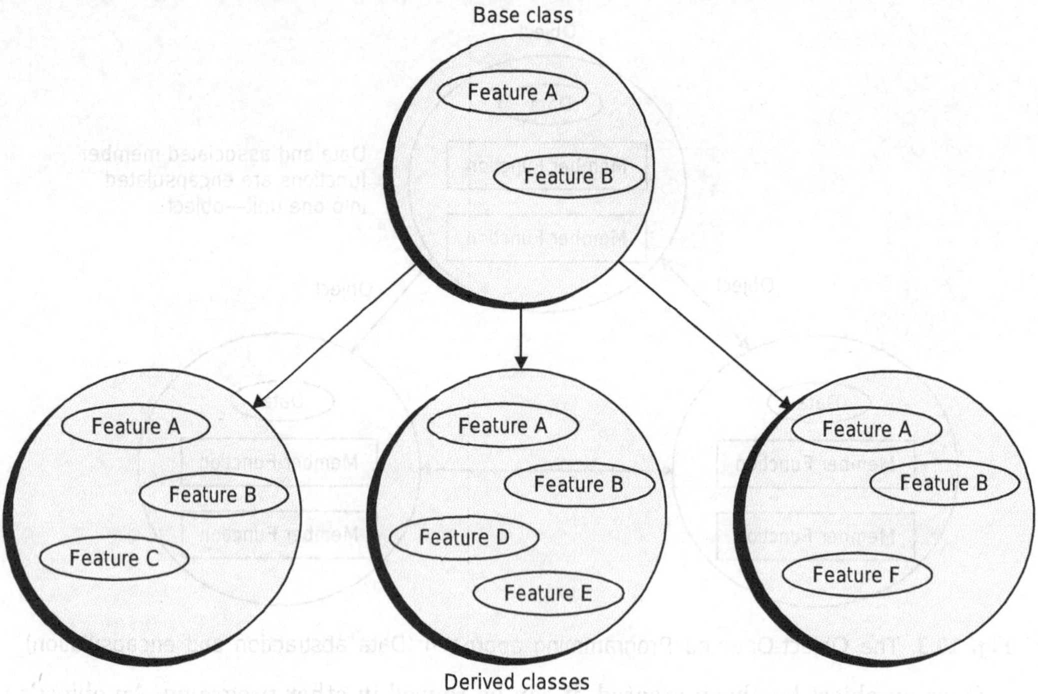

Fig. 10.5. Inheritance

You can observe from Figure 10.5 that features A and B, which are part of the base class, are common to all the derived classes, but each derived class has it's own features as well.

Similary, an OOP class can be divided into subclasses. In C++ the original class is called the *base class*; other classes can be defined that share its characteristics, but add their own as well. These are called *derived classes.* Inheritance can be *transitive* in nature.

> ***Note:*** *A subclass defines only those features which are unique to it.*

3. **Polymorphism.** Polymorphism means the presence of "many shapes." In object-oriented programming, *polymorphism* means that a message (generalized request) produces different results based on the object that it is sent to.

   Figure 10.6 illustrates that a single function name *Area* can be used to handle different number and different types of arguments or parameters. It is something similar to a particular word having several different meanings depending on the

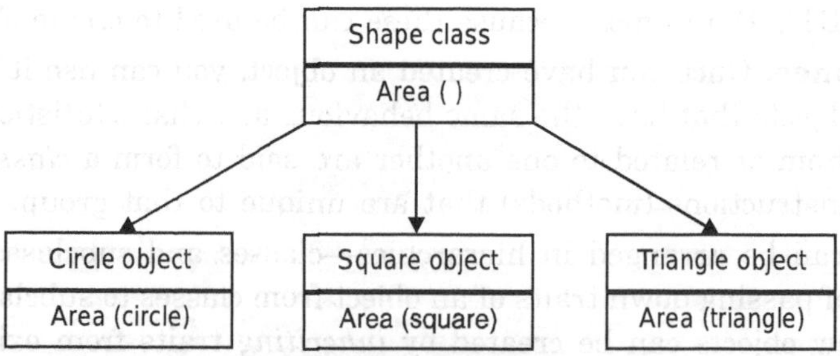

Fig. 10.6. Polymorphism

content. Using a single function name to perform different types of tasks is known as *function overloading*. Polymorphism is extensively used in implementing inheritance.

Polymorphism has important uses. It allows a programmer to create procedures about objects whose exact type is not known in advance but will be at the time the program is actually run on the computer.

An example of an OOP language is **C++ —the plus signs stand for "more than C"— which combines the traditional C programming language with object-oriented capability.** C++ was created by **Bjarne Stroustrup.** With C++, programmers can write standard code in C without the object-oriented features, use object-oriented features, or do a mixture of both.

"Object Oriented Technology is regarded as the ultimate paradigm for the modelling of information, be that information data or logic. The C++ has by now shown to fulfil this goal."

10.3 Advantages and Disadvantages of OOP

OOP offers several advantages over the conventional programming approaches. The principal **advantages** are:

1. It models real world well.
2. The OOP programs are easy to understand.
3. Software security can be implemented using the principle of data hiding.
4. OOP provides classes reusability through inheritance. The redundant code can be eliminated (*i.e.,* the existing classes can be reused) in the derived classes.
5. Saves development time and provides higher productivity as parallel development of classes is possible.
6. The OOP programs are easier to test, manage and maintain.

The OOP technology is still developing. Developing a software that is easy to use makes it hard to build. The **disadvantages** are:

1. OOP takes longer to learn than traditional programming.
2. With OOP, classes tend to be overly generalised.
3. Sometimes the relations among classes become artificial.
4. The OOP programs design can be tricky at times.
5. OOP requires proper planning and proper designing for coding.
6. An OOP programmer requires proper skills like design skills, programming skills, a new way of thinking in terms of objects etc.

REVIEW QUESTIONS AND EXERCISES

1. What is Object-Oriented Programming? How it is different from the procedure-oriented programming?
2. How are data and functions organized in an object-oriented program?
3. Give the advantages and disadvantages of OOP.
4. Differentiate between the following:
   (*i*) Objects and classes. (*ii*) Data abstraction and data encapsulation.
   (*iii*) Inheritance and polymorphism.

❑❑❑

CHAPTER 11

Classes and Objects

11.1 Introduction

Implementation of Object Oriented Programming Concepts in C++

"C with classes" was the original name given by the originator, Stroustrup initially, which nowadays is popularly known as C++. Classes and objects are the most important features of C++. The class implements OOP features and ties them together. A structure groups different type of elements and a function organizes the program actions to perform the desired task.

11.2 Definition of a Class

A class in C++ combines related data and functions together. It makes a data type which is used for creating objects of this type. Classes represent real world entities that have both data type properties (characteristics) and associated operations (behaviour). The syntax of a class definition is shown below :

```
class name_of_class
{
    private     : variable declaration;     // data member
                  function declaration;     // member function (method)
    protected   : variable declaration;
                  function declaration;
    public      : variable declaration;
                  function declaration;
};
```

Here, the keyword **class** specifies that we are using a new data type and is followed by the class name. For example, the following declaration shows the definition of a class **student** :

```
class student
{
  private :
    char reg_no[10];     // data member
```

```
        char name[30];    // data member
        int age;
        char address[25];
    public :
        // inline function definition (inline by default as defined in class)
        void init_data( )       // member function
        {
            cout<<"\n\t\t  Enter data of student ";
            cout<<"\n\n1. Registration Number : ";
            gets(reg_no);
            cout<<"\n\n2. Name : ";
            gets(name);
            cout<<"\n\n3. Age : ";
            cin>>age;
            cout<<"\n\n4. ADDRESS : ";
            gets(address);
        }
        // inline function definition (inline by default as defined in class)
        void display_data( )        // member function
        {
            clrscr( );
            cout<<"Student data is :\n";
            cout<<"\n\n1. Reg. No : "<<reg_no;
            cout<<"\n2. Name : "<<name;
            cout<<"\n3. Age : "<<age;
            cout<<"\n4. Address : "<<address;
        }
    }; // class must have ; (semicolon) as terminator
```

Always remember that the body of the class is delimited by braces and is terminated by a semicolon.

11.3 Members of a Class—Data Members and Member Functions (Methods)

A class in C++ has data members (member variables) and member functions (methods) as its two attributes. Other attributes include class *tagname* that serves as a *type specifier* for the class and *program access levels, that is, private, public*, or *protected* that control access to members in a program. The access levels allow or deny access a class member. For example, in the above class **student** definition the data members are **reg_no, name, age** and **address** and the member functions are

init_data( ) and *display_data( ).*

There are a few restrictions that apply to class members. A non-**static** member variable cannot have an initializer. No member can be an object of that class that is being declared.

(Although a member can be a pointer to the class that is being declared). No member can be declared as **auto**, **register** or **extern.**

> ***Note:*** *A member function of a class is also known as a method.*

11.4 Using private and public Visibility Modes

The body of the class **student** declared in article 11.2 has two keywords namely :

(*i*) *private* (*ii*) *public.*

In C++, the keywords **private** and **public** are called access specifiers. The data hiding concept in C++ is achieved by using the keyword **private**. Private data and functions can only be accessed from within the class itself. Public data and functions are accessible outside the class also. Once an access specifier has been used, it remains in effect until either another access specifier is encountered or the end of the class declaration is reached. Figure 11.1 illustrates *private* and *public* members of a class.

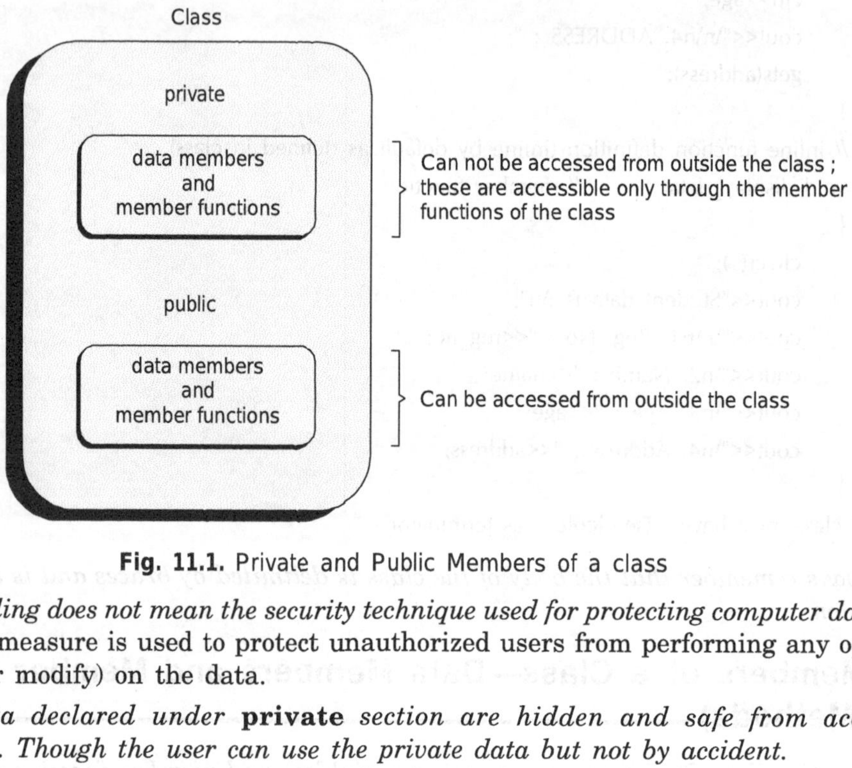

Fig. 11.1. Private and Public Members of a class

Data hiding does not mean the security technique used for protecting computer databases. The security measure is used to protect unauthorized users from performing any operation (read/write or modify) on the data.

The data declared under **private** *section are hidden and safe from accidental manipulation. Though the user can use the private data but not by accident.*

The functions that operate on the data are generally **public** so that they can be accessed from outside the class but this is not a rule that we must follow.

> ***Note:*** *The* **public** *access specifier allows functions or data to be accessible to the other parts of a C++ program.*

11.5 Default Visibility Mode (private)

Data members of a class are generally made **private** and member functions of a class are generally made *public*. Some member functions may be **private** and can be used by the other functions of the class.

Private members are available to only members of class and cannot be accessed by the functions which are outside the class. The default access mode for classes is **private** so that all the members after the class *tagname* and before the first member access specifiers are taken as private. If no access specifier exists the entire data and the member functions of a class are considered as **private**. For example,

```
class bank
{
    int acc_no;       // data members
    char name[30];
    char address[25];
    float balance_amount;
    void init_data( );          // member function prototype
    void display_data( );    // member function prototype
};
```

Here, the access specifier is not mentioned so the data members and member functions are all *private* by default.

> ***Note:** By default, functions and data declared within a class are private to that class and may be accessed only by members of the class.*

11.6 Member Function Definition

The class specification can be done in two parts :

(*i*) **Class definition.** It describes both data members and member functions.

(*ii*) **Class method definitions.** It describes how certain class member functions are coded.

We have already seen the class definition syntax as well as an example.

In C++, the member functions can be coded in two ways :

(*a*) *Inside class definition*

(*b*) *Outside class definition using scope resolution operator (::)*

The code of the function is same in both the cases, but the function header is different as explained below :

11.6.1 Inside Class Definition

When a member function is defined inside a class, we do not require to place a membership label alongwith the function name. We use only small functions inside the class definition and such functions are known as **inline** functions.

In case of inline function the compiler inserts the code of the body of the function at the place where it is invoked (called) and in doing so the program execution is faster but memory penalty is there.

We have already seen the inside class definition of a member function in class student. Here is another example.

Example. *Define a class cricket in C++ with the following description :*

Private members

- Target_score of type integer
- Overs_bowled of type integer
- Extra_time of type integer
- Penalty of type integer
- Cal_penalty( ) a member function to calculate penalty as follows :

  If Extra_time <= 10, Penalty = 1
  If Extra_time >10 but <= 20, Penalty = 2
  otherwise, Penalty = 5

Public members

- A function Extradata( ) to allow user to enter values for Target_score, Overs_bowled, Extra_time.
- A function Disdata( ) to follow user to view the contents of all data members

Solution.

```
class cricket
{
    private :                        //private members
        int Target_score;
        int Overs_bowled;
        int Extra_time;
        int Penalty;
        void Cal_penalty( )
        {
            if(Extra_time <= 10)
                Penalty = 1;
            else if(Extra_time <= 20)
                Penalty = 2;
            else
                Penalty = 5;
        }
    public :                         //public members
        void Extradata( )
        {
            cout<<"\nEnter Target Score : ";
```

```
            cin>>Target_score;
            cout<<"\nEnter Overs Bowled : ";
            cin>>Overs_bowled;
            cout<<"\nEnter Extra Time : ";
            cin>>Extra_time;
            Cal_penalty( );  //function call
        }
        void Disdata( )
        {
            cout<<"\nTarget Score : "<<Target_score;
            cout<<"\nOvers Bowled : "<<Overs_bowled;
            cout<<"\nExtra Time : "<<Extra_time;
            cout<<"\nPenalty : "<<Penalty;
        }
};
```

> ***Note:*** *Functions defined in a class specification are automatically inline.*

11.6.2 Outside Class Definition Using Scope Resolution Operator (::)

In this case the function's full name (qualified_name) is written as shown :

```
name_of_the_class :: function_name
```

The syntax for a member function definition outside the class definition is :

```
return_type  name_of_the_class :: function_name(argument list)
{
    body of function
}
```

Here *the operator :: known as scope resolution operator helps in defining the member function outside the class. Earlier the scope resolution operator (::) was used in situations where a global variable exists with the same name as a local variable and it identifies the global variable.*

> ***Note:*** *The :: operator uncovers a hidden file scope (global) item.*

For example, the outside class definition of functions of class largest given below looks as :

```
class largest
{
    private :
        int num1,num2,num3,big; // data members
    public :
        void enter(int a,int b,int c); //member function prototype
        void max(void); //member function prototype
```

```
        void display(void); //member function prototype
};
// outside class definition of function enter( )
void largest::enter(int a,int b,int c)
{
    cout<<"\nValues assigned to the data members\n";
    num1=a;
    num2=b;
    num3=c;
}
// outside class definition of function max( )
void largest::max(void)
{
    big=num1;
    if(num2>big)
      big=num2;
    if(num3>big)
      big=num3;
}
// outside class definition of function display( )
void largest::display(void)
{
    cout<<"\nLargest number = "<<big<<endl;
}
```

In the above shown class **largest** the function prototyping is done using the declaration :

void enter(int a,int b,int c);

void max(void);

void display(void);

These statements inform the compiler that these are the member functions of the class but will be defined outside the class **largest**.

The statements

void largest::enter(int a,int b,int c)

void largest::max(void)

and **void largest::display(void)**

define the functions **enter( ), max( )** and **display( )** outside the class **largest** using the scope resolution operator.

In case we have the same function name in different classes, the membership label (that is, name_of_the_class ::) resolves the identity and the scope (the part of the program in which a variable or a function can be accessed).

> ***Note:*** *In case we have multiple variables withh the same name, defined in different blocks then the :: operator always refers to the file scope variable.*

11.6.3 Nesting of Member Functions

When a member function of a class calls another member function of the same class, then membership label is not used and is called nesting of member functions.

> ***Note:*** *A member function in C++ can be called only by using an object of the same class.*

11.6.4 Making an Outside Function inline

In C++, an important objective is to separate the implementation details from the class definition. So the member functions are defined outside the class. An outside defined function can be **inline** as shown in the following example :

```
class largest
{
        ------------
        ------------
    public :
        void enter(int a,int b,int c);    //function prototype
        ------------
        ------------
};
inline void largest :: enter(int a,int b,int c)  //function definition
{
    cout<<"\nValues assigned to the data members\n";
    num1=a;
    num2=b;
    num3=c;
}
```

11.7 Declaration of Objects as Instances of a class

The objects of a class are declared after the class definition. One must remember that a class definition does not define any object of its type, but it defines the properties of a class. For utilizing the defined class, we need variables of the class type. For example,

```
largest ob1,ob2; //object declaration
```

will create two objects **ob1** and **ob2** of **largest** class type. As mentioned earlier, in C++ the variables of a class are known as objects. These are declared like a simple variable, that is, like fundamental data types.

In C++, all the member functions of a class are created and stored when the class is defined and this memory space can be accessed by all the objects related to that class.

Memory space is allocated separately to each object for their data members. Member variables store different values for different objects of a class.

Figure 11.2 shows this concept :

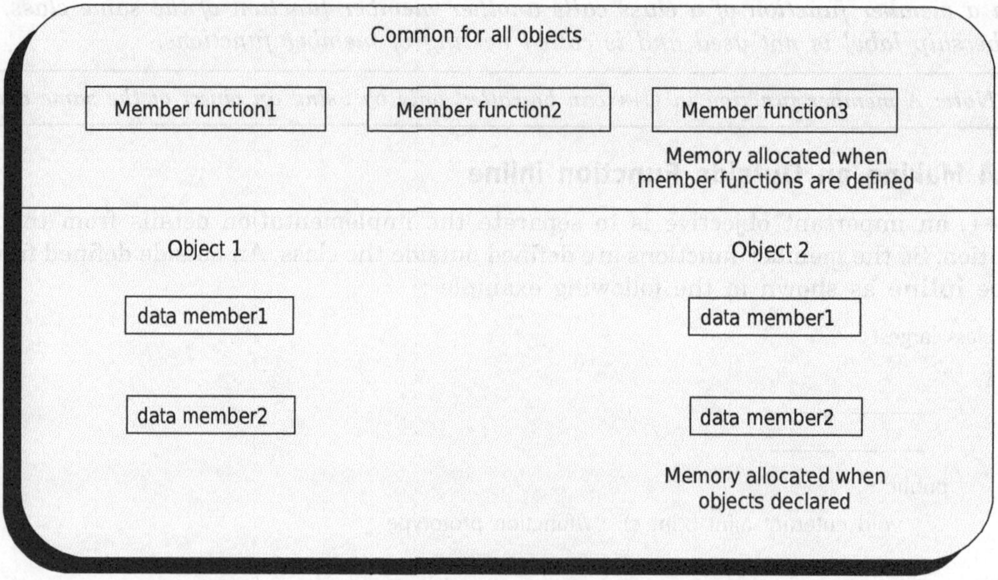

Fig. 11.2. A class, its member functions and objects in memory

> ***Note:*** *A class is a logical abstraction, but an object has physical existence, i.e., an object is an instance of a class.*

11.8 Accessing Members from Object(s)

After defining a class and creating a class variable, that is, object we can access the data members and member functions of the class. Because the data members and member functions are parts of the class, we must access these using the variable we created. For example,

```
class student
{
    private :
        char reg_no[10];
        char name[30];
        int age;
        char address[40];
    public :
        void init_data( )
        {
            - - - - -  // body of function
            - - - - -
        }
        void display_data( )
        {
            - - - - -  // body of function
```

```
            - - - - -
        }
};
student ob;   // class variable (object) created
- - - - -
- - - - -
ob.init_data( );  // access the member function
ob.display_data( );  // access the member function
- - - - -
- - - - -
```

Here, **the data members can be accessed in the member functions** as these have **private** scope, and the member functions can be accessed outside the class, that is, before or after the main( ) function.

The following program illustrates the accessing of members from objects :

Program 11.1

```
// Accessing student data using objects and class
#include<iostream.h>
#include<conio.h>
#include<stdio.h> // for gets( )
class student
{
  private :
    char reg_no[10];
    char name[30];
    int age;
    char address[40];
  public :
    // inline function definition (inline by default as defined in class)
    void init_data( )
    {
        cout<<"\n\t\t  Enter data of student ";
        cout<<"\n\nRegistration Number : ";
        gets(reg_no);
        cout<<"\nName : ";
        gets(name);
        cout<<"\nAge : ";
        cin>>age;
        cout<<"\nADDRESS : ";
        gets(address);
    }
```

```
    // inline function definition (inline by default as defined in class)
    void display_data( )
    {
        cout<<"Student data is :\n";
        cout<<"\nReg. No : "<<reg_no;
        cout<<"\nName : "<<name;
        cout<<"\nAge : "<<age;
        cout<<"\nAddress : "<<address<<endl<<endl;
    }
};
void main( )
{
  student ob1,ob2; // objects declared
  clrscr( );
  ob1.init_data( ); // function call
  ob2.init_data( ); // function call
  clrscr( );
  ob1.display_data( ); // function call
  ob2.display_data( ); // function call
  getch( ); // freeze the monitor
}
```

Output

```
                    Enter data of student
Registration Number : 1001
Name : Dhruv Arya
Age : 25
ADDRESS : 1208, Sector–15, Sonepat
                    Enter data of student
Registration Number : 1002
Name : Shiv Charan
Age : 28
ADDRESS : 104, TP Scheme No. 15, Sonepat
Student data is :
Reg. No    : 1001
Name       : Dhruv Arya
Age        : 25
Address    : 1208, Sector–15, Sonepat
Student data is :
Reg. No    : 1002
```

Name : Shiv Charan
Age : 28
Address : 104, TP Scheme No. 15, Sonepat

In the above program two objects **ob1** and **ob2** have been created which access the member functions **init_data( )** and **display_data( )**. As the data members in the class student are private members so these can't be accessed outside the class directly.

As shown earlier the member functions can be defined outside the class using scope resolution operator (::). The following program defines the member functions using :: and accesses the data members using the member functions which are accessed by the class variables.

Program 11.2

```
// Illustrating use of scope resolution operator(::)
// Store student data using objects and class and display it
#include<iostream.h>
#include<conio.h>
#include<stdio.h> // for gets( )
class student
{
    private :
      char reg_no[10];
      char name[30];
      int age;
      char address[40];
    public :
      void init_data( );   // function prototype
      void display_data( );   // function prototype
};
// function definition init_data( )
void student::init_data( )
{
    cout<<"\n\t\t  Enter data of student ";
    cout<<"\n\nRegistration Number : ";
    gets(reg_no);
    cout<<"\nName : ";
    gets(name);
    cout<<"\nAge : ";
    cin>>age;
    cout<<"\nADDRESS : ";
    gets(address);
}
```

```
// function definition display_data( )
void student::display_data( )
{
    cout<<"Student data is :\n";
    cout<<"\nReg. No : "<<reg_no;
    cout<<"\nName : "<<name;
    cout<<"\nAge : "<<age;
    cout<<"\nAddress : "<<address<<endl<<endl;
}
void main( )
{
    student ob1,ob2; // objects declared
    clrscr( );
    ob1.init_data( ); // function call
    ob2.init_data( ); // function call
    clrscr( );
    ob1.display_data( ); // function call
    ob2.display_data( ); // function call
    getch( ); // freeze the screen
}
```

The output of program 11.2 will be similar to program 11.1.

By now it should be clear that the **private** data of a class can be accessed only by using the member functions of that class. We can use the **public** data by the non-member functions also through the class objects. The **public** member functions of a class are invoked by non-member functions using the class objects.

The syntax of calling a member function is :

```
obj_name.func_name(actual parameters);
```

For accessing the *public* data member, the syntax is :

```
obj_name.public_data_member;
```

For example,

```
class fun
{
    int a,b; //private by default
  public :
    int result;
    int multiply(int num1, int num2)
    {
        int prod=num1*num2;
        return prod;
    }
```

```
        int divide(int num1,int num2)
        {
            int q;
            if(num2) // if num2 is non zero
            {
                q = num1/num2;
                return q;
            }
            else
            {
                cout<<"\nDivision by 0 not possible\n";
                exit(1);
            }
        }
    };
    fun ob1,ob2;
```

Now see the following statements carefully :

```
ob1.result = 50;      //valid as result is a public data member
ob2.result = 75;      //valid as result is a public data member
ob1.a = 100;          //invalid as a being private data member
ob2.b = 200;          //invalid as b being private data member
ob1.multiply(5,8);    //valid
ob2.divide(25,5);     //valid
```

> ***Note:*** *An array can be used as a data member in a class. It can be either* ***private*** *or* ***public****. When it is private, it can only be accessed by the class member functions and when public, it can be used by objects of this type directly.*

11.9 Arrays of Type class

In C++, an array storing **class** type elements is called an **array of objects**. First we define a class and then an array of objects is declared. For example, the following declaration shows it :

```
class BOOK
{
  private :
    int BOOK_NO;
    char BOOK_TITLE[30];
    float PRICE;
    float TOTAL_COST(int N)
    {
        return(PRICE*N);
    }
```

```
public :
   void INPUT( )
   {
        cout<<"\nEnter the book number\n\n";
        cin>>BOOK_NO;
        cout<<"\nEnter the book title\n\n";
        gets(BOOK_TITLE);
        cout<<"\nEnter the price of book\n\n";
        cin>>PRICE;
   }
   void PURCHASE( )
   {
        int N; // N denotes number of copies
        cout<<"\nEnter number of copies to be purchased\n\n";
        cin>>N;
        cout<<"\nTotal cost to be paid is : "<<TOTAL_COST(N);
        cout<<endl;
   }
};
```

BOOK arr[10]; // array **arr** to store 10 objects of **BOOK** type

The array elements being objects store only their data members and member functions are stored separately only once to be used by all class objects.

The above declared array **arr** will be stored in main memory as shown in figure 11.3.

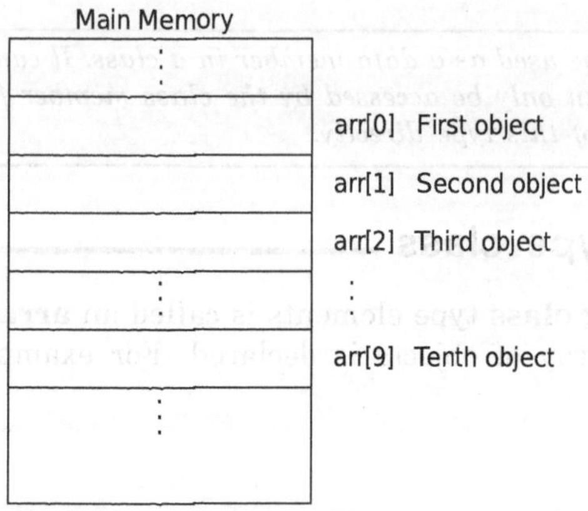

Fig. 11.3. Illustration of storage of array arr having 10 objects

In C++, an array of objects can be used like any other array. The following program illustrates this :

Program 11.3

```
// Illustration of array of objects
#include<iostream.h>
```

```
#include<conio.h>
#include<stdio.h>
#define S 10
class BOOK
{
  private :
    int BOOK_NO;
    char BOOK_TITLE[30];
    float PRICE;
    float TOTAL_COST(int N)
    {
        return(PRICE*N);
    }
  public :
    void INPUT( )
    {
        cout<<"\nEnter the book number\n\n";
        cin>>BOOK_NO;
        cout<<"\nEnter the book title\n\n";
        gets(BOOK_TITLE);
        cout<<"\nEnter the price of book\n\n";
        cin>>PRICE;
    }
    void PURCHASE( )
    {
        int N; // N denotes number of copies
        cout<<"\nEnter number of copies to be purchased\n\n";
        cin>>N;
        cout<<"\nTotal cost to be paid is : "<<TOTAL_COST(N);
        cout<<endl;
    }
};
void main( )
{
  BOOK arr[S]; // array of objects declared
  int i,n;
  clrscr( );
  cout<<"Enter the number of books to be purchased <= "<<S<<endl;
  cin>>n;
  for(i=0;i<n;i++)
  {
      clrscr( );
```

```
            cout<<"Enter the data of book "<<i+1<<endl;
            arr[i].INPUT( ); // function call
            arr[i].PURCHASE( ); // function call
            getch( ); //freeze the monitor
        }
    }
```

Output

```
Enter the number of books to be purchased <= 10
2
Enter the data of book 1
Enter the book number
3648
Enter the book title
MASTERING C++ PROGRAMS
Enter the price of book
325
Enter number of copies to be purchased
10
Total cost to be paid is : 3250
Enter the data of book 2
Enter the book number
5005
Enter the book title
MASTERING C PROGRAMS
Enter the price of book
250
Enter number of copies to be purchased
10
Total cost to be paid is : 2500
```

In the above program first of all the number of books to be purchased are entered. The member functions **INPUT( )** and **PURCHASE( )** are called by objects of type **BOOK** and the desired processing is done.

11.10 Objects as Function Arguments

In C++, an object is treated as a built in data type. An object can be used as a function argument. It can be done in the following two ways :

(*i*) *Pass by value* (*ii*) *Pass by references*

11.10.1 Pass By Value

A copy of the object is passed to the function and any change made is not reflected back. An object may be passed by value to a member function, a non member function and a friend function (to be discussed later on). *The member functions and friend functions are permitted to access the* **private** *and protected members of the passed object. The non member function can only access the* **public** *members of the passed object.*

The following program illustrates this concept :

Program 11.4

```
// Passing objects to function by value
// Here two times are entered in hh mm ss format and then added
#include<iostream.h>
#include<conio.h>
class time
{
  private :
       int hours;
       int minutes;
       int seconds;
  public :
       void enter( ); // member function prototype
       void add_time(time,time); // member function prototype
};
// function definition enter( )
void time::enter( )
{
  cout<<"\nEnter the time :\n\n";
  cout<<"Hours : ";
  cin>>hours;
  cout<<"Minutes : ";
  cin>>minutes;
  cout<<"Seconds : ";
  cin>>seconds;
}
//function definition add_time( )
void time::add_time(time t1,time t2)
{
  int hr,min,sec;
  sec=t1.seconds+t2.seconds;
  min=t1.minutes+t2.minutes+sec/60;
  sec%=60;
```

```
        hr=t1.hours+t2.hours+min/60;
        min%=60;
        cout<<"\nResultant time in \"hh mm ss\" format is :\n";
        cout<<"\nHours       : "<<hr;
        cout<<"\nMinutes     : "<<min;
        cout<<"\nSeconds     : "<<sec;
    }
    void main( )
    {
        time ob1,ob2,ob; // objects declared
        clrscr( );
        ob1.enter( ); // function call
        ob2.enter( ); // function call
        ob.add_time(ob1,ob2); // function call
        getch( ); // freeze the monitor
    }
```

Output

```
Enter the time :
Hours     :     10
Minutes   :     50
Seconds   :     30
Enter the time :
Hours     :     12
Minutes   :     15
Seconds   :     40
Resultant time in "hh mm ss" format is :
Hours     :     23
Minutes   :     6
Seconds   :     10
```

In the above program first of all the class **time**, its member functions **enter( )** and **add_time( )** are declared. Three objects **ob1, ob2** and **ob** are created. The function **enter( )** is called for giving data values of these objects, that is, **ob1** and **ob2**. The **add_time( )** function is called having arguments—objects **t1** and **t2** of type **time**, that is, the objects are passed by value and the function adds the two times and displays the result after addition.

11.10.2 Pass by Reference

The memory address of the object is passed to the function and the called function operates on the original object being passed. No separate memory is allocated for the data members of the passed object. For example, the following program illustrates the concept of passing objects to function by reference :

Program 11.5

```
// Passing objects to function by reference
// Here two times are entered in hh mm ss format and then added
#include<iostream.h>
#include<conio.h>
class time
{
  private :
       int hours;
       int minutes;
       int seconds;
  public :
       void enter(time &);  // member function prototype
       void add_time(time &,time &);  // member function prototype
};
// function definition enter( )
void time::enter(time &obj)
{
  cout<<"\nEnter the time :\n\n";
  cout<<"Hours : ";
  cin>>obj.hours;
  cout<<"Minutes : ";
  cin>>obj.minutes;
  cout<<"Seconds : ";
  cin>>obj.seconds;
}
// function definition add_time( )
void time::add_time(time &t1,time &t2)
{
  int hr,min,sec;
  sec=t1.seconds+t2.seconds;
  min=t1.minutes+t2.minutes+sec/60;
  sec%=60;
  hr=t1.hours+t2.hours+min/60;
  min%=60;
  cout<<"\nResultant time in \"hh mm ss\" format is :\n";
  cout<<"\nHours     : "<<hr;
  cout<<"\nMinutes   : "<<min;
  cout<<"\nSeconds   : "<<sec;
}
```

```
void main( )
{
  time ob1,ob2,ob;   // objects declared
  clrscr( );
  ob.enter(ob1);   // function call
  ob.enter(ob2);   // function call
  ob.add_time(ob1,ob2);   // function call
  getch( );  // freeze the monitor
}
```

The output of program 11.5 will be similar to that of program 11.4 :

In the above program the objects are passed as reference to member functions **enter( )** and **add_time( )**. These functions work on the actual arguments and no separate memory is allocated for the objects passed.

11.11 Functions Returning Object

In C++, objects can not only be passed to functions but object can be returned also from functions. The following program illustrates this concept :

Program 11.6

```
// Illustration of the function returning an object using friend function
#include<iostream.h>
#include<conio.h>
class time
{
    private :
        int hours;
        int minutes;
        int seconds;
    public :
        void enter(int h,int m,int s) //inline function
        {
            hours=h;
            minutes=m;
            seconds=s;
        }
        void display( ) //inline function
        {
            cout<<"\nHours    : "<<hours;
            cout<<"\nMinutes : "<<minutes;
            cout<<"\nSeconds : "<<seconds;
        }
```

```
        friend time add_time(time t1, time t2); //function prototype
    };
//friend function add_time( ) definition
time add_time(time t1, time t2)
{
    time t3; //local object declared
    int temp_sec,temp_min;
    temp_sec=t1.seconds+t2.seconds;
    t3.seconds=temp_sec % 60;
    temp_min=t1.minutes+t2.minutes+temp_sec/60;
    t3.minutes=temp_min % 60;
    t3.hours=t1.hours+t2.hours+temp_min/60;
    return(t3); //return object
}
void main( )
{
    time obj1,obj2,obj3; //objects declared
    int hrs,min,sec;
    clrscr( );
    cout<<"Enter the first time in hh mm ss format\n";
    cin>>hrs>>min>>sec;
    obj1.enter(hrs,min,sec);  //function call
    cout<<"\nEnter the second time in hh mm ss format\n";
    cin>>hrs>>min>>sec;
    obj2.enter(hrs,min,sec);  //function call
    cout<<"\nFirst time is : \n";
    obj1.display( );  //function call
    cout<<"\n\nSecond time is : \n";
    obj2.display( );  //function call
    obj3=add_time(obj1,obj2);  //function call
    cout<<"\n\nResultant time is : \n";
    obj3.display( );  //function call
}
```

Output

```
Enter the first time in hh mm ss format
12  30  55
Enter the second time in hh mm ss format
8  10  45
First time is :
Hours    : 12
```

```
Minutes   : 30
Seconds   : 55
Second time is :
Hours     : 8
Minutes   : 10
Seconds   : 45
Resultant time is :
Hours     : 20
Minutes   : 41
Seconds   : 40
```

Here the friend function add_time ( ) takes two objects of **time** type as parameters and returns an object of **time** type having sum of two passed objects to it. More about friend functions later on in this chapter.

11.12 const Member Function

If a member function does not modify any data in a class, then we may declare it as a **const** member function as given below :

```
void add(int, int) const;        //function prototype
double get_value( ) const;       //function prototype
```

The qualifier **const** is appended to the function prototypes (declaration) and function definition. In case such a function tries to modify the data values, the compiler generates an error message.

11.13 static Class Members

Data members and member functions of a class in C++, may be qualified as static. We can have static data members and static member functions in a class.

11.13.1 static Data Member

It is generally used to store values common to the whole class. The **static** data member differs from an ordinary data member in the following ways :

(*i*) *Only a single copy of the static data member is used by all the objects.*

(*ii*) *It can be used within the class but its lifetime is the whole program.*

For making a data member static, we require :

(*a*) *Declare it within the class*

(*b*) *Define it outside the class.*

For example,

```
class student
{
    static int count; //declaration within class
    ________________
```

```
        ----------------
        ----------------
};
```

The static data member is defined outside the class as :

```
int student :: count; //definition outside class
```

The definition of static data members outside the class is a must as these are stored separately rather than as a part of an object.

> *Note: We must define a static data member outside the class definition.*

We can also initialize the static data member at the time of its definition as :

```
int student :: count = 0;
```

If we define three objects as

```
student obj1, obj2, obj3;
```

Figure 11.4 shows the sharing of a static variable count by all the three objects :

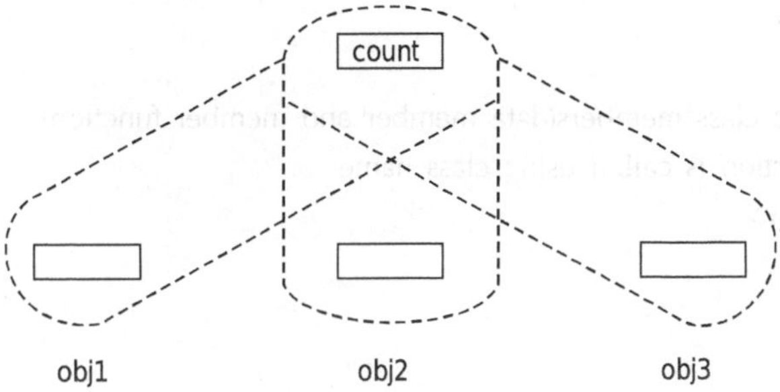

Fig. 11.4

> ***Note:** Remember that you cannot have a static data member inside a local class* i.e., *a class being defined inside a function.*

11.13.2 static Member Function

*A **static** member function can access only the static members of a class.* We can do so by putting the keyword **static** before the name of the function while declaring it. For example,

```
class student
{
    static int count;
    ----------------
    public :
      ----------------
      ----------------
    static void showcount(void) //static member function
    {
      cout<<"count = "<<count<<"\n";
```

```
    }
};
int student :: count=0;
```

Here we have put the keyword **static** before the name of the function showcount ( ).

In C++, a static member function differs from the other member functions in the following ways :

(i) Only static members (functions or variables) of the same class can be accessed by a static member function.

(ii) It is called by using the **name of the class** *rather than an object as given below :*

```
name_of_the_class :: function_name
```

For example,

```
student::showcount( );
```

The following program illustrates the concept of static members of a class :

Program 11.7

```
//Illustration of static class members(data member and member function)
//Static member function is called using class name
#include<iostream.h>
#include<conio.h>
class student
{
  private :
       static int count;  //static data member
       int rollno,marks;
  public :
       void enter(int r,int m)
       {
            rollno=r;
            marks=m;
            count++;
       }
       void show(void)
       {
            cout<<"\nRoll number : "<<rollno<<"\t";
            cout<<"Marks : "<<marks<<"\n";
       }
       static void showcount(void) //static member function
       {
            cout<<"count = "<<count<<"\n";
       }
};
```

```
//a static data member must be defined outside the class
int student :: count=0; //definition of the static data member
void main( )
{
  clrscr( );
  student obj1,obj2,obj3; //all objects share same count variable
  obj1.enter(1001,99); //function call
  student::showcount( ); //static member function call using class name
  obj2.enter(1002,88);
  student::showcount( );
  obj3.enter(1003,100);
  student::showcount( );
  obj1.show( ); //function call
  obj2.show( );
  obj3.show( );
}
```

Output

```
count = 1
count = 2
count = 3
Roll number : 1001 Marks : 99
Roll number : 1002 Marks : 88
Roll number : 1003 Marks : 100
```

Here, function **enter ( )** uses both the ordinary and static members but function **showcount ( )** uses only **static** member.

11.14 Constructors and Destructors

Every object created would have a copy of member data which requires initialization before its use. C++ allows objects to initialize themselves as and when they are created. This automatic initialization is performed through the use of **constructor** functions. **Destructors** are functions that are complimentary to constructors.

11.14.1 Constructor

In C++, a class only creates a data type and the objects of a class are created and initialized as separate. A ***constructor*** *(having the same name as that of the class) is a member function which is automatically used to initialize the objects of the class type with legal initial values.*

Special Characteristics of Constructors

These have some special characteristics, which are given below :

(*i*) *These are called automatically when the objects are created.*

(*ii*) *All objects of the class having a constructor are initialized before some use.*

(iii) *These should be declared in the public section for availability to all the functions.*

(iv) *Return type (not even* **void***) cannot be specified for constructors.*

(v) *These cannot be inherited, but a* **derived** *class can call the base class constructor.*

(vi) *These cannot be static.*

(vii) *Default and copy constructors are generated by the compiler wherever required. Generated constructors are public.*

(viii) *These can have default arguments as other C++ functions.*

(ix) *The address of a constructor cannot be taken.*

(x) *An object of a class with a constructor cannot be used as a member of a* **union**.

(xi) *A constructor can call member functions of its class.*

(xii) *We can use a constructor to create new objects of its class type by using the syntax*

```
name_of_the_class(expression_list)
```

For example,

```
employee obj3 = obj2; //see Program 11.11
```

or even

```
employee obj3 = employee(1002,35000); //explicit call
```

(xiii) *These make* **implicit** *calls to the memory allocation and deallocation operators* **new** *and* **delete**.

(xiv) *These cannot be* **virtual**.

> ***Note:*** *After declaring a constructor, the initialization of the class objects becomes compulsory (mandatory).*

Declaration and Definition of a Constructor

A constructor is defined like other member functions of the class, that is, either inside the class definition or outside the class definition. For example, the following program illustrates the concept of a constructor :

Program 11.8

```
//demonstration of a constructor
#include<iostream.h>
#include<conio.h>
class rectangle
{
   private :
      float length,breadth;          // data members
   public :
      rectangle( ) //constructor definition
      {
         //displayed whenever an object is created
```

```
        cout<<"I am in the constructor"<<endl;
        length=10.0;
        breadth=20.5;
    }
    float area( )    // member function
    {
        return(length*breadth);
    }
};
void main( )
{
    clrscr( );
    rectangle obj; //object declared
    cout<<"\nThe area of the rectangle with default dimensions is : "
        <<obj.area( )<<" sq.units\n";
    getch( ); //freeze the monitor
}
```

Output

```
I am in the constructor
The area of the rectangle with default dimensions is : 205 sq. units.
```

> ***Note:*** *A constructor has no return type in C++. Constructor functions cannot return values.*

In general, constructors are used only to initialize and not for any input or output operation. The constructor is defined inside the class definition in the above program.

The above constructor can also be defined as given below :

```
class rectangle
{
        private :
            float length,breadth;          // data members
        public :
            rectangle( );   //only prototype here
            ___________
            ___________    //other members
};
//Constructor definition outside the class
rectangle :: rectangle( )
{
        //displayed whenever an object is created
        cout<<"I am in the constructor"<<endl;
```

```
        length = 10.0;
        breadth = 20.5;
    }
```

Here the constructor has been coded in the **public** section of the class. It can be defined under **private** or **protected** sections also. *It obeys the usual access rules of a class, that is, a private or protected constructor cannot be accessed by non-member functions.* We cannot create objects of a class in non-member functions.

Example. *Write the output of the following program.*

```
#include<iostream.h>
class Counter
{
    private :
        unsigned int count;
    public :
        Counter( ) {count=0;}
        void inc_Count( ) {count++;}
        int get_Count( ) {return count;}
};
void main( )
{
    Counter C1,C2;
    cout<<"\nC1 = "<<C1.get_Count( );
    cout<<"\nC2 = "<<C2.get_Count( );
    C1.inc_Count( );
    C2.inc_Count( );
    C2.inc_Count( );
    cout<<"\nC1 = "<<C1.get_Count( );
    cout<<"\nC2 = "<<C2.get_Count( );
}
```

Solution. The output of the program will be :

C1 = 0
C2 = 0
C1 = 1
C2 = 2

Default Constructor

A constructor without arguments is known as a **default constructor.** The constructor in the following example is the default constructor for class **Garments**, as it has no arguments. When a constructor is with arguments then the initial values must be passed at the time of creation of the objects.

Example. *Define a class* **Garments** *in C++ with the following descriptions :*

Private Members

GCode	*of type string*
GType	*of type string*
GSize	*of type integer*
GFabric	*of type string*
GPrice	*of type float*

A function Assign( ) which calculates and assigns the value of GPrice as follows

For the value of GFabric as "COTTON",

GType	*GPrice(Rs)*
TROUSER	*1300*
SHIRT	*1100*

For GFabric other than "COTTON" the above mentioned

GPrice gets reduced by 10%.

Public Members

A constructor to assign initial values of GCode, GType and GFabric with the word "NOT ALLOTTED" and GSize and GPrice with 0

A function Input( ) to input the values of the data members GCode, GType, GSize and GFabric and invoke the Assign( ) function.

A function Display( ) which displays the content of all the data members for a Garment.

Solution.

The class definition is given below :

```
class Garments
{
    private :
        char GCode[11];
        char GType[21];
        int GSize;
        char GFabric[21];
        float GPrice;
        void Assign( )
        {
            if(strcmp(GFabric, "COTTON")= =0)
            {
                if(strcmp(GType, "TROUSER")= =0)
                    GPrice=1300;
                if(strcmp(GType, "SHIRT")= =0)
                    GPrice=1100;
            }
```

```
            else
            {
                if(strcmp(GType, "TROUSER")= =0)
                     GPrice=1300*0.9;
                if(strcmp(GType, "SHIRT")= =0)
                     GPrice=1100*0.9;
            }
        }
    public :
        Garments( )    // constructor
        {
            strcpy(GCode, "NOT ALLOTTED");
            strcpy(GType, "NOT ALLOTTED");
            GSize=0;
            strcpy(GFabric, "NOT ALLOTTED");
            GPrice=0.0;
        }
        void input( )
        {
            cout<<"\nEnter the GCode :";
            gets(GCode);
            cout<<"\nEnter the GType :";
            gets(GType);
            cout<<"\nEnter the GSize :";
            cin>>GSize;
            cout<<"\nEnter the GFabric :";
            gets(GFabric);
            Assign( );  //function call
        }
        void Display( )
        {
            cout<<"\nGCode :"<<GCode;
            cout<<"\nGType :"<<GType;
            cout<<"\nGSize :"<<GSize;
            cout<<"\nGFabric :"<<GFabric;
            cout<<"\nGPrice :"<<GPrice;
        }
};
```

> ***Note:** When there is no constructor defined in a class, the compiler automatically supplies a default constructor and if a constructor is declared with arguments it hides the default constructor.*

The default constructor supplied by the compiler does not do anything specific but initializes the data members by any dummy value when the objects are created.

Parameterized Constructors

A constructor with arguments is called a parameterized constructor. With the help of such a constructor the data elements of various objects can be initialized with different values. This is performed by passing different values to arguments of the constructor function while creating an object. For example,

```
class xyz
{
        float a;
    public :
        int b;
        char c;
        xyz(float x,int y,char ch) //parameterized constructor
        {
                a = x;
                b = y;
                c = ch;
        }
        ----------
        ---------- //remaining members
};
```

Once we have declared a parameterized constructor, we must give initial values as arguments. If we do not do so, the compiler reports an error. For example,

```
xyz obj; //not valid
```

For passing initial values while creating an object, we can select any one of the two ways :

(*i*) *Call the constructor implicitly*

(*ii*) *Call the constructor explicitly.*

In case (*i*) we use **xyz obj (10.5, 50, 'A');** It is also called **shorthand** method and it is used frequently.

In case (*ii*) we use **xyz obj = xyz (10.5, 50, 'A');** Here the constructor is called explicitly and object obj is initialized with values 10.5, 50 and 'A' as in case (*i*).

A **temporary instance** or **temporary object** is created when we make an explicit call. A temporary object (without any name) resides in the memory as long as the object is referenced and after that it dies.

Overloaded Constructors

Besides performing the role of member data initialization, constructors are no different from other functions. This includes *overloading* also. In fact, it is very common to find overloaded constructors. For example, consider the following program with overloaded constructors for the *figure* class :

Program 11.9

```
//Illustration of overloaded constructors
//Construct a class for storage of dimensions of circle
//triangle and rectangle and calculate their area
#include<iostream.h>
#include<conio.h>
#include<math.h> //for sqrt( )
#include<string.h> //for strcpy( )
class figure
{
private :
    float radius,side1,side2,side3; //data members
    char shape[10];
public :
    figure(float r) //constructor for circle
    {
        radius=r;
        strcpy(shape,"circle");
    }
    figure(float s1,float s2)  //constructor for rectangle
    {
        side1=s1;
        side2=s2;
        side3=radius=0.0; //has no significance in rectangle
        strcpy(shape,"rectangle");
    }
    figure(float s1,float s2,float s3) //constructor for triangle
    {
        side1=s1;
        side2=s2;
        side3=s3;
        radius=0.0;  //has no significance in triangle
        strcpy(shape, "triangle");
    }
    void area( ) // calculate area
    {
        float ar,s;
        if(radius= =0.0)
        {
            if(side3= =0.0)
                ar=side1*side2;
```

```
                else
                {
                        s=(side1+side2+side3)/2.0;
                        ar=sqrt(s*(s-side1)*(s-side2)*(s-side3));
                }
        }
        else
            ar=3.14*radius*radius;
        cout<<"\n\nArea of the "<<shape<<" is : "<<ar<<" sq. units\n";
    }
};
void main( )
{
    clrscr( );
    figure circle(10.0); // object initialized using constructor
    figure rectangle(15.0,20.6); // object initialized using constructor
    figure triangle(3.0,4.0,5.0); // object initialized using constructor
    circle.area( );  // function call
    rectangle.area( );
    triangle.area( );
    getch( );  // freeze the monitor
}
```

Output

```
Area of the circle is : 314 sq. units
Area of the rectangle is : 309 sq. units
Area of the triangle is : 6 sq. units
```

In the above program the one, two and three argument(s) constructors are called for **circle**, **rectangle** and **triangle** objects respectively for deciding the **shape**. The function **area()** is called using all the three objects one after the other for finding the area of the figure.

So we conclude that *a class can have many constructors each differing in their signature (that is, number and type of arguments).*

Example. *Answer the questions (i) and (ii) after going through the following program.*

```
#include<iostream.h>
#include<string.h>
class Bazar
{
    char Type[20];
    char Product[20];
    int Qty;
```

```
    float Price;
    Bazar( )                // Function 1
    {
        strcpy (Type, "Electronic");
        strcpy (Product, "Calculator");
        Qty=10;
        Price=225;
    }                       // Function 2
public :
    void Disp( )
    {
        cout<<Type<<"-"<<Product<<":"<<Qty
            <<"@"<<Price<<endl;
    }
};
void main( )
{
        Bazar B;            // Statement 1
        B. Disp( );         // Statement 2
}
```

(*i*) Will Statement 1 initialize all the data members for object B with the values given in the Function 1 ? (Yes OR No). Justify your answer suggesting the correction(s) to be made in the above code.

(*ii*) What shall be the possible output when the program gets executed ? (Assuming, if required—the suggested correction(s) are made in the program).

Solution.

(*i*) No, Statement 1 will not initialize all the data members for object B. For initialization of all the data members the constructor

Bazar( ) // Function 1

must be coded in the **public** section of the class Bazar.

(*ii*) The possible output will be :

Electronic–Calculator : 10@225

Copy Constructor

It is of the form **classname (classname &)** *and used for the initialization of an object from another object of same type.* For example,

```
class fun
{
        float x,y;
    public :
        fun ( ) { } //default constructor
        fun(float a,float b)  //constructor
```

```
        {
                x = a;
                y = b;
        }
        fun(fun &f) //copy constructor
        {
                cout<<"\nCopy constructor at work\n";
                x = f.x;
                y = f.y;
        }
        void display (void)
        {
                cout<<x<<" "<<y<<endl;
        }
};
```

Here we have three constructors, one a default constructor, second a parameterized constructor for assignment of initial values given and third a copy constructor for copying data values of a **fun** object to another. Now we can use the following code :

```
fun obj1(3.0,7.0); //obj1 uses second constructor
fun obj2(obj1); //copy constructor used for copying obj1 to obj2
fun obj3=obj2; //copy constructor used for copying obj2 to obj3
```

Also the following statements,

```
fun obj4;
obj4 = obj1;
```

work fine, but do not call copy constructor. Here obj4 being an object of class fun will get values of obj1, member by member.

> ***Note:*** *Initialization using a copy constructor is called* ***copy initialization*** *and is the task of the overloaded (=) assignment operator. A copy constructor takes a reference to an object of the same class as itself as a parameter.*

The following program illustrates the concept of copy constructor :

Program 11.10

```
//illustration of copy constructor
#include<iostream.h>
#include<conio.h>
class fun
{
        int x,y;
    public :
```

```
        fun( ) { } //do-nothing implicit constructor
        fun(int a,int b) //constructor
        {
                x = a;
                y = b;
        }
        fun(fun &f) //copy constructor
        {
                cout<<"\nCopy constructor at work\n";
                x = f.x;
                y = f.y;
        }
        void display(void)
        {
                cout<<x<<" "<<y<<endl;
        }
};
void main( )
{
        clrscr( );
        fun obj1(30,70);  //obj1 is created and initialized
        fun obj2(obj1);   //copy constructor invoked
        fun obj3(obj2);   //copy constructor invoked
        fun obj4;               //obj4 is created but not initialized
        obj4=obj1;        //copy constructor not called
        obj1.display( );
        obj2.display( );
        obj3.display( );
        obj4.display( );
        getch( );  //freeze the monitor
}
```

Output

```
Copy constructor at work
Copy constructor at work
30 70
30 70
30 70
30 70
```

Here *the copy constructor's argument is a reference variable. Value can't be passed to a copy constructor.*

> ***Note:** In case we do not use a copy constructor then the compiler uses its own copy constructor.*

Example. *Answer the questions (i) and (ii) after going through the following program :*

```
class Match
{
        int Time;
    public :
        Match( )                        // Function 1
        {
            Time = 0;
            cout<<"Match commences"<<endl;
        }
        void Details( )                 // Function 2
        {
            cout<<"Inter Section Basketball Match"<<endl;
        }
        Match(int Duration)             // Function 3
        {
            Time = Duration;
            cout<<"Another Match begins now"<<endl;
        }
        Match(Match &M)                 // Function 4
        {
            Time = M.Time;
            cout<<"Like Previous Match"<<endl;
        }
};
```

(*i*) Which category of constructor – **Function 4** belongs to and what is the purpose of using it ?

(*ii*) Write statements that would call the member Functions 1 and 3.

Solution. (*i*) Copy constructor, it is invoked when an object is created and initialized with values of an already existing object of same type.

(*ii*) Match obj1; // call member Function 1, as constructor is called automatically
Match obj2 (90); // call member Function 3

When is a Copy Constructor Called ?

A copy constructor may be called in the following situations :

(*i*) When an object is defined and initialized with other object of the same class.

(*ii*) When we pass an object by value.

(*iii*) In case a function returns an object.

> ***Note:*** *If we do not pass the reference but the value as an argument to a copy constructor (for example, fun(fun) in place of fun(fun &) in program 11.10), the compiler will give an error 'out of memory'. In case of pass by value the copy constructor keeps on calling itself repeatedly for creating copies of the object. By passing reference, no such problem arises.*

Dynamic Initialization of Objects

In C++, the class objects can be initialized at run time (dynamically). We have the flexibility of providing initial values at execution time. The following program illustrates this concept :

Program 11.11

```
//Illustration of dynamic initialization of objects
#include<iostream.h>
#include<conio.h>
class employee
{
        int empl_no;  //data members
        float salary;
    public :
        employee( )  //default constructor
        { }
        employee(int empno, float s)  //constructor with arguments
        {
            empl_no=empno;
            salary=s;
        }
        employee(employee &emp)  //copy constructor
        {
            cout<<"\nCopy constructor working\n";
            empl_no=emp.empl_no;
            salary=emp.salary;
        }
        void display(void)
        {
            cout<<"\nEmp. No :"<<empl_no<<" Salary : "<<salary<<endl;
        }
};
void main( )
{
        int eno;      // variable declaration
        float sal;
        clrscr( );
        cout<<"Enter the employee number and salary\n";
```

```
        cin>>eno>>sal;
        employee obj1(eno,sal);  //dynamic initialization of object
        cout<<"\nEnter the employee number and salary\n";
        cin>>eno>>sal;
        employee obj2(eno,sal);  //dynamic initialization of object
        obj1.display( ); //function call
        obj2.display( );
        employee obj3=obj2;  //copy constructor called
        obj3.display( );
        getch( );  //freeze the monitor
}
```

Output

```
Enter the employee number and salary
1001   15000
Enter the employee number and salary
1002   35000
Emp. No : 1001 Salary : 15000
Emp. No : 1002 Salary : 35000
Copy constructor working
Emp. No : 1002 Salary : 35000
```

Constructors and Primitive Types

In C++, like derived type, that is, class, primitive types (fundamental types) also have their constructors. Default constructor is used when no values are given but when we give initial values, the initialization takes place for newly created instance. For example,

```
float x,y;  //default constructor used
int a(10),b(20);  //a,b initialized with values 10 and 20
float i(2.5),j(7.8);  //i,j initialized with values 2.5 and 7.8
```

Constructor with Default Arguments

In C++, we can define constructors with default arguments. For example, the following code segment shows a constructor with default arguments :

```
class add
{
        private :
            int num1,num2,num3;
        public :
            add(int=0, int=0); //prototype of default argument constructor
                                //to reduce the number of constructors
            void sum( );
```

```
    void display( );
};
//default constructor definition
add::add(int n1,int n2)
{
    num1=n1;
    num2=n2;
    num3=0;
}
//function definition sum( )
void add::sum( )
{
    num3=num1+num2;
}
//function definition display( )
void add::display( )
{
    cout<<"\nThe sum of two numbers is "<<num3<<endl;
}
```

Now using the above code objects of type **add** can be created with no initial values, one initial values or two initial values. For example,

```
add obj1,obj2(5),obj3(10,20);
```

Here, obj1 will have values of data members num1=0, num2=0 and num3=0
obj2 will have values of data members num1=5, num2=0 and num3=0
obj3 will have values of data members num1=10, num2=20 and num3=0

If two constructors for the above class **add** are

```
add::add( ) { } //default constructor
```

and

```
add::add(int=0,int=0); //prototype of default argument constructor
```

then the default argument constructor can be invoked with either two or one or no parameter(s). Without argument, it is treated as a default constructor—using these two forms together causes ambiguity. For example, the declaration

```
add obj;
```

is ambiguous, that is, which one constructor to invoke,

```
add::add( )
    or
add::add(int=0,int=0)
```

So be careful in such cases and avoid such mistakes.

11.14.2 Destructors

These are the functions that are complimentary to constructors. These are used to de-initialize objects when they are destroyed. A destructor is called when an object of the class goes out of scope, or when the memory space used by it is deallocated with the help of **delete** *operator.*

Special Characteristics of Destructors

Some of the characteristics associated with destructors are :

(i) *These are called automatically when the objects are destroyed.*

(ii) *Destructor functions follow the usual access rules as other member functions.*

(iii) *These* **de-initialize** *each object before the object goes out of scope.*

(iv) *No argument and return type (even* **void***) permitted with destructors.*

(v) *These cannot be inherited.*

(vi) **Static** *destructors are not allowed.*

(vii) *Address of a destructor cannot be taken.*

(viii) *A destructor can call member functions of its class.*

(ix) *An object of a class having a destructor cannot be a member of a* **union.**

> ***Note:*** *Destructors should be declared in a program to release memory space for future utilization.*

Declaration and Definition of Destructor

The syntax for declaring a destructor is :

```
~name_of_the_class( )
{
}
```

So the *name of the class and destructor is same but it is prefixed with a ~(tilde). It does not take any parameter nor does it return any value. Overloading a destructor is not possible and can be explicitly invoked.* In other words, a class can have only one destructor. A destructor can be defined outside the class. The following program illustrates this concept :

Program 11.12

```
//Illustration of the working of destructor function
#include<iostream.h>
#include<conio.h>
class add
{
    private :
        int num1,num2,num3;
    public :
        add(int=0,int=0);     //prototype of default argument constructor
                              //to reduce the number of constructors
        void sum( );
```

```
        void display( );
        ~add(void);   //destructor prototype
    };
    //destructor definition  ~add( )
    add:: ~add(void) //destructor called automatically at end of program
    {
        num1=num2=num3=0;
        cout<<"\nAfter the final execution,me,the object has entered in the"
          <<"\ndestructor to destroy myself\n";
    }
    //constructor definition add( )
    add::add(int n1,int n2)
    {
        num1=n1;
        num2=n2;
        num3=0;
    }
    //function definition sum( )
    void add::sum( )
    {
        num3=num1+num2;
    }
    //function definition display( )
    void add::display( )
    {
        cout<<"\nThe sum of two numbers is "<<num3<<endl;
    }
    void main( )
    {
        add obj1,obj2(5),obj3(10,20):  //objects created and initialized
        clrscr( );
        obj1.sum( );  //function call
        obj2.sum( );
        obj3.sum( );
        cout<<"\nUsing obj1\n";
        obj1.display( );  //function call
        cout<<"\nUsing obj2\n";
        obj2.display( );
        cout<<"\nUsing obj3\n";
        obj3.display( );
    }
```

Output

Using obj1

The sum of two numbers is 0

Using obj2

The sum of two numbers is 5

Using obj3

The sum of two numbers is 30

After the final execution, me, the object has entered in the destructor to destroy myself

After the final execution, me, the object has entered in the destructor to destroy myself

After the final execution, me, the object has entered in the destructor to destroy myself

> ***Note:*** *Define a destructor in the public section of class, so that the objects of the class can be (used and then) destroyed in any function of the program.*

For explicit call of a destructor the syntax is : **<object>.<classname>::<destructor>;**

The compiler automatically uses the default destructor to destroy the objects of the class type. For destructing more than one object the destructors are called in the reverse order that of constructors were called.

11.15 Friend Functions

In C++, the concept of data hiding and encapsulation dictate that an object's private or protected data should not be accessed by non-member functions. However, there are situations where such constraints are not acceptable. For accessing the non-public members of a class, C++ has the **friend** facility. A function can be declared a friend in any number of classes by using the **friend** clause before the function declaration. By declaring a function as a friend within a class, does not make this function a member of the class. A friend function can be declared in any one of the three sections that is private, public or protected without affecting its meaning but it must be prototyped within the class(es) of which it is a friend.

The definition of the friend function is somewhere after the class definition, of which it is a friend, like a normal C++ function. The definition of the friend function does not require the keyword **friend** or the scope resolution operator ::. Some characteristics of a friend function are given below :

(*i*) It is not in the scope of the class of which it is a **friend**.

(*ii*) We cannot call a friend function using the object of the class due to the above stated fact.

(*iii*) It can be called like a normal function that is without any object.

(*iv*) It can be declared in any of the three sections without affecting its meaning.

(*v*) It accepts objects as its arguments, generally.

(*vi*) It is oftenly used for operator loading.

(*vii*) It cannot access the member names directly and requires object name followed by dot membership operator with every member.

The syntax of a friend function declaration is shown below :

```
class ONE
{
    . . . .
    . . . .
  public :
    . . . .
    . . . .
  friend int largest(ONE big); //prototype
};
```

The following program illustrates the concept of a friend function :

Program 11.13

```
//to illustrate working of a friend function

#include<iostream.h>
#include<conio.h>

class ONE
{
  private :
    int a, b, c;
  public :
   void enter(void)
   {
        cout<<"\nEnter the values of a, b and c : \n";
        cin>>a>>b>>c;
   }
   friend int largest(ONE big); //friend function prototype
}
//definition of friend function
//friend keyword not required in the definition
//friend function always requires object/objects as it's arguments
int largest(ONE big)
{
   int max;
   max = big.a;
```

```
        if(big.b>max)
          max = big.b;
        if(big.c>max)
          max = big.c;
        return(max);
}
void main( )
{
        ONE obj; //object of class ONE declared
        int result;
        clrscr( );
        obj.enter( );
        result=largest(obj); //object passed to friend function largest( )
        cout<<"\nLargest of three numbers is : "<<result;
        getch( ); //to freeze the screen
}
```

Output

```
Enter the values of a, b and c :
4 6 8
Largest of three numbers is : 8
```

11.16 Friend Classes

In C++, a class can be made a friend to another class. For example,

```
class TWO; //forward declaration of the class TWO
class ONE
{
        --------
        --------
        public:
        --------
        --------
        friend class TWO; //class TWO declared as friend of class ONE
};
```

Now from class **TWO,** all the member of class **ONE** can be accessed. The following program illustrates the concept of a friend class :

Program 11.14

```
// illustration of a friend class

#include<iostream.h>
#include<conio.h>

class TWO; //forward declaration of the class TWO
class ONE
{
    private :
      int x, y;
    public :
      void enter( )
      {
          cout<<"\nEnter the values of x and y\n";
          cin>>x>>y;
      }
      friend class TWO; //class TWO declared as friend of class ONE
      //so all the member functions of TWO can access private data of ONE
};
class TWO
{
    public :
      void show(ONE obj)
      {
          cout<<"\nPrivate data of class ONE is shown below :\n\n";
          cout<<"\nThe numbers x and y are :" ;
          cout<<obj.x  <<"\t"<<obj.y;
      }
};
void main( )
{
    ONE obj1; //object declared
    TWO obj2; //object declared
    clrscr( );
    obj1.enter( );       //function call
    obj2.show(obj1); //function call
}
```

Output

```
Enter the values of x and y
5  10
Private data of class ONE is shown below :
The number x and y are : 5  10
```

11.17 Friends as Bridges

Let us take a situation when a function needs to operate on objects of two different classes. In such a situation a function can be declared as a **friend** function in both the classes. A friend function takes objects of the two classes as arguments for operating on their private data.

For example,

```
class TWO; //forward declaration of the class TWO
class ONE
{
        -------
        -------
    public :
        -------
        -------
    friend int sum(ONE, TWO); //sum( ) declared as friend in ONE
};
class TWO
{
        -------
        -------
    public :
        -------
        -------
    friend int sum(ONE, TWO); //sum( ) declared as friend in TWO
};
```

Now we can easily operate on the objects of both classes ONE and TWO using the function sum ( ). The following program illustrates this concept :

Program 11.15

```
// illustration of the friend functions as bridges

#include<iostream.h>
#include<conio.h>
```

```
class TWO;        //forward declaration of the class TWO
                  //to inform the compiler otherwise an error will be there
class ONE
{
   private :
     int a, b;
   public :
     void enter( )
     {
        cout <<"\nEnter the values of a and b for class ONE\n";
        cin>>a>>b;
     }
     friend int sum(ONE, TWO); //function sum( ) declared as friend in ONE
};
class TWO
{
     private :
        int a, b :
     public :
        void enter( )
        {
              cout<<"\nEnter the values of a and b for class TWO\n";
              cin>>a>>b;
        }
     friend int sum(ONE, TWO); //function sum( ) declared as friend in TWO

};
//friend function sum( ) defined using objects as arguments
//keyword friend not required in the definition

int sum(ONE ob1, TWO ob2)
{
   return(ob1.a + ob1.b + ob2.a + ob2.b); //return the sum
}
void main( )
{
   ONE obj1;
   TWO obj2;
   clrscr( );
   obj1.enter( );     //enter the values for obj1
   obj2.enter( );     //enter the values for obj2
   cout<<"\nSum of the numbers is : "<<sum(obj1,obj2);
}
```

Output

```
Enter the values of a and b for class ONE
1 9
Enter the values of a and b for class TWO
2 6
Sum of the numbers is : 18
```

Here, the friend function **sum ( )** is working as a bridge between classes **ONE** and **TWO** for accessing the private data of both the classes simultaneously.

Let us consider one more example to understood the working of a friend function for multiplying two matrices :

Program 11.16

```
//multiplication of two matrices using a friend function

#include<iostream.h>
#include<conio.h>
#include<iomanip.h> //for formatting
#include<process.h> //for exit( )
#define SIZE 5

class matrix
{
    private :
      int i, j, row, colm, mat[SIZE] [SIZE];

    public :
      void enter( ); //function prototype
      void display( ); //function prototype

    //friend function mat_multiply( ) prototype

    friend matrix mat_multiply(matrix x, matrix y);
};
//function definition enter( )

void matrix :: enter( )
{
    cout<<"Enter the order of matrix <= "<<SIZE<<" * "<<SIZE<<"\n";
    cin>>row>>colm;
    cout<<"Enter matrix of order "<<row<<" * "<<colm<<"\n"'
```

```
    for(i = 0; i < row; i++)
    {
        for(j = 0; j<colm; j++)
        cin>>mat[i][j];
    }
}

//function definition display( )

void matrix :: display( )
{
    for(i = 0; i<row; i++)
    {
        for(j=0; j<colm; j++)
          cout<<setw(8)<<mat[i][j];
        cout<<"\n";
    }
}

//friend function mat_multiply( ) definition
//friend function always takes objects as parameters

matrix mat_multiply(matrix x, matrix y)
{
    matrix z; //object declared of class matrix
    int i, j, k;
    if(x.colm != y.row)
    {
        cout<<"\nMatrix multiplication not possible\n\n"'
        exit(0);
    }
    else
    {
        z.row = x.row;
        z.colm = y.colm;
        for(i=0; i< x.row;i++)
        {
            for(j=0; j< y.colm;j++)
            {
                z.mat[i][j] = 0;
                for(k=0; k<x.colm; k++)
                {
```

```
                    z.mat[i][j] += x.mat[i][k]*y.mat[k][j];
                }
            }
        }
    }
    return(z); //object of type matrix returned
}
void main( )
{
    matrix a, b, c; //objects of class matrix declared
    clrscr( );
    a.enter( ); //function call
    b.enter( ); //function call
    //matrix multiplication
    c = mat_multiply(a,b); //function call
    clrscr( );
    cout<<"***** First matrix is *****\n\n";
    a.display( ); //function call
    cout<<"***** Second matrix is *****\n\n";
    b.display( ); //function call
    cout<<"***** Resultant matrix is *****\n\n";
    c.display( ); //function call
}
```

Output

```
Enter the order of matrix <= 5 * 5
2 2
Enter matrix of order 2 * 2
1 3
2 4
Enter the order of matrix <= 5 * 5
2 2
Enter matrix of order 2 * 2
6 4
9 7
***** First matrix is *****
 1      3
 2      4
***** Second matrix is *****
 6      4
 9      7
```

```
***** Resultant matrix is *****
 33          25
 48          36
```

In the above program first of all order of matrix and the matrix elements are entered and then the order of second matrix and matrix elements are entered using the member function **enter( )**. The friend function **mat_multiply( )** is called using the two objects as arguments, which multiplies two matrices (if possible). The function **display( )** is called three times for printing the original matrices and the resultant matrix.

Solved Problems

Problem 1. *Define a class ITEM in C++ with following description :*

Private Members

- *Code of type integer (Item Code)*
- *Iname of type string (Item Name)*
- *Price of type float (Price of each item)*
- *Qty of type integer (Quantity of item in stock)*
- *Offer of type float (Offer percentage on the item)*
- *A member function GetOffer( ) to calculate Offer percentage as per the following rule:*

If Qty<=50	*Offer is 0*
If 50<Qty<=100	*Offer is 5*
If Qty>100	*Offer is 10*

Public Members

- *A function GetStock( ) to allow user to enter values for Code, Iname, Price, Qty and call function GetOffer( ) to calculate the Offer*
- *A function ShowItem( ) to allow user to view the content of all the data members*

Solution. The class definition is given below :

```
class ITEM
{
private:
    int Code;
    char Iname [40];
    float Price;
    int Qty;
    float Offer;
    void GetOffer( )
    {
        if(Qty< =50)
            Offer=0;
        else if (Qty>50 && Qty < =100)
            Offer=5;
        else
```

```
            Offer=10;
    }
public:
    void GetStock( )
    {
        cout<<"\nEnter Item Code: ";
        cin>>Code;
        cout<<"\nEnter Item Name: ";
        gets(Iname);
        cout<<"\nEnter Price of item: ";
        cin>>Price;
        cout<<"\nEnter Quantity of item in stock: ";
        cin>>Qty;
        GetOffer( ); //function call
    }
    void ShowItem( )
    {
        cout<<"\n Item Code: "<<Code<<endl;
        cout<<"\n Item Name: "<<Iname<<endl;
        cout<<"\n Item Price: "<<Price<<endl;
        cout<<"\n Item Quantity: "<<Qty<<endl;
        cout<<"\n Offer Percentage: "<<Offer<<endl;
    }
};
```

Problem 2. *Define a class named HOUSING in C++ with the following descriptions :*

Private Members :

REG_NO	*integer(Ranges 10 – 1000)*
NAME	*Array of characters(String)*
TYPE	*Character*
COST	*Float*

Public Members :

Function Read_Data( ) to read an object of HOUSING type.

Function Display( ) to display the details of an object.

Function Draw_Nos( ) to choose and display the details of 2 houses selected randomly from an array of 10 objects of type HOUSING.

Use random function to generate the registration nos. to match with REG_NO from the array.

Solution.

```
class HOUSING
{
    private :
```

```
        int REG_NO;  // private members
        char NAME[30];
        char TYPE;
        float COST;
    public :
        void Read_Data( );  // public members
        void Display( );
        void Draw_Nos( );
}   arr[10];  // array 'arr' to store 10 objects of HOUSING type
// function definition Read_Data( )
void HOUSING::Read_Data( )
{
    cout<<"\nEnter the registration number (Range 10–1000)\n";
    cin>>REG_NO;
    cout<<"\nEnter the name\n";
    gets (NAME):
    cout<<"\nEnter the type\n";
    cin>>TYPE ;
    cout<<"\nEnter the cost\n";
    cin>>COST;
}
// function definition Display( )
void HOUSING::Display( )
{
    cout<<"\nRegistration number"<<REG_NO;
    cout<<"\nName"<<NAME;
    cout<<"\nType"<<TYPE;
    cout<<"\nCost"<<COST;
}
// function definition Draw_Nos( )
void HOUSING::Draw_Nos( )
{
    randomize( );
    int regno, count=0;
    clrscr( );  // clears the screen
    while (count !=2)
    {
        // get ranged value for registration number (10 – 1000)
        regno = 10 + random (991);
        if (regno >= 10 && regno <= 1000)
        {
            for (int i = 0; i< 10; i++)
```

```
        {
            if (regno = = are[i].REG_NO);
            {
               count + +;
               cout<<"\n\nDetails of randomly selected house :\n";
               are[i].Display( );  // function call
               break;
            }
         }
      }
   }
}
```

Problem 3. *Answer the questions (i) and (ii) after going through the following class :*

```
class TEST
      {
               int Regno, Max, Min, Score;
      public:
               TEST( )                          //Function 1
               {
                        Regno=101;Max=100;Min=40;Score=75;
               }
               TEST(int Pregno, int Pscore)     //Function 2
               {
                        Regno=Pregno;Max=100;Min=40;Score=Pscore;
               }
               ~TEST( )                                //Function 3
               {
                        cout<<"TEST Over"<<endl;
               }
               void Display( )                  //Function 4
               {
                        cout<<Regno<<":"<<Max<<":"<<Min<<endl;
                        cout<<"[Score]"<<Score<<endl;
               }
      };
```

(*i*) As per Object Oriented Programming, which concept is illustrated by **Function 1** and **Function 2** together ?

(*ii*) What is **Function 3** specifically referred as ? When do you think, **Function 3** will be invoked/called ?

Solution. (*i*) It illustrates the concept of polymorphism through constructor overloading.

(*ii*) Destructor. It will be called when the memory allocated to the object of the class TEST is deallocated.

Problem 4. *Using classes and object, write a program to do the following :*

$$A = B * C + D,$$

where A, B, C, D are 3 × 3 matrices. (PTU 2004)

Solution :

```
// perform A = B * C + D, where A,B,C,D are 3 x 3 matrices

#include<iostream.h>
#include<conio.h>
#include<iomanip.h>
class matrix
{
    private:
        int i,j,k;
    public:
        void input(int mat[3][3]);  // member function prototype
        void display(int mat[3][3]);
        void operation(int a[3][3], int b[3][3], int c[3][3], int d[3][3]);
};

// function definition input( )

void matrix::input(int mat[3][3])
{
    for(i=0;i<3;i++)
    {
        for(j=0;j<3;j++)
            cin>>mat[i][j];
    }
}

// function definition display( )

void matrix::display(int mat[3][3])
{
    for(i=0;i<3;i++)
    {
        for(j=0;j<3;j++)
            cout<<setw(6)<<mat[i][j];
        cout<<endl;
    }
}
```

```
// function definition operation( )

void matrix::operation(int a[3][3], int b[3][3], int c[3][3], int d[3][3])
{
   // perform multiplication of matrices b and c, store the result in a

   for(i=0;i<3;i++)
   {
      for(j=0;j<3;j++)
      {
         a[i][j]=0; //initialize with value 0

         for(k=0;k<3;k++)
         {
            a[i][j] += b[i][k] * c[k][j];
         }
      }
   }

   // perform addition of matrices a and d, store the result in a

   for(i=0;i<3;i++)
   {
      for(j=0;j<3;j++)
         a[i][j]=a[i][j]+d[i][j];
   }
}

void main( )
{
   matrix obj; // object declared
   int A[3][3],B[3][3],C[3][3],D[3][3];
   clrscr( );
   cout<<"Enter matrix B"<<endl;
   obj.input(B); // function call
   cout<<"Enter matrix C"<<endl;
   obj.input(C); // function call
   cout<<"Enter matrix D"<<endl;
   obj.input(D); // function call
   obj.operation(A,B,C,D); // function call
   clrscr( );
   cout<<"Matrix B is : \n\n";
```

```
    obj.display(B); // function call
    cout<<"\nMatrix C is : \n\n";
    obj.display(C); // function call
    cout<<"\nMatrix D is : \n\n";
    obj.display(D); // function call
    cout<<"\nResultant matrix A is : \n\n";
    obj.display(A); // function call

    getch( ); // freeze the monitor
}
```

Review Questions and Exercises

1. What is a class ? How does it accomplish data hiding ? **(PTU 2004)**
2. (*a*) What is a class ?
   (*b*) What are objects ? How are they created ? **(PTU 2004)**
3. Define data members, member function, private and public members with example.
4. How are **public** members of a class different from **private** members of a class ?
5. Illustrate the use of inline function in C++ with the help of an example.
6. When will you make a function inline and why ?
7. What is the significance of scope resolution operator (::) ?
8. Explain the ways of defining member functions in C++ with the help of suitable examples.
9. What do you understand by an array of type class ? Explain with a suitable example.
10. Write a program to maintain library records using array of objects.
11. Write a short note on objects passing as function arguments, with suitable examples.
12. What is the difference between passing the objects as function arguments—pass by value and pass by reference ?
13. What do you mean by static data member of a class ? Explain the characteristics of a static data member.
14. Write a program to register the entrance of people (male or female) using static class data.
15. What is the difference between a **struct** and a **class** in C++ ?
16. Let Item List be a linear array of size N (where N is a user input) where each element of the array contains following fields : Item Code, Item Price and quantity. Declare a class with Item List as data member and member functions that will perform following operations :
    (*i*) Appending an item to the list.
    (*ii*) Given the Item Code, delete an item from the list.
    (*iii*) Printing the total value of the stock.
17. Write a C++ program to perform various operations on a string class without using language supported built-in string functions. The operations on a class are :

(*a*) Read a string (*b*) Display the string

(*c*) Reverse the string (*d*) Copy the string into an empty string

(*e*) Concatenate two strings.

18. A class student has three data members : name, roll number, marks of 5 subjects and member functions to assign streams on the basis of table given below :

Average Marks	***Stream***
96% or more	Computer Science
91%—95%	Electronics
86%—90%	Mechanical
81%—85%	Electrical
76%—80%	Chemical
71%—75%	Civil

Declare the class using the above specifications. Also give the detailed member function definition.

19. Write a C++ program to simulate an arithmetic calculator for integers using a class.

20. Write a C++ program to add two complex numbers using function returning objects method.

21. Write a C++ program to find the roots of a quadratic equation using class method.

22. What do you understand by Data Encapsulation and Data Hiding? Also, give an example in C++ to illustrate both.

23. Define a class STOCK in C++ with following description :

Private Members

- ICode of type integer (Item Code)
- Item of type string (Item Name)
- Price of type float (Price of each item)
- Qty of type integer (Quantity in stock)
- Discount of type float (Discount percentage on the item)
- A member function FindDisc( ) to calculate discount as per the following rule :

If Qty<=50	Discount is 0
If 50<Qty<=100	Discount is 5
If Qty>100	Discount is 10

Public Members

- A function Buy ( ) to allow user to enter values for ICode, Item, Price, Qty and call function FindDisc( ) to calculate the Discount.
- A function ShowAll( ) to allow user to view the content of all the data members.

24. What is the importance of constructor in object oriented programming? Explain with the help of an example.

25. What do you understand by default constructor and copy constructor functions used in classes ? How are these functions different from normal constructors ?

26. What do you understand by constructor and destructor functions used in classes ? How are these functions different from other member functions ?

27. What is a copy constructor ? What do you understand by constructor overloading ?

28. Why is a destructor function required in classes ? Illustrate with the help of an example.

29. List some special characteristics of the constructor and destructor functions.

30. Differentiate between a default constructor and copy constructor, give suitable examples of each.

31. Design a class having the constructor and destructor functions that should display the number of object being created or destroyed of this class type.

32. What is the order of constructor and destructor invocation ? Explain by giving a suitable example.

33. Differentiate between Constructor and Destructor function in context of Classes and Objects using C++.

34. Write a C++ program to evaluate a^b, where a and b are of type real and integer respectively, using a constructor.

35. Write a C++ program to find the factorial of a number using a constructor and a destructor (generating the message "you have done it").

36. Write a C++ program to generate and display the fibonacci series up to N terms using a constructor function. N must not exceed 20.

37. Create a class book which has data members as book name, author name, pages. Initialize all these members first with zero and then with some initial values. Use constructor overloading. Display all results.

38. Answer the questions (*i*) and (*ii*) after going through the following class:

```
class Exam
{
    int Rno, MaxMarks, MinMarks, Marks ;
public :
    Exam ( )                    //Module 1
    {
        Rno=101 ; MaxMarks=100 ; MinMarks=40 ; Marks=75 ;
    }
    Exam (int Prno, int Pmarks)         //Module 2
    {
        Rno=Prno ; MaxMarks = 100 ; MinMarks = 40 ; Marks = Pmarks ;
    }
    ~Exam ( )                   //Module 3
    {
        cout<<"Exam Over"<<endl ;
    }
    void Show ( )               //Module 4
    {
        cout<<Rno<<" : "<<MaxMarks<<" : "<<MinMarks<<endl ;
```

```
            cout<< "[Marks Got]" <<Marks<<endl ;
        }
    } ;
```

(*i*) As per Object Oriented Programming, which concept is illustrated by **Module 1** and **Module 2** together ?

(*ii*) What is **Module 3** referred as ? When do you think, **Module 3** will be invoked/called ?

39. What is copy constructor ? Give an example in C++ to illustrate copy constructor.

40. Is there any limit to the number of arguments that may be used in the constructor? **(PTU Exam)**

41. Create a class date containing int day, int month and int year. Write its constructors. Write a function which checks if a given date is valid or not? Use them in main function. **(PTU Exam)**

42. Create a class distance containing feet and inches as data members. Use getdata( ) function to take data through keyboard and dispdata( ) function to display a distance in the form (feet' inches"), a default constructor, a general constructor, a copy constructor and a destructor. Use them in the main function. **(PTU Exam)**

43. What is a friend function? What are the merits and demerits of using friend functions?

❑❑❑

CHAPTER 12

Basics of File Handling

12.1 Need for a Data File

The first electronic computers were used for calculations in scientific applications. The volume of data in these applications was very small and the number of computations were very large in number. Later on, it was realized that computer could be useful for business applications such as payroll, banking, railway and airline reservation, inventory control, design work etc. where the volume of data is very large in comparison to scientific applications. *The program and data must be brought into main memory before processing takes place.* The computer memory being limited so the entire data may not even fit into main memory. Even if, it fits into memory, the entire data is not processed at a time. Generally, only a small amount of data is processed at a time, so why to keep the main memory occupied with unnecessary data. The unused memory space can be utilized by other programs or data. The above mentioned problems required the use of files.

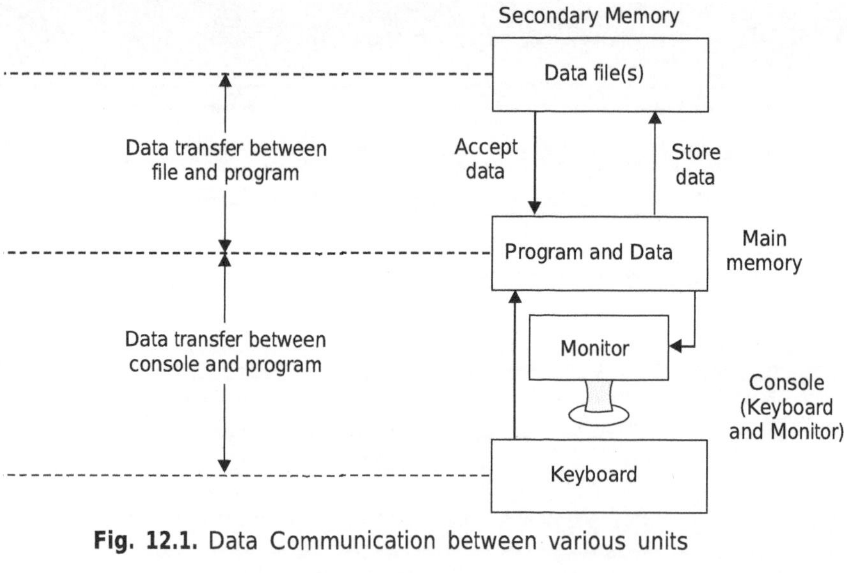

Fig. 12.1. Data Communication between various units

A **file** is a bunch of bytes stored on some storage device like magnetic disk or tape etc. Most of the application programs process large volume of data which is permanently stored in files. We can write programs that can read data from file(s) and write data to file(s). Compilers read source code files and provide executable files. Database programs and word processors also work with files.

Data transfer is generally one or both of the following two types (see figure 12.1) :

(*i*) *Transfer between console unit and the program.*

(*ii*) *Transfer between the program and a file on disk or tape.*

So far we have used the technique of data communication between console unit and the program where the amount of data is very small. Now we are going to describe the important requirements for the need of data storage in files :

(*i*) **Fast response.** There are applications where the required information is needed very fast. In such situations if the data is stored in a file or files it can be utilized immediately without any delay.

(*ii*) **Ease of use.** There are different ways of utilizing the data by different users. If the data stored in a file is in the order we want to process then it becomes very easy to handle it and a lot of time and efforts are saved.

(*iii*) **Constraints on performance.** In real time systems, there are constraints on the performance of the system. The data must be processed very fast, if not so, the data may be lost or may be of no value or there may be serious consequences *e.g.,* in case of natural disasters like earthquakes, floods or chemical industries, space research work, the persons must be informed well in advance so that necessary action may take place.

(*iv*) **Saving of repetitive typing of data.** If the same data is needed again and again for processing, we need not to type it repeatedly. For example, the data of employees in an organization, the data of students in a school is processed many times. The data is stored in a file or files only once and processed for the enquiries on it.

(*v*) **Correctness of data.** The contents of a data file are verified and the errors, if any, can be removed. So the correctness of data is improved which helps in obtaining accurate results.

12.2 Types of Data Files—Text File and Binary File

Files may be classified according to the function they perform in an information system. These are **master file, transaction file, report file, program file, text file** and **binary file**.

Text File. It contains alphanumeric and graphic data input using a text editor program. That is, all information is stored in the same format as it would be displayed on the screen. So 'A' will be written as A onto the file, and the number 336 will be written as the string "336". This means that we can type the file and see the contents on the screen.

Binary File. It allows us to write numeric data to the disk files in less number of bytes as compared to text files. For example, the number 336 will be written as an **int** representation taking up two bytes of space. The number 123.45 will be written as a **float** representation taking up four bytes of space in comparison to six bytes it would take when stored in text format (decimal point is also a character and five digits make it a total of six bytes). So, these files require less storage. But the number cannot be read as they are written in the file. Special commands are needed to read them as discussed later on in this chapter.

12.2.1 Basic File Operations on Text File

The basic file operation on text file are :

1. *Creating an empty file*
2. *Opening a file*
3. *Closing a file*
4. *Writing text into file*
5. *Reading of text from an already existing text file (accessing sequentially)*
6. *Manipulation of text from an already existing text file (accessing sequentially)*
7. *Detecting end-of-file*

1. **Creating an empty file.** First time when a file is created with some valid filename it is empty and therefore it contains no element except that it contains an end-of-file marker and a location pointer pointing to end-of-file.

2. **Opening a file.** A file is opened for performing reading/writing or manipulation of data on it. If the file is not present on the disk it cannot be opened. When an existing file is opened the location pointer points to the beginning of the file.

3. **Closing a file.** After the file is created and data elements are written to it, it should be closed or even if it is opened for reading only. If we don't close it, the opened file is automatically closed when the program using it comes to an end.

4. **Writing text into file.** Once a file with some valid filename has been created, data elements or text can be stored in the file permanently. The already existing file's contents are deleted if we try to write data to it. Rather we can append data to it and keep the existing data.

5. **Reading of text from an already existing text file (accessing sequentially).** An existing file must be opened first and then the data can be read from it in sequential order.

6. **Manipulation of text from an already existing text file (accessing sequentially).** An existing file must be opened first and then the manipulation is done in sequential order. For example, counting of vowels in it.

7. **Detecting end-of-file.** When the data from the file is read in sequential order, the location pointer will reach to the end-of-file. After reaching at the end-of-file no attempt should be made to read data from the file.

All the above operations are implemented in C++ later on in this chapter.

12.2.2 Binary File

Data in computer memory is stored in the binary form. C++ allows a user to store the data in a file without any conversion, such a file is known as a binary file. Binary files need less space for storage of data in a disk file as compared to the text files storing data in text form.

Creation of file. A binary file is always opened in binary mode, for both reading or writing. Upon successful creation, the file pointer is set to the beginning of the file. If the file already exists, its size is reset to 0 (It is essentially the same as deleting the file and creating a new file with the same name).

Writing data into file. A binary file is opened in output mode for writing data in it. A binary file contains non-readable characters in binary code when data has been written. In C++, the function **write( )** writes data to a binary file. Function **write( )** can write all the data members of a class or a structure to a file. The data can be written at the desired location by using the offset. The file must be closed after data has been stored.

Searching for required data from file. A binary file is opened in input mode for searching data from it. The first record (or data item) will be read and it will be checked whether it satisfies the given condition or not. If not, then the successive records will be retrieved till the condition is satisfied. If the desired data is not found in the file, an error message will be displayed. Close the file at the end of searching.

Appending data to a file. Appending data to a binary file means adding the new records (or data items) at the end of the existing file. It is assumed that the data is accurate. The following flowchart illustrates this concept :

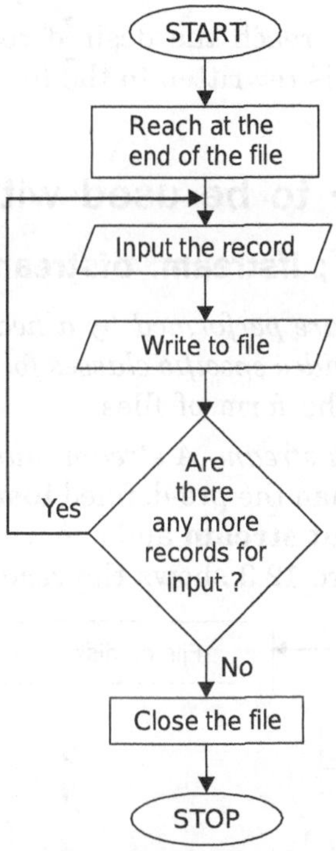

Fig. 12.2. Flowchart for Appending data to a file

Insertion of data in sorted file. The insertion of data in sorted file requires another file. First of all open the given data file which is already sorted in reading mode (input mode) and open a temporary file in writing mode (output mode). As the data in the temporary file must be kept in sorted order, the records from the already existing file, which come earlier to the record to be inserted, are copied to the temporary file. Now copy the given record in it, and after that the remaining records from existing file are copied to the temporary file. Close both the files. Now, rename this temporary file as the master file (a file which is relatively permanent to an organization or person), if needed.

Deletion of data from file. We must know about the data (or record) to be deleted from a binary file. For example, its number or some other key value. There is no way to physically delete the records from a sequentially organized file.

Generally, a special field (say status) is created in each record for the purpose of deletion. This field can have one of the two values 'A' or 'D', 'A' indicating that the record is active and 'D' to indicate that the record is deleted. For processing such a file, access only those records which have their special field value as 'A'. Deletion of records in such a file involves only changing of the special field value from 'A' to 'D'. It is known as **logical deletion**. In a random way, we reach the record directly and make the change in the special field.

Other method is to create a new file and then writing all the records from original file to this file except those records that are to be deleted.

Modification of data in a file. The modification of data in a binary file can be done sequentially or randomly. The sequential modification requires, open the file for Input/Output, retrieval of record (or data), modify it as desired and then it is written back in the same location from which it was read. The modified record must be of the same length as the record retrieved. Close the file at the end of the operation.

In a random way we directly reach the desired record and then make the specified modifications. The modified record is rewritten to the file in the same location. Close the file at the end of the operation.

12.3 Components of C++ to be used with File Handling

12.3.1 Header file : fstream.h ; ifstream, ofstream, fstream classes

In C++ file input/output facilities are performed by a header file **fstream.h** *which exists in the C++ standard library. C++ provides specific classes for dealing with user defined streams.* The user defined streams are in the form of files.

Every file in C++ is linked to a stream. A stream must be obtained before opening a file. These streams are more powerful than the pre-defined **iostreams.** The stream which supplies data to a program is known as **input stream** and one which receives data from the program is known as **output stream.** Figure 12.3 shows the reading and writing of data from files :

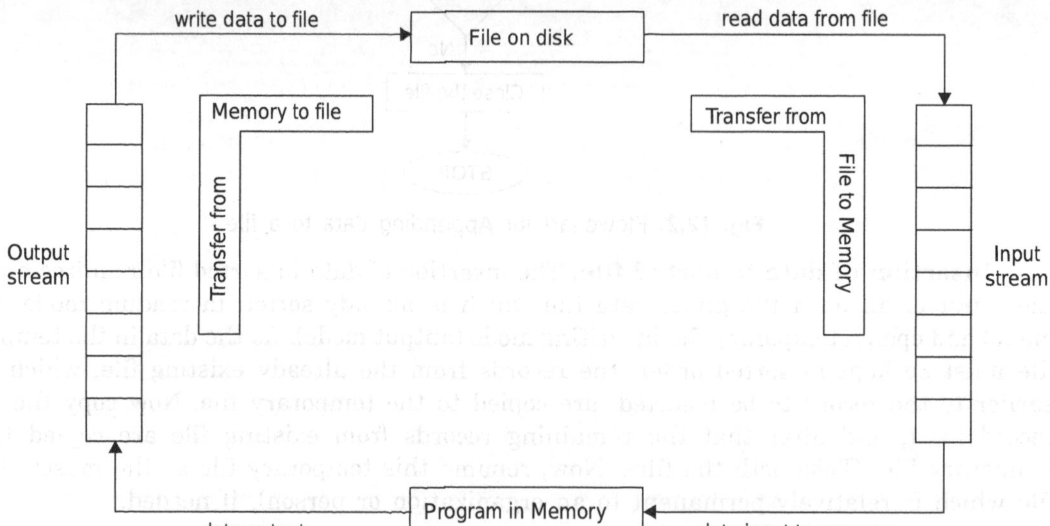

Fig. 12.3. Illustration of file input and output streams

User-defined Streams. The I/O system of C++ has a set of classes for file handling. The definitions of these classes are available in the header file **fstream.h.** The three classes for file input/output are :

(*i*) **ifstream**—derived from istream and used for file input (reading).

(*ii*) **ofstream**—derived from ostream and used for output (writing).

(*iii*) **fstream**—derived from iostream and used for both input and output.

The classes defined in **fstream.h** are derived from the classes in **iostream.h,** the header file for managing console I/O.

Figure 12.4 shows the stream class hierarchy :

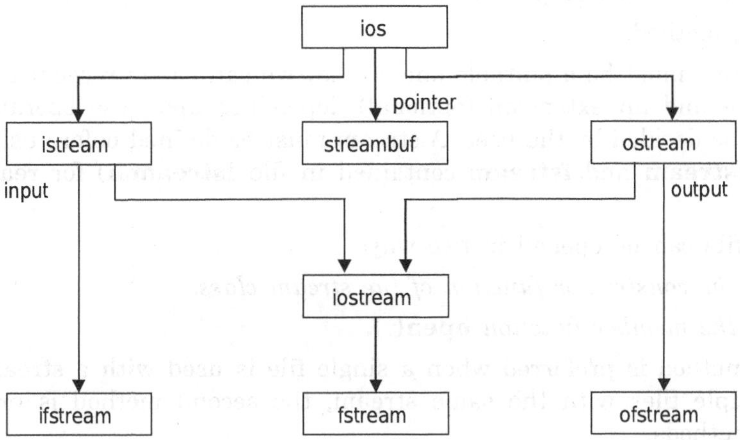

Fig. 12.4. Stream class hierarchy

Table 12.1 gives the details of these classes.

Table 12.1. Stream Classes for Console Operations

Class	*Contents*
ios (General input/output stream class)	• Contains basic facilities that are used by all other input and output classes • Also contains a pointer to a buffer object (**streambuf**) object • Declares constants and functions that are necessary for handling formatted input and output operations.
istream (input stream)	• Inherits the properties of **ios** • Declares input functions such as **get ( )**, **getline ( )** and **read ( )** • Contains overloaded extraction operator >>
ostream (output stream)	• Inherits the properties of **ios** • Declares output functions **put ( )** and **write ( )** • Contains overloaded insertion operator <<
iostream (input/output stream)	• Inherits the properties of **ios istream** and **ostream** through multiple inheritance and thus contains all the input and output functions
streambuf	• Provides an interface to physical devices through buffers • Acts as a base for **filebuf** class used ios files.

Note: ***For complete details of the stream classes, the reference manual of C++ can be referred.***

12.4 Opening a Text File using in, out, and app Modes

Every file on a disk is opened for a specific purpose. The user must decide about the following while using a file :

- Suitable name of file
- Data type and its format
- Type of use (input, output or both)
- Opening method.

The file name must be a suitable one so that we can easily recognize it. It may have a primary name and an extension (optional) depending upon the operating system. Its contents are to be decided by the user. A stream must be defined before using the file (that is **ifstream, ofstream** and **fstream** contained in file **fstream.h**) for reading or writing data.

In C++ a file can be opened in two ways :

(*i*) *using the constructor function of the stream class.*

(*ii*) *using the member function* **open( ).**

The first method is preferred when a single file is used with a stream, however, for managing multiple files with the same stream, the second method is preferred. Let us discuss these methods.

12.4.1 Opening Files Using Constructors

We can use the first method in the C++ programs for managing a single file by creating an object for the stream. For example :

```
ofstream Ofile("BILL.DAT"); //write only
```

will create an output file **BILL.DAT** and creates an object **Ofile** of output stream as shown below :

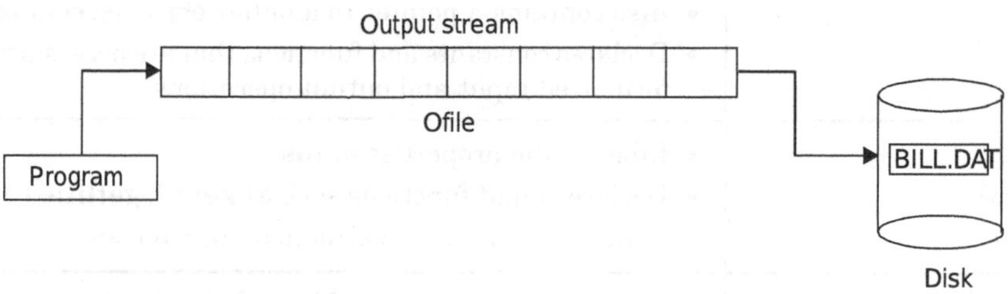

Fig. 12.5. An output stream ofile working on file BILL.DAT

Similarly, the statement

```
ifstream Ifile("BILL.DAT"); //read only
```

declares **Ifile** as an **ifstream** object and it is attached with file BILL.DAT for reading.

In C++, the same file can be used for reading and writing data.

> ***Note:*** *If a file is opened for output using stream class constructor, then a new file is created if the file with the specified name does not exist and if it exists already, the contents are lost and output starts a fresh.*

Closing a File

The connection with a file is closed on the termination of the program. We can also close the connection with a file explicity using the statement like :

```
Ofile.close( ); //close output connection to file
Ifile.close( ); //close input connection to file
```

The streams Ofile and Ifile exist alongwith their buffers and reconnection can be established, if required, with the same file or another file. *When we close a file the flushing of buffer takes place, that is, the existing data in the buffer (output or input stream) is moved out of it in the proper direction (from input buffer to the program or from output buffer to the file on the disk as the case may be).*

> ***Note:*** *Function close( ) flushes the buffer before terminating the connection of the file with the stream associated with it.*

12.4.2 Opening Files using open( ) Function

As mentioned earlier the files were opened so far using the constructor function of the stream class and when the scope of the stream object was over, the destructor of the stream class was automatically called and the file was closed.

We have another way to open files. *In C++, each file stream has an open( ) member function. Opening of more than one file may be required in some situations. If the files are to be processed one by one (that is sequential order), then a single stream can be used with these files after closing a particular file. If more than one files are to be processed together then a stream for each file is required.* For example,

```
ifstream Ifile;  //input stream created
Ifile.open("EMPNAMES");  //stream connected to EMPNAMES
        .
        .
        .
Ifile.close( );  //stream disconnected
Ifile.open("EMPSALARY");  //stream connected to EMPSALARY
        .
        .
        .
Ifile.close( ); //stream disconnected
```

The above code associates a stream with two files one by one. In case we want to operate on the two files simultaneously, then two streams are required. For example,

```
Ifstream Ifile1,Ifile2;          //two input streams created
Ifile1.open("EMPNAMES");         //stream connected to EMPNAMES
Ifile2.open("EMPSALARY");        //stream connected to EMPSALARY
```

```
        .
        .
Ifile1.close( );
Ifile2.close( );
```

Figure 12.6 shows the working of the streams Ofile, Ifile1 and Ifile2 on the files EMPNAMES and EMPSALARY :

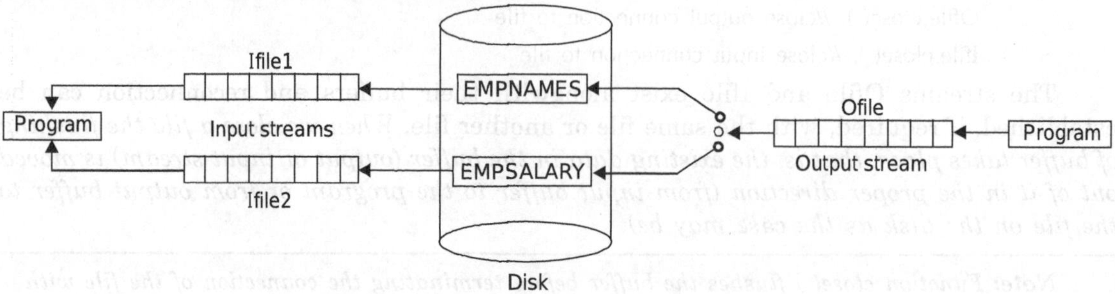

Fig. 12.6. Working of streams on multiple files

> ***Note:** Include the header file **fstream.h** for creating file streams in C++.*

Open( ) Mode Bits

In C++, each stream has a series of bits or flags associated with its operations defined in the **ios** *class. These bits are known as open mode bits and are used for specification of file opening purpose. These bits represent the method of opening the file. If we want to open a file in input mode or output mode, a particular bit is set on.* The syntax of open( ) mode is :

```
stream_object.open("filename", mode);
```

Here, mode is of type int and specifies the purpose of opening the file.

Table 12.2 lists the file opening modes defined in the class **ios.**

Table 12.2 File Mode Constants

Constant	*Purpose*	*Type of Stream*
ios :: in	Open for reading, *i.e.*, in input mode.	ifstream
ios :: out	Open for writing, *i.e.*, in output mode. This also opens file in **ios :: trunc** mode, by default. This means an existing file is truncated when opened, *i.e.*, its previous contents are discarded.	ofstream
ios :: app	Append to end of file. It can be used only with files capable of output.	ofstream
ios :: ate	Go to end-of-file on opening. I/O operations can still occur anywhere within the file.	ofstream, istream

ios :: binary	Binary file. By default, files are opened in text mode. When a file is opened in text mode, various character translations may take place, such as the conversion of carriage return into newlines. However, no such character translations occur in binary mode.	ofstream, istream
ios :: nocreate	Open fails if the file does not exist. It will not create a new file with that name.	ofstream
ios :: noreplace	Open fails if the file already exists, unless *ate* or *app* is set.	ofstream
ios :: trunc	Delete the contents of the file by the same name if it exists.	ofstream

The following examples illustrate the use of the above mentioned modes :

```
ofstream Ofile; //output stream created
Ofile.open("TEMP.DAT", ios::out); //open file for writing
```

which is same as,

```
Ofile.open ("TEMP.DAT");
ifstream Ifile; //input stream created
Ifile.open("TEMP.DAT", ios::in) ; //open file for reading
```

which is same as,

```
Ifile.open("TEMP.DAT");
```

For opening a file TEMP.DAT for both input and output, we write

```
fstream IOfile; //input output stream created
IOfile.open("TEMP.DAT", ios::in|ios::out);
```

The **fstream** class does not provide a mode by default, so we must specify it explicitly while using an object of the **fstream** class. By using **ios::ate** and **ios::app** we move to the end of the file just opened but **ios::app** mode allows us to add data at the end of the file only, while **ios::ate** mode allows to write data anywhere in the file, even data can be written over existing data.

> ***Note:** If open( ) is not successful, the stream object takes NULL (zero) value.*

12.5 Using Cascading Operators for Writing Text to the File and Reading Text from the File

The multiple use of << or >> in one statement is known as cascading. When cascading an output operator (<<), we should provide necessary blank spaces between different data items.

In C++, the file input and output are extensions of the stream extraction and insertion. Input to and output from files can be performed using fundamental and user-defined data types.

12.5.1 File Input and Output using Fundamental Data Types

The following program first creates a file INTEGER.TXT for writing three integers to it. **Ofile** is an object of output stream for writing to file. It is closed before associating a new object **Ifile** of input stream for reading data from the file. The file is again closed after performing the input operation on it. Note that the three integers are displayed on the monitor using **cout.** The write and read operations are performed here using cascading.

Program 12.1

```
//create a file to store integers and display the contents
#include<fstream.h> //for file I/O
#include<conio.h>
#include<process.h> //for exit( )
void main( )
{
    ofstream Ofile("INTEGER.TXT", ios::out); //open file for output
    int x,y,z;
    clrscr( );
    if(! Ofile)
    {
        cout<<"Can't open file for writing\n";
        exit(1);
    }
    else
    {
        cout<<"Enter three integers\n";
        cin>>x>>y>>z;
        Ofile<<x<<" "<<y<<" "<<z;  //write to file using cascading
        Ofile.close( );  //disconnect INTEGER.TXT from Ofile
    }
    ifstream Ifile("INTEGER.TXT", ios::in); //open file for input
    if(! Ifile)
       cout<<"Can't open file for reading\n";
    else
    {
        cout<<"\nThe three integers are :\n";
        Ifile>>x>>y>>z;  //read from file using cascading
        cout<<x<<" "<<y<<" "<<z;  //write to screen
        Ifile.close( );  //disconnect INTEGER.TXT from Ifile
    }
}
```

Output

```
Enter three integers
13      36      24
```

The three integers are :

13 36 24

For checking the contents of the file "INTEGER.TXT", you have created just now through program 12.1, you can opt for any one of the following two ways in Turbo C++ :

(*i*) Select **Open** option under **File** menu and then type the filename "INTEGER.TXT" and press Enter key or click mouse button. You will see the contents, now you can open another file or quit according to your requirement.

(*ii*) Select **DOS shell** option under **File** menu and then on the DOS prompt, type the following command :

Type INTEGER.TXT

On pressing Enter key, you will see the contents of this file. To get back to your program screen, type EXIT at the DOS prompt and press Enter key.

Let us write string type data into a file **TEST.TXT** and then read it back and display on the screen. The following program illustrates this concept :

Program 12.2

```
//writing text to a file and reading it back to display file contents
#include<fstream.h> //for file I/O
#include<conio.h>
#include<process.h> //for exit( )
void main( )
{
	char text[80];
	ofstream Ofile("TEST.TXT",ios::out); //open file for output
	clrscr( );
	if( ! Ofile)
	{
		cout<<"Can't open file for writing\n";
		exit(1);
	}
	else
	{
		Ofile<<"Punjab Technical University\n"
			<<"PROGRAMMING IN C++\n"; //cascading used
		Ofile.close( ); //disconnect TEST.TXT from Ofile
	}
	ifstream Ifile("TEST.TXT", ios::in); //open file for input
	if(! Ifile)
	   cout<<"Can't open file for reading\n";
	else
```

```
        {
            cout<<"\nThe contents of file TEST.TXT are :\n\n";
            while(Ifile)
            {
                Ifile.getline(text,80); //read a line from file
                cout<<text<<"\n"; //display it
            }
            Ifile.close( ); // disconnect TEST.TXT from Ifile
        }
    }
```

Output

The contents of file TEST.TXT are :

Punjab Technical University

PROGRAMMING IN C++

In the above program the file **TEST.TXT** is opened for output using the object **Ofile**. **Ofile** stores the data into the file using cascading. The file is closed and again a new object **Ifile** of input stream is associated with it for reading. The file contents are read line by line using **getline(**) function till end-of-file has reached. The file is again closed when the processing is over. The **getline (**) function is explained later on.

12.5.2 File Input and Output Using Abstract Data Types

We can store and retrieve objects of a user defined class to/from a file. The following program illustrates this concept :

Program 12.3

```
//Illustrating input and output using object
#include<fstream.h>
#include<conio.h>
class bill              //class definition
{
        public :
          int billno;
          float amount;
}; //class definition over
void main( )
{
        bill obj; //class object declared
        clrscr( );
        ofstream Ofile("BILL.DAT", ios::out);
        if(! Ofile)
```

```
            cout<<"\nCan't open source file for writing\n";
        else
        {
            cout<<"Enter bill number and amount for writing to file\n\n";
            //read the object
            cin>>obj.billno>>obj.amount; //cascading used
            //write to file
            Ofile<<obj.billno<<" "<<obj.amount; //cascading used
            Ofile.close( );
            //reading from file
            ifstream Ifile("BILL.DAT", ios::in);
            if(! Ifile)
               cout<<"\nCan't open source file for reading\n";
            else
            {
                //read the object
                Ifile>>obj.billno>>obj.amount; //cascading used
                //write to screen
                cout<<"\n\nData read from the file BILL.DAT is :\n\n"
                    <<"Bill Number "<<obj.billno
                    <<"\nBill Amount "<<obj.amount<<endl;  //cascading
                Ifile.close( );
            }
        }
    }
```

Output

```
Enter bill number and amount for writing to file
101   35080.5
Data read from the file BILL.DAT is :
Bill Number 101
Bill Amount 35080.5
```

In the above program, first of all a file **BILL.DAT** is opened for writing data. The object **obj** accepts the data using cascading and the file object **Ofile** stores the data into file using cascading. The file is closed and then again opened for reading using the **istream** object **Ifile. Ifile** reads data from file using cascading and the data is then displayed on the screen. Finally the file is closed.

12.5.3 open( ), get( ), put( ), getline( ) and close( ) Functions

These member functions present in the file stream classes perform the input/output operations and open and close the C++ data files. The **open( )** and **close( )** functions have been explained earlier. *The* **get( )** *and* **put( )** *functions handle a single character at a time. The function* **getline( )** *handles multiple characters at a time.*

The **get( )** and **put( )** functions are byte oriented, that is, **get( )** reads a byte of data and **put( )** writes a byte of data. The most commonly used forms of get( ) and put( ) are shown below :

```
istream &get(char &ch);
ostream &put(char ch);
```

Here, the **get( )** function accepts a single character from the associated stream and stores it in **ch**. A reference to the stream is returned by it. The **put( )** function writes the contents of **ch** to the stream and a reference to the stream is returned.

The following program prints the contents of a file on the screen by using the **get( )** function which are written to it using a **put( )** function :

Program 12.4

```
//Illustrating working of open( ), put( ), get( ) and close( ) functions
//write a line of text in a file and display the contents
#include<fstream.h>
#include<conio.h>
#include<string.h> //for strlen( )
#include<process.h>
void main( )
{
    char filename[13],ch;
    char str[ ] = "Time is a great teacher but unfortunately it kills all its pupils. Berlioz";
    int i;
    clrscr( );
    cout<<"Enter the name of the file to be opened : ";
    cin>>filename;
    ofstream Ofile; //output stream created
    Ofile.open(filename, ios::out); //open file in output mode
    if(! Ofile)
    {
       cout<<"Can't open file for writing\n";
       exit(1);
    }
    else
    {
       for(i=0; i<strlen(str); i++)
           Ofile.put(str[i]);  //write into the file
       Ofile.put('\0');  //store NULL character into the file
       Ofile.close( );  //disconnect filename from Ofile
    }
```

```
        ifstream Ifile; //input stream created
        Ifile.open(filename, ios::in); //open file in input mode
        if(! Ifile)
          cout<<"Can't open file for reading\n";
        else
        {
          cout<<"\nThe contents of file are :\n\n";
          while(Ifile)
          {
              Ifile.get(ch);
              cout<<ch; //display one character at a time
          }
          Ifile.close( ); //disconnect filename from Ifile
        }
    }
```

Output

Enter the name of the file to be opened : OUT.TXT

The contents of file are :

Time is a great teacher but unfortunately it kills all its pupils. Berlioz

In the above program the **open( )** function is used for opening a file (filename to be given at run time) and associates an **ostream** object **Ofile** with it, that is, the file is opened for output. After opening the file, the contents of the array **str** are written to the file using **put( )** function. The **'\0'** character is also written to file and then file is closed using **close( )** function. The file is again opened for input, *i.e.*, reading and it's contents are displayed using **get( )** function and **cout** inside the **while** loop. The end-of-file is checked in the **while** loop so on reaching the end of file the stream associated with the file becomes zero, that is, **Ifile** becomes zero and the control comes out of the **while** loop. Finally the file is closed using **close( )** function.

To print the output of a program on printer, open file "PRN" as an output file (DOS names printer as PRN file) and write data to it. For example,

```
char filename[13], ch;
cout<<"Enter the name of the file to be printed :";
cin>>filename;
ifstream Ifile(filename, ios :: in);        //open file for input
if(! Ifile)
        cout<<"Can't open file for reading\n";
else
{
        ofstream Ofile;//create output stream
        Ofile.open("PRN"); //open it for printer
```

```
        cout<<"\nThe contents of file are :\n\n";
        while(Ifile)
        {
                Ifile.get(ch);      //read a character from file
                Ofile.put(ch);      //write a character to printer
        }
}
```

> ***Note:*** *The printer must be properly installed and switched on before printing the output of a program on it.*

Now, let us consider the situation when the user wants to copy a text file to another in which multiple blanks are replaced by a single one at all the places. The following program illustrates this concept :

Program 12.5

```
//read a text file and create another file
//in which multiple blanks are replaced by a single one
#include<fstream.h>
#include<process.h> //for exit( )
#include<conio.h>
void main( )
{
        ifstream Ifile;   //input stream created
        ofstream Ofile; //output stream created
        char ch, source[13],target[13]; //two arrays declared to store file names
        clrscr( );
        cout<<"Enter the source file name to be copied : ";
        cin>>source;
        Ifile.open(source,ios::in); //open file in input mode
        if(! Ifile)
        {
                cout<<"\nCan't open source file for reading\n";
                exit(1);
        }
        else
        {
                cout<<"\nEnter the target file name to transfer source file : ";
                cin>>target;
                Ofile.open(target,ios::out); //open file in output mode
                if(! Ofile)
                    cout<<"\nCan't open target file for writing\n";
```

```
        else
        {
            while(Ifile)
            {
                Ifile.get(ch);
                Ofile.put(ch);
                if(ch= =' ')
                {
                    while(ch  = = ' ')  //ignore multiple blanks
                    {
                        Ifile.get(ch);
                    }
                    Ofile.put(ch);
                }
            }
            cout< <"\nSource file has been copied to target file\n";
            cout< <"\nMultiple blanks have been changed to single one";
            Ofile.close( );  //disconnect filename from Ofile
        }
        Ifile.close( );  //disconnect filename from Ifile
    }
}
```

Output

```
Enter the source file name to be copied : ABC.DAT
Enter the target file name to transfer source file : XYZ.DAT
Source file has been copied to target file
Multiple blanks have been changed to single one
```

The other forms of get( ) Function

In addition to the form discussed earlier, the **get( )** function has several other form (*i.e.*, it is overloaded in several different ways). The prototypes for the three most commonly used forms are given below :

istream &get (char *buf*, int *num*);

istream &get (char *buf*, int *num*, char *delim*);

int get( );

The first form reads characters into the array pointed to by *buf* until either *num*–1 characters have been read, a new line is found, or the end of the line has been encountered. For example, the following statements

```
char arr[51];
cin.get(arr, 51);
```

will read characters into **arr** until either 50 characters are read or a new line is found, or the end of file is encountered, whichever occurs earlier. That is, if the user input is as given below :

T20 Cricket has become very popular now.

then **arr** will be storing.

T20 Cricket has become very popular now.

The array pointed to by *buf* (any user defined name) will be null terminated by **get( ).** If the newline character is encountered in the input stream, it is *not* extracted. Instead it remains in the stream until the next input operation.

The second form reads characters into the array pointed to by *buf* until either *num*–1 characters have been read, the character specified by *delim* has been found, or the end of the file has been encountered.

For example, the following statements

char arr [51];

cin.get (arr, 51, '$') ;

will read characters into **arr** until either 50 characters are read or '$' character is found, or the end of the file has been encountered, whichever occurs earlier.That is, if the user input is as given below :

The price of computer is $1000

then **arr** will be storing

The price of computer is

The array pointed to by *buf* (any user defined name) will be null terminated by **get( ).** If the delimiter character is encountered in the input stream, it is *not* extracted. Instead, it remains in the stream until the next input operation.

The third form of **get ( )** returns the next character from the stream. It returns **EOF** if the end of the file is encountered. This form of **get( )** is similar to C's **getc( )** function. For example, the following statements illustrate it :

```
int i;
char ch;
ifstream, Ifile;
.......................
.......................
i = ch = Ifile.get( );
```

If the user input is **a** , then the value of **ch** will be **'a'** and the value of **i** will be 97(ASCII value of **a**).

The getline( ) Function

For reading data we have another function **getline( )** whose prototype is

```
istream &getline(char *buf, int n, char delim = '\n');
```

The function **getline( )** reads characters from input stream and stores them in the array pointed to by **buf** until either **n** characters have been read, or the **delim** specified character is encountered. The default value of the **delim** is the newline character.

The basic difference between the **get**(buf, n, delim) and **getline( )** functions is that **getline( )** removes the newline character from the input stream (if encounted) while reading but the **get( )** function does not remove the delimiter newline character. For example,

Let us assume the input stream is initially as shown below :

D	I	X	I	T		J	\n

Input stream initially

If we use the following statement :

```
get(arr,8); // arr is a character array of size 8
```

then we will have the status of arr and input stream as :

D	I	X	I	T		J	arr

\n								Input stream

The **getline( )** function used as shown below :

```
getline(arr,8); // arr is a character array of size 8
```

has the following effect :

D	I	X	I	T		J	arr

								Input stream

The following program illustrates the concept of working with multiple files and use of **getline( )** function is shown here :

Program 12.6

```
//Illustration of working with multiple files
#include<fstream.h>
#include<conio.h>
#define SIZE 80
void main( )
{
        ofstream Ofile; //create output stream
        char text[SIZE];
        clrscr( );
        Ofile.open("EMPNAMES", ios::out); //connect file to output stream
        Ofile<<"Raman Sharma\n"<<"Disha Grover\n"<<"Pooja Rana\n";
        Ofile.close( ); //disconnect output stream
```

```
    Ofile.open("EMPSALRY",ios::out); //connect file to output stream
    Ofile<<"75000.00\n"<<"10000.00\n"<<"15000.00\n";
    Ofile.close( ); //disconnect output stream
    ifstream Ifile1,Ifile2; //create two input streams
    // connect input stream to first file
    Ifile1.open("EMPNAMES",ios::in);
    // connect input stream to second file
    Ifile2.open("EMPSALRY",ios::in);
    cout<<"The contents of EMPNAMES and EMPSALRY are :\n";
    cout<<"\nEMPNAME                SALARY\n\n";
    Ifile1.getline(text,SIZE);
    cout<<text<<"\t\t";
    Ifile2.getline(text,SIZE);
    cout<<text<<"\n";
    Ifile1.getline(text,SIZE);
    cout<<text<<"\t\t";
    Ifile2.getline(text,SIZE);
    cout<<text<<"\n";
    Ifile1.getline(text,SIZE);
    cout<<text<<"\t\t";
    Ifile2.getline(text,SIZE);
    cout<<text<<"\n";
    Ifile1.close( );
    Ifile2.close( );
}
```

Output

```
The contents of EMPNAMES and EMPSALRY are :
EMPNAME           SALARY
Raman Sharma      75000.00
Disha Grover      10000.00
Pooja Rana        15000.00
```

12.5.4 Detecting end-of-file (with or without using eof( ) Function)

If we want that any attempt should not be made to read data from the file when the end of the file has reached, it can be achieved by using the statement.

```
while(Ifile)
{
    ....
    ....
    ....
}
```

Here, Ifile is an **ifstream** object and returns 0 when any error occurs or end of file has reached.

We can also use the statement

```
if(Ifile.eof( ) != 0) //eof( ) returns nonzero
                      //when end of file reaches
   exit(1);
```

Here **eof( )** is a member function of **ios** class. It returns 0 till file's end is not reached.

12.6 Opening a Binary File using in, out and app Modes

We have already seen various file opening modes when we discussed text files.

When a file is opened (that is, linked with the stream) using constructor, the stream is activated in its default mode. The default modes are :

ios::in —— for input stream **istream**
ios::out —— for output stream **ostream**

For example, the following declaration open the binary file **"DATA.DAT"** for reading, writing and appending respectively :

```
ifstream Ifile; //Declare stream for input (reading)
ofstream Ofile; //Declare stream for output (write/append)
Ifile.open("DATA.DAT", ios::in | ios::binary);      //for reading
Ofile.open("DATA.DAT", ios::out | ios::binary);  //for writing
Ofile.open("DATA.DAT", ios::app | ios::binary);  //for appending
```

When a file is opened in **text mode,** *various character translations may take place, such as the conversion of carriage-return into newlines. But no such translations take place when we open the file in* **binary mode.**

> ***Note:*** *For writing data or reading data from a binary file, we must include* ***ios::binary*** *in addition to the other file mode(s).*

12.7 The open( ), read( ), write( ) and close( ) Functions

The **open( )** function helps in opening a file for processing (that is, writing, reading and appending etc.,) and is associated with a file stream as explained with the opening of binary files in the previous article.

The **read( )** and **write( )** functions are used for handling the data for reading and writing in the binary form. So the data is stored on the disk in the same format as that in the internal memory of the computer. For example,

The integer value 3313 is shown in binary and character formats :

← 2 bytes →

00001100	11110001	Binary Format

← 4 bytes →

3	3	1	3	Character Format

So we see that the binary format represents the number in the exact internal form and no conversions take place while saving the data in much faster way.

The prototypes of the read( ) and write( ) functions are :

```
istream &read((char *) &buf, int sizeof(buf));
ostream &write((char *) &buf, int sizeof(buf));
```

The **read( )** function reads **sizeof(buf)** bytes from the stream associated with it and stores them in the buffer pointed to by **buf.** The **write( )** function writes **sizeof(buf)** bytes from the buffer pointed to by **buf** to the associated stream with it.

The address of the variable must be type cast to type **char** *, that is, a pointer to the character type.

The data written in a file using **write( )** function can only be read accurately using the function **read( ).** For example, the following program illustrates it.

Program 12.7

```
//illustrating use of write( ) and read( ) functions
//Create a binary file to store integers and display contents
#include<fstream.h>    //for file I/O
#include<conio.h>
#include<iomanip.h> //for setw( )
#include<process.h> //for exit( )
void main( )
{
    ofstream Ofile; //output stream created
    //connect file in binary form to output stream Ofile
    Ofile.open("INTEGER.DAT",ios::out | ios::binary);
    int num,choice;
    clrscr( );
    if(! Ofile)
    {
        cout<<"\nCan't open file for writing\n";
        exit(1);
    }
    cout<<"DO you wish to store an integer ?"
        <<"Enter 1 for yes or 0 for no : ";    //Cascading
```

```
cin>>choice;
while(choice)
{
    cout<<"Enter the integer : ";
    cin>>num;
    Ofile.write( (char *) &num, sizeof(int) );   //write num to file
    cout<<"Do you wish to continue ?"
        <<"Enter 1 for yes or 0 for no : ";   //Cascading
    cin>>choice;
}
Ofile.close( ); //disconnect INTEGER.DAT from Ofile
ifstream Ifile; //input stream created
//connect binary file to input stream Ifile
Ifile.open("INTEGER.DAT",ios::in | ios::binary);
if(! Ifile)
{
    cout<<"\nCan't open file for reading\n";
    exit(1);
}
clrscr( );
cout<<"The contents of file INTEGER.DAT are :\n\n";
Ifile.read( (char *) &num, sizeof(int) ); //read from file in variable num
while(Ifile)
{
    cout<<setw(8)<<num; // write num in formatted way
    //read from file in variable num
    Ifile.read( (char *) &num, sizeof(int) );
}
Ifile.close( ); //disconnect INTEGER.DAT from Ifile
}
```

Output

```
Do you wish to store an integer ? Enter 1 for yes or 0 for no : 1
Enter the integer : 336
Do you wish to continue ? Enter 1 for yes or 0 for no : 1
Enter the integer : 3313
Do you wish to continue ? Enter 1 for yes or 0 for no : 1
Enter the integer : 1024
Do you wish to continue ? Enter 1 for yes or 0 for no : 1
Enter the integer : 12
```

```
Do you wish to continue ? Enter 1 for yes or 0 for no : 1
Enter the integer : 1665
Do you wish to continue ? Enter 1 for yes or 0 for no : 1
Enter the integer : 275
Do you wish to continue ? Enter 1 for yes or 0 for no : 1
Enter the integer : 165
Do you wish to continue ? Enter 1 for yes or 0 for no : 0
The contents of file INTEGER.DAT are :
      336      3313      1024      12      1665      275      165
```

In the above program, first of all a binary file **INTEGER.DAT** is opened in output mode, that is, for writing of data. If the file can't be opened then the **exit( )** function terminates the program. The integers are accepted via the keyboard till the user wants and are stored into the file using **write( )** function. The file is closed after that and again opened in input mode, that is, for reading of data and checked for proper opening. The file contents are displayed using the **while** loop, the **read( )** function reads data from the file and **setw( )** prints it in width of 8 per integer. Finally the file is closed when end-of-file is reached.

The binary files can store the user defined data also. This data can be retrieved and desired operations can be performed.

The following program creates a binary file for storing the students records using the **write( )** function :

Program 12.8

```
// creation of a binary file which will store student records
#include<fstream.h>
#include<stdio.h> // for gets( )
#include<process.h> // for exit( )
#include<conio.h>
void main( )
{
    struct student
    {
        char name[31];
        int rollno;
        int marks[5];
        int total;
    };
    student stud; // structure variable declared
    int i,n,j,size;
    char target[13]; // for storing file name
    ofstream Ofile; //output stream
```

```
        clrscr( );
        cout<<"Enter the name of file to be created : ";
        cin>>target;    //Read file name
        //open file in output mode
        Ofile.open(target,ios::out : ios::binary);
        if(! Ofile)
        {
            cout<<"\nCan't open target file for writing\n";
            exit(1);
        }
        size=sizeof(student); // find the size of structure
        cout<<"\nHow many students are there ?\n";
        cin>>n;
        for(i=1;i<=n;i++)
        {
            cout<<"\nEnter the name of student "<<i<<"\n";
            gets(stud.name);
            cout<<"\nEnter the roll number : ";
            cin>>stud.rollno;
            cout<<"\nEnter the marks in five subjects : ";
            for(j=0;j<5;j++)
              cin>>stud.marks[j];
            stud.total=0;
            //compute the total
            for(j=0;j<5;j++)
              stud.total += stud.marks[j];
            //write to file associated with stream Ofile
            Ofile.write( (char *) &stud ,size);
        }
        Ofile.close( ); // disconnect filename from Ofile
}
```

Output

```
Enter the name of file to be created : STUD.DAT
How many students are there ?
2
Enter the name of student 1
Apoorva Dixit
Enter the roll number : 10001
Enter the marks in five subjects : 100 100 99 98 99
```

Enter the name of student 2

Aanchal Dixit

Enter the roll number : 10005

Enter the marks in five subjects : 99 100 99 99 100

In the above program, first of all the name of the file to be opened for writing data is entered. The file is opened in binary form in output mode. The number of records to be entered is asked and inputted. The entered number of records are accepted one by one and stored in the file. Finally the file is closed.

The stored records using the above program can be read back from binary file and displayed on the screen using the **read( )** function. The following program illustrates this concept :

Program 12.9

```
// Print the result of students whose records are stored in a binary file
#include<fstream.h>
#include<process.h>  // for exit( )
#include<conio.h>
void main( )
{
    struct student
    {
        char name[31];
        int rollno;
        int marks[5];
        int total;
    };
    student stud; // structure variable declared
    int size;
    char source[13]; // variable to store filename
    ifstream Ifile; // input stream Ifile
    clrscr( );
    cout<<"Enter the name of file to be read which already stores data : ";
    cin>>source;    //Read file name
    // open binary file in input mode
    Ifile.open(source,ios::in | ios::binary);
    If(! Ifile)
    {
        cout<<"\nCan't open source file for reading\n";
        exit(1);
    }
```

```
    size=sizeof(student); // find the size of structure
    cout<<"\n*************            RESULT  *************\n\n";
    cout<<"NAME                       ROLL NO                         TOTAL MARKS\n\n";
    // read data from file
    Ifile.read( (char *) &stud ,size);
    while(Ifile)
    {
        cout<<"\n"<<stud.name<<"\t"<<stud.rollno<<"\t\t"<<stud.total;
        Ifile.read( (char *) &stud ,size);
    }
    Ifile.close( );
}
```

Output

```
Enter the name of file to be read which already stores data : STUD.DAT
*************            RESULT            *************
NAME                     ROLL NO           TOTAL MARKS
Apoorva Dixit            10001             496
Aanchal Dixit            10005             497
```

From the above two programs it is clear that we need only a single call for reading or writing (to **read( )** or **write( )**) a structure.

> ***Note:*** *The type casts inside the calls to* ***write( )*** *and* ***read( )*** *functions are must when we operate on a buffer not defined as a character array. Because of C++'s strong type checking, a pointer of one type will not automatically be converted into a pointer of another type.*

12.7.1 Reading and Writing Class Objects

The C Input/Output system cannot handle the user defined data types such as class objects. The **read( )** and **write( )** functions in C++ handle the objects as a single unit, using the internal representation of data by the computer.

The **read( )** and **write( )** functions handle a class object byte by byte without conversion. It must be clear that the data members are stored on the disk and not the member functions.

The length(size) of an object is obtained by using **sizeof** operator which is the sum of the lengths of the individual data members of the object. The following program illustrates the storage and retrieval of the class objects using **write( )** and **read( )** functions :

Program 12.10

```
// Appending data to a file
// Illustrating use of open( ),read( ),write( ) and close( ) functions
// Illustrating adding of objects to the bottom of a binary file
```

```
#include<fstream.h>
#include<stdio.h> // for gets( )
#include<process.h> // for exit( )
#include<conio.h>
class JOKE              // class definition
{
        private :
           int Jokeid;                  // Joke identification number
           char Type[5];                // Joke Type
           char Jokedesc[255];          // Joke Description
        public :
           void Newjokeentry( )         // member function
           {
              cin>>Jokeid; gets(Type); gets(Jokedesc);
           }
           void Showjoke( )          // member function
           {
              cout<<Jokeid<<" : "<<Type<<endl<<Jokedesc<<endl;
           }
};
void main( )
{
     void Addjoke( );  // function prototype
     void Dispfile( );  // function prototype
     clrscr( );
     Addjoke( );   // function call
     Dispfile( );   // function call
}
// function definition Addjoke( )
void Addjoke( )
{
     JOKE obj;   // class object declared
     char choice;
     ofstream Ofile;   //output stream created
     Ofile.open("JOKES.DAT",ios::app | ios::binary);
     if(! Ofile)
     {
          cout<<"\nCan't open JOKES.DAT file for writing\n";
          exit(1);
     }
```

```
    while(1)
      {
        clrscr( );
        cout<<"\nDo you wish to add more objects(Y/N) ? \n\n";
        cin>>choice;
        if( (choice= ='Y') || (choice= ='y') )
        {
            cout<<"\nEnter Jokeid, Type and Jokedescription\n";
            obj.Newjokeentry( ); // function call
            // write to file
            Ofile.write( (char *) &obj,sizeof(obj));
        }
        else
          break;
    }
    Ofile.close( );
}
// function definition Dispfile( )
void Dispfile( )
{
    JOKE obj; // class object declared
    ifstream Ifile; // input stream created
    clrscr( );
    Ifile.open("JOKES.DAT",ios::in | ios::binary); // open file
    if(! Ifile)
    {
        cout< <"\nCan't open JOKES.DAT file for reading\n";
        exit(1);
    }
    cout<<"\nContents of file JOKES.DAT are :\n\n";
    // read and display objects from file
    Ifile.read( (char *) &obj,sizeof(obj));
    while( ! Ifile.eof( ) )
    {
      obj.Showjoke( );  // function call
      Ifile.read( (char *) &obj,sizeof(obj));
    }
    Ifile.close( ); // close the file
}
```

Output

```
Do you wish to add more objects (Y/N) ?
y
Enter Jokeid, Type and Jokedescription
1
FUN
Saare Jahan Se Achha Hindustan Hamara !
Do you wish to add more objects (Y/N) ?
y
Enter Jokeid, Type and Jokedescription
2
SAD
Ramu married Miss World and lives a HAPPY daily life !
Do you wish to add more objects (Y/N) ?
n
Contents of file JOKES.DAT are :
1 : FUN
Saare Jahan Se Achha Hindustan Hamara !
2 : SAD
Ramu married Miss World and lives a HAPPY daily life !
Do you wish to add more objects (Y/N) ?
y
Enter Jokeid, Type and Jokedescription
3
FUN
ALL CORRUPT POLITICIANS WILL LEAVE INDIA BY 2025 !!!
Do you wish to add more objects (Y/N) ?
N
Contents of file JOKES.DAT are :
1  :  FUN
Saare Jahan Se Achha Hindustan Hamara !
2  :  SAD
Ramu married Miss World and lives a HAPPY daily life !
3  :  FUN
ALL CORRUPT POLITICIANS WILL LEAVE INDIA BY 2025 !!!
```

In the above program the file **"JOKES.DAT"** is opened using open( ) function in **app** mode as a **binary** file. An infinite **while** loop is used for adding more objects, depending on the user's choice, to the file using **Addjoke( )** function. The while loop terminates and the file is closed when user does not want to add an object. The function **Dispfile( )** is called for displaying the contents of the file using the file in input mode. The functions **write( )** is used for writing to file and **read( )** function reads data from it while displaying it. The file is closed again after the input operation is over, using **close( )** function.

12.7.2 Detecting end-of-file (with or without using eof( ) Function)

The end-of-file in binary file can be checked in two ways like text file. For example,

```
while(Ifile)
{
    ------
    ------
    ------
}
```

The **Ifile** is an **ifstream** object and returns 0 when any error occurs or end of file has reached.

We can also use the statement

```
if(Ifile.eof( ) !=0) // eof( ) returns nonzero when end of file reaches
   exit(1);
```

or, the statement used in the last program as checks for end-of-file

```
while( ! Ifile.eof( ))
{
    ------
    ------
    ------
}
```

Here **eof( )** is a member function of **ios** class. It returns 0 till file's end is not reached.

The following program inserts data in a sorted file and detects the end-of-file as well :

Program 12.11

```
//Insertion of data in sorted file
//Inserts data of an employee in a sorted file on employee number
//Checks for duplicate employee number while inserting
#include<fstream.h>
#include<conio.h>
#include<string.h>
#include<iomanip.h>    //for setw( )
#include<stdio.h>    //for rename( ) and remove( )
#include<process.h>
```

```
class employee
{ int empno;
  char empname[31];
  float salary;
  public :
    employee( )//constructor
    {
      empno=0;
      strcpy(empname,"");
      salary=0.0;
    }
    void enter( );      // function prototype
    void display( );
    int getempno( );
} obj,newobj;   // Objects declared
//function definition enter( )
void employee :: enter( )
{
    cout<<"\nEmployee number : ";
    cin>>empno;
    cout<<"\nEmployee name : ";
    gets(empname);
    cout<<"\nEmployee salary : ";
    cin>>salary;
}
//function definition display( )
void employee :: display( )
{
    cout.setf(ios::fixed); //set flag for setprecision( )
    cout<<setw(10)<<empno<<setw(30)<<empname
        <<setw(20)<<setprecision(2)<<salary<<endl;
}
//function definition getempno( )
int employee :: getempno( )
{
    return(empno);
}
void main( )
{
    void addrec( ); //function prototype
```

```
void dispfile( );
void dupcheck( );
char flag = 'y'; //for checking whether new record
clrscr( ); //clears the screen
cout<<"Enter the data in sorted order of employee numbers\n";
addrec( );  //function call
cout<<"\nPress any key to continue ...\n";
getch( );
clrscr( );
cout<<"\nEMP.DAT contains the following data\n\n";
cout<<setw(15)<<"Employee Number"<<setw(25)
   <<"Employee Name"<<setw(25)<<"Employee Salary\n\n";
dispfile( );
cout<<"\nPress any key to continue ... \n";
getch( );
clrscr( );
cout<<"\nEnter details of employee whose record is to be inserted\n";
newobj.enter( );
dupcheck( );  // function call for checking duplicate employee number
ifstream Ifile ("EMP.DAT,"ios::in);
ofstream Ofile ("TEMP.DAT",ios::out);
if(! Ifile || ! Ofile)
{
   cout<<"\nCan't open file(s)\n":
   exit (1);
}
//copy objects  from EMP.DAT to TEMP.DAT
//also insert new data at appropriate position
Ifile.read( (char *) &obj, sizeof(obj) );
while(! Ifile.eof( ) )
{
   //newobj is new object and obj is object from EMP.DAT file
   if( newobj.getempno( ) < obj.getempno( ) )
   {
      // add the new data
      Ofile.write(char *) &newobj,sizeof(newobj) );
      flag = 'N';
      break;
   }
   else
      Ofile.write( (char *) &obj,sizeof(obj) );
```

```
            Ifile.read( (char *) &obj,sizeof(obj) );
        }
        if(flag == 'y')
            Ofile.write( (char *) &newobj,sizeof(newobj) ); // add the new data
        else if( ! Ifile.eof( ) )
        {
            while( ! Ifile.eof( ) )
            {
                Ifile.read( (char *) &obj,sizeof(obj) );
                Ofile.write( (char *)&obj, sizeof(obj));
            }
        }
        Ifile.close( ); // close file
        Ofile.close( );
        // remove the old EMP.DAT file and rename TEMP.DAT as EMP.DAT
        remove("EMP.DAT");
        rename("TEMP.DAT","EMP.DAT");
        Ifile.open("EMP.DAT", ios:: in);
        clrscr ( ); // clears the screen
        if( ! Ifile)
        {
            cout<<"\n Cannot open EMP.DAT file for reading\n";
            exit(1);
        }
        cout<<"\nEMP.DAT now contains the following data\n\n";
        cout<<setw(15)<<"Employee Number"<<setw(25)
              <<"Employee Name"<<setw(25)<<"Employee Salary\n\n";
        dispfile( ); //function call
        cout<<"\nPress any key to continue ...\n";
        getch( );
}
// function definition addrec( )
void addrec( )
{
        char choice;
        ofstream Ofile("EMP.DAT",ios::out : ios::binary);
        if( ! Ofile)
        {
            cout<<"\nCannot open EMP.DAT file for writing\n";
            exit (1);
        }
```

```
    while(1)
    {
        cout<<"\nDo you wish to add employee record(y/n)?\n":
        cin>>choice;
        if(choice == 'Y' || choice == 'y')
        {
            obj.enter( ); // function call
            // write to file
            Ofile.write( (char *) &obj,sizeof(obj) );
            clrscr( );
        }
        else
            break;
    }
    Ofile.close( );
}
// function definition dispfile( )
void dispfile( )
{
    ifstream  Ifile("EMP.DAT",ios::in | ios::binary);
    if( ! Ifile)
    {
        cout<<"\nCannot open EMP.DAT file for reading\n";
        exit(1);
    }
    // read and display data from file
    Ifile.read( (char *) &obj,sizeof(obj) );
    while( ! Ifile.eof( ))
    {
        obj.display( );
        Ifile.read( (char *) &obj,sizeof(obj) );
    }
    Ifile.close( ); // close the file
}
// function definition dupcheck( )
void dupcheck( )
{
    ifstream Ifile("EMP.DAT", ios::in | ios::binary);
    if( ! Ifile)
    {
        cout<<"\nCannot open EMP.DAT file for reading\n";
```

```
        exit(1);
    }
    // check whether duplicate employee number
    Ifile.read( (char *) &obj,sizeof(obj) );
    while( ! Ifile.eof( ) )
    {
        // newobj is new object and obj is object from EMP.DAT file
        if( newobj.getempno( ) = = obj.getempno( ) )
        {
            cout<<"\n\nSorry ! duplicate employee number exists\n";
            getch( );
            exit(1);
        }
        Ifile.read( (char *) &obj,sizeof(obj) );
    }
}
```

Output

Enter the data in sorted order of employee numbers

Do you wish to add employee record (*y/n*) ?

Y

Employee number : 1001

Employee name : DINESH SHARMA

Employee salary : 20000.00

Do you wish to add employee record (*y/n*) ?

Y

Employee number : 1007

Employee name : PREETI GUPTA

Employee salary : 25000.000

Do you wish to add employee record (*y/n*) ?

N

Press any key to continue ...

EMP.DAT contains the following data

Employee Number	Employee Name	Employee Salary
1001	DINESH SHARMA	20000
1007	PREETI GUPTA	25000

Press any key to continue ...

Enter details of employee whose record is to be inserted

Employee number : 1004

Employee name : DEEPIKA CHOPRA
Employee salary : 70000.00
EMP.DAT now contains the following data

Employee Number	Employee Name	Employee Salary
1001	DINESH SHARMA	20000
1004	DEEPIKA CHOPRA	70000
1007	PREETI GUPTA	25000

Press any key to continue ...

12.8 File Pointers and their Manipulators

The C++ input and output system associates two pointers known as file pointers. These pointers are :

get pointer (input pointer)—specifies the position of next read or input operation.

put pointer (output pointer)—specifies the position of next write or output operation.

These can be thought of as the current position for read and write operations, respectively. When an input or output operation takes place, the sequential advancement of the appropriate pointer is automatically made.

The file pointers are not like normal C++ pointers (which represent the address of variables).

12.8.1 Default Actions While Reading or Writing

Oftenly we want to start reading an existing file from the beginning and continue sequentially until the end of the file has reached. This is shown below :

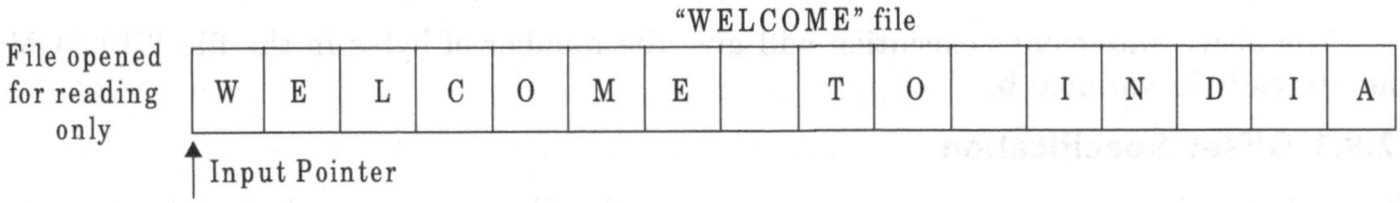

When we want to append some data, the file is opened in 'append' mode and the file pointer is moved to the end of the file, that is, at the end of the stored contents as shown below :

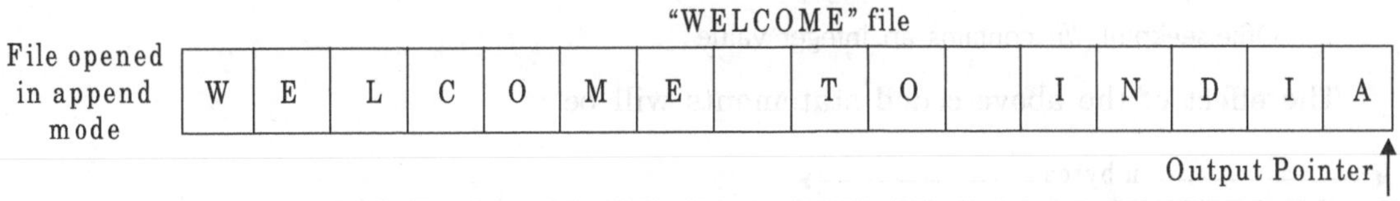

Similarly, when we want to write data to a file, its contents (if exist) are deleted and the output pointer is placed in the beginning of the file as shown below :

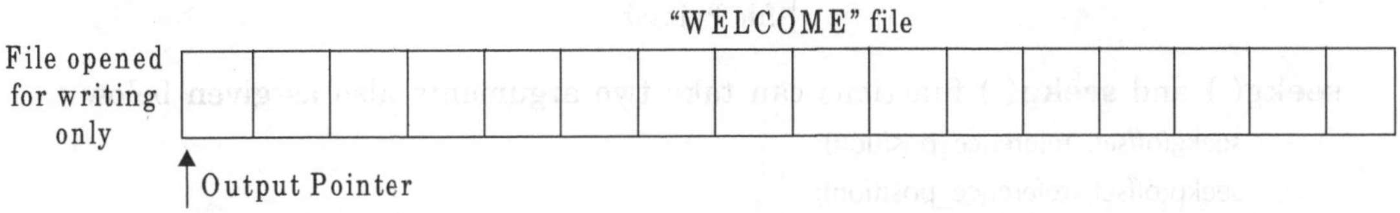

These figures represent the default actions and no manipulation of pointer is required.

12.8.2 File Pointers Manipulation Functions (tellg( ), tellp( ), seekg( ), seekp( ) Functions)

There are situations when we must manipulate the file pointers for reading from and writing to, an arbitrary position from the file. For setting and examining the get pointer there are **seekg( )** and **tellg( )** functions and we have **seekp( )** and **tellp( )** functions for the same actions on the put pointer. So a file can be accessed non-sequentially or **randomly** using these four functions.

The tellg( ) and tellp( ) functions can be used for finding the current position of the file pointer in a file. We can reposition all stream classes using one of the functions seekg( ) or seekp( ). The seekg( ) and seekp( ) functions move the get and put pointers to an absolute address in a file, to a desired location. For example,

```
ifstream Ifile;
Ifile.open("WELCOME",ios::in | ios::binary);
Ifile.seekg(7);
```

This statement moves the get pointer 7 bytes from the beginning. As the byte numbers starts from 0, so the above statement makes the pointer, point to the 8th byte in the binary file WELCOME.

Consider one more example,

```
ofstream Ofile;
Ofile.open("WELCOME",ios::app | ios::binary);
long int b = Ofile.tellp( );
```

The above statement's execution will give the number of bytes in the file WELCOME and stores it in variable **b**.

12.8.3 Offset Specification

The seek function using a single argument moves the file pointer to a desired location. For example,

```
ofstream Ofile;
Ofile.open("WELCOME",ios::binary | ios::out);
Ofile.seekp(n); //n contains an integer value
```

The effect of the above coded statements will be :

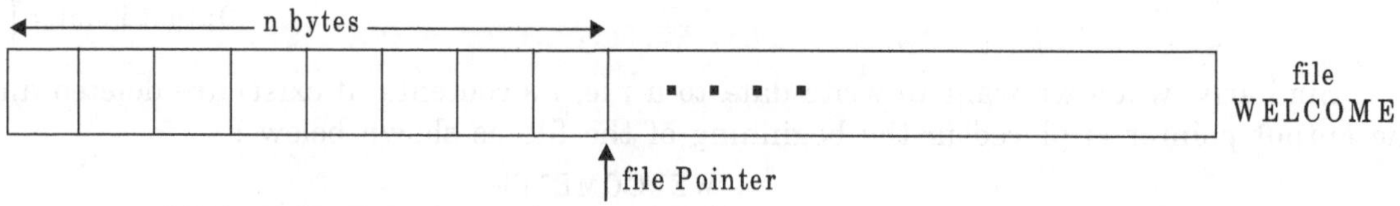

seekg( ) and **seekp( )** functions can take two arguments also as given below :

```
seekg(offset, reference_position);
seekp(offset, reference_position);
```

Here, the first argument offset specifies the number of byte positions and the second argument is the reference position. There are three reference positions defined in the **ios** class :

(*i*) **ios::beg** — the beginning of the file

(*ii*) **ios::cur** — the current position of the file pointer

(*iii*) **ios::end** — the end of the file

For example,

```
ifstream Ifile;
Ifile.open("WELCOME", ios::in : ios::binary);
Ifile.seekg(–12, ios::end); //backup 12 bytes from the end of file
Ifile.seekg(10, ios::cur); //goto 10 byte from the current position
Ifile.seekg(15); //ios::beg taken as default
```

The **tellg( )** member function, does not have any argument and returns the current byte position of the get pointer relative to the start of the file. For example,

```
//current position of get pointer stored in p
long int p = Ifile.tellg( );
```

The **seekp( )** and **tellp( )** functions are used with the put pointer and are defined in the **ostream** class and the **seekg( )** and **tellg( )** member functions are defined in the **istream** class. For example,

The following program illustrates the use of **seekg( )** and **tellg( )** functions :

Program 12.12

```
// Find size and number of records in an already existing file STUD.DAT
#include<fstream.h>
#include<process.h>
#include<conio.h>
void main( )
{
    struct student
    {
        char name[31];
        int rollno;
        int marks[5];
        int total;
    };
    student stud;  // structure variable declared
    fstream file;  // file pointer for input/output
    int n,size=0;
    clrscr( );
    file.open("STUD.DAT",ios::in | ios::binary);
    if(! file)
```

```
    {
        cout<<"\nCan't open file\n";
        exit(1);
    }
    file.seekg(0,ios::end); // reach at the end of file
    size=file.tellg( );
    n=size/sizeof(stud); // find number of records
    if(n>0)
    {
        cout<<"\nSize of file STUD.DAT is : "<<size<<endl;
        cout<<"\nNumber of records : "<<n<<endl;
    }
    else
        cout<<"\nNo record in file STUD.DAT\n";
    file.close( );
}
```

Output

```
Size of file STUD.DAT is : 90
Number of records : 2
```

12.9 Random Access

In C++, random access is achieved by using **seekg( ), seekp( ), tellg( )** *and* **tellp( )** *functions for manipulating the file pointers. Updation is required in a data file for various operations.* It includes one or more of the following :

(i) Insertion of a new item

(ii) Deletion of an existing item

(iii) Modification of an existing item

(iv) Display a particular record or entire file contents.

The file pointers can be moved to the desired location (that is to the item/object to be processed). It is an easy task if all the items/objects in the file are of equal lengths. The size of each object is given by the following statement :

```
int obj_len = sizeof(obj);
```

We can find the location of a particular object as follows :

```
int loc = (n - 1) * obj_len; //n denotes the number of object
```

Here, **loc** provides the byte number of the first byte of the nth object. Now the **seekg( )** or **seekp( )** functions can be used for reaching this byte. The total number of objects can be found using the length of the object calculated earlier and the **file_size** as given below :

```
int no_of_objects = file_size/obj_len;
```

Here, file_size can be found by using the function **tellg( )** or **tellp( )**, when the file pointer has been moved to the end of the file as given below :

```
fstream file;
......
......
file.seekg(0,ios::end); //reach at end of file
int file_size = file.tellp( );
```

The following program illustrates the updation of a file randomly. A file **"EMPREC.DAT"** *is created while performing the following operations :*

(*i*) Addition of a record

(*ii*) Modification of a record (if exists)

(*iii*) Display a record (if exists)

(*iv*) Delete a record (if exists)

(*v*) Save the active records in a temporary file "TEMP.DAT".

(*vi*) Delete file "EMPREC.DAT" by issuing command :
remove ("EMPREC.DAT");

(*vii*) Rename file "TEMP.DAT" as "EMPREC.DAT" as follows :
rename("Temp.DAT", "EMPREC.DAT");

With minor changes, we can use this program on different data files created using this program or even source and target files can be supplied by the user of his/her choice.

Program 12.13

```
// Updating a binary file randomly
// Add, modify,display and delete employee records
#include<iostream.h>
#include<conio.h>
#include<fstream.h>
#include<string.h>
#include<process.h>
#include<stdio.h>
int count = 0; // initially no record assumed
class emp
{
        char empname[41];
        char desig[31];
        float salary;
        char status;    // for active or deleted record
                        //status is ' ' for active and '*' for deleted record
    public :
        void enter(void); //function prototype
```

```
        int display(void);
        void modify(void);
        void del(void);
        int copy(void);
};
//function definition enter( )
void emp::enter(void)
{
        int i;
        clrscr( );
        //fill the empname with blanks
        for(i = 0; i < 41; i++)
            empname[i] = ' ';
        //fill the desig with blanks
        for(i = 0; i < 31; i++)
            desig[i] = ' ';
        salary=0.0;
        cout<<"\nAdd Employee Data : ";
        cout<<"\n\nRecord Number : "<<(++count)<<endl;    //count is global
        cout<<"\nEmployee Name : ";
        gets(empname);
        cout<<"\nDesignation : ";
        gets(desig);
        cout<<"\nSalary : ";
        cin>>salary;
        status=' ';
}
//function definition display( )
int emp::display(void)
{
        if(status != '*') //if active record
        {
                clrscr( );
                cout<<"\nEmployee Details : ";
                cout<<"\nName : "<<empname;
                cout<<"\nDesignation : "<<desig;
                cout<<"\nSalary : "<<salary;
                return 1;
        }
        else
        {
                cout<<"\nEmployee record not available\n";
```

```
            return 0;
        }
}
//function definition modify( )
void emp::modify(void)
{
        int i;
        char tempname[41];
        char tempdesig[31];
        //fill the tempname with blanks
        for(i = 0; i < 41; i++)
           tempname[i] = ' ';
        //fill the tempdesig with blanks
        for(i = 0; i < 31; i++)
           tempdesig[i] = ' ';
        float tempsal=0.0;
        clrscr( );
        cout<<"\nEmployee Details : ";
        cout<<"\nName : "<<empname;
        cout<<"\nDesignation : "<<desig;
        cout<<"\nSalary : "<<salary;
        cout<<"\n\nEnter new details\n";
        cout<<"\nIf you wish to retain the old name or designation\n";
        cout<<"\nPress ENTER key\n";
        cout<<"\nName : ";
        gets(tempname);
        cout<<"\nDesignation : ";
        gets(tempdesig);
        cout<<"\nSalary : ";
        cin>>tempsal;
        if(strlen(tempname) != 0)
           strcpy(empname,tempname);
        if(strlen(tempdesig) != 0)
           strcpy(desig,tempdesig);
        if(tempsal >= 0)
           salary=tempsal;
}
//function definition del( )
void emp::del(void)
{
        if(status == '*') //if record is already deleted
           cout<<"\n\nRecord does not exist\n\n";
```

```
        else
            status='*';      //change the status from ' ' to '*'
                             //logical deletion
}
//function definition copy( )
int emp::copy(void)
{
        if(status == '*') //if deleted record
            return 0;
        else
            return 1;
}
void main( )
{
        int choice,offset,temp,flag;
        char ch;
        clrscr( );
        emp obj; // object of class emp created
        fstream fio; // input/output stream created
        fio.open("EMPREC.DAT",ios::in | ios::out | ios::binary);
        if(! fio)
        {
                cout<<"Can't open file\n";
                exit(1);
        }
        fio.seekg(0,ios::end); //reach at the end of file
        int file_size=fio.tellp( ); //find the length of file
        count=file_size/sizeof(emp); //find number of records stored
        while(1) //infinite loop
        {
                clrscr( );
                cout<<"\nMain Menu\n";
                cout<<"\nAdd Record        1.";
                cout<<"\nModify Record     2.";
                cout<<"\nDisplay Record    3.";
                cout<<"\nDelete Record     4.";
                cout<<"\nSave and Exit     5.";
                cout<<"\n\nEnter your choice (1-5) : ";
                cin>>choice;
                switch(choice)
```

```
{
    case 1 : //for adding a record
            obj.enter( );
            temp = count;
            offset = ((temp–1)*sizeof(emp));
            fio.seekp(offset,ios::beg);
            fio.write((char *)&obj,sizeof(emp));
            break;
    case 2 : //for modifying a record
            if(! count)
            {
              cout<<"\nNo Entry Available ";
              getch( );
              break;
            }
            cout<<"\nEnter record number <= "<<count<<endl;
            cin>>temp;
            if(temp > count)
            {
              cout<<"\nInvalid Employee Number";
              getch( );
              break;
            }
            else
            {
              offset = (temp – 1) * sizeof(emp);
              fio.seekg(offset,ios::beg);
              fio.read((char *)&obj,sizeof(emp));
              flag=obj.display( );
              getch( );
              if(flag)
              {
                cout<<"\n\nModify this record [y/n] : ";
                cin>>ch;
                if(ch == 'y' || ch == 'Y')
                {
                  cout< <"\nEnter New Values\n";
                  obj.modify( );
                  fio.seekg(offset,ios::beg);
                  fio.write((char *)&obj,sizeof(emp));
                  cout<<"\n\nNew Values Replaced\n";
```

```
                    getch( );
                }
            }
        }
        break;
    case 3 : //for displaying a record
        if(! count)
        {
            cout<<"\nNo Entry Available\n";
            getch( );
            break;
        }
        cout<<"\nEnter Record Number to be displayed : ";
        cin>>temp;
        if(temp > count)
        {
            cout<<"\nInvalid Record Number\n";
            getch( );
            break;
        }
        else
        {
            offset = (temp - 1) * sizeof(emp);
            fio.seekg(offset,ios::beg);
            fio.read((char *)&obj,sizeof(emp));
            obj.display( );
            getch( );
        }
        break;
    case 4 : //for deleting a record
        if(! count)
        {
            cout<<"\nNo Entry Available\n";
            getch( );
            break;
        }
        cout<<"\nEnter Record Number to be deleted : ";
        cin>>temp;
        if(temp > count)
        {
            cout<<"\nInvalid Record Number\n";
```

```
            getch( );
            break;
        }
        else
        {
            offset = (temp - 1) * sizeof(emp);
            fio.seekg(offset,ios::beg);
            fio.read((char *)&obj,sizeof(emp));
            flag=obj.display( );
            getch( );
            if(flag)
            {
                obj.del( );
                fio.seekg(offset,ios::beg);
                fio.write((char *)&obj,sizeof(emp));
                cout<<"\n\nNow the record is deleted\n";
                getch( );
            }
        }
        break;
case 5 : //for copying the undeleted records to "TEMP.DAT"
        fstream fio1; //create input/output stream
        fio1.open("TEMP.DAT",ios::in | ios::out | ios::binary);
        if(! fio1)
        {
            cout<<"\nCan't open file\n";
            exit(1);
        }
        fio.seekg(0); //move to beginning of file
        fio1.seekp(0); //move to beginning of file
        emp tempobj; //create temporary object
        do
        {
            //read the object from file
            fio.read((char *)&obj,sizeof(emp));
            if(! fio) //if no record left in file
              break;
            flag=obj.copy( ); //check status of record
            if(flag)
            {
                tempobj=obj;
```

```
                    //write the record to file
                    fio1.write((char *)&tempobj,sizeof(emp));
                  }
                } while(fio);
                fio.close( ); //delink the file
                fio1.close( ); //delink the file
                remove("EMPREC.DAT"); //delete file
                rename("TEMP.DAT", "EMPREC.DAT");//rename file
                exit(0);
            default :
                cout<<"\nWrong Choice, Range(1-5)\n";
                getch( );
                break;
          } //switch statement ends here
      } //while loop ends here
}
```

Output

```
Main Menu
Add Record        1.
Modify Record     2.
Display Record    3.
Delete Record     4.
Save and Exit     5.
Enter your choice (1-5) : 1
Add Employee Data :
Record Number : 1
Employee Name : J. B. DIXIT
Designation : LECTURER
Salary : 35000
Main Menu
Add Record                1.
Modify Record             2.
Display Record            3.
Delete Record             4.
Save and Exit             5.
Enter your choice (1-5) : 1
Add Employee Data  :
Record Number : 2
```

```
Employee Name : RUCHI
Designation : LECTURER
Salary : 30000
Main Menu
Add Record            1.
Modify Record         2.
Display Record        3.
Delete Record         4.
Save and Exit         5.
Enter your choice (1–5)  : 1
Add Employee Data :
Record Number : 3
Employee Name : RAMAN SHARMA
Designation : MANAGER
Salary : 80000
Main Menu
Add Record            1.
Modify Record         2.
Display Record        3.
Delete Record         4.
Save and Exit         5.
Enter your choice (1–5) : 2
Enter record number <= 3
1
Employee Details :
Name : J. B. DIXIT
Designation : LECTURER
Salary : 35000
Modify this record [y/n] : Y
Employee Details :
Name : J. B. DIXIT
Designation : LECTURER
Salary : 35000
Enter new details
If you wish to retain the old name or designation
Press ENTER key
Name :
Designation :
Salary : 40000
```

```
New Value Replaced
Main Menu
Add Record            1.
Modify Record         2.
Display Record        3.
Delete Record         4.
Save and Exit         5.
Enter your choice (1–5) : 3
Enter Record Number to be displayed : 1
Employee Details :
Name : J. B. DIXIT
Designation : LECTURER
Salary : 40000
Main Menu
Add Record            1.
Modify Record         2.
Display Record        3.
Delete Record         4.
Save and Exit         5.
Enter your choice (1–5) : 1
Add Employee Data :
Record Number : 4
Employee Name : KULDEEP DAHIYA
Designation : PRINCIPAL
Salary : 36000
Main Menu
Add Record            1.
Modify Record         2.
Display Record        3.
Delete Record         4.
Save and Exit         5.
Enter your choice (1–5) : 4
Enter Record Number to be deleted : 1
Employee Details :
Name : J. B. DIXIT
Designation : LECTURER
Salary : 40000
Now the record is deleted
```

Main Menu

Add Record	1.
Modify Record	2.
Display Record	3.
Delete Record	4.
Save and Exit	5.

Enter your choice (1–5) : 3

Enter Record Number to be displayed : 1

Employee record not available

Main Menu

Add Record	1.
Modify Record	2.
Display Record	3.
Delete Record	4.
Save and Exit	5.

Enter your choice (1–5) : 5

12.10 Error Handling Functions for File I/O

In C++, we have a large number of functions to handle the errors that may occur during file input/output operations. These errors may include :

(*i*) *Attempt to read a non-existing file.*

(*ii*) *Attempt to read past the end-of-file.*

(*iii*) *Attempt to create a file that already exists on the disk.*

(*iv*) *Non-availability of space on the disk for storing a file.*

(*v*) *Use of invalid filename.*

(*vi*) *Attempting an input/output operation on a file without opening it.*

In C++, a file stream inherits a 'stream-state' member (provided by ios class). This member function records the status of the file in use. Bit fields are used for the above stated errors by the stream state member function. The current state of the I/O system is held in an object of type **iostate**, which is an enumeration defined by **ios** that includes the following members :

Name	Meaning
ios :: goodbit	No error bits set
ios :: eofbit	1 when end-of-file is encountered; 0 otherwise
ios :: failbit	1 when a (possibly) nonfatal I/O error has occurred; 0 otherwise
ios :: badbit	1 when a fatal I/O error has occurred ; 0 otherwise

For obtaining I/O status information, you can call the **rdstate( )** function. It has the following prototype:

```
iostate rdstate( );
```

It returns the current status of the error flags. As you can probably guess from looking at the preceding list of flags, **rdstate( )** returns **goodbit** when no error has occurred. Otherwise, an error flag is turned on.

Table 12.3 lists the error handling functions provided by ios class.

Table 12.3. Error Handling Functions

Function	*Purpose*
bad( )	checks for invalid I/O operations and for unrecoverable errors. Returns a non-zero value if an invalid operation on a file is performed or if an irrecoverable error has occurred.
good( )	Returns a non-zero value if the stream state is alright.
fail( )	Returns a non-zero value, if the last file I/O operation has failed or if an irrecoverable error has occurred.
eof( )	Returns a non-zero value (true) if the end-of-file has reached. Otherwise returns zero (false).
clear( )	Returns no value but removes errors from a stream, if any error has occurred.
rdstate( )	Returns the state of a stream.

For example,

```
ifstream Ifile;
Ifile.open("TEMP.DAT", ios::in);
while(! Ifile.fail( ))
{
    ........
    ........    //process the file
}
if(Ifile.bad( ))
    cout<<"Unrecoverable error\n";
```

When any invalid I/O operation is performed on a file the function bad( ) returns a non-zero value and the message is displayed on the screen.

Similarly, the statement

```
Ifile.clear( );
```

resets the error state so that further file I/O operations can be performed.

Some of the features have already been used in the earlier programs, such as :

```
while(Ifile)
{
    ........
    ........
}
```

and

```
while(Ifile.read(....))
{
    ........
    ........
}
```

Here, **Ifile** will be zero (false) when the end-of-file is reached and **eof( )** returns non-zero (true).

The above stated functions can be used by us at the proper places in the program code for obtaining the status of a file stream and then take appropriate action (if required).

Solved Problems

Problem 1. *Write a C++ program to copy a text file to another.*

Solution.

```
// copy a text file to another
#include<fstream.h>
#include<conio.h>
void main( )
{
    char source[13],target[13]; //to store filenames
    char ch;
    clrscr( );
    cout<<"Enter the source file name to be copied : ";
    cin>>source;
    ifstream Ifile(source,ios::in); //open file in input mode
    if( ! Ifile)
        cout<<"\nCan't open source file for reading\n";
    else
    {
        cout<<"\nEnter the target file name to transfer source file : ";
        cin>>target;
        ofstream Ofile(target,ios::out); //open file in output mode
        if(! Ofile)
            cout<<"\nCan't open target file for writing\n";
        else
        {
            while(Ifile)
            {
                Ifile.get(ch);
                Ofile.put(ch);
            }
```

```
                cout<<"\nSource file has been copied to target file\n";
                Ofile.close( ); //disconnect target file from Ofile
            }
            Ifile.close( ); //disconnect source file from Ifile
        }
    }
```

Problem 2. *Write a C++ program to store roll number and marks of students using objects and then display the file contents.*

Solution.

```
//Create a file of objects and display the objects stored
#include<fstream.h>
#include<conio.h>
#include<iomanip.h> //for formatting of data
class student //class definition
{
        private :
            int rollno,marks;
        public :
            void getdata(void); //function prototype
            void putdata(void); //function prototype
}; //class definition over
void student :: getdata(void) //function definition
{
        cout<<"\nEnter Rollno and Marks\n\n";
        cin>>rollno>>marks;
}
void student :: putdata(void) //function definition
{
        cout<<setw(6)<<rollno<<setw(22)<<marks<<"\n";
}
void main( )
{
        fstream file; //create stream
        student obj; //class object declared
        int i,n;
        char filename[13]; //variable to store filename
        clrscr( );
        cout<<"Enter the name of file for data storage and retrieval : ";
        cin>>filename;
        file.open(filename, ios::in | ios :: out);
        if(! file)
```

```
    cout<<"\nCan't open file for writing\n";
  else
  {
      cout<<"\nHow many objects are to be entered ? \n";
      cin>>n;
      for(i=1;i<=n;i++)
      {
          clrscr( );
          cout<<"\nEnter object number : "<<i<<"\n\n";
          //read the object
          obj.getdata( );
          //write to file
          file.write( (char *) &obj,sizeof(obj));
      }
      file.seekg(0); //reset to start of file
      clrscr( );
      cout<<"\nThe contents of file "<<filename<<" are : \n\n";
      cout<<"\nRoll Number"<<"\t\tMarks\n\n";
      for(i=1;i<=n;i++)
      {
          file.read( (char *) &obj, sizeof(obj) );
          obj.putdata( );
      }
      file.close( );
  }
}
```

Problem 3. *Observe the program segment given below carefully, and answer the question that follows :*

```
class Applicant
{
    long AId;           //Applicant's Id
    char Name[20];      //Applicant's Name
    float Score;        //Applicant's Score
public :
    void Enroll( );
    void Disp( );
    void MarksScore( ); //Function to change Score
    long R_AId( ) {return AId;)
};
void ScoreUpdate (long Id)
{
    fstream File;
```

```
        File.open("APPLI.DAT",ios :: binary | ios : : in | ios :: out);
        Applicant A;
        int Record=0, Found=0;
        while(! Found && File.read((char*)&A, sizeof(A)))
        {
            if(Id==A.R_AId( ))
            {
                cout<<"Enter new Score";
                A.MarksScore( );
                ________________                    //Statement1
                ________________                    //Statement2
                Found=1;
            }
            Record++;
        }
        if(Found==1) cout<<"Record Updated";
        File.close( );
    }
```

Write the Statement1 **to position** the File Pointer at the beginning of the Record for which the Applicant's Id matches with the argument passed, and Statement2 **to write** the updated Record at the position.

Solution.

```
File.seekg(-1*sizeof(A),ios::cur);          //Statement1
File.write((char *)&A, sizeof(A));          //Statement2
```

Problem 4. *Write a function in C++ to count the number of lowercase alphabets present in a text file "BOOK.TXT".*

Solution. The function definition is given below :

```
//function definition count_lowercase( )
void count_lowercase( )
{
    char ch; //local variable
    int count=0;
    ifstream Ifile("BOOK.TXT", ios::in);
    if(! Ifile)
    {
        count<<"\nCannot open the file BOOK.TXT \n";
        exit(1);
    }
    while (! Ifile.eof( ) )
    {
        Ifile.get(ch);
```

```
        if( Ifile.eof( ) )
            break;
        if(ch >= 'a' && ch <='z')
            count++;
    }
    count<<"\nNumber of lowercase alphabets is : "<<count;
    Ifile.close( );
}
```

Problem 5. *Given a binary file PHONE.DAT, containing records of the following structure type*

```
class Phonlist
{
    char Name[20];
    char Address[30];
    char AreaCode[5];
    char PhoneNo[15];
public :
    void Register( );
    void Show( );
    int CheckCode(char AC[ ])
    {
        return strcmp (AreaCode, AC);
    }
};
```

Write a function TRANSFER( ) in C++, that would copy all those records which are having AreaCode as "DEL" from PHONE.DAT to PHONBACK.DAT.

Solution. The function definition is given below :

```
//function definition TRANSFER( )
void TRANSFER( )
{
    Phonlist P;
    ifstream Ifile("PHONE.DAT", ios::in | ios::binary);
    ofstream Ofile("PHONEBACK.DAT", ios::out | ios::binary);
    if(! Ifile || ! Ofile)
    {
        cout<<"\nFile(s) cannot be opened\n";
        exit(1);
    }
    while (! Ifile.eof( ))
    {
        Ifile.read((char *)&P, sizeof(P));
```

```
        if(strcmp(P.AreaCode,"DEL") = =0)
            Ofile.write((char *)&P, sizeof(P));
    }
    Ifile.close( );     //close file
    Ofile.close( ); //close file
}
```

Problem 6. *(a) Observe the program segment given below carefully and fill the blanks marked as Line 1 and Line 2 using fstream functions for performing the required task.*

```
#include <fstream.h>
class Library
{
    long Ano ;              //Ano – Accession Number of the Book
    char Title [20] ;       //Title – Title of the Book
    int Qty ;               //Qty – Number of Books in Library
public :
    void Enter (int) ;      //Function to enter the content
    void Display ( ) ;      //Function to display the content
    void Buy (int Tqty)     //Function to increment in Qty
    {
        Qty + = Tqty;
    }
    long GetAno ( ) return Ano ; }
} ;
void BuyBook (long BANo, int BQty)
                    //BANo → Ano of the book purchased
                    //BQty → Number of books purchased
{
    fstream File ;
    File. open ("STOCK.DAT", ios : : binary ¦ ios : : in ¦ ios : : out);
    int Position = – 1 ;
    Library L;
    while (Position = = – 1 && File.read ((char *) & L, sizeof (L) ) )
        if (L.GetAno ( ) = = BANo)
        {
            L.Buy (BQty) ; //To update the number of Books
            Position = File.tellg ( ) – sizeof (L) ;
            //Line 1: To place the file pointer to the required
            position __________ ;
            //Line 2: To write the object L on to the binary file
            ____________ ;
        }
        if (Position = = – 1)
```

```
        cout<<"No updation done as required Ano not found.." ;
    File.close ( ) ;
}
```

Solution. File.seekp (Position, ios : : beg)

File.write ((char *)&L, sizeof(L))

(b) Write a function COUNT_TO( ) in C++ to count the presence of a word 'to' in a text file "NOTES.TXT".

Example :

If the content of the file "NOTES.TXT" is as follows :

It is very important to know that smoking is injurious to health. Let us take initiative to stop it.

The function COUNT_TO ( ) will display the following message :

Count of -to- in file : 3

Note : In the above example, 'to' occurring as a part of word stop is not considered.

Solution. The Function definition is given below :

```
//function definition COUNT_TO ( )
void COUNT_TO ( )
{
    char str [80] ;
    int count = 0 ;
    ifstream Ifile ("NOTES.TXT", ios :: in) ;
    if (! Ifile)
        cout<<"\nCannot open NOTES.TXT file for reading\n" ;
    else
    {
        while (! Ifile.eof ( ) )
        {
            Ifile>>str ;
            if(strlen(str) ==2)
            {
                if(toupper(str[0] == 'T') && (toupper(str[1] == 'O') )
                    count++ ;
            }
        }
        cout<<0"\nCount of -to- in file : "<<count ;
        Ifile.close ( ) ;
    }
}
```

(c) *Write a function in C++ to read and display the detail of all the members whose membership type is 'L' or 'M' from a binary file "CLUB.DAT". Assuming the binary file "CLUB.DAT" contains objects of class CLUB, which is defined as follows :*

```
class CLUB
{
    int Mno ;            //Member Number
    char Mname [20] ;        //Member Name
    char Type ; //Member Type : L Life Member M Monthly Member G Guest
    char Phone_No [15] ;
public :
    void Register ( ) ;//Function to enter the content
    void Display ( ) ; //Function to display all data members
    char WhatTpye (  ) { return Type ; }
} ;
```

Solution. The function definition is given below :

```
//function definition Display_details ( )
void Display_details ( )
{
    CLUB obj ; //object declared
    ifstream Ifile ; //file stream
    char Mtype ;
    int count = 0 ;
    Ifile.open ("CLUB.DAT", ios :: in | ios :: binary) ;
    if(! Ifile)
        cout<<"\nCannot open CLUB.DAT file for reading\n" ;
    else
    {
        int size = sizeof(CLUB) ;       //find size of object
        cout<<"\nMembers whose membership type is 'L' or 'M' : \n";
        Ifile.read ((char *), & ob], Size) ;
        while (Ifile)
        {
            Mtype = obj.WhatType ( ) ;          //function call
            if (Mtype == 'L' || Mtype == 'M')
            {
                count++ ;
                obj.Display( ) ; //function call
                cout<<'\n' ;
                Ifile. read ( ( char *) &obj, size) ;
            }
        }
```

```
    if (! count)
        cout<<"Is not present in the file CLUB.DAT\n" ;
    }
}
```

Problem 7. (*a*) **Observe the program segment given below carefully and fill the blanks marked as Statement 1 and Statement 2 using tellg( ) and seekp( ) functions for performing the required task.**

```
#include <fstream.h>
class Client
{
        long Cno; char Name [20], Email [30];
public:
        //Function to allow user to enter the Cno, Name, Email
        void Enter( );
        //Function to allow user to enter (modify) Email
        void Modify( );
        long ReturnCno( ) {return Cno;}
};
void ChangeEmail( )
{       Client C;
        fstream F;
        F.open("INFO.DAT", ios: :binary|ios: :in|ios: :out);
        long Cnoc; //Client's no. whose Email needs to be changed
        cin>>Cnoc;
        while (F.read((char *)&C, sizeof(C)))
        {
            if (Cnoc= =C.ReturnCno( ))
            {
                C.Modify( );
                                    //Statement 1
                int Pos=__________  //To find the current position of file pointer
                                    //Statement 2
                _______________     //To move the file pointer to write the
                                    //modified record back onto the file
                                    //for the desired Cnoc
                F.write((char *)&C, sizeof(C));
            }
        }
        F.close( );
}
```

Solution. F.tellg ( ) – sizeof (C);

F.seekp (Pos, ios::beg);

(b) Write a function in C++ to count the words "this" and "these" present in a text file "ARTICLE.TXT".

[Note that the words "this" and "these" are complete words]

Solution. The function definition is given below:

```
//function definition Count-Words( )
void Count_Words( )
{
        void str[31];   //assuming maximum word length 30
        int count=0;
        ifstream Ifile("ARTICLE.TXT", ios::in);
        if(! Ifile)
            cout<<"\nCannot open ARTICLE.TXT file for reading \n";
        else
        {
                while (! Ifile.eof ( ))
                {
                        Ifile>>str;
                        if((strcmpi(str,  "this")==0)||(strcmpi(str,"these")==0))
                        {
                        count++;
                        }
                }
                cout<<"\nCount of this and these in file="<<count;
                Ifile.close( );
        }
}
```

(c) Write a function in C++ to search and display details of all flights, whose destination is "Mumbai" from a binary file "FLIGHT.DAT". Assuming the binary file is containing the objects of the following class.

```
class FLIGHT
{
        int Fno;                //Flight Number
        char From[20];                  //Flight Starting Point
        char To[20];            //Flight Destination
public:
        char * GetFrom( ) {return From;}
        char * GetTo( ) {return To;}
        void Enter( ) {cin>>Fno;gets(From);gets(To);}
        void Display( ) {cout<< Fno<<":"<<From<<":"<<To<<endl;}
};
```

Solution. The function definition is given below:

```
//function definition Search_Display( )
void Search_Display( )
{
    FLIGHT obj; //object declared
    ifstream Ifile; //file stream
    int count=0;
    Ifile.open ("FLIGHT.DAT", ios :: in | ios :: binary);
    if(! Ifile)
        cout<<"\n Cannot open FLIGHT.DAT file for reading \n" ;
    else
    {
        int size=sizeof(FLIGHT);          //find size of object
        cout<<"\nDetails of flights is/are";
        Ifile.read ((char *), & obj, size) ;
        while (Ifile)
        {
            if(strcmpi(obj.To,"Mumbai")= =0)
            {
                count+ +;
                obj.Display( ); //function call
                Ifile. read ( ( char *) &obj, size);
            }
        }
        if (! count)
            cout<<" not present in file FLIGHT.DAT \n";
        Ifile.close ( );
    }
}
```

Problem 8. *Write a C++ program that takes input of two matrices A and B from an input file and find their product in C, give the output in an output file.* **(PTU Exam)**

Solution :

```
// an input file contains two matrices A and B
// find their product in C, give the output in an output file

#include<fstream.h>
#include<iomanip.h>
#include<stdlib.h>
#include<conio.h>
#define S 5
```

```
void main( )
{
    char source[13],target[13]; // for input and output files
    int A[S][S],B[S][S],C[S][S],row1,colm1,row2,colm2,i,j,k,data;
    clrscr( );
    cout<<"Enter the source file name : ";
    cin>>source;
    fstream Sfile(source,ios::in | ios::out); // open source file
    if( ! Sfile)
        cout<<"\nCan't open "<<source<<" file \n";
    else
    {
        cout<<"\nEnter the target file name : ";
        cin>>target;
        fstream Tfile(target,ios:: in | ios::out); // open target file
        if(! Tfile)
        {
            cout<<"\nCan't open "<<target<<" file for writing\n";
            Sfile.close( ); // disconnect source from Sfile
        }
        else
        {
            // store the data from keyboard to source file

            cout<<"\nEnter the order of matrix A : ";
            cin>>row1>>colm1;
            Sfile.write( (char *) &row1,sizeof(int) );
            Sfile.write( (char *) &colm1,sizeof(int) );
            cout<<"\nEnter the order of matrix B : ";
            cin>>row2>>colm2;
            Sfile.write( (char *) &row2,sizeof(int) );
            Sfile.write( (char *) &colm2,sizeof(int) );
            cout<<"\nEnter matrix A rowwise :\n";
            for(i=0;i<row1;i++)
            {
                for(j=0;j<colm1;j++)
                {
                    cin>>data;
                    Sfile.write( (char *) &data,sizeof(int) );
                }
            }
```

```
cout<<"\nEnter matrix B rowwise :\n";
for(i=0;i<row2;i++)
{
        for(j=0;j<colm2;j++)
        {
                cin>>data;
                Sfile.write( (char *) &data,sizeof(int) );
        }
}
Sfile.seekg(0,ios::beg); // reach in the beginning of file

// read order of matrices from source file

Sfile.read( (char *) &row1,sizeof(int) );
Sfile.read( (char *) &colm1,sizeof(int) );
Sfile.read( (char *) &row2,sizeof(int) );
Sfile.read( (char *) &colm2,sizeof(int) );

if( colm1 != row2 )
{
        cout<<"\n\nMatrix multiplication not possible\n";
        Sfile.close( ); // disconnect source from Sfile
        Tfile.close( ); // disconnect target from Tfile
}
else
{
        // read matrices from source file

        for(i=0;i<row1;i++)
        {
                for(j=0;j<colm1;j++)
                    Sfile.read( (char *) &A[i][j],sizeof(int) );
        }

        for(i=0;i<row2;i++)
        {
                for(j=0;j<colm2;j++)
                    Sfile.read( (char *) &B[i][j],sizeof(int) );
        }
```

```
            // perform matrix multiplication

            for(i=0;i<row1;i++)
            {
               for(j=0;j<colm2;j++)
               {
                  C[i][j]=0;
                  for(k=0;k<colm1;k++)
                  C[i][j] += A[i][k] * B[k][j];
               }
            }

            // store the product matrix C in target file

            for(i=0;i<row1;i++)
            {
               for(j=0;j<colm2;j++)
               Tfile.write( (char *) &C[i][j],sizeof(int) );
            }
            clrscr( );
            cout<<"\nProduct matrix C stored in "<<target<< " file is :\n\n";

            Tfile.seekg(0,ios::beg); // reach in the beginning of file

            for(i=0;i<row1;i++)
            {
                  for(j=0;j<colm2;j++)
                  {
                        Tfile.read( (char *) &data,sizeof(int) );
                        cout<<setw(8)<<data;
                  }
                  cout<<"\n";
            }
            Sfile.close( ); // disconnect source from Sfile
            Tfile.close( ); // disconnect target from Tfile
        }
     }
  }
  getch( ); // freeze the monitor
}
```

Problem 9. *In a file of text, write a program to find the number of vowels in the text.* **(PTU 2004)**

Solution :

```
// find the number of vowels in the text ( in a file of text )

#include<fstream.h>
#include<conio.h>

void main( )
{
    char source[13];
    char ch;
    int vowel_count=0;
    clrscr( );
    cout<<"Enter the source file name of text : ";
    cin>>source;

    ifstream Ifile(source); //open file in input mode

    if ( ! Ifile)
        cout<<"\nCan't open "<<source<<" file for input\n\n";
    else
    {
        while (Ifile)
        {
            Ifile.get(ch);
            If( ch=='a' || ch=='A' || ch=='e' || ch=='E' ||
                ch=='i' || ch=='I' || ch=='o' || ch=='O' ||
                ch=='u' || ch=='U' )
            Vowel_count++;
        }
        cout<<"\nNumber of vowels in "<<source<<" file : "<<vowel_count;
        Ifile.close( ); // disconnect filename from Ifile
    }
    getch( ); // freeze the monitor
}
```

REVIEW QUESTIONS AND EXERCISES

1. Why do we need a data file ?
2. What are the types of data files ? Explain.
3. What are the basic file operations on text files ? Explain.
4. Write short note on sequential input/output operations. **(PTU Exam)**
5. Write a short note on the following :

   (*i*) Creating a text file. (*ii*) Writing text into file.

   (*iii*) Reading and Manipulation of text from an already existing text file.
6. What is a binary file ? What is the basic difference between a text file and a binary file ?
7. Write a short note on the following taking into consideration binary file :

   (*i*) Creation of file. (*ii*) Writing data into file.

   (*iii*) Searching for required data from file. (*iv*) Appending data to a file.

   (*v*) Insertion of data in a sorted file. (*vi*) Deletion of data from file.

   (*vii*) Modification of data in a file.
8. What is a stream ? Name the streams generally used for file I/O in C++.
9. Why is it necessary to include the file **iostream.h** in all the C++ programs ?
10. What is a file mode ? Explain the various file modes (in , out, app) available in C++ with reference to a text file.
11. State the type of data for which binary files are more suited. In what respect binary files are better than text files ?
12. Write a C++ program to read an existing text file and display words of this file on screen (one word per line) in the order they appear in the file. Assume that successive words are separated by one or more white space characters.
13. Write a C++ program to append the contents of a file named as TRY1.TXT to another similar file TRY2.TXT.
14. Describe how would you determine the number of bytes in a file. When do you need such information ?
15. What are the different ways of detecting end-of-file ? Explain with suitable examples.
16. Describe the opening of a binary file using **in, out** and **app** modes.
17. Write syntax of **write(**) and **read(**) functions. For what type of disk files these functions are used ? Illustrate your answer by means of suitable examples.
18. Write short note on the following functions :

    (*i*) seekg( ) (*ii*) tellg( )

    (*iii*) seekp( ) (*iv*) tellp( )
19. Write a C++ program which generates a new file having one blank line inserted after every line of a given file. Names of input file and output file will be specified by the user always.
20. Write a C++ program to delete white spaces such as horizontal tab, vertical tab space, linefeed, newline and carriage return from a text file and to store the contents of the file without spaces on another file. Names of input file and output file will be specified by the user always.
21. A hospital wants to create a database regarding its indoor patients. The information to store include

    Name of the patient

    Date of admission

Disease

Date of discharge

Create a structure to store the date (year, month and date as its members). Create a base class to store the above information. The member function should include functions to enter information and display a list of all the patients in the database. Create a derived class to store the age of the patients. How will you list the information about all the pediatric patients (less than 12 years in age) ?

22. Write statements using seekg( ) for the following :

(*i*) To go to byte number 40 in the file.

(*ii*) To go backward by 17 bytes from the end.

(*iii*) To move the pointer by 10 positions backward from the current position.

(*iv*) To move to the beginning of file after completing an operation.

23. Write a function in C++ to count the number of lines present in a text file "STORY.TXT".

24. "Global Tours" is a renowed tour and travel company. It takes the customers on three types of tours :

Discover World

Pilgrimage Package

Honeymoon Bash

These tours start every month. A customer can select a tour of any category for a month specifying the number of tourists with him/her.

Design a class tourist having following data members :

Customer name (string–30 char)

No. of people accompanying (int)

Package Category (D/P/H)

Cost (float)

Tour month (string–10)

Use the concept of insertion and extraction to write and read data in a file called TOURIST.DAT. Open the file in output mode and append data to it (if the file exists). Get data for the object using a member function called **getdata( )** until the user desires. Now close the file and open it in input mode for reading and displaying the values using a member function **putdata( )** until the end of the file has reached.

Write a C++ program to implement the above stated tasks.

25. Modify the tourist class given in exercise 23 to include a function called **browse( )** for accepting a record number from the user and display the requested record (using read( ) and write( ) functions for the earlier stated member functions getdata( ) and putdata( )).

Write a C++ menu driven program having the following options for the user's choice :

Insert data

Display data

Query data

Exit

26. Write a C++ program that creates a file named "TELEPHON.DAT". Using an object of the class telephone having the following members.

protected data members

telephone_number

name

address

public member functions

get_data( ) to accept data

show_data( ) to show data

After creating the file, the program should read the file and display its contents.

27. Write a function in C++ to count the number of alphabets present in a text file "NOTES.TXT".

28. Write a function in C++ to add new objects at the bottom of a binary file "STUDENT.DAT" assuming the binary file is containing the objects of the following class.

```
class STUD
{
        int Rno;
        char Name[20];
    public :
        void Enter( ) {cin>>Rno; gets(Name);}
        void Display( ) {cout<<Rno<<Name<<endl;}
};
```

29. Write a function in C++ to count the number of uppercase alphabets present in a text file "ARTICLE.TXT".

30. (*i*) What functions enable a file pointer to be set for read operations? **(PTU Exam)**

(*ii*) Which flag when set flushes all stream after insertion? **(PTU Exam)**

31. Write a short note on file pointers. **(PTU Exam)**

32. (*a*) What class function enables opening a file in write mode? **(PTU Exam)**

(*b*) What error conditions are tested on a file pointer? **(PTU Exam)**

(*c*) What are the three modes in which a file can be opened? **(PTU Exam)**

(*d*) How random access is done for files? **(PTU 2004)**

❑❑❑